The Age of the Baroque in Portugal

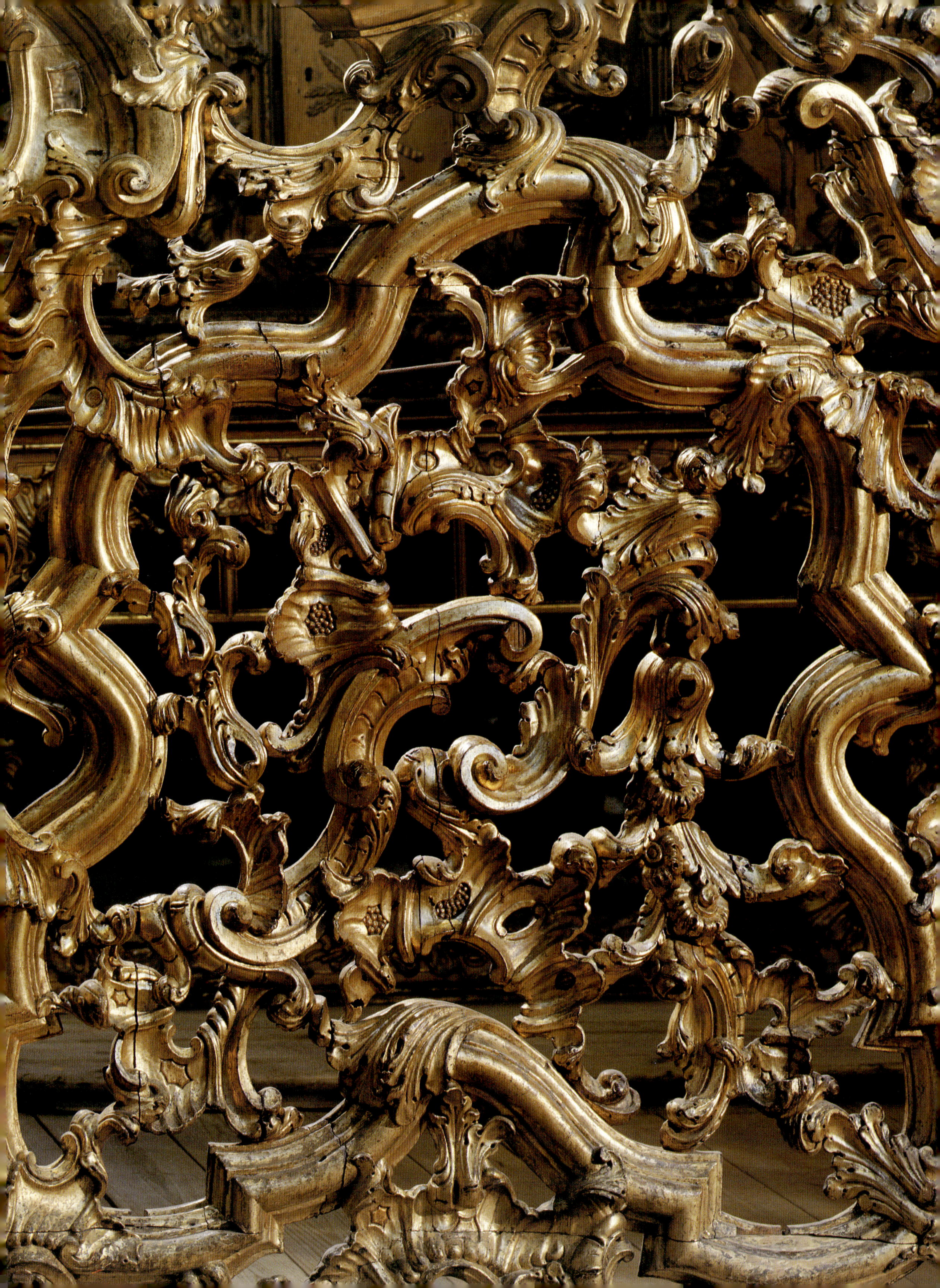

The Age of the Baroque in Portugal

Edited by Jay A. Levenson

NATIONAL GALLERY OF ART, WASHINGTON
YALE UNIVERSITY PRESS, NEW HAVEN AND LONDON

The Age of the Baroque in Portugal
7 November 1993–6 February 1994

Organized by the National Gallery of Art and the Portuguese Secretary of State for Culture through the Instituto Português de Museus

with the assistance of
Ministério do Comércio e Turismo
Secretaria de Estado das Comunidades
Gabinete de Relações Culturais Internacionais
Embassy of Portugal in Washington

The exhibition is made possible by generous grants from

Pacific Telesis Foundation
Espírito Santo Financial Holding S.A.

Banco Comercial Português
Banco Totta & Açores

The Calouste Gulbenkian Foundation
Luso-American Development Foundation

*The National Gallery of Art and the Instituto Português de Museus
are grateful for the support of*
Instituto Camões
The Orient Foundation
Investimentos e Participações Empresariais, S.A.

International Corporate Circle of the National Gallery of Art

An indemnity for this exhibition has been granted by the Federal Council on the Arts and the Humanities.

All photos were supplied by the Arquivo Nacional de Fotografia, Instituto Português de Museus, Lisbon (photographers: José Pessoa, Giorgio Bordino, Vítor Branco, Pedro Ferreira, Francisco Matias, Carlos Pombo da Cruz Monteiro, Manuel da Palma, Luís Pavão, Arnaldo Soares, Mario Soares) or by the owners of the works of art, except the following: Conway Library, Courtauld Institute of Art, Carvalho figs. 2, 4, 5, Delaforce figs. 1, 4, 10, 11, França fig. 4, Wohl figs. 3–6, 9, 10, 12, 13, Montagu figs. 2, 3, 4; José Gomes Ferreira, Carvalho fig. 3; Tria Giovan, courtesy *Art & Antiques Magazine*, Wohl fig. 1; Gulbenkian Foundation, Silva Fernandes, Wohl fig. 20, Luís Felipe Oliveira, Wohl fig. 17, Robert C. Smith, Wohl figs. 7, 8, 16; Photo Camera, Wohl fig. 2.

Produced by the Editors Office,
National Gallery of Art
Editor-in-Chief, Frances P. Smyth
Editor, Jane Sweeney
Designer, Phyllis Hecht

Typeset in Adobe Caslon by
General Typographers, Inc., Washington
Printed by Arti Grafiche Motta, Arese, Italy
The clothbound edition is distributed by
Yale University Press

Cover: detail, cat. 27
Facing title page: detail, cat. 113

Library of Congress
Cataloging-in-Publication Data
The Age of the baroque in Portugal / edited by Jay A. Levenson.
  Includes bibliographical references.
  1. Art, Portuguese—Exhibitions. 2. Art, Baroque—Portugal—Exhibitions. 3. Art, Rococo—Portugal—Exhibitions. 4. Portugal—History—Modern, 1580–   I. Levenson, Jay A.
N7126.5.B37A35   1993
709'.469' 074753—dc20   93-5425
                                   CIP

ISBN (paper) 0-89468-198-2
ISBN (cloth) 0300-058-411

PRINTED IN ITALY

Contents

Lenders to the Exhibition

Jorge de Brito, Cascais

Câmara Municipal de Oeiras

Coimbra Cathedral Chapter

Fundação Berardo, Funchal

Fundação Ricardo do Espírito Santo Silva, Lisbon

Igreja de Nossa Senhora da Conceição dos Cardais, Lisbon

Igreja de São Domingos, Macao

Igreja de São Francisco, Évora

Igreja de São Francisco, Oporto

Lamego Cathedral Chapter

Lisbon Cathedral Chapter

Ministry of Foreign Affairs, Lisbon

Museu da Fábrica da Vista Alegre, Ílhavo

Museu de Física da Universidade de Coimbra, Gabinete de Física Experimental

Museu Nacional de Arte Antiga, Lisbon

Museu de Aveiro

Museu de São Roque, Santa Casa da Misericórdia, Lisbon

Museu Nacional de Soares dos Reis, Oporto

Museu Nacional do Azulejo, Lisbon

Museu Nacional dos Coches, Lisbon

Museu Nacional Machado de Castro, Coimbra

Palácio Nacional da Ajuda

Palácio Nacional de Queluz

Private Collections

Solar Collection, Lisbon

Foreword

This year marks the two hundred and fiftieth anniversary of the birth of perhaps the most eminent representative of eighteenth-century rationalism in America, Thomas Jefferson. One of his greatest friends in later life was the Abbé Correia da Serra, Portugal's second ambassador to the United States and an equally distinguished representative of the Portuguese enlightenment. Their friendship reminds us of the longevity of the ties between our country and its nearest neighbor in Europe, a relationship that this exhibition appropriately celebrates.

The Age of the Baroque in Portugal is the first exhibition at the National Gallery of Art organized entirely from Portuguese collections, but it is not the first time that major treasures from Portugal have been shown here. Visitors to our quincentenary exhibition, *Circa 1492: Art in the Age of Exploration*, will remember the extraordinary works of art that documented the Portuguese travels to Brazil, Africa, India, and the Far East in the fifteenth and sixteenth centuries. Such was the level of interest generated by these objects that we were delighted when our colleagues in Portugal proposed an exhibition devoted to another great age of their country's history.

Our goal this year is to introduce audiences in our country to the eighteenth century in Portugal, a remarkable period for both history and the history of art. While the masterpieces of baroque Portugal have long been prized by specialists—in fact, two eminent American art historians, George Kubler and the late Robert Smith, played major roles in modern scholarship on baroque art and architecture in Portugal—the field has long been difficult to study for anyone unable to visit that country. With relatively few exceptions, these works, whether created there or commissioned abroad, have remained in Portuguese collections, both public and private. Thus our exhibition would have been impossible without the extremely generous cooperation and support of our Portuguese colleagues and lenders, to whom we extend our heartfelt gratitude.

The Age of the Baroque in Portugal, a collaborative undertaking between the National Gallery of Art and the Portuguese Secretary of State for Culture, echoes a marvelous survey of the eighteenth century entitled *Triomphe du Baroque*, which was the centerpiece of a series of highly successful exhibitions for the 1991 Europalia festival in Belgium and subsequently inaugurated the exhibition galleries of the Centro Cultural de Belém in Lisbon. Our exhibition adds works in other media as well, in particular jewelry and scientific instruments, and introduces the Portuguese baroque to an entirely new audience here. Moreover, in view of the limited literature in English on Portuguese history and art of the eighteenth century, we have included in this catalogue essays by prominent scholars dealing with many aspects of this fascinating subject, some of which were commissioned expressly for our publication.

It is my special privilege to recognize the contribution to this project of the Prime Minister of Portugal, Aníbal Cavaco Silva, for his personal support of our exhibition, wholly in keeping with his longtime regard for our country. We also wish to thank Minister of Foreign Affairs José Manuel Durão Barroso and Minister of Trade and Tourism Fernando Faria de Oliveira for the support of their ministries. It was the vision of Secretary of State for Culture Pedro Santana Lopes that made this show possible. He has been our enthusiastic and supportive partner in this enterprise from the start, as has Dr. Simonetta Luz Afonso, commissioner of the Europalia exhibitions and subsequently the highly energetic director of the Instituto Português de Museus, who expertly coordinated all organizational matters in Portugal. We are also indebted to Dr. José de Monterroso Teixeira of the Fundação das Descobertas, the Portuguese curator of the exhibition, who, in addition to writing the majority of the catalogue entries, wisely chose the history of the baroque period as the best approach to understanding its art.

Two members of the prime minister's cabinet, Ambassador António Martins da Cruz, Foreign Affairs Adviser, and Dr. Isabel Teixeira da Mota do Amaral, Cultural Adviser, expertly and sympathetically guided our progress from Lisbon, and, with the assistance of Dr. José Menezes Teles and Dr. Patricia Salvação Barreto of the Secretariat of State for Culture, were especially helpful in bringing the Coach of the Embassy of the Marquês de Fontes to Washington. We would also like to extend our deep gratitude to the Portuguese diplomatic corps in Washington. Both Ambassador Francisco Knopfli and his Cultural Counsellor, Professor Graça Almeida Rodrigues, have provided unfailing and tireless guidance.

Among the many who worked on this show at the National Gallery, I would like to single out Jay A. Levenson, guest curator of the exhibition and editor of the catalogue, as well as Gaillard F. Ravenel and Mark Leithauser of the Department of Design and Installation, who played a crucial role in the selection of the works of art to be exhibited as well as imaginatively tailoring the installation to the special requirements of the baroque. We are also indebted to my predecessor, Director Emeritus J. Carter Brown, who took the all-important first steps toward realizing this project.

Exhibitions would remain just a concept without generous benefactors. We are particularly indebted to our broad-based consortium of corporations and foundations. From the earliest stages, Tony Coelho, President and Chief Executive Officer of Wertheim Schroder Investment Services Inc., has been an unwavering advocate on our behalf; his guidance has helped us form the crucial funding partnerships necessary to realize the exhibition. The American sponsor, Pacific Telesis Foundation, has embraced the project as an unprecedented tribute to the important cultural heritage of Portugal, and we especially wish to recognize the enthusiastic support of Sam Ginn, Chairman and Chief Executive Officer of Pacific Telesis Group.

The Portuguese business community also has endorsed the project: Espírito Santo Financial Holding S.A., along with its foundation, the Fundação Ricardo do Espírito Santo Silva, with the leadership of its chairman, Dr. Ricardo Espírito Santo Silva Salgado; Banco Totta & Açores; and Banco Comercial Português. Additional assistance was provided by Investimentos e Participações Empresariais, S.A.

Other Portuguese foundations also have supported the exhibition. The Luso-American Development Foundation, led by its President, Dr. Rui Machete, and its Administrator, Dr. Bernardino Gomes, was the exhibition's first benefactor, providing development funds and a contribution toward the transportation of the coach; the distinguished Calouste Gulbenkian Foundation and its Trustee, Dr. José Cordeiro Blanco, has generously supported the exhibition, the catalogue, and the opening dinner's musical program. The Orient Foundation provided additional exhibition assistance. The symposium would not have been possible without the aid of the Instituto Camões. Portugal's Secretary of State for Culture has given critical financial as well as organizational help. The Federal Council on the Arts and the Humanities in Washington provided support in the form of an indemnity.

We thank all who have participated in making this project a reality.

Earl A. Powell III
Director
National Gallery of Art

Acknowledgments

A true transatlantic collaboration, this exhibition would not have been possible without the help of many colleagues and friends in Portugal and the United States. I wish to extend my deepest gratitude to the many people, only a few of whom can be named here, who deserve significant credit for this accomplishment. Our partner in this undertaking from the start has been the Portuguese Secretary of State for Culture, and the organizational work for the show has been the special responsibility of the Instituto Português de Museus. At the Instituto, Maria de Jesus Monge worked tirelessly on the innumerable details of the exhibition and the catalogue, aided by Inês Ferro, director of the Palácio Nacional de Queluz, Miguel Soromenho, Isabel Cordeiro, Cecília Pereira, and Rui Afonso Santos. For the photography, we are grateful to the Arquivo Nacional de Fotografia, to José Pessoa and Vitória Mesquita, who served as coordinators of our project, assisted by Emília Tavares and Sofia Costa Ferrão.

Many officials in the Portuguese government helped with different aspects of the exhibition. In the Ministry of Trade and Tourism in Lisbon, I would especially like to thank Secretaries of State Alexandre Costa Relvas and António de Sousa. From the Instituto do Comércio Externo de Portugal (ICEP), I wish to thank Miguel Athayde Marques, President, Luís Manuel M. Correia da Silva, Miguel Fialho de Brito, Alberto Marques, and Teresa Figueiredo de Carvalho, as well as Pedro Antunes de Almeida of the Empresa Nacional de Turismo. In the New York office of ICEP, I am grateful to José Vital Morgado, Jorge Felner da Costa, who organized and hosted the press tour of baroque Portugal, Maria da Encarnação Mello, and Ana Maria Osório. At the Foreign Ministry in Lisbon, Secretary of State Luís Sousa de Macedo provided valuable counsel, as did Vasco Graça Moura of the Commission on the Discoveries.

Our lenders' generosity has made this exhibition possible: Isabel Silveiro Godinho and Ana Maria Batalha Reis of the Museu do Palácio Nacional da Ajuda; Maria Lobato Guimarães of the Museu de Aveiro; João Castelo-Branco Pereira of the Museu Nacional do Azulejo; Ana Brandão, Leonor d'Orey, Maria Helena Mendes Pinto, and Rafael Calado of the Museu Nacional de Arte Antiga; Silvana Costa Macedo of the Museu Nacional dos Coches; Maria José Sampaio of the Museu Nacional Machado de Castro; Laura Mónica Bessa Luís Baldaque of the Museu Nacional de Soares dos Reis; Ambassador Afonso de Castro of the Ministry of Foreign Affairs; Luís Alte da Veiga and Décio Ruivo Martins of the Museu de Física of the University of Coimbra; Dom António dos Reis Rodrigues, Dom Albino Cleto, and Cónego Manuel Lourenço of Lisbon Cathedral; Dom António de Castro Xavier Monteiro of Lamego Cathedral; Cónego Leal Pedrosa and Padre Aurélio de Campos of the New Cathedral of Coimbra; Nuno Vassallo e Silva of the Santa Casa da Misericórdia, Lisbon; the Provedor of the Ordem Terceira de São Francisco, Oporto; Cónego Luís Adriano of the Igreja de São Francisco, Évora; the Provedor of the Convento dos Cardais, Lisbon; Maria João Espírito Santo Bustorff Silva, Alexandra Bettencourt Jardim de Oliveira, and Pedro Severim de Melo of the Fundação Ricardo do Espírito Santo Silva; Bernardo Vasconcellos e Souza of Vista Alegre; J.Berardo and Francisco Capelo of the Fundação Berardo; Manuel Leitão of Solar; José Brito; and the anonymous lenders.

Along with the many individuals acknowledged in the Foreword for their roles in the distinguished consortium of corporate and foundation sponsors, the following were crucial to this undertaking: C. Lee Cox, President and Chief Executive Officer, PacTel Corporation; Jan Neels, President and Chief Executive Officer of Pacific Telesis International, and Ronald F. Stowe, Vice President of Washington Operations, and Lucie Gikovich, Director of Federal Relations, Pacific Telesis Group; at Espírito Santo Financial Holding S.A., Manuel Villas-Boas, Senior Vice President and U.K. Representative, Jackson Gilbert, Director, and Teresa de Souza, Vice President; at Banco Totta & Açores, José Alfredo Holtremann Roquette, President, and Luís de Castro e Almeida, Director of Public Relations; at Banco Comercial Português, Jorge Jardim Gonçalves, President, José Manuel Pinto Bastos, Secretary General, Pedro Libano Monteiro, Managing Director, and Maria de Los Angeles Sanchez, Deputy Director; at Investimentos e Participações Empresariais, S.A., José Manuel de Morais Cabral and Pedro Geraldes, Administrators; at the Luso-American Development Foundation, Luís dos Santos Ferro, Director; at the Gulbenkian Foundation, Maria Clara Farinha; at the Orient Foundation, Carlos Monjardino, President, João de Deus Ramos, Trustee, and João Rodrigues Calvão, Deputy Director; at the Instituto Camões, Luís Adão da Fonseca, President. At *Fortune* magazine, Fran Hall made it possible to include two exhibition-related pages in the April 1993 *Portugal* advertising supplement.

Many other colleagues and friends in Portugal who supported the project must be singled out: Fernando Albuquerque, Conde de Mangualde, his wife, Maria Amélia, and his daughter Inês; Augusto de Athayde; Maria Manuel Godinho de Almeida and Duarte Cabral de Melo; Alain Demoustier; Florindo Ferreira dos Santos; Helena Geraldes; José Maria Jorge and his family; João Marques Pinto; Jorge Lopes; Paulo Pereira; Maria João da Silva Pertana; and Elisabeth Plaister. Outside Portugal, the project received important help from Silvio Bedini, Miguel Bensaúde, Daniel J. Boorstin, Gabriele Borghini, Wolfram Koeppe, George Kubler, Claire Le Corbeiller, Susan Davidson, Chris Leone, Pedro Pinto da Silva, William Rieder, Nicolas Sapieha, Rita Varela Silva, and Michael Teague of the American Portuguese Society. Angela Delaforce and Kenneth Maxwell were helpful in countless ways, the latter assisted by Alberto Vourvoulias-Bush.

At the National Gallery, I am especially grateful to Director Earl A. Powell III for his warm support. Recognition should be given also to D. Dodge Thompson, Cameran G. Castiel, and Diane Martini Richard of the Exhibitions Department for their invaluable contributions; Elizabeth A. C. Perry, Corporate Relations Officer, who astutely managed the fund raising, ably assisted by Susan Davis; Daniel J. Herrick, Treasurer, and Joseph J. Krakora, External Affairs Officer; Gordon Anson and John Olson of the Department of Design and Installation; Ruth Kaplan, Information Officer, and Deborah Ziska and Nancy Soscia of her staff; Genevra Higginson of the Office of Special Events; Michelle Fondas of the Registrar's Office; Mervin Richard of the Conservation Division; and Susan Arensberg and Gail Feigenbaum of the Division of Education. In the Editors Office, Frances P. Smyth, Editor-in-Chief, Jane Sweeney, and Phyllis Hecht patiently shepherded this catalogue to completion. Isabel Dervaux, Gilberta Dantas, Jerry Mallick, Thomas F. J. McGill, Chris Vogel, Philip Walsh, Karen Weinberger, and Jeffrey Weiss were also of assistance. I wish to extend my warmest personal gratutude to Mr. and Mrs. Paul Mellon, Anita Engel, Michon Ornellas, Catherine Levenson, Claire Levenson, and Mary Schuette.

Jay A. Levenson

Preface

Portugal made her first grand appearance on the world stage during the Age of the Discoveries, the period that began in the mid-fifteenth century with the series of state-supported voyages that ultimately brought her merchants as far east as Japan. While the Portuguese trading empire languished in the later sixteenth and early seventeenth centuries, when the kings of Spain ruled Portugal, the international dimension to her commerce and culture never entirely disappeared. The wealth flowing into Portugal in the first decades of the eighteenth century from the discovery of phenomenal deposits of precious metals and gems in the colony of Brazil enabled her once again to become a major world power.

During the reign of Dom João V (1706–1750), the royal court became among the most brilliant in Europe. The earthquake that devastated Lisbon in 1755 brought this period of buoyant optimism to a sudden end, but it also helped to usher in the enlightenment. Under the rule of the marquês de Pombal, the all-powerful minister during the reign of Dom José I (1750–1777), the structure of government, commerce, and education underwent thoroughgoing reform. The destroyed center of Lisbon was rebuilt, following a rational design that reflected new concepts of city planning. The remarkable collection of scientific instruments assembled at the University of Coimbra, examples of which are included in this exhibition, attests to the spirit of this new age.

The visual arts thrived during this century of affluence. In general, the age of João V is associated with the baroque style, that of José I with the austere Pombaline style as well as with the rococo. Portugal's long-standing tradition of internationalism ensured that patrons of the arts looked to both domestic and foreign sources of production, encouraging a diversity of styles among the works they purchased and commissioned. Sculpture and the decorative arts, in particular, flourished; painting, which functioned mainly for portraiture and decoration, tends to be of lesser interest. The entries in this catalogue have been organized by the type of patronage represented—secular, royal, or religious—to give a sense of the various milieus in which the works exhibited originally functioned.

For the adornment of their households the nobility and the wealthy bourgeoisie could select from the finest objects the world had to offer. In the case of furniture, Portuguese dominance was assured by the ready supply of Brazilian hardwoods and the virtuosity with which cabinetmakers adapted foreign styles to local tastes. Portugal's traditional taste for the exotic is reflected in the popularity of lacquer decoration. The success of domestic jewelers was facilitated by the extensive import into Portugal of gemstones from Brazil. Also principally Portuguese were the design and production of animated compositions in the blue-and-white painted tiles known as *azulejos*, which decorated private and public interiors. For their tables the Portuguese commissioned elaborate services of Chinese export porcelain. The royal family had access to all these sources as well as to the ultra-luxurious silversmiths and goldsmiths of Paris, with whose works they vied to outshine the commissions of the French king himself.

The deeply devout João V began a tradition of lavish patronage of religious art that lasted through the century. His commissions brought works by the most famous late baroque sculptors and goldsmiths of Italy to the churches of Portugal, where they served as models for local artists. Religious buildings were also decorated with elaborate gilded woodcarving, polychromed statuary, and exuberant *azulejos*, creating a type of decorative ensemble that remains uniquely Portuguese.

The final section of the catalogue is devoted to a sumptuously decorated coach commissioned in Rome for João V's celebrated embassy to the Vatican in 1716. It is a characteristic example of the monarchy's use of the visual arts in support of political and social goals. The embassy was an essential element of a campaign to obtain concessions from the pope that would consolidate the king's power over the church in Portugal at a time when matters of church and state were central concerns for the kings of Catholic Europe. Like so many of the works in this exhibition, it is also a reminder that the masterpieces from this period have survived almost exclusively in Portugal's own public and private collections.

Jay A. Levenson
José de Monterroso Teixeira

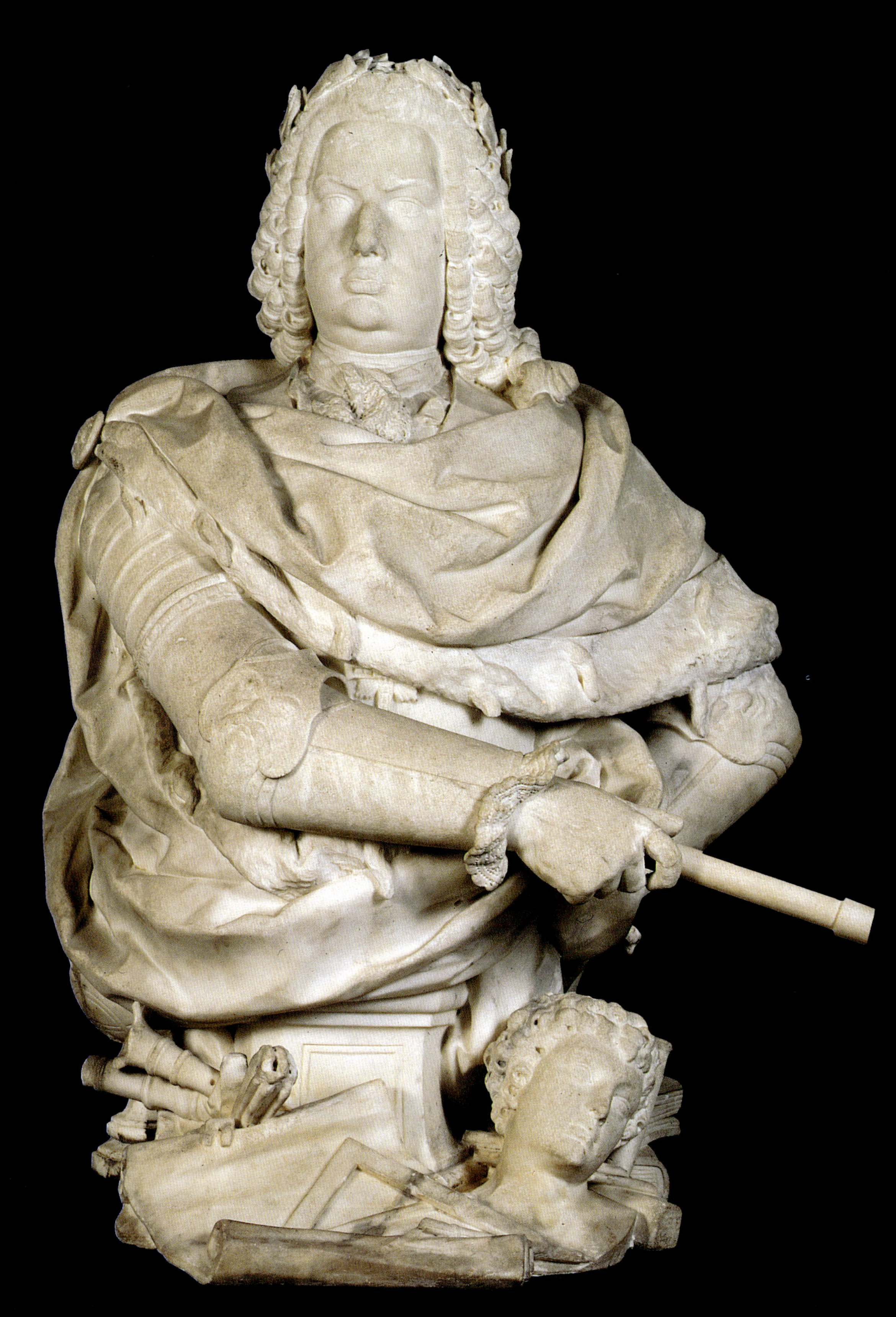

Portugal and the World in the Age of Dom João V

A. J. R. Russell-Wood

*I*n 1716, at age twenty-seven, Dom João V left Lisbon for his country palace at Vila Viçosa to convalesce from a bout of depression brought on by the realization that reasons of state, financial exigency, and his precarious health would prevent him from fulfilling his ambition to make the grand tour of Europe. Indeed, at no time during his long reign did the king leave Portuguese territory, a deeply felt lacuna for someone whose intellectual and cultural formation, and the diplomatic and commercial policies he pursued, enabled one of the smallest nations of Europe to be represented at international council tables and her king to be admired and respected in the courts of Europe. During Dom João V's reign, Lisbon continued as one of Europe's gateways to a wider world in the exchange of European goods for imports from Africa, America, and Asia. The imprint of the monarch was felt on every facet of his nation's life, on European diplomacy, and in areas as distinctive as China and Brazil. Internationalism was a strong feature of Portugal during his reign.

Circumstances of birth, family, education, upbringing, and personal inclination disposed Dom João to a vision that transcended his small country. The eldest son of Dom Pedro II of Portugal, his mother was Maria Elizabeth of Palatinate Neuburg. He married (1708) Maria Ana of Austria, and their offspring married the children of Philip V of Spain: José, heir to the Portuguese throne, married Maria Ana Victória; and Maria Bárbara married Fernando and became queen of Spain on his accession as Fernando VI. Dom João's brother, Manuel, spent nineteen years abroad, fought in the service of Prince Eugene of Savoy against the Turks, and was proposed as a possible king of Poland or of a kingdom of Sardinia and Corsica to be created by Charles VI of Austria. The greatest personal influence on Dom João was not from kith or kin, but from Louis XIV, "Le Roi Soleil." The Portuguese monarch aspired to emulate Louis' absolutism and the cultural prominence he achieved for France.

Versed in the languages and literature of France, Spain, and Italy, Dom João was an avid student of mathematics and sciences and a lover of music and the fine arts. He was a fellow of the Accademia dell'Arcadia in Rome. Dom João looked to European models for cultural institutions. The examples of the

fig. 1. Alessandro Giusti, *Bust of Dom João V*, 1748, marble. Palácio Nacional de Mafra

Académie Française and Academia Española spurred him to create (1720) the Academia Real de História Portuguesa, whose publications included the first attempt to catalogue Portuguese materials in Simancas. Dom João promoted the arts and *belles lettres* and was Maecenas to individual artists. The royal will was reflected in cultural contacts and exchanges between Portugal and other European countries.

Bibliophile and collector, Dom João commissioned his ambassadors, notably in Paris and Rome but also in London and Holland, to purchase manuscripts, music, rare books, missals, maps, atlases, and prints for the royal library. He ordered the copying of documents in Vatican archives relating to Portugal, comprising 222 volumes preserved in the Biblioteca da Ajuda in Lisbon. In addition to travel books about Portugal, French interest was reflected in histories of Portugal by Lequien de Neufville (1700) and La Clède (1735) published in France. The king's personal interest was shown by a royal appointment to and membership in the Order of Christ for de Neufville. Attributable to the king was the presence in Portugal (1723–1726) of the Swiss physician Merveilleux. Dom João commissioned Merveilleux to work in the royal mint, to write a natural history of Portugal, and to organize a museum of natural history for the king, who requested civil servants in Africa, India, and Brazil to send specimens. Under the royal patronage were published Johann Friedrich Pfeffinger's *Nouvelle Fortification,* a treatise on French, Spanish, Italian, and Dutch military architecture, and Rafaël Bluteau's *Vocabulário Portuguez e Latino* (1712–1721), a landmark in European lexicography. Acknowledgment of the importance of foreign languages was shown by publication in Portugal of Italian and Dutch grammars and the first English-Portuguese dictionary. This reaching for new linguistic horizons suggested a demand stemming not only from the book trade to Portugal of works in a variety of European languages, but also from intense diplomatic, commercial, and cultural interaction with countries beyond the Pyrenees whose nationals, in increasing numbers, resided in Portugal for extended periods. For the less gifted or less diligent, there were Portuguese translations from French, English, and Italian. The appearance (1715) of the weekly *Gazeta de Lisboa* removed any excuse not to be *au courant* with developments in Europe.

A hallmark of the reign of Dom João V was the commissioning of art, providing work for artists and ateliers in several countries. Italians and the French had the lion's share of such commissions. Few rivaled the commission to the Italian architects Luigi Vanvitelli and Nicola Salvi in Rome of a chapel dedicated to Saint John the Baptist, rich in eighteen types of marble, four types of alabaster, ormolu, porphyry, agate, lapis lazuli and amethysts, gilded bronze figures, gilded wood, mosaics, and paintings. This was finished in 1744 and transported to Lisbon for the church of São Roque, accompanied by Italian master craftsmen (see cats. 106–108). In the first decades of his reign, the king commissioned works from British silversmiths; but, such was the growing reputation of Thomas Germain that from the late 1720s the king patronized his *galeries du Louvre* and commissioned chandeliers, crowns, crosses, altar furnishings, and domestic silver including a huge silverware set, virtually all of which disappeared in the earthquake of 1755. For churches in which he had a special interest the king imported from Italy gilded silver pieces in the baroque style. The excellence of Portuguese tiles did not inhibit him from importing tiles from Holland. Nor did the presence of skilled coach builders in Portugal prevent the king from spending exorbitant sums on construction of coaches in Rome and elsewhere. He purchased materials from Italy, Holland, and France. Dom João also counted on Portuguese territories overseas and access to a multi-oceanic and multicontinental trade network to provide a rich and varied medley of media for artistic expression: diamonds, gold, and fine woods from Brazil, silver from Spanish America, silks from China, precious stones and ebony from India and Ceylon, and ivory from Africa.

Dom João V was a collector of people, notably foreign artists who found in the king a generous employer and in Portugal a hospitable cultural climate. Conspicuous was the Bavarian-born and Italian-trained architect João Frederico Ludovice, in whose erudition the king must have found a kindred spirit. Established in Lisbon as a goldsmith, Ludovice submitted the winning design for Mafra. Later he was appointed chief architect of the realm. In and around Oporto, the Tuscan architect and painter Nicolau Nasoni completed numerous works of which the most visible is the tower and church of the Clérigos. To the south the Hungarian-born and Italian-trained engineer and architect Carlos Mardel, who came to Portugal in 1733, designed the palaces of Oeiras, Junqueira, and Salvaterra, the convent of São João Nepomuceno, and even fountains. The Italian sculptor Alessandro Giusti came to Lisbon in 1747 to oversee assembly of the chapel of Saint John the Baptist and stayed to direct the school of sculpture in Mafra.

For painters and engravers, the king turned to France and Italy. There was a cohort of distinguished French engravers. Guilherme F. L. Debrie left some eight hundred prints created in the years 1729–1754, eclectic in their variety and including portraits of royalty and the aristocracy, and contributed to Caetano de Sousa's *História Genealógica da Casa Real Portuguesa*. Pierre Massar de Rochefort came to Lisbon in 1728, accompanied by his engraver son Charles, to make engravings for publications of the academy of history and also contributed to *História Genealógica*. Pierre played a major role in the history of printing in Portugal by selecting engravers to be invited to Lisbon to work in the new typography. Pierre-Antoine Quillard was the most prominent French painter in Portugal. Inspired by Watteau and with a precocious talent, he came to Portugal to illustrate the works of Merveilleux on natural history, undertook commissions for the dukes of Cadaval and portraits of the royal family, and painted ceilings and religious subjects. Other artists included Jean Ranc, French portraitist to Philip V, who visited Portugal to paint members of the royal family, and the Savoyard Giorgio Domenico Duprà whose portraits of royalty hang in the Bragança palace in Vila Viçosa. From Genoa came Giulio Cesare di Femine, who executed religious paintings, notably in the Convento da Graça, was elected to the governing body of the artists' guild of Saint Luke, and whose disciple was the Portuguese André Gonçalves. For the internal decoration of churches and altars, the Portuguese turned to Italy, as in the case of Francesco Trevisani whose Virgin and Saint Anthony can be seen in the *capela mor* of Mafra. Furniture of the Joanine era shows English influence in the Queen Anne style, the popularity of gate-leg tables, and skilled imitations of Chippendale, and French influence in addition to the popular *fauteuils*. Works by foreign artists were destroyed in the Lisbon earthquake of 1755. Victims included several *quadratura* ceilings by the Florentine artist Vincenzo Baccarelli, whose perspective painting lived on in the works of his pupil António Lobo. Other works did not come to fruition, as was the fate of designs for the church of the Patriarchate and new palace in Lisbon by the famous Turin architect Filippo Juvarra during six months in Portugal in 1719.

During the Joanine era Portugal received foreign artists and foreign influences whose legacy went beyond individuals or specific works of art. In architecture, Mafra, from its baroque dome to steeples, inspired derivative works. Neo-Palladianism of the chapel of Saint John the Baptist had a ripple effect on architecture in Lisbon and the south of Portugal, finding imitations in painted wood and on canvas. In the north Nasoni's interpretation of Italian baroque and of Italian-style villas had an impact. The introduction of the rococo has been attributed to the French painter Quillard and French engravers. The Frenchman Claude de Laprade breathed life into funerary sculpture, and imports by the king of marble statues from Italy had a major impact on carving in wood and stone. Even that most Portuguese of arts, tile work, depicts fountains in the form of statues whose introduction into Portugal has also been attributed to Nasoni. Imported Dutch tiles influenced the *albarrada* themes of Portuguese tiles, design of cheaper tiles each of which was a complete picture in its own right, and large scenes in churches reminiscent of tapestries. Be it in architecture, sculpture in wood and stone, perspective painting or portraiture, ceramics, silver, and furniture, the Joanine era was redolent with the impact of foreign influences and styles.

Other dimensions to this transmission are represented by music, the sciences, and metallurgy. The Neapolitan Domenico Scarlatti, preeminent harpsichordist, fine organist, and fecund composer, came to Lisbon to direct the Capela Real. With the elevation of the royal chapel to a Patriarchate, he headed the newly created musical seminary. During his nine years in Portugal (1720–1729), Scarlatti composed music for the court and was tutor to the Infanta Maria Bárbara. His most distinguished pupil was José Carlos de Seixas. Another musical seminary, that of Santa Catarina de Ribamar, was directed by a Venetian cleric. Italian music had already been introduced into Portugal, but its greater prominence was directly attributable to the king who invited Italian musicians and whose interest was demonstrated by the construction of an opera house (1737) and the organization of a musical library that was destroyed in the 1755 earthquake. From Spain came the popular *zarzuela*. Royal interest in mathematics was reflected not only in the importation of instrumentation but of three professors of mathematics from Italy: Pe Francesco Musarra and the Jesuits Domenico Capaci and Giovanni Battista Carbone. Carbone was tutor to the Infanta Maria Bárbara and became influential at court. Also from Italy came Bernardo Santucci to hold the chair of anatomy from 1732–1747. After suspension of anatomical dissections, he was reduced to teaching theory. He created a school of anatomy whose leading lights were Caetano Alberto and Santos Gato who became professors at the University of Coimbra. Santucci also published the first anatomy text in Portuguese in Portugal. Three botanists who achieved international reputations were born in the reign of Dom João: the Jesuit João de Loureiro, who spent thirty-six years in Cochin China and whose *Flora Cochinchinensis* was published in 1790; Félix de Avelar Brotero whose botanical compendium was published in Paris in 1788; and José Francisco Correia da Serra who opened a botanical seminar in Philadelphia in 1813 and became Portuguese minister plenipotentiary to the United States.

In addition to exponents of fine arts and of theoretical or applied sciences, foreigners were vehicles for technology transfer. The French opener of the seals Antoine Mengin fell within this category. Brought to Portugal in 1721 to work in the royal mint, he specialized in coins, commemorative medallions, and portraits. At Mafra the Frenchman Nicolau Levache established a foundry to make the bells, although the carillons were made in Antwerp. A glass factory at Coina was directed by an Irishman. When the king promoted a national silk industry, he turned to French horticulturalists for advice on planting mulberry trees and to Robert Godin as first director (1734) of the royal silk factory in the Rato. Such technocrats trained Portuguese to become proficient in their skills. Dom João was reluctant to countenance European nationals in Portuguese territories overseas. An exception were French textile workers on São Miguel in the Azores in the first part of the eighteenth century.

There were foreign influences present at the court bearing on the history of intimacy in Portugal. From France came wigs and perfumes. French fashions, dress, and even speech were mimicked. There was an influx of furniture: sideboards, secretaries, tables, gilded *talha,* beds gilded in silver and gold, chairs, and personal items such as silver-topped canes and timepieces.

Portugal exerted a centrifugal as well as a centripetal force in the transmission of the arts, sciences, technology, and people. The king encouraged Portuguese artists, scientists, and scholars to study abroad. About 1720 he established the Accadèmia di Belle Arti Portoghese in Rome. Among artists, the painter known as Vieira Lusitano (Francisco Vieira de Matos), who resided in Rome where he studied with Benedetto Lutti and Trevisani, was destined to achieve the most fame. In 1727 he was made an *accademico di merito* of the academy of Saint Luke in Rome. Later he lived in England and Seville before being appointed royal painter in Lisbon. Among Portuguese sculptors who went to Italy the most distinguished was José de Almeida who studied with Carlo Monaldi and carved with equal skill in wood and in marble and whose most important work is the *Crucified Christ between Angels* in the church of Santo Estevão in Lisbon. Musicians who studied in Italy included João Rodrigues Esteves, António Teixeira, and Francisco António de Almeida whose operas were well received. Portuguese scholars taught in European universities. In distant Beijing, Portuguese missionaries were making astronomical observations.

The intellectual and cultural Europeanization of Portugal gave rise to the *estrangeirados* (foreignized). These were Portuguese who lived for extended periods outside Portugal and became steeped in economic and political thought, literature, and the arts beyond the Pyrenees. They returned to Portugal with new ideas and concepts. Two examples will illustrate the breed. The autodidact Martinho de Mendonça de Pina e Proença visited Spain, Italy, Germany, and France, was mathematical tutor to the Infante Dom Manuel, organized the royal library, was ambassador in Madrid, interim governor of Minas Gerais, and director of the Torre do Tombo archive in Lisbon. Another was Alexandre de Gusmão, born in Santos in Brazil (1695), educated at the Jesuit college in Bahia and at the University of Coimbra, who was private secretary to the Portuguese ambassador in Paris and studied law at the Sorbonne. He returned to Coimbra to receive a degree in canon law and resided in Rome before becoming private secretary to Dom João V. Their intellectual brilliance, culture, wit, and cosmopolitan mien recommended these men for high office. Some men of science did not return. Dr. Jacob de Castro Sarmento and Dr. António Nunes Ribeiro Sanches fled to England to escape the Inquisition; the former was elected a fellow of the Royal Society. Another aspect of this intellectual internationalism were students from overseas, overwhelmingly from Brazil, who studied at Coimbra and took holy orders or entered the civil service or magistracy and who stayed in Portugal or received overseas postings.

Although geographically remote, Portugal has a long history of participation in European affairs. Dom João V pursued diplomacy intensely. He inherited the diplomatic tangle and war born of disputes over Spanish succession between the houses of Bourbon and Habsburg after the death of Charles II of Spain in 1700. The Grand Alliance (1701) of Britain, the United Provinces, Austria, and some German states had declared war on France. Portugal had been forced to take a stand and had joined the alliance on behalf of the Austrian Archduke Charles. Allied access to Portuguese ports was decisive. In 1704 Franco-Spanish forces had attacked Portugal and been repelled. Seesaw campaigns, border raids, and counter raids in 1705 and 1706 raised hopes of a successful allied outcome with the Portuguese marquês de Minas commanding the army that took Madrid in 1706, saw the acclamation of Charles III, and moved on to Catalonia. At this juncture the seventeen-year-old Dom João came to the throne. Portugal's allegiance to the alliance was strengthened by his marriage to Archduchess Maria Ana of Austria. Campaigns in 1707 and afterward saw progressive erosion of the allied position, defeat at Almansa, demoralization of the Portuguese army, food shortages and famine, lost hope of launching invasions from Valencia or Portugal, battlefield defeats, and reverses often attributable to poor judgment and allied dithering. Spanish forces battered the Alentejo, Beira, and Minho, and Portuguese entered Andalusia and León. Portuguese lost and retook (1711) Miranda do Douro and heroically defended (1712) Campo Maior. The raison d'être for the alliance, namely to prevent Bourbon domination of Europe, was replaced by the specter, following the death of Emperor Joseph I in 1711 and the choice of Charles to succeed to the imperial throne, that, should Charles also become king of Spain, there would be a revived and dominant Habsburg empire. England pulled out of the alliance, but not without having secured Portugal's position at the bargaining table at Utrecht. The Spanish people had not taken kindly to Charles. Philip V was firmly ensconced on the Spanish throne. In 1712 peace discussions opened at Utrecht. Portugal signed a peace treaty with France (1713) and with Spain (1715). The failure of the alliance was a blow. Portugal had counted on fulfillment of promises made by the allies in 1703. The country had been ravaged by war and the treasury was depleted.

The lesson was well learned. The Spanish capture of Sardinia and Sicily in 1717 and 1718 led to the Quadruple Alliance of France, Britain, the United Provinces, and Austria against Philip V. Dom João V remained neutral, resisting English and French pressures seeking to benefit from Portugal's strategic position, but did press to be included at discussions to be held at Cambrai. In 1725 Portugal remained neutral in the dispute of the Maritime Powers against Spain and the emperor. British opposition to the marriages that would unite the houses of Spain and Portugal, and Dom João's own wish to avoid any damage to Portugal's alliance with George I, were made moot by the ingenious proposal that the marriage issue should be discrete from negotiations taking place in Vienna.

A decade elapsed before Europe was again embroiled, this time over the issue of Polish succession in 1732. Promoting his father-in-law Stanislaw Leszczynski, Louis XV allied himself with Spain and Sardinia against Austria and Russia. Dom João was heavily courted. The emperor offered Sicily and Corsica to Dom Manuel and the prospect of marriage between the Portuguese prince Dom Pedro and an archduchess whose dowry would include the duchies of Parma and Tuscany, should Dom João support his brother as the candidate. England offered Galicia if Portugal opposed Spain. But Dom João adhered to a policy of neutrality. Walpole's declaration of war on Spain in 1739 over free navigation in American waters raised Franco-Spanish fears that Portugal would align with England. Portugal again adopted a position of neutrality, asking in return for concessions in South America.

The death of Emperor Charles VI in 1740 plunged Europe into the War of Austrian Succession. Portugal remained uninvolved during these years of European upheaval; however, acting either in response to an initiative proposed by the French foreign minister, the marquis d'Argenson—endorsed by the warring powers—or as the result of a suggestion made by Dom João V to the French chargé d'affaires in Lisbon expressing willingness to act as mediator, Dom João did draw up preliminary articles for a settlement. When these were rejected by France he withdrew, but a momentum of expectation was built leading to the Peace of Aix-la-Chapelle in 1748.

Portugal's studied neutrality in Europe-wide disputes after 1715 did not preclude intense bilateral diplomacy. Dom João's religious convictions and his ambition to promote Portugal as a major power led him aggressively to pursue relations with the Vatican. Only two major disagreements, attributable to excessive royal pressure for exceptional concessions and to the seriousness with which the king accepted his duty to defend the concept of *Padroado Real,* respectively, marred cordial relations. The first concerned the appointment of Monsignor Vincenzo Bichi as papal nunzio in Lisbon in 1710. Already in 1707 Dom João had instructed his ambassador in Rome to press for the extension to Portugal of a privilege enjoyed by papal nunzios in Madrid, Paris, and Vienna, namely that nunzios to Lisbon receive cardinals' hats and that no appointment be made unless a list of nominees had previously been submitted to the king and received his approval. A poor diplomat who disobeyed instructions, Bichi was not a good test case. The pope refused this concession, whereupon Dom João broke off diplomatic relations with the Vatican in 1728. Relations were restored when one of the first acts of Clement XII was to raise Bichi to the cardinalate. The second concerned *Padroado Real,* those rights and privileges granted by the papacy in the fifteenth century to Portuguese monarchs to promote the spread of the Gospel overseas. Since 1622 the Congregatio de Propaganda Fide in Rome had encouraged popes to infringe on the *Padroado.* Papal appointments had been made and prelates and missionaries dispatched to Asia directly from Rome. Questions over the China mission prompted a 1711 Portuguese embassy to Rome to seek clarification over jurisdiction. In all other matters Dom João supported the Vatican. Doctrinal controversies within the French church attributable to Jansenism prompted the papal bull *Unigenitus dei filius* (1713) condemning the 101 propositions contained in the *Réflexions morales*. A document authored by doctors of the University of Coimbra unequivocally supported the pope. This support could take a more practical turn. Turks under Sultan Ahmed III had retaken the Peloponnesus and the Venetian fortress on Crete and the sultan declared war on Venice and Austria. The doge appealed to the pope who, in turn, appealed to other Catholic nations. In 1716 Dom João dispatched a squadron of six warships and support vessels and 2,581 soldiers to Corfu, but already the Turks had retreated and the vessels returned to the Tagus untested. The continuing threat merited sending another armada in 1717. This became part of a joint allied force that defeated the Turks at the battle of Cape Matapan. Portugal played a very different role when Dom João acted as mediator between the Vatican and Maria Theresa of Austria, which led to papal recognition of Francis I as emperor.

Such support did not go unrecognized. On the occasion of the births of Maria Bárbara (1711) and Dom Pedro (1712), Pope Clement sent swaddling clothes he had blessed, a highly prized gift commemorating the garments in which Jesus had been wrapped by the Virgin. The greatest concession granted by Rome was the Patriarchate of Lisbon, created by papal bull in 1716. Dom João's further efforts to aggrandize the church in Portugal were rewarded in 1737 when the pope granted a cardinal's hat to the patriarch of Lisbon. Creation of the Patriarchate in Lisbon caused a sensation in Europe. These were the highlights of a mutually beneficial relationship that saw numerous papal bulls favoring Portugal. The greatest personal accolade garnered by Dom João V came nineteen months before his death. By a papal bull of 23 December 1748, Benedict XIV granted him the title of "Most Faithful." The king of Portugal could stand shoulder to shoulder with the "Most Christian" king of France and the "Most Catholic" king of Spain.

Relations with France were suspended during the War of Spanish Succession but restored at Utrecht. The French refusal to accede to Portugal's request for a seat at Cambrai led Portugal to downgrade diplomatic representation from ambassador to envoy but not to suspend relations. A dispute over protocol postponed an exchange of ambassadors until 1739. The abbé de Livry was named in 1724 by Louis XV as French ambassador to Portugal. The abbot's perspective that in the hierarchy of European powers France ranked higher than Portugal led to disagreement between the ambassador-designate and the Portuguese secretary of state Diogo de Mendonça Corte Real as to who should be the first to call on the other. The outcome was the departure of the abbot without presenting his credentials. Periodically Dom João protested to the French king about predations by French corsairs against Portuguese vessels.

The issue of diplomatic jurisdiction also provoked tense relations with Austria. The custom whereby ambassadorial jurisdiction extended beyond embassies to the immediate neighborhood had been abolished by Dom Pedro II. In 1709 the emperor's ambassador instructed his staff to prevent Portuguese from entering the proximity of his embassy. Embassy staff obstructed passage of a constable escorting a prisoner who was subsequently given asylum in the embassy. Portuguese authorities downplayed the incident, but the ambassador, believing he had found weakness and anticipating support from the queen, an Austrian, lodged a formal complaint and incited other ambassadors to join him. He received an official reprimand. There was a similar incident in 1710. The secretary of state ensured that the Austrian ambassador could not reach the queen, and forced him and his cronies to accept the Portuguese position.

At Utrecht, Portugal and Spain agreed to return what each had captured. Portugal returned the frontier garrisons of Puebla de Senabria and Albuquerque; Spain returned the castle of Noudar and the river island of Verdoejo. Spain proved recalcitrant in complying with five other terms of the treaty. In addition to Spanish-American issues, there were three points that soured relations between the two countries. One concerned compensation claimed by the Portuguese Companhia Real da Guiné in accordance with the terms of the contract for providing slaves to Spanish America and repayment of a loan to Charles II. The former was waived but the Spanish crown agreed to pay six hundred thousand *escudos*. Spain claimed compensation for three vessels homeward bound from Buenos Aires: two entered Rio de Janeiro and were confiscated in 1704; the third went aground off the Algarve. Spain overlooked the fact that in 1703 it had captured Portuguese vessels but was now challenging Portuguese assertions that the same conditions prevailed.

Relations between Portugal and Spain were greatly enhanced by the marriages of the offspring of Dom João V and of Philip V agreed to in 1725, with final exchange of the princesses in 1729, but all was not smooth sailing. The friendship of Pedro Álvares Cabral, Portuguese ambassador to the Spanish court, with the prince of Asturias and his Portuguese bride provoked the jealousy of Isabella Farnese, second wife of Philip V, and exacerbated tensions already present between Philip V and his son and anti-Portuguese sentiment at court. In 1735 a chance incident in Madrid proved inflammatory. A convict escaped his escort and sought asylum in the Portuguese embassy. Spanish authorities alleged that he had been assisted by embassy staff and troops attacked the embassy, retook the convict, and arrested and jailed nineteen staff members. This breach of diplomatic immunity sparked a parallel response in Lisbon. Portuguese troops invaded the Spanish embassy and arrested nineteen employees. Both ambassadors were recalled and both armies were put on alert. Treaty obligations led Britain to send twenty-six naval vessels under Admiral Norris to the Tagus where they stayed for two years. Fearing that Portugal might seek alliance with England and Austria against Spain, and seeing an opportunity to reopen relations with Portugal, Louis XV mediated a settlement signed in Paris in 1737. The strong influence of Maria Bárbara on her husband and her closeness to her father were critical to Luso-Hispanic relations, especially after the accession of Fernando to the throne of Spain in 1746 and the ouster from the court of Isabella Farnese.

Britain had been a long-standing ally of Portugal, and from the Portuguese perspective was important because of her maritime strength, which deterred Franco-Spanish pretensions, and as a commercial partner. Furthermore, Dom João recognized that Portugal was well served by stability in the Mediterranean. Papal entreaties aside, this may have led him to support Venice against the Turks. It also led Portugal to support British occupation of Gibraltar. Commercial ties also united England and Portugal, the most recent being the Methuen Treaty of 1703. Throughout the reign of Dom João V, Britain outdid Portugal as the major beneficiary of the Brazil trade. One aspect of what became a high degree of dependency concerned wheat supplies to Portugal. Following a bad harvest in Britain, exports were suspended in 1740, which led to tension between the two countries.

Struggles between European powers were often played out on stages in America, Africa, and Asia. As the richest jewel in the Portuguese crown, Brazil was a magnet for foreign interlopers. French corsairs menaced the Brazilian coast, and Rio de Janeiro was the object of two attacks. In 1710 Du Clerc, backed by Louis XIV, landed, fought his way to the city center, and only capitulated after losing half his force in a bloody fight. Du Clerc was murdered while under house arrest. In 1711, the Breton pirate Duguay-Trouin's bombardment forced evacuation of the city and capitulation. After occupying Rio for two months, he departed with full holds. Fernão de Noronha, an island off the Brazilian coast and a penal colony, also attracted corsairs. In 1738 Portugal reaffirmed its hold by landing soldiers and taking as prisoners some twenty French and other nationals. All the while the lure of Spanish silver ensured lively British interest in the Río de la Plata, and anticipation of contraband Brazilian gold led to the presence of British vessels off the Brazilian coast.

In South America, ill-defined or absent boundaries were the prime source of Portuguese disagreements with France and Spain. The 1713 agreement at Utrecht resolved the dispute between France and Portugal that had resulted from French expansionism from Cayenne. France renounced rights to lands granted by the 1701 treaty to Cabo do Norte, a region bordered to the south by the Amazon and to the north by the River Oyapock, and recognized Portuguese navigation rights on the Amazon and sovereignty of both its banks. France also agreed not to send missionaries into Portuguese territory. Portugal was thus able to rebuild forts demolished by the French and the River Oyapock became the boundary between France and Portugal in South America.

Portuguese disputes with Spain in America had their genesis in the 1494 Treaty of Tordesillas. Portuguese adventurers had infiltrated into regions west of the meridian set by Tordesillas with general impunity and apparently tacit acceptance by Spain. But Spain was highly sensitive about Río de la Plata and the region between the rivers Paraná and Uruguay. Dom Pedro II had tried to formalize the north bank of Río de la Plata as Brazil's southern border by incorporating this region into the jurisdiction of the bishop of Rio de Janeiro and establishing a colony in 1680 at Sacramento opposite Buenos Aires. This set the scene for protracted diplomatic negotiations in Europe and hostilities between Spanish and Portuguese troops in America. At Utrecht, Spain recognized the north bank of Río de la Plata as Portuguese and as the southern border of Brazil. Portugal was confirmed in its possession of Sacramento and contiguous lands. At issue was not only that Sacramento was a Portuguese needle in the side of the Spanish governor of Buenos Aires, but the broader strategic concern of Portuguese maritime access to Río de la Plata and the politico-commercial dimension of contraband. There was also the delicate issue of Portuguese expansionism into the area of Jesuit missions on the River Uruguay and along the north coast of La Plata east of Sacramento. Spanish governors in Buenos Aires resented a Portuguese presence on their doorstep, and sought to thwart, or only grudgingly acknowledged, diplomatic agreements. The 1720s and 1730s witnessed establishment of Portuguese settlements such as Montevideo and Spanish counteroffensives to oust them. In 1735 the governor of Buenos Aires blockaded Sacramento by sea and bombarded it from the land and a two-year siege was only lifted after Portuguese reinforcements arrived. Though an armistice was signed in Paris in 1737, only with the death of Philip V could progress be made. A Portuguese princess as queen of Spain and Brazilian-born Alexandre de Gusmão as Dom João's personal secretary made settlement of boundary disputes viable. Six months before Dom João V's death a treaty was signed at Madrid (13 January 1750) fixing the boundaries of Spanish and Portuguese America. Based on the principle of *uti possidetis,* the treaty gave sanction to Portuguese settlements west of the Tordesillas meridian. Portugal gave up Sacramento and contiguous lands and navigation rights on the Río de la Plata and Spain renounced claims to navigation rights on the Amazon and to the region occupied by seven mission stations to the east of the River Uruguay. Signing of the treaty brought neither immediate implementation nor peace but instead ushered in a further quarter century of hostilities only resolved by the Treaty of San Ildefonso in 1777.

Although Portuguese America had achieved a position so preeminent in the Portuguese-speaking world as to lead a seasoned adviser to the king to suggest transferral of the court to Brazil and appointment of a viceroy for Portugal, there was also a Portuguese territorial presence in Africa, Asia, and the Indonesian archipelago. Mazagão was all that remained of an earlier strong Portuguese presence in Morocco. In Africa, Portuguese interests focused on Angola, and there were trading posts on the Guinea coast and Gulf of Guinea. In East Africa, the Portuguese flag flew over the Mozambique coast and inland. On the west coast of India, the Província do Norte extended from Bombay to Daman and included Chaul, Bassein, Diu, Daman, some islands and a trading post at Surat, and the Província do Sul comprised Goa, Salsette, and Bardez. Macao in China and parts of the Indonesian islands of Timor and Solor were also under Portuguese control. Portugal counted numerous trading posts and islands, of which by the eighteenth century the most important were the Atlantic archipelagoes of the Cape Verdes, Azores, and Madeira and, in the Gulf of Guinea, São Tomé and Príncipe, Fernando Pó, and Annobón.

A Portuguese presence in Africa and Asia was a source of hostilities between Europeans. The French sacked Benguela (1705), São Tomé and Príncipe (1709) and plundered Ribeira Grande and Praia in the Cape Verdes (1712). In 1723 the Portuguese destroyed a fort raised by the British engaged in the slave trade in Cabinda, but Dutch and British corsairs resisted Portuguese attempts to oust them from the Costa da Mina and Angolan coast. It was much the same story in East Africa. Attracted by hopes of gold, Dutch and British focused on the region around Lourenço Marques in the 1720s and 1730s and were joined by French corsairs. In the Indonesian archipelago, the Dutch incited the local populace against the Portuguese. Throughout the reign of Dom João V, French, Dutch, and British corsairs harassed Portuguese in the waters of the Atlantic, Indian, and Pacific oceans.

The multicontinental nature of the Portuguese empire led to diplomatic relations with non-Europeans. The Portuguese were representing not only national interests but Christianity. This was the case of relations with China, which were akin to walking on eggshells and conducted at two levels: between Lisbon and Beijing as ruler to ruler and between Macao and Canton as captain to viceroy. Gifts sent by Emperor Kangxi to Dom João V were lost when the vessel carrying them burned in Rio de Janeiro in 1722; in 1725 Dom João V dispatched an embassy led by Alexandre Metelo de Sousa de Meneses that arrived in Beijing in May 1727 and was well received. The ambassador conveyed the royal condolences to Emperor Yongzheng on the death of his father and presented gifts from Dom João. Two months passed in audiences, banquets, and visits outside Beijing and were characterized by goodwill and improved conditions for missionaries. Yongzheng's anti-Western stance found practical application in harassing trade in and out of Macao and imposing Chinese customs. On the grounds that Chinese in Macao were exempt from Portuguese laws, the Chinese insisted on appointment of a mandarin in Macao in 1736 to pass judgment on Chinese infractors. A Chinese penal code was introduced into Macao in 1749. Despite the best efforts of the captain, city councilors, and bishop of Macao, tense relations with the authorities in Canton prevailed, often attributable to high-handed enforcement of imperial edicts or to local initiatives calculated to inconvenience the Portuguese.

In India, the Portuguese faced a multiplicity of rulers with whom an attempt was made to have reasonably harmonious relations. As viceroy, the count of Ericeira was particularly diligent to maintain cordial relations with the shah of Persia and the Great Mughal. Across the Indian Ocean, in East and West Africa, much of the Portuguese effort was directed toward diplomatic maneuvering between competing local interests and rivalries. There were two exceptional instances in which local leaders took diplomatic initiatives. So apprehensive was the king of the island of São Lourenço because of Dutch and British vessels in the Mozambique channel, that in 1722 he sent an embassy to Portugal. The three ambassadors were received by Dom João, and the Portuguese were granted freedom to trade from the island's ports and establish trading posts. The 1720s also saw the sultan of Pate sending an embassy to Goa seeking alliance with the Portuguese for protection against the intrigues and rivalries of sultanate politics on the Swahili coast. In Portuguese America, sporadic peace settlements, as with the Tapuia of northeastern Brazil, were short-lived or coerced. In the Maranhão, the chiefs of the warrior Barbados, Arua and Guarané, offered peace and friendship in the 1720s and swore allegiance to Dom João. Other peoples resisted and were massacred after surrendering, whereas still others, such as the Bororo in Mato Grosso, allied themselves with the Portuguese in wars against fellow native Americans.

Portuguese overseas often found themselves in conflicts with non-Europeans. In Brazil, the reign of Dom João saw Portuguese moving into the interior to raise cattle and seek gold. Exploratory and punitive expeditions destroyed indigenous peoples and committed atrocities. Not all such offensives were the fruits of settlers on an uncontrolled rampage. Dom João was directly involved in some decision making. In 1708 the king declared war on the Anaperu and other tribes of the Maranhão and later approved the declaration of "just war" against the Paiaguá and other peoples of Cuiabá. Contracts for offensives against native peoples in Brazil were funded by the royal exchequer.

In Africa, regions of conflict were Morocco, Angola, and Mozambique. In Morocco, the fort and town of Mazagão was isolated and made dependent on Lisbon for supplies; its inhabitants were victims of skirmishes, ambushes, and harassment. Only in 1745 was the sultan of Meknes repelled after two decades of attacks against the Portuguese outpost. In Angola, the Portuguese had three priorities: to maintain a presence despite local offensives; to bring local rulers to cooperate, if not to submit; and ensure as little disruption as possible to the slave trade. Garrisons were repeatedly threatened, invaded, and even occupied before counteroffensives reinstated the Portuguese. Portuguese expansion inland brought war from 1739 to 1744 with the state of Matamba. The volatile mixture of indigenous rivalries, expanding areas for procuring slaves, British suppliers of firearms and gunpowder, and European and African opportunism and greed provoked violence. In East Africa, Mombasa, Pate, Pemba, Zanzibar, and Malindi had been lost to the Omani in 1698. Mombasa was retaken in 1728 by an expeditionary force from Goa, but within two years the Omanis regained control of the Swahili coast and Mombasa.

The Indian Ocean and west coast of India saw Portuguese warring on sea and on land. In 1719, Portuguese under Admiral António Figueiredo Utra scored resounding naval defeats against Arab fleets. Land campaigns were characterized by heavy loss of life and massive destruction of property inflicted by the Portuguese, as illustrated by two examples. During the viceroyalty (1712–1717) of Vasco Fernandes César de Meneses, the raja of Kanara reneged on a treaty to provide Goa with rice at a fixed price and alleged that Portuguese had insulted him. The viceroy dispatched eleven vessels carrying soldiers who destroyed boats, burned pagodas, razed coastal villages, and bombarded Mangalore. The raja asked for peace, which the Portuguese granted on humiliating terms. Meneses' successor as viceroy, the count of Ericeira, launched an expedition against Popotane near Diu, which had refused to pay tribute—reducing it to ashes, killing some 1,500 people, and forcing payment of enormous financial indemnity. The Maratha menace intensified and gained the upper hand in the late 1730s. Peshwa Baji Rao I founded the north Maratha empire in part at the expense of the Portuguese Província do Norte and destroyed a Portuguese fleet. If the Portuguese had not agreed to pay tribute, Goa would also have been lost. The count of Ericeira, returning to India as viceroy in 1741, headed an expeditionary force of six ships and two thousand soldiers to wage war against the Marathas. Despite reverses, the Portuguese achieved restoration of lands and forts, gained new territories, and secured a peace that lasted to the 1790s. Another dimension to such hostilities was when Portuguese became engaged in disputes between indigenous rulers, as occurred in East Africa and the Malayan archipelago where the Portuguese officially threw their support behind one sultan against rivals.

Commerce was the glue that bound the national, intra-European, and global dimensions of Portugal during the reign of Dom João V. Portugal continued a lively trade with European neighbors and with her principal trading partner, Britain. France, Germany, and Spain were also major trading partners in a trade diaspora extending to Ireland, the Baltic, and Italy. This network should not blind one to the fact that, of goods exported by Portugal to European nations, the proportion by volume or value originating in Portugal was small. A high proportion of Portuguese exports originated beyond Europe, and a high proportion of goods imported into Portugal from Europe had extracontinental destinations, especially Brazil. Throughout his reign Dom João faced a trade deficit in which imports exceeded exports. Had it not been for Brazilian gold, diamonds, and sugar this deficit would have been greater. If England were the prime beneficiary of Brazilian gold and diamonds, it was not alone. By a trickle-down process, Brazilian gold permeated the European economy.

This is not the place for detailed discussion of the extra-European dimension of the Portuguese trading diaspora. Suffice it to say that there were maritime routes transporting commodities between Portugal and Morocco, the Atlantic islands, East and West Africa, Brazil, Indian Ocean ports, Macao, Solor, and Timor. Most lucrative were the *carreira da India* and the *carreira do Brasil,* both of which had Lisbon as a terminal. There were also trade networks without a European component: in the Atlantic between Brazil and West Africa, in the Indian Ocean between the Persian Gulf and Mozambique and India, and beyond India to Ceylon, Malacca, Macao, and Indonesia. Madeira, the Azores, and the Cape Verdes were points of articulation between Europe, America, and Africa, as too was São Tomé in the Gulf of Guinea. Portuguese ports and trading posts on the Atlantic seaboard of West and Central Africa, the Indian Ocean, the Malay Straits, and China Sea were points for procurement and redistribution of European and indigenous products. The variety of this multicontinental trade cannot be overemphasized. Contraband was prominent, be it silver from Spanish America carried by the Portuguese to Europe and India or Brazilian gold that arrived in England and Amsterdam. Regulations prohibiting non-Portuguese vessels from putting into Brazilian ports were disregarded or unenforceable. The Atlantic islands were points of convergence for contraband originating in and whose final destinations were Africa, Asia, the Caribbean, and North America. Concessions to non-Portuguese to trade in the Cape Verde Islands, São Tomé, and other ports were granted in the hope of lessening contraband, but met with mixed results.

There were other aspects of this international trade diaspora. Portuguese collaborated in commercial ventures with non-Europeans and non-Christians, be it for venture capital, obtaining transportation, and acquiring and distributing commodities. This cross-cultural dimension, especially noticeable in India and Asia, continued a long-standing practice. Non-Portuguese traded between ports under Portuguese control. There was limited authorized residence by nationals of other European nations in Portugal and her overseas territories. Merchants predominated. Oporto counted a flourishing British colony, and the commercial community of Lisbon was international as regards Europeans. Reference has been made to French and British technicians in Portugal. As for Brazil, permission had been granted for a small number of Dutch and British merchants to reside in Bahia, Rio, and Pernambuco. There were British and French consuls in Portuguese ports overseas. Foreigners included men of the cloth. Most in evidence were Jesuits, often in strategically sensitive regions as in parts of Brazil. There were incidents in frontier areas of Spanish Jesuits inciting native Americans to leave Portuguese territories, refusing to acknowledge boundaries set by Portugal or Spain, and instigating rebellions.

It can be argued that the reign of Dom João V was the golden age of Portugal. This was true in the sense that during his reign about five hundred tons of Brazilian gold were landed on the wharves of Lisbon. There also accrued to the royal coffers large sums derived from taxes, tariffs, dues, and "voluntary contributions." On the debit side were heavy expenses for the upkeep of metropolis and empire. Whatever he undertook, Dom João V did in great style. His ambassadors were not only heard from Beijing to Utrecht, but were highly visible. The Manchu court was dazzled by the splendor of the embassy of Sousa de Meneses. Before the chapel dedicated to John the Baptist was transported to Lisbon in 1747, it was on display in the church of Sant'Antonio dei Portoghesi in Rome at the express wish of Pope Benedict XIV whose visit was the occasion for a magnificent reception. Ostentation was part of the portfolio of every ambassador. That foreign policy was not built on style alone but had substance was shown by the admission of Portugal to the council chambers of Europe and the successful preservation of Portuguese neutrality. From Timor to Morocco, Portuguese negotiated, accommodated, and maneuvered to gain advantage, but the king and his representatives did not shy from warfare against non-Europeans and Europeans threatening Portuguese interests. This policy of aggrandizement of king and country, coupled with his own intellectual breadth of interests, led Dom João V to make Portugal receptive not only to the arts, literatures, fashions, and styles of Europe but also a repository for works of art from beyond Europe. Testimony to the international hallmark of the reign of Dom João V and a legacy more enduring than treaties and diplomatic protocols is the international provenance of works of art dating from the first half of the eighteenth century whose richness and variety can be appreciated by visitors to the churches, palaces, and museums of Portugal.

Dom João V awaits his biographer in English, but there is much material on his internationalism as represented in cultural exchanges and artistic influences on Portugal, diplomacy, and commerce. Essays and monographs of the life and times genre are light on the life, with the exception of his conventual loves, and heavy on the times. This is the case of the work of Manuel Bernardes Branco, *Portugal na épocha de D. João V* (Lisbon, 1885) and Mário Domingues, *D. João V. O homem e a sua época. Evocação histórica* (Lisbon, 1964). A good overview is provided by Eduardo Brazão, *D. João V. Subsídios para a história do seu reinado* (Oporto, 1945). Essays in *D. João V. Conferências e estudos comemorativos do segundo centenário da sua morte (1750–1950)* (Lisbon, 1952) provide an introduction, with those of Reinaldo dos Santos and Mário de Sampayo Ribeiro focusing on art and music respectively. The best introduction to Portuguese art remains Robert C. Smith, *The Art of Portugal, 1500–1800* (New York, 1968). For Italian artists in Portugal, see Emilio Lavagnino, *Gli artisti italiani in Portogallo* (Rome, 1940), especially chapter 5. Diplomacy during his reign has been well described by Eduardo Brazão, *Portugal no Tratado de Utrecht, 1712–1715* (Lisbon, 1933), *Dom João V e a Santa Sé: As relações diplomáticas de Portugal com o governo pontifício de 1706 a 1750* (Coimbra, 1937), *Relações externas de Portugal, Reinado de D. João V*, 2 vols. (Oporto, 1938), and *Subsídios para a história do Patriarcado* Bebiano, *D. João V. Poder e espectáculo* (Aveiro, 1987). For intellectual exchanges, see Manoel Cardozo, "The Internationalism of the Portuguese Enlightenment: the Role of the Estrangeirado, c. 1700–c. 1750" in A. Owen Aldridge, ed., *The Ibero-American Enlightenment* (Urbana, 1971), 141–207. Vitorino Magalhães Godinho, *Mito e mercadoria, Utopia e Prática de navegar. Séculos XIII–XVIII* (Lisbon, 1990) sets the global commercial scene. See also his essay "Portugal and Her Empire, 1680–1720," in *The Rise of Great Britain and Russia*, ed. J. S. Bromley, vol. 6 of *The New Cambridge Modern*

History (Cambridge, 1970). For overseas, see Charles R. Boxer's *The Portuguese Seaborne Empire, 1415–1825* (London, 1969) and A. J. R. Russell-Wood, *A World on the Move. The Portuguese in Africa, Asia and America, 1415–1808* (New York, 1992). A good read on Brazil is Boxer's *The Golden Age of Brazil, 1695–1750* (Berkeley and Los Angeles, 1969). Excellent histories by Portuguese scholars are A. H. de Oliveira Marques, *History of Portugal*, vol. 1, *From Lusitania to Empire* (New York, 1972) and Joaquim Veríssimo Serrão, *História de Portugal*, vol. 5, *A restauração e a monarquia absoluta, 1640–1750*, 2nd rev. ed. *de Lisboa, 1716–1740* (Oporto, 1943). To place these in the broader context of Portuguese diplomacy, see Pedro Soares Martínez, *História diplomática de Portugal* (Lisbon, 1986). Royal capacity for ostentation is documented in Rui Bebiano, *D. João V. Poder e espectáculo* (Aveiro, 1987). For intellectual exchanges, see Manoel Cardozo, "The Internationalism of the Portuguese Enlightenment: the Role of the Estrangeirado, c. 1700–c. 1750" in A. Owen Aldridge, ed., *The Ibero-American Enlightenment* (Urbana, 1971), 141–207. Vitorino Magalhães Godinho, *Mito e mercadoria, Utopia e Prática de navegar. Séculos XIII–XVIII* (Lisbon, 1990) sets the global commercial scene. See also his essay "Portugal and Her Empire, 1680–1720," in *The Rise of Great Britain and Russia*, ed. J. S. Bromley, vol. 6 of *The New Cambridge Modern History* (Cambridge, 1970). For overseas, see Charles R. Boxer's *The Portuguese Seaborne Empire, 1415–1825* (London, 1969) and A. J. R. Russell-Wood, *A World on the Move. The Portuguese in Africa, Asia and America, 1415–1808* (New York, 1992). A good read on Brazil is Boxer's *The Golden Age of Brazil, 1695–1750* (Berkeley and Los Angeles, 1969). Excellent histories by Portuguese scholars are A. H. de Oliveira Marques, *History of Portugal*, vol. 1, *From Lusitania to Empire* (New York, 1972) and Joaquim Veríssimo Serrão, *História de Portugal*, vol. 5, *A restauração e a monarquia absoluta, 1640–1750*, 2nd rev. ed. (Lisbon, 1982).

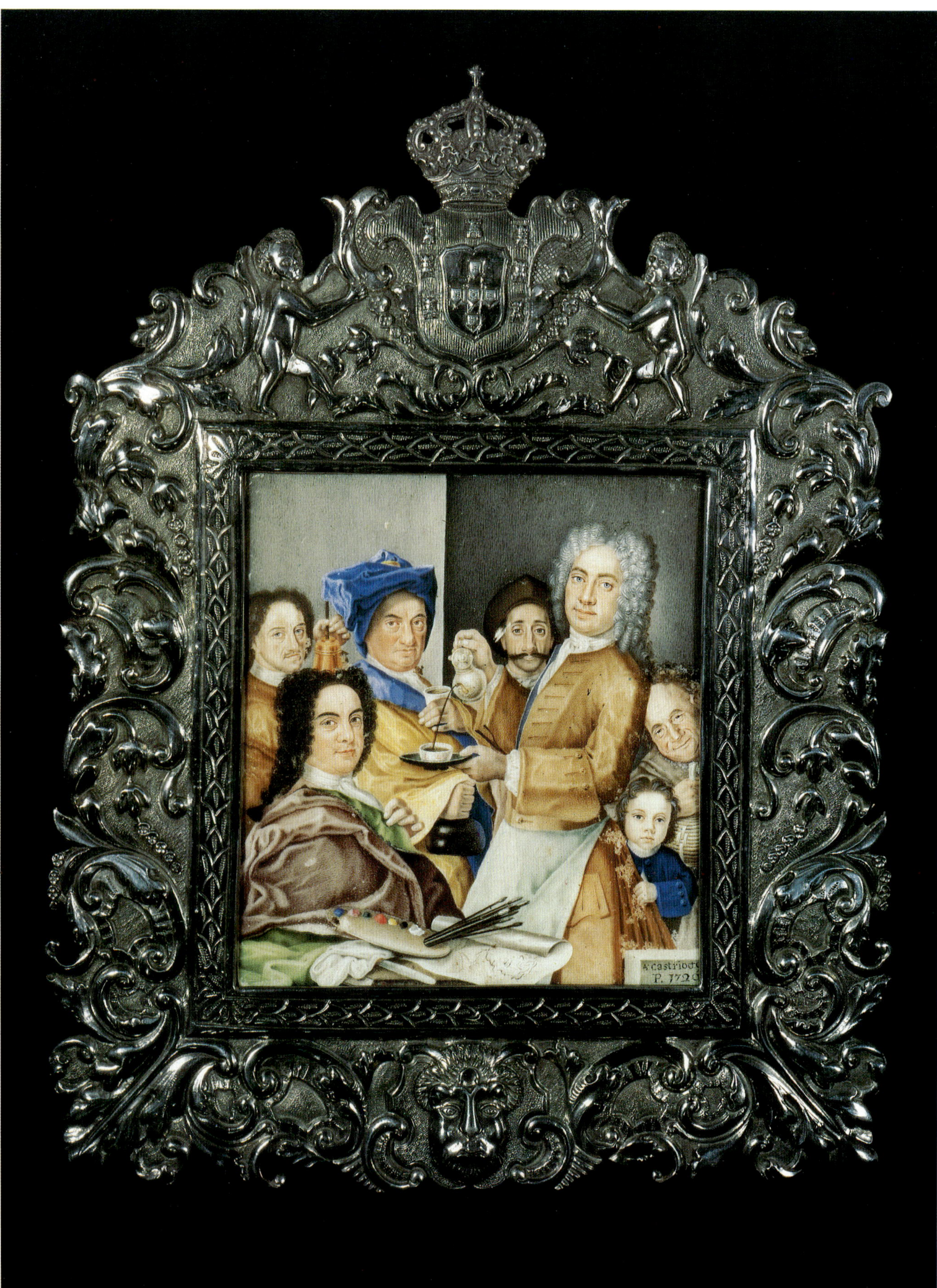

Dom João V and the
Artists of Papal Rome

A. Ayres de Carvalho

During the seventeenth century, artistic movements brought to Portugal from France and Italy survived the turbulent period of the restoration of the monarchy in 1640 and a further twenty-eight years of interminable warfare. Skilled military engineers constructed fortresses and strongholds along the length of Portugal's coast, embellishing and adorning them with martial and symbolic ornament. Successive artists were appointed to execute royal commissions, and the architecture class taught in the royal palace (the Paço da Ribeira) continued virtually unchanged from the reign of Dom João IV (r. 1640–1656), who believed that the arts and music were integral parts of culture. The final quarter of the century was the end of the old era as most of the talented artists and engineers who had constructed the great monuments of the period died.

By 1689 Portuguese artists had succeeded in breaking away from the medieval guilds and thus were no longer subject to their restrictions. Grouped around their patron saint Luke in the manner of the Roman or Florentine academies, Portuguese artists enthusiastically joined classes given by the priests of the Society of Jesus and instruction at the palace from the master architects inspired by the treatises of the Roman theorists Vitruvius, Serlio, and Vignola. Thus a new Santa Engrácia, Portugal's most beautiful baroque monument, was begun in 1682 by João Antunes, a master stone mason who became a highly efficient and prolific architect. And the year 1689 brought the birth of a son, the future Dom João V, to Dom Pedro II and his wife, Maria Sofia Isabel of Bavaria.

The early eighteenth century saw the death of João Antunes in 1712, before he could finish the magnificent dome of Santa Engrácia. The jealousies and intrigues of contemporary stone masons and architects impeded its completion, and the few who did consider continuing the work were uncertain whether the supporting walls could support the weight of the dome. Nothing was done until 1713, when, through the intervention of the French consul Du Verger, the facade was strengthened with buttresses ending in volutes that are virtually

fig. 1. A. Castriotto, *Dom João V Drinking Chocolate with the Infante Dom Miguel*, 1720, oil on ivory, silver frame. Museu Nacional de Arte Antiga, Lisbon

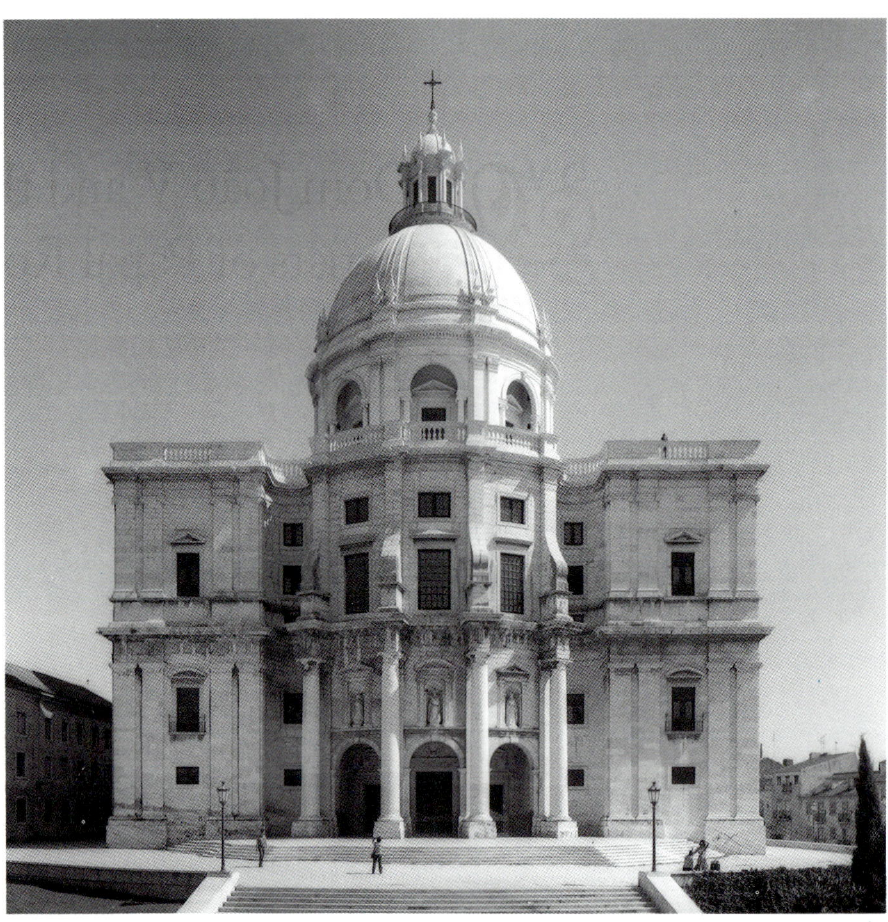

identical to those designed by Le Muet for the Val-De-Grâce convent. This modification was authorized by Dom João V (r. 1706–1750), young and inexperienced as he was and surrounded by artistic advisers who were doubtless more interested in new and larger projects and clearly showed a lack of interest in this monument begun in the previous century. It was unfortunately not to be concluded, and then with regrettable lack of finesse, until recent times (fig. 2).

The king's enthusiasm for all that came from abroad was well known. But few of the engineers and architects who fled the France of Louis XIV, after his disastrous revocation of the Edict of Nantes, made their way to Lisbon. For fear of the Inquisition, Protestants dared not cross the borders of Portugal and Spain. They took refuge instead in such countries as Germany, Switzerland, the Netherlands, or England. And thus it was that these countries, particularly the two latter, were the source of outstanding works of art, particularly furniture, silverware, jewelry, tapestries, and even the coaches of the embassy to Vienna in connection with the king's marriage to Maria Ana of Austria.

With the arrival of the German-speaking queen, many of the monotonous customs of the court of the times of Dom João IV and the Filipes were dropped, "and now there was entertainment on Sunday nights, celebrations and musical concerts, attended by the Royal Couple and the entire aristocracy" in enthusiastic imitation, endorsed by the queen, of what went on in foreign courts. Even the king was influenced by this breath of fresh air and entertainment, and elevated several young men who were proficient musicians to the noble ranks. Another novelty introduced by the queen was "always to eat with the king, necessitating full pomp and ceremony," a custom that had fallen into disuse upon the death of Dom João IV, according to Da Silva.[1]

Apparently, for all her virtues, Maria Ana of Austria had reason for sadness in the king's infidelities, which were a source of great concern to the nobility, the clergy, and even the common people. After she had been in Lisbon three years without producing an heir, rumors of her infertility circulated. The year 1710 saw the foundation of a religious order that numbered among its possessions a picture of the Infant Jesus said to be miraculous. The queen must have been aware of the foundation of the order and, when word spread that she was with child, the hope arose that the image of the Infant Jesus would work the desired miracle of an heir to the throne. The nuns were surprised and delighted when, on 4 July 1711, the king himself and his court appeared not only to lay the first stone of the future hospital, the retreat where the nuns were to perform their nursing duties, and the church that would be devoted to the worship of Mary, but also to leave a sizable donation toward the furtherance of construction. Five months later, on 4 December 1711, instead of the son so eagerly desired by the king, a princess was born, Maria Bárbara who was to become queen of Spain through her marriage to Ferdinand VI, son and heir of Philip V.

The church of the Menino Deus (Infant Jesus) remains the most representative example of architectural knowledge of the time and one of the few monuments of Lisbon to remain virtually intact after the earthquake of 1755 (fig. 3).[2] Despite the fact that the dome was never completed and notwithstanding the twenty-six years it took to reach even that unfinished stage, this was the first construction financed by Dom João V, perhaps in fulfillment of a vow made by his queen. The entire design must certainly have been created and developed in the workshops of the palace. There, under the direction of the venerable master architect Father Tinoco and with the advice and experience of his long-

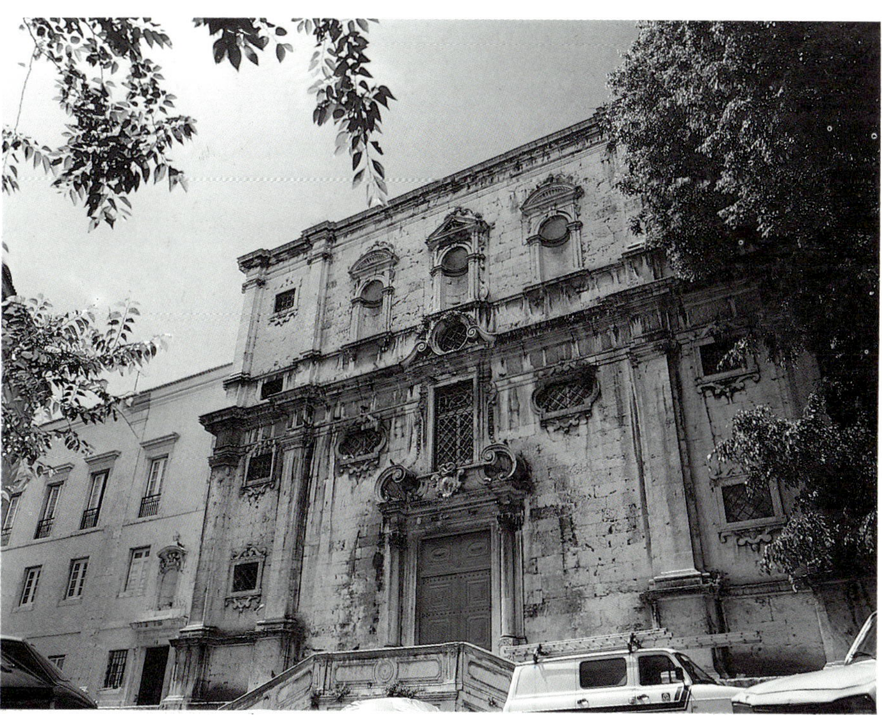

fig. 3. Attributed to Father Tinoco and João Antunes, *Igreja do Menino Deus*, Lisbon

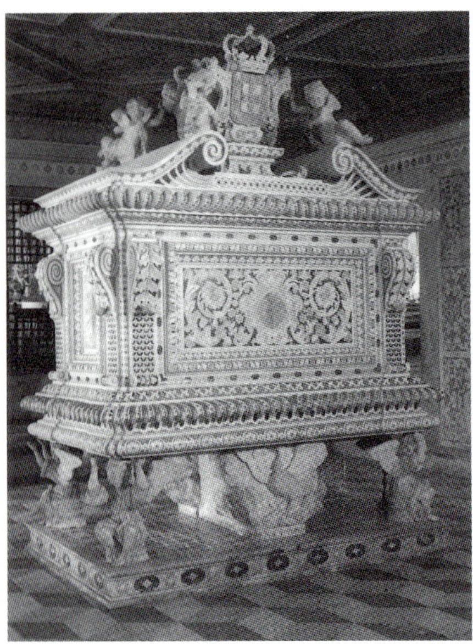

fig. 4. *Tomb of Princesa Joana,* Mosteiro de Jesus, Aveiro

standing disciple, architect João Antunes,[3] and under the attentive eye of the king, the plans and elevations of the beautiful structure of the Menino Deus were developed. This was the first artistic creation in Lisbon in which an Italian influence is apparent.

While João V and Maria Ana were building a church in honor of the Infant Jesus, the tomb of the holy Princesa Joana was being completed in the Mosteiro de Jesus, Aveiro (fig. 4). This splendid coffin, encrusted with precious stones in Florentine style, is a product of the imagination of a painter rather than an architect. Its funereal and decorative motifs display a poetry and symbolism comparable only to one of the first known works of art in the Church of São Roque, the reredos of the Capela da Trindade, commissioned in Rome about 1620 by Gonçalo Pires de Carvalho, purveyor of royal works.

The Franciscans and the landowners of Mafra had long and ardently wished to see a small monastery erected on this cold and windswept plain northwest of Lisbon, to offer the poor inhabitants of the area a little more spirituality and religion. The townspeople of Mafra were renowned for the spiritual backwardness and the dire poverty in which they had lived since the sixteenth century, not only because the town's founders had condemned it to neglect, but also on account of the disregard of the clergy who held the benefice of the Colegiada de Santo André.[4]

The birth of Princesa Maria Bárbara did not fulfill the dynastic expectation of the royal couple, and so it was that, despite the Mafra landowners' insistence that the monastery to Saint Anthony and the Virgin be situated there,[5] one reads of no more talk of miracles or vows until a male heir was born on 19 October of the following year as the Franciscan António de São José from Vila de Cheleiros had predicted. Príncipe Pedro's birth revived Dom João V's enthusiasm for carrying out a vow marking his special devotion for Saint Anthony by founding a monastery accommodating thirteen monks dedicated to him in Mafra "with the declaration that this monastery will belong to the Franciscan Order of Arrabidos."[6]

In 1712, when the male succession had been assured, and also because of differences of opinion as to the proper site for the monastery, the king resolved to go with his closest attendants to Mafra, where the visconde de Vila Nova de Cerveira owned a palace and estates abutting the collegiate church of Santo André.

The location chosen by the king for the tiny monastery was in the area called A Vela. The site commanded the town's highest point, an altitude of some two hundred meters, with an unimpeded view of Ericeira and the Atlantic Ocean. Even in early 1713, many pieces of land were still being valued and purchased for the crown, to the despair of the poverty-stricken local inhabitants who were no longer allowed to till the lands that had provided their livelihood.

As fate would have it, Príncipe Pedro survived for only two years and ten days, and on 29 October 1714 he died. However, the blow was cushioned by the birth, a few months earlier, on 6 June of that same year, of another prince, the future Dom José I.

The most reliable historian of the eighteenth century, Frei Cláudio da Conceição, described one of the medals struck to commemorate the laying of the first stone, on 17 November 1717, of the church and monastery of Mafra. The medal "depicted a magnificent Temple that was being consecrated, showing two tall towers on the sides with the dome in the center, the doors of the church to the west and the monastery on the left side." This was indeed how the construction had been planned initially, although it was to be changed substantially.[7]

The Swiss naturalist who visited Portugal in 1726, Charles Frédéric de Merveilleux, left a document that gives the flavor of the project.

Sovereigns are always surrounded by flatterers and individuals who seek only to seduce in order to line their own pockets at the expense of the Sovereign, and Dom João was no exception. The members of his court persuaded him that a great king should carry out a project that would render his memory eternal; that he should consult his ambassador in Rome and ask him to send suitable construction plans for a building of dimensions that would demonstrate His Majesty's zeal in proclaiming God's glory. This advice was heeded, and a plan was ordered from Rome for a building even more magnificent than the Escorial. In the center of the construction was a superb church entirely in marble. Behind the choir, premises to accommodate two hundred monks with good incomes who would serve as chaplains in this magnificent church. The right wing of the building was a huge palace for the king, royal family, and the grandees of court. The left wing, another magnificent palace for the patriarch and his twenty-four false bishops or mitered canons. Intrigue was rife among the royal engineers to secure the appointment to oversee this prodigious construction. A goldsmith called Fridericks [...] was appointed to supervise the works in Mafra. He was an unsophisticated German who had some skill as a draftsman. He was also in charge of producing all the silverware for the patriarchal church, which he made of very low quality alloy, over-adorned with ill-finished decorations but solid because labor was paid by the ounce. No goldsmith ever made so much money, and he grew extremely wealthy. The king was sent a miniature replica of Saint Peter's of Rome, which occupied an entire large room, including models of all the monuments of that city.

Construction began on the church which is entirely in marble, in a desert of sand, where there is not a drop of water. I saw the nave completed and it appeared that the finished building would be magnificent, although so over-adorned with superfluous decoration that it merely detracted from its beauty. I saw two blocks of black marble of astonishing size beside the main altar; they were so beautifully worked and so highly polished that, it was said, a few days previously the king had dressed before these marbles, which served him as a mirror.

The fact is that three quarters of the king's treasures and gold brought by the fleets from Brazil were transformed into stone. The king forbids anyone to visit Mafra without his permission because he lives informally among his craftsmen, to whom he has apprenticed so many Portuguese disciples that there will be no shortage of stone masons and carvers in the coming years, to the extent that he could even lend them to neighboring countries. His Majesty's unswerving concentration on carrying out his project guarantees that it will be perfectly executed; this building will truly be worthy of such a magnificent and pious king.[8]

At the same time that the first stone was laid at Mafra in 1717, the king's persistence and religious fervor bore fruit in Lisbon's elevation to the rank of patriarchal see. The marquês de Fontes, who had been Dom João's vain and autocratic ambassador to Rome since 1712 and who was a greater megalomaniac than even the king himself but possessed of uncommon artistic vision, had undertaken to prepare his embassy with all pomp and ceremony. Fontes commissioned monumental and splendid coaches from Roman artisans for the embassy that favorably impressed the pope and his court and were remembered for more than a century by the Romans (see the essay by Apolloni in this volume). Fontes made a contribution to Dom João's artistic aspirations by discovering in Rome and bringing to Portugal a twelve-year-old boy of considerable promise: the talented Francisco Vieira de Matos, who was to become the painter better known as Vieira Lusitano.

In 1718 the monastery for thirteen monks and its church at Mafra were placed under the responsibility of the German-born silversmith João Frederico Ludovice, who was to become the most prolific architect of this period and of the reign of the king called "the Magnanimous." Ludovice was assisted by an exceptional master stone mason who had long worked for the Jesuits, the Italian Carlos Baptista Garvo, who had executed the beautiful reredos of the Jesuit church in Santarém in 1713. The Mafra construction was speedily to rise from its foundations on its inhospitable and arid site, without water and virtually without vegetation as Merveilleux noted at the time of his visit in 1726 (fig. 5).

Following the Peace of Utrecht and the end of the Wars of Succession, Dom João V implanted a new and glorious artistic vision in the stony soil that was Portugal. In Brazil, the new El Dorado, ships were loaded with gold and precious gems. They sailed up the Tagus to the awe of the local Portuguese, who caught but a glimpse of this gold transformed into doubloons stamped

fig. 5. João Frederico Ludovice, *Palace-Convent*, Mafra

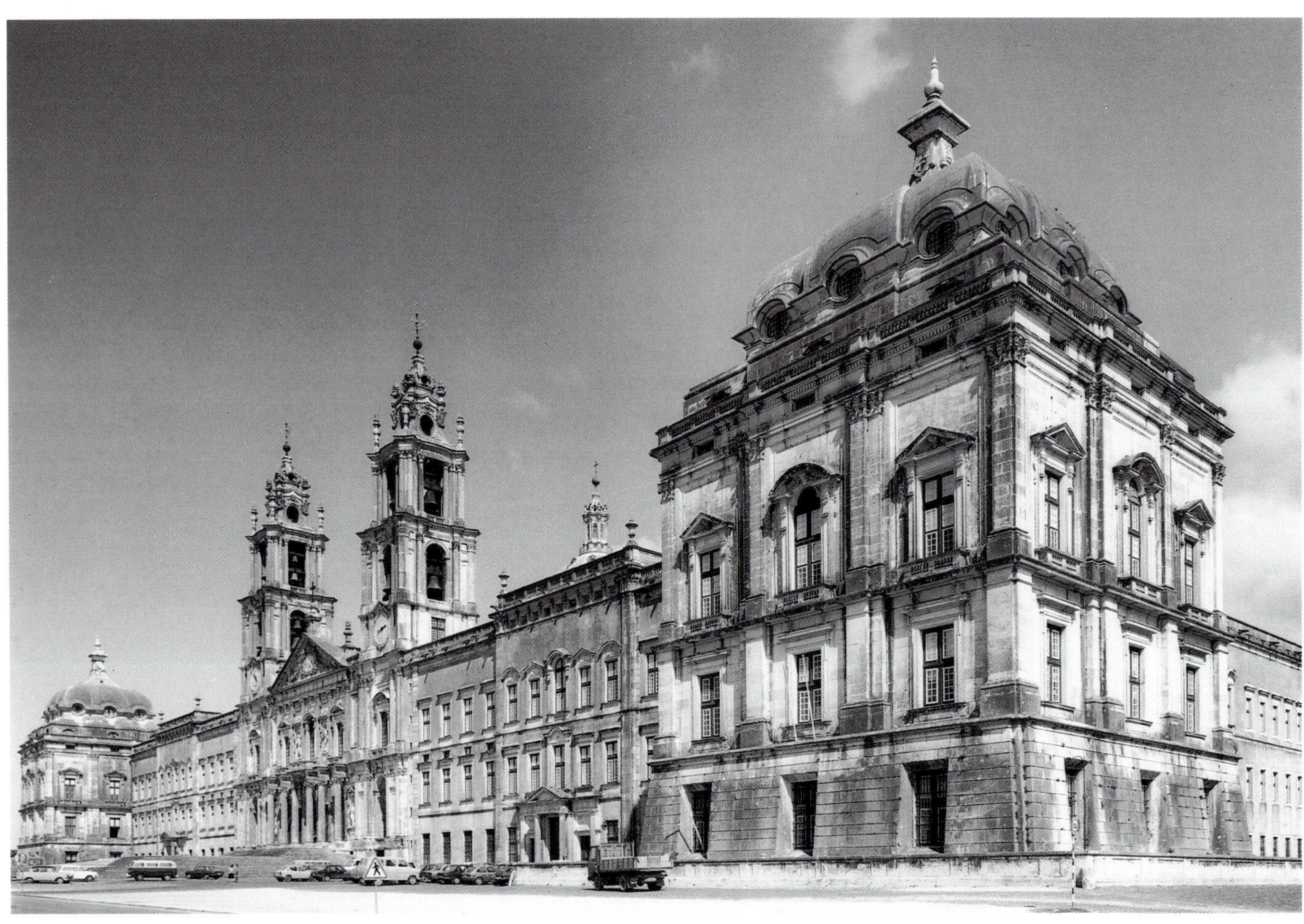

with the king's laurel-crowned head as though a hero of ancient Rome. From as far afield as Lorraine the duque de Cadaval summoned a great master of mintage, Antoine Mengin, who gradually converted the gold of Brazil into coins and medals that no one ever saw, as they were buried in the foundations of the Mafra basilica. They bore Vieira Lusitano's rendering of the king's head. These pieces of gold assisted the king in winning over the papal court.

In the royal chapel attached to the Paço da Ribeira in Lisbon, plans were laid for installing the new mitered canons and the supreme head of the church of Portugal, Patriarch Tomás de Almeida. The gold of Brazil would gild the carvings and sculptures with which Portuguese artists lavishly adorned reredos, credenzas, altars, and holy statues in every church in the land. If the fame of Portuguese wealth failed to attract prominent foreign artists, they were summoned by the king, the Society of Jesus, or the religious organizations and engaged to work on the immense projects that were planned: palaces, churches, chapels, and altars.

An important event in 1719 was the arrival in Lisbon of the great architect from Messina, Filippo Juvarra, engaged by the court of Savoy but summoned by Dom João V expressly to collaborate in his project of constructing a patriarchal see. Juvarra remained in Portugal only six months, designing, drafting projects, and doubtless setting a fine example for local architects. But Ludovice had firmly entrenched himself at court, not only with his work as silversmith but also as architect, complying with the wishes of the canons of Évora cathedral in irretrievably destroying the centuries-old main chapel and modernizing it in the style of Borromini in the Lateran in Rome.[9] He was assisted in this work by another Italian artist, Giovanni Antonio Bellini from Padua, a sculptor rather than an architect who worked for the Jesuits on the construction of Santo Antão. Subsequently, in the 1740s, he turned the main chapel of the São Domingos church into a museum housing his "sculpture," which was totally destroyed in a recent fire. Insight into Bellini's renown in his own day is given in an account written in 1740 by the historian Luís Montez Mattozo, who ascribed the chapel and a gem-encrusted reredos of Nossa Senhora da Boa Morte to "the great architect Antonio de Padua." This must have been the same sculptor who worked with Ludovice[10] in creating the wooden models for the silver saints of the altar ensemble for Coimbra cathedral (cats. 100, 101).

Ludovice was no doubt the organizer and decorator of the famous Corpus Christi procession, which may well have been witnessed by Juvarra, since it took place during the period of his stay in Lisbon. Decorative, religious, and secular sculptures by the Provençal Claude de Laprade[11] and his sculptor companions, Manuel Machado and Domingos da Costa e Silva, were displayed under canopies designed by Ludovice with paintings by the Genoese Júlio Cesar de Temine, who is said to have taught the Portuguese artist André Gonçalves.

By this time, the canons of São Vicente had dismissed the famous painter of perspectives and architecture, the Florentine Vicente Baccherelli, who had for years been engaged in decorating the ceilings, choir stalls, and naves of Lisbon's churches in the style of Andrea Pozzo, including the church of São Francisco, creating a school of painters and decorators that survived to the end of the century. The entrance hall of São Vicente de Fora is the best-known example of his work.

The foundation of the Academia Real de História Portuguesa in 1720 was a great historical moment in Dom João V's reign. Under the king's patronage, cultural activity in Portugal flourished from this time onward. An unending flow of artists from many countries began to arrive in Portugal, especially engravers, as the publications of the academy had to be illustrated. These artists included Débrie, Harrewyn, Rochefort, Leboiteux, and, most particularly, the outstanding painter and etcher Pierre Antoine Quillard, who left behind Watteau-style pictorial renderings of *fêtes galantes* and insights into lively popular celebrations, public events, fireworks displays, and crowds watching the launch of a ship in the Tagus in the presence of the royal family.

Juvarra's plans for Mafra were grandiose in the extreme and therefore costly. The king would not have hesitated to carry them out were it not for the thirty long years that it would have taken to complete the project, for João did not expect to live that long. He was a hypochondriac and suffered from melancholia, convinced that he was subject to every conceivable illness. The king was criticized for his readiness to squander money on building a patriarchal see and for the fact that the vow to Saint Anthony, consisting of a tiny monastery and a small church, was becoming ambitious to an extent that dwarfed the Escorial. The thirteen monks had multiplied to three hundred, to the great satisfaction of the king's favorite Fontes, who had become the marquês de Abrantes, while the palace for the royal family and a second palace for the patriarch and his mitered canons had likewise increased considerably in scale.

It was decided that the likeness of the king and the royal family should be preserved for posterity. From Rome came a portraitist, Giorgio Domenico Duprà, a disciple of Trevisani and a colleague of Vieira Lusitano, and from Naples a miniaturist, Alessandro Castriotto. As a young man, the latter had traveled to many countries, and his fame went before him. But in Lisbon he left the most beautiful and revealing example of his art, together with an eloquent pictorial gibe at both the king and the papal nunzio Vincenzo Bichi, who ultimately caused relations between the Portuguese court and the papal court to be severed.

The work in question (fig. 1), certainly a commission, was a miniature dated 1720 in which the king is shown posing to a portraitist, no doubt Duprà who was beginning work on the royal commission at that time and who remained in Portugal until the 1730s. The artist's palette and brushes are to be seen beside the king, who is about to drink a cup of hot chocolate prepared by a court favorite and, beside Duprà, the miniaturist Castriotto with brushes behind his ear. In the background are one of the castrati of which there were such numbers in Rome and, beside him, the gleeful smirk of the nunzio Bichi, holding in one hand a Florentine flask that he appears to be offering to the king.

It was this nunzio who caused the break between the king and the Vatican. Although João V poured so much gold into every crack and cranny of Rome in the hope that, like the French and Spanish monarchs, he might be granted the privilege of placing a cardinal's biretta on his nunzio's head, the churchman had such a poor reputation that three popes refused to accept his candidacy. The king blustered and protested, expelling all citizens of the papal state from Lisbon and recalling every Portuguese resident in Rome, thus sparking a war of prestige and diplomacy.

A single member of the clergy, Frei José Maria da Fonseca e Évora, remained in Rome as ambassador, continuing to spend freely in attempts to smooth ruffled feathers and win over cardinals and popes, but to no apparent avail. The king must have learned of the ironical miniature portraying the smirking nunzio whose Florentine anecdotes and wit would certainly have amused the sovereign. The miniaturist Castriotto had came from Spain bearing a recommendation to the Portuguese court from Queen Isabel Farnese, a great enemy of Dom João V, and thus the artist may well have been put up to playing such a trick on her Portuguese rival.

Three interminable years passed, from 1728 to 1731, during which Frei Fonseca e Évora tirelessly traveled Italy from end to end, commissioning paintings and marbles from Carrara, ordering enormous statues from the best artists of the day, but all "in secret" as recommended by the king's secretary, José Correia de Abreu, because it was all for Mafra and was part of the extravagance of the king of Portugal.

It appears, however, that work in Mafra had actually ground to a halt. Despite the endless plans copied from the churches in Rome—plans by Vignola and Bernini, Maderno and Borromini, and details and more details sent to Lisbon and assembled by the most famous architects of the time such as Fontana or his disciple Tomazzo Mathey, Salvi, Vanvitelli, Juvarra, or Canevari, not forgetting the Maltese Carlos Gimac, the famous author of the rebuilding and restoration of Sant'Anastasia in Rome,[12] it had become obvious that Ludovice, the unfortunate German goldsmith who had been elevated to the position of architect, although ably assisted by the Garvos, father and son, was not equal to the task with which he had been entrusted.

During his visit to Portugal in 1719, Juvarra had left plans and designs for the Patriarchate in the style of the elevations and views of the award-winning royal palace that he had designed for the Clementine competitions in 1705 to the admiration of his teacher, Carlo Fontana. These served as a fine source of inspiration to Ludovice for the massive roofs of the Mafra towers. Some say that Ludovice's designs are an echo of the fort attached to the Paço da Ribeira, which was still standing at that time, or an imitation of Vignola, the admired architect of the Villa Farnese at Caprarola. However, Ludovice's drawings for Mafra appear to be a proud imitation of Juvarra's designs for the Clementine competitions. Thus the king and Ludovice were given some notion of how to design an imposing construction without having to ape the grandiose Saint Peter's, of which, according to Merveilleux, a perfect copy stood in the most prominent position in the ambassadors' hall in the Paço da Ribeira. As late as 1728, shortly before the consecration of the basilica at Mafra, no final decision had been taken regarding the facade of the church or the pediment. Was there to be a repetition of the circumstances of the Menino Deus or Santa Engrácia, left without pediment or bell towers, neither completed, forgotten as soon as their outstanding architect died? And what about the towers of Mafra? Would they promptly collapse like those Bernini built for Saint Peter's? Surely the great Roman architect Antonio Canevari, Salvi's teacher whose designs had already been realized in Rome, including the famous and original Accademia dell'Arcadia (see the Delaforce essay in this volume), would have been capable of meeting Dom João V's requirements.

Meanwhile, important marriages were about to take place. Agreements had been signed for the unions between the Portuguese royal children and those of

Spanish king Philip V. Thus Princesa Maria Bárbara, who had always been pushed into the background by the death or births of her sibling heirs to the throne, would one day became queen of Spain. Great festivities ensued, with cannon salutes and fireworks, triumphal arches in which Canevari was an expert, tolling bells, and endless processions to Caia, the much-publicized and memorable exchange of princesses. Maria Bárbara was to go to Spain to hear the famous castrato Farinelli or talk with Isabel Farnese and be loved by the future king of Spain, Ferdinand VI. Mariana Vitória, who had been passed over by Louis XV, was to proceed to Lisbon to marry the heir to the Portuguese throne, Príncipe José, spending her days criticizing the court and the king in the letters she wrote daily to her mother.

The senate resolved to approach the king to persuade him to heed the popular demand to bring water to Lisbon. Chief Magistrate Cláudio Gorgel de Amaral declared to the king in 1728 that "he had an obligation to attend to the public needs of the city." It was finally agreed that only the king, "with his sublime and royal understanding, could arrive at the most appropriate and comfortable means." All agreed "that this project was so enormous that only his immense generosity of spirit could allow such a construction to be successfully essayed in that day and age, which would be of great and obvious usefulness to all dwellers in the Bairro Alto of Lisbon, and particularly in the monasteries, palaces, and stately homes situated there."[13]

The royal decision was somewhat simplistic and almost ironic when one bears in mind the quantities of gold that were transformed into stone for the marble colossus in Mafra, demanding the sweat and sacrifice of thousands of laborers who worked as slaves under military supervision and the foreman's whip. As ships sailed from Rome laden with statues bedded upon woolen mattresses or well protected with beautiful embroidered trappings, the immense church bells arrived from Flanders and were blessed by the patriarch in Tojal.

Canevari and the patriarch had designed an immense and magnificent aqueduct and a monumental fountain for Lisbon, with a palace to accommodate the monarch. The peoples of the patriarch's land at Tojal already had fountains and drinking water, which were an incentive and an example for the king. Dom João V informed the senate that it could "impose taxes on any item they considered appropriate, during any given year, at a level they considered necessary to finance the channeling of the 'águas-livres' [the 'free waters' that were to be brought into the city from the surrounding countryside] or of water from any water source that they could introduce or incorporate."

Work began on construction of the imposing aqueduct, but it was paid for out of the common people's pocket. Taxes were levied on wine, olive oil, and meat. Canevari was the first to begin work on the aqueduct and, despite the fact that the Tojal fountain had fallen into disrepair, it served as a blueprint for the Portuguese and foreign architects of all that was most modern and elegant in Rome. (Nicola Salvi, Canevari's disciple, began almost simultaneously, in Rome, to build one of the largest and most beautiful scenographic and pictorial creations of the century, the Trevi Fountain, which was to set the scene for prodigious festivities, eighteenth-century displays, aquatic games, and fireworks of fantastic proportions.)

Soon after completing his plans and constructing the first arches of the aqueduct, Canevari found himself the target of ridicule and malicious criticism by his former emulators Ludovice and Manuel da Maia. He was to be unceremoniously dismissed for failing to build the arches higher. And, as was reported sarcastically by Milizia, a middle-ranking architect but in reality more of an archaeologist and art critic, Canevari returned to his homeland humiliated.

It is not known exactly what part Ludovice played in Canevari's dismissal, but, judging by his determination to direct the aqueduct project and the influence he always had at court as well as on the monks of Santo Antão and even on the king himself, and according to a statement by the prior of São Nicolau in Lisbon, Ludovice persuaded Dom João V to dismiss Canevari in 1732. Although thwarted, Ludovice was always ambitious and even drafted designs for the aqueduct, which were never used. Many years later, in 1746, without rivals to overshadow him, Ludovice wrote a letter to the aforementioned prior of the church of São Nicolau, a veritable outburst of hate and spite against Canevari, Manuel da Maia, Custódio Vieira, and even Carlos Mardel, the talented designer of many fountains and wells that survive in Lisbon to this day. It is readily apparent how unfair Ludovice was to Mardel if one visits the Museu da Cidade in Lisbon and views the beautiful plans for numerous fountains, including those constructed in Rato, Esperança, São Pedro de Alcântara, as well as two projects for a fountain-monument devoted to Dom João V and approved by Dom José I, his son. These projects date from 1752, just after Dom João's death, and, since "out of sight is out of mind," all projects honoring João were promptly shelved after the earthquake.

Giovanni Antonio Bellini from Padua, the well-known sculptor who worked with Ludovice, in 1737 described a "written" project for a grandiose fountain-monument devoted to João V that sounds so familiar that it almost appears that Padua had the audacity to place himself on a par with the great Bernini or Borromini in conjuring up the fountains of Piazza Navona. The decoration is lavish and highly baroque, depicting the continents, the figure of Minerva, a dragon, mermaids, dolphins and tritons, a Pegasus pounding the rocks, and two shackled slaves, the figure of Lisbon and of "old Tagus." A sculptural group in the style of Bernini surmounts the whole, with an "elephant, symbol of Prudence," carrying a large obelisk and finally, rising out of the surging waters, Dom João V dressed as a Roman warrior, crowned with laurels and riding a proud horse.[14]

The much-quoted architect Ludovice, with his talents and outrageous vanity, wrote a famous letter to the prior of São Nicolau about a new project for the Patriarchate, which the king had given up in 1719 as a hopeless cause. Documentation on this early project exists in the sketches made by Juvarra while he was in Lisbon. From Ludovice's letter, one may conclude that soon after 1736 the king must have given renewed thought to completing his Patriarchate project. Ludovice's ideas no doubt fell short of the grandiose style desired by the king, who was probably thinking of something more along the lines of the majestic plans drawn up with such magnificence, taste, and refinement by the incomparable Juvarra.

The patriarchate designed by Juvarra was never built. The king instead improved and enlarged the royal chapel in the Paço da Ribeira so that it could indeed be used for purposes for which it had originally been built. In 1728, following Canevari's arrival, new life was breathed into the project, and the old tower that had fallen into disrepair was demolished and replaced by another, elegant and well-proportioned, designed by the Roman architect. Several engravings of the time show what came to be known as the Gamenha (clock tower), as it was called by Portugal's Vieira Lusitano when his admiration for Canevari led him to write verses lamenting the fact that this Roman architect had not designed Mafra.

It is interesting to note Ludovice's approach to designing the Patriarchate, which, in its magnificence, would have rivaled Saint Peter's in Rome. Ludovice wrote an intriguing and enlightening history of a second patriarchate, the old architect's designs for which were once more frustrated for very implausible reasons on the part of the king who apparently no longer held much store by Ludovice's self-interested and spiteful observations.

His Majesty ordered that a site be selected for a patriarchal church. I considered that the only potential site lay between the Noviciado da Cotovia and the Convento de Jesus, which was more than sufficient for a church the size of Saint Peter's of Rome, and its churchyard... a plan for which I submitted to His Majesty... and the said building would stand the width of Rocio Square distant from the Noviciado. This would not only give the fathers a broad view of the sea but also a view of a beautiful building. His Majesty answered that everything should be done to ensure that the fathers did not lose any of the sea view they presently enjoy, and that I should persevere with this project.[15]

Ludovice's reflections and his ambition to construct a building to rival Saint Peter's in Rome would be laudable were it not for the fact that, had he really been the author of the grandiose design for Mafra, he would have referred first to "his work" that had already been realized and that was also intended to imitate and rival Saint Peter's.

Certain documents concerning the chapel of Saint John the Baptist give us a better insight into Ludovice's personality, which is also evident in his correspondence between 1742 to 1744 in which he passed on his opinions to the Roman architects at the king's prompting. It would appear that, after Salvi and Vanvitelli, Canevari was the person best placed to shed light on Ludovice's personality. Ludovice had certainly been passed over yet again by Dom João V, who opted to have such an important commission executed in Rome. The architect's criticisms make it clear not only that there was little justification for his differences of opinion with his Roman colleagues, but also that there was a degree of inconsistency in the way he presented his opinions, and finally that he was at least thirty years behind artists such as Canevari, Salvi, and Vanvitelli.

On one occasion Ludovice filled more than twelve pages with scathing remarks on the works of great artists such as Vignola, Bernini, Borromini, Michelangelo, and others and then turned his attention to the authors of the beautiful chapel of Saint John the Baptist. However, he never sent a single sketch or plan that could elucidate or guide the Italian artists in rectifying the shortcomings on which he harped with such malice.

For the Patriarchate project, Ludovice continued to dream of making use of the unfinished palace in Cotovia commissioned by the conde de Tarouca from João Antunes. Meanwhile, as Baptista de Castro reported, the old royal chapel of the Paço da Ribeira had "an extensive and admirable collection of countless relics of Saints for each day of the year." It also possessed a Roman object, "a baptismal font… with meticulously worked gilt bars surrounding it, and a very fine painting of Christ's baptism, executed in Rome by the outstanding Agostinho Massuci [sic] in 1745." He tells, moreover, that many of the precious objects belonging to the patriarchal church were lost, "consumed by the devastating fire following the earthquake" and that only "a small amount of melted silver was recovered, of the original thirty thousand marcs." After the earthquake, Ludovice's son João Pedro, working together with the architect of new Lisbon, Eugénio dos Santos, incorporated the masonry of the unfinished palace built by João Antunes for the conde de Tarouca in Cotovia in the late seventeenth century in their plans for the new Patriarchate, but this church was also destroyed by fire several years later.

Letters and documents relating to the chapel of Saint John the Baptist reveal a great deal about the art of the time of Dom João V. In Dom João V's records is confirmation of the bestowal of the position of chief customs officer on José Correia de Abreu on 19 July 1729, greatly facilitating reception of items arriving daily from Italy and France. He subsequently embarked on the study of law, became one of the "Treasurers of the Furniture Store," later "Steward for Supplies and Treasurer for Freight in the Department of Trade."

The king had placed a huge order for statues in Italy to decorate the fifty-eight niches of the facade, porch, and chapels of the basilica at Mafra, an essential decorative conclusion of this magnificent work of architecture that, for unknown reasons, was not completed until early 1730. Could it be that Dom João V originally thought that he could commission the Portuguese and foreign sculptors then in Lisbon to execute this magnificent gallery of figures in stone? The most famous artists living in Lisbon at that time were Claude de Laprade and Manuel Dias, who were wood carvers rather than stone sculptors, and José de Almeida, who had recently arrived from the Roman academies after pitting his skills against those of Pietro Bracci and Filippo della Valle in the Clementine competitions. According to Cirilo Wolkmar Machado, an eighteenth-century painter who chronicled the lives of his fellow artists and architects, he was the only Portuguese sculptor at that time who was able to work in marble. Giovanni Antonio Bellini of Padua was also skilled in carving marble. It is known that Laprade executed some ornamental elements in wood that were then transposed to marble by sculptors, and Almeida made sculptural compositions in wood for the high altar that were sent to Genoa to be sculpted by Schiafino as well as models for the facade for the basilica, to be carved in stone by the sculptor Giuseppe Lironi in Rome.

By 1732 the first nineteen statues commissioned by the king were finally ready; eleven of them were executed in Florence and eight in Carrara. Also completed were paintings for the altars of the basilica, most of which had been commissioned in Rome by Taddeo Ludovico Olivieri, an Italian master woodworker of the king's confidence who, like so many other artists and craftsmen, had come to Portugal from Rome at the instigation of Fontes and had been appointed master carpenters for works at the royal palace in 1723. These artists had taken Portuguese citizenship in 1728 following the rift between the Portuguese court and the papacy. José Correia de Abreu's letters reveal the king's unprecedented enthusiasm for the magnificent statues that he had commissioned from the most "illustrious" Italian sculptors of his day. Abreu repeatedly emphasized "the king's magnificent taste and involvement in this project" and his "desire to see the statues perfectly finished and placed in their niches."

The orders given by Correia de Abreu were carried out by a modest Franciscan monk, José Maria da Fonseca e Évora, who had taken part in the marquês de Fontes' famous embassy in 1716. The pope had finally agreed to place the cardinal's biretta personally on Nunzio Bichi's head and was now curious to see the magnificent works commissioned by the king of Portugal. Bernardo Corso Procaccio had been entrusted to "take the magnificent Cross and the Candlesticks manufactured in Florence to Rome to be viewed by the Pope." In July 1732 the objects commissioned by the king were dispatched by sea under the watchful eye of Gaetano Grassi, a goldsmith who was much later engaged in creating silverware for the chapel of Saint John the Baptist in São Roque and who accompanied the "candlesticks to Lisbon by coach from Florence to Livorno, remaining six days at an inn since contrary winds prevented his departure." More altar candlesticks by goldsmiths Pozzi and Zappatti, together with embroidered vestments executed by the distinguished Giuliano Saturni, were dispatched by ship from Rome to Livorno in three crates.

A master carpenter by the name of Giuseppe Domini was charged with the delicate task of transporting the statues. He was instructed to "accompany these works from Florence to Livorno by way of the Arno within the ten days that are necessary if you stopped in that City to clear customs and pack all the statues and packages in the vessel, since the Master was well qualified to undertake all that was necessary." A considerable sum was likewise paid to Giuseppe Borgagni, a "packer, to settle his account for the packing of the large candlesticks, numbering seventeen in all, urns, and other items dispatched in the vessel." Finally, in Portuguese mixed with Italian, the account tells of the trials and tribulations experienced by Captain Falleri in sailing down the Arno River, which was virtually dry, from Florence to Livorno, transporting not only the magnificent packages of the candlesticks, but also the item of greatest value, the finest treasure that Dom João V could have acquired at the court of Florence. The Italian captain encountered many difficulties in the transportation and the care of these precious items. Correia de Abreu reported payment "to Navicellaro Falleri for the transportation from Florence to Livorno of twenty-two packages: namely, the packages containing the candlesticks and the clock and the Madonna by Raphael of Urbino on their way to Lisbon but, being large packages, they had to be handled with utmost care and, sending them by barge from Ponte Signa and later reloading them because there was little water in the Arno and it was difficult to sail down the river and so the total cost of this task was set at forty-four escudos per package." Finally an additional four *escudos* were paid for the barge and stevedores to put the packages on board in the river at Livorno where the ship was anchored.

In December 1732 new instructions were received from the nobleman Correia de Abreu to the effect that "the task should be suspended until new orders and Antonio Arrighi should go to Rome with his team."

As early as May 1730, Correia de Abreu had already given thought to all that had to be done when the statues were ready to be dispatched. The friar, who was now virtually an ambassador, would have the responsibility for the marbles and for choosing them, and it was recommended that he begin to give thought to "the easiest and safest way to transport said statues, remembering also that subsequent to their arrival in Portugal, they will have to be taken to

Mafra on poor roads, for which reason they should be packed in strong cases to protect them from any mishap, down to the last toe, for which reason they should be well packed, and Your Reverence should use all care and precautions; and if necessary you should have ordinary mattresses made of wool which will provide more support than straw which is gradually crushed and turns to dust. The arms, hands and fingers of the statues will not be completely detached from the stone from which they are carved, and the remaining supports will be cut here and finished, when your Reverends consider appropriate, because otherwise the statues will not be safe and we wish to deliver them to Mafra without any damage whatsoever. Your Reverends will send two engineers with the said Statues in order to facilitate transportation."

He concluded, "it would appear that I have dwelt at sufficient length on the transportation of the statues and on the five main points of this task which are perfection, speed and appropriateness of prices, honesty and due care in handling…and I have assured our lord and master to this effect, observing his great pleasure and involvement in this entire project, which is a mere trifle in the presence of his greatness, and today his mind is much occupied with the desire to see the project finished to perfection and the statues placed in their positions by the feast day of Saint Francis next year."

It is regrettable that some of the letters from José Correia de Abreu concerning this period have been lost or stolen. The missing letters would no doubt have thrown light on his assessment of the clock, as meticulously executed as a piece of Florentine furniture with its classical and understated carving, which was very different from the work of Portuguese carvers such as Miguel Francisco or Laprade, intended to frame a "painting of a Madonna by Raphael of Urbino." Originally from Florence and either presented by a Medici to the king of Portugal or purchased by him, there is no way of knowing whether this painting was an original or merely a copy. The fact is that it was not just the candlesticks inlaid with lapis-lazuli and precious stones that required the greatest care and "good handling…given that these are important packages," but also the clock and the Madonna by Raphael.

Correia de Abreu returned from Rome upon completion of his mission as a director of Portugal's academy of fine arts, together with all the Portuguese artists such as Vieira Lusitano, José de Almeida, Domingues Nunes, and Inácio de Oliveira Bernardes, when Portugal broke off relations with the papal court. A connoisseur of art, he had passed on commissions to Italian artists with great meticulousness. Évora was responsible for all the hard work and anxiety of executing the king's orders, and he was generously compensated when the king appointed him bishop of the city of Oporto. He was alternately admonished and extravagantly praised by Correia de Abreu. One of the paintings for the Mafra altars most admired by Évora was that of the Holy Family painted by Masucci, while he also praised the same subject painted by Vieira Lusitano. He indiscriminately mixed paintings and medicine when he received a huge collection of canvases and a "St. Nicolas salve" to deliver to the cardinals.

According to accounts by the Italians who traveled to Portugal to assemble the chapel of Saint John the Baptist in São Roque, in June 1748 the ailing king propelled himself in his chair from Paço da Ribeira to the Casa da India to see the beautiful mosaics for the chapel that had just been unloaded from the vessels arriving from Italy. The mosaics were displayed, and the king was lost in

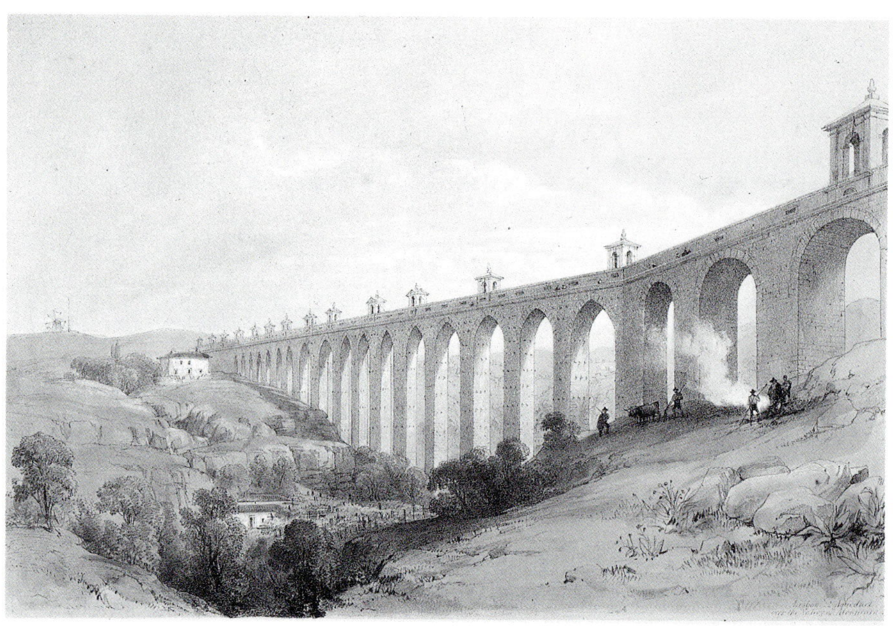

fig. 6. *Old View of the Aguas Livres Aqueduct,* colored print. Museu da Cidade, Lisbon

admiration and began to pray aloud with great fervor and devotion. Afterward he exclaimed repeatedly, as he touched the beautiful images with delicacy and admiration, "beautiful, beautiful."

Alexandre de Gusmão was summoned and a message was sent to Ludovice who came immediately to confirm His Majesty's words: "beautiful, so beautiful, there is nothing comparable in the whole kingdom," adding that they would remain unknown because only His Majesty had seen and admired them. Next the entire royal household came to view the mosaics, followed by every last member of the nobility. Alexandre de Gusmão and the second marquês de Abrantes remained no more than a moment, but the king returned on Sunday, 9 June, and on Tuesday, 11 June, lost in admiration of the works of art that he had commissioned from the Roman artists.

Meanwhile, it never occurred to the king to visit the monumental aqueduct magnificently spanning the Alcântara valley over ogival arches rising from the colossal supports (fig. 6) dreamed of by Francisco de Holanda and made reality by Custódio Vieira, the "Herod" of the aqueduct as Ludovice called him. A few months before water began to flow along the aqueduct and beside the triumphal arch that Mardel designed and erected to perpetuate the memory of the king for finally consenting to the project, the facade of the famous royal fountain, the Chafariz d'El-Rei, which had been described and admired by the Venetian nobility when they came to congratulate the king of Spain on his conquest of Portugal, collapsed in spectacular fashion.

1. José Soares da Silva, *Gazeta en forma de carta* (Lisbon, 1933), items 1701 to 1709, MS 512-B.8–25.

2. A. Ayres de Carvalho, *D. João V e a Arte do seu Tempo*, 2 vols. (Lisbon, 1960–1962).

3. A. Ayres de Carvalho, *As Obras de Sta Engrácia e os seus Artistas* (Lisbon, 1971).

4. Unpublished documents give some conception of the backwardness of these populations of old. See "Visitações na Igreja e colegiada de Santo André, em Mafra" (manuscript, National Library of Mafra).

5. Viscondes de Vila Nova da Cerveira.

6. Frei João de S. José do Prado, "Monumento Sacro," 1751.

7. Frei Cláudio da Conceição, *Gabinete Histórico*, vol. 8 (Lisbon, 1820).

8. Attributed to the Swiss naturalist Charles Frédéric de Merveilleux, *Memoires Instructifs pour un voyageur dans les divers Etats de L'Europe*, 2 vols. (Amsterdam, 1738).

9. In the mid-seventeenth century, the Lateran Basilica became a target for the aesthetic and artistic attentions of Pope Innocent X, who appointed the great architect Francesco Borromini. The architect sought to maintain the original while introducing several novelties in the baroque taste. Fifteenth-century frescos by Gentile da Fabriano and by Pisanello were destroyed and twelve niches were created to accommodate the statues of the Apostles. Pope Clement XI took it upon himself to find the patrons to pay for the statues to complete the work of Borromini and Pope Innocent X. A letter from Pope Clement XI to Dom Pedro II reveals that Dom Pedro II, Dom João V's father, was one of the first patrons, generously agreeing to pay for the statue of Saint Thomas, which was sculpted by the French sculptor Pierre Le Gros (1666–1719). Le Gros came to Lisbon under contract to the Society of Jesus to execute the grandiose sacrarium of the main altar of Santo Antão. Ajuda Library (49-VII-16-301a, book on statues of Saint John Lateran and respective payments between 1704 and 1735).

10. Ludwig, better known as João Frederico Ludovice, was German and had won fame in Rome for his enormous silver figure of Saint Ignatius for the Gesù, in Rome, modeled by Pierre Le Gros. Subsequently, in Lisbon, he imitated Bernini's style, which won him fame and celebrity in Portugal. The sculptor from Padua, Giovanni Antonio Bellini, was Ludovice's colleague, also employed by the Jesuits on the reconstruction of Évora cathedral and the São Domingos project in Lisbon. When Ludwig arrived in Lisbon in the late seventeenth century, he found that many masons had become self-styled "architects," including João Antunes who had attended the class given in the Paço da Ribeira, as disciple of Father Tinoco, and built churches and reredos from his own plans. When João Antunes died in 1712, Ludwig was presented with a golden opportunity to make his name as an architect and take charge of the immense Mafra project.

11. The artist-sculptor Claude Courrat de Laprade, who was born in 1682 in the outskirts of Avignon, came to Portugal as a young man to complete the sculptures and decoration of the Capela da Vista Alegre near Aveiro.

12. The Maltese architect Carlos Gimac, trained in Rome, was summoned to Portugal in the late seventeenth century at the request of António Correia de Sousa Montenegro, commander of Leça (1618–1696), a Portuguese nobleman belonging to the Order of Malta. Gimac was to design and construct a palace on the Novões estate. In the early eighteenth century, Gimac came to Lisbon to work for the royal household. He was one of the artists who constructed triumphal arches for the king's marriage to Maria Ana of Austria. He accompanied the marquês de Fontes on the embassy sent to Pope Clement XI, and in 1712 while in Rome rebuilt the church of Sant'Anastasia with great originality for Cardinal da Cunha as well as building the chapel that served as his last resting place when he died in Rome in 1730.

13. From "Anno Noticioso e Histórico" by Luíz Montez Mattozzo, vol. 1, Lisbon, 10 March 1740. "Work is proceeding on the magnificent Águas Livres aqueduct, and the water is bought from the Parish of Bellas, which has a spring, and it is channelled along the magnificent and sturdy aqueduct, designed by Brigadier Manuel Da Maya, which came into operation on August 6, 1738: the water from a second spring is channelled in only 1800 paces distant from the beginning of the aqueduct and it proceeds on its way, either over arches or under ground, to reach the Bayrro Alto, crossing at the Ribeira de Alcantara over extremely high arches of worked stone. The water runs through a channel that is 7 'spans' across and 14 deep, with a walkway running beside it, and on each side a stone wall."

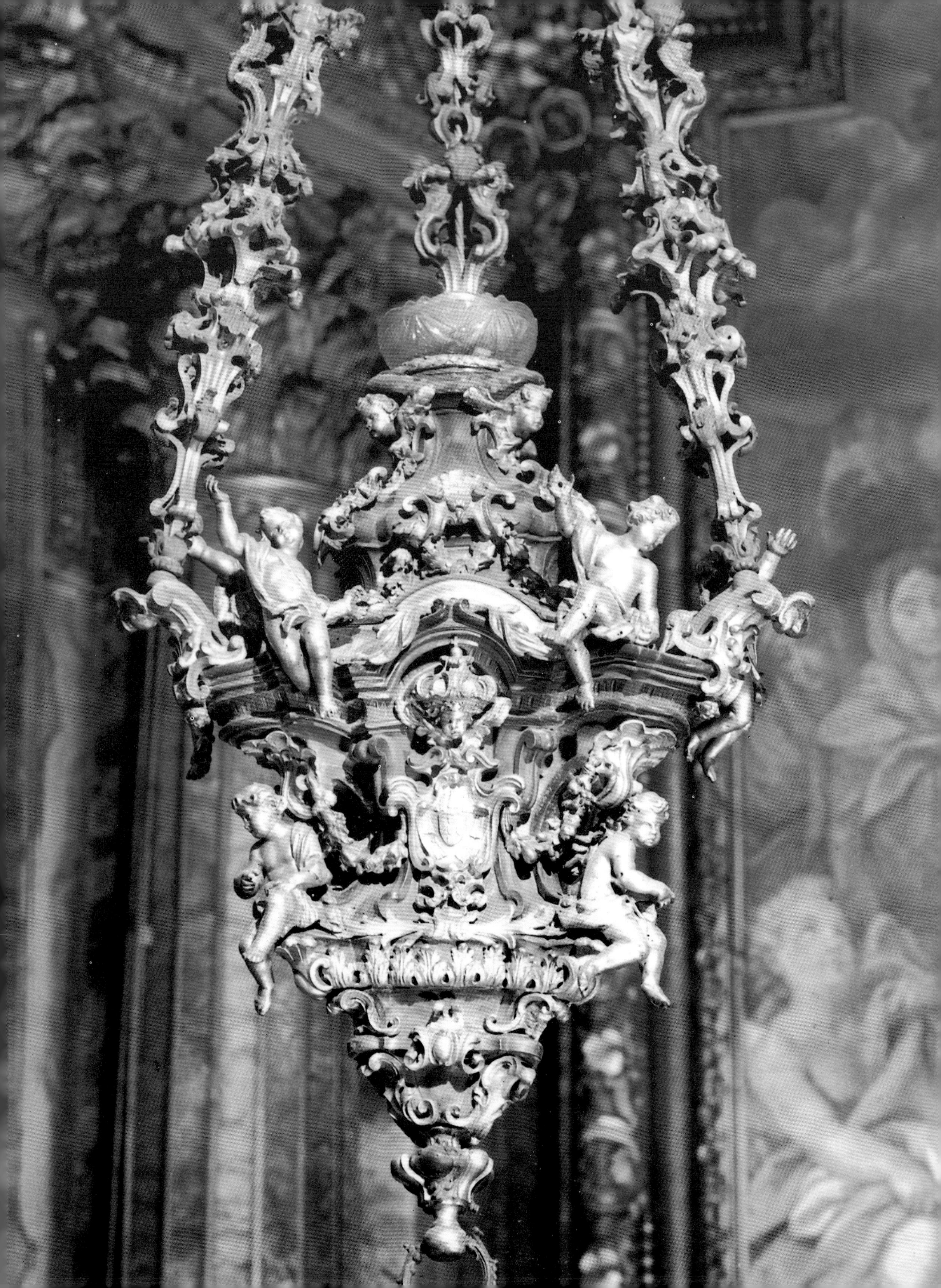

Lisbon, 'This New Rome'

Dom João V of Portugal and Relations between Rome and Lisbon

Angela Delaforce

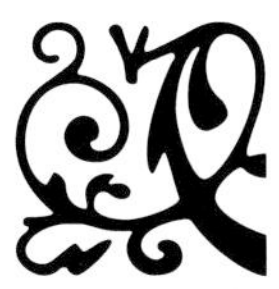

A Roman triumphal arch that was originally named after the Emperor Domitian and that became known as the Arch of Portugal once stood in Rome by the church of San Lorenzo in Lucina in Via Flaminia. Although it was demolished in 1662, throughout the eighteenth century this great monument continued to be recorded as the Arco di Portogallo in engravings, as in Blaeu's *Nouveau Theatre* of 1704.[1] It was during the eighteenth century through the well-defined policies of that absolute monarch, the Bragança Dom João V (r. 1706–1750), that Portugal was to establish an even more vivid identity and forceful presence in the political and cultural life of the Eternal City.[2] The first steps in this rise to greater influence had been established by the king's father, Dom Pedro II (r. 1683–1706).

At the turn of the seventeenth century and in the early years of the eighteenth, Portugal was represented at the Holy See by the Jesuit priest António de Rego based at her church in Rome, Sant'Antonio dei Portoghesi. In 1700 the architect Carlo Fontana, at this date factotum to that noted patron and friend of Portugal, Cardinal Benedetto Pamphili, was also active in the service of Dom Pedro II. His first documented work for the Portuguese crown was the design of the Sepolcro del Giovedi Santo erected during Holy Week of 1700 in the Portuguese church. This ephemeral structure was described as taking the form of a colonnaded temple with a *Deposition of Christ* set before a view of Jerusalem.[3] Far more significant in its permanence, however, was the contribution of Dom Pedro II to the most important sculptural project in Rome in the early eighteenth century, an undertaking from 1703 by the newly elected Albani pope, Clement XI (1700–1721). He became one of the greatest art patrons of the age, and besides his many public works he sponsored the Concorso Clementino, a competition associated with the Academy of Saint Luke that was a major incentive to young artists.[4] Twelve great marble statues of the Apostles, which line the nave of Saint John in Lateran, were carved by many of the leading sculptors in Rome for the gray marble niches designed by Francesco Bor-

fig. 1. *Hanging Lamp from Chapel of Saint John the Baptist, São Roque*, Lisbon, 1742–1744

romini that had been completed in 1650. From 1699, the year when Cardinal Pamphili became archpriest, he was closely associated with the basilica and its decorative program.[5] As architect to the pope, Fontana was responsible for determining the scale and balance of these statues within their architectural setting. The powerful and expressive figure of Saint Thomas (1705–1711), carved by the French sculptor Pierre Le Gros the Younger, was paid for by Dom Pedro II in 1704 with the sum of 5,000 *scudi*. The apostle is shown bearing the *sasso,* or stone, and a cross, symbolic of the legend that Saint Thomas carried Christianity to Goa and that part of India that, from the early years of the sixteenth century, belonged to the Portuguese crown, and where what is thought to be the apostle's crucifix is preserved in the cathedral of Meliapur.[6] Portugal's association with this major papal project in Rome's Lateran basilica was not only highly prestigious, but was also an appropriate and symbolic statement. Both the attributes of the saint and the statue's iconography recall Portugal's long and historic tradition of religious crusades that were an integral part of the great maritime voyages of discovery of the fifteenth and sixteenth centuries, and they allude as well to the nation's continuing spiritual mission in Asia. A prominent feature of the cultural program of Clement XI was the embellishment of Rome's early Christian basilicas. The financial contribution of the Portuguese king to this costly project was politically astute in the difficult economic climate that, as has been shown by Gross, currently faced the papacy.[7]

The reports of the papal nunzio, Monsignor Michelangelo Conti, writing back from Lisbon to the Holy See (1698–August 1710), give perceptive details of life at court under Dom Pedro II, and his observations of the heir, the prince of Brazil, are astute and sympathetic.[8] Conti was made a cardinal in 1706, became Cardinale Protettore del Portogallo at the papal court from 1710, and was elected Pope Innocent XIII on 8 May 1721. His succession raised considerable optimism and hope for Portugal's long-term interests and her relations with Rome. These were not to be fulfilled, however, as the pope was ill throughout much of his brief reign and died in 1724. Earlier the energetic Nunzio Conti seems to have had considerable influence in Lisbon, in particular with the queen, Maria Ana of Austria (1683–1754), daughter of Emperor Leopold I and sister of Emperor Joseph I, who arrived in Lisbon in October 1708. Her dynastic marriage to the prince of Brazil, arranged in 1703, was intended to strengthen the new alliance between Portugal and the imperial Empire[9]; this is explicit in the imagery of an engraving, *Allegory of the Marriage of Dom João V and Maria Ana of Austria* c. 1708 by Peter van der Berge (Biblioteca Nacional, Lisbon, inv. E55R). A few years earlier Valesio had reported in *Diario di Roma* for July 1701 that whereas the French and Spanish ministers in Lisbon were finding it hard to conduct negotiations at court, Conti's persuasive and diplomatic skills were far more successful.[10] Conti's accounts stress the close ties of the royal family and nobility with the long-dominant Jesuits, their great devotion to Jesuit saints such as San Francisco Xavier, and frequent attendance at the church of Saõ Roque, noted for its magnificent ceremonial, lighting, and music. Jesuit influence, in particular among the queen's confessors and advisers, pervaded the reign of Dom João V. Although he came to favor clerical reform and wished to broaden the educational practices of the Jesuits, the king had a life-long allegiance to the society because of his own education by their priests. He was to give generously to the order in both Lisbon and Rome, where in

1739 he made a payment of 2,000 *scudi* for new paving in the mother church of the Gesù.[11] Politically, Conti's period as nunzio in Lisbon was dominated by the long, drawn-out theological question over the unconventional "Riti Cinesi," the Chinese rites, that were contrary to papal decree. João V defended the Jesuits of the China mission in their disputes with the college of the Propaganda Fide in Rome, a stand that was further complicated by Portugal's insistence on protecting her valuable commercial interests in China.[12] During his years in Lisbon, Nunzio Conti also observed closely the character of the prince of Brazil, the future Dom João V. Even before his succession in December 1706, the seventeen-year-old prince had taken an active part in public life during the long final illness of his father. Conti's accounts to Rome praise the prince's maturity and lively intelligence and express optimism for his potential and for a new beginning. But above all the nunzio emphasized the prince's extreme piety and religious devotion. Dom João V was to be the most punctilious and devout of all Portuguese monarchs.[13]

In Rome, elaborate allegorical funerary decorations, designed by Carlo Fontana, were erected on 13 September 1707 in Sant'Antonio dei Portoghesi after Dom Pedro's death. The commemoration was widely reported.[14] The central catafalque, the scenographic effects of which recall Bernini, is documented in a sketchlike drawing made by Filippo Juvarra, who may also have assisted on the project. The "apparato funebre" was surmounted by a great crown and royal mantle in the form of a *baldacchino* (Biblioteca Nazionale, Turin).[15] Accompanying the text published to honor the event were engravings illustrating the decorations and a series of painted reliefs representing the virtues of Pedro II as an exemplary Christian monarch. The frontispiece displays four allegorical figures representing the four Continents over which Portugal possessed vast dominions. Through the church and the extended network of Roman Catholic missions in Africa, Asia, and Brazil, the Portuguese monarchy, in a union of the cross and the crown, had long exercised and guarded rights of ecclesiastical patronage, the *Padroado Real*. The imperial theme dominated the decorations in the church; it was expressed in a lunette on the west wall and on the church facade, where reference was made to the great voyage of Vasco da Gama that opened the sea route to India in 1497–1498.[16] Fontana was the most acclaimed architect of his day, official architect to Clement XI and a *principe* of the Academy of Saint Luke. Valesio recorded that he served Dom Pedro II as *Architetto Reggio* for many years and that the king made him a knight of the prestigious Military Order of Christ (Ordem do Christo).[17] No other projects by Fontana for Dom Pedro II have been traced, but it has been suggested that he sent drawings of Roman buildings to Portugal. Fontana died in 1714, but his name has also been connected with a design by his pupil Tomasso Mattei for the palace, church, and monastery of Mafra (foundation decreed in 1711 and building begun 1717), obtained in Rome by the ambassador, the marquês de Fontes, and sent to Lisbon sometime before 1717. There is no documentary evidence for recent attributions to Fontana of the plans for Mafra. It is generally accepted that these were by the goldsmith-architect Johann Friedrich Ludwig, a German trained in Italy, who, significantly, worked as a goldsmith for the Jesuits at Sant'Ignazio in Rome between 1696 and 1700. He came to Portugal in 1701 to work for the Jesuits and there became known as João Frederico Ludovice.[18]

In 1751, the year after Dom João V's death, Lisbon, with the Patriarchate he

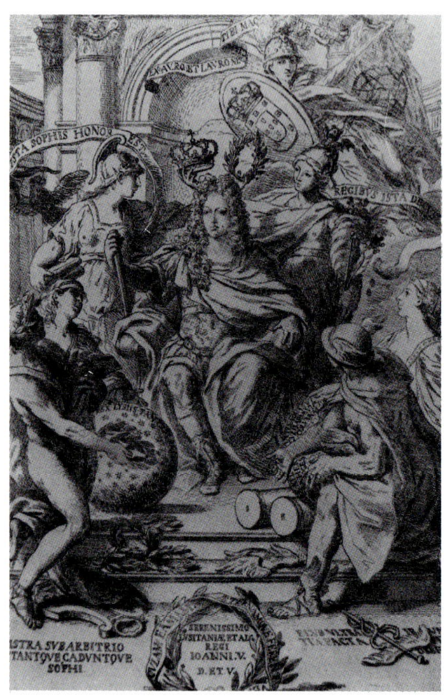

fig. 2. Francisco Vieira Lusitano, *Allegory of the Reign of Dom João V,* engraving. Biblioteca Pública, Colleção de Estampas, Évora, P III, no. 76

had created, was being likened to a miniature pontifical court, and the city was described as a new Rome, "esta nova Roma."[19] Throughout Europe the court had become famous for its church decoration and displays of the finest vestments and church plate, especially commissioned from Italian, French, and Portuguese sources. Many accounts speak of the exceptional beauty of the Italian church music performed and the extraordinary magnificence of the ceremonial and processions in the patriarchal church, which the king had modeled closely on the ritual, splendor, and etiquette of Saint Peter's at Rome.[20] Many nunzios' reports in the period describe the long and elaborate celebrations of saints' days, such as Saint Peter's, and feast days, such as the Purification of the Virgin, both of which were particularly venerated. At court it seems as if there was no shade of difference between many of the secular state ceremonies and those held in the patriarchal church, and indeed its siting, attached to the royal palace in the Terreiro do Paço, can be seen as symbolic. Any distinction between the political and the religious appears to become blurred in rituals such as the liturgical act of *The Washing of the Feet of the Poor by Dom João V.* The ceremony in the palace on Maundy Thursday of 1748, in which the king took a leading part, is recorded in an engraving by Guillaume Debrie. The dedication underlines the divine right of kings, João V's role as protector and defender of the faith as a "Principe do Ceo e da terra," and makes plain his development of a religion that evolved around the monarchy.

The crown was now greatly enriched by its revenues from the newly discovered Brazilian gold and diamonds, resources that first began to be exploited in the 1690s. Using this vast wealth, the king sought to inaugurate a new golden age in Portugal. He wanted to place his court on a standing equal to those of the principal European capitals, Paris, Madrid, and the imperial court of Vienna. His ambition was accompanied by an ever-deepening desire to emulate the pomp and grandeur of the papal court. João V started by raising his chaplain to the dignity of patriarch and then building a magnificent new patriarchal church. Then for the Capuchin friars, a reformed branch of the Franciscan Order, he founded the ex-voto monastery and palace at the remote site of Mafra; all these buildings were to be the setting for a display of late Roman baroque painting and sculpture.[21] The king intended to create an official state art that would reflect a new image of the kingdom and that would celebrate the prestige and glory of the absolutist monarchy he had created. In many ways Dom João V modeled his style and philosophy on that of the Sun King, Louis XIV. His policy was clearly defined, even though the underlying philosophy was ambivalent. The great quantities of *arte sacra* imported at vast expense from Italy were essentially to be used in the service of religion and for the elaborate ceremonies that were the obsessive but very genuine acts of devotion of a pious monarch; Nunzio Bichi described his "gran Pietà e delicatezza di Coscienza." The king used art also as a political instrument, as a form of patronage employed consistently and with considerable intelligence and determination to realize his ambitions, and especially, as will be seen, for establishing a position of considerable prestige in Rome. Art and spectacle were to express power. This is made clear in an undated engraving by Francisco Vieira Lusitano, *Allegory of the Reign of Dom João V* (fig. 2), in which, wearing antique Roman costume, the king is crowned by Minerva, is accompanied by Bellona who bears the royal arms of the Bragança dynasty, and the armillary sphere, emblem of the Portuguese crown, and is flanked by Ceres (?) with the heraldic dragon of the Braganças. He is further attended by the gods Apollo, Urania, and Mercury, and at his feet are the columns of Hercules. This was also the king's avowed intention in determining the grand scale and splendor of Mafra. The nunzio specifically recorded that the building was to demonstrate royal greatness and the king's generosity as a benefactor of the church. In October 1717 he wrote that Mafra, "quel magnifico Tempio," was to be a reflection of this, "volendo il Re che li opera sià degna dalla sua grandezza e generosità." Through the course of his reign the king showed an increasing love of spectacle and worldly display alongside an ever deepening religious faith. That these trends coexisted was noted by the Swiss naturalist Charles Frédéric de Merveilleux, who, in 1726, spoke of the king as "un roi aussi magnifique et aussi rempli de piété."[22]

The vast scale of Dom João V's endowment of churches and the Patriarchate and his promotion with unlimited funds of a religion of considerable visual splendor and *"luxo"* are only comprehensible in a historical perspective. His philosophy may appear to be based on an illusion, to be alien in an age of enlightenment, but the king's attitude was not an isolated one, nor was he a religious fanatic. Many of his deeds, which can be seen to have had little direct benefit on Portugal as a whole or on its economic development and to have had a limited effect on its infrastructure, were in fact a calculated and integral part of state policy. His policy was shared and articulated also by his ministers, by contemporary historians, nobility, and clergy, and was a positive expression of the ideology of the age and of Portugal's colonial history. The discovery of ever-increasing amounts of gold in Brazil at the end of the seventeenth century was seen as a veritable gift of God, newly revealed, an act of divine providence. From this belief it followed essentially that, in accordance with divine will, the greater part of these riches should be rendered directly back to the church, should be used in the ritual of public worship and thereby would benefit society and ultimately the spiritual well-being of the nation as a whole.[23]

Beyond Dom João V's desire to bring magnificence to the church in Portugal, to attain international prestige for his country, and behind his vast expenditure on art in France and Italy, there is something more profound and as enduring. By all accounts the king had a genuine and sophisticated love of art and collecting, an interest in academic and intellectual pursuits and, according to Merveilleux, better taste than all of his subjects. At the end of the reign, Francisco Xavier da Silva also testified to the king's discrimination when, in 1750, he described "o grande e preciosa tesouro, que ajuntou mais ao seu bom gosto, que o desejo de conservar preciosidades."[24] An informal royal visit to an artist's studio is suggested by the miniature *Dom João V Drinking Chocolate with the Infante Dom Miguel* by A. Castriotto (see Carvalho, fig. 1). The loss in the 1755 earthquake of the royal collection and library, and of a remarkable collection of tapestries, paintings, drawings, and engravings, together with the palace of Terreiro do Paço, makes it hard either to visualize or define this with any precision or to characterize Dom João V as a connoisseur. But there exists ample documentary evidence of the king's lifelong fascination with Rome: with her architectural past, with contemporary Italian art, and with Rome's taste and skills. It can also be seen how his antiquarian pursuits were wholly in accord with the ideas of the European enlightenment, and his extensive collection of Roman antiquities, antique medals, busts, and other rare objects is recorded. His love of antique Roman and Italian culture appears to have been far deeper than some passing royal fancy, and it endured and gathered momentum during the reign. There is frequent association with imperial history in literature of the period, as in 1729, when an entry at court by Dom João V is likened to the triumphs of Caesar, and the Portuguese spirit of conquest is compared to that of Alexander the Great during his glorious campaigns.[25]

These interests expanded to the conservation and documentation of Portugal's historic past. A royal decree signed by the king in 1721 was intended to preserve the fabric of all ancient, medieval, and classical buildings, sculpture, and antique inscriptions up to and including those of the reign of the penultimate Aviz monarch, Dom Sebastian (d. 1578). This meant that no Renaissance building could be destroyed. The decree can be linked to the aims of the newly founded Real Academia de Historia of 1720, whose seat was the palace of the duques de Bragança, and which was directed by such members of the nobility as the marquêses de Abrantes, Fronteira, and Alegretti and the conde de Ericeira, who was renowned for his erudition. The foundation was commemorated by a medal whose iconography, devised by the marquês de Abrantes, was based on an imperial model from the period of Vespasian (Lisbon, Casa da Moeda, inv. 2968). Over the years the nunzios told of the many learned orations and panegyrics given in honor of the monarch by the Real Academia. More significant, however, for the methodology and its study of archival material was their twelve-volume *Storia Genealogica della Casa Reale di Portogallo* by the Theatine António Caetano de Sousa (vol. 1, 1735), the sixth volume of which was presented to João V in a ceremony witnessed by Nunzio Oddi in January 1741.[26]

The first of the cultured and intelligent men chosen by Dom João V to represent him at the Holy See, that "prima Corte del Mondo," was André de Mello e Castro, who was created conde das Galveias in 1718. He was made envoy (Enviado Extraordinario) on 20 August 1707, became ambassador in June 1718, and served until 1728 when he was recalled following the break in diplomatic relations with Rome over the Bichi affair. Late in 1707 Mello e Castro took up residence. He lived with considerable style, first in the seventeenth-century Palazzo Cavallerini all'Argentina, Via Barbieri, for which he commissioned paintings, until 1719, when he moved to the Palazzo Cesarini. Mello e Castro loved music and the theater, and frequented Cardinal Ottoboni's theater at the Palazzo Cancelleria and the Capranica and Ruspoli theaters.[27] It is evident that Dom João V was now concerned to present a new Lusitanian image on the Roman stage. The emphasis was to make it more aristocratic and sophisticated. The change from representation previously by a Jesuit minister to a high-profile diplomatic presence is highly significant. The envoy made his first official entry into Rome in 1709, in six carved and gilded baroque coaches made in Rome. In the Portuguese tradition the imperial theme was displayed in the imagery, with allegories of the voyages of discovery and Portugal's extended dominions. The Portuguese crown's long spiritual mission worldwide was articulated on the first coach, where a figure representing Religion was placed between those of Africa and America. Even the spokes of the carriage wheels were symbolic, in the shape of a staff *(cetro)*, which alluded, it was said, to the authority of the king invested in the envoy.[28]

Nunzio Conti's first account from Lisbon in the year 1707 was made shortly after the coronation of Dom João V on New Year's Day. This was held in what was described as the galleria of the royal palace and was decorated with the finest and most precious tapestries from the royal collection, their subjects not specified.[29] The fine portrait bust of *Dom João V* wearing the cross of the Order of Christ by the Genoese Domenico Parodi and Francesco Biggi shows the youthful features of the king at this time (c. 1708, Palácio Nacional da Ajuda). Conti reported the king's preoccupation with increasing royal control over ecclesiastical affairs that came to dominate the reign, and one that eventually became more important for him than any form of government, political or temporal. This policy was initiated very early on. Nunzio Conti reported that the new king was seeking ways of celebrating the divine cult with greater splendor, majesty, and decorum than before, and, he said, the royal chapel, a "rica e maestosa cappella" that adjoined the palace, was already more like a church than a private chapel. A new chapel, dedicated to the Blessed Sacrament, was being created in one of the lateral naves of the building and painted and gilded at great expense.[30] By May 1710 part of Mello e Castro's mission in Rome had borne results. On 5 May, Conti conveyed to Rome the king's pleasure at the Papel Breve from Clement XI that gave the title of collegiate to the royal chapel. It was to be dedicated to Saint Thomas, and Monsignor Nuno da Cunha de Ataide (made cardinal in 1720) became the Cappellano Maggiore. The nunzio emphasized that this was a personal concession from the pope and one that had been procured by the king. This title had been awaited with increasing impatience since 1707, and evidently pressure had been placed on the nunzio to convey the king's demands to Rome.[31]

It was probably this delay, the slow reponse to his demands, that led the king to believe in a more forceful presence, as well as greater investment, in Rome. On 13 September 1709, Nunzio Conti first informed the secretary of state in Rome of the decision to send Dom Rodrigo Aires de Sà e Meneses, marquês de Fontes (1673–1733), as Ambasciatore Straordinario to Clement XI.[32] The mission was intended primarily to resolve differences that had arisen with the papacy concerning the *Padroado Real,* as well as the standing question of the "Riti Cinesi." The ambassador was also charged with realizing the king's deep ambition for an enlarged royal chapel and its elevation to the status of Patriarchate. The ancient privileges that accompanied this title would bring greater prestige and dignity to the court. The marquês de Fontes was the perfect courtier, close friend and counselor to the king, and he resided in the royal palace. In 1690 he had married Isabel de Lorena, the only daughter of one of Dom João V's ministers, the premier duque de Cadaval, another aristocratic family very close to the crown; she had died in 1699.[33] For two years the departure of the embassy was eagerly anticipated at court, but in January 1711 the marquês was still in Lisbon. One reason for the delay was over the compensation he demanded to maintain a suitable state of magnificence and *"decoro"* in Rome, all of which was reported at length by the nunzio.[34] Eventually in January 1712 the marquês de Fontes sailed to Italy in a Genoese ship, the *Nostra Signora delle Vigne.*[35] It was not, however, until July 1716 that negotiations led to any diplomatic success and the ambassador was given his first public audience by Clement XI at the Quirinale. Again there had been considerable impatience in Lisbon at the delay.

Meanwhile during the intervening years it seems that the skilled diplomacy of Clement XI's representative, Monsignor Giuseppe Firrao, and his good relations with the Portuguese secretary of state, Dom Diego de Mendoza Corte Real, had contributed toward a better understanding between the papacy and Lisbon, though the question of the Riti Cinesi, which were contrary to this pope's decree, was not yet resolved.[36] Monsignor Firrao (nunzio in Lisbon 1721--1728) had been sent to Lisbon as Nunzio Extraordinario in 1714 in order to deliver the *fasce benedette*, the symbolic swaddling bands that by long tradition were given by the pontiff to the heirs of Catholic monarchs.[37] In 1715 the Infante Dom José (born 6 June 1714, heir following the death in October 1714 of the Infante Dom Pedro), was ceremonially honored, and Clement XI gave the king a splendid Italian carved, gilded, and painted coach (Museu dos Coches, Lisbon). For the first time, evidence of João V's intense diplomatic activity in Rome was now witnessed in Lisbon. On the coach, an angel symbolizing Charity is shown leading the allegorical figures that personify the four Continents and flanked by sea horses they celebrate Portugal's imperial history, symbolism that can be seen to signify the developing accord between Rome and Portugal.[38]

In the following year, 1716, a part of the mission of the marquês de Fontes was accomplished. This came about as a result of wider European events, when in February 1716 the buildup of Turkish forces in the Mediterranean and the grave threat to the papal states led to a further request for naval support from a beleaguered Clement XI to the Portuguese king.[39] João V was receptive to such a demand, and the pope's call to fight the infidel and defend the papacy met with immediate response. From March 1716 preparations for a Portuguese fleet of twelve vessels were begun and it sailed from the Tagus on 4 July of that year. It took an important part at Corfu and in the decisive victory over the Turks at Cape Matapan in 1717, and the king's reward followed.[40] The dispatches of 1716 and 1717 from Nunzio Bichi make very clear that the papal concession to transform the royal chapel in Lisbon into a cathedral and grant it the title and status of Patriarchate was given personally to Dom João V, "che… si fara alla M^{ta} Sua, non alla Nazione, ne alla Corona." It was made in recognition of the king's support in dispatching the flotilla and of his special devotion to the church, "supponendo S. M^{ta} di posere meritar qualche cosa anche per il suo gusto, e genio particolare, essendo figlio piu ubbidiente della Chiesa, amante e veneratore di Sua Beat$^{mo.}$…." With the *Bollo Aurea in Supremo Apostolatus Solio* of 1716, Clement XI divided the city and diocese of Lisbon in two parts, the east with an archbishopric and the west with a metropolitan archdiocese in which the archbishop would hold the title and prerogative of patriarch.[41] The first patriarch was the aristocratic and influential Dom Tomás de Almeida (1670–1754), formerly bishop of Lamego (1705) and Oporto (1709), of whom there are two similar full-length portraits by Vieira Lusitano (Lisbon, Patriarcado).[42]

The ceremonial entry into Rome by the marquês de Fontes was eventually held on 8 July 1716, the feast day of the Portuguese queen, Saint Isabel. His spectacular progress through the streets to the Quirinale for his public audience with Clement XI remained indelible in the Roman memory, and was hailed in Lisbon as a veritable Roman triumph, the gilded carriages seen as standing in the historic tradition of the triumphal cars of antiquity. The reports

tell how during the three days of festivities all the papal court flocked to his illuminated palace at Piazza Colonna, where refreshments were served on the
finest Japanese porcelain. The cultured marquês, known for his humanistic and
historical studies, devised the decorative program for the magnificent baroque
coaches that were made in Rome (all in the Museu dos Coches, Lisbon). The
program, notable for its erudition, is expressed through literary reference, symbolism, and through elegant allegorical figures.[43] It can be read emblematically
as an illustration in three interrelated parts of the proud title of all Lusitanian
monarchs: Lord of the Conquest, of Navigation, and of Commerce in Ethio-
pia, Arabia, Persia, and India. The symbols are divided thematically between
the three principal coaches. The life-size carved figures convey the fantasy and
drama, the sheer theatricality of the event, a sense of which is conveyed by the
printed accounts. On the ambassador's coach the beautiful and regal allegorical
figure of Lisbon is shown crowned by Fame and flanked by Abundance (see
cat. 115). She has at her feet the figures of Africa and Asia (these have also been
seen as representing a Moor and a Turk), and below the recent success at
Corfu is further represented by a quiver with arrows and, on a half-moon, a
snarling, winged dragon, the emblem of the Braganças. The dramatic quality
is notable again in the third coach where Apollo, the sun god, rises above allegories that represent the Indian and Atlantic oceans holding hands, a vivid and
poetic image that refers to the 1488 voyage of Bartolomeu Dias and his round-
ing of the Cape of Good Hope at the union of these seas (see Apolloni, fig. 1).
The carved seashells, the sea horses, and the serpents and monsters all represent the Conquest of the Seas. This ornament, which is at once realistic and
fantastic, looks back to the iconography of the sea in Manueline architecture,
which celebrated the very recent voyages of discovery in sixteenth-century Portugal. The sea gods and heroes of antiquity depict literary imagery from *Os
Lusíadas* (Lisbon, 1582), the epic poem by Luís de Camões, which, inspired by
Virgil's *Aeneid*, immortalized this great adventure in Portugal's history.[44] The
sea goddess Thetis represents Navigation and traces the Portuguese sea routes
with dividers on a globe of the universe (Canto 10, see Apolloni, fig. 5); the
giant Adamastor personifies the Cape of Storms (Canto 5); also shown is the
Roman goddess of war, Bellona (Canto 1).

The entry of the marquês de Fontes in 1716 was said at the time to have
been of a perfection and good taste not seen before in Rome. From all accounts, the unity of form and content was complete; it was an occasion when,
as was noted, a Lusitanian concept was realized through the style and gesture
of magnificent Roman baroque figures, "feita pelo gosto Romano."[45] It was, of
course, apt that the 1716 entry before a papal audience should emphasize cru-
sading and religious motives, the spiritual mission that was an integral part of
Portugal's oceanic voyages, and thus demonstrate the way this spirit was alive
and continuous, as with the fleet very recently sent against the Turks. The program stands in a tradition that can, for example, be related back to the wording
of all fifteenth-century papal bulls granted in favor of the Portuguese monarchs. The 1716 entry also exploited an image of Portugal's unique colonial tradition, one that distinguished her historically from other European states. Two
centuries earlier, in 1514, a wealth of rare and exotic imagery, representing the
dazzling new Portuguese conquests in Asia, had been seen in Rome in the embassy of Dom Manuel I to Leo X.[46] By the eighteenth century Portugal's im-

perial tradition had developed something of its own mystique, which was seen in 1716 when once again the lustrous image of the nation was used to powerful political advantage and was magically conjured up to display Portugal's standing in the world to a Roman audience.

The marquês de Fontes continued his intense diplomatic activity. In February 1717 the papacy issued an *Aviso Segreto* setting out the form of ceremonial and worship to be used in the new patriarchal church. In Lisbon, in the same month, triumphal arches were erected for the solemn entry of the first patriarch archbishop, Dom Tomás de Almeida, when he took possession of his cathedral; the nunzio described the magnificent procession, "ne si poteva vedere cosa più grandiosa per la richezza, maestà ed ordine." In Rome at an audience in March 1717, the ambassador gave Clement XI an account of this and was successful in his petition for further privileges for the administration of the Patriarchate. In Lisbon on 2 March 1717 the nunzio first reported that Dom João V was planning to build a new patriarchal church and palace which, he said, would be of magnificent proportions.[47] The marquês de Fontes was back in Lisbon in April 1718 and was created marquês de Abrantes in recognition of his decisive role in interpreting royal policy. His success was only seen as partial, however, and he was criticized for failing to resolve the dispute over the "Riti Cinesi," a matter on which the king was eventually to concede and to retract the measures that enforced them.[48] By all accounts Portugal's presence in Rome had been greatly enhanced by the ambassador's distinctive personality. A letter of January 1718, written by Cardinal Annibale Albani, the pope's nephew and minister who was closely involved in the cultural life of Rome, spoke of his high reputation and of "le rara qualità e persona del S Marchese de Fontes."[49] Portugal's interests in Rome were furthered over a long period by Cardinal Albani, as in 1712 when he intervened in support of Monsignor Nuno da Cunha de Ataide (1664–1750), Portugal's grand inquisitor, when he was made a cardinal. A portrait of the cardinal, who was a distinguished participant in the political and religious activities of the period, is recorded in an engraving that also shows his titular church in Rome, Sant'Anastasia (Lisbon, Biblioteca Nacional, inv. E249P).[50] It was further noted in Rome how following his public audience on 8 July 1716, the marquês de Fontes had called on Clement XI's secretary of state, Cardinal Paolucci, and on the pope's minister, Cardinal Albani, who had supported his mission. In 1739 the cardinal was generously rewarded with gifts for his continued assistance with Portuguese affairs of state.[51]

For six years the marquês de Fontes had lived in Rome surrounded by a small court of poets, artists, architects, and musicians, among whom was Domenico Scarlatti as his Maestro di Cappella. He was such a generous patron and so involved with the artistic life of the city that his critics back in Lisbon said this had distracted him from his political mission.[52] The marquês clearly saw himself as a protector of the arts, a role in which he evidently had royal support. The allegorical figure of Minerva, goddess of wisdom, of learning, and the arts, which was placed prominently beside his coat of arms on his state coach in the 1716 entry, makes this clear.[53] Francisco Vieira (known as Vieira Lusitano), who accompanied the embassy to Rome, often spoke of the generosity of his patron, his Maecenas, in his *O Insigne Pintor* (Lisbon, 1780).[54] The young and gifted Vieira, who made drawings of the 1716 entry intended for en-

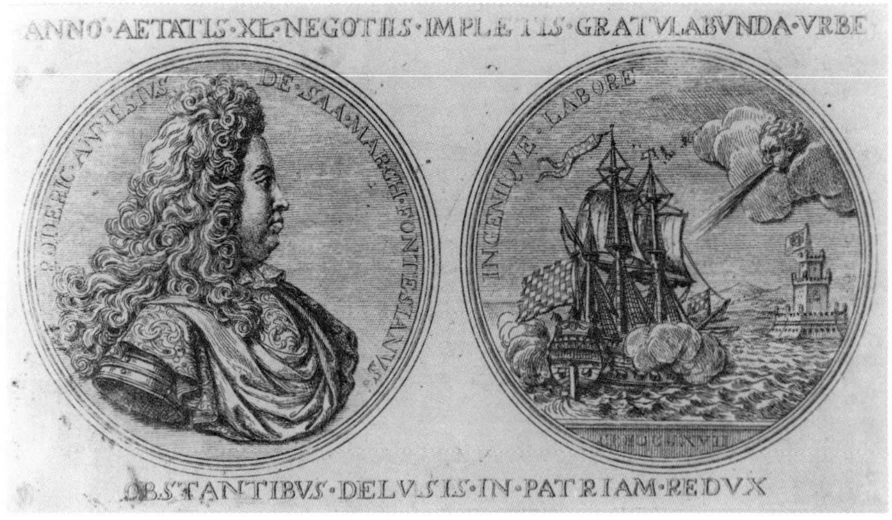

fig. 3. Francisco Vieira Lusitano, *Project for a Medal Dated 1717 Commemorating the Embassy to Rome of the Marquês de Fontes,* engraving. Biblioteca Pública, Colleção de Estampas, Évora, p iii, no. 8

gravings (untraced) and who may also have assisted, designed a medal to commemorate the event. An engraving for the medal has on the obverse a profile bust of the marquês de Fontes dressed in court armor and wearing a luxuriant wig (fig. 3).[55] This image, impressive despite its small size, reflects something of his vital personality and the qualities that led to his immediate rapport with the cultural life of Rome. There the marquês moved within the rarefied circles of the Accademia dell'Arcadia, Rome's leading cultural institution, and, in 1723, was to become a Pastore Arcade with the name Logindo Artemisio.[56] Also recorded are events such as in January 1716, when the marquês de Fontes took part with cardinals Conti and Albani in the Arcadia's delayed celebrations of Christmas 1715 held in Cardinal Ottoboni's Palazzo Cancelleria.[57] The marquês was reputed to be a connoisseur of painting, but his primary interest was architecture, in which he had experience of planning military fortifications. This and his literary talent were recognized by a founder-member of the Arcadia, Giovanni Maria Crescimbeni, who in 1722 wrote of him as a "Gentiluomo grandemente versato non solo nelle materie d'Architettura, ma anche nelle erudite e nelle lettere amene."[58] The marquês laid the groundwork and from Rome made many of the contacts that first established and sustained Dom João V's artistic policy. In Rome he hired the portraitist from Savoy, Giorgio Domenico Duprà, who in Portugal (active 1719–1730) gave new vigor to this genre. Duprà established the grand official image of Dom João V in the state portrait that is the focal point of the magnificent library (built 1716–1728), the gift of the king to the university at Coimbra (see Wohl essay, fig. 4). The form and decoration of the library, with its richly painted and gilded surfaces, is characteristic of the very best of Joanine art, the official courtly style named after Dom João V. The king's policy was pursued and fulfilled over subsequent decades by his envoys in Rome, and it culminated in that most refined and luxurious miniature monument, the chapel dedicated to Saint John the Baptist for the Lisbon Jesuit church of São Roque (1742–1747).[59]

On his return to Portugal in 1718, the newly created marquês de Abrantes continued to be dominant at court. He acted as the royal artistic adviser, and his ability to think on a grand scale may have encouraged the king's aim to revitalize Portuguese art, and, after a period of relative isolation, to follow artistic developments elsewhere in Europe. The marquês was also involved in devising

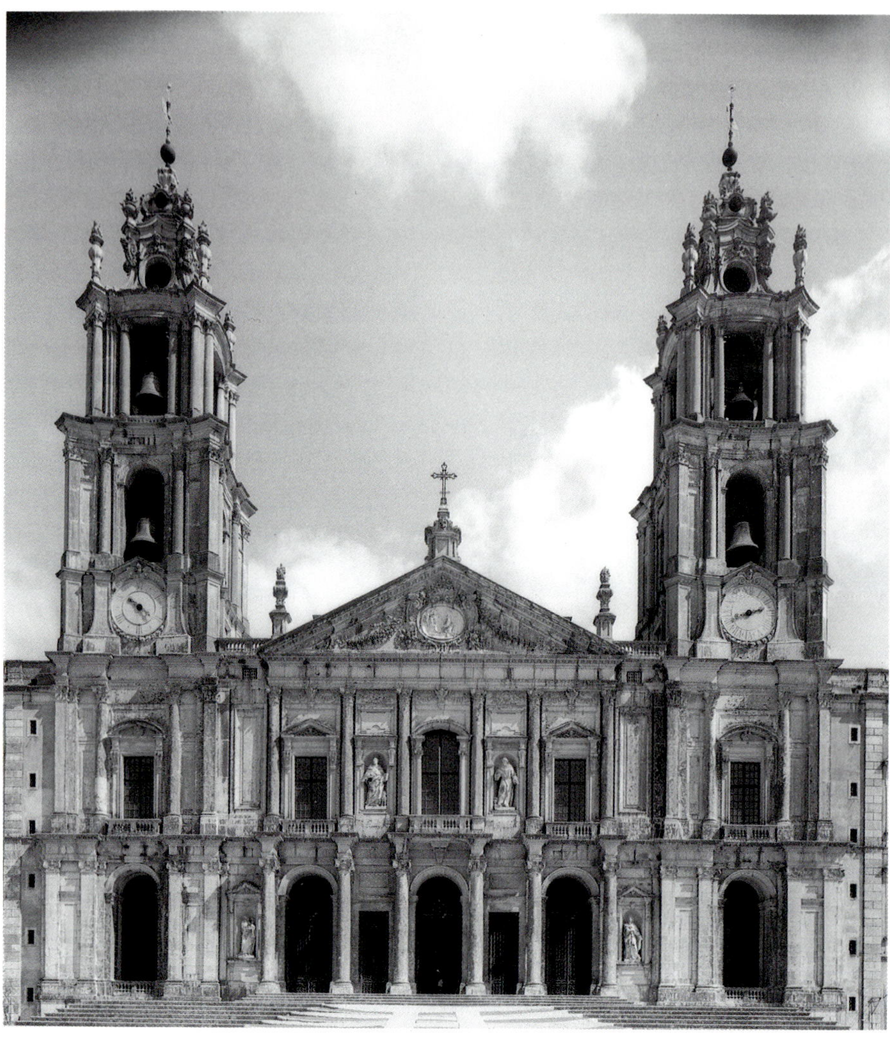

the elaborate ceremonies for the new patriarchal church, which now began to be modeled on those he had witnessed at Saint Peter's in Rome and which he recounted in detail to the king. By 1719 the nunzio reported that the liturgy conformed to that in Rome, it was "tutto al uso Romano." The magnificence on solemn feast days was said by Merveilleux in 1726 to surpass even those celebrations before the pope.[60] On 14 September 1719, Domenico Scarlatti, appointed Maestro de Cappella, and a group of Italian singers and musicians arrived in Lisbon. Their appointment to the service of the Portuguese king had been initiated in Rome by the marquês de Abrantes and came though the intervention of the papal vice-chancellor, Cardinal Ottoboni. Though the use of "musica all'Italiana" had first been noted by Nunzio Bichi in 1710, the novelty and beauty of Scarlatti's compositions and the form of music he introduced to the patriarchal church seem to have caused something of a sensation at court.[61]

The marquês de Abrantes, sharing the king's enthusiasm for architecture, accompanied him to Mafra on frequent visits to monitor progress on the building. During 1718 the massive reinforced foundations of the basilica there were being laid by an army of workers, and by October the nunzio also reported that the measurements of its ground plan were modeled on those in Rome's Jesuit church of Sant'Ignazio (by Orazio Grassi, partly completed by 1650).[62] In his designs for the elevations of Mafra, the architect Ludovice introduced various elements that derived from his study of seventeenth-century buildings in Rome: the front of the church (fig. 4) suggests Carlo Maderno's Saint Peter's (completed 1614), and the church towers, Sant'Agnese by Francesco Borromini (1653–1657). The marquês' firsthand knowledge of these buildings was invaluable. At this time it is probable that he also encouraged the king to give a more dynamic direction to the arts by sending promising Portuguese artists to study in Rome, including the sculptor José de Almeida and the painter Ignácio de Oliveira Bernardes (both in Rome from 1720). The strong Italian character of the Joanine, or late baroque, style in Portugal was directly determined by this dispatch of artists to Rome as well as by the Italian paintings and sculpture imported by the king for Mafra, for the new chancel of Évora cathedral begun in 1721 to the design of Ludovice with commissions placed in Rome of sculpture by the Paduan G. A. Bellini and a painting by Agostino Masucci of the *Assumption of the Virgin* (completed 1736), and for other buildings elsewhere.[63]

For Dom João V, Rome was always the ideal artistic and cultural model. In 1712, the architect, poet, and scholar Carlos Gimac, who accompanied the marquês de Fontes' embassy, compiled a journal for the king describing many of Rome's religious and secular buildings. But when the *Diario* was sent to Lisbon in August 1712 it was found to lack sufficient detail.[64] This frustration can only have increased the king's desire to visit the city himself. His wish to resolve his political and ecclesiastical interests more immediately could also have been a factor in his plans. For on 27 September 1715, the nunzio reported that the king was to travel incognito through Europe as far as Rome for Christmas, and then on to Jerusalem.[65] The end of the War of Spanish Succession (1702–1713), the Treaty of Utrecht signed with France in 1713 and Spain in 1715, and a Europe now at peace made this an attractive possibility. Like the historic tour of eastern Europe made by Tsar Peter the Great (1682–1725) between 1697 and 1698, it was motivated by the desire to witness European culture and progress at first hand. But although the journey was opposed by factions at court, and was interrupted by preparations for the fleet against the Turks, the idea persisted in the king's mind. Preparations for the never-to-be-realized *gran viaggio* continued. In 1716 the plan was for the king to witness Holy Week in Rome, there would be visits to Florence and Venice, but according to Nunzio Bichi, the ultimate most tantalizing destination was Rome, "essendo il suo unico e principale oggetto il portari in Roma."[66]

By the end of his reign, the king of Portugal had conjured up his own private vision of Rome. Dom João V lived in the royal palace of Terreiro do Paço surrounded by a re-creation of the Grand Tour he never made and of the city of Rome he never saw. There were endless salons filled with a series of large models of Rome's buildings, a remarkable display of her palaces and churches.[67] There were numerous architectural plans, paintings, and drawings, such as of the facade of Saint John in Lateran or of libraries in Rome, made by Carlos Gimac, and drawings of liturgical objects and apparatus used there in religious processions. There were volumes of engravings, such as those by Vasi of Rome's churches, altars, and chapels, palaces, antique triumphal arches, and obelisks, gardens, and fountains.[68] There was a magnificent silver model of Bernini's *Fountain of the Four Rivers* (1651), which, symbolizing the four continents, stands in Piazza Navona.[69] Teams of artists and craftsmen were involved in making full-scale models, such as the reconstruction of Saint Peter's and the Vatican palace and gardens, the entire complex made from meticulous drawings by Antonio Canevari (1722–1723) under the direction of the architect Giuseppe Marchetti, and sent to Lisbon, together with a model of the Lateran baptistry, in 1728. In March 1723 Charles Poerson, the director of the French academy in Rome, described this large and beautiful model made in walnut, which was so detailed that more than 8,000 rooms could be counted.[70] In 1729 a plan and model in wood and metal of the Palazzo del Quirinale, then called the Palacio de Monte Cavallo, reached Lisbon. In 1745 there arrived a large model of the altar in the Cappella Gregoriana in Saint Peter's made by Antonio Ravasi.[71] In the palace all these models may have joined the wooden model of Rome's Colosseum made in 1547 for the Aviz Dom João III (r. 1521–1557), himself an amateur architect. In any case all were destroyed in 1755, five years after the death of Dom João V, and only documents bear witness to this rare and seemingly romantic collection. But the intention was not merely to reconstruct Rome in order to satisfy the king's curiosity. Many of these models and drawings were intended as working material, an aim that becomes increasingly evident from the repeated demands to Rome for greater accuracy, detail, and measurements.[72] The drawings of libraries, such as that of the Biblioteca Apostolica Vaticana, can be connected with the planning of the library at Mafra.[73] Just before the consecration of the church at Mafra on 22 October 1730 there was further intense activity and many requests for drawings, which could be used during the concluding stages of construction as well as for decorating and furnishing the building. By this time the specific nature of the demands shows how well-informed the Lisbon court was on the latest architectural developments in Rome. During 1729 and 1730 drawings were urgently requested of Roman altarpieces, such as those in Santa Maria Maggiore and Saint John in Lateran, and of the most "modern" sacristies, such as those in Santa Maria in Vallicella, Sant'Ignazio, Bernini's Sant'Andrea al Quirinale, and the newly restored Santissimi Apostoli. At the same time there were requests for drawings of the ciborium and holy water stoops and for a plan of the Cappella Papale and its fittings, all in connection with the sacristy and other parts of Mafra.[74] In 1740 it is recorded that wooden models were made of Bernini's *baldacchino* and *cathedra petri* (1657–1666), and another made to the same measurements of the tabernacle used for the Holy Sacrament, all in Saint Peter's.[75]

Of the Italians who went to Portugal to work for Dom João V, the most gifted was the architect of Turin, Filippo Juvarra (1685–1736), who arrived in Lisbon in January 1719.[76] At this date his brilliance and creativity were already very apparent, but in Portugal his potential for new and advanced design was not to be realized. Juvarra's first link with Portugal was in 1707, when, as Fontana's pupil, he may have been involved in creating the funeral decorations for Dom Pedro II. His visit to Portugal was initiated by the marquês de Abrantes, who was moving in the Roman circles of Juvarra's influential patron, Cardinal Pietro Ottoboni. The cardinal is also known to have furthered Portugal's political affairs, for which he was rewarded with gifts by João V in 1739. Cardinal Ottoboni was a nephew of the short-lived Pope Alexander VIII (d. 1691), but he continued under successive regimes to hold the post of papal vice-chancellor, and until his death in 1740 his palace of the Cancelleria was the center of the most enlightened patronage in Rome.[77] There the scenery of the cardinal's theater was managed by Juvarra, who produced stage settings of exceptional vitality.[78] Juvarra's drawings for projects for Cardinal Ottoboni, such as *Oratory for Holy Week* (Biblioteca Nazionale, Turin), give some idea of those he created in Lisbon for Holy Week in April 1719. There the king, court, and all the foreign envoys flocked to the Italian church of Madonna di Loreto to admire his novel freestanding design with its deep perspective and dramatic lighting. The nunzio wrote of "la novità del sepolcro Isolato, e degli Altari tutti chiusi, come se fosse un gran sepolcro, tutta la chiesa illuminata con sopra 700 grossi lumi di cera e torcia dentro e fuori del prospetto principale."[79] Of the many religious processions for which the reign was renowned, that of Corpus Domini became the most famous, with people coming from all over the Iberian Peninsula to witness it. The king always walked in the procession carrying a lighted flare. Juvarra may have advised on the scenographic effects for Corpus Domini in June 1719; they were modeled on accounts brought back from Rome by the marquês de Abrantes. Even Nunzio Conti had never witnessed anything like it, and wrote that no words could describe either the extraordinary magnificence with which all Lisbon had been transformed or the beauty of the colonnades that were hung with series of tapestries worked in gold thread from the royal collection.[80]

The nunzio made plain that Juvarra's visit was not connected with Mafra, as the building was already well advanced. It was, he says, specifically for planning the new patriarchal church, a project that had first been considered in March 1717. The existing church had become too small for its new function and the large number of clergy who now presided. The ideal had already been determined, and the building was intended to follow the Roman model, with the church and palace linked, "all'uso di Roma." It was to have a special symbolic and ideological significance, with palace and church united in celebration of the special relationship between the Portuguese monarch and the church.[81] Previously in Rome in 1717, Juvarra had been asked to revise and develop a project for the royal palace and Patriarchate, which had been made by the marquês de Abrantes himself, "un modello di sua invenzione."[82] This has not been traced, but it may be the designs for the building of which the nunzio wrote in Lisbon on 2 March 1717 (note 47 above). In any case this collaboration dates to after the ambassador's arrival in Rome in 1712, the year in which Juvarra became a Pastore Arcade through the support of his patron and prince of the Arcadia, Cardinal Ottoboni.[83] During this Roman period, Juvarra was working on an unrealized project for a new facade for Saint John in Lateran (1715) and on his only work in Rome, the beautiful Cappella Antamoro (1708–1710) in San Girolamo della Carità. The permission from Vittorio Amadeo II of Savoy for Juvarra to work in the service of the king of Portugal is in a letter dated 14 August 1719 and can be related to the newly restored political and diplomatic relationship between Turin and Portugal.[84]

A close collaboration and accord developed between patron and architect during the six months in Lisbon. Nunzio Conti reported how Juvarra always traveled with the king in his carriage as they conferred over the planning of the new building, and he wrote of the king's intense application to the task. At court there was an excited air of anticipation as the advantages of each possible site were debated, including the first, which was to be beside the Tagus at Terreiro do Paço (plans made by 14 March 1719). When Juvarra sailed from Lis-

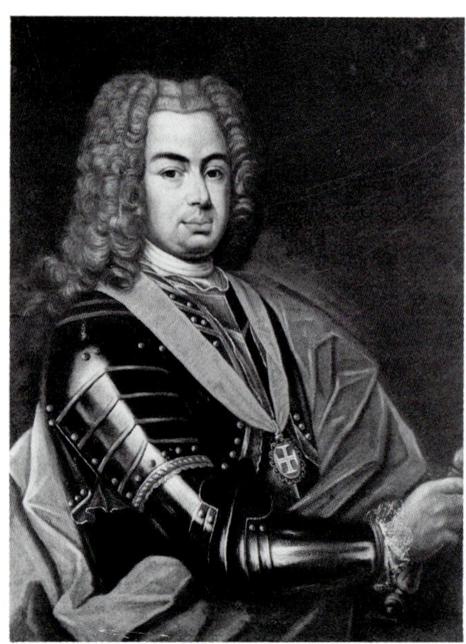

fig. 5. Attributed to Pier Leone Ghezzi, *Dom João V as Pastore Arcade Wearing the Order of Christ*, 1721, oil on canvas. Museo di Roma

bon on 20 July 1719, he had completed plans and drawings, "delle bellisime piante e disegni magnificentissimi," for two sites, the second building being on a larger scale and suitable for the terrain in the area known as Buenos Aires at Alcântara. Of these only sketchlike drawings have survived (Museo Civico, Turin) for the second site, which was the one finally chosen. Significantly it was away from the traditional waterside setting of the Portuguese monarchs beside the port, the Casa da India and the Arsenal. These drawings show how the new building would have dramatically dominated the city, set high on elevated slopes with fine views to the river and out to sea.[85] They show a centrally planned building with a high cupola and four lateral bell towers, and they contain elements of ideas conceived by Juvarra earlier in Rome. It does appear as if Juvarra intended to rework plans he had submitted to the academy of Saint Luke for his admission on 3 April 1707 *(in situ)*. Both sets show a similar design and both were inspired by Roman baroque buildings, especially Sant'Agnese in Piazza Navona (begun 1653, by Borromoni and Carlo Rainaldi).[86] It can also be seen from the sketches for Lisbon how the setting for the patriarchal church evokes the reconstruction made by Juvarra of the ancient Roman Campidoglio, recorded in his drawing of 1709 (Biblioteca Nazionale, Turin).[87] On 25 April 1719 it was reported that the king might be reconsidering such a major conception in view of the unsettled state of Europe and, the nunzio speculated, in the absence of general peace. It is also likely that the king, who always had a very strong sense of his own mortality, was reluctant to begin a building he might never see completed. The planning resumed in May and preparation of the site continued until September but was then finally abandoned. It was a scheme that would have transformed the city of Lisbon and one that would have created an opportunity, which in artistic terms is perhaps comparable to Bernini's great abandoned project for the Louvre of 1665.[88] Juvarra with his practice of drawing after the antique was, however, able to delight and maybe flatter the king's imperial aspirations with a separate design for a column imitating those made for the emperors of Imperial Rome, "sullo stile antico," and with the royal coat of arms (untraced), a project that also reflects the antiquarian interests of the Arcadia in Rome in these years.[89]

The Lusitanian presence was felt even more forcefully in Rome during the first half of the 1720s. Dom João V began to make a significant and more public investment in ecclesiastical projects not directly connected with the Holy See. He also moved toward a broader promotion of the arts: of literature, theater, and music. He became involved with the celebrated Accademia dell'Arcadia, which since its foundation in 1690 had received the support of Clement XI and his entourage. In November 1721, following the death of Clement XI, the Arcadia, in a move promoted by Prince Ruspoli and its first custodian general, Giovanni Maria Crescimbeni, canon of Santa Maria in Cosmedin, resolved that Clement XI's place and pastoral name of Arete Melleo should be taken by Dom João of Portugal. It was also voted that in honor of the concession and title of Patriarchate given to Lisbon by Clement XI in 1716, the king of Portugal should become a patron of the Arcadia. A portrait of Dom João V shown as Pastore Arcade marks the event (fig. 5).[90] Cultural and political divisions that had shaken the roots of the Arcadia in 1711 were completely healed, and it has been shown how this form of international papal diplomacy was a determining factor in the Arcadia's gradual rise in importance. In the privileged ambient of the Arcadia, Portuguese diplomats and clergy were able to move at the center of Rome's ecclesiastical, artistic, and intellectual life, to develop contacts and increase their influence. The king could carry out his cultural program more fully by employing artists attached to the academy of Saint Luke who were also accredited to the associated Arcadia, such as Francesco Trevisani, Agostino Masucci, and the architect Antonio Canevari. Canevari was to work in Portugal between 1727 and 1732, for a short while on the great aqueduct of Aguas Livres, which the king gave to the city of Lisbon, on designs in the palace that included a clock and bell towers (destroyed 1755), and most success-fully in his design for the elegant summer palace and church assigned by the king to the first patriarch, Dom Tomás de Almeida, and his successors at Santo Antão do Tojal, outside Lisbon.[91]

The election in May 1721 of Cardinal Conti as Pope Innocent XIII was marked in Lisbon by a *Te Deum* sung in the patriarchal church.[92] In Rome it was soon apparent, however, that the new pope did not intend to deviate from the hard line of his predecessor, Clement XI, over granting a cardinalate to Nunzio Bichi, as Dom João V had long since requested. Nevertheless Conti was an accomplished diplomat and he continued to maintain good relations with Portugal and her envoys in Rome at a different and less official level. The acceptance of Dom João V into the Arcadia in November 1721, under the aus-pices of Innocent XIII's papacy, and all the celebrations accorded to the king, can be interpreted in this context. And on 16 November 1721, in honor of the new pope, the Ambassador Mello e Castro staged the pastorale *La Virtù negl'amori* with music by Alessandro Scarlatti and with stage sets by the cele-brated Francesco Galli-Bibiena. This spectacle at the Teatro Capranica con-cluded with a staging of the great chariot of the sun, and an apotheosis of João V and the newly elected pope, which was, it was said, "a dimostrazione del Vaticinio loro assegnato dai mitologi."[93]

Portugal's increased commitment to a policy of diplomacy, united with pa-tronage of the arts, had become evident after the arrival in Rome in July 1721 (even if a little late for the conclave) of the Portuguese cardinals Pereira de Lacerda (made cardinal in 1720) and Nuno da Cunha, accompanied by the theologian Canon Pedro da Motta e Silva (made Enviado Extraordinario in Rome in 1722, cardinal in 1727).[94] The two cardinals lived in Rome in great style and opulence. They became Pastori Arcadi, so acquiring their plots of mythi-cal land in Arcadia. In August 1721 they attended the Arcadia's celebrations for the new pope, Innocent XIII, the *Giuochi Olimpici* held in the gardens of Prince Ruspoli on the Aventine.[95] By July 1721 Cardinal da Cunha had begun the major restoration of his titular church of Sant'Anastasia (rebuilt 1606, fa-cade 1636) following the designs prepared by Carlos Gimac. The emphasis on restoration in Rome's early churches, such as at Santissimi Apostoli, had, as been shown, received active support from Clement XI, and this ideology con-tinued to be promoted by the Arcadia. In the nave of Sant'Anastasia the cardi-nal's coat of arms and lengthy inscriptions prominently record the Lusitanian connection. He commissioned a series of eight paintings of saints connected with Portugal, such as of *Beata Juana, Princess of Portugal* by Michelangelo Cerruti, and a large painting by the same artist of the *Martydom of Saint Anas-tasia* in perspective set into the coffered ceiling of the nave (all, 1722). Two new altarpieces were dedicated to Saint George, to whom the castle of Lisbon is

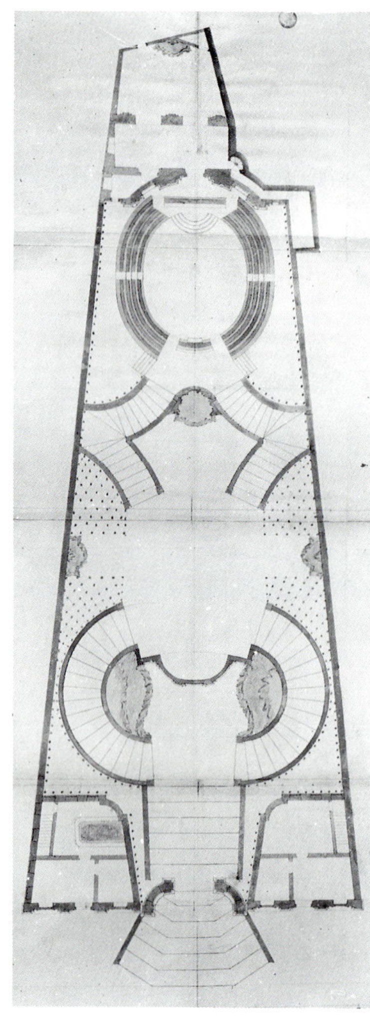

fig. 6. Antonio Canevari, *Plan of the Bosco Parrasio dell'Arcadia,* Rome, drawing. Accademia di San Luca, Rome

dedicated, and to Saint John the Baptist, namesake of the king.[96] In 1721 the intense Portuguese activity continued when Cardinal Pereira de Lacerda celebrated the saint's day on 16 August of his titular church, Santa Susanna (early church, remodeled 1593 and facade 1597 by Carlo Maderno), with festival decorations by Antonio Canevari on the triumphal arch over the choir. Several events were devoted to the theater, including the entertainment financed by the cardinal for the Accademia dei Cavalieri and held in the courtyard of the Collegio Clementino with allegorical stage sets by Francesco Galli-Bibiena.[97]

The Accademia dell'Arcadia had led an uncertain and nomadic existence since its formation in 1690; one of their open-air meeting places had been in the idyllic Orti Farnesiani.[98] The gift of 4,000 *scudi* to the Arcadia by Dom João V on 24 September 1723 made possible their first permanent seat. It is documented in the *Fatti degli Arcadi* that by December 1723 a site had been chosen for the Bosco Parrasio on the Gianicolo, a legendary plot sacred to Apollo. The plan was commissioned from Antonio Canevari, and the drawing shows his brilliant use of the very narrow site and a subtle play on a series of curvilinear forms (fig. 6).[99] Ambassador Mello e Castro both advised the king and encouraged the project in meetings with the custodian and leading Arcadians.[100] The king's patronage of the prestigious Arcadia was imaginative. At the time it was acknowledged as showing the king's gratitude to Clement XI for granting the Lisbon patriarchial church. In Rome Dom João's benefaction to the Arcadia was reported in the *Diario di Roma* following the opening on 9 September 1726, and, in 1751, following the king's death, in an elegant *Orazione* (fig. 7). His generosity is recorded for posterity in the conspicuous inscription on the marble monument at the entrance of the Bosco Parrasio. Above this monument it was once intended to erect a statue of Apollo, with his symbols of lyre and mask, as the embodiment of the Greek classical spirit.[101]

The Arcadia had grown out of the private academy formed by the exiled Queen Christina of Sweden, the members of which had been leading figures among Rome's prelates and laity, including Cardinal Giovanni Francesco Albani, subsequently Clement XI. In associating himself with the Arcadians, Dom João V would have been very conscious of their by-now legendary founder, whose presence in Rome was still vividly recalled and whose dramatic abdication and conversion to Roman Catholicism was seen as a living symbol of the triumph of faith over heresy. She died in 1689, but her tomb by Fontana in Saint Peter's was completed only in 1702 under Clement XI. It is fitting that the Arcadia's permanent seat, the Bosco Parrasio, should overlook the gardens of the Palazzo Riario, now the Palazzo Corsini, where Christina lived from 1662 until her death.[102] The design for the Bosco Parrasio follows in the tradition of the open-air theaters in the gardens of Roman villas of antiquity. The steep slope is divided into three successive levels, connected by curved symmetrical flights of steps that pause at a grotto and then lead up to a small amphitheater. The arrangement of the steps can be connected to contemporary designs in Rome such as that for the Spanish Steps by Francesco de'Sanctis (1723–1728); and the first level resembles the ingeniously curved steps added by Alessandro Specchi to the Porta di Ripetta in 1707 (destroyed). The miniature villa of the Bosco Parrasio is like a stage set, its convex facade acting as a backdrop to the small theater where the Arcadians gathered to recite their compositions. An engraving after Canevari's design shows the pairs of statues of the

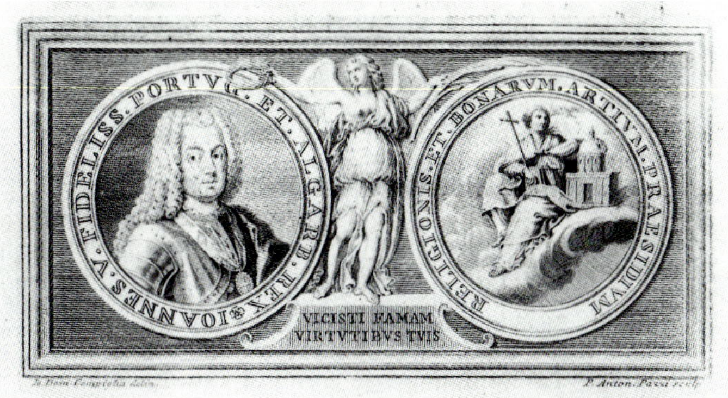

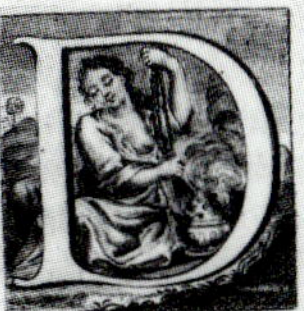

gods Pan and Syrinx and Pallas and Mercury, all connected with the arts and literature, that were once above the entrance. On either side were fountains incorporating statues of river gods, the Tevere and Arno, representing the Latin and Tuscan poetry that was declaimed by the Arcadians. In a grotto once stood the figure of Alceo, the image for Greek poetry and emblematic of a lost golden age, a sense of which still pervades this enclosed garden (fig. 8).

Life in Arcadia was overshadowed, however, by political reality. There were increasing difficulties between Rome and Lisbon relating to the nunciature of Vincenzo Bichi (nunzio 1710–1721). In view of Portugal's very real financial contribution to the church, Dom João wanted a precedent established, one obtaining in Vienna, Paris, and Madrid, that the reward for service as nunzio in Portugal should be a cardinal's hat. The king had made repeated requests to Clement XI, Innocent XIII, and the Orsini pope Benedict XIII (1724–1730) for this favor, but Bichi had associated his interests too completely with those of the Portuguese government to please Rome. His generosity with special temporary indulgences in Lisbon against the wishes of Rome had also made him ineligible.[103] Finally in January 1728, after two years of threats and endless rumors, Dom João V, always preoccupied with his personal prestige, was reported to be gravely offended by the pope's stand. He ordered Ambassador Mello e Castro and Cardinal Pereira de Lacerda to leave Rome and declared a formal break with the Holy See. At the same time, Bichi, who since 1721 had refused to leave Lisbon, and Nunzio Firrao were obliged to remove the pontifical arms

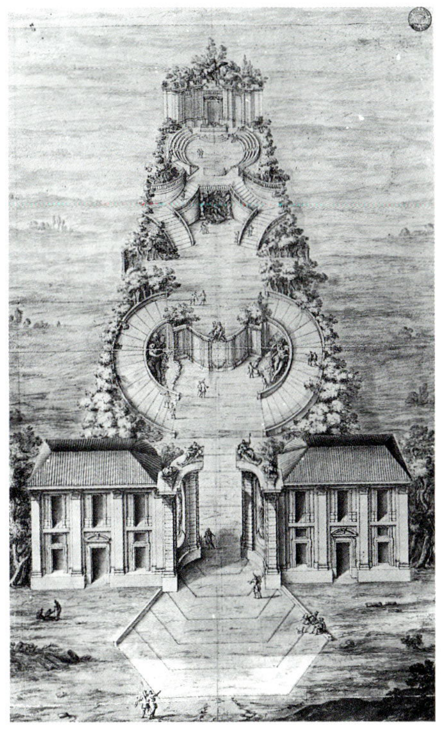

from their residence and ordered to leave Portuguese territory.[104] In Rome, the repercussions of the *rotura,* the break in diplomatic relations, were immediate. By May 1728 the Portuguese academy had been closed and its directors and pupils departed.[105] This academy, which had been formed in about 1720, with the Lisbon Real Academia de Historia established in that same year, was part of the cultural reformation initiated by João V in this period.[106] By 1725 the Portuguese academy, which it was said with some scepticism wished to emulate the stability of the prestigious French academy in Rome, was based in the Palazzo Magnani, beside San Lorenzo in Lucina, and directed by Paolo de Matteis.[107] A lack of continuity in its activities and direction always meant that its presence had little impact in Rome, though in 1725 José de Almeida won a prize in the prestigious Concurso Clementino in competition with Rome's leading sculptors.[108] The break in 1728 also meant the suspension of commissions for Portugal, although some silversmiths moved to Florence and outside the papal state in order to complete the work in hand. The loss of Portugal's considerable spending in Rome soon began to be felt.[109]

The election of the Florentine Lorenzo Corsini as Pope Clement XII, on 24 September 1730, opened the way to a compromise and brought an end to the two-year-old diplomatic break. Bichi received his cardinalate in 1731, and in the following year Dom João V sent the new cardinal more than 25,000 *cruzados,* enabling him to enter Rome with befiting magnificence.[110] In 1730 the energetic and scholarly Franciscan, Frei José Maria da Fonseca e Évora (1690–1752), became minister for Portugal in Rome. Throughout the crisis he had been trying to resolve the situation with the papacy by using his influence among the cardinals of the curia.[111] Fonseca e Évora had first arrived in Rome in 1712 in the suite of marquês de Fontes and remained there until 1741, when years of dedication were rewarded by his appointment as archbishop of Oporto. His long and distinguished activity in Rome was focused on the church of Santa Maria in Aracoeli. There, with funding by the Portuguese crown, he built a library (1733), and he had restored the chapel of Saint Francis, formerly Savelli, in the right transept of the church, with the architect Filippo Raguzzini, and commissioned the altarpiece, a painting of *Saint Francis in Ecstasy* by Francesco Trevisani (1728), which with the chapel had been consecrated by Benedict XIII on 4 October 1728.[112] On 25 September 1728, Fonseca e Évora, who was a master at staging ceremonies, had transformed Santa Maria in Aracoeli in celebration of the canonization of Margherita of Cortona; the spectacular decoration of the nave and facade were by the Portuguese architect active in Rome, Manuel Rodrigues dos Santos (1733-1771); these are recorded in engravings (fig. 9) and a drawing by Giacomo de Santi.[113] Fonseca e Évora also rebuilt the Franciscan church and monastery of Santa Maria di Palazzola, which still bears the Lusitanian coats of arms (completed 1735 by architect Domenico Navone), and he laid out the surrounding garden in the beautiful setting on the shores of Lake Albani, facing across the lake the papal summer residence of Castel Gandolfo. At Palazzola he entertained members of the Corsini household, and the close relationship he developed with them and with the curia is revealed in a group portrait attributed to Agostino Masucci that once hung in his library. It shows *Padre Fonseca e Évora with Cardinals Passeri, Corsini, and Gentili,* and portraits of Clement XII and Dom João V of Portugal hang on the wall behind (Biblioteca Nazionale Centrale Vittorio

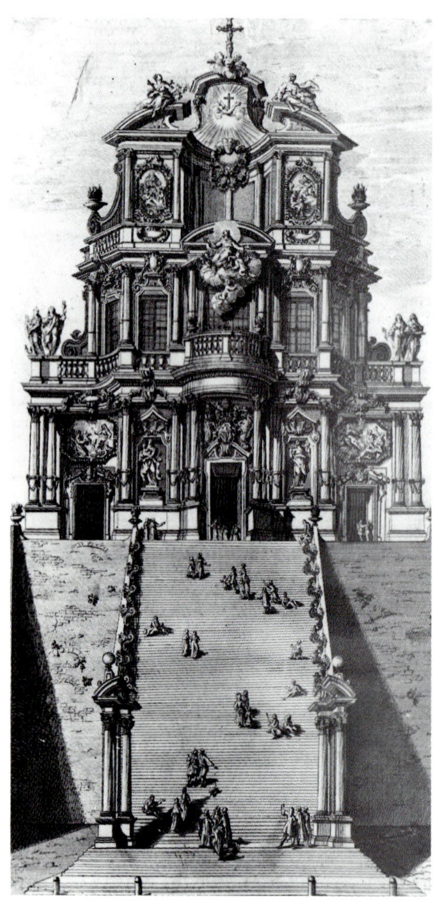

fig. 9. F. Nasconi, *Facade of Santa Maria in Aracoeli Decorated for the Canonization of Santa Margarita di Cortona on 25 September 1725,* engraving after a design by Manuel Rodrigues dos Santos

Emanuele II, Rome). The event recorded is the consistory of 20 December 1737, when, finally and only due to the patient diplomacy of Fonseca e Évora and Cardinal Neri Corsini, it was agreed that the patriarch of Lisbon, Dom Tomás de Almeida, would be nominated as cardinal and that the name of his successors should be put forward by the Portuguese crown. This was a concession that the king had long been determined to get and that had been debated among the curia since the early 1730s.[114] Fonseca e Évora was also responsible for the major task of placing and coordinating all the commissions in Italy for paintings, sculpture, altar plate, and other furnishings for Mafra, and these are recorded during the 1730s in correspondence with Frei José Correa de Abreu, superintendent of royal works at Mafra.[115] The paintings for the altars of the basilica are all by Roman masters; they include a *Pentecost* and a *Crucifixion* by Corrado Giaquinto, an *Immaculate Conception* by Giovanni Odazzi, another *Immaculate Conception* by Sebastiano Conca, and the *Coronation of the Virgin* by Francesco Mancini (all 1730, Museum, Palácio Nacional de Mafra).

Cardinal Neri Corsini (d. 1770), nephew of Clement XII, became Protettore del Regno di Portogallo in 1739, but, as has been seen, he was already closely associated with João V's sustained artistic and political initiative in Rome during this decade. The pope and his nephew collaborated and shared an interest in art and scholarship that was reflected in the gatherings at the Palazzo Corsini. In 1736 Ferdinando Fuga was commissioned by the cardinal to transform the former Palazzo Riario to house their picture gallery, important library, and print collection.[116] They built the beautiful Corsini Chapel (design of Alessandro Galilei, 1732–1736) in Saint John in Lateran, of which the cardinal was archpriest. There, the lavish nature of the decoration is everywhere tempered by a restrained quality in light and color and by the sober classicism of the ornament, all qualities that have led the chapel to be seen as epitomizing Roman art of this transitional period from baroque to early neoclassicism.[117] Many of the sculptors active in the Corsini Chapel were also working for Dom João V on the sculpture he imported for the very different and isolated setting at Mafra, a commission on a scale that was without precedent in the eighteenth century. It can therefore be seen how closely the Mafra commission was defined by the taste of the Corsini in Rome. More than fifty over-life-size figures of saints from the most prestigious Roman and Florentine masters were intended for the facade, portico, and the niches of colored marble in the vestibule (or narthex) and along the nave of the basilica at Mafra, and when installed they formed a magnificent gallery of contemporary sculpture in the *barocchetto* style, a display unparalled outside Italy (see Montagu essay in this volume). The vestibule is particularly fine, with perfect equilibrium between architecture and sculpture, the play of light and reflection and the effects of the material creating scenographic effects that are so characteristic of João V's reign. The correspondence from 1730 between Lisbon and Rome suggests that speed, perfection of finish, and appropriate iconography were the dominant criteria; it gives little evidence of a formal thematic program.[118] Among sculptors in the service of the Corsini who also worked for Mafra was their Florentine protégé, Filippo della Valle (*Saõ Jeronimo*) along with Guiseppe Rusconi (*Saõ Benedetto* and *Saõ Bernardo*), Giovan Battista Maini (*Saõ Chiari, Santa Elisabetta,* among several) and Carlo Monaldi, also much favored by the Portuguese, who carved five of the statues, including *Saõ Domenico* and *Saõ*

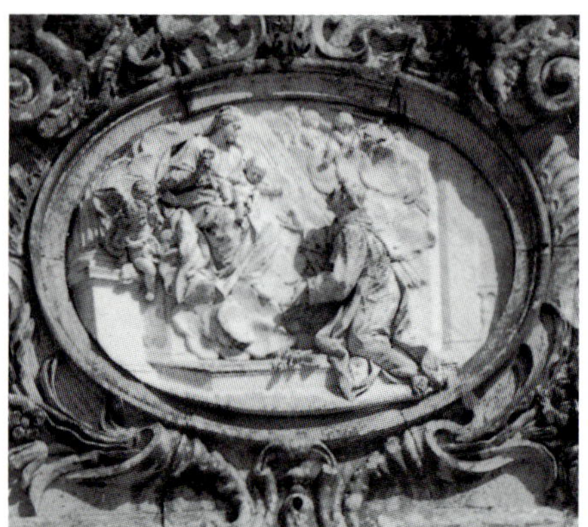

fig. 10. Carlo Monaldi, *Madonna and Child with Saint Anthony*, 1730–1733, marble, basilica at Mafra

Francesco and made the relief of the *Madonna and Child with Saint Anthony* (fig. 10) for the dedication for the portico (all Mafra, in situ, commissioned 1730, sent 1732 and 1733).[119]

Monaldi's marble bust of *Frei José de Fonseca e Évora* (1740, Collegio Romano, Rome) marks his departure from Rome and records the important diplomatic role of the Franciscan in healing relations with the Corsini Clement XII following the breach with Portugal. During this period Monaldi also carved the allegorical figure of *Magnificence* that stands beside the bronze *Clement XII* by Maini in the Corsini Chapel in Saint John in Lateran and celebrates this other great patron of the arts. In one hand the statue holds a marble sheet of the plan by Galilei chosen for the new facade (1733–1735); the other points to this plan of the most important artistic project of the Corsini papacy.[120]

The last decade of the reign of Dom João was distinguished by his close relationship with the Bolognese Lambertini pope, Benedict XIV, elected on 17 August 1740. Benedict XIV's private letters written to Cardinal de Tencin convey his almost paternal feeling toward the Portuguese king, who responded by sponsoring a new edition of a work close to the heart of the scholarly Prospero Lambertini, his *Martirologia Romano* (1748).[121] The reconciliation with the papacy was complete. In the same year the king's remarkable political success with the Holy See was crowned when, in recognition of his very real contribution to the church, Benedict XIV granted Dom João V and his successors the title of *Rei Fidelissimo,* an act that was "in benemerenza di quanto ha fatto, e fa continuamente quel Re in benefizio della Religione e di questà S Sede." The title (signed 23 December 1748) granted new dignity to the Portuguese crown and equality with the titles of the Spanish and French monarchs, respectively *Rei Católico* and *Cristianissimo.*[122] Through Portugal's new ambassador in Rome, Manuel Pereira de Sampaio (1681–1750), minister plenipotentiary from 1740, her interests and demands for further benefits and ecclesiastical titles for the church were zealously promoted with ever more lavish payments and gifts, all, in the apt phrase of Valesio, in accordance with the pious extravagance of the king. These included a gold chalice emblazoned with the Portuguese arms given in 1742 to Saint Peter's, and in December 1745 the king's generous contribution to the funds of that basilica. All this munificence coincided with the arrival in Lisbon of the greatest quantity of gold and diamonds from Brazil; these shipments were assiduously noted by, among several, Nunzio Oddi in June 1740 and by Nunzio Tempi, to the secretary of state, Cardinal Valenti Gonzaga, in 1745 and 1747.[123]

There is an account of the king in his last years rising early to watch the fleet departing for India from a window of the palace. Throughout the reign, the nunzio would report on the arrival of ships from Asia and Brazil, not only with currency in the form of gold and diamonds, but with a whole array of exotic objects: 899 ivory elephant tusks, rare woods from the American Indies and the Brazilian wood called *legno santo,* Chinese and Japanese porcelain, Chinese silks, lacquer panels, Indian textiles, precious stones such as a magnificent pearl sent to the king by the emperor of China, and rare animals and birds. In Rome the Portuguese envoys and cardinals became known for their lavish gifts of these highly desirable objects from every part of the empire to the papacy, the curia, and Roman nobility, as on 28 April 1722 when Cardinal da Cunha gave the pope's brother, Cardinal Conti, "une quantité prodigieuse de porcelaine de la Chine and du Japon, avec des coffres, cabinets, des sièges et autre raretez des Indes."[124]

By the 1740s reports from Lisbon by Nunzio Tempi (1739–1744) and Jacopo Oddi (1744–1754) reveal that court life had become dominated by public prayers and processions for the king after he became seriously ill in May 1742. On 2 October 1742 he suffered a further epileptic stroke and paralysis and was not expected to live.[125] It is significant that the order sent to Rome for the nave chapel of the late sixteenth-century Jesuit church of São Roque in Lisbon, to be dedicated to the Holy Spirit and Saint John the Baptist, was made on 26 October 1742. The timing indicates that the chapel was an ex-voto made by the king, fearful of death, just as earlier a new chapel, dedicated to the Madonna, at the Palácio de Necessidades was said by the nunzio to be a votive building given by the king in June 1742 in thanks for his recovery.[126] The making of the chapel of Saint John the Baptist is documented in detail. It was to be designed,

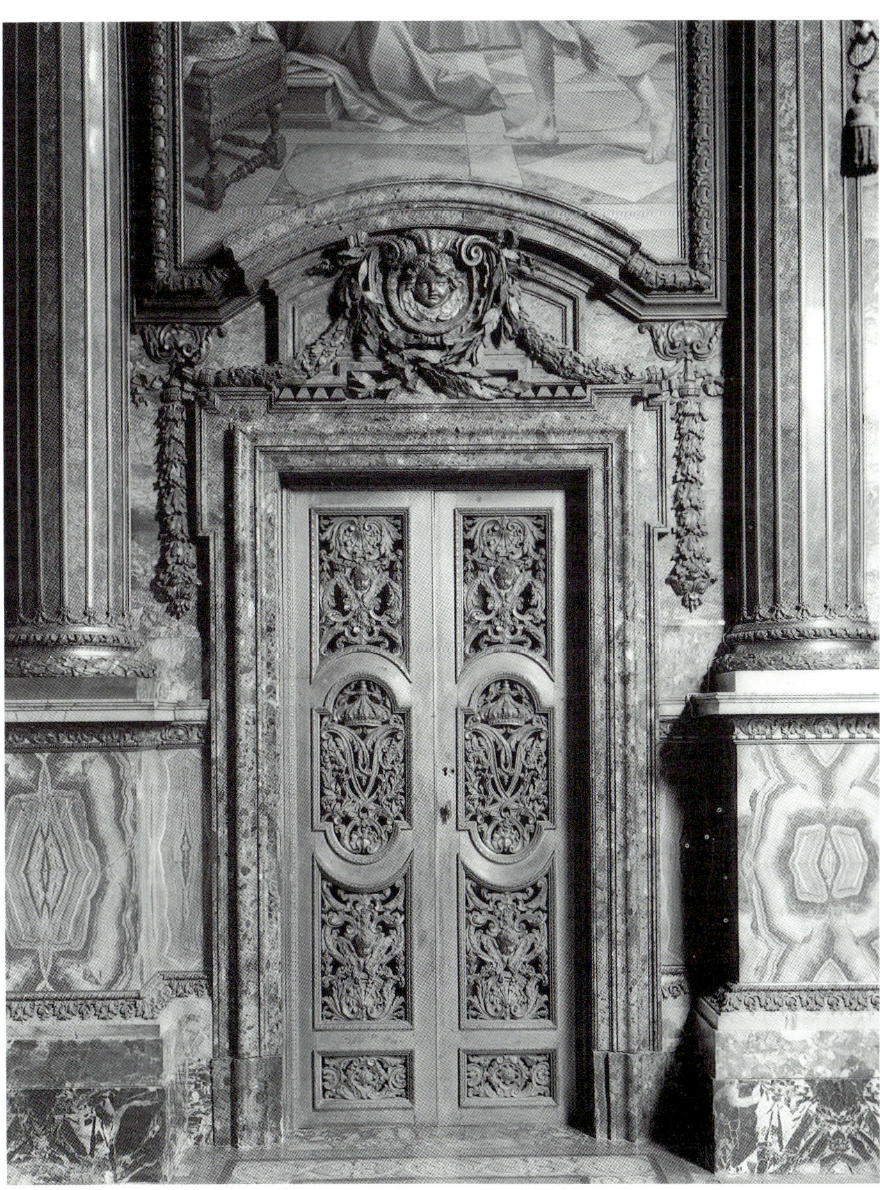

fig. 11. Luigi Vanvitelli and Nicola Salvi, *Chapel of Saint John the Baptist, São Roque,* Lisbon, side door, 1742–1744

at the king's request, by the best architect to be found in Rome, Luigi Van-vitelli, and by Nicola Salvi. The paintings by the king's favorite Italian artist, Agostino Masucci, depicting the *Baptism of Christ,* the *Annunciation,* and the *Pentecost* were in the final project replaced in mosaic.[127] Before being shipped to Lisbon, the chapel and all its accompanying liturgical objects were set up in the Palazzo Capponi-Cardelli in Via Ripetta where, on 23 April 1747, it was blessed by Benedict XIV who afterward joined many of the cardinals and nobility at a lavish reception given by Ambassador Sampaio who had supervised the project.[128] All Rome was said to wonder at the magnificence of this Italian creation destined for Lisbon. Made of rare and precious materials possessing the rich surfaces beloved by the king, such as agate, porphyry, amethyst for the altar, lapis lazuli for the columns, ormolu, gilded bronze for the cornice, mosaics for the floor, and silver, the chapel is the finest of the building and decorative programs he initiated. The chapel epitomizes royal taste and aspirations. It also marks a stylistic transition of the courtly Joanine art toward a more restrained and refined neoclassicism. There is in Rome no comparable ensemble capable of demonstrating so clearly the elegance and high technical and artistic achievement in the city in the mid-eighteenth century during the pontificate of Benedict XIV (fig. 11). In 1747 the sculptor Alessandro Giusti went to Lisbon to direct the installation of the chapel in São Roque. The king's long career as a Maecenas is commemorated in his marble bust, *Dom João V* (see Russell-Wood, fig. 1). The aged sovereign is shown in court armor, crowned with a laurel wreath and with symbols of the arts and sciences.[129]

In his last years Dom João V was said to think of nothing but the Patriarchate, while affairs of state were left to Providence: "Di questa Corte non ho da communicarla cose interessanti, perchè il Re e quello che vuol far tutto, e non pensa ad altro che alla sua Patriarcale lasciando gl'altri affari alla Providenza" (13 October 1744).[130] In the 1740s the enlargement of the Patriarchate was projected once again. Though the nunzio wrote of the "architects" for the new design, they are not named. It has been concluded that the plan was by

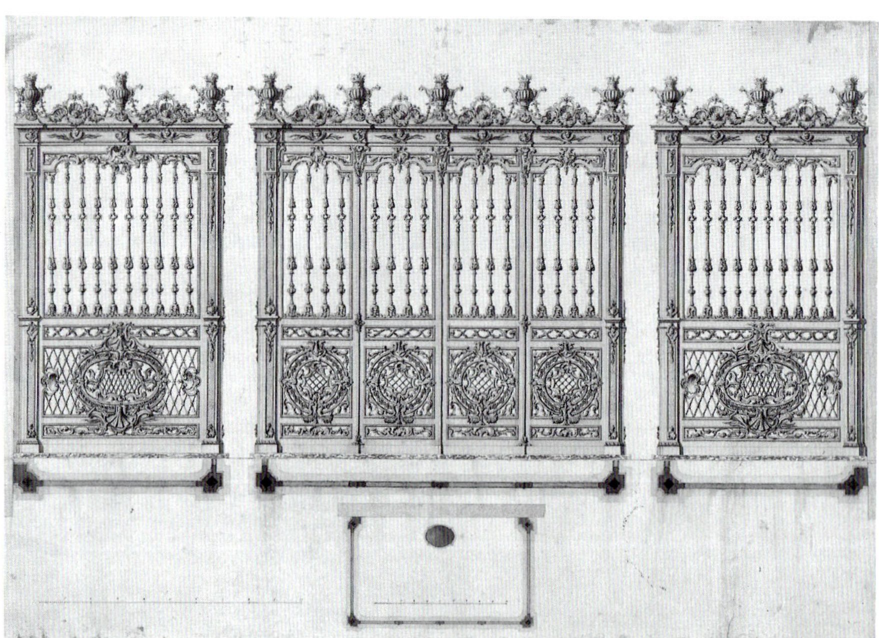

fig. 12. Andrea Valadier, *Design for the Gates of the Baptistery of the Patriarchate in Lisbon with Plan,* c. 1744–1747, pen and ink with wash over graphite. Artemis Group, London

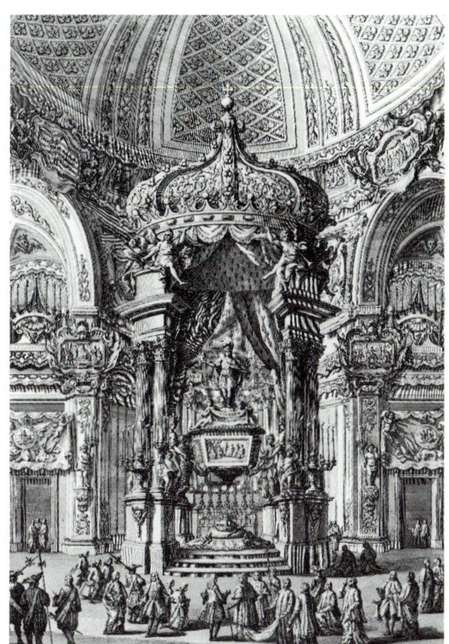

fig. 13. Giuseppe Vasi, *Funeral Decorations for the Memorial Service for Dom João V Erected in Sant'Antonio dei Portoghesi, Rome,* engraving dated 1751 after a design by Manuel Rodrigues dos Santos, with statue of Dom João V by Pietro Bracci. Bibliotèca Hertziana, Rome

Ludovice and that his model for the patriarch's residence is known to have been the Vatican apartments. In May 1741 work was shortly to begin on measuring the terrain and clearing the site, which involved the destruction of 600 houses. As the documentation in March 1745 shows, the king was increasingly dependent on the arrival of Brazilian gold to pay for the massive building. By August 1745 he commanded that the building be complete by Christmas, and to this end was said to have borrowed money from the Dutch.[131] The church was consecrated in 1746, and among the quantity of objects documented as coming from Rome were copies of all the candlesticks in Saint Peter's (ordered June 1741) and a statue in silver (arrived Lisbon, March 1746).[132] A drawing attributed to Luigi Vanvitelli is the only record of the magnificent baptismal font, commissioned in Rome in 1743, and made of antique marbles, alabaster, and lapis lazuli with gilded bronze decoration, destined for the baptistery of the patriarchal church (Museu Nacional de Arte Antiga, Lisbon). The font was enclosed by great gilded bronze gates designed and made in Rome by Andrea Valadier (1744–1747) and known from three drawings (fig. 12).[133] The last commissions for Lisbon displayed in Rome were the remarkable monumental candlesticks for São Roque (see cat. 107), made from the design of G. B. Maini by Giuseppe Gagliardi and Francisco Giardoni, and the life-size gilded silver statue of the *Immaculate Conception* also by Maini and Gagliardi for the high altar of the Patriarchate, a figure of special devotion to Dom João V (destroyed 1755). After a ceremony of papal blessing in Sampaio's residence in the Palazzo Contestabile Colonna in October 1749, Benedict XIV was moved to describe the extraordinary beauty and fine craftsmanship of the two candlesticks and statue in a letter to Cardinal Tencin.[134]

Dom João V died on 31 July 1750. In Rome his death was solemnized by elaborate funeral decorations, the "castrum doloris" in the church of Sant'Antonio dei Portoghesi designed by Manuel Rodrigues dos Santos (fig. 13), and by a catafalque in Santissimi Apostoli beside Palazzo Colonna.[135] For nearly fifty years the Portuguese king had paid homage to Rome and had sought to identify himself and his country with the papal city by emulating her magnificence and grandeur. It was a vision most vividly reflected at Mafra. There on the facade is a balcony of benediction, which was modeled on that of Saint Peter's in the city of the popes and yet was intended for a king. His dream was to endure in a monument that continued to stimulate the imagination. In 1787 William Beckford wrote from the desert landscape of Mafra, "we entered the church, passing through its magnificent portico, which reminded me of the entrance to Saint Peter's, and is adorned by colossal statues of saints and martyrs carved with infinite delicacy out of blocks of the purest marble... never did I behold such a profusion of beautiful marble as gleamed above, below, and around me."[136]

The research on which this text is based was carried out in Rome and the Archivio Segreto Vaticano and was made possible by a fellowship from the Calouste Gulbenkian Foundation, Lisbon. I am deeply grateful to the Foundation and to their Director, Dr. José Blanco, for this support.

The following abbreviations are used throughout:
ASV Portogallo; Seg.: Archivio Segreto Vaticano, Segretaria di Stato, Nunziatura di Portogallo; Segnatura
BN Lisbon: Biblioteca Nacional, Lisbon
Ajuda: Palácio Nacional da Ajuda, Lisbon

In the quotations the original orthography has been retained.

1. *Disegno e Pianta dell'Arco detto di Portogallo* 1662, Biblioteca Apostolica Vaticana, Cod. Chigi, PVII, 13, fol. 32. M. Vasi, *Roma del Settecento, Itinerario Istruttivo di Roma* (Rome, 1763), ed. Rome, 1970, from ed. of 1794, 49. Blaeu, *Nouveau Theatre d'Italie*, 4 (1704), tav. 22 and 24 in *Roma aeterna Petri Schenkii* (Amsterdam, 1705), tav.7.

2. F. G. Cancellieri, *Roma Lusitana* (1817), ed. Milan, 1926. E. Brazão, *D. João V e a Santa Se. As relações diplomaticas de Portugal com o Governo Pontificio de 1706 a 1750* (Coimbra, 1937). E. Brazão, *Relações externas de Portugal, Reinado de D. João V;* 2 vols. (Lisbon, 1938). Padre J. de Castro, *Portugal em Roma* (Lisbon, 1939). A. de Carvalho, *D. João V e a Arte do seu Tempo;* 2 vols. (Lisbon, 1962). V. E. Giuntella, *Roma nel Settecento* (Bologna, 1971). Y. Bottineau, "Le gout de Jean V; Art et Gouvernment," *Bracara Augusta* 27 (Braga, 1973), no. 64 (76), 341-353. *Roma Lusitana-Lisbona Romana,* exh. guide; Rome, San Michele a Ripa, 1990-1991; Sandra Vasco Rocca, Gabriele Borghini, Paola Ferraris, *Triomphe du Baroque* [exh. cat. Palais des Beaux-Arts] (Brussels, 1991), José Teixeira and others.

3. Cancellieri 1926, 133. For Carlo Fontana (1634-1714) see A. Braham and H. Hager, *The Drawings of Windsor Castle* (London, 1977). The patronage of art and music and of the Colegio Clementino of Benedetto Pamphili (1653-1730), made cardinal in 1681, is in Lina Montalto, *Un Mecenate in Roma Barocca, Il Cardinale Benedetto Pamphili* (Florence, 1955).

4. Gian Francesco Albani of Urbino was elected Pope Clement XI on 23 Nov. 1700 (d. 1721). See C. M. S. Johns, "The Art Patronage of Pope Clement XI Albani," unpublished diss., University of Delaware, 1985.

5. Montalto 1955, 264, n. 13 and the connection of Pamphili with Portugal; "Taluni artisti e artigiani romani che lavorano fra la 2ª meta del sec. XVII e il primo trentennio del XVIII anche per il Pamphili troviamo ricordati operanti in Portogallo." E. Lavagnino, *Gli Artisti Italiani in Portogallo* (Rome, 1940).

6. A. Baldeschi and G. Crescimbeni, *Stato della SS Chiesa Papale Lateranense nell'anno mdccxxiii* (Rome, 1723), 11-12. F. Den Broeder, "The Lateran Apostles: The Major Sculptural Commission in Eighteenth Century Rome," *Apollo* 63 (1967), 360-365. R. Enggass, *Early Eighteenth-Century Sculpture in Rome* (University Park, Pa., 1976), 2:20-21, 142, 143.

7. S. F. Ostrow and C. M. S. Johns, "Illuminations of S. Maria Maggiore in the early Settecento," *Burlington Magazine* 132, no. 1049, (August 1990), 528-534. H. Gross, *Rome in the Age of Enlightenment: The Post Tridentine Syndrome and the Ancient Regime* (Cambridge University Press, 1990), "Public Finance," chap. 5, 116-151.

8. ASV Portogallo, in particular Seg. 57, 1700; Seg. 58, 1701; Seg. 59, 1702; Seg. 60, 1702-1705.

9. Innocent XIII (b. 1655, d. 7 March 1724). L. von Pastor, *Storia dei Papa* (Rome, 1933), 15, 413-486. Padre Francisco da Fonseca, *Embaixada do Conde de Villarmayor, Fernando Telles da Sylva de Lisboa à Corte de Vienna, e Viagem da Rainha Nossa Senhora D. Maria Anna de Austria à Corte de Lisboa* (Vienna, 1717).

10. F. Valesio, *Diario di Roma* (ed. Milan, 1977), 1:432, 6 July 1701.

11. ASV Portogallo; Seg. 59, fol. 153r, 21 Feb. 1702; Seg. 63, fol. 520r, 9 Dec. 1705; Seg. 70, fol. 519r, 13 Dec. 1712. For accounts of Jesuit ceremonies at São Roque see ASV Portogallo; Seg. 75, fols. 4r and v, 3 Jan. 1719. For the king's education see R. Bebiano, *D João V, poder e espectaculo* (Aveiro, 1987), 4 ff. Valesio 1977, 6:213, 25 March 1739.

12. Archivio di Stato di Torino, Sez. I. Lettere Ministri, Roma, Cartella 151, n. 144, 28 Sep. 1715. In the use of the Chinese rites, Jesuit missionaries had attempted, in their quest for converts, to reconcile Chinese Confucian ethics with the principles of the Catholic church in order to make the Christian faith more accessible to both the Chinese emperor and his people. See also Brazão 1937; Boxer 1991, chapter 10 (note 16 below).

13. ASV Portogallo; Seg. 64, fols. 443r and 444v, 13 Dec. 1706.

14. Valesio ed. 1977, 3:827; see 881 for the visit of Clement XI to the Portuguese church on 8 Sep. 1707, 884-887 for an account of the funeral.

15. Braham and Hagar 1977, 98-103, nn. 241-284. For biography of Fontana and his project for the tomb of Dom Pedro II see G. M. Crescimbeni, *Notizie Istoriche sugli Arcadi morti* (Rome, 1720), 2:345-349. For the Juvarra drawing see M. Viale Ferrero, *Scenografo e architetto teatrale* (Turin, 1970), 16. *S. Antonio dei Portoghesi, Archivi del Catalogo,* Rome I, Istituto Centrale per il Catalogo e la Documentazione (Rome, 1992), A 22-A 44, 219-225, includes Fontana's plans and drawings for the project.

16. *Funerale Celebrato nella Chiesa di Santo Antonio Della Nazione Portoghese in Roma per la morte del Re di Portogallo, Don Pietro Secondo l'Anno MDCCVII.* with engravings by Giovanni Girolamo Frezza and Domenico Franceschini. The symbols and allegories were described by the Jesuit priest Miguel Dias, who gave the sermon. See "The Crown Patronage and the Catholic Missions," chap. 10, 228-248, in C. R. Boxer, *The Portuguese Seaborne Empire, 1415-1825*

([London], 1991): "The Portuguese *Padroado* can be loosely defined as a combination of the rights, privileges and duties granted by the Papacy to the Crown of Portugal as patron of the Roman Catholic missions and ecclesiastical establishments in vast regions of Africa, of Asia, and in Brazil."

17. Valesio 1977, 885. For Dom Pedro II as a patron of architecture, see Carvalho 1962, 2:101–203.

18. Carvalho 1962, 2:307. C.-F. Merveilleux, *Memoires Instructifs pour un Voyageur dans les Divers Etats de l'Europe* (Amsterdam, 1738), in Carvalho 1962, 1:268-269. The first notice by Nunzio Bichi to Rome of the foundation at Mafra by Dom João V, and said to honor "un voto" made by his father Dom Pedro and to be dedicated to Saint Anthony, is in ASV Portogallo; Seg. 74, fol. 186r, 14 Sep. 1717, and fols. 208v–209r, 26 Oct. 1717. The foundation stone was laid by the king, and the ceremony on 17 Nov. 1717 is described by the nunzio in ASV Portogallo; Seg. 74, fols. 220r and v, 23 Nov. 1717. A good account of Mafra and its Italian sources is R. C. Smith, "The Building of Mafra," *Apollo* 97 (April 1973), 360-367.

19. F. A. de Costa de Barbosa, *Élogio funebre do Padre João Baptista Carbone da Companhia de Jesus* (Lisbon, 1751), 15, "a miniatura da corte pontificia."

20. The ceremonial, with exquisite Italian music and a "mesa solenne de Roma . . . la quale da un virtuoso alla Città e stato ridotta in qualche passe allo stile e modo dicantare de'musici di questa Nazione," is in ASV Portogallo; Seg. 71, fols. 12r and v, Jan. 1713. For correspondence with Rome on the form of ceremonial see ASV Portogallo; Seg. 74, fols. 14r–17v, 16 Feb. 1717. For the form of the rites used in the patriarchal church, "tutto al uso Romano," see ASV Portogallo; Seg. 75, fol. 71r, 11 April 1719.

21. In this connection see the quote from Merveilleux in Carvalho 1962, 1:270, "Il est certain que les trois quarts des Trésors du Roi et de l'or que portoient les Flottes du Brazil étoient métamorphosés en pierres."

22. ASV Portogallo; Seg. 69, fol. 109r, 6 June 1711; Seg. 74, fol. 209r, 26 Oct. 1717. Merveilleux in Carvalho 1962, 1:270.

23. L. V. Ribeiro Salgado de Oliveira, "O Significando do Luxo no Reinado de D João V, alguns aspectos," *Bracara Augusta* 28 (Braga, 1974), nos. 65–66 (77-78) Tomo III, 299-312. The reasons behind the endowment by the king of the cardinals of the Patriarchate is defined in the contemporary account of Frei Claudio da Conceição: "E havendo Deos Nosso Senhor augmentado as minhas rendas com o ouro, e sendo justo, que dos rendimentos dos quintos se tire alguma porção, para se applicar a Igreja, em reconhecimento daquelle beneficio," quoted on p. 303 of this article.

24. Merveilleux in Carvalho 1962, 1:81. F. Xavier da Silva, *Élogio funebre e historico de . . . . D. João V* (Lisbon, 1750).

25. Xavier da Silva 1750. Gross 1990, 1–12 and chap. 14, "Antiquarianism and neoclassicism," 310-330. M. Coelho da Graca, *Breve noticia das entradas… nesta Corte de Suas Magestades com os Serenissimas Principes do Brazil e Altezas* (Lisbon, 1729), 8.

26. ASV Portogallo; Seg. 77, fol. 312r, 30 Sep. 1721; Seg. 75, fol. 526r, 24 Dec. 1720; Seg. 79, fol. 274r, 19 Dec. 1724; Seg. 96, fol. 14v, 10 Jan. 1741.

27. Brazão 1938, vol. 2, chap. 9, 7-23. Ajuda: MS 49,IX, 11, sn Jan. 1711.

28. De Bellebat, *Relation du voyage de Monseigneur André de Mello de Castro a la Cour de Rome, en qualité de Envoye Extraordinaire* (Paris, 1709). J. Castel-Branco Pereira, *Viaturas de Aparato em Portugal* (Lisbon, 1987), 53-55.

29. ASV Portogallo; Seg. 65, fols. 17r–18v, 5 Jan. 1707.

30. ASV Portogallo; Seg. 65, fol. 5r, 5 Jan. 1707; fols. 260r and v, 20 Sep. 1707; Seg. 66, fol. 40r, 22 March 1708, fol. 160r, 20 June 1706. M.-T. Mandroux-França, "La Patriarcale du Roi Jean V de Portugal," *Coloquio-Artes* (Lisbon, 1990), Plan E, no. 42.

31. ASV Portogallo; Seg. 68, fols. 154r–155r, 5 May 1710; fol. 186v, 27 May 1710. The promotion and celebrations for Cardinal Nuno da Cunha and the arrival of the Berretta from Rome are ASV Portogallo; Seg. 70, fol. 243r, 17 June 1712; fols. 390r and 391v, 23 Sep. 1712; fol. 415r, 4 Oct. 1712; fols. 434r and v, 18 Oct. 1712. E. Brazão, *Subsidios para a História do Patriarcado de Lisbon, 1716-1740* (Lisbon, 1943), 51.

32. ASV Portogallo; Seg. 67, fol. 261r, 13 Sep. 1709.

33. BN Lisbon, *Memórias da Casa de Abrantes*, F G Cod. 418, fol. 25, 55 ff. Marquês de Valenca, *Élogio. . . . ao Marquez de Abrantes* (Lisbon, 1745). A. Lamas, *A Casa Nobre de Lazaro Leitão;* Lisbon, transcribes material from BN Lisbon, Col. Pombalina, MSS 157. Dr. Lazaro Leitão Aranha was secretary to the embassy of the marquês de Fontes. Brazão 1943, 69 ff. His instructions over the "Riti Cinesi" are pp. 70-79. Carvalho 1962, 2:281–311; and the will made by the marquês de Fontes is 284-286. For the rights and duties of the *Padroado Real* see also S. J. Miller, *Portugal and Rome c. 1748–1830, An Aspect of the Catholic Enlightenment* (Rome, 1978), 30-32.

34. ASV Portogallo; Seg. 69, fol. 30v, 31 Jan. 1711; fol. 54r, 10 March 1711; fol. 58v, 20 March 1711; fol. 186r, 4 Sep. 1711. The meeting of the marquês de Fontes with the nunzio is Seg. 69, fol. 69r, 1 April 1711.

35. The departure from Lisbon of the marquês de Fontes is ASV Portogallo; Seg. 70, fol. 26r, 18 Jan. 1712.

36. Von Pastor 1933, 466 ff.

37. Marquês MacSwiney de Mashanaglass, *Le Portugal et le Saint-Siège, Les linges benits envoyés par les Papes aux Princes Royaux de Portugal* (Portugal, 1899), 3. Brazão 1938, vol. 2, *A Missão Extraordinario de Monsenhor Firrao*, 62-78.

38. Castel-Branco Pereira 1987, 16-17.

39. Brazão 1938, 2:79–80. ASV Portogallo; Seg.

73, fol. 64r, 27 Feb. 1716; fols. 95r and 100r, 19 March 1716.

40. ASV Portogallo; Seg. 73, fol. 183r, 13 June 1716: Lista da Esquadra que S Mag. he servido mandar de socorro a santidade do Papa Clemente a favor das Armas de Igreja. The departure of the fleet is Seg. 73, fol. 214r, that contains *Gazeta de Lisboa*, no. 28, 11 July 1716.

41. ASV Portogallo; Seg. 73, fol. 59r, 19 March 1716; fol. 156v, 11 June 1716 (for quote), fol. 282r, 6 Oct. 1716; Seg. 74, fol. 8r, 16 Feb. 1717. The papal bull *In Supremo Apostolatus,* 1716, is ASV Archivio della Legazione di Portogallo presso la S. Sede, cassa 9, mazzo 2, MS no. 1.

42. Fernando A. da Costa, *Élogio Histórica, Vida e Morte do Eminentissimo e Reverendissimo Senhor Cardeal D. Thomas da Almeida* (Lisbon, 1754), in Brussels 1991, 264, 266–271 with plates. The establishment of the Patriarchate is documented in ASV Portogallo; Seg. 73; fol. 282r, 6 Oct. 1716; fols. 340r and v, 342r, 344r, 8 Dec. 1716; fol. 348r, 15 Dec. 1716; fol. 361r, 29 Dec. 1716.

43. ASV Portogallo; Seg. 73, fol. 239r, 11 July 1716, with copy of *Gazeta de Lisboa,* no. 34, no. 173, 22 Aug. 1716; fol. 265v, 8 Sep. 1716. L. Chracas, *Ragguaglio del sontuoso treno delle carrozze con cui ando all'udienza l'Illustrissimo ed Eccellentissimo Signore Don Rodrigo Annes de Saa Almeida e Meneza, Marchese de Fontes Commendatore di S Pietro di Faro…ambasciatore appresso la Santità di Nostro Signore Papa Clemente XI in Roma 1716,* in which the program is attributed to Fontes, "pensieri e geroglifici conceptit ed ideati dalla gran mente dell'Eccellenza Vostra…." F. Vieira Lusitano, *O Insigne Pintor e leal esposo* (Lisbon, 1780), 204–212. Brazão 1943, 85–100, gives a Portuguese account based on Chracas. Castel-Branco Pereira 1987, 56–64.

44. For literary images in the 1716 entry from Camões, see a contemporary account of the ambassador's coach, quoted in Brazão 1943, 90: "a parte posterior da carroça representava a horrivel cabeça de hum monstro, qual era Adamastor hum dos gigantes filhos da terra o qual com cantou O Poeta Portuguez, ambicioso do Imperio do mar, e de amor de Thetis, descorria furiosam.te por aquelles mares…."

45. Brazão 1943, 89–90. The carriages of the marquês de Fontes returned to Lisbon in three ships. The first to arrive in April 1719 on a French ship was accompanied by two carvers, one carpenter, and a painter, presumably to repair any damage from the voyage. The two other ships had not yet arrived though they had sailed earlier from Livorno and there were fears at court that the remaining coaches had been sunk in a storm. The first report of their use is on New Year's Eve 1719 when the queen attended a Te Deum at São Roque, "La Regina con Treno magnifico composta la sua vanguardia di tutte le ricchissima carrozze portate di Roma dal Sig. Marchese d'Abrantes." ASV Portogallo; Seg. 75, fol. 72v, 11 April 1719; fol. 308, 2 Jan. 1720.

46. Damião de Goïs, *Chronica de el Rei, D.*

Manuel (Lisbon, 1909–1912), 12 vols., chap. 55.

47. The *Aviso Segreto* and Lisbon celebrations are documented in ASV Portogallo; Seg. 74, fols. 14r–17v, 16 Feb. 1717; fols. 43r and 44v, 2 March 1717; the account of the papal audience is fol. 92r, 16 March 1717 with copy of *Gazeta de Lisboa* Num. 17, 125 for 29 April 1717; fol. 44r, 2 March 1717, "meditando adesso La M.ta Sua di fabbricare di pianta la nova Chiesa Patriarcale con il Palazzo del Patriarca magnifico a proporzione, havendone di già nelle mani i disegni, alcuni de'quali passarano la spesa di 12 Milioni di Cruciata."

48. ASV Portogallo; Seg. 74, fol. 299r, 22 April 1718; fol. 312r, 26 April 1718; fols. 352r and v, 5 July 1718. Brazão 1943, 151–153.

49. ASV Portogallo; Seg. 74, fol. 240r, 4 Jan. 1718.

50. ASV Portogallo; Seg. 70, fol. 72, 23 Feb. 1712, records Annibale Albani made cardinal in that year. For his intervention with regard to Mons. Nuno da Cunha receiving the berretta see ASV Portogallo; Seg. 70, fols. 390r and v, 23 Sep. 1712, fols. 243r and 247r, 17 June 1712; fols. 415r, 421r, 434r and v, 4 and 8 Oct. 1712.

51. ASV Portogallo; Seg. 73, fol. 239r, 11 July 1716. Valesio ed. 1977, 216, 2 April 1739.

52. Carvalho 1962, 2:292, 296.

53. Chracas 1716, note 43 above. Carvalho 1962, 2:301.

54. Vieira Lusitano 1780, 51 ff, 279: "Aquelle eximio Maecenas dos virtuosos talentos…."

55. L. Xavier da Costa, *Francisco Vieira Lusitano, Poeta e Abridor de Aguas-Fortes* (Coimbra, 1929), 62–63.

56. A. M. Giorgetti Vichi, *Gli Arcadi dal 1690 al 1800* (Rome, 1977), 169. G. M. Crescimbeni, *Catalogo de'Pastori Arcadi per Ordine di Annoverazione* (Rome, 1690–1728), vol. 3 (1722), no. 80.

57. Rome; Biblioteca Angelica, Arch. Acc. Arcadia, Atti Arcadici, fol. 218.

58. G. M. Crescimbeni, *L'Istoria della Basilica di S. Anastasia, Titolo Cardinalizio* (Rome, 1722), 28.

59. A. de Carvalho, *Domenico Duprà, 1689–1770,* Connoisseur Year Book (London, 1958), 78–85. R. Sousa Viterbo and R. Vicente d'Almeida, *A Capela de S João Baptista* (Lisbon, 1900). M.-J. Madeira Rodrigues, *A Capela de S João Baptista e as suas colecções* (Lisbon, 1988).

60. Merveilleux in Carvalho 1962, 1:157-159.

61. ASV Portogallo; Seg. 68, fol. 397r, 12 Dec. 1710; Seg. 74, fol. 312r, 26 April 1718; Seg. 75, fol. 215r, 20 Sep. 1719; fol. 405r, 2 July 1720; fol. 425r, 6 Aug. 1720 and fol. 486v for a performance of his *Trionfo delle Virtù* on 29 Oct. 1720. Scarlatti's departure from Lisbon is recorded in ASV Portogallo; Seg. 84, fol. 32r, 28 Jan. 1727.

62. ASV Portogallo; Seg. 74, fol. 358r, 19 July 1718; fol. 413v, 8 Nov. 1718; for plan; "dovendo essere della stessa misura p tutti i lati della Chiesa di S. Ignazio di Roma" see ASV Portogallo; Seg. 74, fol. 402r, 25 Oct. 1718.

63. José de Almeida is documented in Rome in 1725, but was probably there earlier. See

Carvalho 1962, 2:299-300. R. Smith, *The Art of Portugal* (London, 1968), 166-167.

64. Carvalho 1962, 2:293-294. For the Maltese Gimac's long collaboration with Portugal in Lisbon and Rome see the same reference, 241-296.

65. ASV Portogallo; Seg. 72, fols. 329r, 330r, 331r, 339r, 351r and 363r, 27 Sep. to 10 Dec. 1715.

66. ASV Portogallo; Seg. 73, fols. 7 r and v, 8r, 7 Jan. 1716; fol. 135r, 21 April 1716; fol. 187r, 23 June 1716; Seg. 60, fol. 198r, May 1716; for quote see Seg. 72, fol. 363r, 10 Dec. 1715.

67. Xavier da Silva 1750.

68. Ajuda; MSS, VII, 1 n. 9 (1724), n.11 (1724), n. 63 (1724). The request for an engraving of the obelisk erected at the Lateran by Sixtus V is Ajuda; MSS 49, VII, 1, n. 108 (1725).

69. Xavier da Silva 1750.

70. A. de Montaiglon et J. Guiffrey, editors, *Correspondance de l'Académie de France*, 18 vols. (Paris, 1887-1912), vol. 6, 1896. Nos. 2382 (7 Oct. 1721), 2483 (2 March 1723), 2499 (4 May 1723), 2502 (11 May 1723). Ajuda; MSS 49 VI, 20n, 49y (1722); MSS 49 VII, 1 nn. 66, 74 and MSS 49, VII, 8 (1724); MSS 49, VII, 1, nn. 90, 110b, 164 (1725). Merveilleux in Carvalho 1962, vol. 1, writing in 1726 recorded an earlier model: "on envoya au Roi S Pierre de Rome executé en petit, mais qui occupe un grand sale, avec tous les modèles des raretés de Rome."

71. Ajuda; MSS 49, VII, 13 nn, 230, 232, 239, 250, 253, 257, 263, 267, 269, 273, 285, 294, 296, 298, 322 (1729); VIII, 26, fols. 104v-133v (1745).

72. Carvalho 1962, 2:399-424, for correspondence from 1728-1734, and fundamental source for the royal commissions for Mafra, in particular, p. 402, 7 Dec. 1729; p. 408, 30 May 1730; p. 410, 4 July 1730.

73. Ajuda; MSS 49, VII, 15 nn. 32, 43 (1728). Gimac's drawing of the Biblioteca Apostolica Vaticana was completed in 1731 by Carlo Marchionni. Ajuda; MSS 49, VII, 15, nn. 158-159, n. 256b (1729, 1730).

74. For altars see Carvalho 1962, 2:404, 11 Aug. 1729; 403, 24 Jan. 1730. For sacristies, see the same source, 402-403, 19 Jan. 1730.

75. Ajuda; MSS 49 IX 22, ff 40 (1740); MSS 49 VIII, 26 ff 3, 7-81 ff (1741).

76. ASV Portogallo; Seg. 75, fol. 18r, 31 Jan. 1719.

77. For Cardinal Ottoboni see F. Haskell, *Patrons and Painters, Art and Society in Baroque Italy* (New York and London, 1971), 164-166. For his patronage of Francisco Trevisani, active in Arcadian circles and for Portugal, see A. Griseri, "Francesco Trevisani in Arcadia," *Paragone* (1962), no. 153, 28-37. For gifts to Ottoboni from Dom João V in 1739 see Valesio ed. 1977, 216.

78. Juvarra's activity for Ottoboni is in Viale Ferrero 1970.

79. ASV Portogallo; Seg. 75, fol. 71v, 11 April 1719. Drawing for an *Oratorio per la Settimana Santa* for the Palazzo della Cancelleria (Turin, Biblioteca Nazionale, Ris. 59, 4, f81 [1]), is reproduced in A. E. Brinckmann, *Filippo Juvarra* (Turin, Milan, 1937-1938), 1:295.

80. ASV Portogallo; Seg. 75, fol. 123r and v, 23 May 1719; fols. 138r and v, 5 June 1719; fols. 160r and v, 20 June 1719.

81. ASV Portogallo; Seg. 75, fol. 18r, 31 Jan. 1719, fol. 25r, 14 Feb. 1719.

82. Anonymous biography of Juvarra, 1737, "Vita del Cavaliere don Filippo Juvarra, Abbate de Selve e Primo architetto di S. M. di Sardegna," *Mostra di Filippo Juvarra* (Messina, 1966), 26-28.

83. Crescimbeni 1690-1728; vol. 2 (1712), for Filippo Juvarra who acquired the name Bramanzio Feesseo.

84. L. Masini, "La vita e l'arte di Filippo Juvarra," *Atti Soc. Piemont archeol. e B.A.* 9, fasc. 2 (1920), 197.

85. ASV Portogallo; Seg. 75, fol. 18r, 31 Jan. 1719; fol. 25r, 14 Feb. 1719; fol. 37r, 28 Feb. 1719; fol. 47r, 14 March 1719; fol. 63r, 28 March 1719; fols. 63r and v, 28 March 1719, which describe the beauty of the Buenos Aires site, and the proposed garden and zoo: fol. 104v, 9 May 1719. Juvarra's departure, laden with honors and the Ordem do Christo, is fol. 175r, 18 July 1719; fol. 182r, 25 July 1719.

86. P. Marconi, A. Cipriani, E. Valeriani, *I disegni di architettura dell'Archivio Storico dell'Accademia di San Luca* (Rome, 1974), nos. 140-142.

87. The design for reconstruction of the Campidoglio is reproduced in Brinckmann 1937-1938, 1:14.

88. ASV Portogallo; Seg. 75, fol. 208v, 12 Sep. 1719; fol. 87r, 25 April 1719: "e porrebbe essere che i presenti torbidi dell'Europa...."

89. Anonymous, *Vita del Cavaliere don Filippo Juvarra* (Mostra, 1966), 27; "una colonna sullo stile antico ad imitazione di quelle che si vedono in Roma, con l'arme del re in mezzo retta da due fame—per imitare le opere degli antichi imperatori...."

90. Rome, Biblioteca Angelica, Arch. Acc. N. Arcadia Fatti III, fol. 496, 25 Nov. 1721. The king's letter, before 29 February 1722, thanking the Arcadia is Fatti IV, fol. 56: "si perché mi vien offerta la successione ad un Luogo che fu onorato dalla Persona del Santo Pontefice Clemente XI, di gloriosa memoria, come perché mi si dà l'occasione di prendere sotto la mia reale protezione un'Accademia tanto conosciuta in Europa e tanto giustamente Stimata, quanto è quella degli Arcadi di Roma."

91. G. M. Crescimbeni, *Sonnetti ed orazione in lode delle nobili arti del disegno, pittura, scoltura ed architettura* (Rome, 1764). A. Scotti, "L'Accademia degli Arcadi in Roma e i suoi rapporti con la cultura portoghese nel primo ventennio del 1700," *Bracara Augusta* 27 (Braga, 1973), no. 64 (76), 115-130. A. Griseri, "Arcadia; Crisi e trasformazione fra sei e settecento," *Storia dell'Arte Italiana dal '500 al '800*, vol. 2 (ed. 1981), 562-596. P. Ferraris, "L'Arcadia nella Diplomazia Internazionale, Il Bosco Parrasio Gianicolense," *Arcadia, Accademia Letteraria*

Italiana, Atti i Memorie; Ser. 3, vol. 8, Fasc. 4 (Rome, 1986–1987), 227–268. V. Golzio, "Antonio Canevari e Vincenzo Mazzoneschi, Artisti Romani all'Estero," *Roma,* Fasc. XI, (1938), 18:464–467. J. Fernandes Pereira, *A acção artistica do primeiro Patriarca de Lisboa* (Lisbon, 1984).

92. ASV Portogallo; Seg, 76, fol. 73v, 10 June 1721.

93. Chracas 1716, no. 681, Rome, 29 Nov. 1721, 19–21. Two engravings of the sets dated 1722 by Federico Mastrozzi and Filippo Vasconi are published in *Meravigliose scene Piacevoli inganni; Galli-Bibiena* [exh. cat. Palazzo Comunale] (Bibbiena, 1992) by Deana Lenzi, nos. 36, 37 and for the iconography of the piece.

94. ASV Portogallo; Seg. 75, fol. 309r, 6 Jan. 1720; fol. 334r, 27 Feb. 1720; Seg. 76, fol. 79r, 1 July 1721.

95. Rome, Biblioteca Angelica, Arch. Acc. N. Arcadia, Fatti IV, fol. 21, 24025, 27. Giorgetti Vichi 1977, 219, 262.

96. Crescimbeni, *S Anastasia* 1722, 28 ff. F. Cappello, *Brevi Notizie, S Anastasia di Roma* (Rome, 1722). E. Tormo, *Monumentos de espanoles en Roma, y de Portugueses* (Rome, 1940), 2:305–309. Valesio ed. 1977, 4:762, for account of reconsecration, 30 Dec. 1726.

97. Chracas 1716, no. 639. Rome 16 Aug. 1721, 4 for the decoration with "il manto reale che facea cascata." For the Collegio Clementino see Chracas 1716, no. 666, Rome 18 Oct. 1721, and L. Montalto, *Il Clementino* (Rome, nd), 179.

98. G. M. Crescimbeni, *Storia dell' Accademia degli Arcadi* (Rome, 1712, London, 1804). G. M. Crescimbeni, *Notizie istoriche degli Arcadi Morti* III (Rome, 1721). G. M. Crescimbeni, *Dell'istoria della volgar poesia,* vol. 6 (Venice, 1730), dedicated to Lorenzo Corsini, Clement XI. M. G. Morei, *Vite degli Arcadi Illustri* (Rome, 1751). M. G. Morei, *Memorie Istoriche dell'Adunanza degli Arcadi* (Rome, 1761). E. Portal, *L'Arcadia* (Palermo, 1921).

99. Rome, Biblioteca Angelica, Arch. Acc. N. Arcadia, Fatti IV, fols. 104, 105, 107–109, 111–113, 114v–115v. C. D'Onofrio, *Storie romane tra Cristina di Svezia, piazza del Popolo e l'Accademia d'Arcadia,* "Roma val bene un'abiura" (Rome, 1976). Ferraris 1986–1987, 233 ff.

100. Ambassador Mello e Castro became a Pastore Arcade as Ramiro Maiadeo in 1723; Giorgetti Vichi 1977, 218.

101. V. Giovardi, *Notizia del nuovo teatro degli Arcadi aperto in Roma l'anno 1726* (Rome, 1727). *Racconto della Funzione fattasi nel Getto della Prima Pietra ne'Fondamenti del Nuovo Teatro degli Arcadi* (Rome, 1725). *I Giouchi Olimpici celebrati dagli Arcadi per l'ingresso dell'Olimpiade DCXXVI in lode della Sacra Real Maestà di Giovanni V Re di Portogallo* (Rome, 1726). M. G. Morei, *Adunanza tenuta dagli Arcadi per la morte del Fedelissimo Re di Portogallo Giovanni V* (Rome, 1751), dedicated to Cardinal Neri Corsini, Protettore de I Regni di Portogallo.

102. L. Lotti, "Cristina di Svezia; L'Arcadia e il Bosco Parrasio," *Quaderni dell'Alma Roma* 16 (Rome, 1977), 21 ff.

103. Brazão 1937, 304, 314, 321, 322. Brazão 1938, 2:307–323. Miller 1978, 35–36.

104. Valesio ed. 1977, 4:901, 31 Jan. 1728; 909, 12 Feb. 1728; no. 984, 18 Aug. 1728. ASV Portogallo; Seg. 85. The nunzio's last report from Lisbon is March 1728, see Badajoz, fol. 115r, 6 April 1728. Carvalho 1962, 2:402–410.

105. Montaiglon *Correspondance* 1887–1912, 7: no. 2913, 4 July 1725; no. 3145, 420, 27 May 1728. Valesio ed. 1977, 4:900, 27 Jan. 1728, where the Portuguese academy is described as "l'Accademia del disegno."

106. ASV Portogallo; Seg. 75, fols. 506v and 526r, 10 and 24 Dec. 1720; Seg. 76, fol. 84v, 15 July 1721, gives meeting of Real Academia, in honor of Innocent XIII, when the conde de Ericeira recited "Un Orazione Panegirica. . . ."

107. Ajuda; MSS 49, VII, 13 n. 266 (1725).

108. Rome, Archivio Accademia S. Luca, vol. 48, fol. 141v.

109. Valesio ed. 1977, 1022, 23 Nov. 1728; 14 Dec. 1728, 1029.

110. Montaiglon *Correspondance* 1887–1912, no. 3505, 302, 20 Feb. 1732.

111. Valesio ed. 1977, 4:915, 3 March 1728.

112. P. F. Casimiro Romano, *Memorie Istoriche della Chiesae e Convento di S Maria in Aracoeli* (Rome, 1736). C. Frascarelli, *Iscrizioni Portoghesi* (Rome, 1868), 32, 73, 74. Montaiglon *Correspondance* 1887–1912, 8:3354, 14 Sep. 1730; 3464, 10 Oct. 1731. Valesio ed. 1977, 5:457, 20 March 1732, for Frei Fonseca e Évora's audience with the pope and with Cardinal Corsini regarding Portuguese affairs of state. 6:400, 30 Oct. 1740, gives the minister's departure from Rome and comments on the considerable sums of money spent by the Portuguese on Santa Maria in Aracoeli and Santa Maria di Palazzola.

113. Rome, Biblioteca Nazionale, Fondo Nazionale, no. 11726, reproduced in L. Bianchi, *Disegni di Ferdinando Fuga* (Rome, 1955), 110 and fig. 34. M. Tafuri, "Un 'Fuoco' Urbano della Roma Barocca," *Quaderni dell'Istituto de Storia dell'Architettura,* Serie XI, fasc. 61 (1964).

114. Valesio ed. 1977, 5:816, 10 Oct. 1735, for the meal offered at Palazzola by the Portuguese to the Casa Corsini. Brazão 1943, 195 ff.

115. Carvalho 1962, 2:399–424.

116. F. Caraffa, "Capella Corsini nella Basilica Lateranense 1731-1799," *Carmelus* 21 (Rome, 1974). Gross 1990, 35, 277, 280, 326, 353, 361.

117. Enggass 1976, 1:16–19.

118. Carvalho 1962, 2:409, 413–415, and 416–417 for shipping in 1732. Montaiglon *Correspondance* 1887–1912, no. 3354, p. 142, 14 Sep. 1730: "le roy de Portugal occupe icy plus de vingt sculpteurs, ce que tarit Rome d'ateliers."

119. A. de Carvalho, *La Escultura de Mafra* (Mafra, 1956), 14–18, 20. R. Enggass, "Bernardino Ludovisi III, His work in Portugal," *Burlington Magazine* 110 (Nov. 1968), 613–618. Enggass 1976, 1:184, 189 ff.

120. Enggass 1976, 1:184 ff, no. 6. A. Blunt, *Guide to Baroque Rome* (London, 1982), 52. In

1741 an engraving was made for João V by Giuseppe Palms of the *ciborio* in the Cappella Corsini, part of a set of drawings of the *apparati processionale* of the Lateran; Ajuda; MSS 49, VIII, 12 n. 199.

121. A. Schiavo, "Notizie e giudizi de Benedetto XIV su due Ambasciatori accreditati presso la sua Corte," *L'Urbe* (Rome, 1975), n. V, 24–30. E. Morelli, ed., *Le lettere di Benedetto XIV al Cardinale de Tencin* (Rome, 1955, 1965), 2 vols. L. Samoggia, "Carteggio fra Benedetto XIV e Giovanni V di Portogallo," *Atti del Convegno Internazionale di Studi Storici*, vol. 2. Fondazione Baraffaldi. *Martirologia Romano, Sanctissimi Domini Nostri Benedicti XIV P.O.M. Litterae apostolicae de nova martylogi romani, editione ad Joannem V Portugalliae et Algarbium regem illustrem 1 Julii 1748.* Morelli ed. 1955, 1965, 2:73, 7 Aug. 1748.

122. Morelli ed. 1955, 1965, 2:152, 30 April 1749. Brazão 1938, vol. 2, *Rei Fidelissimo*, 241–245.

123. Valesio 1977, 6:468, 27 April 1741; 497, 18 July 1741, for the quote, "…secondo le pie stravaganze de quel re." Chracas 1716, no. 3888, 3891 (1742). Schiavo 1975, 24: "L'aver poi alla mani una borsa piena di denari che si spandano per Roma in ogni sorte di persone per i lavori che ad esse si commettono, il continuo regalare…." ASV Portogallo; Seg. 104 A, fols. 94r–89r, 28 Dec. 1745. ASV Portogallo; Seg. 95A, fol. 139r, 7 June 1740; Seg. 100, fol. 49r, 9 March 1745; Seg. 102, fols. 27r and v, 31 Jan. 1747; fol. 287v, 31 Oct. 1747.

124. ASV Portogallo; Seg. 104, fol. 87r, 22 April 1749; Seg. 68, fol. 346v, 24 Oct. 1710; Seg. 79, fol. 104r, 16 March 1723; Seg. 81, fol. 124r, 15 Aug. 1724; Seg. 78, fol. 407r, 29 Dec. 1722. Montaiglon *Correspondance* 1887–1912, 6: no. 2416, p. 136, 28 April 1722.

125. ASV Portogallo; Seg. 97, fols. 153v and 154v, 15 May 1742; fols. 309r and v, 2 Oct. 1742.

126. Sousa Viterbo 1900, 105–106, 26 Oct. 1742. ASV Portogallo; Seg. 97, fol. 223v, 10 July 1742.

127. See Sousa Viterbo 1900, for documentation. M. S. Briggs, "St. John's Chapel in the Church of St. Roque, Lisbon," *Burlington Magazine* 28 (Nov. 1915), 50–56, 88–93, for the lost *Book of Sketches of the Designs of Works proposed which are being made in Rome by order of the Court*; Patriarcale, Lisbon MDCCLV. A. Schiavo, *La Fontana di Trevi e la altre opere di Nicola Salvi* (Rome, 1956), 197–219. Enggass 1968, 617–618.

128. Chracas 1716, no. 4644, 9–11, 29 April 1747.

129. A. de Carvalho, "A Escola de escultura de Mafra," *Belas Artes* 19 (Lisbon, 1963), 27–42.

130. ASV Portogallo; Seg. 104A, fol. 13r, 13 Oct. 1744.

131. ASV Portogallo; Seg. 96, fol. 125r, 9 May 1741; fol. 213r, 1 Aug. 1741; Seg. 100, fol. 49r, 9 March 1745; fol. 182r, 24 Aug. 1745.

132. Valesio ed. 1977, 6:487, 25 June 1741. ASV Portogallo; Seg. 99, fol. 357r, 22 Nov. 1744. Seg. 101, fol. 119r, 31 March 1746.

133. For the baptismal font see Schiavo 1956, 221–224. Mandroux-França 1990. Valadier, [exh. cat. Artemis Group] (London, 1991) 22–23.

134. Morelli ed. 1955, 1965, 2:205, 8 Oct. 1749. Chracas 1716, no. 4914, 5001, Oct. 1749.

135. E. Assemani, *Iscrizioni in occasione delle solenni esequie alla memoria del re Giovanni V* (Rome, 1752). I. M. da Costa Mascarenhas, *Oração Funebre, Panegyrica e Historica Nas Reães Exequias… A Saudosa memoria do Serenissimo e Fidelissimo Senhor Rey de Portugal D. João V* (Lisbon, 1751).

136. *The Journal of William Beckford in Portugal and Spain 1787–1788*, ed. B. Alexander (London, 1954), 176.

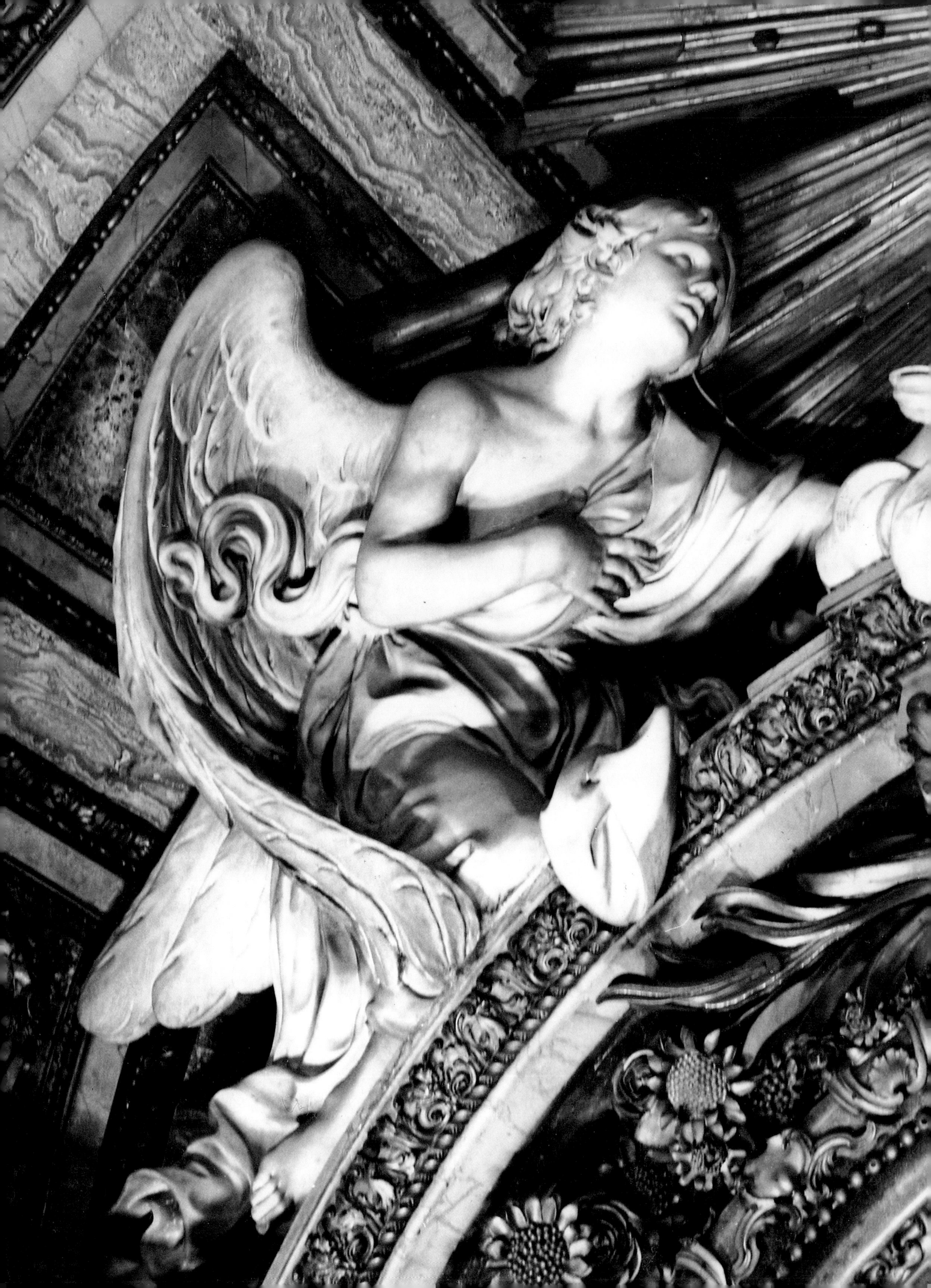

João V and Italian Sculpture

Jennifer Montagu

For anyone in the early eighteenth century wishing to commission sculpture of the highest quality and style, Italy and especially Rome was the obvious place to look. This had been the case for more than a hundred years. The attraction of Rome was all the greater for Dom João V of Portugal, whose active ecclesiastical building program was consciously modeled on the great churches of the Eternal City and whose ministers incessantly demanded information on papal church ceremonies.

Yet in our own day the Italian sculptors of the fourth and fifth decades of the eighteenth century have been understudied and undervalued. This is not altogether surprising, since, coming between the death of Camillo Rusconi in 1728 and the emergence of Pietro Bracci as the leader of the sculptural field in the mid-1740s, sculptors of the 1730s and 1740s could be characterized as continuing in the stylistic modes of their teachers and predecessors, refining and elaborating pre-established manners. Although it is undeniable that they developed their own individual sculptural personalities, they were not sufficiently innovative to inspire much art historical interest. Those who did evolve a particularly striking individual style found no followers. These Italian artists of this period suffer from the general scholarly neglect of the settecento, compounded by an even more general neglect of sculpture; the lighter, rather prettier form of the baroque practiced throughout most of Italy at this time, well described by the term *barocchetto,* never achieved the perfection of the northern rococo, and was seen by the historians of the next generation as a tired and degenerate prelude to neoclassicism.

Yet in their work for Portugal at Mafra and in the chapel of Saint John in São Roque in Lisbon one can see that there was not only a high level of sculptural competence, but also a great deal of individual talent of the highest order.

The great convent church of Mafra, begun in 1717 in fulfillment of a vow by Dom João V and consecrated in 1730, was adorned with no fewer than fifty-eight statues of standing figures (fifty-four saints and four angels), not to mention some reliefs and a crucifix adored by angels, all sent from Italy and all produced in a few years after 1730.[1] This alone would be sufficient to make it a showcase of Italian sculpture, but the marble reliefs subsequently produced by local sculptors under the direction of the Italian sculptor Alessandro Giusti,

fig. 1. Peter Anton von Verschaffelt, *Angels above the Altar of the Baptism.* São Roque, Lisbon

the so-called school of Mafra, can be seen as an intriguing offshoot of the
Roman tradition.

Frei José Correa de Abreu, in a letter from Lisbon of 10 May 1730, established an order of priority, commissioning first the crucifix with its glory and a
pair of adoring angels, followed by a relief of the Virgin and Child with Saint
Anthony, and then the statues for the facade and vestibule (fig. 2).[2] These were
to represent saints Dominic, Francis, Clare, and Elizabeth of Hungary on the
facade, while those in the vestibule should include saints Vincent and Sebastian.

By May 1730 a number of drawings had already been sent from Italy, and
more were to follow. These drawings, none of which appear to have survived,
provided the basis on which sculptors were accepted or rejected. Comments
were made on the costumes or attributes proposed for the figures. The same
letter requested that, as the sculptors would make small models (as well as
large ones), these, which should be about three *palmi* high (about 28 inches),
should be well packed and sent to Lisbon so that they could be placed above
the shelves in the library. This may be the origin of the small models that still
exist in the palace of Mafra. However, there is no suggestion that they were
sent as examples of the proposed work, and, with no record of their arrival, we
may assume that they followed or accompanied the larger marbles.

It was the Portuguese ambassador, Frei José Maria de Fonseca e Évora,
upon whom fell the task of finding sculptors to execute this immense command, about which all too little is known despite the number of documents
that have been published. Letters from Lisbon list some of the saints to be included but provide no hint of a coherent program. They give some advice on
how they were to be represented, but not enough to suggest that the matter
had been fully thought through, and they suggest some sculptors and criticize
drawings sent by others. It was left to the ambassador, as the man on the spot,
to find those artists who would be able to produce the statues to the required
standard in the required time. On two things the king insisted: that the statues
should be "fit to do honor to the artists who made them, and worthy of the
temple for which they are destined," and they should be done quickly, with a
reminder that Pierre Le Gros had taken only eight months to carve his great
relief of *Saint Luigi Gonzaga in Glory* in Sant'Ignazio in Rome.[3]

The insistence that only well-respected and expert sculptors should be employed recurs frequently in the correspondence, together with questions about
the standing of the artists proposed. Le Gros, whose statue of Saint Thomas
in the Lateran in Rome had been paid for by the Portuguese crown, was, of
course, dead. Of the sculptors who are known to have worked for the Portuguese, Domenico Parodi (who had carved a bust of João V) was not to work
for Mafra; and the name of Giuseppe Lironi, who had carved the mask on the
inscription tablet at the entrance to the Bosco Parrasio and prepared a model
of Apollo to go over it, does not appear on any of the Portuguese statues.[4] Fonseca e Évora, as a member of the Franciscan order, had played a part in commissioning the statue of Saint Francis from Carlo Monaldi for the series of the
founders of orders in Saint Peter's.[5] He clearly viewed Monaldi with favor,
commissioning no fewer than five statues from him, more than from any other
single sculptor, including the saints Sebastian and Vincent for the vestibule[6]
and the marble relief of the Virgin and Child with Saint Anthony (see Delaforce, fig. 10).

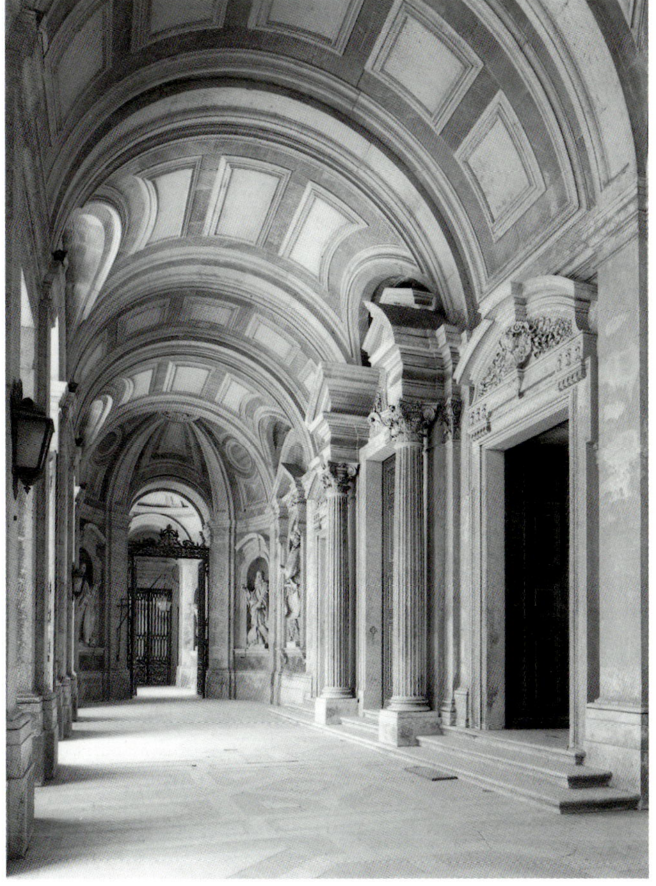
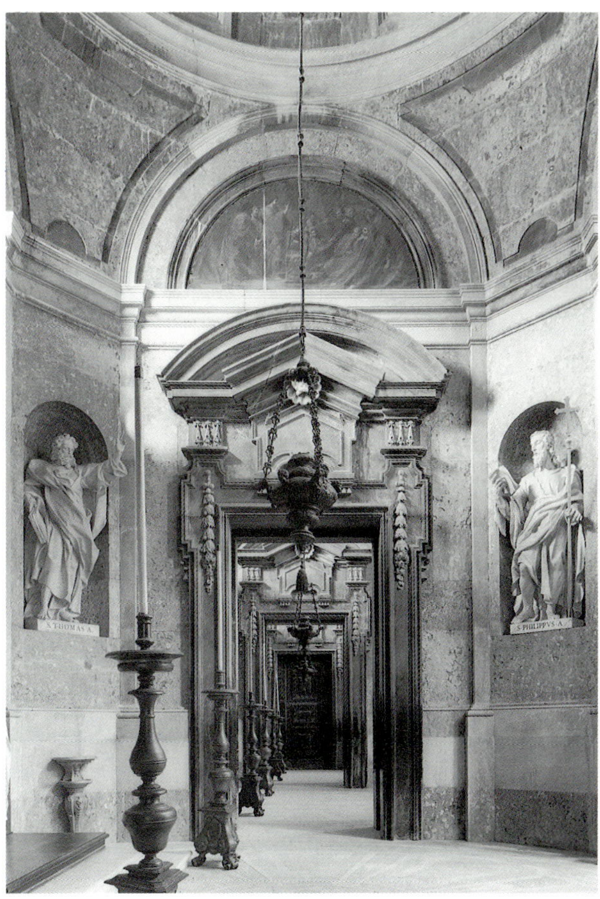

fig. 2. *Statues in the Vestibule of the Basilica,* Mafra

fig. 3. Simone Martinez, *Saint Thomas,* and unsigned *Saint Philip* from a side chapel, Mafra

Nothing is known of Monaldi's education, and he appears to have belonged to no particular school, experiencing difficulty in gaining acceptance by the sculptors' guild, because he was, at the same time, also an artilleryman. Another sculptor whom Fonseca e Évora proposed was Agostino Cornacchini, a Florentine working in Rome and one of the most original and eccentric of the sculptors there. It may have been that his drawings of saints Vincent and Sebastian sent to Lisbon did not please the authorities, or perhaps they had heard of the controversy that had surrounded his equestrian statue of Charlemagne, set up in the atrium of Saint Peter's in 1725. Whatever the reason, the king's ambassador was told that Cornacchini was not to be used unless it was really necessary.[7]

In fact, the choice of the sculptors seems to be as lacking in any precise program as the selection of the subjects. It was proposed from Lisbon that each sculptor should carve two figures, and in most cases this proposal seems to have been followed. Other suggestions were less practical: Correa de Abreu had heard of the sculptor Massimiliano Soldani Benzi and had instructed Fonseca e Évora to find out whether he was capable of working for the convent. But when it was learned that he specialized in bronze, he was not employed.

Rome furnished more of the sculptors than any other center, though any analysis of the patronage for Mafra is subject to the caveat that so many of the statues are unsigned that such attempts as have been made to attribute them are not entirely convincing and in some cases are manifestly wrong. Moreover, some of the signatures are of artists of whom little or nothing is known. Giovanni Battista Maini carved four statues, including two for the facade, and Pietro Bracci, who, like Maini, had been a pupil of Rusconi, made two. Bernardino Ludovisi and Giovanni Battista Rossi each carved two statues, and Bartolommeo Pincellotti signed only one; Simone Martinez, born in Messina but working in Rome, signed the statue of Saint Thomas Aquinas (fig. 3), and Agostino Corsini of Bologna, who was also established in Rome, the saints John of God and Ignatius. Filippo della Valle, a Florentine established in Rome, carved the impressive *Saint Jerome,* and was to be commissioned by Neri Corsini to carve the two reliefs on the side walls of the burial chapel of Manuel Pereira Sampaio in Sant'Antonio in Rome. Another Florentine in Rome, Antonio Montauti, carved the saints *Peter* and *Paul.* Montauti was later to be commissioned to carve a *Virgin and Child* for the patriarchal church in Lisbon, a figure that came to grief in transit when, due to defective packing, the head of the Christ Child broke off. Montauti also was to make a grille for the Patriarchate that led to considerable complaint as, owing to insufficient funds, he had used a poor quality bronze that drank up an unexpected and un-acceptable amount of gold when it was gilded. This complaint prompted as-surances from Rome that he was, indeed, a highly regarded sculptor, both in marble and in bronze.[8]

Most of the leading Florentine sculptors were also employed at Mafra; with the exception of the rather older Giuseppe Piamontini, the teacher of Mon-tauti, they were, like della Valle and Montauti, members of the second genera-tion of the sculptors who had been sent by the Grand Duke Cosimo III de' Medici to the Florentine academy in Rome to acquire the new baroque manner.

Although "Schiaffino" (presumably the Genoese sculptor Francesco Maria Schiaffino, who had studied in Rome with Rusconi) was mentioned frequently in correspondence regarding the *Crucifix with Adoring Angels,* it may have been the need to acquire marble from Carrara that put Fonseca e Évora in contact with members of the Vacca and Baratta families, though, with the exception of Giovanni Baratta, the sculptors of those names who worked at Mafra are not otherwise known. So far as can be judged from the signatures, Fonseca e Évora does not appear to have looked for sculptors farther afield than these artistic centers.

The task these sculptors were set was a standard one, the standing statue in a niche. It required the ability to create a figure that filled the restricted field without leaving too much empty space and that projected out to the spectator, either physically or emotionally. The fact that the statues were set above eye level also demanded that, even if they were not looking down, they should at least be fully legible from below. Such figures should fit the restrictions of their settings without being cramped by them, and, above all, they should animate the building in which they were placed without conflicting with the appear-ance of solidity and stability of the wall. Given these fairly simple and familiar requirements, the statues of the convent church of Mafra provide a fascinating conspectus of the ways in which the sculptors invented variations on the theme and the degrees of success with which they achieved it. Saint Peter's in Rome can offer a comparable number of such figures, but only in Mafra can one ex-amine figures carved within so short a space of time and from such a variety of cities.

Battista Maini's four statues at Mafra may not strike the modern viewer as particularly exceptional. However, they were the ones that best satisfied the demands of the patrons in Lisbon, so much so that, on the basis of these sculptures together with the Saint Philip Neri in Saint Peter's, he was recommended to make the model of the oval relief of the Virgin and Child for the Patriarchate, which was cast in bronze by Francesco Giardoni to replace the marble by Montauti that had broken in transport and was in any case judged unsatisfactory as the relief had not been high enough to be properly visible at a distance. The letter concerning this bronze is particularly interesting as an example of the very specific demands that were made concerning the iconography, the style, and the facture. Instructions were given about the exact disposition of the Virgin, Child, and globe, including a special warning that the genitals of the Christ Child should be covered with a veil, something that "excellent artists often showed nude and uncovered." The sculptor was to follow the style of Carlo Maratti or Agostino Masucci, "avendo essi un singolarissimo gusto nelle Imagine referita" (since they have a very distinctive taste in such images)[9] and he was to remember that, as the bronze had to fit a preexisting frame, the model should be somewhat larger as the bronze would shrink in casting. Since the sculptor and founder would certainly have been aware of this well-known technicality, one can only imagine that it was spelled out so that, should the bronze turn out to be the wrong size, the Portuguese would have grounds for rejecting it.

In 1744 Maini was again selected as the preferred artist for the statue of the Virgin of the Immaculate Conception for the same church, for which almost equally precise instructions were sent.[10] At the same time, when it was planned to place a lamb adored by two angels over the altar of the chapel of Saint John in the church of São Roque, this too was to be made by Maini "or others as good as he."[11] In fact the idea of a lamb, much criticized in Rome, was abandoned, and Maini was not involved in the sculpture of the chapel, although he did model the body of Christ for the crucifix of the altar ensemble, the so-called *muta nobile;* and, as has been argued here (see cat. 107), Maini almost certainly designed the great silver candlestick cast by Gagliardi, very probably also the whole of the altar ensemble, and quite possibly the reliquaries as well.

The chapel of Saint John (see cat. 106) is less interesting as an example of Portuguese patronage in that it was designed in Rome by the architect Luigi Vanvitelli (even if with much critical comment from João Frederico Ludovice). It was no doubt Vanvitelli who selected the sculptors as well. The most important marbles are two oval medallions, the *Visitation* by Carlo Marchionni and the *Preaching of Saint John the Baptist* by Bernardino Ludovisi, with their accompanying putti carved by Agostino Corsini and Ludovisi; the angels over the altar of the Baptism adoring the cross, which were carved by Peter Anton von Verschaffelt (see fig. 1); and the pair of angels on the wall of the nave over the entrance to the chapel by Antonio Corradini. Ludovisi had worked at Mafra (and he also modeled the bronze putti at either side of the silver and lapis-lazuli altar frontal, which was cast by Antonio Arrighi from a model by Agostino Corsini, another sculptor who had been employed at Mafra). But Verschaffelt, having been born in 1710 and belonging to a younger generation, had not been part of the team at Mafra; during the early 1730s Verschaffelt had not yet arrived in Rome, and Corradini had been working in northern Europe. Why L'Estache was not employed at Mafra (unless, indeed, he merely ne-

fig. 4. Carlo Marchionni, *The Visitation,* with angels carved by Agostino Corsini and Bernardino Ludovisi, Chapel of Saint John, São Roque, Lisbon

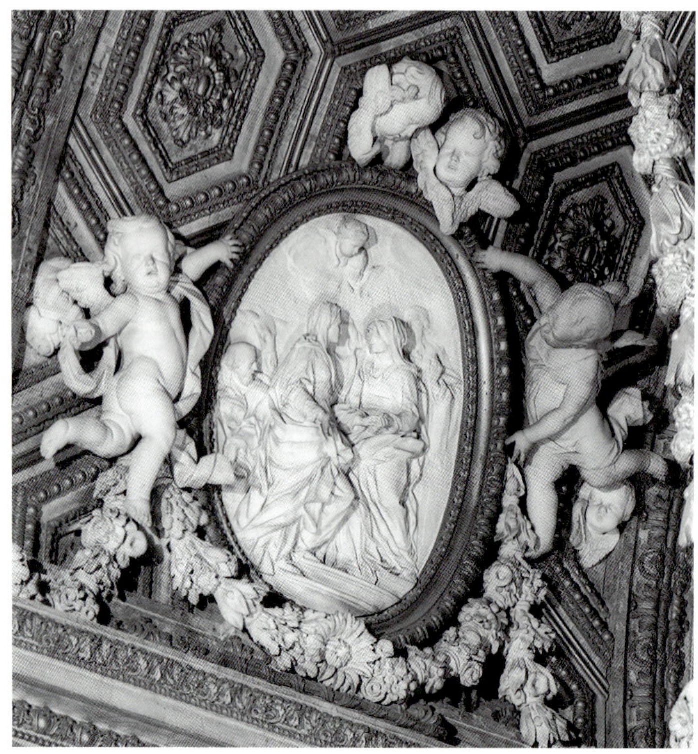

glected to sign his sculpture) is less evident. A number of other sculptors were responsible for the cherub heads on the vault of the chapel.

The style of this marble sculpture is very much in keeping with Portuguese taste, being reminiscent of the art of Masucci and, behind him, of Carlo Marrati, as is particularly evident in Marchionni's *Visitation* (fig. 4), which is closely dependent on Maratti's print of the same subject.[12] Ludovisi, treating in the *Preaching of Saint John the Baptist* a subject that required a far deeper view into the distance, was less successful, overloading the composition to suggest the crowd of listeners and failing to overcome the problem of handling deep recession with a number of overlapping planes in a relief. The overall effect is typical of the art of the period of Pope Benedict XIV in its rather heavy late baroque classicism (quite different from the neoclassicism that was to succeed it), combined not entirely happily with the lighter touches of the *barocchetto* in the proliferation of cherub heads, garlands, and elaborate moldings. To some extent this conflict can be seen as the result of the divergent tastes of Ludovice and Vanvitelli.

No consideration of the chapel can ignore the importance of the gilded metal in creating its richness and splendor. Although the names of the founders and silversmiths are known, and much of the superb quality of this work is due to their skills, quite possibly a sculptor provided models for the great garlands of gilded bronze that lighten the effect of the architecture, and certainly the silversmiths could not have produced their work without such assistance. We are fortunate in knowing that Corsini and Ludovisi provided the models for the *paliotto,* and the documents provide evidence that Maini made those for much, and very probably all, of the great torchères, just as they also suggest his responsibility for those of the *muta nobile* with its figures copied from prints after Bernini. It must be acknowledged that the altar furniture is indubitably sculpture, and any account of João V and Italian sculpture should include the contribution of those who made the models for the reliquaries, mass cards, thuribles, and incense boats, even if their names remain to be discovered. Indeed this metal work, not merely because of the fortuitous fact that it has survived when so much similar work for Italy has been melted down, represents the highest point of Italian eighteenth-century sculpture in Portugal.

Among the sculptors who carved clouds and cherubs for the chapel was Alessandro Giusti, and he was also among the artisans sent to Portugal to install this work, which had been prefabricated in Rome. Giusti remained in Portugal to found the school of local sculptors who continued the work at Mafra, carving lunettes and altarpieces to replace canvases that had rotted in Mafra's damp sea air. He therefore became the most important of all the Italian sculptors for the later development of the art in Portugal, and it is perhaps not without significance that he was trained by Giovanni Battista Maini. Apart from this virtually nothing is known of his previous career beyond the fact that he had been employed on the altar of Sant'Apollinare, being paid by the founder Filippo Valle "ottonaro" (brass worker, not to be confused with the sculptor Filippo della Valle) s.140.90 "di diversi modelli fatti di stucco per vedere il composto dell'altare e altri in greta ordinati dal sudetto Signor Cavaliere [Fuga]" (for various models made of stucco to show the ensemble of the altar and others in clay [*greta*] ordered by the above-mentioned Cavaliere [Fuga]).[13] His own accounts do not survive, so it might be argued that he merely produced a model to show the appearance of the work. However, the very attractive cherub heads that have been attributed to the sculptor Filippo della Valle[14] are manifestly in an entirely different style, and can therefore be safely attributed to the young Giusti.

These reliefs that proliferate over the interior of the church at Mafra are entirely Roman in derivation. Giusti's ability can best be judged from the models, as the marble figures are all-too-often stiff and stilted in their movements and lacking in expression, a result of the less expert hands of the carvers. They are for the most part conceived on the surface, with little attempt to explore the possibilities of relief composition in depth, a characteristic that they share with Roman work of the mid-century; in their greater ambition to rival the effects of painting and include a multitude of figures, they tend to a fatal lack of focus. But Giusti and the school of Mafra are beyond the period of João V and the great age of Portuguese patronage of Italian sculpture.

1. A. Ayres de Carvalho, *A Escultura em Mafra*, 2nd ed. (Mafra, 1956).

2. A. Ayres de Carvalho, *D. João V e a Arte do seo Tempo* (Lisbon, 1962), 404-407.

3. Carvalho 1962, in particular 399-430, and the general studies of the subject, Carvalho 1956, and Pierpaolo Quieto, *Giovanni V de Portogallo e le sue commettenze nella Roma del XVIII secolo (la pittura a Mafra,Évora, Lisbona)*, ([Bologna], 1988), 63-78.

4. Carvalho has attributed the figure of Saint Bruno to Lironi (1956).

5. Carvalho 1962, 389; Quieto 1988, 19.

6. Carvalho (1956) also ascribed to him the saints Francis and Dominic on the facade, where the other two statues are by Maini.

7. Carvalho 1962, 405.

8. Ajuda 49-VIII-6, fol. 112.

9. Ajuda, ms 49-VIII-29, fol. 65r.

10. Ajuda, ms. 49-VIII-29, fol. 72v.

11. Francisco Viterbo, Marquês de Sousa, and R. Vicente d'Almeida, *A Capella de S. João Baptista* (Lisbon, 1902), 115.

12. Bartsch XXI.90.3.

13. A.S.V., S.P.A., Computisteria vol. 997, fol. 312r.

14. Vernon Hyde Minor, "Filippo della Valle as Metalworker," *Art Bulletin* 66 (1984), 511-514.

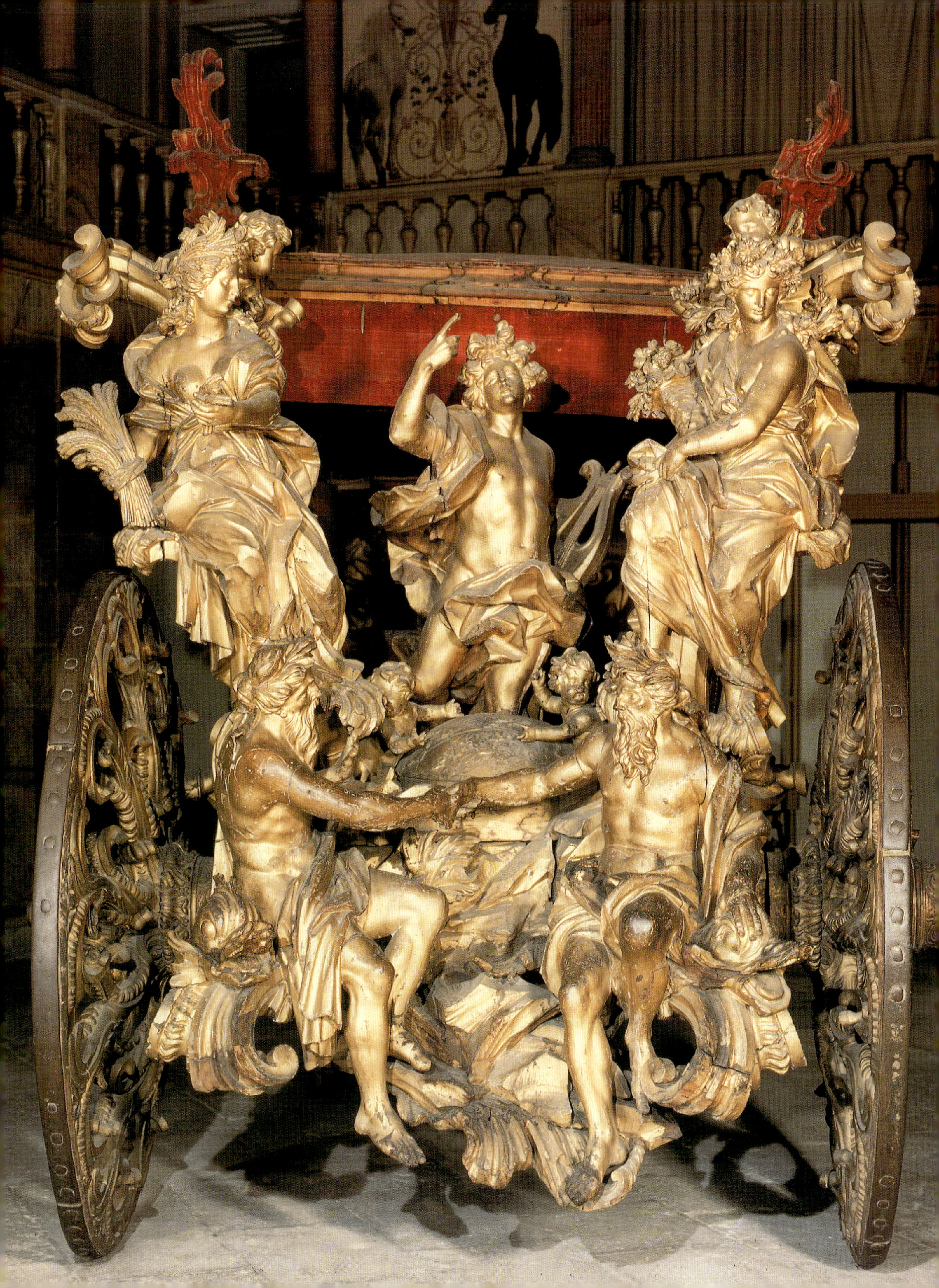

Wondrous Vehicles

The Coaches of the Embassy
of the Marquês de Fontes

Marco Fabio Apolloni

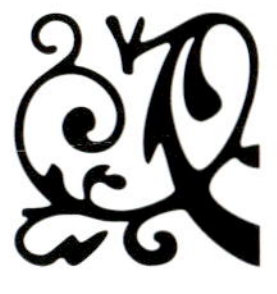

hree survive of the four coaches built in Rome for the official entrance of the ambassador extraordinary of Portugal to the papal court, Dom Rodrigo Annes de Sà, Almeida e Menezes (1676–1733), marquês de Fontes. Later, on his return to Portugal, he was named marquês de Abrantes, the title by which he is more commonly known.[1]

The official entrance was the most formal and magnificent occasion in the Roman diplomatic ceremonial, and the preparations for it could sometimes take years. This was indeed the case with the marquês de Fontes, who arrived in Rome on 21 May 1712, but only on 13 April of the following year went to kiss the sacred slipper of Pope Clement XI, in an entrance at court that was not yet the formal presentation of official diplomatic credentials. The marquês de Fontes succeeded the envoy extraordinary André de Mello e Castro; the latter stayed in Rome for the entire tenure of his fellow countryman and then in turn succeeded the marquês, making his official entrance in 1718, a year after Dom Rodrigo had left Rome.[2]

The biographer of the marquês de Abrantes, José Barbosa, wrote: "As was the custom at the Roman court and up to that time had been scrupulously observed, ministers could not transact the business of their sovereigns until after the ceremony of official entrance, which at Court today is neglected or dispensed with."[3] It is not known exactly what subtle formalities led the marquês to delay for so long his official entrance, which took place on 8 July 1716, but Barbosa reported that he had very little time to prepare as sumptuously as he did, both to astound the Roman public with his pomp and to reinforce the prestige of his king, João V.[4] The mission of the marquês de Fontes had been elaborately prepared and his departure from Lisbon delayed at length by the ambassador himself because of the question of the amount of money necessary for the journey and his early expenses, for which in the end forty thousand *cruzeros* were appropriated.[5] His expenses in Rome are not known, but the cost of preparing his official entrance must have been enormous. The marquês paid

fig. 1. *Rear View of the Last Coach in the Procession,* 1716. Museu Nacional dos Coches, Lisbon quite a sum out of his own pocket, as he had to ask his butler to pawn diamonds that decorated the hilt of his sword in order to pay some of his officers.[6]

Such great expenditures to dazzle Rome and the ambassadors from other courts attest to Portugal's ambition to take her place in the new European scheme after the Treaty of Utrecht (1713). Just as strong was the wish to influence her relationship with the Holy See in order to obtain privileges and ecclesiastical concessions that could not only placate the vanity of João V, but also consolidate the power of the monarchy over the church in Portugal, while at the same time maintaining all the sanctions of a very strong devotion.

The marquês de Abrantes was one of the principal agents and inspirations for this policy. A traveler in Portugal noted around 1722–1723 that "the marquês de Abrante, [João V's] *camerista* [gentleman in waiting], infatuated with the grandeur of Rome, did everything he could to persuade the king to go to kiss the foot of the Pope" but this was "to free his state and crown from the persecutions of the papal court and to suppress the fury of the Inquisition."[7]

For its part, Portugal had two inducements to influence the pope to grant the privileges it requested: material aid in the form of men and ships for the war against the Turks that Clement XI was promoting, and the attractive prospect of evangelizing the peoples of Asia, where the Portuguese colonies could well serve as points of reference for a future conversion to Christianity.[8] These two themes received major emphasis in the symbolic program of the decoration of the coaches. The sculptural groups in gilded wood decorating the coaches were traditionally dedicated to the glorification of the virtues and power of the reigning dynasty that the ambassador represented, but in the case of Fontes' embassy they took on a much more studied and meaningful allegorical complexity than had been the custom until then. The program[9] guiding the execution of these symbolic coaches—a type invented by the Roman baroque, which, despite its unlimited fantasy, had maintained almost unchanged the methods of representation—was in this case dictated by the ambassador himself.[10] Luca Antonio Chracas wrote that he would explain "thoughts and hieroglyphics conceived and created by the great mind of Your Excellency," that is, the marquês to whom the account is dedicated. Even if this is a case of excessive flattery and the concepts expressed in the sculptures and decoration of the coaches were invented by a learned man in the ambassador's service, nonetheless it is certain that the man was Portuguese, since the references to Luís de Camões' epic poem *Os Lusíadas (The Lusiads)* are so many and so exact that we must assume familiarity with the themes and words of the text hardly within the realm of an Italian.

Very little is known of the culture and patronage of Dom Rodrigo Annes de Sà, but it was certainly not limited to the coaches of his Roman embassy.[11] Various witnesses agree in calling him an expert on painting and above all a practical connoisseur of civil and military architecture, as is confirmed by his familiarity in Rome with the architect Filippo Juvarra, to whom the idea for Fontes' coaches has sometimes been attributed.[12]

It is not certain who designed Fontes' coaches or who actually built them. The conception and design could certainly be the work of just one artist, but the execution necessarily would have been entrusted to a veritable army of artisans and workers who were divided into categories according to their specializations. Artists' bills relative to Mello e Castro's embassy are useful for an understanding at least of how the work proceeded. Among them are scattered payments to artists and artisans who worked on the coaches for his official entrance of 1718, and a few rare instances of work done earlier for Ambassador de Fontes, but unfortunately of very little account.[13] The names mentioned in the documents are all of otherwise unknown artisans, and there is no mention of a known painter, sculptor, or architect involved in the execution of Mello e Castro's coaches. From what one can extrapolate, the largest part of the work was done by Giovanni Tommaso Corsini, "sculptor and carver," who presented first of all "the Model of said coach, with very fine wheels"; whether a drawing or a clay sketch is not specified. Figures or parts of figures were first realized in clay as were the decorations to be executed in wood by other artisans, and wax was used for the buckles with grotesque masks or other details in metal, from which molds could be made for either the bronze casters or the sword makers, depending on whether they were to be cast in bronze or iron. A canopy is mentioned that seems to have been singularly complicated; this was the ceiling of the coach, for which a clay model was made "life size," and from this were then made the plaster molds into which were poured "ground clay... and cardboard." While Giovanni Tommaso Corsini is the man responsible for the design and sculptural groups, one also finds Francesco Tibaldi, carver, who worked for Mello e Castro beginning in 1716–1717 carving various minor elements such as the vases decorating the roofs of the coaches, or assembling pieces that had already been done, or roughing out some wooden elements, but, as is specified, "excepting the sculpture which is the responsibility of the sculptor." Tibaldi must have had a number of workers under him, as he presented a bill for "many work-days." He also made "designs and models for the first coach... the embroidered ornaments in the style of the carvers for the use of the embroiderers" (the wooden supports, probably, for the embroidery in high relief) and also "the drawings of the two floors" that were executed in inlay by other carpenters.

The bodies of the coaches and the load-bearing structures of the frames, axles, and wheels were the work of the *facocchi* (coach builders), divided according to their specialization into fine or rough workers, to which was added the work of the *ferracocchi* (iron workers) for those parts in metal that made up the functional structure of the vehicle. The names include *Mastro* Giovanni Prestinari *Facocchio*, Benedetto Prestinari *facocchio e ferracocchio*, and Orazio Rossi and Filippo Valmori, *facocchi d'arte sottile* (coach builders for the fine work, that is builders of the bodies). Also mentioned were the names of the gilder, bronze worker, sword maker, painter, saddle maker, crystal worker, and the embroiderer who must have had dozens of other needleworkers under her direction.[14]

It is necessary to note this division of labor not only as a point of historical precision, but also because it is important for understanding the global effect of the work on the spectators of the time. Beyond their immediate general impression at the sight of the coach or an examination of the symbolic groups, they knew very well how much work and money went into all the rest: the embroidery in gold, the curtains in gold and silver, the upholstery and padding in brocade and velvet. Chracas' obsessive attention to these elements, parts of which are now lost, was not a coincidence, because the cost of golden thread alone in Fontes' coach probably was higher than any piece of sculpture. And too, the general effect of the whole coach in motion was based on all the decorations seen as a whole, including the waving plumes that completed the top of the carriage.

One might wonder what happened to the artists' bills relative to Fontes' embassy: that is if they were lost by chance or if they were kept separately, distinct from other accounts, perhaps because the ambassador may have considered them personal expenses even if made in the interest of the crown. The brief interval between the official entrance of 1716 and that of 1718 and the impression of a continuing working relationship that seems to emerge from the existing accounts suggest the hypothesis that the same artisans who made Fontes' coaches also worked on those for the entrance of Mello e Castro. But since these latter carriages have not survived and there are no known documents of their appearance, it is impossible to make any comparison and thus verify the idea.

The study of Roman coaches as works of art is still in its early stages; moreover only those in the Museu Nacional dos Coches in Lisbon have survived. There is little documentation about these, while paradoxically many of the carriages that are now lost are represented in sketches and preparatory drawings or commemorative prints.[15] At least for the second half of the seventeenth century, Giulia Fusconi[16] has very providentially begun to put the material in order, concentrating mainly on the coaches for gala occasions designed by the painter Ciro Ferri (1643–1689), whose production of carriages was the first to be engraved in a commemorative series created especially to spread the fame of these solemn and ceremonial entries.

In one of these series, that celebrating the official entrance of Lord Castelmaine, envoy of James II of England (1687), along with the name of the draftsman and engraver of the prints is the name of Ciro Ferri with the word "invenit," which is appropriate for the painter who designed the inventions and symbolic groups of the coaches depicted there. Along with Ferri there appears however also "Andrea Cornely fecit," who must have done the actual construction of the coach and carved the gilded wooden sculptural groups. In other prints from the same series, where coaches of minor importance are represented, one reads instead "Andrea Cornely inv. et fecit," indicating thus a highly specialized profession, that of builder of triumphal coaches, which seems to be very similar to the work of Giovanni Tommaso Corsini as it appears from documents.[17]

In the Roman drawings for coaches catalogued by Giulia Fusconi, especially in those that are not finished presentation drawings or preparatory drawings for prints but instead freely expressed sketches, one can actually perceive the creative process according to which, from Bernini on, coaches were conceived in Rome, starting not from the symbolic groups of statues, but from the functional parts of the coach: frame, axles, tie-rods, wheels. In a word, it is the skeleton of the carriage—a faint pencil line—onto which is then forcibly superimposed a vivid naturalization, masking every element with rock, tufts of reeds, trunks, garlands, sheaves of palm leaves, and other similar imitations of the world of nature, on the one hand forcing nature into the forms required by the mechanisms of a carriage, and on the other trying to make these mechanisms almost unrecognizable except as natural elements.[18] A splendid example of this practice is provided by the wheels of the main coach (fig. 2) of Fontes'

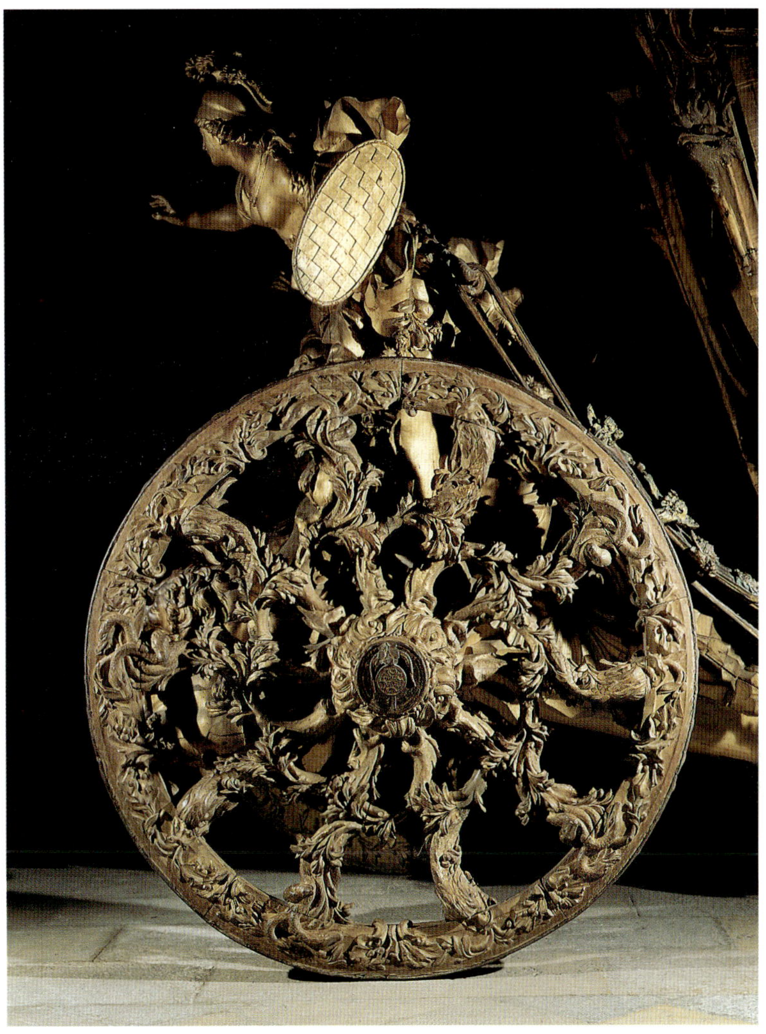

embassy, whose spokes are alternately snakes entwined with laurel branches and dolphins, all attached to the wooden rim completely carved with shells and laurel leaves, and to the hub on the opposite side, which was carved as a group of dolphins' heads and whose metal wheel cap is also decorated by smaller leaping dolphins.

Every other structural element of the main coach is similarly camouflaged as a natural form, while those of the other two coaches are developed according to different decorative principles, which transform the motifs from the vegetable world or the valves of shells into abstract forms that are almost completely artificial, purely decorative, innervated into *C-* or *S*-shaped scrolls with smooth sharp edges, twisted into complicated curls, or decorated with a kind of picturesque roughness distantly inspired by the rough surface of oyster shells. It is possible that this substantial stylistic difference was intentional, its purpose being to single out more distinctly the coach in which the ambassador rode—the richer, more elaborately gilded one with a floor inlaid in ivory (fig. 3)—from the two that were relatively less sumptuous. However, it is difficult not to think that this is a case of different styles altogether when one compares also the nature of the carved allegorical figures, more expressive and detailed on the main coach and more abstract and simplified, almost idealized, on the other two. To claim to be able to distinguish various "hands" in the three

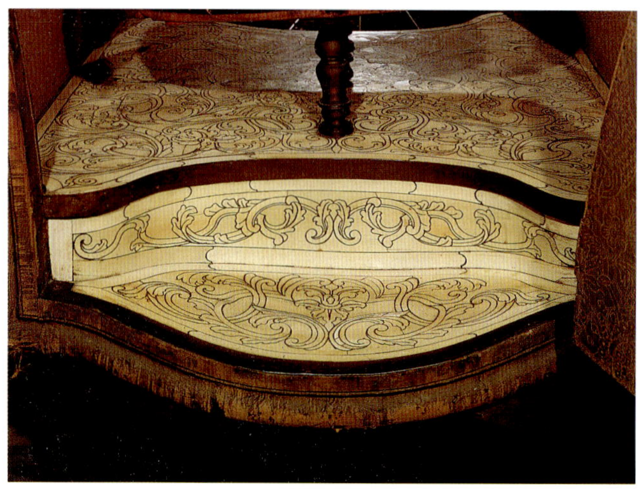

fig. 3. *Inlaid Ivory Floor of the Main Coach,* detail. Museu Nacional dos Coches, Lisbon

coaches is a vain hope at this stage of knowledge, but one should nonetheless be aware of the difference if other elements come to light to confirm it.

Even though it can be misleading to compare wooden sculptures with contemporary works in marble or stone, these carriages show a kinship with the fountains of the period of Pope Clement XI, which carried into the eighteenth century the tradition of imitation of nature of Bernini. The fountain by Carlo Monaldi in the courtyard of Palazzo Venezia, just slightly later than Fontes' coaches, shows a number of analogies with the sculptures of the main coach in particular that cannot be explained solely by their common iconography of marine elements, tritons, and shells.[19] It is much more difficult to make a comparison with wooden sculptures in churches, both because of the completely different, secular nature of the coaches and because of the real difficulty in finding a work in a church decorated close to the years 1714–1716. Analogies could be found with Roman furniture, which could have in common with these coaches the secular, mythological repertory, but as for chronology and attribution, even less is known of these objects than of Fontes' coaches.

The symbolic program of the three coaches is expressed in perfect harmony. Originally there was a fourth coach as well, called the *carrozza di rispetto,* which had no passengers and came first in the procession and which has not survived. It carried "the glorious Coat of Arms of His Excellency [the marquês de Fontes], topped by a princely crown" to which were attached "two large outstretched wings, indicating very aptly those of Fame."[20] The ambassador's self-glorification seems more evident than the homage usually paid to the reigning house that he represented: from reports and prints of other official entrances, Fontes' ostentation seems to have been without precedent. On the main coach the de Sà coat of arms appears on the shield carried by the flying figure of Bellona at the right on the back, checkered in silver and blue, even if here it is obviously in solid gold, and the heraldic colors of the marquês were borne during the entry on the rich livery of his escort of pages and lackeys. A proportionally more modest position was assigned to the heraldic dragon of the house of Bragança, which was placed on the top of the roof of the main coach and was mixed in with the other allegorical figures on the back.

As Chracas explained at length, the general theme of the sculpture, echoed also in the decoration of the embroidery, is that of Portugal's glorious discoveries and conquests in the fifteenth and sixteenth centuries, which had already been immortalized by Camões in *Os Lusíadas* and were here celebrated as something eternal and insuperable: Portugal's mastery of navigation, her triumph over Islam and paganism, the emphasis on her role as a Christian and civilizing nation that brought the Gospel and commerce to barbarous lands across the seas. This theme of land and sea is announced on the front of the main coach by a satyr, representing the land, harnessing with a garland of flowers a wild sea horse (fig. 4), while on either side of the driver's box appear Minerva and Hope, referred to by the Latin word *spes,* a sophisticated archaeological allusion to the coin struck by the Emperor Claudius at the birth of his son Britannicus.[21] João V, too, had a male heir, and the ambassador was making the official announcement of this event even though it had happened two years earlier and had already been recognized by the pope, who had blessed and sent the ceremonial swaddling bands to the newborn infante.[22]

The entire outside of the coach was resplendent with cloth richly decorated with spoils of war embroidered in low relief. In the middle of the coach's roof

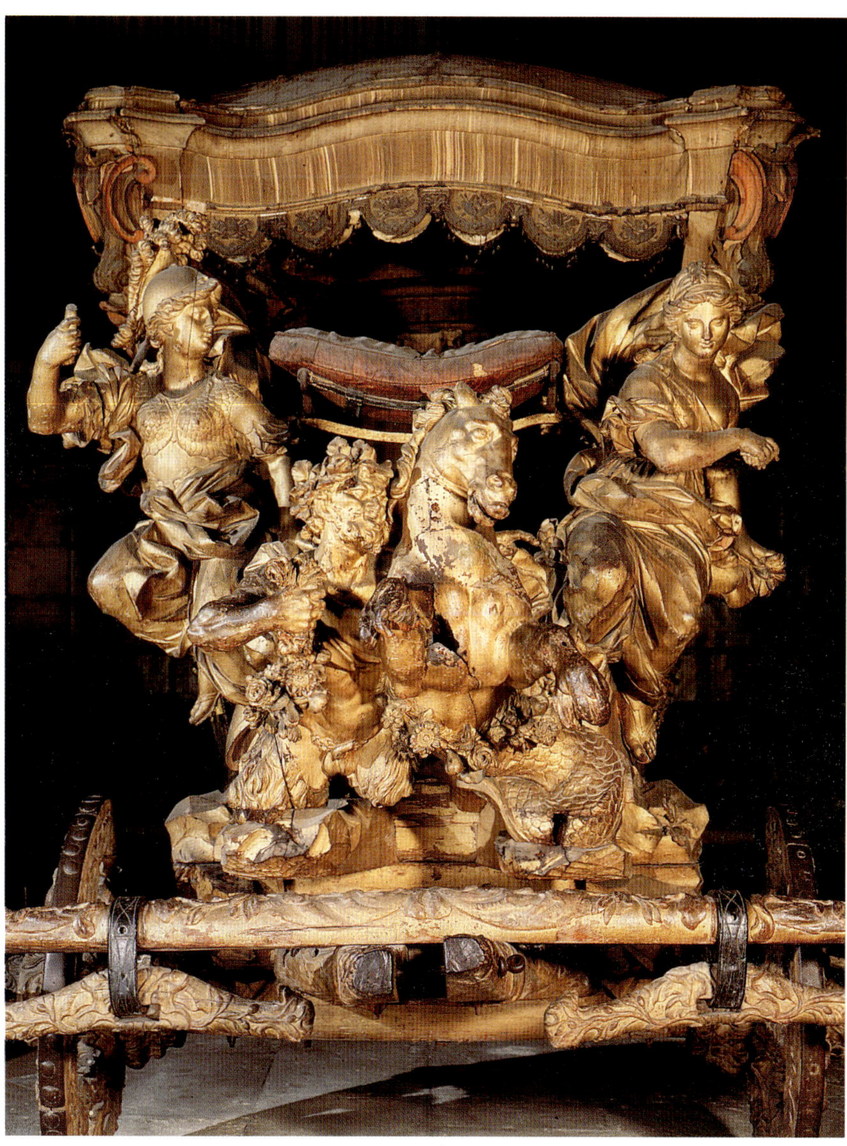

fig. 4. *Front View of the Main Coach.* Museu Nacional dos Coches, Lisbon

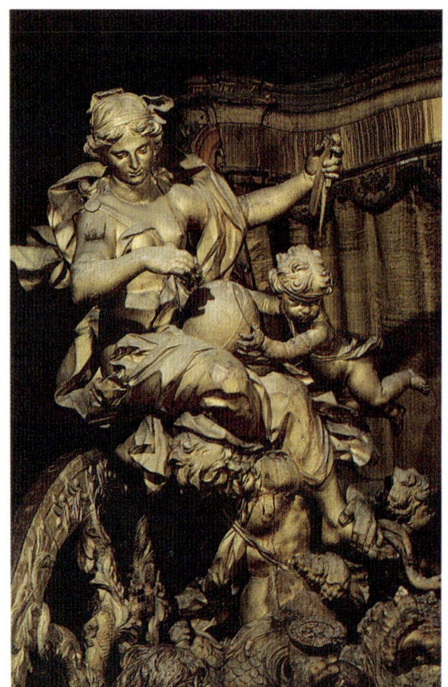

fig. 5. *Rear View of the Main Coach,* detail of
Thetis. Museu Nacional dos Coches, Lisbon

BELOW: fig. 6. *Side View of the First Coach*
(cat. 115), 1716. Museu Nacional dos Coches,
Lisbon

was originally the Bragança dragon on a pile of arms and surrounded by a rim
of gilded oak branches and other spoils of war in classical style. Each pile of
armor was topped with large waving plumes. The back of the coach rested on a
horrible monster, Adamastor, described by Camões as the petrified personification of that insurmountable African cape that, after the passage of Vasco da
Gama, was rechristened with the name of the virtue riding next to the driver:
Good Hope. A bearded hippo-triton, Palemon, benign guardian of ports, lies
stretched out on a dolphin, holding up a compass on which can be seen
strange figures: a human skull marks the north, a bull the west, and two others
that can no longer be distinguished represent the other two cardinal points.[23]
On the left a young man holding a bouquet of flowers in his left hand falls
back, attacked by a lion; the wild beast represents Portuguese virtue, which
overcomes weakness, the natural temptation of the exotic delights of India. On
the left there is a group composed of an old triton with a shell bugle around his
neck, leaning against the prow of an ancient ship with a winged siren as its fig-
urehead. He represents the storm, and is mastered by Navigation, personified
by the goddess Thetis (fig. 5) who sits on his back. Wrapped in a sail fluttering
in the wind, she holds nautical instruments in her left hand while her right
hand measures with a compass a celestial globe held for her on his lap by a
Zephyr who has a lifted blindfold on his forehead, probably signifying the far-
sightedness that had been acquired by the science of navigation. In flight on
the other side is Bellona, patroness of military endeavors, and beneath her is a
delightful baby satyr with a garland of herbs and flowers symbolizing the benign and fruitful nature of the soil of the Indies. At the center a cherub holds
up the ancient Roman *fasces,* symbol of justice, while another cherub with a
serpent around his neck, symbol of prudence, helps him bear his burden.

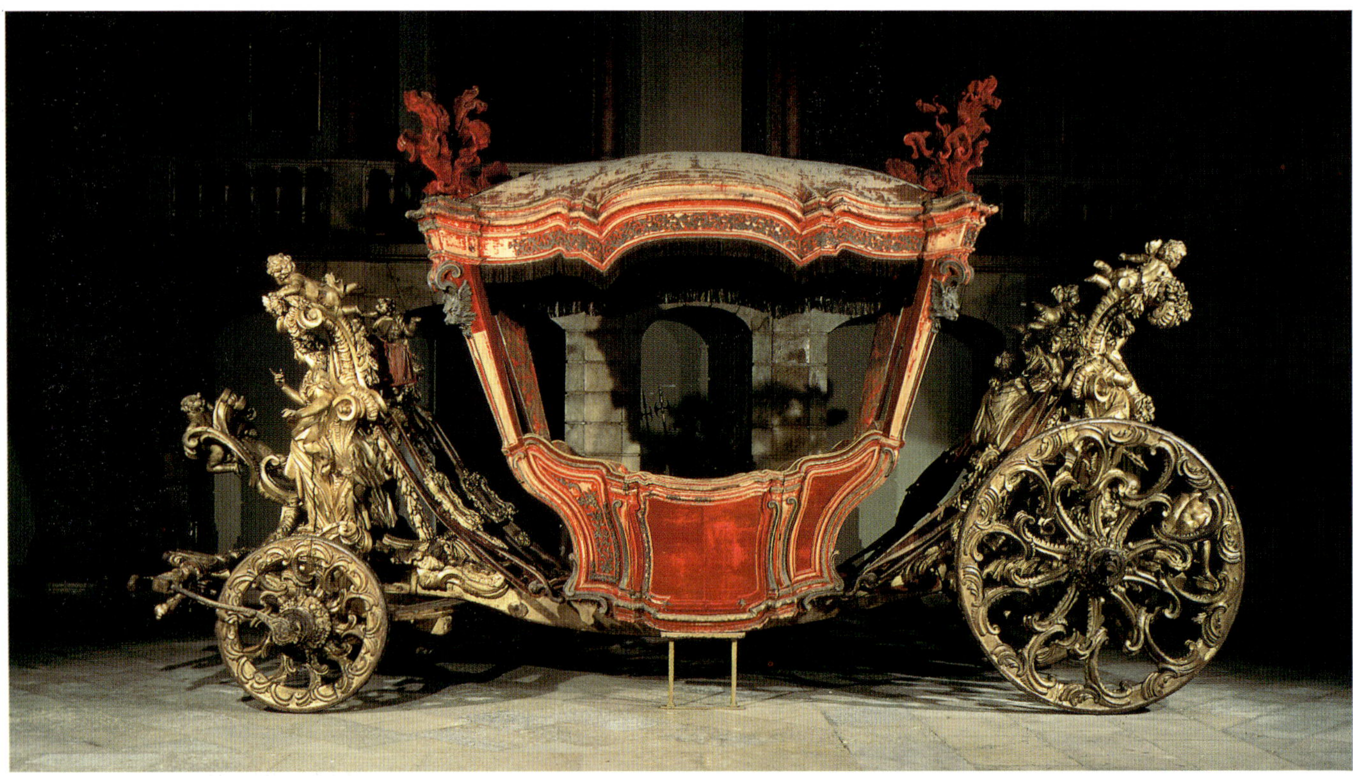

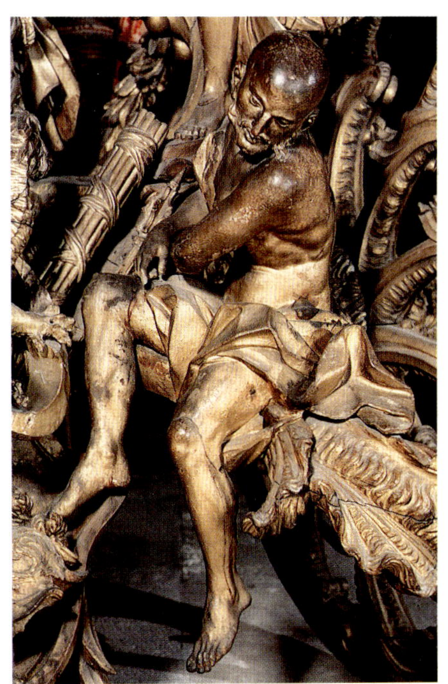

fig. 7. *Rear View of the First Coach* (cat. 115), detail. Museu Nacional dos Coches, Lisbon

The first noble coach of the entourage (fig. 6), the one exhibited here, bears at the top of each of its upper four corners zephyrs with laurel garlands. At the sides of the driver's box are, on the left, a youth crowned with a laurel wreath, "certainly a hieroglyphic of Love of Heroic Virtue," and, on the right, a woman crowned with sun rays, with a luminous sun on her breast and around her waist a snake biting its tail, symbol of immortality, here attributed to the illustrious name of the Portuguese nation. At the center of the rear of the coach sits the personification of the city of Lisbon, wrapped in a regal mantle and wearing the armor of an ancient Roman general; on her right "the glory of princes" holding the trumpet of fame suspends above her head a turreted civic crown, while on the left is Abundance with her cornucopia turned upside down so that its fruits spill out. At the feet of Lisbon a very lively Bragança dragon has momentarily left off tearing apart an Ottoman crescent between his claws and turns to look at Lisbon as though seeking her assent. Below, seated among scattered weapons, are chained prisoners, a Turk (fig. 7) looking down as though unable to bear the light of the true faith and a Moor looking up as if illuminated by the beginnings of a conversion.

The last noble coach, a twin of the preceding one in its decorative motifs and the arrangements of the sculpture, bears at the four sides four more zephyrs, beneath each of them the female personification of a season: Winter and Autumn on the front of the coach and Summer and Spring on the rear (see fig. 1), flanking an Apollo interpreted here as the personification of the sun and its seasonal course, floating above the sphere of the world held by two small genies — "the two intelligences attending the two poles" — at the feet of which, a little lower in the position occupied by the Turk and Moor in the preceding coach, sit the Atlantic and Indian oceans, amicably shaking hands, once again signifying their ideal communion achieved by the passage of the Portuguese navigators, the first in the modern age, from one sea to another around the Cape of Good Hope.

1. Summary information about the marquês de Abrantes can be found in António Caetano de Sousa, *Memórias históricas e genealógicas dos Grandes de Portugal…* (Lisbon, 1775). However, he is not even mentioned in the *Dicionário de história de Portugal*, ed. J. Serrão (Lisbon, 1979). His biographer was his contemporary Dom José Barbosa, whose *Élogio*, published soon after Abrantes' death, was not available to this author. In compensation, however, the "Coleção Pombalina" in the National Library in Lisbon (Cod. 418) contains the manuscript of the work, along with the author's notes and various transcriptions of documents of the time that he used in writing the *Élogio*. This material served also as the source for the summary of the story of Abrantes' trip from Lisbon to Rome in 1712 (fols. 55–56). This voyage was particularly difficult and tormented; the memory of it certainly influenced him to make the return trip in 1718 by land.

The marquês left Lisbon on a Genoese ship in a strong gale on 17 January 1712. Continuing bad weather forced a stop at Gibraltar almost a month later. The vessel embarked once more but was seized by an even more furious storm. The marquês, fearing shipwreck, made a vow to Our Lady of Bonaria, a sacred image honored in a sanctuary near Cagliari in Sardinia. The weather cleared and the party stopped at Cagliari on 19 March so that the marquês could fulfill the vow, walking barefoot to the sanctuary on painfully sharp sand and offering to the shrine a valuable gold bar. He was received by the viceroy of Sardinia before setting sail for Genoa, where he stayed for a month and a half before going to Leghorn on 18 May. He marked his arrival in Rome on the 21st by attending a ceremony in Saint Peter's proclaiming the canonization of five new saints. His host in the Eternal City was André de Mello e Castro until he took up residence in Piazza Colonna, whence his splendid train of coaches departed for the papal palace four years later, in July 1716.

2. The first official entrance of André de Mello e Castro as envoy of Portugal had been made to the Vatican on Sunday, 14 April 1709. It was first mentioned on that day in Francesco Valesio, *Diario di Roma*, ll. 7–8, vol. 4, ed. G. Scano

(Milan, 1978), 259: "They were very beautiful, shaped like covered coaches with huge glass windows, the first with the body carved with figures representing Portugal and the four parts of the world and the body gilded and painted with a top of red velvet.... The second also gilded but without figures, but decorated with lace and fringes of gold of unbounded width; and the third with top of turquoise velvet with smaller gold lace. These were followed by three other gilded and black coaches." A report of this entrance exists in *Relation du Voyage de Monseigneur de Mello e Castro à la Cour de Rome, en qualité de Envoyé Extraordinaire du Roi de Portugal Don Jean V, auprès de S.S. Clemente XI* (Paris, 1709). This is accompanied by illustrations of the coaches, drawn by Pietro Zerman and engraved by Giovanni Battista Siries, which are reproduced in Joaquim Maria Pereira Botto, *Promptuario analytico dos carros nobres da Casa Real Portuguesa e das carruagens de gala*, vol. 1 (the only one published) (Lisbon, 1909), plates on pages 230–231, 232–233, 234–235. According to Pereira Botto (230, no. 9, and 307, no. 24), the coaches were designed by D. Manuel Gonçalves Ribeiro, a gentleman in waiting to Mello e Castro, who painted also the pictures on the sides of the carriages, while the sculptures were carved by José Machado. Botto named also António Selci Selleiro, the last word being perhaps an indication of his profession (saddle maker) rather than his surname.

Mello e Castro's second official entrance as ambassador was in 1718, and Pereira Botto reported a hypothetical contribution by the very young sculptor José de Almeida (1700?–1769). Cancellieri (see A. de Faria, *Roma Lusitana, manoscritto inedito dell'Abate Francesco Cancellieri* [Milan, 1929]), reported other entrances or solemn audiences made by Mello e Castro on 8 July 1719, "with seven coaches," on 26 August 1719, "with a train of honor [treno de' Fiochetti]," and again on 14 September 1720. On 4 October 1721, the official entrance after the elevation to the throne of Innocent XIII took place. For each of these, Cancellieri cited the *Diario Ordinario* of Chracas under the corresponding date.

As for the official entrance of 1718, A. Raczynski, *Dictionnaire Historico–Artistique de Portugal* (Paris, 1847), 5, cited, in the entry for the sculptor José Almeida, "le livre intitulé *Embaixada de Mello e Castro*, 1 vol. in fo. On voit dans le livre les dessins de ces carrosses (Communication de M. le vicomte de Juromena)." No trace of this book has been found by this author.

3. Barbosa, "Élogio," fol. 56r.

4. Because of the questions regarding their alliance in the war against the Turks, the ambassadors of the empire and of Venice had already made their entrance at court. See Luca Antonio Chracas, *Ingresso fatto in Roma dall'Ecc.mo Sig. GIO.VINCESLAO di GALLAS…Ambasciatore Ordinario di detta Maestà Cesarea, e Cattolica alla S. Sede. Il 13 Maggio 1714* (Rome, 1714). See also Chracas, *Descrizione del Corteggio fatto per la prima udienza pubblica data dalla Santità di N.S. Papa Clemente XI.Il 22 Maggio 1714 all'Ecc.mo Signore GIO.VINCESLAO GALLAS* (Rome, 1714). Regarding the Venetian ambassador, see *Relazione del…pubblico ingresso…in Roma…e pubblica udienza avuta l'30 settembre 1714 da…Nicolò Duodo Ambasciatore Ordinario per la Serenissima Repubblica di Venezia appresso… Clemente XI* (Rome, 1714). The Gran Bali of the Order of Malta and the Spanish ambassador made their official entrances at the same time.

5. A. Ayres de Carvalho, *D. João V e a arte do Seu Tempo. As memórias D'El Rei D. João V pelo naturalista Merveillieux* (Lisbon, n.d. [1962]), 1:21.

6. Barbosa, "Élogio," fol. 67.

7. Carvalho 1962, 1:20–21, cited *Memoires Instructifs pour un voyageur dans les divers Etats de l'Europe . . .* (Amsterdam, 1738), attributed to the Swiss traveler, naturalist, and adventurer Charles Frédéric de Merveilleux (c. 1685–1749), who visited Portugal in the years 1720–1723, where, if the memoirs are his, he met the marquês de Abrantes.

8. For the war against the Turks, F. Pometti, "Studi sul Pontificato di Clemente XI, 1700–21," *Archivio della Società Romana di Storia Patria* (2), 22 (1899), 109–179; (3 and 4), 23 (1900), 239–275, 449–515. On the evangelization of the Orient, see *Memoriale al Papa Clemente XI presentato dall'Ambasciatore Straordinario del Re del Portogallo Marchese de Fontes, con cui si offre per parte del Re del Portogallo João V la dote per tre nuovi vescovati in Cina* [Rome, c. 1716]. This author consulted the copy in the Biblioteca Casanatense in Rome marked "Vol. Misc. 221.2."

9. The program is referred to as "note of erudition" in the documents of payment for the coaches of the Mello e Castro embassy.

10. Luca Antonio Chracas, *Distinto Ragguaglio del sontuoso Treno delle Carrozze con cui andò all'Udienza di Sua Santità il dí 8 luglio 1716 l'Illustrissimo, ed Eccellentissimo Signore Don Rodrigo Annes de Saa, Almeida e Meneses, Marchese di Fontes, Conte di Pennaghiano, Capitano Maggiore e Alcaide Maggiore della Citta di Porto, e della Fortezza di S. Giovanni della Foce del Doro, e di N.ª Signora delle Nevi in Leza di Matosigno, Signore del Consiglio di Sevèr, Pennaghiano, Fontes, Gudim, e Godomar. Signore di Villanuova, Terra di Vaca, e Aghiar di Souza, Bensas, Gaja, e della Honra di Sobrado, Signore della Casa di Abrantes, e delle Ville de Sardoal. Alcaide Maggiore delle Ville di Abrantes, Pugnete, Amendoa, e di Massam. Commendatore di S. Giacomo, Gentiluomo della Camera della Maestà del Re di Portogallo, e del Suo Consiglio, e Suo Ambasciatore Straordinario appresso la Santità di Nostro Signore Papa Clemente XI* (Rome, 1716). In the dedication to the marquês de Fontes, Chracas mentioned "the honor that my presses have received from Your Excellency's kind orders for the printing of various materials." This indication, along with Barbosa's concerning the works dedicated to the ambassador, "from single sheets and small works . . . to the dedication of entire volumes," should put scholars on the trail

of other printed pieces hidden in Roman libraries. The report is certainly true to its title, as it is very detailed and precise in its descriptions. It gives such a confident and careful explanation of the symbolism of the coaches as to lead us to think it was based directly on the "note of erudition" that had served for their construction.

11. Carvalho 1962, 21–22, reported the opinions of Dom Francisco de Portugal, marquês de Valença (1745), according to which Dom Rodrigo "drew with incredible skill the plans for squares and palaces, and was no less eminent in civil architecture than in military…," and of José Barbosa, according to whom he "knew Geometry perfectly, especially concerning civil and military architecture, so that the plans he drew were perfect, and the squares he mapped out were regular. He knew the Italian and Flemish schools as well as a professor of the art of painting, distinguishing with perspicacity copies from originals." In José-Augusto França, *Lisboa Pombalina e o Iluminismo* (Lisbon, 1977), 50 and 214, the marquês is mentioned as "Artistic Mentor" of João V and promoter of the erection of a public monument in front of the arsenal of Lisbon (destroyed in the earthquake of 1755) dedicated to his king, the work of Giovanni Antonio Bellini, the sculptor from Padua.

One would like to know if he bought works of art in Rome, and which ones, during his embassy. See in Cancellieri 1929 a footnote by Carlo Fea in the Roman edition of the *Storia delle Arti del Disegno presso gli antichi, di Giovani Winkelmann* (Rome, 1784), 3:29–30, n.(A), which says that the statues "of Caracalla…and of his mother Julia," which were located in the "Circus of Caracalla" (that is, of Massenzio), during the pontificate of Clement XI were "bought by the duke of Abrantes ambassador of Portugal to Rome." Cancellieri added that the architect Tommaso De Marchis sold them to the ambassador.

The tradition according to which it was the very young painter Francisco Vieira de Mattos (1699–1783), called "Vieira Lusitano," who designed Fontes' coaches (see Luciano Freira, *Catalogo do Museu Nacional dos Coches* [Lisbon, 1923]), is difficult to credit because of the artist's age. And it is also hard to believe he would not have boasted about it in his autobiographical poem *O insigne pintor e leal esposo Vieira Lusitano, historia verdadeira que ele escrive em cantos lyricos…* (Lisbon, 1780). In it the marquês is remembered as "Maecenas" and "arquitecto." We must keep in mind, however, that Vieira was also an engraver, and he could have been involved in the project of illustrating Fontes' coaches after the official entrance. Why this was never done is in fact one of the most tantalizing mysteries among the many still unresolved questions concerning these coaches.

12. Attribution to Filippo Juvarra of the plans for Fontes' coaches has been proposed by Max Terrier, "La Mode des Espagnolettes, Oppenord et Juvarra," *Antologia di Belle Arti* (1985), n.s., 123–146, nos. 27–28. This hypothesis, although intriguing, nonetheless awaits corroborating evidence, even if it seems an arduous task to

recognize Juvarra's style in the decorations of the coaches. The only certain and important fact is the familiarity that had been achieved in Rome between the architect and the ambassador. As Terrier recalled, Juvarra's anonymous eighteenth-century biographer clearly wrote: "While Don Filippo was staying in Rome, he had contracted a very close working relationship with the ambassador of the king of Portugal the marquês de Fontes, who dabbled in architecture with such a foundation of knowledge that few professional architects could keep up with him," and again when he was directing the construction of the basilica of Superga, "Don Filippo used in the winter months, when work was suspended, … to come to Rome to see his relatives and to stay with them, and when he went to pay his respects to the ambassador, the ambassador showed him a model of his own invention, of the patriarchal church of Lisbon and the royal palace."

Juvarra went to Portugal, with the permission of the court of Sardinia, at the request of João V during the years 1719–1720, when the marquês de Abrantes was at court. See Emilio Lavagnino, *L'Opera del Genio Italiano all'Estero. Gli Artisti in Portogallo* (Libreria dello Stato, 1940), which mentioned a picture painted by Gaspar Van Wittel from plans drawn by the ambassador and Juvarra of an ideal view of Lisbon and sent to João V. A strange fact is recorded by Barbosa ("Élogio," fol. 66v): "Em todo o tempo do seo ministerio na Corte de Roma fez huma vida digna de admiração; era secular no exterior e religioso no animo. Todas as semanas hia confessar-se a S. Jerónimo da Charidade, com o P.e João da Guarda Portuguez…." Juvarra's only work in Rome, in San Girolamo della Carità, was the Antamoro Chapel, finished in 1710.

13. See *Manuscritos da Ajuda, Guia* 1, Centro de Estudos Históricos Ultramarinos (Lisbon, 1966), 535: "49-VI-15 a 28. Contas e recibos de pagamentos feitos em Roma aos Artistas que trabalharam para Portugal, por ordem do Conte das Galveas, Andre de Mello e Castro, Embaixador naquella Corte, 1715 a 1726."

The patient transcription of these documents, made on the occasion of an exhibition in Rome in 1990, *Roma Lusitano,* has been very graciously placed at my disposition by Dr. Gabriele Borghini. This is a small mine of information from which we have taken an extract by kind concession, leaving a more complete use of the work to the person who has the right to it.

14. Useful information on the Roman corporations can be found in Antonio Martini, *Arti Mestieri e Fede nella Roma dei Papi* (Bologna, 1965). The Società o Università dei Falegnami (guild of woodworkers) included twenty-five "corpi d'arte" (specializations), among them coach builders, workers in inlay, and carver-sculptors. These last were not, however, considered the colleagues of sculptors in marble. In this regard, for this period, see the interesting case of Carlo Monaldi, for whom the academy of Saint Luke made as a condition of his entry that "the same detach himself completely from the Company of Woodworkers"; see Robert

Enggass, *Early Eighteenth-Century Sculpture in Rome* (State College, Pa., 1976), 1:183 ff.

15. Among the many visual documents, one can point out as stylistically quite similar to the Fontes coaches an anonymous drawing in Berlin of a coach topped by a royal crown, with the precise indication of its scale in "Roman palms." See Sabine Jacob, *Staatliche Museen Preussischer Kulturbesitz. Italienische Zeichnungen der Kunstbibliothek Berlin. Architektur und Dekoration 16–18 Jahrhunderts* (Berlin, 1975), no. 787, ill.

16. See Giulia Fusconi, "Per la storia della scultura lignea in Roma: le carrozze di Ciro Ferri per due ingressi solenni," *Antologia di Belle Arti* (1984), n.s., 80–97, nos. 21–22.

17. The prints of the "Veduta laterale e treno posteriore della prima carrozza del seguito di Lord Castelmaine" (side and rear views of the first coach in the entourage of Lord Castelmaine) are reproduced in "Disegni Decorativi del barocco romano," figs. 21–22. Others from the same series appear in H. Kreisel, *Prunkwagen und Schlitten* (Leipzig, 1927).

18. See the coach designs attributed to Ludovico Gimignani in "Disegni Decorativi del barocco romano," nos. 39–46r.

19. Enggass 1976, 2: figs. 190–195.

20. Chracas 1716, 7–8.

21. For this archaeological source, which it would have been completely impossible to recognize without the unexpected but precise mention of it in Chracas 1716, see *Enciclopedia dell'Arte Antica* under the entry "Spes," and the note by Carlo Fea in the Roman edition of the *Storia delle arti del disegno…* (1783), 1:177–178, n.(h).

22. The coach of the "blessed bands" sent to João V can be seen, albeit subsequently reworked, in the Museu Nacional dos Coches in Lisbon, but aside from the learned illustration provided in Botto 1909, 89–98, its history, still very unclear, merits careful study.

23. Very similar figures, especially the skull— perhaps a reference to the highly venerated relic of Saint Vincent's jawbone—can be seen sculpted on the keystone of the vault in the Manueline church of the Jerónimos in Belém.

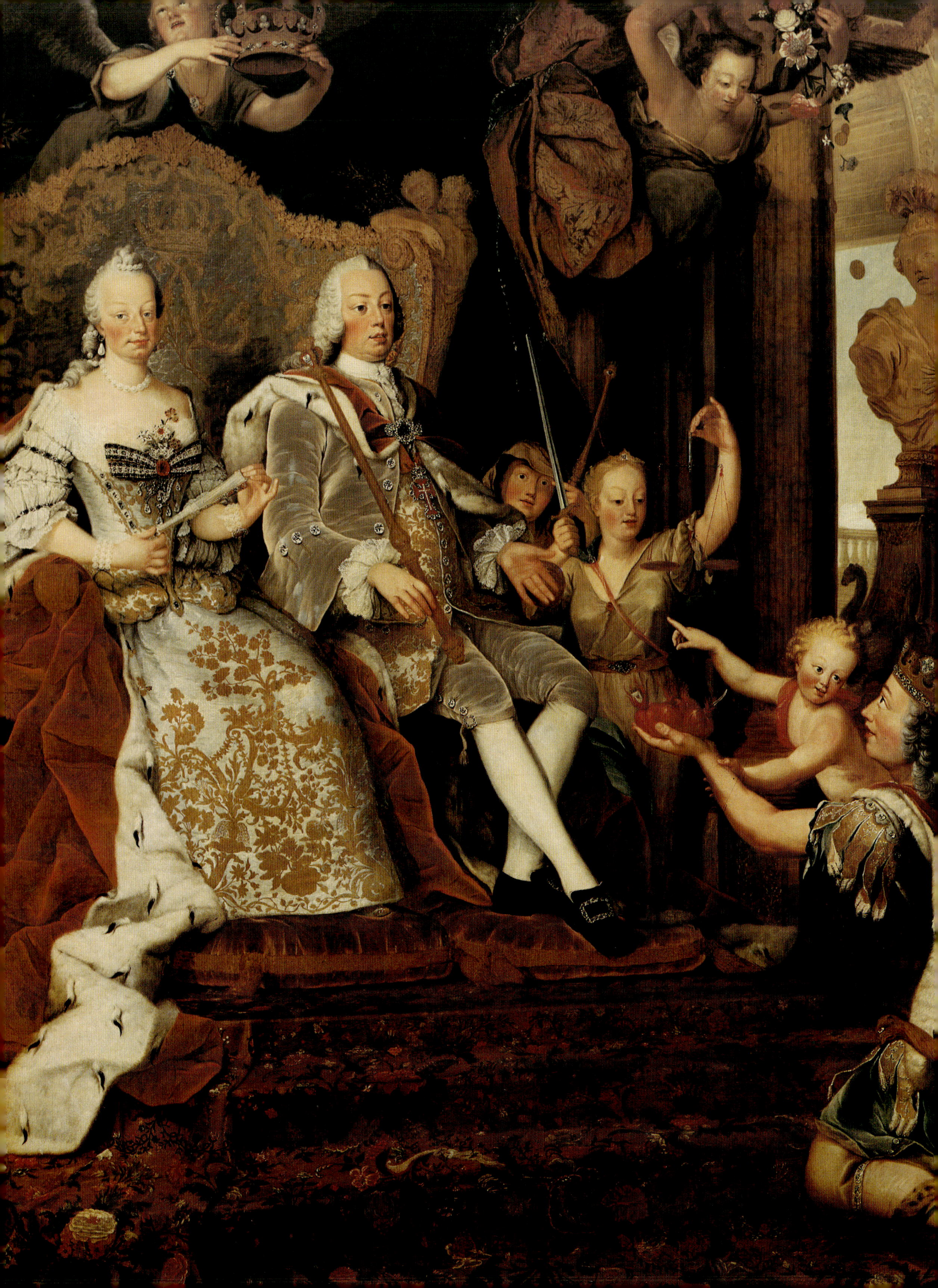

Eighteenth-Century Portugal

Faith and Reason, Tradition and Innovation During a Golden Age

Kenneth R. Maxwell

Despite Portugal's great wealth and opulence during the eighteenth century, the country had a sorry image in the rest of Europe. The European writer who needed a stereotypical example of a lack of rationalism almost invariably turned to Portugal. Voltaire summed up the attitude well. Writing about the gold-rich Portuguese monarch Dom João V (1707–1750), he observed: "When he wanted a festival, he ordered a religious parade. When he wanted a new building, he built a convent, when he wanted a mistress, he took a nun."[1]

The contrast between the views of foreigners and the image of the eighteenth century within Portugal, however, is striking. The period, especially after the 1750s, is seen in Portugal as being the very embodiment of the enlightenment. Among the elements emphasized is the legislative activity that left few aspects of Portuguese life untouched. This included the establishment of the first system of public, state-supported education, the root and branch reform of the ancient university at Coimbra, the reduction of the Inquisition's power, the modernization of the military, the abolition of slavery in Portugal (but not in the colonies), and the ending of the distinction between so-called "old" and "new Christians" (the new Christians were the descendants of Portuguese Jews who had "chosen" to embrace Christianity in 1497 rather than face expulsion). In addition, a royal treasury with centralized accounting systems and uniform taxing powers was established, and its first lord was designated, following British practice, the king's chief minister. Above all, the reconstruction of Lisbon after the devastating earthquake of 1755 is held up as a model of enlightenment town planning. In the colonies, Brazil most especially, the reform of the whole administrative structure can be claimed: the creation of joint stock companies and the outlawing of discrimination against Amerindians in Portuguese America and Asians in Portuguese India.[2] Portuguese historians will agree that eighteenth-century Portugal was governed by an absolutist regime. It is argued, however, that it was a regime inspired by an absolutism of reason, and its authoritarianism was essential to the revitalization of state

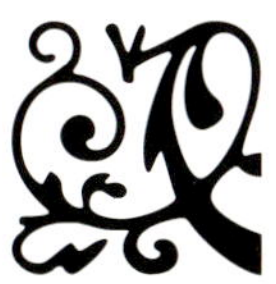

fig. 1. Attributed to Francisco Vieira Lusitano, *Allegory of the Acclamation of Dom José I*, detail, c. 1750, oil on canvas. Ministry of Foreign Affairs, Lisbon

power and to the process of reestablishing national control over the economy.

Even the opulent and licentious Dom João V himself, the would-be Portuguese *roi soleil,* has recently been reappreciated. Historians have discerned behind the smog of religious incense, the fires of the Inquisition, and the expensively encased reliquaries a surprisingly eclectic, proto-scientific, even open-minded monarch intent in his genuine piety and with his great wealth on building a new Rome on the Tagus.

The long Portuguese eighteenth century began during the late 1660s. Portuguese independence had been achieved in 1640 when Spanish rule was thrown off, but it was recognition by the major European maritime powers (England in 1654 and 1662, the Netherlands in 1661 and 1667) that was decisive in forcing Spain itself to reluctantly follow suit in 1668. And this long Portuguese eighteenth century ended in the climactic winter of 1807–1808 when Napoleon's armies under Général Junot seized Lisbon and the Bragança dynasty fled across the Atlantic to establish its seat in Brazil.

Within these broad chronological parameters unfolded the struggles of the eighteenth century: the clash of tradition with the forces of change and innovation, the struggle between the old religion and the new rationalism of the age of reason, the desire to be great again on the basis of the wealth of South America yet the ever-present nostalgia for glories past in the Orient, the conflict between despotic means and enlightened objectives. And it was within this framework that the great events that punctuated the epoch occurred: the exploration of the interior of South America, the discovery of gold in Brazil, the magnificent ceremonials of the new Patriarchate, the cruel spectacles of the Inquisition, the earthquake of 1755, the expulsion of the Jesuits, the reconstruction of Lisbon.

Three monarchs ruled Portugal during the eighteenth century. The reign of Dom João V covered the first half of the century, during which great wealth flowed into Lisbon from the Brazilian territories. In 1750 Dom João V was succeeded by his son Dom José I, a monarch who preferred hunting and opera to the arduous task of government and whose reign was marked by the long predominance in affairs of state of Sebastião José Carvalho de Melo, known after 1769 as the marquês de Pombal. And, the pious and later mad Dona Maria I succeeded her father in 1777. Dona Maria was declared incompetent in 1792 when her portly son João became de facto regent. He became the prince regent formally in 1799, which he remained until the death of his mother in 1816 when he was acclaimed in Rio de Janeiro as Dom João VI of the United Kingdom of Portugal, Brazil, and the Algarves.

The eighteenth century was, for Portugal, a period of demographic growth. During the first quarter of the century the Portuguese population had been increasing, and in 1732 was in the range of 2 million people. By 1758 the population reached $2\frac{1}{2}$ million and increased to 3 million by the 1780s. Lisbon, however, which had been the largest city in the Iberian Peninsula in the mid seventeenth century, was overtaken by Madrid in the eighteenth century. At the time of the 1755 earthquake Lisbon's population numbered some 150,000, a figure at which it remained until 1780. Oporto, the second city in the country, by way of contrast grew rapidly, from twenty thousand in 1732 to forty thousand in 1787.[3]

Portugal's economy throughout the eighteenth century was marked by the preeminence of colonial, mainly Brazilian staples in its European re-export trades. In many respects, the prosperity of metropolitan Portugal depended directly on the fluctuations of its colonial commerce. The gold, sugar, and tobacco of Brazil formed the basis of a South Atlantic-based commercial complex, with sugar and tobacco providing profitable re-exports to Spain and Brazilian gold a means for balancing Portugal's unfavorable trade with northern Europe and paying for the import of wood and grain.[4]

Since the late seventeenth century the focus of Portugal's imperial interest had shifted decisively westward from the trading-post thallasocracy of the Indian Ocean first established in the early sixteenth century to the plantation-based colonies of the South Atlantic. The trade in African slaves and Brazilian sugar, which had predated the Asian empire and thrived even while overshadowed by the Asian spice trade, came fully into its own. Within the South Atlantic system itself, integrated by the triangular interdependence of Lisbon, the slaving enclaves of the west and central African coast, and the expanding colonies of European and African settlements in Portuguese America, imperial priorities were reordered to favor support of Portugal's territorial empire in Brazil.

The most dramatic and decisive consequence of Portuguese exploration of the interior of South America was the discovery of gold. The search for precious metals had brought many of the first Europeans to the Western hemisphere and also provoked the most audacious explorations of the vast interior of South and North America. The Spanish had been well rewarded for their early explorations. Within months of Columbus' landfall, gold had been discovered in Hispaniola. And during the 1540s in the barren mountains of the Andes, the Spaniards came upon a vast mountain of silver at Potosí, in present-day Bolivia, and in Mexico along the eastern slope of the Sierra Madre they were no less successful in exploiting silver ore. The Portuguese, on the other hand, were less fortunate. For almost two hundred years after Portugal laid claim to the territory that became known as Brazil, they had to make due with more prosaic commodities: Brazil-wood used to produce red dye, sugar, hides, cacao, and tobacco, worthy and valuable products all, but not the precious metals the early settlers had hoped for.

At the end of the seventeenth century, however, half-Indian frontiersmen from the small inland settlement of São Paulo struck it rich. São Paulo was a resource-poor community that made its living by capturing and selling Indian slaves and raiding the prosperous Jesuit missions in Paraguay. The Paulistas were ever on the lookout for booty. In the 1690s, after years of searching, they came across rich deposits of alluvial gold in the streams that flowed from the Mantiqueira Mountains. Three hundred and fifty miles inland from the port city of Rio de Janeiro, the Mantiqueira range marked the watershed for the great north-flowing San Francisco River as well as for the tributaries that flowed south into the vast La Plata River basin. As word spread, speculators used both river systems to reach the goldfield, and within a decade of the discovery the first great gold rush of modern history was in full swing.

These discoveries had political as well as material consequences. Gold from Brazil, for example, allowed the Portuguese monarchs the luxury of avoiding recourse to the nation's ancient representative (and tax granting) institution. It is no accident that the last parliament met in 1698 and was not to meet again until 1820. The eighteenth century, therefore, saw the apogee of the absolutist state in Portugal.[5] The material consequences, however, were significant. The gold remittances from Brazil increased steadily over the course of the first half of the eighteenth century, reaching their apogee in the early 1750s. After 1729 diamonds were added to the riches flowing to Lisbon and on to Amsterdam from the interior of Portuguese America.[6] A major mechanism linking the Portuguese South Atlantic colonial system to a developing world economy was Anglo-Portuguese commerce. By the Methuen Treaty of 1703 English woolen goods entered Lisbon and Oporto free of duty and, in return, Portuguese wines received advantages on the English market. During the first half of the eighteenth century trade was greatly in Britain's favor and the profits for individuals high.[7] Woolen cloth made up two-thirds of total British exports to Portugal.[8] After the early 1730s the great influx of gold and diamonds from Brazil exaggerated the imbalance of Anglo-Portuguese exchange.[9] Deficits could be made up and the purchase of foreign goods facilitated by the outflow of bullion.

The British factory in Oporto had initiated the wine trade in 1678 as a substitute for the re-export trade in Brazilian sugar and tobacco, which they had lost to British West Indies competition. As a result of pressure on Parliament in London, the English merchants in Portugal obtained a tariff beneficial to them in 1697 and, under the terms of the Methuen Treaty, Portuguese wines paid a rate one-third below those of French wines. Wine exports increased dramatically over the course of the eighteenth century: from a yearly average of 632 barrels in 1678–1687, to 17,692 in 1718–1727, to 40,055 in 1788–1789.[10] By the end of the eighteenth century, nine-tenths of all Port wine exported went to England where Portuguese wine dominated seventy to seventy-five percent of the English market.[11] The value of the Portuguese trade to Britain was obvious. However, Portugal's own industry suffered from this development of commerce. Its growth and decline over the course of the century was directly linked to the rise and fall of Brazilian gold production. Portuguese domestic manufacturing thrived prior to 1700 and again after 1770, but languished during the golden age.[12]

Portugal remained a chronic grain importer throughout the eighteenth century, from northern Europe at the beginning of the century and later from North America, especially Virginia and the Carolinas. North America also became an importer of Portuguese wines, a factor that helped develop North American taste for Port and Madeira wine, which became as much favored by such founders of the American republic as George Washington and Thomas Jefferson as they were by the Tory squirearchy in England.[13]

The eighteenth century also saw the rise of influential foreign merchant communities in Lisbon and Oporto, which, protected by treaties, enjoyed special legal status. The British merchants in those cities were not the only foreign merchants in Portugal, to be sure, nor the only foreign merchants enjoying special concessional privileges, but they were the most prominent by far.[14] The British factories in Lisbon and Oporto were, throughout the eighteenth century, privileged commercial communities possessed of a legal status dating from the seventeenth century and operating important institutions of their own: churches, graveyards, hospitals, assembly rooms. The treaty of 1654 between Portugal and Cromwellian England guaranteed the English not only

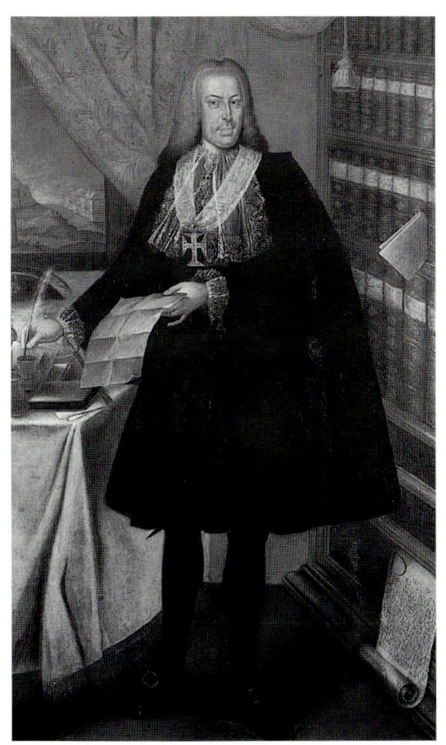

fig. 2. Attributed to Joana do Salitre, *Portrait of the Marquês de Pombal*, c. 1769, oil on canvas. Museu da Cidade, Lisbon

the "same liberties, privileges, and exemptions as the Portuguese in metropolitan and colonial commerce," but also provided for religious toleration and, by a secret article, prohibited the raising of customs duties on British goods above twenty-three percent. Parts of the treaty had always remained dead letters, particularly those related to the presence of English merchants in the Portuguese possessions, but the 1654 and subsequent treaties provided a favorable environment for the creation of the state of semicolonial dependency in which mid-eighteenth-century Portugal found herself with relation to her northern ally. Great prosperity, given the privileged position of the British and foreign merchant corporations in Lisbon and Oporto, encouraged the penetration of foreign credit and goods throughout the Luso-Brazilian system.

The eighteenth century was also framed by the ongoing diplomatic and military struggle between France and Britain for hegemony, especially as far as this affected the naval, commercial, and colonial affairs of the Atlantic where Portugal's vital economic and strategic interests now lay.

Lisbon tried to accommodate both France and Britain, but by its very Atlantic nature and because of the central economic role of Brazil within the Luso-Atlantic commercial system, Portugal was tied inextricably to Britain and, though it always sought to remain neutral and retain thereby the prosperous *entrepôt* function of Lisbon for the re-export of colonial products, it was very rarely able to maintain neutrality long. This need for external political and military support in Europe was of course at the core of the commercial concessions Portugal had made to England in the 1640s. And Portugal was reminded of the need for outside assistance during the Seven Years War when British troops had been required to ward off a Spanish invasion. As a consequence a major program of military reform was introduced in Portugal during the 1760s. Sporadic warfare with Spain in South America was recurrent throughout the eighteenth century, especially over the disputed Southern borderlands.

The role of Brazil in Portuguese calculations and diplomacy thus held a high priority throughout the century. Preoccupation with the development of the Portuguese Atlantic empire on the one hand, and with Portugal's diminished stature and apparent backwardness on the other, permeated the Portuguese political and intellectual milieu of the age.

Like Portugal itself, the marquês de Pombal (fig. 2), de facto ruler from 1750 to 1777, also has a very curious historical image. Even before he took power, Pombal's contemporaries were divided in their views about him. The political testament of Dom Luís da Cunha, Pombal's patron and mentor, recommended Pombal for his "patient and speculative temperament."[15] Others were not so complimentary. Sir Benjamin Keene, who had been the British envoy in Lisbon from 1745 to 1749, wrote of him, "it is a poor Coimbrian pate as ever I met with, to be as stubborn, as dull, is the true asinine quality... I shall only say that a little genius who has a mind to be a great one in a little country, is a very uneasy animal."[16] To some Pombal is a great figure of enlightened absolutism, comparable to Catherine in Russia, Frederik in Prussia, and Joseph II in Austria-Hungary; to others he is little more than a half-baked philosopher and a full-blown tyrant.

When Pombal entered office, he did so with a well-formulated set of ideas that built on a generation of discussion among Portuguese officials and diplo-

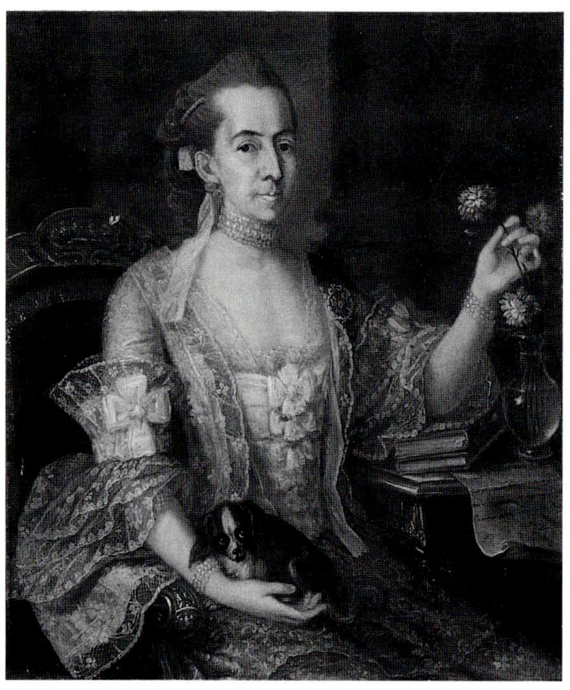

fig. 3. Pierre Jouffroy, *Maria Leonor Ernestina, Countess of Daun, Marquesa de Pombal,* 1770, oil on canvas. Private Collection, Évora

mats who had given much thought to what they perceived as Portugal's decadence and to the imperial organization and the mercantilist techniques that they believed had brought about the startling and growing power and wealth of France and Great Britain, two nations that had now eclipsed the Iberian powers themselves.[17] In these concerns Pombal's preoccupations reflected those of his colleagues. He had served, moreover, in London from 1739 to 1744 and in Vienna from 1744 to 1754.

In London, Pombal, who had become a member of the Royal Society in 1740, set out to investigate the causes, techniques, and mechanisms of British commercial and naval power. Among the books in his London library were those of Thomas Mun, William Petty, Charles Davenant, Charles King, Joshua Gee, and Joshua Child as well as select reports on colonies, trade, mines, and woolen manufactories; specialized tracts on sugar, tobacco, and fisheries; parliamentary acts on tonnage and poundage; shipping and navigation; fraud in customs houses; the book of rates; ordinances of the British marine; and, above all, a heavy concentration of works on the English trading companies.[18] He used his extensive reading to formulate his famous critical account of the unfair advantages the British enjoyed in Lisbon and Oporto, advantages for which Portuguese merchants in Britain had gained no reciprocal privileges. Also included in his London library were several works prohibited in Portugal by the Inquisition.[19]

In Vienna, Pombal found a well-placed ally when he became the very intimate friend of Manuel Teles da Silva, a Portuguese émigré of aristocratic lineage who had risen high within the Austrian state. Manuel Teles da Silva, who had been created Duke Silva-Tarouca by Austrian Emperor Charles VI in 1732, was president of the councils of the Netherlands and of Italy. "For eight years Your Excellency observed with a vision more secure than that of corporal eyes the constitution of Great Britain, of her forces and accidental riches," Duke

Silva-Tarouca wrote to Pombal in 1757, "and for another period of five years in Vienna of Austria[,] Your Excellency with equal judgment and perspicacity observed the non-accidental riches and forces of these most fertile states."[20] Silva-Tarouca, a confidant of Empress Maria Theresa, served as a principal sponsor at the marriage of Pombal to Maria Leonor Ernestina, countess of Daun (fig. 3), in 1746.[21]

The importance of Pombal's Austrian experience to his reform program has been insufficiently appreciated. The impact was clearest, of course, in the relationship with Silva-Tarouca. But the influence of the Austrian sojourn can be shown even in domestic architecture. Pombal's palace at Oeiras is a neoclassical country house that was influenced by the Hungarian Carlos Mardel, who collaborated with Pombal in the rebuilding of Lisbon. The plan dates from 1750 following Pombal's return from Vienna and bears a striking resemblance to Duke Silva-Tarouca's country estate in Bohemia. Silva-Tarouca had been superintendent of the architectural remodeling of the summer palace of the Habsburgs at Schönbrunn. As can be seen from the visiting book of the Portuguese mission to Vienna, which has survived, Pombal received a wide array of visitors while Portuguese envoy to Maria Theresa's court, including Gerhard van Swieten, who was his personal physician as well as being that of the empress.[22] The reforming Dutch doctor was a principal agent of Maria Theresa's measures to reform the Austrian educational system. In Vienna Pombal had also been in contact with the enlightened Portuguese "new Christian" physician, António Nunes Ribeiro Sanches. Van Swieten and Ribeiro Sanches were friends and correspondents, both having worked under the great Dutch doctor Boerhaave.[23] While in Vienna Pombal had been involved in delicate diplomacy concerning the papacy.[24]

Following the death of João V in late July 1750, news of Pombal's ascendancy in the government reached Vienna that September. Duke Silva-Tarouca wrote at once to Lisbon. "We are not slaves of fashion and foreign practices," he told his old friend. He recalled their "intimate conversations" and recommended that "when great new dispositions are necessary they should always be put forward by ancient names and in ancient clothing."[25] "Great new dispositions" Pombal clearly had in mind, and Duke Silva-Tarouca's recommendation of the need for subterfuge is in many ways a succinct description of the methods Pombal was to make his own. It was a policy of reform, disguised, when prudence dictated, by traditional institutions and language.

Pombal built on two distinct but interrelated aspects of the intellectual environment in eighteenth-century Portugal. First was an intense debate over fundamental questions concerning philosophy and education, and second was a considerable body of thought about aspects of Portugal's political economy.

As elsewhere in Europe, the stimulus to the philosophical debate in Portugal was provided by the intellectual achievements of Descartes, Newton, and Locke, who, during the seventeenth century, had promoted a bold break with the tradition of authority, be it biblical or Aristotelian, and promoted the merits of reason, experience, and utility. The most important works to emerge from this intellectual school in Portugal included those of Martinho de Mendonça de Pina e Proença, who attempted to adapt to Portugal some of Locke's theories; the writings of the new Christian Dr. Jacob de Castro Sarmento, who introduced Newtonian ideas in Portugal; and the works of Ribeiro Sanches,

Pombal's acquaintance in Vienna. Ribeiro Sanches had developed plans for the reform of medical teaching in Portugal as early as 1730, though his personal history reflected the vicissitudes that freethinkers, especially those of Jewish origin, still faced in eighteenth-century Portugal. With the Inquisition hard on his heels, Ribeiro Sanches had left Portugal in 1726, working thereafter in England, Holland, Russia, and finally in France where he lived from 1747 until his death in 1783. In Paris he was a collaborator of the encyclopedists, and wrote on medicine, pedagogy, and economics. Jacob de Castro Sarmento, a new Christian like Ribeiro Sanches, sought to develop relationships between the Academia Real de História Portuguesa in Lisbon and the Royal Society in London. He began the translation of Francis Bacon's *Novum Organon* and wanted to see a botanical garden established at the University of Coimbra. He had dedicated his *Cronologia Newtoniana epitomizada* (1737) to the Dom José, future king of Portugal, and his *Matéria médica-physico-histórica-mecânica* to Marco António de Azevedo Coutinho, Pombal's uncle.

Sarmento's works, together with his *Teorica verdadeira das marés*, which eulogized the "incomparable Newton," were all part of the "first serious attempt," according to Banha de Andrade, "to implant practical studies in place of abstract theories" in Portugal.[26] The most influential of all these scholars was the Oratorian Luís António Verney (1713–1792), who lived most of his adult life in Italy where he was a friend of the leading Italian encyclopedist Ludovico Antonio Muratori (1672–1750). Verney served for a time as secretary to the Portuguese envoy to the Vatican, Francisco de Almada e Mendonça, who was a relative of Pombal's first wife. Verney was the extremely influential author of *O Verdadeiro Método de Estudar* (The True Method of Education), first published in Naples in 1746. Paraphrasing Newton, Verney wrote that "philosophy is to know things by their causes, or to know the true cause of things."[27]

The most immediate consequence of this philosophical debate in Portugal was to call into question the influence of the Society of Jesus. This was because the Jesuits held a near monopoly of higher education and were, in the view of their opponents, the principal upholders of a dead and sterile scholastic tradition ill-suited to the age of reason. In Portugal the Jesuits held the exclusive right to teach Latin and philosophy at the college of arts, the obligatory preparatory school for entrance into the faculties of theology, canon law, civil law, and medicine at the University of Coimbra. The only other university in Portugal, at Évora, was a Jesuit institution. In Brazil the Jesuit *colégios* were the principal avenues of secondary education. And in what remained of Portugal's empire in Asia the Jesuits had been a dominating force from the early years of Portuguese expansion in the Orient.

As elsewhere in Europe much substantive discussion took place in private debating or philosophical societies. One major circle of critics of the status quo in Portugal had, since the turn of the century, centered around the Ericeiras, a family made famous by the third conde, Luís de Meneses (1632–1690), a proponent of mercantilist development and Colbertian economic policies in Portugal during the late seventeenth century. Dom Francisco Xavier de Meneses, fourth conde de Ericeira (1674–1743), maintained close contact with scientists outside Portugal and had provided the means of communication between Dom João V and Sarmento, which led to the consultation with Sarmento over the reform of medical studies at Coimbra.[28] Ericeira had been nominated a member of the Royal Society of London in 1738. Writing to Dom Luís da Cunha in 1741, he observed sardonically: "As a new member of the Academy of London I abjure Cartesianism for Newtonianism...." He read widely, he told Dom Luís, in the works of "Mr. Voltaire."[29]

Several short-lived conclaves of individuals, organized to discuss scientific and philosophical questions, had developed under the Ericeiras' protection. One of them, the *Academia dos Ilustrados,* met during 1717 at the Lisbon house of Pombal's uncle. The fourth conde de Ericeira was one of the most distinguished members of the *Academia dos Ilustrados* as well as a director of the *Academia Real de História Portuguesa,* founded in 1720. He had sponsored Pombal's election to the academy on 24 October 1733. Pombal was the author of a eulogy of the fifth conde de Ericeira, which appears to have been first published in London.[30]

Priests also played an important role in the introduction of new ideas in Portugal. Unlike northern Europe, where proponents of "modern" rationalistic philosophy and scientific experimentation became harsh critics of the church and religion, in Portugal some of the most outspoken advocates (as well as practitioners) of educational reform came from within the religious establishment. The activity of the Oratorians to which Verney belonged was notable. The congregation of the Oratoria de São Felipe de Nery, a society of secular priests, had taken the lead in Portugal, as they had elsewhere in Catholic Europe, in the introduction of scientific experimentation. The Oratorians possessed an excellent library of some thirty thousand volumes with an experimental laboratory. They were leading opponents of the Jesuits in the debate over pedagogical models. The Oratorians were strong promoters of the natural sciences and also stressed the importance of the Portuguese language, grammar, and orthography, which they believed should be studied directly and not via Latin.[31]

In addition to this philosophical debate, which was characteristic of Catholic Europe in this period, there existed an important current of thinking specific to Portugal. This was a body of ideas and discussion about governance, economy, and diplomacy that emerged in the first half of the eighteenth century among a small but influential group of Portugal's overseas representatives and government ministers. An old conundrum had faced Portugal's rulers since the fourteenth century: the need to protect its national interests in the face of military challenges from land-based enemies, yet at the same time contain the commercial challenges of maritime allies whose support rarely came cost-free. Sometimes members of this group were pejoratively called the "foreignizers" [*estrangeirados*] because of their supposed infatuation with foreign models.[32] Yet their preoccupations were in fact intimately a product of a Portuguese milieu.

Ericeira's correspondent, Dom Luís da Cunha, successively Portuguese ambassador to the Dutch republic and to France, was the most formidable of these thinkers and author of a comprehensive analysis of Portugal's weaknesses and the means to remedy them. These discussions, unlike the disputations of the philosophers and pedagogues, in the main took place in private and were built on the longer tradition of Portuguese economic and diplomatic thinking that had emerged from experience in the decades following the reestablishment of Portugal's independence from Spain in 1640. Less concerned with the specific impact of the discovery of Brazilian gold on Portugal, this debate focused on the broader parameters of Portugal's location in the international system and confronted directly both the constraints and the options with which a small country like Portugal, part of Iberia but independent of Spain, had to live. Central to these discussions was the problem of retaining and exploiting the considerable overseas assets that Portugal controlled in Asia, Africa, and America and developing a mechanism to challenge English economic domination without weakening the political and military alliance that was needed to contain Spain.

Dom Luís da Cunha's sophisticated critique of Portugal's international relations and social and mental condition was contained both in his "instructions" for Marco António de Azevedo Coutinho (1738) and in his political testament (1748). Here the link to Pombal's thinking was direct. Azevedo Coutinho, who was secretary of state for foreign affairs, had previously been ambassador in London (1735–1738) and before that ambassador in Paris (1721–1728). Pombal and Azevedo Coutinho were cousins, although Pombal referred always to his distinguished relative as "uncle," and it was at his "uncle's" designation that Pombal embarked on his diplomatic career.

Dom Luís da Cunha placed Portugal's problems in the context of its relationship with Spain, its dependence on and economic exploitation by England, and on what he believed were Portugal's self-inflicted weaknesses in terms of low population and spirit of enterprise. This sad mental and economic condition he attributed to the excess number of priests, the activity of the Inquisition, and the expulsion and persecution of the Jews. The Treaty of Methuen (1703) had been, in his view, an arrangement beneficial only to England. He praised Ericeira's short-lived attempt to introduce manufacturing industry in Portugal during the late seventeenth century. He proposed the creation of monopolistic commercial companies on the Dutch and English models.[33]

So acute had Portugal's reliance on Brazil become during the early eighteenth century that Dom Luís da Cunha foresaw the eventual transfer of the Portuguese court to Rio de Janeiro. The king would take the title "Emperor of the West" and appoint a viceroy to rule in Lisbon. In his 1738 "instructions" for Marco António de Azevedo Coutinho, Luís da Cunha envisioned a Portuguese empire in America extending from the Río de la Plata and Paraguay to north of the Amazon estuary. "It is safer and more convenient to be where one has everything in abundance," he wrote, "than where one has to wait for what one wants." Pombal, who also demonstrated a special concern for Brazil's importance and potential, believed that the state had a central role in promoting economic well-being and drew models from his interpretation of the experience of the more developed European countries. The diminished stature of the Iberian nations in the eighteenth century, despite their continuing role as overlords of vast overseas territories, generated among both Spanish and Portuguese statesmen of Pombal's generation the acute consciousness that governmental efficiency and imperial consolidation were essential if either country was to regain its influence and power in an increasingly competitive and jealous world.

Geopolitical concerns in South America, a constant theme to the Portuguese eighteenth century, provide the occasion for one of the great events and continuing controversies of eighteenth-century Portuguese history: the expulsion of the Jesuits from Portugal and its overseas territories in 1759, which began the process that saw the Jesuits later expelled from Spain and France, and the Society of Jesus itself suppressed by the pope in 1773.

The Treaty of Madrid signed between Spain and Portugal in January 1750 and its negotiation, which had preoccupied the last decade of João V's reign, sought to delineate the landward frontiers of their colonial territories in South America in their entirety and replaced the vague and long-violated line of demarcation established by the Treaty of Tordesillas some three hundred years before. In essence, Portuguese claims to the Amazon were upheld by the treaty, particularly the fluvial interior boundary of the Guaporé-Mamoré-Madeira rivers. These frontier demarcations were of great sensitivity for the missionary orders, especially the Jesuits, since the Jesuit missions were strategically placed deep in the interior between Spanish and Portuguese territories or along the key river systems in the interior of South America.

With the new definition of frontiers and the growing awareness of the strategic value of control over the interior, particularly sensitive to the Portuguese since the Brazilian goldfields lay beyond the Tordesillas boundaries, it was perhaps inevitable that the great complex of Spanish and Portuguese Jesuit missions, which stretched from the mouth of the Amazon to the Río de la Plata, should begin to appear as a threat to the interests of both the dominant powers in South America.

Under the terms of the treaty, the thirty thousand Indians in the mission communities were expected to migrate with all their movable goods from what is now part of Brazil's state of Rio Grande do Sul into lands now occupied by Argentina and Paraguay. Rather than leave the lands they had inhabited and tended for three generations, the Indians chose to resist. The response from both European powers to this defiance was rapid. In January 1756, an allied Portuguese and Spanish military force of 3,700 men and nineteen pieces of artillery invaded the territory of the Seven Missions to enforce the treaty stipulations, crushing the christianized Amerindian combatants who never numbered more than two thousand.[34]

Yet the image of militarized Indians under Jesuit control, unilaterally opposing the mandates of the Iberian monarchs, had a significant impact on the European mind and provided much grist to Pombal's anti-Jesuit propaganda mill. In *Candide,* Voltaire portrayed a sword-wielding Jesuit riding on horseback.[35] And the events surrounding the attempted implementation of the Treaty of Madrid served to fortify Pombal's conviction that the presence of the Jesuits in Portuguese lands was an impediment to the realization of his imperial designs.

To protect the national economic interests, Pombal had thrown his support behind the established Portuguese merchants in the metropolis against the interlopers and contrabandists whom he saw as little more than agents of foreigners. Following the recommendations laid out by Dom Luís da Cunha in his political testament and the ideas of his brother who had been sent to Brazil as governor of the Amazonian territory, in 1755 Pombal established the Companhia de Grão Pará and Maranhão, which was given the exclusive right to all commerce and navigation of the captaincies for a period of twenty years. Pombal hoped that by granting special privileges and protection via such a mechanism, national merchant houses would be able to accumulate sufficient capital in Lisbon to compete more effectively with British merchants in the Portuguese colonial trade as a whole and, by extension, in Portugal proper.[36]

In 1756, with similar objectives in mind, Pombal established a general company for the agriculture of the vineyards of the Upper Douro, the *Companhia de Agricultura das Vinhas de Alto Douro.* The objective of the Upper Douro company was essentially to protect vineyard owners there from the vast expansion of vine cultivation by smaller producers that had occurred over the previous decades. The title of the company is almost invariably mistranslated, indeed it is very often mistranscribed even in Portuguese, transforming *vinhas* (vineyards) into *vinho* (wine), thus misrepresenting entirely the major objective of the company. The most important innovation was that the company established a restricted production zone and exclusive name *(nom d'appellation)* of Port wine almost a century before the French were to do the same with their wines.[37]

This intervention by the Portuguese state in the entrepreneurial situation of the northern wine-producing region was not unlike Pombal's manipulation in the colonial entrepreneurial nexus. Using state intervention to protect the large export producers, Pombal aimed at stabilizing prices and market conditions. The purpose of the company was not to seize the Port wine trade from the British Port wine exporters. The privileged position Port enjoyed in English markets was, after all, a result of English tariff manipulation (in favor of Portuguese wine), and was exactly the sort of reciprocal and mutually beneficial trading of which Pombal approved. He had no intention of disrupting this access to the English markets. But, he did hope the monopoly company would encourage the development of a Portuguese merchant class that could compete with the British merchant houses in Portugal.

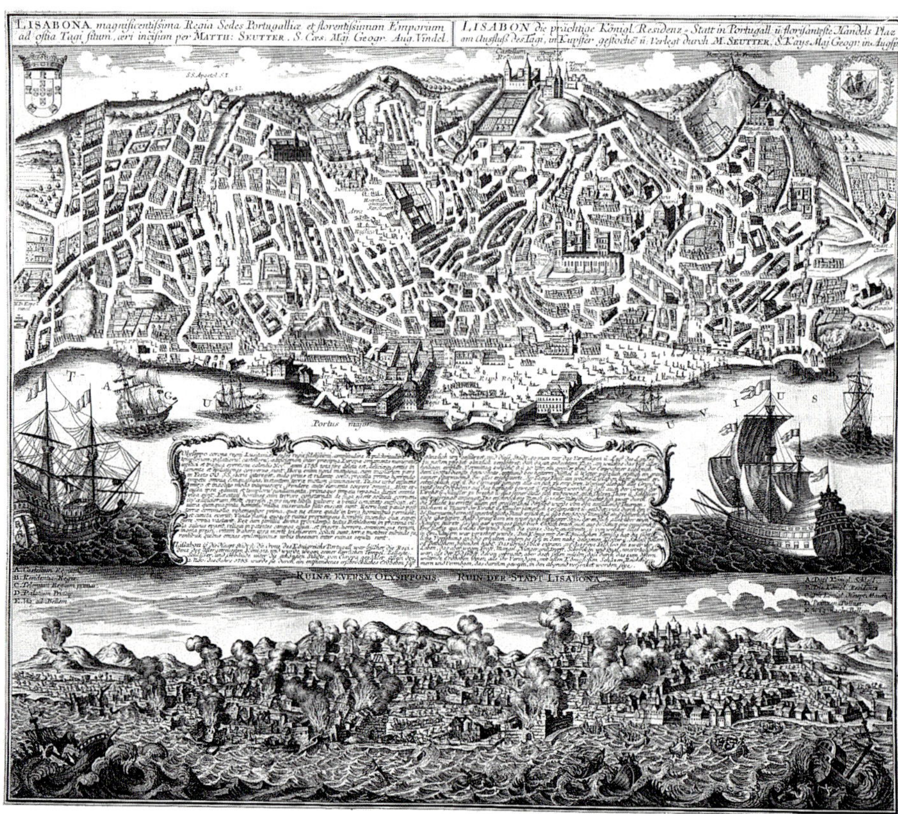

fig. 4. Mateus Sautter, *Lisbon before and during the Earthquake,* c. 1750–1800, intaglio print. Museu da Cidade, Lisbon

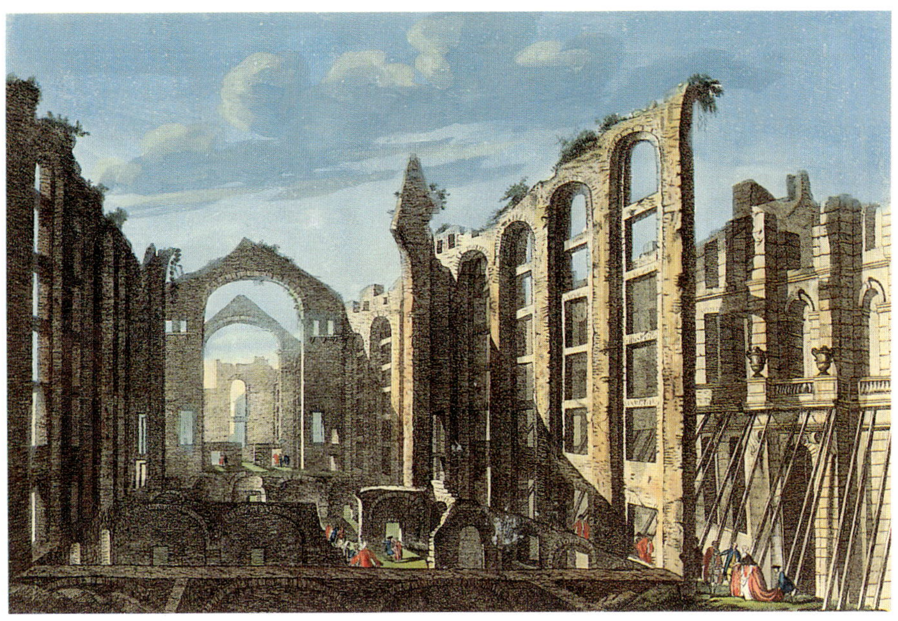

fig. 5. Jacques Philippe Le Bas, *Ruins of the Royal Opera House, Lisbon, after the Earthquake*, 1757, colored print. Museu da Cidade, Lisbon

A further cause of the fractured image of eighteenth-century Portugal was undoubtedly the impact of the Lisbon earthquake of 1755.[38] The great earthquake of All Saints Day (fig. 4) reduced one of the richest and most opulent cities of the epoch to ashes and provoked an extraordinary philosophical debate about optimism, God, and natural phenomena.

The English consul Edward Hay, writing to London two weeks after the earthquake, provided a concise eyewitness account of the event. "The first shock began about a quarter before ten o'clock in the morning, and as far as I could judge, lasted six or seven minutes, so that in a quarter of an hour, this great city was laid in ruins. Soon after, several fires broke out, which burned for five or six days. The force of the earthquake seemed to be immediately under the city.... It is thought to have vented itself at the quay which runs from the Customs House towards the king's palace, which is entirely carried away, and has totally disappeared. At the time of the earthquake, the waters of the river rose twenty or thirty feet."[39] About one-third of the city was totally destroyed by the quake and flood.

Estimates of casualties ranged from ten to forty thousand. At the time the latter estimate was widely believed though the true figure was probably closer to fifteen thousand, no small number for a city of 150,000. The royal family, who were at Belém, outside the city, escaped what would have been certain death in their collapsed palace in Lisbon. The bewildered and frightened king placed full authority in the hands of his only minister who showed any capacity to deal with the catastrophe, Pombal.

The scope of the destruction was colossal. The royal opera house, completed only a month before, was in ruins (fig. 5). Of Lisbon's forty parish churches, thirty-five had collapsed, many onto parishioners who had been at mass when the earthquake struck, crushing them to death within the ruins. Only three thousand of Lisbon's twenty thousand houses were habitable. The palace of the Inquisition on the Rossio had crumbled and many townhouses and palaces of the aristocracy were destroyed. At one mansion alone two hundred paintings were lost, including a Titian and a Rubens and a library of eighteen thousand books and a thousand manuscripts. Seventy thousand books in the king's library perished.

It was the earthquake that propelled Pombal to virtually absolute power, which he was to retain for another twenty-two years until the king's death in 1777. He took quick, effective, and ruthless action to stabilize the situation. Looters were unceremoniously hanged, bodies of the earthquake victims were quickly gathered and, with the permission of the Lisbon patriarch, taken out to sea, weighted, and thrown into the ocean. Rents, food prices, and the cost of building materials were fixed at pre-earthquake levels. No temporary re-building was permitted until the land was cleared and plans for new construction drawn up.

Military engineers and surveyors, headed by General Manuel da Maia (1672–1768), the eighty-three-year-old chief engineer, Colonel Carlos Mardel (1695–1763), and Captain Eugénio dos Santos (1711–1760), were charged with making inventories of property rights and claims and implementing the myriad of practical decisions to assure that sanitary and leveling operations were carried out safely. They were also charged with drawing up plans for the new city.[40] (See also França essay in this volume.)

It was these practical-minded engineer officers who, under the closest scrutiny from Pombal, developed the economical Pombaline architecture and grid of streets and the great waterfront square that make Lisbon to this day a classic example of eighteenth-century town planning. The idea to set an important square on the waterfront as the focal point of the scheme came from dos Santos. It was also highly significant that the new square, placed on the old royal plaza, was to be called, as it remains, the *Praça do Comércio,* the place of commerce (see França, fig. 1). The new Lisbon was thus intended to be a preeminently mercantile and administrative center. As the rest of Europe debated the meaning of the earthquake for the philosophy of optimism, engaging Voltaire, Goethe, Rousseau, and John Wesley among others, the reaction in Portugal was more prosaic. Pombal's architectural and city planning was intended to celebrate national economic independence and a modern, well-regulated, utilitarian state.

Lisbon's reconstruction is something of a paradigm for much of Pombal's activities in government and represented a good example of the role the Portuguese enlightened absolutist wished to see the state perform. It was a role deeply rooted in a pragmatic assessment of options, a mixture of eclectic borrowing and innovation and the selective intervention by the state in society to promote what was conceived to be the national interest.

The events in South America and Pombal's intervention in the Portuguese metropolitan and colonial economies, of course, did not go unopposed. State intervention in favor of the Upper Douro producers and the enforced rationalization of the entrepreneurial structure of the Luso-Brazilian commercial community provoked repercussions throughout Portuguese society. The state had chosen to support elements within patterns of conflicting interests and the result was to force those groups not favored into opposition and, at times, into collusion and conspiracy. Pombal's measures hurt many vested interests and the reaction was swift and angry.

The promulgation of the Companhia de Grão Pará and Maranhão's monopoly privileges and removal of Jesuit tutelage over the Indians provoked an immediate response from the dispossessed traders and Jesuits. Both found an organ for agitation in the Mesa do Bem Commum, a rudimentary commercial association. Meanwhile from the pulpit of the basilica of Santa Maria Maior in Lisbon, the Jesuit Manoel Ballester delivered a vehement attack on the monopoly, proclaiming that "he who entered it would not be of the company of Christ our Lord."[41]

Pombal acted swiftly in the face of these provocations. He immediately dissolved the Mesa do Bem Commum as "prejudicial to the royal service, common interest, and commerce," and the deputies who had protested to the king were condemned to penal banishment. Meanwhile a serious popular reaction to the Douro company was developing in the north of Portugal, especially in Oporto. Anger at the company was concentrated within several occupational groups adversely affected by the establishment of the Upper Douro monopoly. The coopers, for example, whose guild had exclusive rights to cask production, feared the company's power to requisition their services. The company had been granted a monopoly of supply to the taverns and employed inspectors to control the quality of the wine sold at retail (and to verify that the wine sold was indeed company wine).

On 23 February 1757, according to the account of the municipal government, some five thousand rioters besieged the house of the judge conservator of the Douro company. The mob next stormed the mansion of the company's director and ransacked the company's archives along with the mansion.[42] Pombal reacted to the uprising, which dissipated as quickly as it had arisen, with ferocity —treating the event as an act of *lèse majesté*.

The special court set up to investigate the uprising condemned 375 men, 50 women, and young boys: a total of 442 people. Some escaped and were hanged in effigy, but on 14 October 1757, 13 men and a woman were hanged, their quartered limbs placed on spikes for fifteen days. Oporto was placed under a state of siege; townspeople were prohibited from holding meetings after dark, from wearing capes, carrying arms, or loitering. To enforce these restrictions two thousand troops were billeted in Oporto in addition to twenty-four hundred troops already in the city.[43]

These popular disturbances took place in concert with increasing aristocratic anger at Pombal's measures. Oliveira Marques has pointed to the division of the nobility into two groups in the eighteenth century. On one side stood a sector whose members were, in their own view, the defenders of blood and lineage, the old methods of government, and were linked to landed property and agriculture. On the other side stood a more open-minded group that accepted the elevation of men of letters, even businessmen and bureaucrats, to noble status, and that looked to trade and profit and saw England and Holland, not Spain and France, as their models.

Dom João V's reign had witnessed the beginning of a reassertion of state and hence bureaucratic power at the expense of the old nobility. This process of change in favor of the new nobility was greatly accelerated by Pombal. In the twenty-seven years of Pombal's rule, twenty-three new titles were granted and twenty-three old titles were extinguished. In this way, about one-third of the nobility was of new blood by 1777.[44]

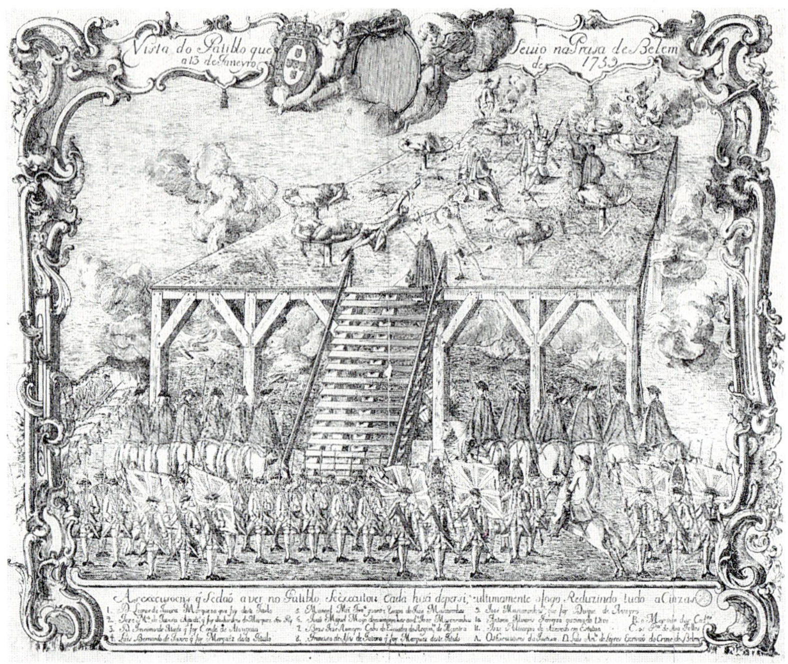

To the old aristocracy Pombal himself was an upstart. In the face of virulent opposition he had married into the Arcos family. His activity at the academy of history had been interpreted as an insidious attempt to gain intelligence on the ancient houses of Portugal.[45] Even the Austrian envoy complained that only one of Pombal's diplomatic representatives was a "person of distinction."[46] The opposition to Pombal's social engineering was strongest among the self-styled puritanos of the Portuguese nobility. "Puritanism" in Portugal referred to the old concept of "purity of blood," that is, the absence of Jewish or Moorish ancestry, a condition that since 1496 was required for office holding and state honors. Yet Pombal sought to raise taxes "without differences and without privileges whatsoever."[47] And, like his mentor, Dom Luís da Cunha, Pombal believed the expulsion of the Jews and the discrimination against new Christians had stunted Portuguese enterprise. The statutes of all his commercial companies used the allure of ennoblement as an incentive to invest.[48] The favors bestowed on Pombal's collaboration served in effect to create an identity of interest between the discontented nobles, the Jesuits, and the small interlopers who had suffered from the monopolies and privileges given to Pombal's collaborators among the larger merchants.

Out of this discontent emerged the most serious crisis of Pombal's rule: the attempted regicide in September 1758. Dom José was returning to his palace when his carriage was fired upon. The king was wounded sufficiently seriously for the queen to assume the regency during his recuperation. There was official silence on the incident until early December, when, in a large dragnet operation, a substantial number of people were arrested, including a group of leading aristocrats. The most prominent prisoners were members of the Távora family and the duque de Aveiro. The residences of the Jesuits were simultaneously placed under guard. The king appointed a commission of inquiry on 9 December 1758, granting the presiding judge wide authority to remove even the minimal protections afforded by the Portuguese legal code.[49] With such broad terms of reference, the tribunal acted with dispatch. The interrogations were carried out before the secretaries of state, including Pombal himself in his role as secretary of the kingdom (*reino*).[50]

On 12 January 1759 the prisoners were sentenced. The duque de Aveiro was to be broken alive, his limbs and arms crushed, exposed on a wheel for all to see, burned alive, and his ashes thrown into the sea. The marquês de Távora Velho was to suffer the same fate. The marquesa de Távora was to be beheaded. The limbs of the rest of the family were to be broken on the wheel, but they were to be strangled first, unlike the marquês and the duque, whose limbs were to be broken while they were still alive (fig. 6). The sentences were carried out the next day in Belém.

The treatment of the conspirators was not out of keeping with eighteenth-century European practice. In 1757, the unsuccessful assassin of Louis XV of France, Robert-François Damiens, was subjected to every form of physical punishment then in use until the *coup de grâce* was finally administered hours later. What was unusual in the case of the Távoras and Aveiro was the status of the victims. Aveiro, the most powerful noble in Portugal after the royal family, was head of the court nobles and president of the supreme court. The marquês de Távora Velho was a general, director general of the cavalry, and had served as viceroy of India.

The Távora case provoked much interest and comment in the rest of Europe. George II of England was especially intrigued and asked the British envoy in Lisbon, Mr. Hay, for a report. Mr. Hay wrote to London on 10 February 1759: "There is a circumstance that seems to have been industriously concealed, but is not therefore the less credited, and which is the only one that accounts for the treacherous behavior of the Távora family... The king's intimacy with the young marquês' wife, which began during the time the general was viceroy of India...." Mr. Hay added that "...when the rest of the relations were confined, this lady was sent to a convent, not a very strict one, where it is said she lives very much at her ease."[51] The relationship was, in fact, even more complicated than Mr. Hay intimated, since the young marquês' wife was also the king's paternal aunt, an arrangement by no means uncommon among the Portuguese high nobility and the royal family itself. In 1760, in fact, the king's daughter, Maria, was married to his brother, Pedro.

The day before the spectacular punishment of the aristocrats and others found guilty of attempted regicide, eight Jesuits were arrested for alleged complicity, among them Padre Gabriel Malagrida, a missionary and mystic. Malagrida, who had been born in Italy, had gone to Brazil in 1721, working in Maranhão. After a brief sojourn in Lisbon between 1749 and 1751, he returned to Brazil where he ran afoul of Pombal's brother. Malagrida had also published a pamphlet on the Lisbon earthquake, *Juizo da Verdadeira Causa do Terremoto* (The True Cause of the Earthquake), attributing the disaster to divine wrath. Pombal had gone to great effort to explain the earthquake as a natural phenomenon. Pombal personally denounced Malagrida to the Inquisition, at the head of which he had installed his brother, Paulo de Carvalho.[52]

During 1758 the temporal power of the Jesuits was suppressed throughout Brazil and the directory system of Indian secular control designed by Mendonça Furtado, Pombal's other brother, for Grão Pará and Maranhão was made applicable in all of Portuguese America. On 3 September 1759 the Portuguese government decreed the proscription and expulsion of the Society of Jesus from the whole empire, prohibiting any communication, either verbal or in writing, between Jesuits and Portuguese subjects. The order's vast properties in Brazil, Portugal, and throughout the Portuguese empire were expropriated.[53]

Pombal's conflict with the Jesuits, like the Lisbon earthquake, brought Portuguese affairs to the center of European concerns. The Portuguese were the first to begin a movement that would bring about the expulsion of the Jesuits from all of Catholic Europe and led to the suppression of the order by the pope himself. The spark for these extraordinary repercussions had been set by a combination of factors, including Pombal's plan for economic regeneration through the rational exploitation of the colonies and the challenge to Britain's economic power. A geopolitical conflict over frontiers and the security of the empire, in which the Jesuit Guarani missions in particular opposed Portugal's decisions by force of arms, had aggravated the conflict. The security of the regime itself was jeopardized by the attempted regicide.

But it was the conflict with Pombal that began the process that led to the Jesuits' demise. They met their match in a powerful and ruthless minister who would not tolerate dissent, for whom *raison d'état* was supreme policy, and who did not hesitate to act when challenged. That a dispute in Portugal served as a catalyst for the expulsion of the Jesuits from Spain and later France, and the suppression of the Society of Jesus by Pope Clement XIV in 1773, owed much, of course, to the receptivity to Pombal's actions by European enlightened opinion, the intricacies of church politics, and the diplomatic acquiescence of the Catholic monarchs. But European opinion alone would not necessarily have been sufficient to destroy so powerful a religious order. The Catholic monarchs were quick to follow Portugal's example, to be sure, but it is not at all clear that any of them would have acted had Portugal not acted first. On 6 June 1759 the future marquês de Pombal was granted the title of conde de Oeiras by Dom José for services rendered in the judgment of the would-be assassins.[54]

In no other European country had the Counter-Reformation been so thoroughly embedded, or the order that so exemplified the ultramontane claims of papal supremacy, the Jesuits, been so warmly received, or the control of the Jesuits so strongly established over the education of the elite. The Vatican, for its part, was thoroughly horrified by developments in Portugal. The papal nunzio in Madrid, Lazzao Opizo Pallevicini, was instructed (1760) by cipher to warn the Spanish monarch, Charles III, that "in that Kingdom [Portugal] . . . occult Hebrews and obvious heretics . . . benefit in every way from the greatest favor of the minister [Pombal]."[55]

Pombal's drastic measures cleared the way for government action on several fronts. The 1760s thus marked a period of consolidation and amplification of the reforms initiated during the first decade of Pombal's rule. These included the erection of a new system of public education to replace that of the fallen Jesuits; the assertion of national authority in religious and church administration; the stimulation of manufacturing enterprise and entrepreneurial activity; and the strengthening of the state's taxing authority, military capabilities, and security apparatus. In each case the legislation needed for these measures was encapsulated within a reformed, codified, and systematized set of public laws where the reasoning was clearly outlined, justified, and explained. Pombal also

fig. 7. Anonymous, *Auto da Fé in the Terreiro do Paço*, c. 1741, intaglio print from Juan Álvarez de Colmenar, *Annales d'Espagne et du Portugal,* vol. 7 (Amsterdam), 252–253. Biblioteca Nacional, Lisbon

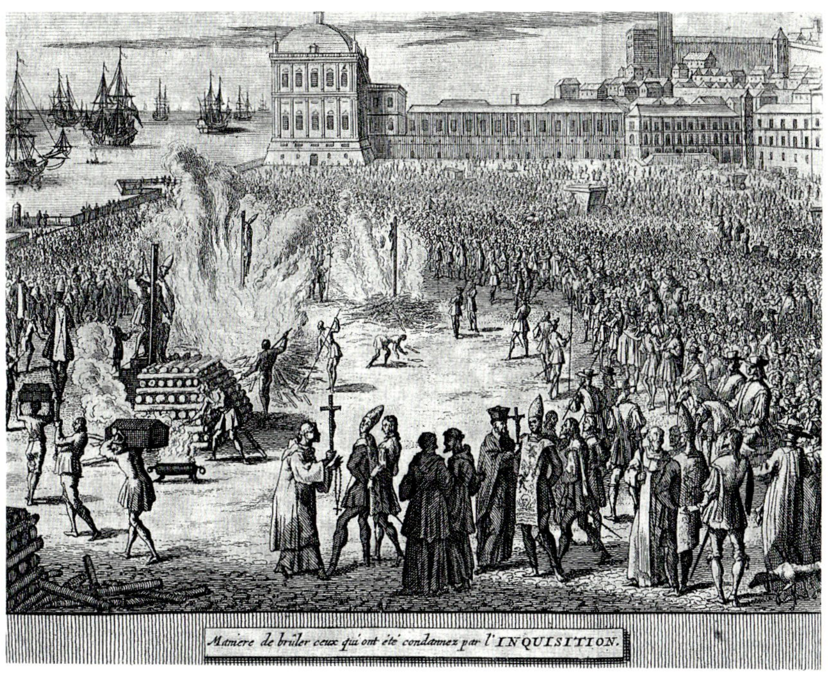

fortified his own position. The crime of *lèse majesté* was expanded to include attacks against the king's ministers. And Pombal obtained for himself a personal corps of bodyguards, something unseen in Europe since the primacy of Richelieu in France.

The creation in Lisbon of a royal treasury (*Erário Régio*) in 1761, however, was the key element in Pombal's overall effort of rationalization and centralization. Here all the crown's income was to be concentrated and recorded. Pombal appointed himself inspector general of the treasury, a position that was designed to be closest to the monarch and by implication that of chief minister.[56] The aim of the treasury was to centralize jurisdiction for all financial matters in the exchequer and make it solely responsible for all the different sectors of fiscal administration, from customs house revenues to the farming of royal monopolies. The creation of the royal treasury marked the culmination of Pombal's reform of the revenue and collection machinery of the state.

Just as the Pombaline state engaged in propaganda to enhance its image and influence opinion elsewhere in Europe, so too did its legislation outline in sometimes tiresome detail for domestic audiences the objectives and antecedents of the policy changes as well as the substance of the measure itself. In this respect the corpus of legislation establishing secular authority over the areas that had previously fallen under papal or ecclesiastical jurisdiction required special argumentation.

The occasion for the break with Rome, as so often in such cases of regalist and ultramontane conflict, was a dispute over a papal dispensation for the marriage of Maria, princess of Brazil and the heir apparent, to her uncle, the king's brother, Dom Pedro. In the face of Roman foot-dragging the papal nunzio was expelled from Portugal on 15 June 1760. Pombal used this occasion to place the church firmly under state control.[57]

Equally important was Pombal's secularization of the Inquisition (fig. 7). From 1684 to 1747, 4,672 persons were sentenced by the Inquisition and 146

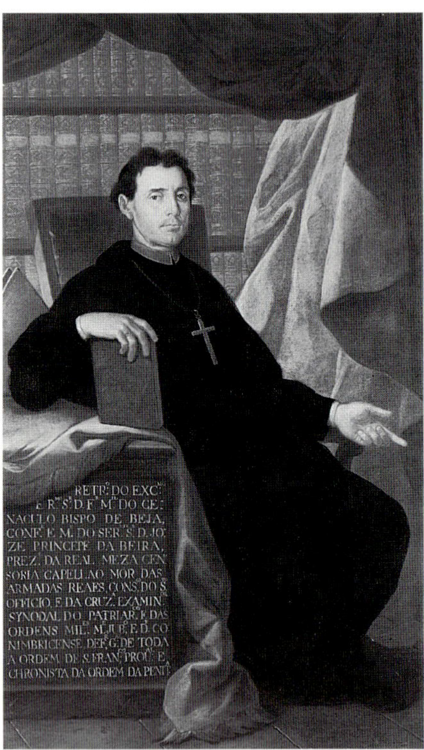

fig. 8. António Joaquim Padrão, *Portrait of Frei Manuel de Cenáculo Vilas Boas (1724–1814),* c. 1770–1771, oil on canvas. Museu Rainha D. Leonor, Beja

burned at the stake. From 1750 to 1759, there had been 1,107 sentences and 18 burnings. Pombal abolished the distinction between old and new Christians in 1768. And in 1769 he moved against the Inquisition itself, destroying its power as an independent tribunal and making it dependent on the government. Public *autos da fé* ceased, along with the death penalty. Ironically, it was the Jesuit Malagrida who was the last victim, burned in 1761.[58]

The book censorship role, previously the responsibility of the Inquisition, was now assigned to by a newly created royal censorship board. The Inquisition's police powers had already been appropriated by a new general intendant of police of the court and kingdom in 1760. These measures gave the state the organizational means to combat crime and banditry as well as provide surveillance over enemies of the government. The intendant Pina Manique, who was to hold the office for twenty years, also brought public lighting to Lisbon and founded the famous *Casa Pia* of Lisbon for the education and shelter of orphans.[59]

The expulsion of the Jesuits had left Portugal bereft of teachers at both the secondary and university levels. Not surprisingly, the establishment of a state-sponsored secondary education system and the reform of the University of Coimbra drew directly on the recommendation of the Jesuits' old enemies, the Oratorians and Luís António Verney, the latter by now a paid consultant to the Portuguese government. Ribeiro Sanches, on Pombal's demand, wrote a paper on how to reform the study of medicine (1763). The subtitle of Verney's famous work, the *Verdadeiro método de estudar,* in fact, summed up the radicalism as well as the limitations of his educational philosophy. It was a method "intended to be useful to the Republic, and the Church, commensurate to the style, and necessity of Portugal."[60]

To implement the educational reform, Pombal had first established a position of director of studies to oversee the establishment of a national system of secondary education. Later a junta for the provision of learning *(Junta da Providência)* was formed to prepare for the reform of higher education. A leading figure in these educational innovations was Frei Manuel de Cenáculo Vilas Boas (1724–1814) (fig. 8). The son of a candle maker, Cenáculo was educated by the Oratorians in Lisbon. He had joined the third order of Saint Francis in 1739. From 1740 he was a resident in Coimbra where he became a tutor of theology in 1749. He became part of the reaction against scholasticism, embracing the ideas of Descartes and Newton. In 1750 he visited Rome and in 1755 moved to Lisbon.[61] Cenáculo was a brilliant scholar and an expert in Greek, Syrian, and Arabic. In the area of educational reform, Cenáculo was one of Pombal's closest collaborators, becoming president of the royal censorship board, confessor and preceptor to the heir apparent Príncipe Dom José, and first bishop of Beja. He was also a major influence in the reform of the University of Coimbra.

The royal decree creating the state-run educational system envisioned 526 positions of instructor and 358 professors (236 of Latin, 38 of Greek, 49 of rhetoric, 35 of philosophy). The instructors were to receive stipends of between forty and sixty thousand *reis* depending on location, whereas a full professor of Latin in a town, for example, was to earn one hundred thousand *reis.* These were not generous sums. The minimum needed to sustain a peasant's family in the Alentejo in this period was estimated at about twenty-five thousand *reis.* In some places the new state schools were successful. The whole system was to be financed by a new tax, a literary subsidy [*subsídio literário*] based on a tax on wine and *eau de vie* in Portugal and the Atlantic islands. In Asia and America the literary subsidy was based on a tax on meat and *eau de vie.*

In Vienna, the principal mechanism of educational reform had been the creation of the book censorship commission instituted in 1760 under Pombal's friend from his Vienna days, van Swieten. In Portugal the Real mesa censória (the royal censorship board), established in 1768, was intended to provide a mechanism to secularize the long-standing religious control and prohibitions that had governed the introduction of new ideas into the country. Thus the Real mesa censória superseded the Inquisition and became the judge of what was deemed acceptable for the Portuguese reading public. The censorship of the state in this instance was paradoxically intended to provide a means of stimulating enlightenment. The *mesa* often released books to their owners or booksellers that had been condemned previously by the Inquisition—among them Voltaire's *Oeuvres* (theater), Richardson's *Pamela,* Montesquieu's *Esprit des Lois,* and Locke's *Essays on Human Understanding.* But the limitations placed on readership are also illuminating. Works that were deemed harmful to religion remained excluded, and the principal censors were drawn from the reforming wing of the church—including the erudite Frei Cenáculo. In his role of president of the royal censorship board, Cenáculo took on the functions of what J. Marcadé defined as "if not a ministry then certainly a veritable commission of national education." [62]

As in other areas Pombal took from the example of others what suited him. Despite claims and fears in Rome and more traditionalist circles, the royal censorship board carefully analyzed the literary production of the high enlightenment (and some works of a less elevated nature) and carefully removed from the Portuguese editions whatever they deemed detrimental to Catholic dogma. Sometimes they restricted circulation to those whom they believed should be aware of the offending works in order to be better able to refute their message. The Portuguese reformers were not free-thinkers to be sure; they were seeking to promote what they believed would be useful to the state. In the context of northwestern Europe this cautious approach appeared self-defeating, but in the context of eighteenth-century Portugal it was a major innovation.

In 1768 Cenáculo was chosen as confessor to the prince, Dom José, and in 1770 his preceptor, a position he held for seven years. Dom José became prince of Brazil and heir apparent after the succession of his mother to the throne in 1777. The curriculum Frei Cenáculo prepared for the prince included geometry, geography, and law at the king's request. Cenáculo personally taught geometry and the history of Portugal. In the prince's library Cenáculo placed *Les aventures de Télémaque* of Fénelon, *Verborum* of Erasmus, *De copia l'historie universelle* of Bossuet, and *Histoire ecclesiastique* of the abbé Racine.[63] Dom José retained a high regard for his tutor. After Cenáculo's semi-disgrace following Pombal's downfall, he made a point of commenting in public that, "other than being born a prince, everything else that made me respectable in the eyes of the world I owe to that great man." [64]

The Pombaline educational reform had a highly utilitarian purpose: to produce a new corps of enlightened officials to staff the reformed state and church hierarchy. It was to be here among these freshly minted bureaucrats that the Pombaline reforms would find their perpetuators and defenders. And it is no accident that the classic statement of purpose for this process of enlightened reform should have come from the pen of Francisco de Lemos, installed by Pombal as the reformer of the University of Coimbra:

One should not look on the university as an isolated body, concerned only with its own affairs, as is ordinarily the case, but as a body at the heart of the state, which through its scholars creates and diffuses the enlightenment of wisdom to all parts of the monarchy, to animate and revitalize all branches of the public administration and to promote the happiness of man. The more one analyzes this idea, the more relationships one discovers between the university and the state: the more one sees the mutual dependency of these two bodies one on the other, and that science cannot flourish in the university without at the same time the state flourishing, improving and perfecting itself. This understanding arrived very late in Portugal, but at last it has arrived, and we have established without doubt the most perfect and complete example in Europe today.[65]

Pombal regarded his reform of the university as his single most important measure. And the plans were indeed ambitious and exceptionally advanced for the period: new laboratories for physics, chemistry (fig. 9), and anatomy, and an observatory and a botanical garden, as well as a thorough revamping of the curriculum.

There were weaknesses to the Pombaline reform program. In his economic reforms Pombal always faced the problem of Portugal's limited entrepreneurial capacity. No less critical were the problems of finding suitably qualified people to carry forward the transformation of the educational and administrative structures of the country. In the area of educational reform he tried to make use of foreigners, especially Italians. Yet the shortage of personnel meant he was forced to rotate from institution to institution the few modern-minded individuals he had at his disposal. The professors contracted in Italy for the new college of nobles, established in 1768, for example, were later moved to Coimbra following the reform of the university.

The creation of human capital was a slower process than the accumulation of wealth via the manipulation of tariffs or the concession of lucrative monopolies. The effort made by Pombal to create an enlightened generation of bureaucrats and officials was to benefit his successors, but in his own administration he relied on a very small group of collaborators. These included a handful of enlightened gentry and aristocrats such as the morgado de Mateus and the marquês de Lavradio, reform-minded clergy of modest origins or colonial backgrounds such as Cenáculo and Francisco de Lemos, and foreign experts such as the Italians Dominici Vandelli and Giuseppe António dalla Bella (see cat. 63) and the English porcelain entrepreneur William Stephens. Many of these men accumulated several positions just as his business associates accumulated positions in the management of fiscal and commercial affairs.

Cenáculo's multiple jobs, for instance, meant that the supervision of some of his responsibilities proved to be impossible. His secretary, Alexandre Ferreira de Faria Manuel, was accused of selling off books deposited with the royal censorship, including "six *Belisaires* by Masmontee," "six *Letters persanes*," and "five *Historie des Indes de l'abbé Raynal*" for a total of 103,000 *reis*. The latter, curiously, was a book prohibited in Portugal.[66]

Pombal found that there were also limits to what could be accomplished by

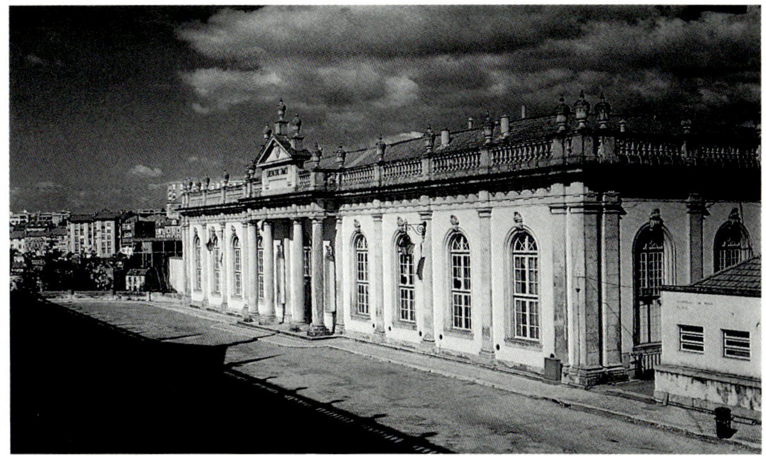

fig. 9. Guilherme Elsden, *Chemistry
Laboratory,* University of Coimbra. Cat. 59
is a contemporary depiction in painted tiles
of this building

legislation. António Ribeiro Sanches, reviewing a copy of the law prohibiting
discrimination against those of Jewish origin like himself, wrote in his diary,
"but can this law extinguish from the minds of a people, ideas and thoughts
they have acquired from their earliest years."[67] Sanches, of course, hit on the
key point of weakness of enlightened social engineering. The legal formula-
tions of the Pombaline state were justified as an application of natural law, a
secularized system that was a logical construct based on reason, not faith or
custom. Pombal even enacted this in 1769 as the *Lei da Boa Razão* (Law of the
Good Reason), instructing that henceforth all law was to be construed on the
basis of "good reason" without which it would not be valid.[68] Yet in practice the
explicit constructs of the state were underpinned by the unstated networks of
personal relationships, clientelism, and self-interest. Such self-interest was
clearly seen by Pombal as a means to fortify the objectives of the state in economic policy as well as in administration. To work, this required a vision that
set the national interest above private interests. While Pombal ruled, this overall objective prevailed. But it did so at the cost of continuous personal intervention and much repression. And as Pombal grew older, and as his brothers
died, he became more and more repressive, suspicious of even his closest collaborators should they show too much independence or oppose his desires.

The Pombaline state continued to reward with noble titles the heads of the
new great merchant dynasties it had so carefully stimulated and aided since
1750. The attack on the practice of *puritanismo,* the caste-like exclusivity of the
hereditary aristocracy, was part of the process that had seen the ennoblement
of Pombal's collaborators among the businessmen and participants in his state-
supported economic enterprises. In 1768, puritanism was formally outlawed by
royal decree. The Cruz family, from which Pombal had drawn several of his
closest collaborators, was judiciously rewarded. Joaquim Ignácio da Cruz obtained the entailed estates and title of Sobral, an ex-Jesuit possession, and the
title passed to his brother Anselmo on his death. José Francisco da Cruz obtained the *morgado,* or entailed estates of Alagoa, a title that became that of his
sons, aspiring pupils at the college of nobles. When in 1775 an equestrian statue
of Dom José I, the centerpiece of the great new commercial square on Lisbon's
waterfront, was inaugurated in a lavish ceremony, Anselmo José da Cruz stood
at the right hand of the beplumed and ceremonious marquês de Pombal.[69] By
1777, in fact, the great merchant houses Pombal envisioned twenty years before

and had sheltered and nurtured with direct and indirect state assistance for two decades had come of age. By state intervention and economic circumstance the Pombaline oligarchy had been created. The opulence of these Portuguese noble businessmen of the last quarter of the eighteenth century was praised by poets and pamphleteers and impressed visiting literati. "The large and magnificent houses" of the Quintellas, Braamcamps, and Bandeiras were noted by the English poet Robert Southey at the turn of the century. And the ever-caustic William Beckford noted their "clearing display of false taste and ill-judged magnificence."[70] "Is there anyone who does not do business?" asked Bernardo de Jesus Maria in his *Arte e diccionario do comércio e económia portuguesa,* published in Lisbon in 1783. "Good customs and much money," ran the contemporary jingle, "make any kind of knave a gentleman."[71]

Pombal's vast powers had always depended on the king's support. This was both his strength and his weakness, a link the conspirators against the king's life had seen in the late 1750s. And, following the death of the king in 1777, Pombal's position became at once untenable. The new monarch, Maria I, had been for long the focus of hope of Pombal's enemies. The pent-up frustrations of those interests long discredited, the merchants who did not benefit from the special privileges and protections of Pombal's collaborators, the ultramontane clergy, the aristocrats who had not compromised with the regime, and the English all found receptive audiences for their complaints in the changed political environment.

Many though not all of Pombal's closest associates were removed from office following his fall from power. Frei Cenáculo was ordered to resign as the prince's tutor and was required to take up residence at his bishopric of Beja. The reformer of the University of Coimbra, Francisco de Lemos, was dismissed, and Pombal's sister, the abbess of the convent of Santa Joana, was deposed. The Jesuits incarcerated since 1760 were released as were the surviving aristocratic conspirators. In all, some six thousand political prisoners were set free under Rainha Maria's clemency decisions.[72]

Pombal's fall from grace was rapid. The situation became sufficiently threatening in Lisbon for him to withdraw first to Oeiras and then to move north to his properties near Pombal. He was forced to travel incognito, but his empty coach was stoned. Troops were called out to prevent his Lisbon house from being burned, and the crowd had to be satisfied with burning his effigy instead. There was an explosion of denunciation and satires. Abandoned by many of his allies (though not all, by any means), Pombal prepared to face his enemies both in the juridical proceeding that the queen instituted and through the systematic written defense of his policies and actions.[73]

Pombal lived five years beyond his fall from power. He died in 1782, a forlorn, sick, but still defiant old man. His immediate successors judged him harshly, but by the turn of the century many of his acolytes returned to positions of power. Portuguese historians, like Pombal's contemporaries, remain divided as to his merits and the importance of his reforms. And it was a century and a half before he received national recognition in the form of a great statue that now dominates Lisbon at the end of Avenida da Liberdade.

Several dilemmas marked the Portuguese eighteenth century, and ultimately none of them was fully resolved. The most fundamental rested in the dependency of Brazil, since it was the South Atlantic dimension that set the chronological framework for the whole epoch. For historical reasons initially and then for reasons related to the growing imbalance between Brazil and Portugal, the relationship between the two throughout this whole period was never merely that of a colonial servant and European master. The historical reasons went back to the period between 1580 and 1640 when Portugal had fallen under the rule of the Spanish Habsburg monarchy and a substantial section of Brazil's most prosperous northeastern sugar-producing region had been seized by the Dutch. The struggle to reestablish Portuguese sovereignty in Brazil had been largely a Brazilian affair.

Once Portugal regained its own independence and the duque de Bragança had been recognized as king of Portugal, the value of Brazil to Portugal's recuperation of its position in Europe, most especially by the utilization of Brazilian wealth, played a large part in the calculations of the great Jesuit polymath and statesman Padre António Vieira in the immediate post-restoration years. The more astute Portuguese leaders from the late seventeenth century until the early nineteenth were aware that the Brazilians had contributed mightily to the restoration of Portuguese sovereignty in South America and had mobilized against other foreign threats when they had presented themselves, particularly against the French in the early years of the eighteenth century and against the Spaniards over the whole period. As a consequence, they were careful to treat the Brazilians with suitable respect and caution. Pombal, in particular, while ferocious in his defense of royal privilege and authority in Portugal itself, sought to co-opt and integrate Brazilians into the mechanisms of government both in Brazil and in Portugal. Yet Portugal was in the final analysis a small country with a large empire, and the notion that Brazil would eventually surpass Portugal in population and wealth led several leading figures, Dom Luís da Cunha among them, to foresee the eventual move of the seat of government across the Atlantic.

Brazilian gold provided the means to consolidate the Portuguese absolutist state. The role of the parliament had been important in the days of penury and weakness following the restoration of independence in 1640. And the claim to the throne had emerged out of an act of rebellion and from among the upper reaches of the Portuguese aristocracy. The relationship of the Braganças to the upper nobility was thus a complicated one and the Portuguese monarchy had as a consequence often drawn its most intimate advisers from other sources. The Jesuits from the time of Vieira until the 1750s played a key role as confessors and as special advisers and agents for the crown. Colonials had performed a similar role both in the reign of Dom João V, as in the person of his influential Brazilian-born private secretary, Alexandre de Gusmão. Later on Francisco de Lemos, another Brazilian, worked intimately with Pombal and was the reforming rector of the University of Coimbra. Toward the end of the century Pombal's godson, Francisco de Sousa Coutinho, drew from the ideas of a de facto Brazilian brain trust in his ambitious plans to get the Pombaline reform program back on track at the turn of the century.

A fundamental objective of Pombal's education reforms, his creation of a college of nobles, and the provision of the education of the provincial nobility at Coimbra was intended precisely to create a service nobility, free, as the statutes of the college of nobles put it, "from the pernicious notion that they could live free of virtue." But here the dilemmas facing such social engineering were profound. The traditional nobility was small, intermarried, and intensely traditionalist. The Inquisition and its obsession with purity of blood, with ferreting our subversion, with Judaism and heresy was a powerful bastion against reform. Yet the Inquisition was also a powerful arm in the defense of the state, and the monarchs were faced here with their own ambiguities. Dom João V, as Angela Delaforce shows in her essay in this volume, was proud of his title of "most faithful" *(fidelíssimo),* with his plans for the Patriarchate of Lisbon, with his expensive promotion of religious ceremonial, and not least his project at Mafra. Yet the Braganças had also permitted, or had been forced to permit because of the need for defensive alliances with the Protestant maritime powers, the practice of the Protestant religion within their own capital. And their more thoughtful royal advisers, from the Jesuit António Vieira to Dom Luís da Cunha to Pombal, had all believed that Portugal needed to recuperate the new Christian and Jewish wealth and business expertise lost to Portugal because of the Inquisition's depredations.

There was, of course, an element of paranoia to these views, since they were sometimes a mirror image in their expectation of Jewish and new Christian entrepreneurial perspicacity, of the Inquisition's fear of it. But these tentative steps in the direction of social reform and toleration were part of a wider clash between the traditional values of the Counter-Reformation and a reform program that aimed at reestablishing national control over the economy, at shoring up the power of the state, and at the education of a new generation of skillful businessmen and enlightened aristocrats. And here the ambiguity of the crown's own response to these conflicting tendencies was most acute. Dom João V wanted initiative and orthodoxy to flourish at the same time, which they could not. Pombal, by contrast, had thrown the state's support wholeheartedly behind reform but with a ferocity and despotism that left his measures dangerously dependent on his personal power and left them vulnerable, therefore, to reversal and rejection after his fall. And he had in a curious way so fused authoritarianism to reform that the succeeding reign of the ultra-pious Dona Maria I recalled at times the less rigorous eclectic confusion of her extravagant grandfather. So that as the queen retreated into the pastoral fantasies of her palace at Queluz and set out to build the great basilica at Estrela, both in inspiration and style as far removed from the utilitarian neoclassicism of the new Pombaline Lisbon or the designs of Colonel William Elsden for the new laboratories and observatories of Coimbra as could be imagined, she also permitted the new royal academy of sciences to be inaugurated and encouraged the great "philosophical" expeditions of Alexandre Rodrigues Ferreira and his colleagues who set out to record the natural history of the Amazon, Angola, and Mozambique. Once the regency was formally declared in 1799, many of Pombal's acolytes returned to office, including Francisco de Lemos who returned to Coimbra to continue his interrupted work.

The second great dilemma of the long Portuguese eighteenth century involved the conflicting interests of trade and industry. When gold began to flow from Brazil, it became cheaper to import finished goods than to manufacture them at home. Thus the gold of Brazil helped kill off the infant industries that the conde de Ericeira had tried to develop in the late seventeenth century.

Conversely, when gold remittances declined, the changed economic environment helped to stimulate the new manufactories set up by the Pombaline regime. So subtle had been Pombal's approach and so powerful were the incentives to Portuguese manufacturing, that by the end of the century Portugal was benefiting both from its own manufactured products, which came to comprise a significant portion of Portuguese exports to Brazil, and from a surge in colonial re-exports, such as sugar and cotton. This brought a true reciprocity to Portugal's commercial dealings with the rest of Europe and with Britain in particular, something that had been the aim of mercantilists in Portugal since the restoration of Portuguese independence in the mid-seventeenth century.

But here again the classic constraint of the long eighteenth century came into play. The age of mercantilism was passing. In England the industrial revolution was beginning. The free traders were pushing for a removal of barriers and special relationships. Adam Smith in fact made the Anglo-Portuguese commercial relationship in general, and the Methuen Treaty in particular, the classic example of restraint on trade. The Lancashire cotton textile producers and exporters were pushing the government in London for a direct relationship with the lucrative markets of the Americas. Thus just as the mercantilist dream had been achieved, the context within which mercantilism worked, as far as the Portuguese were concerned, was about to be overthrown.

This denouement came about as a result of the third dilemma of the long Portuguese eighteenth century, the invidious role of Portugal within the struggle for hegemony in the Atlantic between France and Britain. In the climactic moments of that long struggle, the revolutionary and Napoleonic wars, the final break occurred. It was France and not Britain that provoked the rupture when Napoleon decided that Portuguese neutrality could not be tolerated and that the port of Lisbon provided too serious a breach in his Continental system. Napoleon miscalculated the degree to which the Portuguese monarchy had prepared for the move to Brazil or the willingness of the British to facilitate this historic transfer of the seat of government from metropolis to colony in their own commercial interest in establishing a direct relationship with Brazil.

The fundamental problem for Portugal arose from the logic of the Brazil-based Atlantic system. In the final analysis, Brazil would inevitably become the dominant partner within the Portuguese-speaking empire. If the political constraints, which had governed the whole period from the 1660s to the end of the eighteenth century, also changed, that is if, for example, Great Britain no longer saw it in its own interest to protect Portugal from her Continental neighbors, then the British might opt for a direct relationship with the colony rather than with the mother country. Since the whole basis of Portugal's prosperity had been built on the manipulation of colonial monopolies, cash-crop exports, colonial markets, and colonial gold, such a rupture would bring fundamental change and would close an epoch. The French seizure of Lisbon in 1807 collapsed the structure of the Luso-Atlantic system as it had existed since the 1660s, and direct access between Europe and the Brazilian ports destroyed Lisbon's role as a required intermediary. Thus 1807 brought the long Portuguese eighteenth century to an end. Left unresolved, however, was the old conflict between innovation and tradition, and as the nineteenth century opened without the cushion that the wealth of Brazil provided, this struggle became bitter indeed.

1. Cited by Susan Schneider in *O marquês de Pombal e o vinho do Porto; dependência e subdesenvolvimento em Portugal no século XVIII* (Lisbon, 1980), 8.

2. See the excellent summary of historiography by Jorge Borges de Macedo in *Dicionário de história de Portugal*, 6 vols. (Oporto, 1979), 5:113-121.

3. Oliveira Marques, *History of Portugal*, 2 vols. (New York, 1979), 1:380.

4. For the Portuguese grain trade, see Vitorino Magalhães Godinho, *Prix et Monnaies au Portugal 1750–1850* (Paris, 1955), 147-149; for Spanish-Portuguese trade, see Jean François Bourgoing, *Voyage de ci-devant duc du Chatelet en Portugal…* 2 vols. (Paris, 1798, 1808), 1:228; comments on the importation of wood from northern Europe, Francisco Xavier de Mendonça Furtado to Sr. Fernando de Lavra, 26 January 1752; and Mendonça Furtado to Pombal, 15 July 1757 in *A Amazônia na era Pombalina, correspondência inédita do governador e capitão-general do estado do Grão Pará e Maranhão, Francisco Xavier de Mendonça Furtado 1751–1759,* 3 vols. (Rio de Janeiro, 1963), 1:214-215; 3:1119-1120.

5. For the period between the 1660s and 1700, a good overview is provided by Carl A. Hansen, *Economy and Society in Baroque Portugal, 1668–1703* (Minneapolis, 1981). See also Carl A. Hansen, "D. Luís da Cunha and Portuguese Mercantilist Thought," *Journal of the American Portuguese Society* 15 (1981), 15-23.

6. Vitorino M. Godinho, "Portugal, as frotas do açúcar e as frotas do ouro (1670-1770)," *Revista da história* 15 (São Paulo, 1953); Virgilio Noya Pinto, *O ouro brasileiro e o comércio anglo-português* (São Paulo, 1979); Kenneth R. Maxwell, *Conflicts and Conspiracies: Brazil and Portugal, 1750–1808* (Cambridge, England, 1973).

7. Background on the Methuen Treaty, A. D. Francis, *The Methuens and Portugal, 1691–1708* (London, 1966); and Alan K. Manchester, *British Preëminence in Brazil* (Chapel Hill, 1933), 24. For an account of an individual merchant involved in the Portugal trade, Lucy S. Sutherland, *A London Merchant 1695–1774* (Oxford, 1933).

8. A. B. Wallis Chapman, "The Commercial Relations of England and Portugal 1487-1807," *Transactions of the Royal Historical Society,* 3rd series (1907), 177; Jorge Borges de Macedo, *Problemas de história da indústria Portuguesa no século 18* (Lisbon, 1963), 48.

9. "Destinations of exports from England and Wales," Table V and "Sources of imports into England and Wales," Table VI, Elizabeth Boody Schumpeter, *English Overseas Statistics* (Oxford, 1960), 17-20; Macedo 1963, 46-47, 53; H. E. S. Fisher, "Anglo-Portuguese Trade 1700-1770," *The Economic History Review*, 2nd series, 16 (1963), 229 (republished in W. E. Minchinton, ed., *The Growth of English Overseas Trade in the 17th and 18th Centuries* (London, 1969), 144-164; C. R. Boxer, "Brazilian Gold and British Traders in the First Half of the Eighteenth Century," *Hispanic American Historical Review* 49, 3 (August 1969), 455-472.

10. Marques 1979, 1:385.

11. H. E. S. Fisher, *The Portugal Trade* (London, 1971).

12. Macedo 1963.

13. Albert Silbert, *Do Portugal de antigo regime ao Portugal oitocentista* (Lisbon, 1977), and Godinho 1955.

14. On the role of the British factories, see John Delaforce, *The Factory House at Oporto* (London, 1983); and A. R. Walford, *British Factory* (Lisbon, 1940), 20.

15. "Maximas sobre a reforma…dirigidas ao…Sr. D. José…por D. Luís da Cunha…" Biblioteca Nacional de Lisboa, Pombal collection (BNLCP) cód. 51, fol. 178v.

16. Benjamin Keene to Abraham Castres, October 1745, in Sir Richard Lodge, ed., *The Private Correspondence of Sir Benjamin Keene, K. B.* (Cambridge, 1933), 72. Keene had been in Lisbon from 1745 to 1749 before his appointment as envoy in Spain. Abraham Castres was (from 1746) British consul in Lisbon.

17. Manuel Nunes Dias, "Fomento ultramarino e mercantilismo: A Companhia Geral do Grão Pará e Maranhão 1755-1778," *Revista de história (RHSP)* 66 (São Paulo, April-June 1966), 426; Moses Bensabat Amzalak, *Do estudo e da evolução das doutrinas económicas em Portugal* (Lisbon, 1928), 88-98; Teles da Silva to Pombal, Vienna, 3 November 1755, *Anais da academia Portuguesa da história*, ed. Carlos da Silva Tarouca, S. J., 2nd series (Lisbon, 1955), 6:346-348.

18. Based on the catalogue of Pombal's books in London, BNLCP códs. 165, 167, 342, 343.

19. For an excellent discussion of Pombal's service in London and the background of the "Relação dos gravames que ao comércio e vassalos de Portugal se têm inferido e estão actuamente inferindo por Inglaterra," see Sebastião José de Carvalho e Melo, *Escritos económicos de Londres, 1741–1742,* selected and with introduction by José Barreto (Lisbon, 1986). The original manuscript of the "Relação dos gravames" is in cód. 635 BNLCP with annotations and corrections in Pombal's own hand.

20. [Silva Tarouca] to [Pombal], Schönbraunn, 25 July 1757, "Correspondência entre o duque Manuel Teles da Silva e Sebastião José de Carvalho e Melo," Academia Portuguêsa 1955, 379.

21. For Pombal's Austrian period see Maria Aleina Ribeiro Correa, *Sebastião José de Carvalho e Melo na Corte de Viena de Austria, 1744–1749* (Lisbon, 1965).

22. The names of visitors are contained in BNLCP cód. 718.

23. David Willemse, "António Ribeiro Sanches, elevé de Boerhaave et son importance pour la Russie," *Janus: Revue internationale de l'historie del sciences et de la medicine*, vol. 6 (Leiden, 1966).

24. See Ribeiro Correa 1965, 31-71.

25. [Silva Tarouca] to [Pombal], Vienna, 25 September 1750, Academia Portuguêsa 277-422, citations from 313-315.

26. António Alberto de Andrade, *Vernei e a*

cultura do seu tempo (Coimbra, 1966), 126-127.

27. For a brief introduction see A. A. Banha de Andrade, *Verney e a projecção da sua obra*, which contains in an appendix extracts from Verney's correspondence with Muratori (Lisbon, 1980).

28. Andrade 1980, 136-139.

29. Andrade 1980, 139.

30. See Barreto's introduction to Carvalho e Melo 1986.

31. For a discussion of the Oratorians and more generally the reformist tendencies in eighteenth-century southern European Catholicism, see Samuel J. Miller, *Portugal and Rome c. 1748-1830: An Aspect of the Catholic Enlightenment* (Rome, 1978).

32. See discussion in Macedo 1979.

33. Academia das Sciências de Lisboa, *Instruções inéditas de D. Luís da Cunha a Marco António de Azevedo Coutinho, revistas por Pedro de Azevedo e prefaciadas por António Baião* (Coimbra, 1929), 139, 211, 214, 215; Charles R. Boxer, *The Golden Age of Brazil, 1659-1750* (Berkeley and Los Angeles, 1962), 323-324.

34. For disputes along southern borderlands, see David Alden, *Royal Government in Colonial Brazil with Special Reference to the Administration of the Marquis of Lavradio, viceroy 1769-1779* (Berkeley and Los Angeles, 1968).

35. Voltaire, *Candide*, trans. and ed. Robert M. Adams (New York, 1966), 30-31.

36. Kenneth Maxwell, "Pombal and the Nationalisation of the Luso-Brazilian Economy," *Hispanic American Historical Review* 58, no. 4 (Nov. 1968), 608-631.

37. Schneider 1980.

38. T. D. Kendrick, *The Lisbon Earthquake* (London, 1956) and *The Lisbon Earthquake of 1755: British Accounts*, introduction and translation Judith Nozes (London, 1990).

39. Cited in Charles R. Boxer, *Some Contemporary Reactions to the Lisbon Earthquake of 1755* (Lisbon, 1956).

40. A classic account is José Augusto França, *Lisboa Pombalina e o Iluminismo* (Lisbon, 1977).

41. Conde de Carnota (John A. Smith), *Marquis of Pombal*, 2nd ed. (London, 1871), 166-167; and Lucio d'Azevedo, *Estudos de história Paraense* (Parà, 1983), 60.

42. Fernando de Oliveira, *O motim popular de 1757; uma página na história da época pombalina* (Oporto, 1930).

43. "Sentença de Alçada que o Rei Nosso Senhor mandou conhecer da rebelhão sucçedada na cidade de Porto em 1757" (Lisbon, 1758), BNCLP cód. 456.

44. See discussion in Marques 1979.

45. João Lucio d'Azevedo, *O Marquês de Pombal e sua época*, 2nd ed. (Lisbon, 1922), 148-149.

46. Azevedo 1922, 125-126.

47. See Jorge Borges de Macedo, *A situação económica no tempo de Pombal* (Oporto, 1950), 50.

48. "Alvará porque … he servido declarar que todos os ministros, e officiaes de justiça e fazenda ou guerra he permitido negociar por meyo da companhia geral do Grão Pará e Maranhão, e qualquer outros por V.M. confirmados…" 5 January, 1757. BNLCP cód. 456, folio 138.

49. For a discussion of the Távora case, see *Pombal: O processo dos Távoras*, ed. Pedro de Azevedo (Lisbon, 1921); and Joaquim Verissimo Serrão, *Pombal: o homen, o diplomata e o estadista* (Lisbon, 1982).

50. The interrogations comprise the bulk of the *Processo do Távoras* (Azevedo 1921). For Pombal's role, see 11.

51. John Smith, *Memoirs of the Marquis of Pombal*, 2 vols. (London, 1843), 213-214.

52. Serrão 1982, 108-109.

53. "Ley porque Vossa Magestade he servida exterminar, proscrever, e mandar expulsar dos seus Reinos e Domínios, os Religiosos de companhia denominada de JESU…" 3 September 1759, BNLCP, cód. 453, folio 291-294.

54. Azevedo 1921, 214.

55. Cited by Samuel J. Miller, *Portugal and Rome, 1748-1830: An Aspect of the Catholic Enlightenment* (Rome, 1978), 109.

56. "Compendio histórico: politico das honras e magnificencas que são inherentes do caracter de primer ministro de grandes cortes de Europa," BNLCP, códs. 10510, 10568.

57. See *Collecção dos negócios de Roma no reinado de El-Rei Dom José I, ministério do marquês de Pombal*, 2 parts (Lisbon, 1874).

58. Marques 1979, 1:402.

59. Marques 1979, 1:394.

60. "para ser útil a Republica, e a Igreja, proporcionado ao, estilo, e necessidade de Portugal." Verney, *Verdadero metodo* (Naples, 1746).

61. J. Marcadé, *Frei Manuel do Cenáculo Vilas Boas (1770-1814)* (Paris, 1978), 5-16.

62. Marcadé 1978, 67.

63. Marcadé 1978, 60-65.

64. Marcadé 1978, 66.

65. *Relação geral do estado da universidade, 1777* (Coimbra, 1983), 232.

66. Marcadé 1978, 78.

67. Cited by António José Saraiva, *Inquisição a cristãos-novos*, 4th ed. (Oporto, 1969), 317.

68. Marques 1979, 1:407.

69. "Parallelo de Augusto Cesar e de Dom José O Magnanimo Rey de Portugal," Lisbon, 1775, BNLCP, cód. 456, folio 44.

70. Robert Southey, *Journal of a Residence in Portugal 1800-1801*, ed. A. Cabral (Oxford, 1900), 137-139; and William Beckford, *The Journal of William Beckford in Portugal and Spain 1787-1788*, ed. Boyde Alexander (London, 1954), 257-258.

71. Cited in Macedo 1963, 216.

72. Serrão 1982, 167-171.

73. Serrão 1982, 167-171.

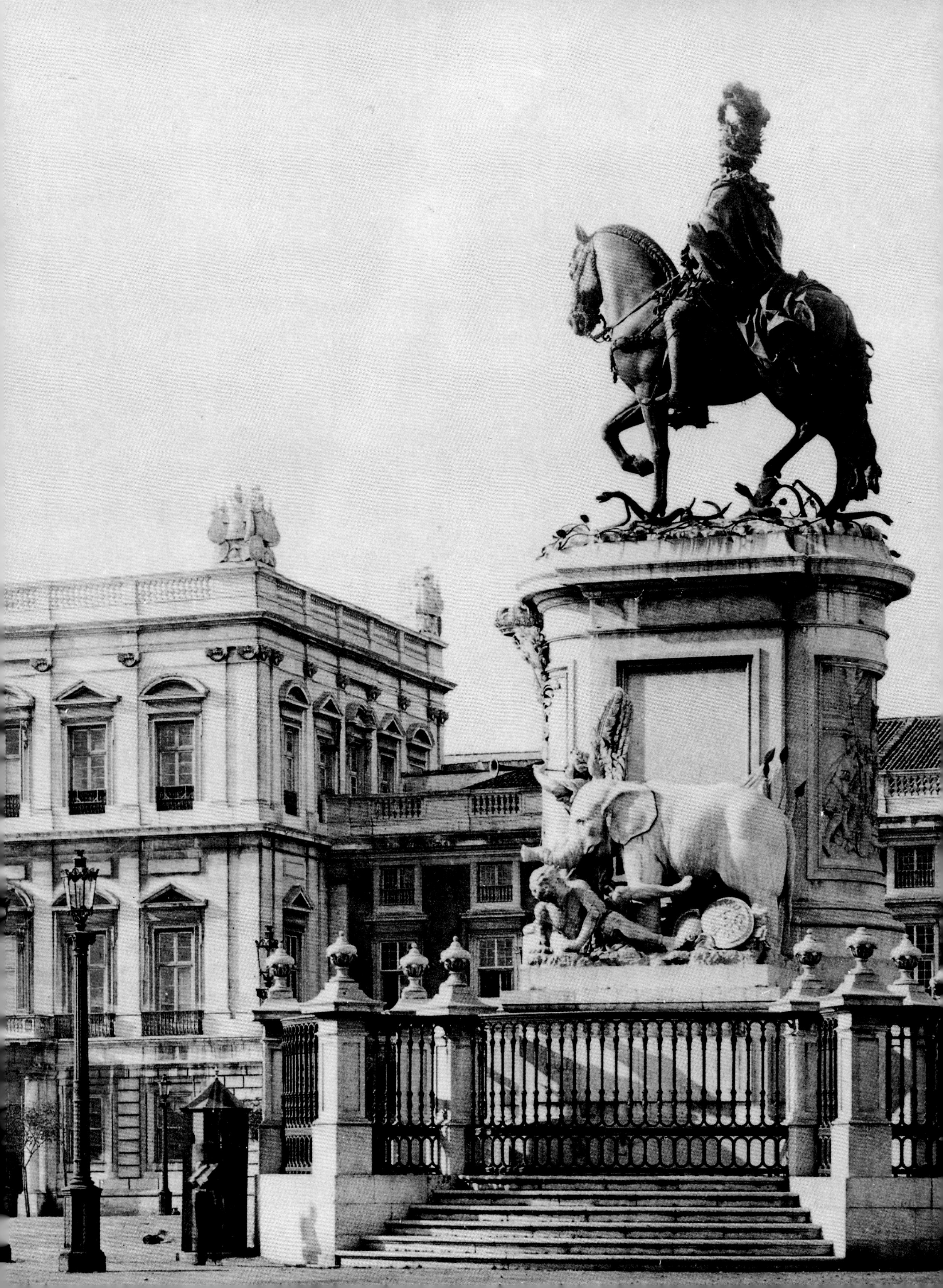

Lisbon, the Enlightened City
of the Marquês de Pombal

José Augusto França

After the Age of the Discoveries during the late fifteenth century, the Lisbon earthquake in the mid-eighteenth century was one of the central turning points in the history of Portugal. Two architectural styles provided the aesthetic and ideological parameters for these historical events. The lavish, late-Gothic embellishment of monuments in the Manueline style, named after Dom Manuel I, is associated with the discoveries; and, at the dawn of the age of neoclassicism, the rational layout and sober facades of the new Pombaline area of the city are consequences of the earthquake.

On 1 November 1755, the city of Lisbon, with 250,000 inhabitants, suffered an earthquake of unprecedented proportions, followed by a fire that completed the destruction begun by the elements.[1] With ten thousand dead and two-thirds of the houses reduced to smoking rubble, the old capital was left a desert of stones and debris stalked by terror.

Sebastião de Carvalho, the future marquês de Pombal, was to take the lead in dealing with the situation, his jealous and ferocious energy preventing anyone else, even Dom José I himself, from taking action. This man of fifty-six years proved to be the person equal to a challenge that he ultimately turned to his advantage. The tragic circumstances offered him the means to fulfill his destiny as strong man, dictator, and enlightened despot.

The earth had barely ceased shaking when Pombal began to dream of a rebuilt Lisbon that could become a new city, capital of his own kingdom, the stage on which he was to play out his drama of reform. Pombal worked within the framework of enlightened thought, although circumscribed by the memory of the career of Colbert in France and the intrinsic contradictions of an empirical opportunism. Yet Pombal's urban dream was more readily definable than that of Colbert, since the ruined Lisbon gave the Portuguese architects free rein. It was a matter of rebuilding a symmetrical city on a place in which everything had been burned to the ground.

Pombal was of a practical nature and surrounded himself with a team equal to the task he had set. Three men, belonging to three different generations, headed his staff. Manuel da Maia, chief engineer of the realm, had began his

fig. 1. *Praça do Comércio*, Lisbon, detail of a photograph by Francisco Rocchini, 1872. The statue of Dom José I (1771–1775) by Joaquim Machado de Castro is in the foreground

professional life on the fortifications of the village of Vauban; in 1755 he was eighty years old and had been trained in the ways of Portuguese seventeenth-century architecture, which still bore the traces of Spanish mannerism. Karoly (called Carlos) Mardel was a colonel of engineers, a sixty-year-old Hungarian who had taken up residence in Portugal twenty years before and so was, by contrast, a man of central Europe. He introduced the discreet charms of the rococo style into Portuguese architecture. Eugénio dos Santos, captain of engineers, forty years of age, represented a new outlook and a new taste. He was part of Pombal's team by virtue of his belief that a degree of utilitarianism, a "modern" element, should be introduced into architecture.

Three military engineers thus took on the task of rebuilding Lisbon. There was no element of speculation in their approach; they were foremen dealing with technical problems requiring immediate and economical solutions. Time was nonexistent, and the empty state coffers imposed major limitations. The approach adopted by the three men reflected a combination of forces that merit comment. Santos represented new, pragmatic sociocultural schemes, creating an architectural language suited to the situation. Mardel introduced into the project a refined and erudite system of architecture. The elderly Maia expressed the real nature of the situation created by Pombal: a sound empirical sense that was in keeping, during this, the age of reason, with the architectural precepts formulated in France by Blondel.[2] The product of their work could have provided examples for J. N. L. Durand's courses at the Ecole Polytechnique de Paris half a century later, had Durand been aware of them. But because of an unfortunate misunderstanding, an article commissioned from the Lisbon Academy of Sciences by the editor of the Methodical Dictionary of 1784 was never published. Thus Pombal's project remained virtually unknown outside Portugal, although the natural disaster preceding it had moved the whole world, from Voltaire to Rousseau, from Kant to Sade.

Immediately after the tragedy of the earthquake, Chief Engineer da Maia submitted three successive reports to Pombal. These extremely important documents illustrate an approach to urban planning that advances from the traditional structures of the sixteenth and seventeenth centuries toward modern functional models. The old engineer put forward four possible solutions: to rebuild the city as it was; to rebuild it with broader main streets; to remodel completely the central, low-lying section (called the Baixa) after razing what little remained; or to abandon the ruins and build a new city a few kilometers farther west in the direction of Belém, an area on the banks of the Tagus that had been spared by the earthquake. Pombal selected the third option, which was to introduce a new aesthetic in the very heart of the city. Thus, Blondel's ideals of "simplicity, proportion, and harmony" underlay the organization of the new urban plan for Lisbon, which was also influenced by the need to comply with the financial constraints of the time.

Six proposals drawn up by as many engineers' officers illustrate da Maia's approach. Again Pombal selected the best, which was also the most radical, designed by dos Santos, who died in 1760, and by Mardel, who in turn died three years later (fig. 2).

A harmonious integration of the new urban ground plan and the continuance of the old city was provided by a symmetrical but dynamic grid of streets crossing each other at right angles, which extends between two beautiful pre-

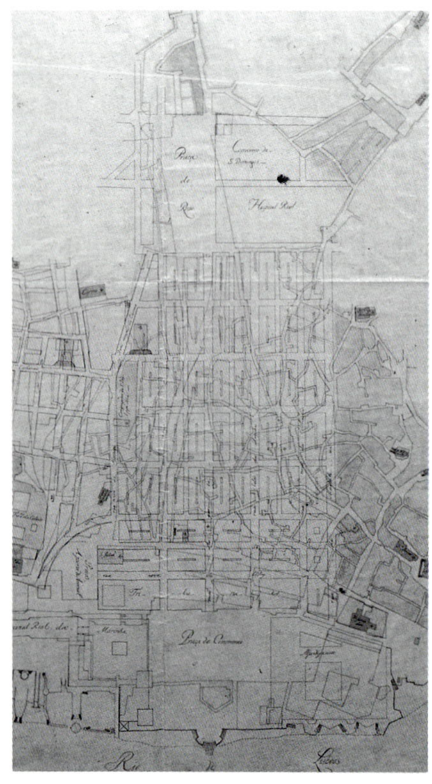

fig. 2. João Pinto Ribeiro, *Plan of the City of Lisbon in Accordance with the New Alignment Planned by the Architects Eugénio dos Santos and Carlos Mardel* (detail of the Baixa), ink and watercolor. Instituto Geográfico e Cadastral, Lisbon

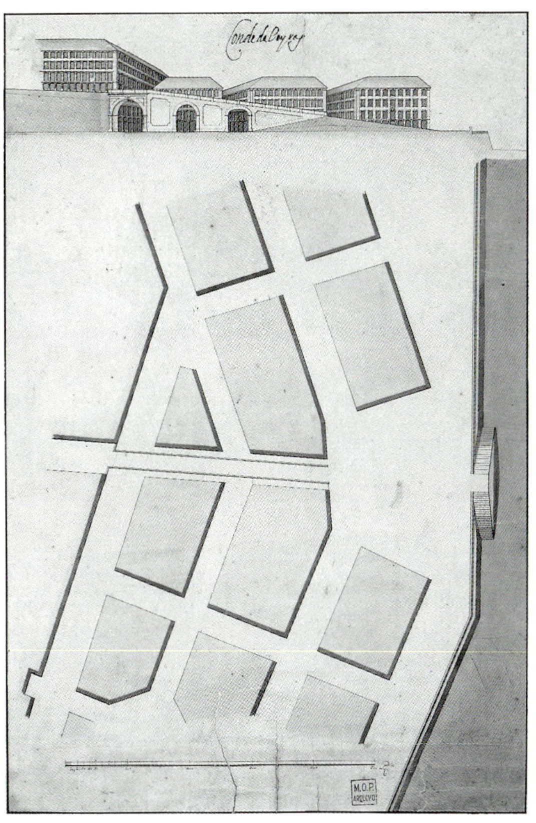

existing squares that were given a more regular shape in the rebuilding project. These squares mark the southern point (Terreiro do Paço) and the northern limit (Rossio Square) of this new area. To the east, at the foot of the medieval castle-fortress of Saint George, lay the labyrinth of the old Alfama quarter, which was virtually unscathed by the earthquake. Its location admirably illustrates the contrast, then and now, between the old and the new city: between its Gothic past and the new style of the enlightenment.

Da Maia also studied the possibility of urbanizing two uninhabited areas on the outskirts of the city. However, this was an overambitious project that could not be realized. Nevertheless, it reflected the desire for regular organization that was prominent during the Pombaline period. Da Maia looked to the future. He had tried to obtain information on the renovations of London and Turin (to him the most famous of the courts of Europe) and reached the conclusion that the Lisbon project was markedly superior to either. Nor was his plan at all Utopian, unlike those proposed by the theoretical architects of the Renaissance—Alberti, Filarete, Palladio—or by Fénelon's teaching, since the task at hand was a matter of rebuilding a city.

A law of May 1758 set down the necessary legal framework for the building of the new city. The document reconciled property owners to the plan that had been approved, guaranteeing their rights and establishing their obligations. In order to avoid speculation, they were to exchange their property or pay and receive compensation according to meticulously calculated property values. They were also required to build within a certain generally lengthy period of time.

The regularity of the urban grid was echoed by the regularity of the facades likewise proposed by da Maia. "Every road should maintain the same symme-

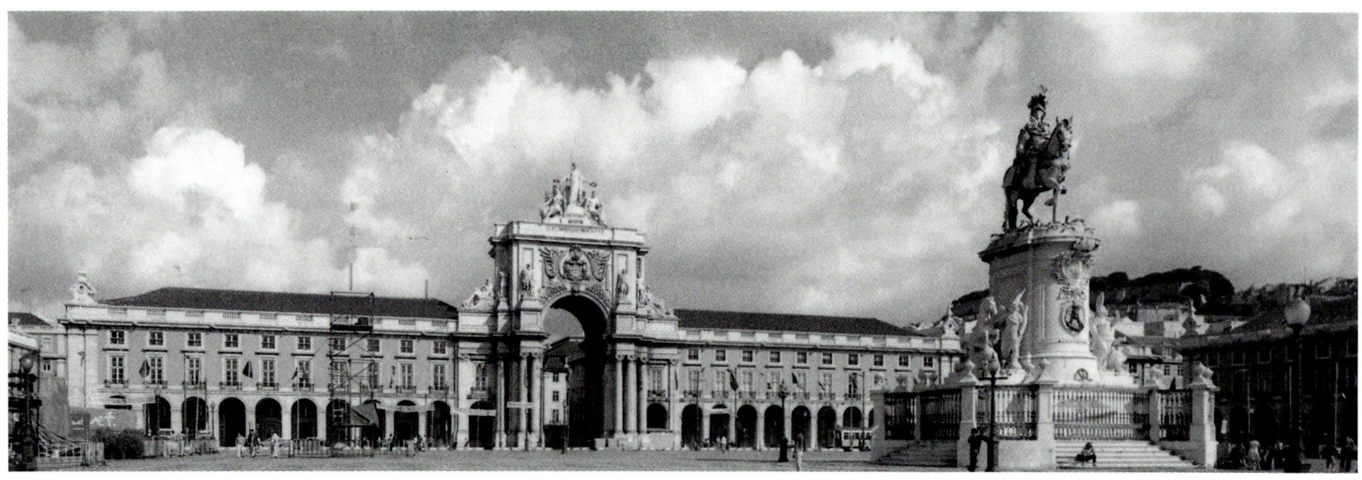

tries in doors, windows, and elevations," he wrote.[3] The facades of the streets of the Baixa, designed by dos Santos, and those of the Rossio, designed by Mardel, are of a utilitarian monotony that, though the subject of criticism, is nonetheless striking (fig. 3). Mardel added a taste for double roofs to the style that evolved, and dos Santos contributed a simple differentiation in degree of ornamentation in accordance with the importance of the streets that is also apparent in their width. The entire Baixa district was built with three-story apartment houses. As the area was slowly rebuilt, a satisfied and dynamic middle class moved in and invested capital, which provided the financing for reconstruction that consisted of such buildings. The aristocracy was as good as ruined.

Rational as it was, did this type of architecture constitute a style? Recently emerging from an uncertain past, the country's taste for the simple style of the Portuguese seventeenth-century pre-baroque was apparent, while the so-called Pombaline style remained fairly vague. It might instead be called a Pombaline type, applied exclusively to apartment buildings. Solid, unadorned, monotonous, bourgeois in their very severity, these buildings symbolized the rise of the middle class to prominence. It should therefore be thought of as an ideological architecture within the context of social evolution precipitated by the disastrous earthquake of 1755, which laid low the foundations of baroque power.

Praça do Comércio (fig. 4), square of commerce, was the new name given to the ancient Terreiro, the enormous monumental space on the northern bank of the Tagus around which new urban structures were assembled. There in 1500 Dom Manuel I had built his palace, which Filipe II had modernized and which João V, the "sun king" of Portugal, continued to embellish with the proceeds of the gold and diamonds brought from Brazil until the eve of the earthquake. Dos Santos gave the square a fringe of arcades and colonnades, a triumphal arch, and an equestrian statue of Dom José I (see fig. 1), this last a masterful finishing touch to the Pombaline program, creating a noble setting for the seat of new power: ministries and courthouses, stock exchange and customs office. This French-style *place royale,* rechristened Praça do Comércio in keeping with the new political philosophy, formed the transition between the area of the city of functional design and the area of more decorative buildings, which represented, to some extent, a ransom paid to the court and the church, both dominated by the all-powerful Pombal. The royal palace, which was allowed to remain as a special concession, and the Roman baroque style of the series of churches of the new Lisbon, which were not to be completed for some time, look back to a formal period on which Dom João V, who died in 1750, had left his lavish mark. This same taste, contrasting with the style of Pombal's city, is evident in the construction of the palaces in Queluz, the princely retreat that had just been begun a few leagues distant from Lisbon shortly before the earthquake. And the city was soon to witness the appearance of a large basilica in the Estrela district in fulfillment of a royal vow. However, since Pombal fell from power in 1777, the style of the basilica marked a return to the Romanesque. At this time, the Pombaline bourgeoisie was manifesting its new social role with the construction of an opera house (the São Carlos theater), which was designed along the best Italian neoclassical lines. Particularly prominent at the turn of the century was the royal palace, which was finally begun in the suburb of Ajuda, originally a baroque design abruptly replaced by a neoclassical plan submitted by two young architects (Costa e Silva and F. S. Fabri), admirers of the palace of Caserta.

The history of the reconstruction of Lisbon would not be complete without mention of the unprecedented circumstance that large buildings, standing on an original anti-earthquake structure of wood, were standardized. Work on the sites was supported by a network of shops producing standardized materials, a phenomenon that transcended the technical and the economic spheres to enter into the aesthetic, brought about by a socio-cultural situation of the utmost significance. Pombaline Lisbon was the last of the old cities that still bore a baroque stamp. It was also the first of the modern cities, in an empirical compromise of styles within a paradoxical system that is typical of the European enlightenment.

1. For additional information on the earthquake, see the essay by Kenneth Maxwell in this volume.

2. Jacques-François Blondel, *L'Architecture français*, ed. Jombert, vol. 2 (Paris, 1752).

3. "Dissertação de Manuel da Maia," in José-Augusto França, *Une ville des Lumières, la Lisbonne de Pombal*, 2nd ed. (Paris, 1988), 291-305.

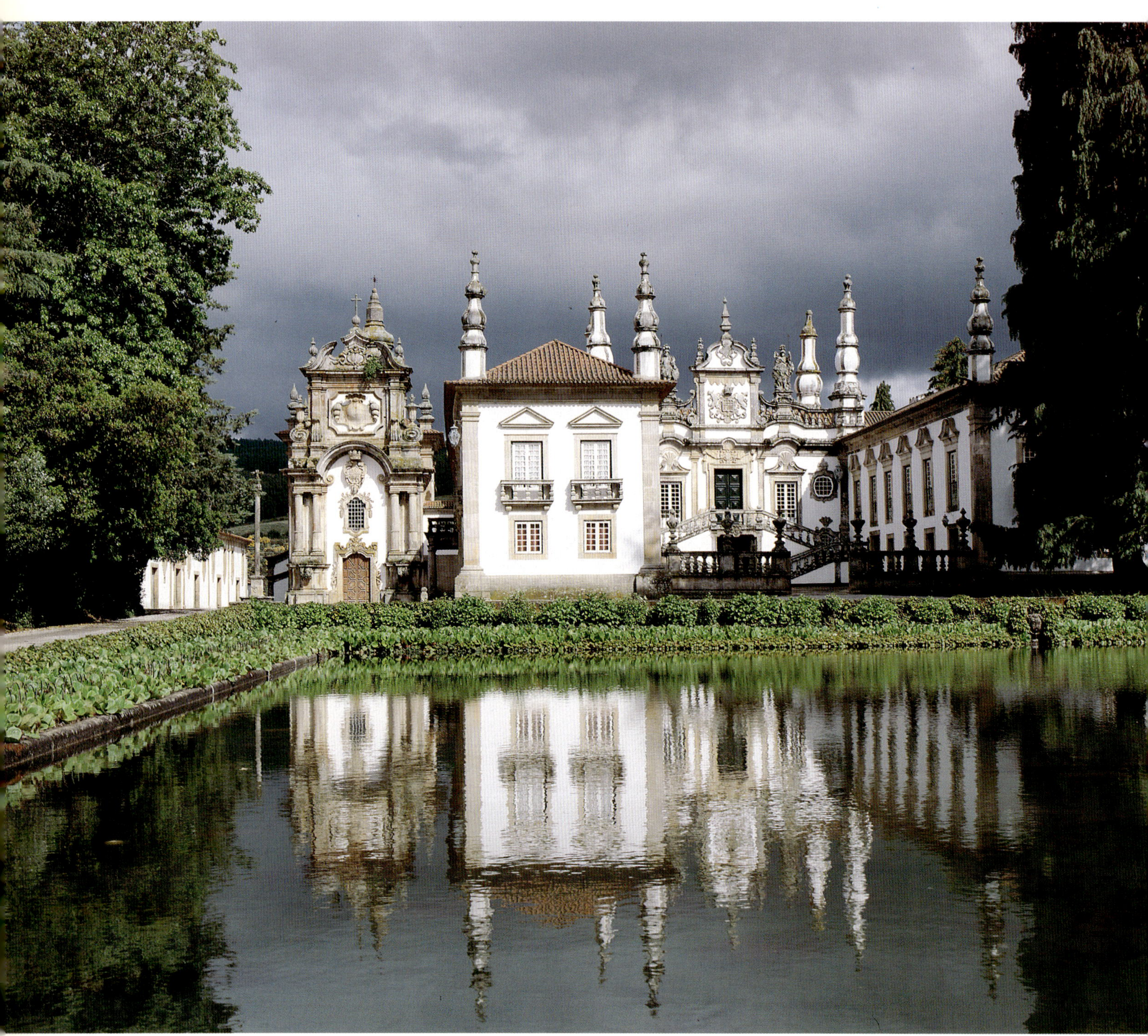

Portuguese Baroque Architecture

Hellmut Wohl

The baroque style had its origin in Italy and spread from there to the rest of Europe and to the Spanish and Portuguese dominions in the Americas. The different forms it assumed wherever it took hold were in large measure shaped by the traditions it inherited. In the architecture of Portugal the baroque made its appearance at the beginning of the eighteenth century. It was the heir of what has been aptly called the plain style of the sixteenth and seventeenth centuries, a tradition of flat walls and sparse ornament with exterior walls of white plaster trimmed with stone and interiors lined with *azulejos* (painted tiles). Although the Portuguese baroque, like any style, appears in diverse forms and variations, its most salient, clearly identifiable trait is the application to these flat surfaces of systems of rich ornamentation: in cut stone on the exterior of buildings and in gilded carved woodwork in interiors, characterized by vigor, opulence, and exuberance and charged with sculptural energy.

The flowering of Portuguese baroque architecture took place in and emanated from the northern Portuguese regional centers of Oporto and Braga during the second and third quarters of the eighteenth century. Its slightly earlier appearance in the country's southern region between Coimbra and Lisbon followed upon the accession to the throne in 1706 of Dom João V. In comparison with the flair and flamboyance of the northern Portuguese baroque, eighteenth-century architecture in the southern part of the country is restrained and conservative. A case in point is the large, drafty, votive church of Milagres near Leiria to the south of Coimbra, begun by the architects José and Joaquim da Silva in 1732. It is the masterpiece and the last example of a group of churches that combine two-tower facades with colonnaded verandas along the flanks. At Milagres the veranda also runs along the facade in the form of a narthex, a solution that unifies the design and contributes to its largeness of scale.

The restrained character of the southern Portuguese baroque was in large measure determined by the Lisbon office of royal architects, the Aula de Arquitetura Civil dos Paços da Ribeira. Established at the end of the sixteenth century following the annexation of Portugal by Spain in 1580, architects working for the crown continued to be trained there after the restoration of Portugal's independence in 1640. But for its pragmatic orientation, this office was the equivalent of an architectural academy, setting standards of design by ex-

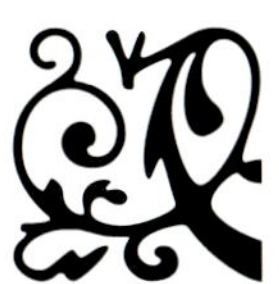

fig. 1. Nicolau Nasoni, *Casa de Mateus,* Vila Real, 1739–1743

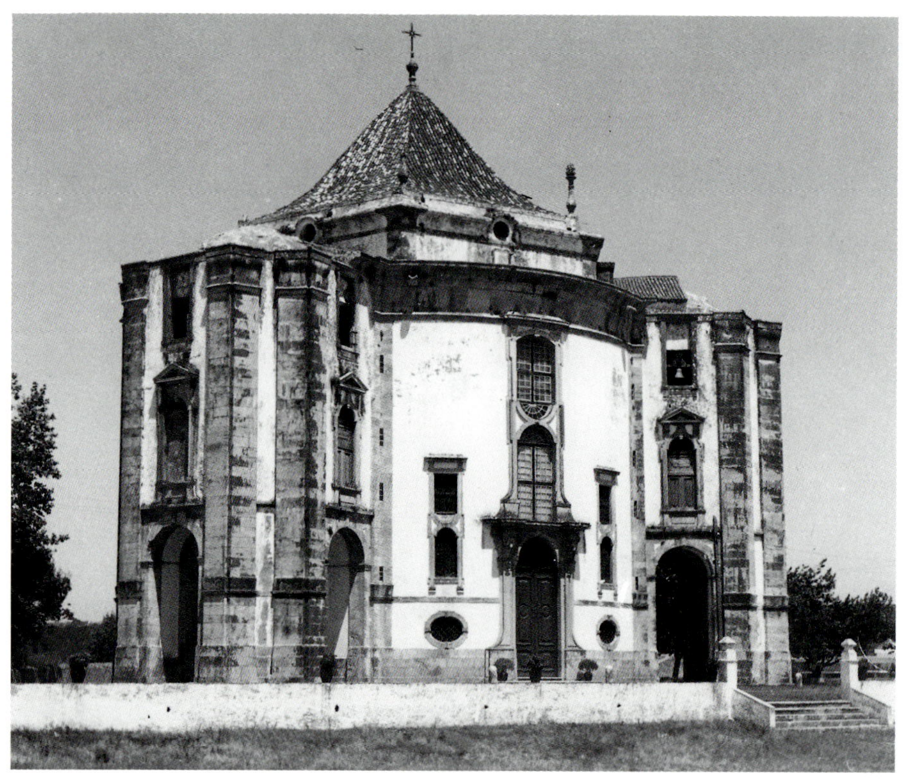

ample and precedent rather than by decree. Its members were military and civil engineers appointed by the crown and holding military rank. Both their training and the bulk of their commissions—the planning and construction of warehouses, fortifications, docks, and aqueducts—inclined them toward designs that stressed efficiency and economy. One member of the Aula, Captain Rodrigo Franco, designed for João V in 1740 and left incomplete in 1747 the massive church of Senhor da Pedra (fig. 2) outside the walls of Óbidos as a way station where the king could rest and attend mass on his way from the capital to the north. On each side of its hexagonal plan is a three-story pavilion with open passages at ground level providing shelter for men, horses, and carriages, rooms on the second floor, and bell lofts at the top. A curved curtain wall connecting the two pavilions forms the facade.

In matters of the faith no more prodigal monarch has sat upon a European throne than Dom João V of Portugal. In matters of architecture João V looked to Rome. The lists of artists employed by him are studded with the names of Italian or Italian-trained architects, sculptors, and goldsmiths. In this way he succeeded in deflecting Portuguese architecture to some extent from the tradition of the plain style. Early in his reign the king vowed to found a Franciscan convent at Mafra (see Carvalho, fig. 5) to the northwest of Lisbon if his queen, Maria Ana of Austria, should bear him a male heir. The future José I was born in 1714, and work on the religious complex, which instead of housing a small community of Franciscans grew into an immense palace-convent, began in 1717 on the design of João Frederico Ludovice, a silversmith from Regensburg who had been trained in Augsburg and Rome and who came to Lisbon in 1701 to work for the Jesuits. By the time Mafra was completed in 1735 it had come to include a basilica with a two-tower facade, a great library, a royal palace, and a convent occupied by three hundred monks. To the English traveler William Beckford, who visited Mafra in 1794, it "looked like the palace of a giant, and the whole country around it as if the monster had ate it desolate." When the French physician Charles-Frédéric Merveilleux visited the site in 1726, he called it "this desert where King John is building a second Escorial." The quantity of marble that Merveilleux saw being cut and polished left him with the impression that "three-quarters of the king's treasure and the gold brought by the fleets from Brazil have been metamorphosed into stone."

On 22 September 1730 Lord Tyrawley, the British ambassador in Lisbon, wrote a report on Mafra to the British secretary of state, the duke of Newcastle. "I must inform your grace," the ambassador wrote,

that for some months past, the whole business of Portugal has stood quite still, and this, wholly upon account of a church and convent, that the king is building six leagues from Lisbon. It is now some months that the king will not hear of anything else. We compute there may be employed there about fifty thousand men, who work day and night. This has drained the whole country of their laborers, and, consequently, half their lands this year have been left untilled, and has also taken up all sorts of tradesmen in Lisbon for building, finishing, and furnishing this convent. To raise money for this immense expense, the king has taxed all sorts of provisions, some twenty, some thirty, some fifty per cent, which makes it so extravagant living here that I hardly know which way to support myself. But the greatest misfortune is that neither the king nor the secretary of state are to be spoke about any business, because that His Majesty is busy about Mafra.[1]

Impressive as it may be, Mafra is something of a medley of architectural ideas over which Ludovice, a silversmith before he was an architect, did not have firm control or command. Its most distinguished design is also its simplest, the ground level of its three courtyards surrounded by arcades, where the Italian Renaissance formula of arches on piers surmounted by an entablatures resting on engaged columns receives the spatially novel, baroque variation of columns emerging in full roundness surmounted by an enblature with a forcefully projecting cornice. The conception of Mafra as a whole, as well as the flat facade and the narthex of the church in the center of the facade, is derived from the Escorial. The corner pavilions with finialed square domes repeat the corner pavilion of Manuel I's royal palace on the Lisbon waterfront that was rebuilt and enlarged by Felippo Terzi for Philip II in 1581 and was destroyed in the earthquake of 1755 (see cat. 2). The common source for both are the corner towers in an engraving of the Château de Verneuil in Jacques Androuet Du Cerceau's *Premier volume des plus excellents bastiments de France* of 1576. The twin towers of the basilica at Mafra are elaborations of Borromini's towers on the facade of Sant'Agnese in Piazza Navona in Rome. Among Ludovice's assistants at Mafra was Mateus Vicente de Oliveira, who at the end of the eighteenth century, on the commission of Dom João V's granddaughter Maria I, repeated Ludovice's design of the church at Mafra on a smaller scale in the basilica of the Sacred Heart, known as the Estrêla, in Lisbon.

From the time of the accession of Maria I to the throne in 1777 until the Portuguese court moved to Brazil thirty years later, the principal royal residence was the palace of Queluz a short distance to the west of Lisbon (fig. 3). The palace was begun in 1747 by Dom João V's younger son Pedro. The architect in charge of the first building campaign, which ended in 1752, was

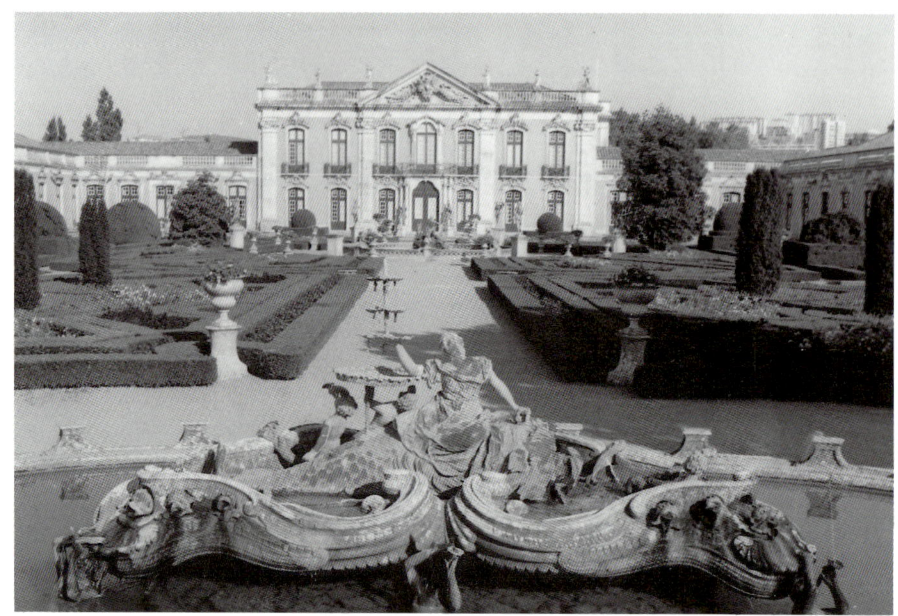

Oliveira. The garden entrance is flanked by two rearing horses mounted by riders holding aloft brass trumpets. The entrance is on axis with the central pavilion, which at ground level contains a glittering hall for official receptions and celebrations. It was there that in 1794 Príncipe João received Beckford. Facing the garden on the north is the pavilion housing the magnificent throne room, a masterpiece of rococo ornament and illusionistic ceiling paintings designed during a second building campaign that was begun in 1758 by the Lisbon wood sculptor Silvestre de Faria Lobo and the French decorator Antoine Collin. The south wing on the opposite side, its corner piers crested by stone sculptures of cannons and military emblems, was constructed during the second campaign in a more severe, classically inspired style by Jean-Baptiste Robillon, who had worked in Paris for the great silversmith Thomas Germain.

The pavilions and wings of Queluz are components of an overall design that includes a series of formal gardens on two levels and a canal, lined with violet and yellow *azulejos,* that is crossed by a bridge in imitation of the canals of Venice. There are two pools with statues of Neptune: one, in the lower garden, carved in stone in which the figure stands on a shell supported by dolphins and tritons in the tradition of Bernini and another, in bronze, in the upper garden in front of the central pavilion, where the statue is surrounded by mythological figures on stone pedestals. On the evening of 14 June 1794, William Beckford recorded "a mysterious kind of fête" in the gardens at Queluz at which

cascades and fountains were in full play; a thousand sportive *jets d'eau* were sprinkling the rich masses of bay and citron, and drawing forth all their odors, as well-taught water is certain to do upon all such occasions. Amongst the thickets, some of which received a tender light from tapers placed low on the ground under frosted glass, the Infanta's nymph-like attendants, all thinly clad after the example of her royal and nimble self, were glancing to and fro, visible one instant, invisible the next, laughing and talking all the while with very musical silvertoned voices. I fancied now and then I heard gruffer sounds; but perhaps I was mistaken.[2]

At such a fete on the day of Saint Peter in 1759, Lord Kinnoul, the British envoy extraordinary to José I, accompanied the royal party

to a pavilion beside a canal on which rode three galleys richly decorated. In one were allegorical personages representing Jupiter and Juno, with Hymen on the stern; in another, Plenty accompanied by Ceres and Cupid, who each recited a speech suited to their character and to the occasion. The entertainment concluded with a grand illumination of the arcade surrounding the garden, round which three illuminated chariots were drawn by horses.[3]

The interior furnishings at Queluz, as at other royal palaces, were at best makeshift except for the ceremonial trappings of the rooms of state. During the nearly eight centuries of the monarchy, the court resided at one time or another in thirteen palaces. When the royal family moved from one of· their many palaces to another they took what furniture they had with them. "Shabby enough they were," Beckford wrote of the antechambers at Queluz in 1794,

bare as many an English country church, and not much less dingy. The beings who were wandering about in this limbo, or intermediate state, belonged chiefly to that species of living furniture which encumber royal palaces — walking chairs, animated screens, commodes and conveniences, to be used by sovereigns in any manner they liked best; men who had little to feed on beside hope and whose rueful physiognomies showed plainly enough the wasting effects of that empty diet.[4]

But when "His Royal Highness was graciously pleased to grant me an audience," Beckford went on, it was in "the long state gallery where the prince habitually receives the homage of the court upon birthdays and festivals — a pompous, richly gilded apartment, set round with colossal vases of porcelain, as tall and as formal as grenadiers."

The most grandiose interior of the southern Portuguese baroque is the royal library of João V presented to the University of Coimbra (fig. 4). The design has been attributed to Ludovice, but comparison with Ludovice's documented buildings does not support this. On the basis of style it is more likely that the designer of the library as a whole, as well as of its sumptuous, elaborate gilded woodcarving, was the French sculptor Claude Laprade, who came to Portugal at the end of the seventeenth century and was active in Aveiro and Coimbra before moving to Lisbon in 1705. Work on the library is recorded from 1716 to 1728. The interior consists of three high rooms connected in the center by arches ornamented with gilded brackets, garlands, and pointed projections at the soffits. A portrait of João V in the center of the third room is flanked by putti holding curtains in simulated polychromed wood. The walls are lined with bookcases in two tiers: the supports of the lower stage were ornamented in 1725 by the Lisbon painter Manuel da Silva with green, scarlet, and gold *chinoiserie* decorations, the same year in which two other painters from Lisbon, António Simões Ribeiro and Vicente Nunes, decorated the ceiling with illusionistic architectural perspectives.

Among Dom João V's religious foundations in Lisbon was the refurbishing of the church at the convent of Madre de Deus (fig. 5), founded by a decree of Manuel I in 1509. Between 1730 and 1750 its plain barrel-vaulted nave was encased in blue and white painted *azulejos*, gilded carved retables, and oil paint-

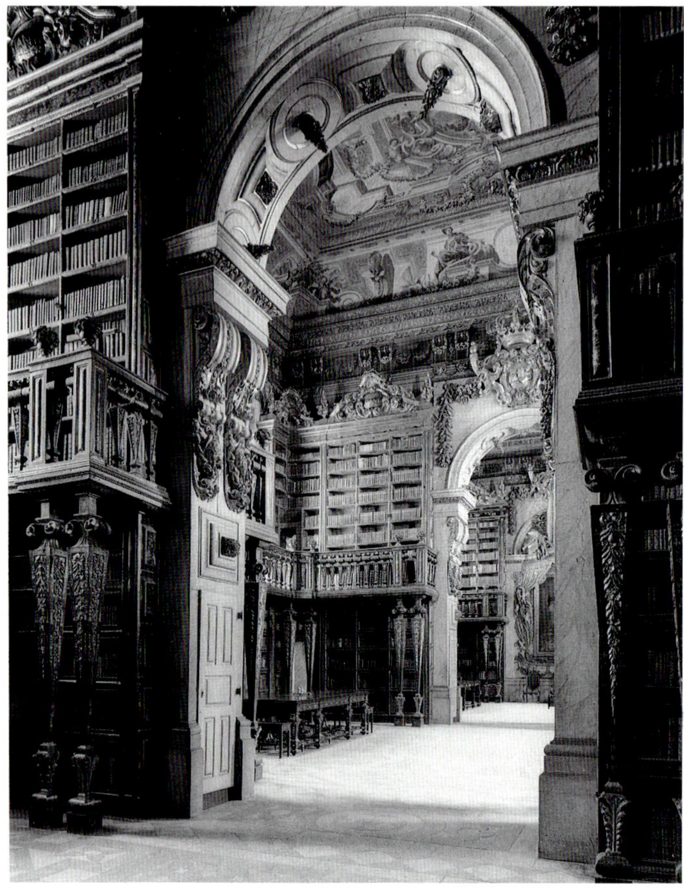

ings in the coffers of the vault. The crossing and apse received gold trim on paneled white surfaces, and the triumphal arch was emblazoned with the royal coat of arms. The western choir loft of the church is overrun with gilding containing paintings of the lives of Franciscan saints. The rich, complex ornamental revetment of the pulpit in the nave of the church, derived from engravings of decorative patterns in Andrea Pozzo's *De perspectiva pictorum et architectorum*, published in Rome in 1693, offers a foretaste of the lavish ornamental vocabulary of the baroque style that evolved in northern Portugal in the second quarter of the eighteenth century.

The northern Portuguese baroque owes its inception to two unrelated phenomena: the spread from Lisbon to Oporto of the style of gilded wood carving that flourished under the patronage of Dom João V, as in the retable with Solomonic columns encircled by vine leaves in the apse of the Madre de Deus, and the arrival in Oporto in 1725 of the Italian-born architect Nicolau Nasoni. An early, enormously influential installation of gilded wood sculpture in Oporto was the decoration in 1730 of the apse of the Gothic church of Santa Clara by the Lisbon wood carver Miguel Francisco da Silva, who moved there in 1726, one year after Nasoni's arrival. The wall panels in the interior of Santa Clara are filled with stylized patterns of husks and garlands and projecting figures of putti below the window zone of the pilasters. Volutes framing cartouches with concave centers above the windows document a link with the early work of Nasoni. The heavy cornices and lambrequins imitating damask and brocade hangings over the doors and windows were to become standard devices in the repertory of designers in the northern provinces.

All the characteristics of the northern Portuguese baroque came into play on the grandest possible scale in the gilded woodwork of the third quarter of the eighteenth century in the originally Gothic interior of São Francisco in Oporto (fig. 6). We can distinguish a sequence of three styles: the closely spaced, small-scale ornament on the arches and ceiling of the nave employs a vocabulary found throughout eighteenth-century Portugal; the central throne of the altar has the flaring lines and graceful rhythms that are distinctive of the north; and the chancel arch and the frame of the high altar, with Solomonic columns girdled in vine leaves, display the style associated with the patronage of João V in Lisbon. The interior as a whole has the aspect of a theatrical, bombastic, gilded stalactite cave.

Shortly before 1725, master carvers from Oporto lined the interior of the apse in the church of the sixteenth-century Dominican convent of Jesus at Aveiro with a sheath of closely woven gilded woodwork that, in the ceiling, simulates late Gothic vaulting of the Portuguese Manueline style of the late fifteenth and early sixteenth centuries, an explicit reference to the affinity between the Manueline and the eighteenth-century styles of architectural decoration. Both arose during periods of sudden, enormous wealth. Both were patronized by and reflected the ambitions of sovereigns: Manuel I, the recipient of the riches that resulted from the discovery by Portuguese navigators of the sea route to India, and João V, the beneficiary of the gold and diamonds of Brazil. Both were espoused by monarchs who wished to celebrate their own and their nation's prosperity in works of architecture. And both the Manueline style and the Portuguese baroque coincided with epochs during which reperto-

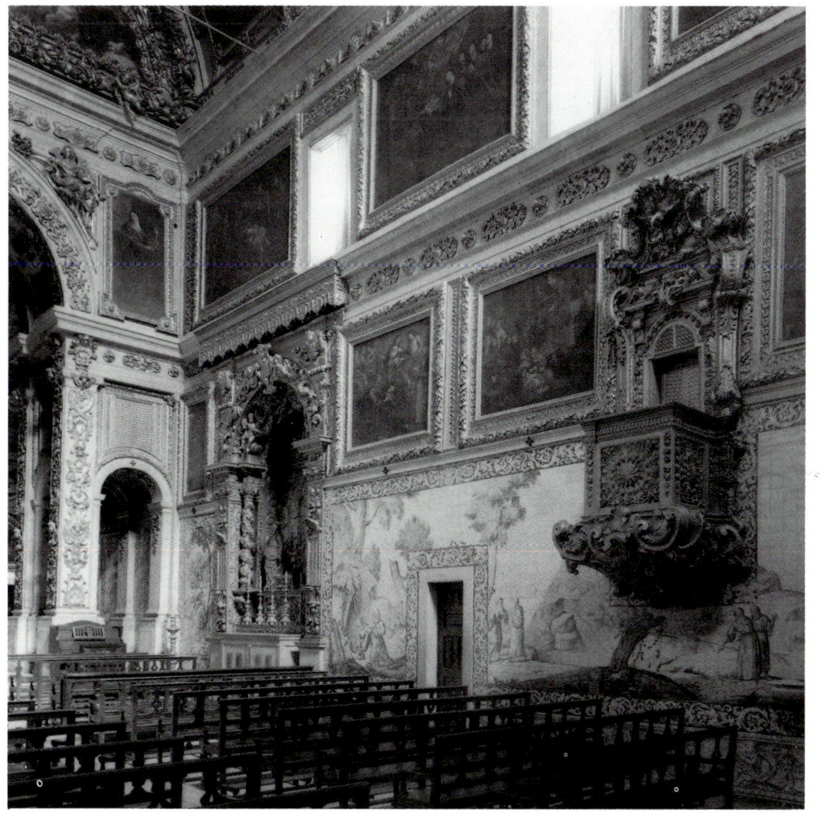

fig. 5. *Madre de Deus*, Lisbon, interior as redecorated 1730–1750. The pulpit is visible at the right

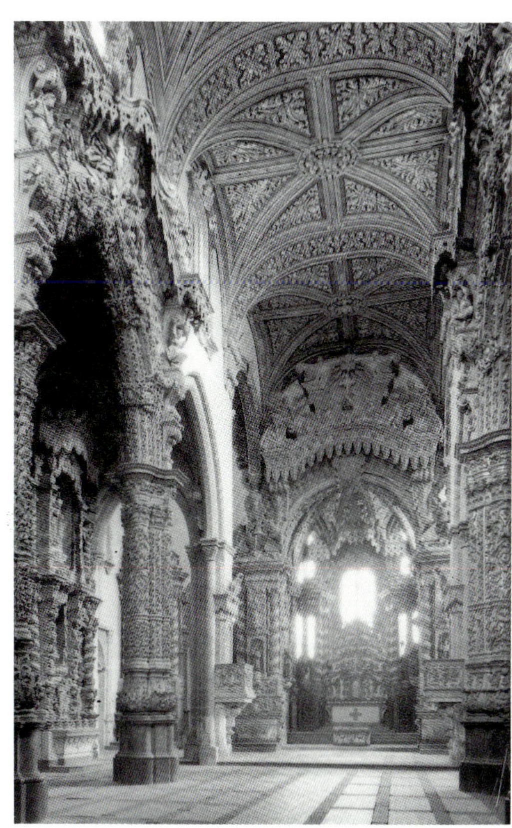

fig. 6. *São Francisco*, Oporto, showing the woodwork dating from the third quarter of the eighteenth century

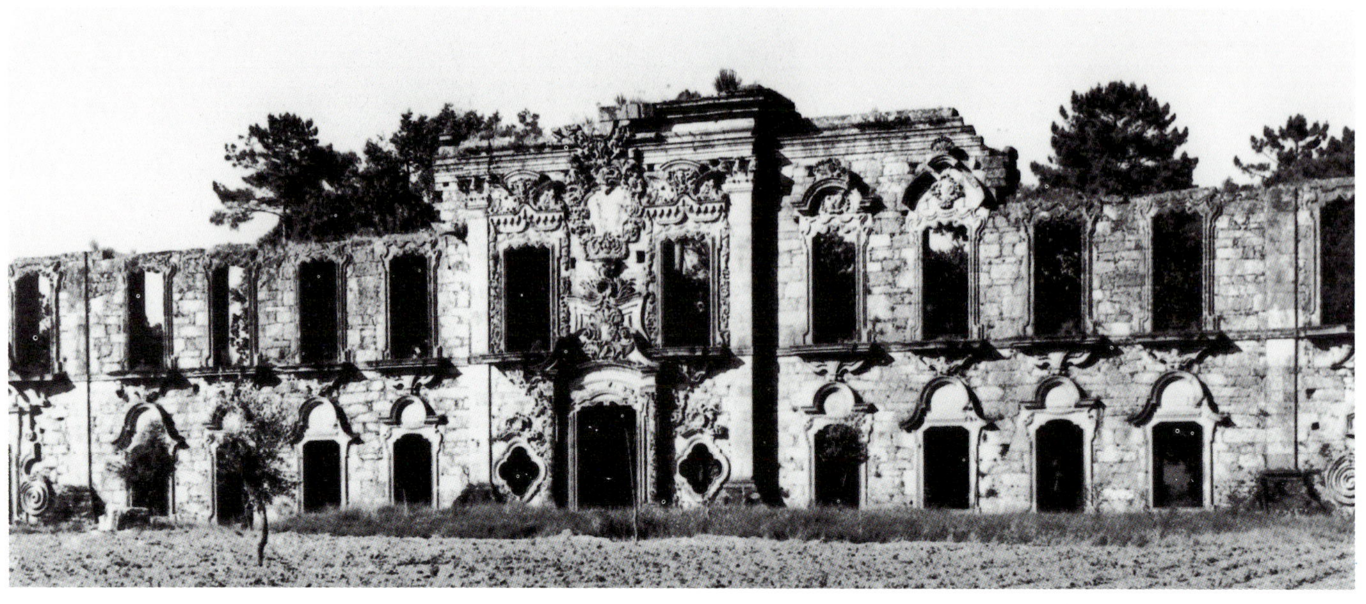

fig. 7. *Facade of Portocarreiro Residence,* Vila Boa de Quires, c. 1745–1750

ries of elaborate ornament were in vogue in Europe and available to Portuguese designers in the form of engravings.

The most astonishing and bizarre monument of the Portuguese baroque (fig. 7) is a wall that divides fields of hay and potatoes on one side from a grove of trees on the other in Vila Boa de Quires, a village northeast of Oporto. Here an unknown Spanish architect worked from 1745 to 1750 on a palatial country residence for the Portocarreiro family. The first thing he built was not the foundations on which the structure would rest, but the facade. Before it was finished the project was abandoned. The intricately ornamented facade is thus all of the project that remains, a ruin of what never came into being. It is the backdrop for a scenario composed not of stately coaches, uniformed footmen, and bewigged lords and ladies, but of a peasant family planting and harvesting hay and potatoes. The facade's teeming surcharge of ornamentation is the direct heir in stone of the fantastic shells, vegetative motifs, overhanging cornices, and lambrequins of Oporto woodcarving. Only the frame for the coat of arms over the central portal has been left empty.

A very different concept of ornament governs the facade of the Lobo Machado house built by an unknown architect in Guimarães, the birthplace of the Portuguese nation, between 1750 and 1775. Introduced to Portugal by Nasoni, this concept was developed with dazzling virtuosity by the great architect of the city of Braga, André Soares. It depends for its effectiveness not on the encrustation or masking of the wall with a screen of overall decoration as at Vila Boa de Quires, but on the contrast between the lightness of white or tiled walls and the weight of banded layers of ornamented granite applied to and framing them. It is characterized by monumental scaling and by the tendency of ornament to dominate its architectural support, escaping the logic of tectonic constraints to the point of assuming the function of a structural shell or body. The decoration of the Portocarreiro facade is a translation into stone of the gilded woodwork in the interior of Oporto churches. The ornament at the Lobo Machado house has more diverse origins. Its vocabulary of decorative motifs is borrowed, by way of engravings, from the repertory of late seventeenth-century *rocaille* patterns, from the forms of Italian cabinetmakers and

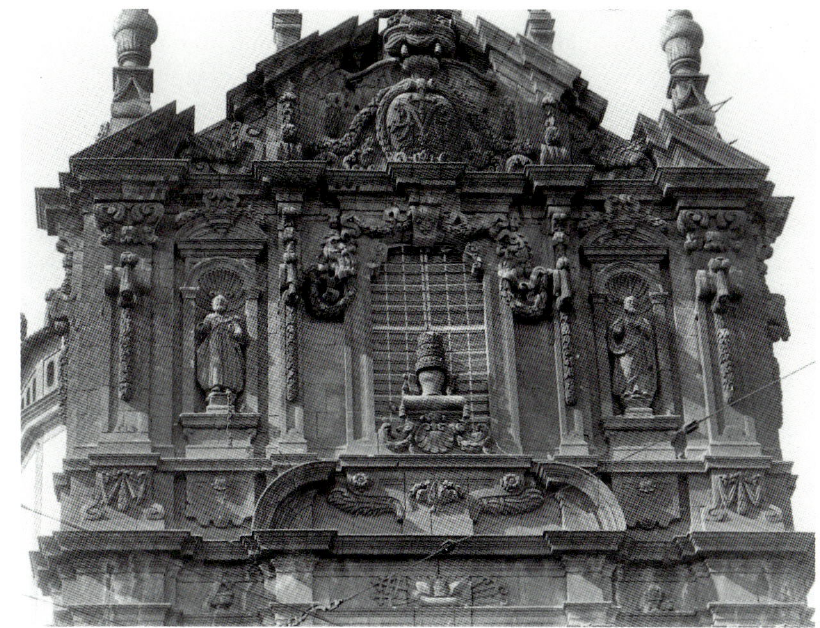

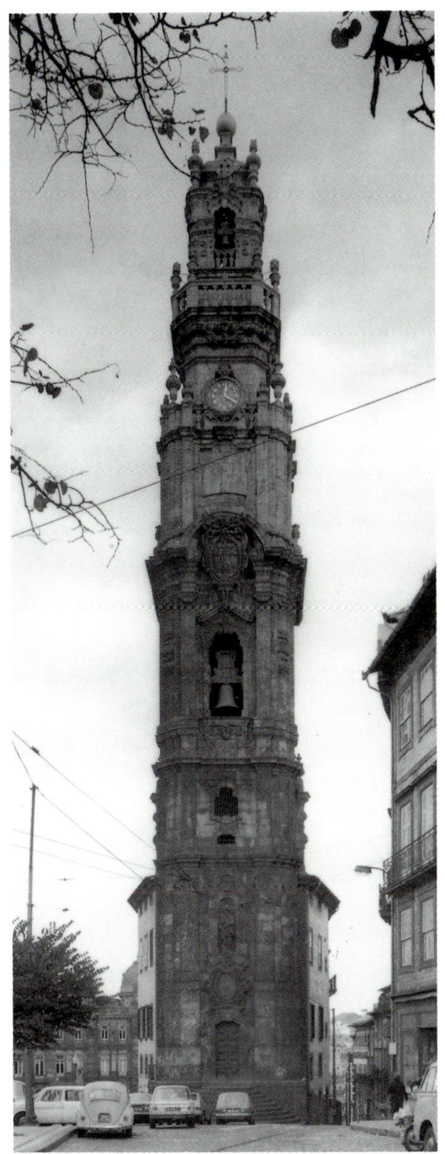

silversmiths, and from the German *Ohrmuschelstil,* an inflated variant of the French *rocaille* specializing in asymmetrical shellwork and foliage. The concept of ornament as a structural shell or body, however, is Portuguese. It is implied in the massive bands of granite on plain white walls of such northern Portuguese seventeenth-century buildings as the parish church at Anadia near Viseu, and it has its roots in the sixteenth- and seventeenth-century Portuguese tradition of cellular wall structures, such as the great late sixteenth-century Palladian cloister by Diogo de Torralva at the convent of Christ at Tomar or the ten-foot-thick lateral walls of the late seventeenth-century church of Santa Clara-a-Nova at Coimbra. Guimarães is on the way from Oporto to Braga, and the ornamentation of the exterior of the Lobo Machado house repeats variations of motifs developed in both cities. The volutes and the inverted pediments over the windows belong to the style of Nasoni at Oporto, while the swinging lines of the cornice are characteristic of facades by André Soares at Braga.

Nicolau Nasoni was a native of San Giovanni Valdarno in Tuscany. He was trained as an architect and illusionistic ceiling painter in Siena. He then worked in Malta and came to Oporto in 1725 at the invitation of a family associated with the order of Malta in order to modernize the city's Romanesque cathedral. His chief contribution to it is the massive, bizarre porch on its northern flank. In 1731 the Brotherhood of the Clergy at Oporto chose Nasoni as the architect for their new church on a site that slopes down toward the west. Nasoni took advantage of this by designing a tall western facade preceded by a double staircase, placing the *campanile* at the site's highest point to the east, and connecting the two with the continuous white, granite-trimmed exterior walls of an oval nave, a rectangular sanctuary, and a house of the clergy in the form of a hairpin. Not the least original component of the Clérigos church, on which Nasoni was active until 1750, is the combination of the low oval nave and rectangular sanctuary with the high facade pavilion. The design of the facade is derivative of Roman seventeenth-century churches. Its indented pediment is a specific citation of Carlo Rainaldi's facade of Santa Maria

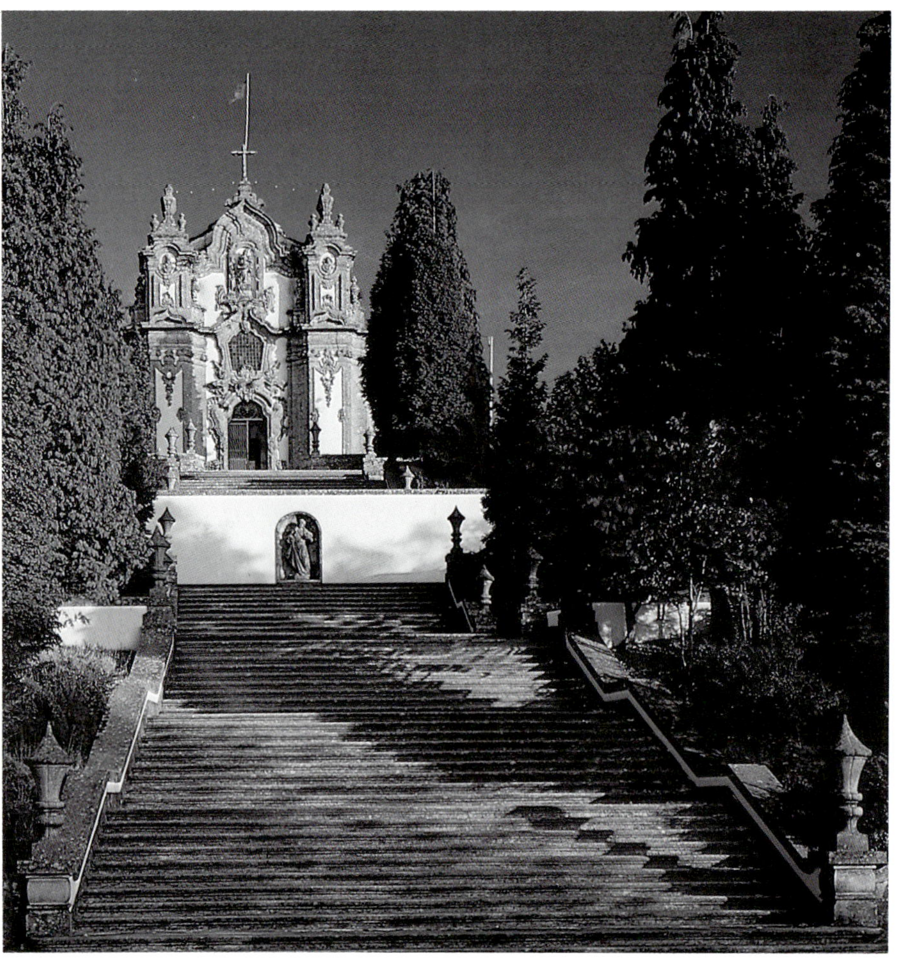

in Campitelli. To it, however, Nasoni added the tall, cone-shaped pinnacles that are characteristic of northern Portuguese churches. Because of the sloping site, the floor of the nave is at the level of the upper landing of the double staircase, and the entrance to the nave is behind the facade at the right. The lower door on the level of the platform in the center of the double staircase gives access to the crypt.

Three types of ornament appear in the decoration of the facade (fig. 8): the oval disk in the pediment with the monogram of the Virgin and garlands, volutes, acanthus brackets, and panels with shells and rosettes related to the vocabulary of illusionistic ceiling painting; the frieze between the lower and upper stories with liturgical emblems — a censer, an incense boat, a hyssop bowl, episcopal croziers, and papal crosses — modeled on silver vessels; and the baldachin in the upper story with realistically carved curtains and tassels under the broken cornice taken from the repertory of gilded wood carving in the interiors of Oporto churches. Under the baldachin a metal papal tiara rests on a stone cushion, a reference to the papal brief by which in 1710 Clement XI authorized the formation of the Brotherhood of the Clergy. The *campanile* (fig. 9), built in six sections to a height of 250 feet, punctuates the skyline of the city like a giant pin. In contrast to the facade, its design is not embroidered with rich ornament, but emphasizes the elegant articulation of its volumes and shapes. The corners on the side toward the house of the clergy are rectangular. On the side facing away from the church they are rounded, providing an occasion for the application of a series of handsome moldings that accompany the tower's upward thrust. Within the shell of its exterior walls an inner octagonal core rises to a corbeled balcony that encircles the terminal belfry. These crowning elements, as well as the tower's independence from the church and isolation against the sky, recall the tower of the Palazzo Vecchio in Florence and other *campanili* in Nasoni's native Tuscany.

Nasoni was also the architect of one of Portugal's most magnificent country houses, the Casa de Mateus (see fig. 1), a magnificent *solar* in the province of Tras-os-Montes that he designed between 1739 and 1743. The *solar,* a word derived from the Latin *solium,* meaning ground, is the residence of the Portuguese nobility, usually but not invariably in the country. It is also the emblematic and symbolic expression of the family's identity, unity, and continuity. The institution of the *solar* originated soon after the foundation of Portugal as an independent nation in the thirteenth century, when each nobleman had control over a district called a *terra,* a word that signifies both the land and the place where one comes from. The first half of the eighteenth century, coinciding with the reign of João V, was the golden age of the Portuguese nobility and of the *solar.* Nasoni built several besides the Casa de Mateus. Others *solares* were influenced by his designs, such as the Casa do Cabo in Santo João da Pesqueira. There the family crest over the central portal is modestly scaled in comparison with its proud and lofty display at the Casa de Mateus. But the family *escudo* can assume even greater prominence. In the Casa de A Barros at Moimento da Beira, for example, the inflected curved pediment at the center of the facade bearing the family crest is of truly regal proportions, so that its size and decorative opulence, when seen from the round landing below the double staircase leading to the central portal, dominate and overshadow the rest of the facade.

The plan of the Casa de Mateus is a variant of the U-plan of Italian sixteenth-century villas and seventeenth-century French townhouses. A ground-level vaulted passage in the center of the main block connects an open exterior court of honor with an enclosed interior courtyard. At either side of this passage a double staircase ascends to the central portal of the facade at the level of the *piano nobile.* To the left of the main block is the chapel. Pinnacles of the proportion of minarets, scaled to the ample dimensions of the plan, stand like sentinels at the corners of the cornice, providing vertical accents that act as a counterpoint to the building's predominant horizontality. In contrast to the rich ornamentation of the facade and the roofline of the central pavilion, the inner and outer flanks are relatively plain. A balcony, from which members of the family could assist at religious processions on their way to the chapel, projects from the outer left flank of the court of honor. The facade of the chapel, encased by a triumphal arch with a single span resting on paired columns and surmounted by a massive frontispiece, rises to the height necessary for it to hold its own in relation to the house when seen from a distance. A simpler and smaller version of the chapel by an anonymous architect, which shows the influence of Nasoni especially in the ornament surrounding the oculus above the entrance portal, is the Capela Nova of the Brotherhood of the Clergy in nearby Vila Real.

Beginning in the last quarter of the seventeenth century, Braga became a center for the employment of *appliqué* or *accroché* patterns of exterior ornament

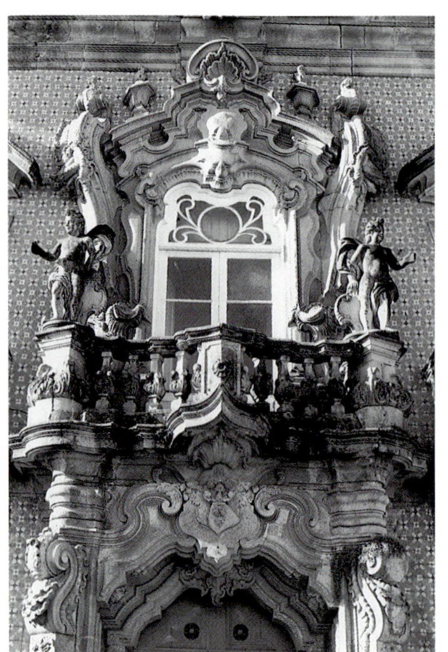

fig. 11. André Soares, *Casa do Raio*, Braga, detail of facade, c. 1753–1755

designed to disguise and mask the severity of church facades and interiors. At São Vicente, for example, large stone swags and garlands festoon the windows and tablets of an otherwise perfectly plain rectangular facade. In the early eighteenth century, craftsmen from Braga carved a hanging of gilded woodwork for the triumphal arch of the chilly, austere interior of São Bento da Vitoria in Oporto. The tradition at Braga of architects and craftsmen who clothed and encased the plain walls of contemporary and earlier churches in massive, luxurious systems of ornamentation had its most brilliant and original exponent in André Soares. Among his early works, built between 1753 and 1755, are the pilgrimage chapel of Santa Maria Madalena do Monte da Falperra (fig. 10), just outside Braga, and the townhouse known as the Casa do Raio, designed for Manuel Duarte de Faria, the paymaster of the religious brotherhood that awarded Soares the commission for the Falperra chapel. The Falperra chapel is designed on a septagonal plan with a false front and projecting twin towers. The ornamentation of the facade is a sophisticated, bold fusion of the two components that were instrumental in forging the novel concept of ornament as a structural shell or body: the Portuguese tradition of thick, cellular walls and the convoluted patterns of the French *rocaille* and the German *Ohrmuschelstil*. In the Casa do Raio (fig. 11) the powerfully projecting decoration of portals and windows anticipates the designs of Antonio Gaudí, a century and a half later, in suggesting that the stability of the building is called into question by the ornament's surge and flow. In the doorway, variously shaped frilled fans, bosses, and volutes sheathed in corrugated shellwork extend beyond their frames in a multiplicity of planes like tropical vegetation.

André Soares also worked as a designer of gilded woodwork, a medium in which he achieved his greatest triumph in the interior of São Martinho (fig. 12) at Tibães, the Portuguese headquarters of the Benedictines. Its monumental decorations were designed by Soares in 1756 and 1757 and carved by his collaborator José Álvarez from 1757 to 1760. With the emblem of the Benedictines displayed under the oculus at the top of the valence that masks the bare profile of the triumphal arch, the interior of Tibães is a flamboyantly theatrical expres-

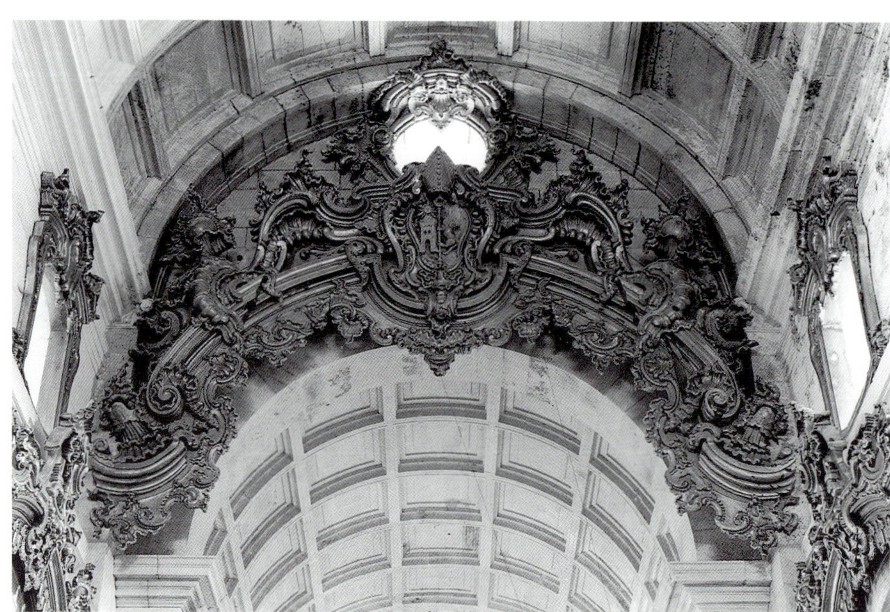

fig. 12. André Soares, *São Martinho*, Tibaes, detail of woodwork carved by José Álvarez, 1756–1760

fig. 13. Carlos Luís Ferreira Amarante, *Nossa Senhora do Popolo*, Braga, 1775–1780

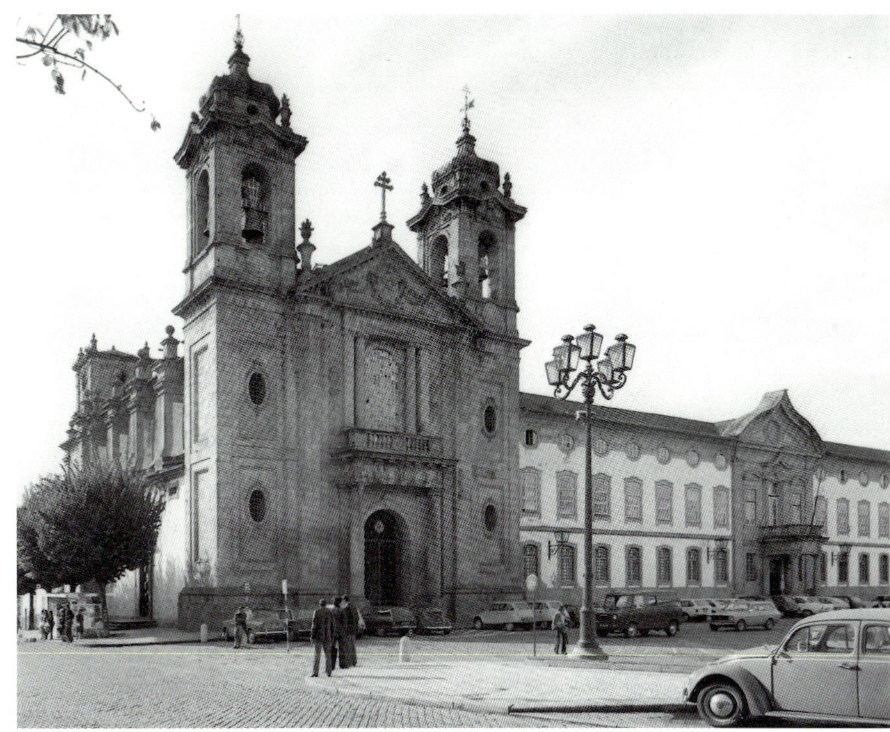

sion of the Benedictine order's power and wealth. It is also the finest ensemble in Portugal of baroque gilded wood sculpture. When, on the other hand, the civil authorities of Braga asked Soares in 1753 to build them a new town hall, he demonstrated that his mastery of the restrained, traditional plain style equaled his command and inventiveness as a designer of ornament. Constructed between 1753 and 1756, the Casa da Camara at Braga shows restraint even in the embellishment of the facade's central axis. Giant volutes project on either side of the portal, and in the second story a canopy in the form of a huge leaf surmounts the niche containing a statue of the Virgin.

Following the deaths of Soares in 1769 and of Nasoni in 1773, there was a shift away from baroque forms in northern Portugal. In large measure the English wine merchants at Oporto, and especially the British consul John Whitehead, an amateur architect who favored a clean, Palladian, neoclassical vocabulary, influenced this change. In 1786 Whitehead built, for the English colony in the city, the neoclassical British Factory House. The impact of these developments can be seen in the work of the Braga architect Carlos Luís Ferreira Amarante, whose design of Nossa Senhora do Populo (fig. 13), built between 1775 and 1780, employs a neoclassical repertory of Doric and Ionic columns framing the central portal and window, and of rectangular, undecorated paneling in the zone of the towers. Only the towers themselves retain something of the exuberance of the baroque.

Amarante was also the designer of the last stages of the ceremonial pilgrimage staircase and of the church at Bom Jesus do Monte (fig. 14), north of Braga. The church was begun in 1784 and completed in 1811, the year in which the duke of Wellington drove the French from Portuguese soil. The double staircase with nine landings that leads up to the church is flanked at ground level by two unornamented octagonal chapels. The balustrades of its nine landings are surmounted by stone urns and by statues of Christian allegorical

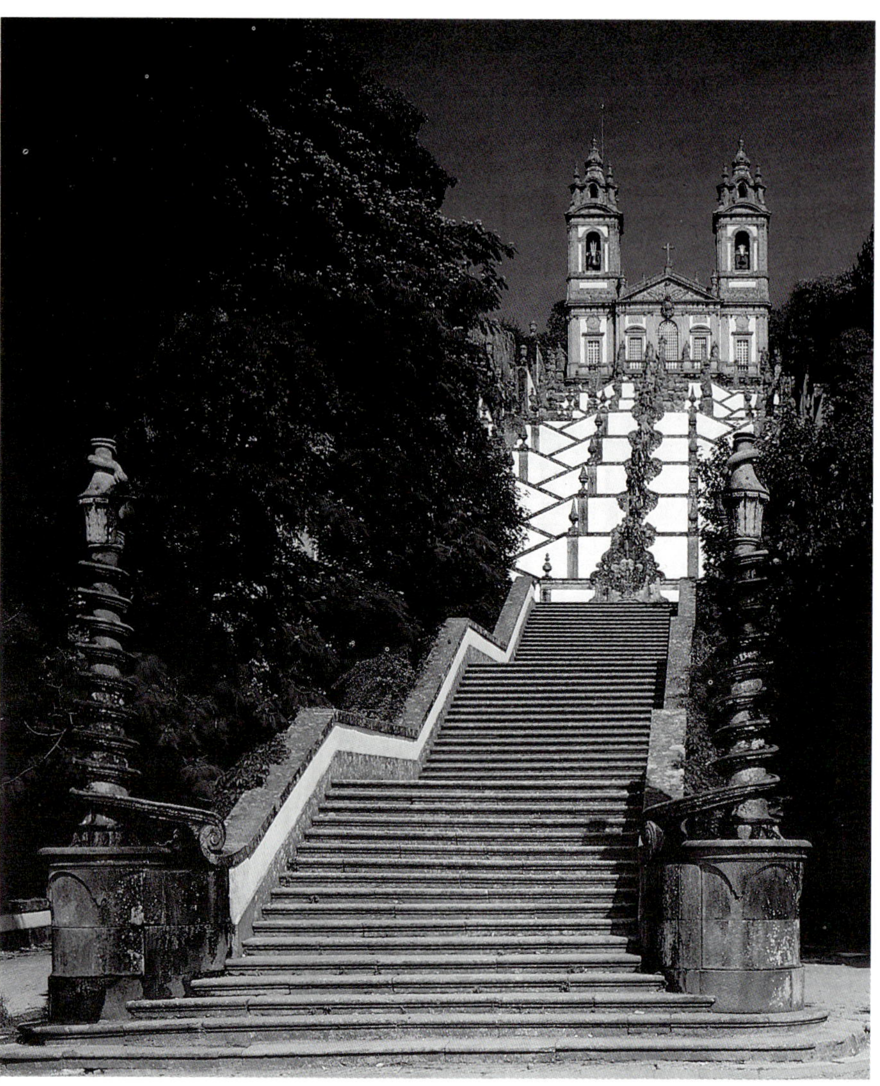

personifications. The church facade, with its Doric entrance portal, straight cornices, undecorated window frames, and Ionic pilasters in the upper story, is an instructive example of the adaptation of neoclassical forms to the persistent tradition of the Portuguese plain style. At another pilgrimage site, dedicated to Nossa Senhora dos Remédios (fig. 15) and constructed between 1750 and 1760 on a high wooded hill outside Lamego to the east of Oporto, a similar double staircase with nine landings and with white walls trimmed in granite ascends to a circular court surrounded by granite pillars crowned with stone figures of Old Testament kings in exotic hats and classical togas. In the center a tall obelisk rises from a scalloped fountain, and at the east end of the court the staircase continues upward toward the terrace in front of the church. Its facade is decorated with a flattened, routine version of the ornamental repertory of the baroque of Oporto and Braga.

After the waning of the baroque in the two regional centers of Oporto and Braga, its curvilinear ornamental forms persisted in centers of northern Portugal that in matters of architecture took their cue from and thus lagged behind them. The Misericórdia church at Viseu (fig. 16) to the south of Lamego, begun in 1775, is related to Nossa Senhora dos Remédios in the swinging forms of the crowning central pediment and in the flattened treatment of the orna-

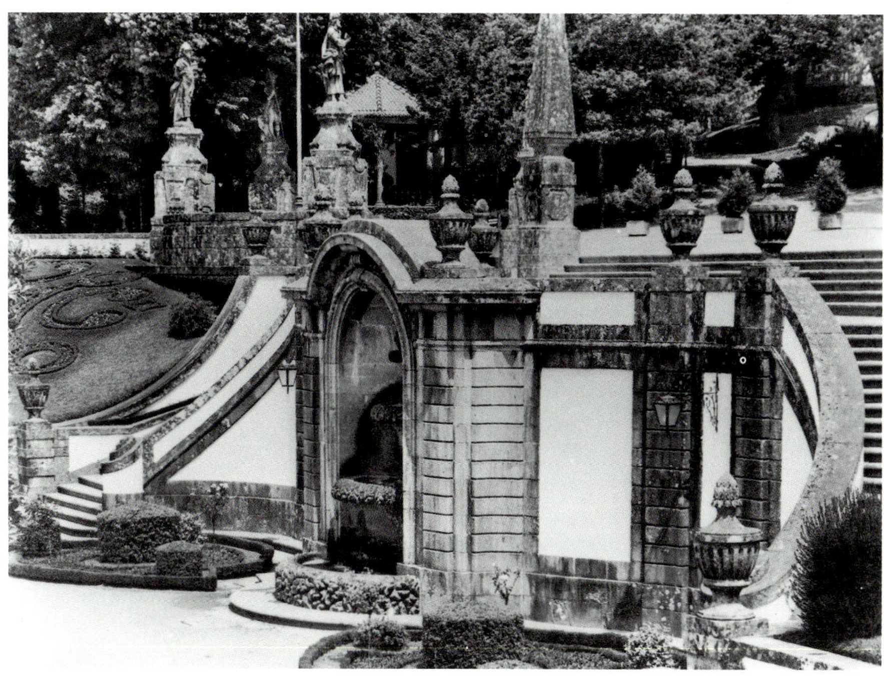

fig. 15. *Nossa Senhora dos Remédios*, Lamego, 1750–1760

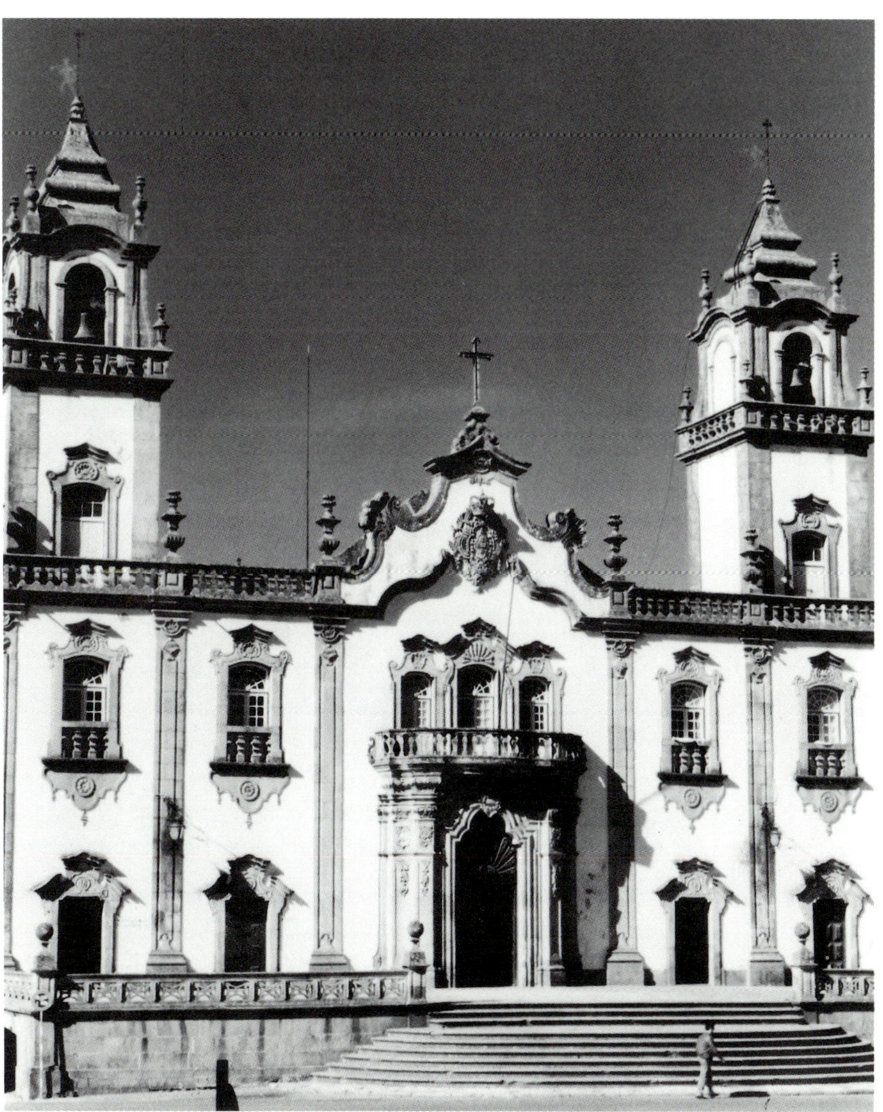

fig. 16. *Church of the Misericórdia*, Viseu, begun 1775

mental surrounds of the facade. It is, however, a far more successful and unified design than the Remédios church, and in this respect it is a fine example of the innate, intuitive feeling of Portuguese designers and builders for the justness of scale and proportion.

The flattening and simplification of ornament that are general characteristics of Portuguese architecture at the end of the eighteenth century were accompanied in the treatment of exterior walls by great elegance in the shaping and spacing of dark granite trim in relation to the whitewashed surfaces that it frames and contains. The chapel of São Bartolomeo outside Trancoso, east of Viseu, was built in 1786 to 1787 on the site of an earlier structure in front of which the Portuguese king Dinis married Isabel of Aragon in 1282. Both simple and sophisticated, the chapel itself is a kind of marriage, harmonious and lighthearted, of the Portuguese traditions of the plain style and the northern baroque.

The prosperity of the regional centers of northern Portugal during the second half of the eighteenth century was due not only to the favorable trade terms with England, but also to the policies of the remarkable Portuguese statesman who became known as the marquês de Pombal. In 1737 he inherited from his uncle Paolo de Carvalho e Ataide, an archpriest of the Lisbon Patriarchate, a property at Oeiras on the northern bank of the Tagus to the west of Lisbon on which he constructed a spacious palace in the midst of gardens, vineyards, pools, and farmlands (fig. 17). The upper and lower levels of the garden are connected by a double staircase containing a fountain lined in blue and white *azulejos* and surmounted on either side of its balustrade by allegorical marble statues. By 1739, construction of the palace was under way. For his personal emblem, Pombal retained the eight-pronged star that had also been the

fig. 17. Carlos Mardel, *Palace of the Marquês de Pombal,* Oeiras, after 1739

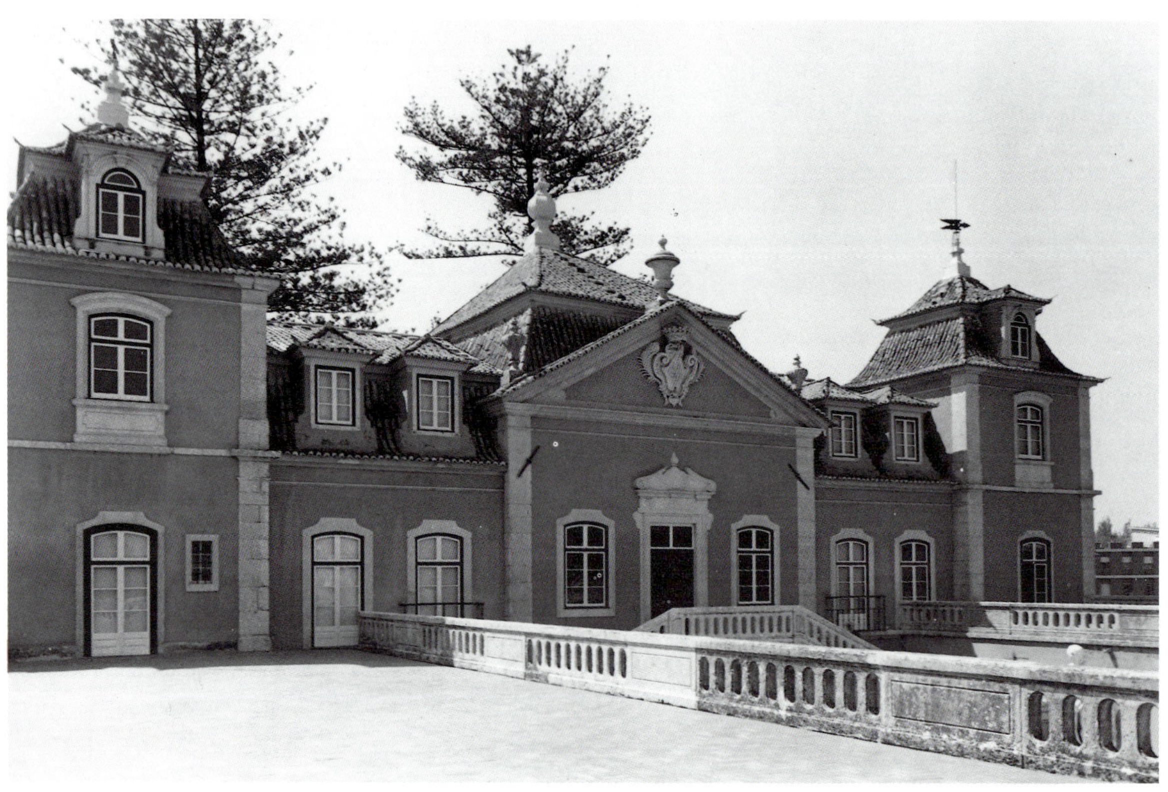

device of his uncle. It appears under a cardinal's hat and a bishop's miter on the wall enclosing the court of honor of the palace at Oeiras in testimony of the fact that when the palace was built ownership of the property was still in his uncle's name. The local land register did not list the owner as the "conde e senhor de Oeiras" until 1767. The roofs of the court of honor that precedes the main block of the palace serve as terraces for the *piano nobile,* which is reached at the center of the facade by a double staircase. The block of the facade is divided into five units, with windows in groups of two, three, and two in the three central bays, and turrets surmounted by concavely planed double-hipped roofs, a motif imported from Central Europe, at the corners. Over the doors at the sides of the court of honor are Pombal's eight-pronged stars, now unencumbered by the uncle's ecclesiastical emblems. At the western end of the formal garden is the handsome *adega* that was used for the making, aging, and storing of wine, with busts of Roman emperors on the exterior piers. The most spectacular of the palace's outlying structures is a monumental staircase flanked by granite pylons topped by stone urns and flanked by blue-and-white tiled walls. Above the staircase is a cascade, and below it, enclosed by walls decorated with mural-sized *azulejo* compositions of marine subjects, is a pool that in the eighteenth century was stocked with fish.

The architect of Pombal's palace was Carlos Mardel, a native of Hungary who had taken part in the wars of the Habsburg Empire and had worked in Poland, England, and France. Like his Portuguese contemporaries he had been trained to design buildings in both a formal baroque and a straightforward, utilitarian vocabulary. He possessed remarkable sensitivity for the aesthetic properties of each. In 1739 he designed for João V the Galvao-Mexia house—legend has it that the king built it for his mistress Soror Paula — in the northern outskirts of Lisbon. Construction appears to have been completed by 1744, the date on one of the *azulejo* panels in the interior. The composition of the facade, thirteen bays divided into five groups by colossal pilasters with an ascending curved pediment over the central segment, became a prototype for eighteenth-century townhouses and *solares* throughout Portugal. Reduced to nine bays in groups of three, it is the scheme of André Soares' great Casa da Camara at Braga.

Mardel arrived in Portugal in 1733. In 1735 he received his first royal appointment, an assignment to work as military and civil engineer with the rank of Sergeant-Major on the Lisbon aqueduct, which had been begun in 1732 under the direction of the Italian architect and engineer Antonio Canevari. From 1745 until his death in 1763 Mardel was the architect in charge of the aqueduct and of other works connected with the distribution of water in the city of Lisbon. In 1745 he submitted to the crown a plan for the Cais Novo, a redevelopment project for the Lisbon docks. He was named architect of the royal palace in 1747, and architect of the military orders and of the Lisbon fortifications in 1749. The first report to the crown signed by Mardel as architect in charge of the aqueduct is dated 4 June 1745 and deals with the majestic pointed arches spanning the Alcântara valley. These were declared finished in 1746. By September 1748, six lanterns had been installed over the arches, the triumphal arch framing one of the terminal arches had been built, and work was in progress on the reservoir (fig. 18). Its interior, composed of nine cross vaults of equal height resting on plain walls and on four freestanding square piers that rise

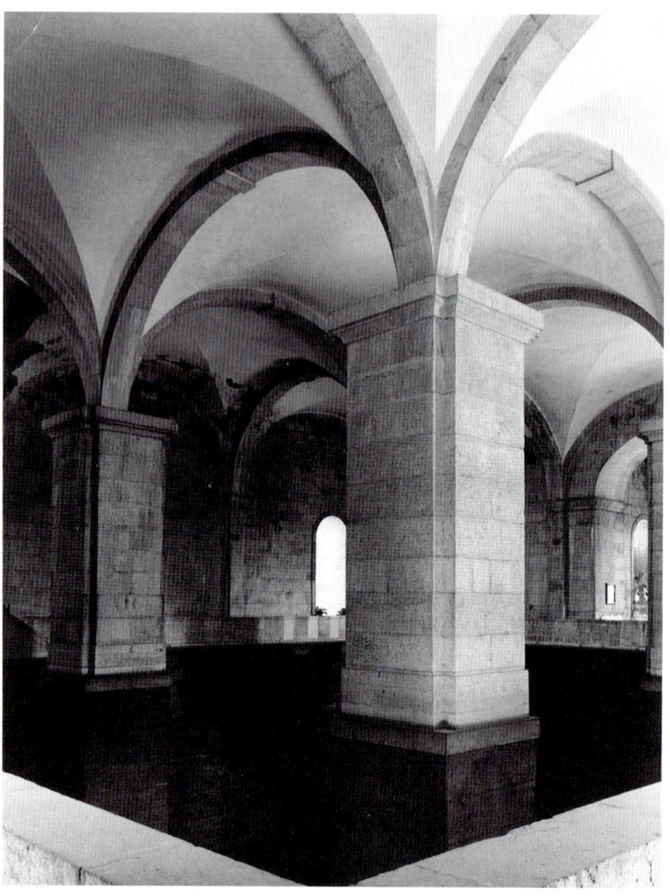

from a deep basin surrounded by walks on four sides, recalls the design of Portuguese hall churches of the first half of the sixteenth century. The construction of the interior piers and walls is described in the report of 23 October 1750. Activity at the reservoir is reported for the last time on 12 June 1754.

On 15 November 1752, José I approved plans and elevations signed by Mardel for four fountain projects for the distribution of water in various parts of the city. Only two of these were built. The simpler of the two is the Rato fountain within sight of the reservoir. It is surmounted by a lantern that is an unornamented version of one that crowns Mardel's nearby triumphal arch. The reports to the crown place its construction between April and November 1753, and it is mentioned as in operation in a royal decree of 24 August 1754. The fountain at the Largo da Esperança (fig. 19), constructed between December 1756 and May 1758, is of the same type, with a lower basin at street level and an upper basin on a raised platform reached by stairs at either end and protected by a balustrade in front. In its carefully phrased interplay of site, massing, and detail, placed against a house front, with a pediment on flat pilasters providing a transition between the highly articulated spatial forms of the fountain and the plain surface against which it stands, the Esperança fountain is one of Mardel's most surefooted works.

His most brilliant, sophisticated fountain design, however, is in the Rua do Seculo, to the east of the reservoir. The fountain is not mentioned in the reports to the crown, but its composition and the vocabulary of its aedicule—smooth Tuscan pilasters placed against strips of rustication, sections of a Doric frieze with sharply cut triglyphs and guttae, and a forcefully projecting pediment recessed in the center—leave no doubt that Mardel was its author. Within the taut geometry of these forms, curvilinear, scalloped rococo frames surround fields of polished stone. Like the Esperança fountain, the design shows Mardel's sensitivity in adapting the structure to its site. The fountain is placed at the end of a square cut into steeply rising terrain. Three sides of the square are lined with high walls of smooth, finely cut stone (the fourth is open to the street). Mardel placed the fountain at the center of the end wall in the form of a flat aedicule and a single low basin set on a wide pentagonal platform with five steps. The fountain was in operation by 7 September 1760, when a royal decree assigned the overflow from it to the palace in the Rua do Seculo, the Lisbon residence of Sebastião de Carvalho, not yet named marquês de Pombal but by then the most powerful man in Portugal.

Pombal had great power from the time of his appointment as minister of war and foreign affairs in 1750. But it took an extraordinary event to make him dictator of his country. At 9:30 on the morning of All Saints Day in 1755, when much of the population of Lisbon was in church, a rumbling sound was heard. Then there was a pause. Then a violent two-minute shock brought roofs, walls, and facades crashing down. Another pause, and a third shock completed the destruction. A dark fog of dust arose from the ruins, and the brilliant day turned to night. An hour later, three enormous waves reared up offshore and plummeted over the devastated city. All light structures on the shore were washed away; ships were torn from their moorings and smashed. But in the end it was the fires that destroyed most of the city's material wealth; fanned by a brisk northeast wind, they burned for a week. Between ten and fifteen thousand people were crushed, burned, or drowned in the earthquake and the ensuing holocaust. Pombal moved quickly, in the words of the marquês de

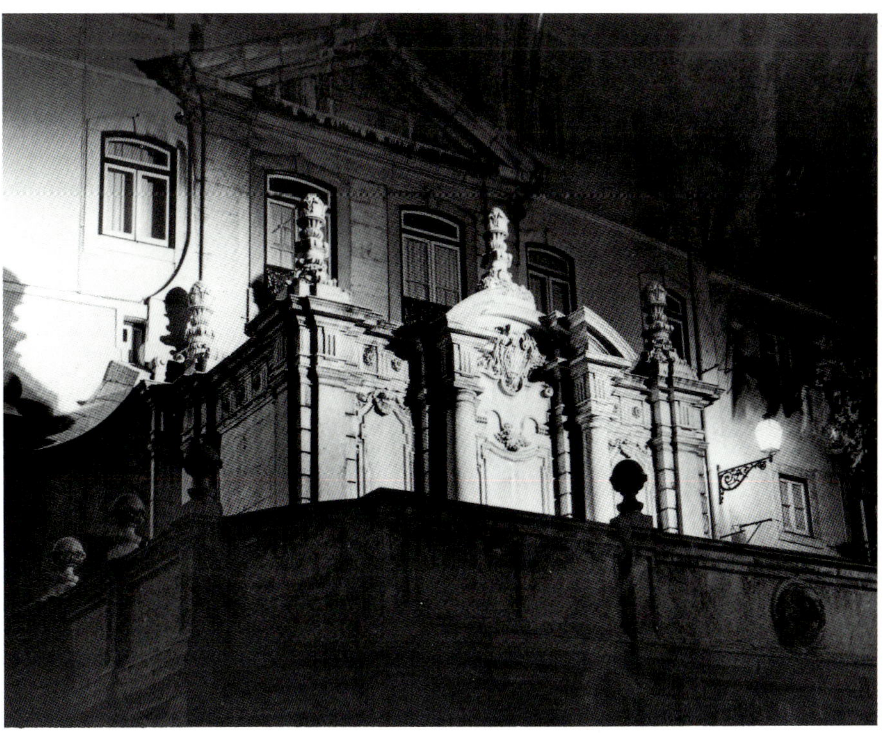

fig. 19. Carlos Mardel, *Largo da Esperança Fountain,* Lisbon, 1756–1758

Alorna, to "bury the dead, care for the living, and close the ports."[4] He organized the relief of the city and he brought in the royal engineer-architects Manuel da Maia, Eugénio dos Santos, Carlos Mardel, and others, first to deal with the disaster and then to rebuild the destroyed central part of the city according to an efficient, rational plan. The new center of Lisbon, rising from its ashes in uniform blocks of five-story buildings, broad, straight, paved, and well-lit streets, and with a well-functioning sewage system, was the first large-scale standardized urban reconstruction program in Europe.

Construction on the royal palace at Queluz had come to a halt between the end of the first building campaign in 1752 and the beginning of the second campaign in 1758, the same year in which Pombal approved the final plan for the rebuilding of Lisbon. The contrast between Queluz and the new Lisbon of Pombal goes to the heart of a conflict in Portuguese eighteenth-century architecture and society that came to the fore following the earthquake of 1755. The palace and gardens and Queluz correspond less to present needs than to the wish symbolically to express and perpetuate the idea of royalty. The architecture of the court, no less than religious building of the time, was governed by ritual and ceremony, constituting a domain apart from the world around it. In contrast, the new Lisbon of Pombal was not an ideal project, but an empirical solution to a disaster.

The fact that Manuel da Maia, Eugénio dos Santos, and Carlos Mardel were civil and military engineers offered them singular advantages for the task before them. Manuel da Maia, the chief engineer of the kingdom, with experience in city planning and in problems of construction relating to the safety and hygiene of streets, prepared a proposal on the rebuilding of the city that he presented to Pombal in three installments in 1755 and 1756. In the first part of his proposal da Maia suggested four alternative approaches to the reconstruction. The first, to rebuild the destroyed section as it had been, seemed inadvisable because it would not improve the city and would not render it less vulnerable to future earthquakes. The second, to improve the existing plan by widening its streets, had massive economic and practical disadvantages. The third alternative was to rebuild the destroyed center of the city with a new plan. The fourth proposed a new city on the banks of the Tagus to the west. Da Maia himself favored the last suggestion, which would have connected the new city with a new royal residence that would have replaced the waterfront palace destroyed by the earthquake. Pombal preferred the third solution. Accordingly, it was decided that the *baixa*, the central section of the city from the river northward, should be rebuilt. Less than three weeks after da Maia had submitted his first report, he received orders from Pombal to study the downtown site and the embankment where it meets the river.

In the second installment of his proposal, da Maia addressed the practical problem of razing, clearing, and expropriating property and of relocating residents. There he first proposed the concept of uniformity for the new city. The third part of the proposal was accompanied by six plans for the new *baixa*. Da Maia had appointed three teams, each charged with working out new plans on the basis of existing conditions. Numbered from one to six, they were presented to José I on 19 April 1756. Plan one, prepared by the team headed by Gualter de Fonseca, follows the general disposition of the old city. Plan two by the team of Captain Poppe substituted for existing streets a more regularized scheme. Plan four, drawn up by Fonseca without the collaboration of his team, proposed a grid system for an entirely and radically new design. Plan six, drafted by Captain Poppe independently of the team that worked on plan two, suggested the same solution but with greater imagination. Plan three by the team headed by Eugénio dos Santos is notable for its emphasis on the distinction between narrower streets and wider thoroughfares and for the importance it gives to the riverfront square, the site of the destroyed royal palace and patriarchal church and of the future Praça do Comércio. Fonseca's and Poppe's grid plans included a rebuilt patriarchal church at its former location. Dos Santos eliminated the patriarchal church, and was thus able greatly to enlarge the square on the river. None of these five plans were implemented.

The plan that was approved was the fifth, signed by dos Santos and Mardel. It was sent by Pombal to the president of the Lisbon supreme court with an order to execute it on 12 June 1758. Two years had been taken up with settling legal matters of expropriation, relocation, and the transfer of titles. It took another year, until landlords were ordered to assume responsibility for their redistributed properties, for the actual reconstruction to begin. The plan by dos Santos and Mardel that was put into execution was in the form of a grid notably superior in intelligence and practicality to the rectilinear schemes of Fonseca and Poppe (see França, fig. 2). It provided for forty rectangular blocks with axes from north to south, twelve blocks aligned from west to east, and three squares: one in front of the town hall to the west of the riverfront square, another, the already existing but enlarged Rossio to the north, and the Praça do Comércio to the south.

The new plan subordinated the Rossio, which had been the principal public space in the city prior to the earthquake, to the Praça do Comércio. Known prior to the rebuilding as the Terreiro do Paço, or palace yard, its new name and the fact that both the royal palace and the patriarchal church were banished from it were emblematic of Pombal's vision of transforming his country into a modern mercantile society. The buildings on the east, west, and north of the Praça do Comércio (see França, fig. 4) were and still are occupied by government ministries. The first design for the square was submitted to Pombal by da Maia in April 1756 and was not accepted. Then in June 1759 construction of the new square began according to the design of Eugénio dos Santos, with facades on arcades of the same height as the buildings in the adjoining streets, with the exception of the slightly higher corner towers. Only the triumphal arch in the center of the north side interrupts the standardized uniformity of the buildings on the square's west, east, and north sides. The corner towers repeat the single, low, wide tower that Felipe Terzi had added to the destroyed royal palace in the late sixteenth century, though for Terzi's square dome dos Santos substituted flat terraces. The form of the square dome was retained in the corner towers in an alternate project for the Praça do Comércio by Mardel, courtly and grandiose rather than plain and practical, that was rejected. The senate moved into the west wing of the Praça do Comércio in 1774, and in the following year the completion of the great square was commemorated by the dedication at its center of an equestrian statue of José I bearing on its base a bronze relief with the portrait of Pombal. Work on the statue, the first monumental equestrian bronze in Portugal, began in 1770. A model based on Charles Lebrun's monument to Louis XIV was made by Eugénio dos Santos

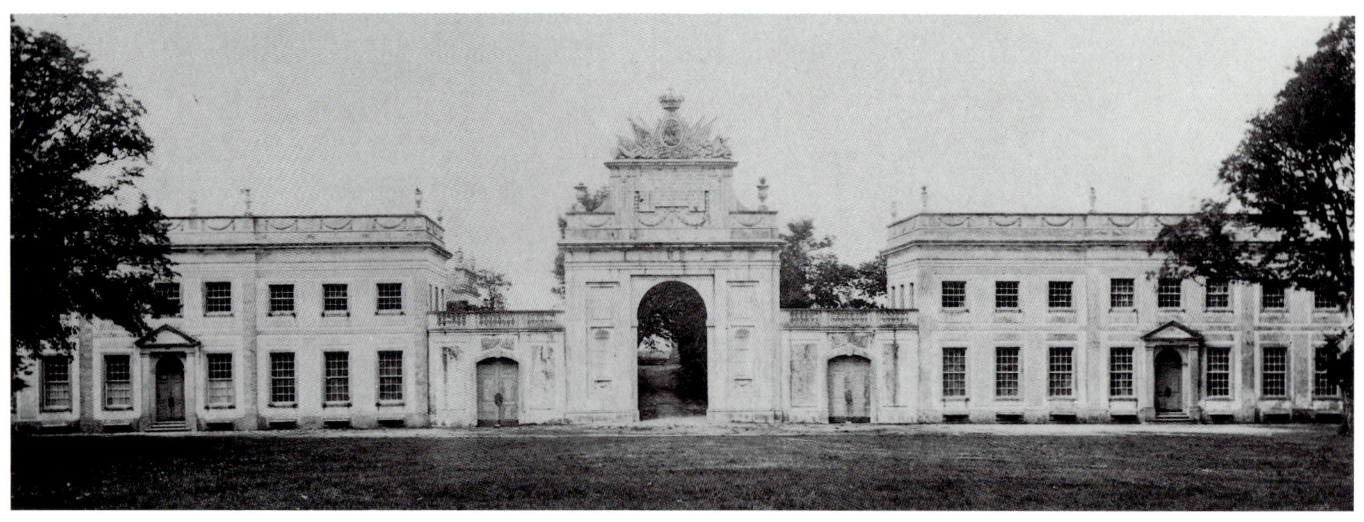

and was modified by Joaquim Machado de Castro, Portugal's foremost sculptor of the time, who modeled and cast the work.

The blocks to the north of the Praça do Comércio had been completed by 1770. The decree of 1758 ordering the work to begin included minute instructions for the width of streets, the facades of buildings, the repartition of appropriated properties, and measures for public safety, sewage disposal, and fire prevention. The necessary speed of construction led to innovations in the organization of designers, draftsmen, and building crews guaranteeing a rational, standardized mode of production. The *casa do risco* (planning office) learned how to design parts that could be manufactured cheaply and quickly and that could fit into any building. The standardization of design affected all phases of production, including the *azulejos* that lined the public spaces of the new five-story blocks, which consisted of repeated, uniform floral patterns, one to a tile, rather than of the narrative compositions that had appeared on the walls of courtly and religious buildings. For the interior framework of the new row houses the planning office devised a mode of construction in the form of a wooden cage, a *gaiola,* which provided the necessary flexibility for withstanding the tremors of earthquakes. Mardel ordered a detachment of soldiers to march across a trestle placed on such a *gaiola* put up in the Praça do Comércio in order to test the structure's resilience.

The sources of the simple, disciplined Pombaline style of the buildings in the new *baixa* can in large measure be found in seventeenth-century Lisbon palaces with arcades at street level. For the sake of the maximum utilization of space Pombaline designers eliminated and filled in these arcades. They were retained only in the facades of the Praça do Comércio. The harsh, rational economy of the designs of dos Santos and the other architects of the *baixa* are also a consummate expression of the tradition of the plain style that is the common denominator of much Portuguese building from the early sixteenth century on. But while the functional spirit of the Lisbon of Pombal was an expression of the dictator's policies and vision for the future, it was also the product of the practical orientation and efficiency of the office of royal architects in which dos Santos had been trained and which was directed by Mardel at the time of the rebuilding of the *baixa.*

The Pombaline idiom was adopted in large-scale urban projects throughout Portugal. It is reflected on a smaller scale in one of the last *solares* of the eighteenth century. The two pavilions comprising the palace of Seteais at Sintra (fig. 20), one of the most elegant examples in Iberia of the neoclassical style, were built for the Dutch consul Daniel Gildemeester in the early 1780s. By 1794, when British traveler William Beckford stayed there, the palace had been sold to the marquês de Marialva. In 1802 a triumphal arch connecting the two pavilions was erected to commemorate the visit of the prince regents of Brazil, the future João VI and his consort Carlota Joaquina. The arch, a reference to Eugénio dos Santos' monumental triumphal arch on the north side of the Praça do Comércio, is purely Italian in its decorative vocabulary of neoclassical garlands, urns, and military emblems. The Latin inscription on its frontispiece proclaims the desire for peace in calamitous times *(calamitosis temporibus),* not by invincible imperial arms *(non tantum armis imperi ab omni aevo semper invictus),* but by wisdom, prudence, and justice *(sed ex sapientia, prudentia et justitia).* It is a sentiment culled from the rhetoric of Roman imperial invocations of society's noblest aspirations. But like the arch on which it is inscribed, it also commemorates the enlightenment ideals of the marquês de Pombal.

Although there are excellent monographs on Portuguese architecture of the sixteenth and seventeenth centuries by Albrecht Haupt, *De Baukunst der Renaissance in Portugal* (Frankfurt, 1890-1895, 2 vols.), and George Kubler, *Portuguese Plain Architecture: Between Spices and Diamonds, 1521-1706* (Middletown, 1972), a comparable, comprehensive work on Portuguese eighteenth-century architecture has yet to be written. Closest to it is França 1965. Surveys of a general nature in languages other than Portuguese can be found in Raul Lino, *L'Evolution de l'architecture domestique au Portugal* (Lisbon, 1937); Germain Bazin, *L'Architecture religieuse au Portugal et au Brésil à l'époque baroque* (Lisbon, 1949) and "Reflexions sur l'origine et l'évolution du Baroque dans le Nord du Portugal," *Belas Artes* (1950); John B. Bury, "Late Baroque and Rococo in North Portugal," *Journal of the Society of Architectural Historians* (October 1956); George Kubler and Martin Soria, *Art and Architecture in Spain and Portugal and Their American Dominions, 1500 to 1800* (Harmondsworth, 1959); Flavio Gonçalves, "The Architecture and Wood Sculpture of the North of Portugal, 1750-1850" in *Portugal and Brazil in Transition* (Minneapolis, 1967); and Smith 1968. Articles in English on eighteenth-century architects active in and near Lisbon (no specialized studies on eighteenth-century Portuguese architecture exist in French, German, Italian, or Spanish) are Robert C. Smith, "João Frederico Ludovice, an Eighteenth-Century Architect in Portugal," *Art Bulletin* (September 1936) and "The Building of Mafra," *Apollo* (April 1973), and Hellmut Wohl, "Carlos Mardel and His Lisbon Architecture," *Apollo* (April 1973). Books in Portuguese on eighteenth-century architects, regional centers, and building types published between 1960 and 1973, including important monographs by Ayres de Carvalho on the architectural patronage of João V and by Robert C. Smith on Nicolau Nasoni and André Soares, are discussed in Hellmut Wohl, "Recent Studies in Portuguese Post-Medieval Architecture," *Journal of the Society of Architectural Historians* (March 1975).

1. Robert C. Smith, "The Building of Mafra," *Apollo* (April 1973), 363–364.

2. William Beckford, *Excursion à Alcobaça et Batalha* (Paris, 1956), 210.

3. Marcus Cheke, *Dictator of Portugal: A Life of the Marquis of Pombal 1699–1782* (London, 1938).

4. Beckford 1956, 216.

5. Some authorities attribute to Alorna the famous remark usually credited to Pombal. See C. R. Boxer, *The Golden Age of Brazil* (Berkeley and Los Angeles, 1969), 363.

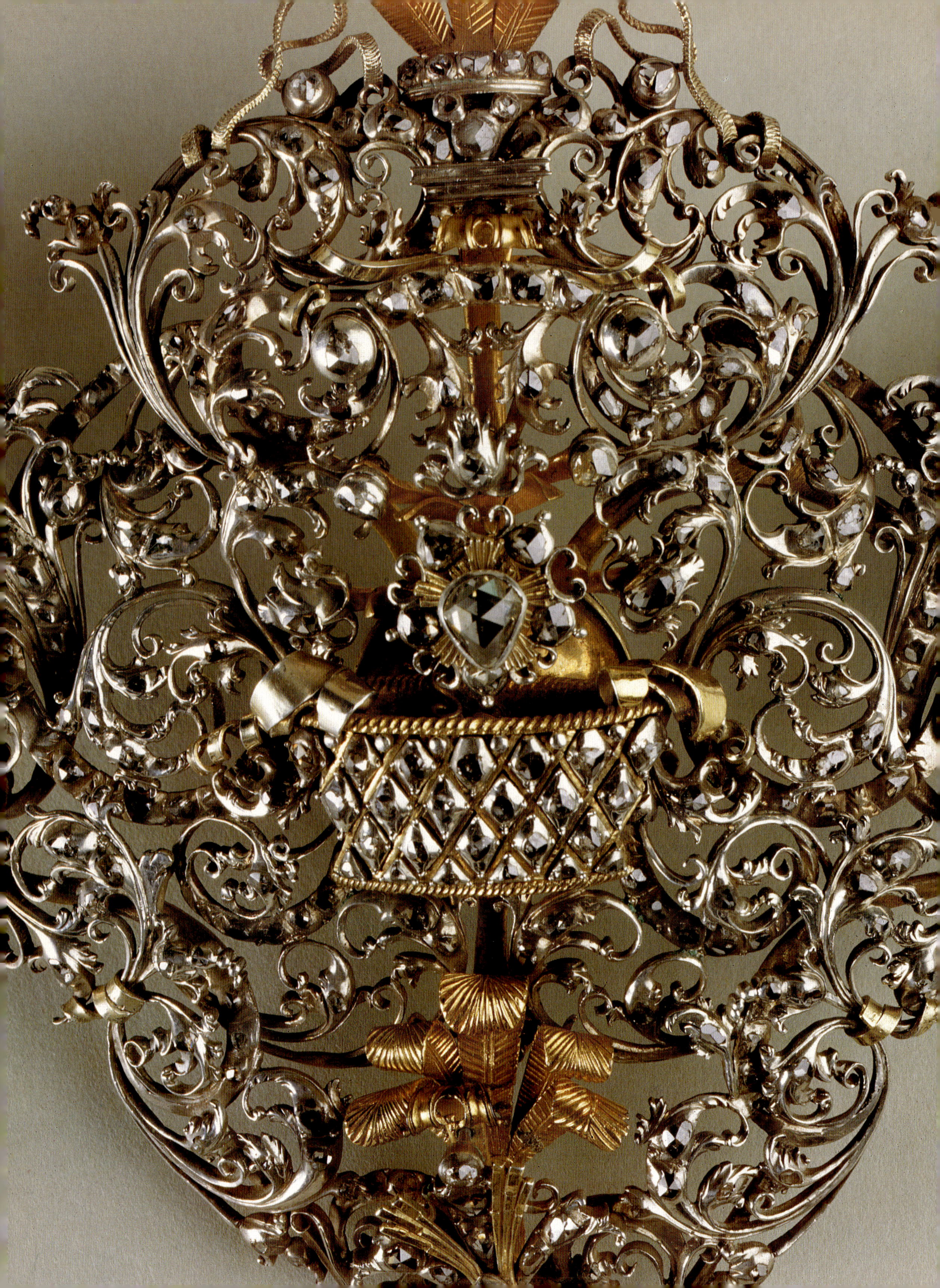

Portuguese Jewelry of the Eighteenth Century

Leonor d'Orey

*I*n the early eighteenth century, Portugal was bathed in an unprecedented euphoria by the gold flooding in from the enormous deposits in Brazil, followed in 1729 by the discovery of fabulous diamond mines and other precious and semiprecious stones. The Portuguese were all too ready to believe that this source of wealth was infinite. And indeed, day after day, for almost a century, Brazil remained the world's leading diamond producer, while the deposits in the Orient, which had originally been the main source of this precious gem, were gradually exhausted. Deposits of other stones were discovered within that immense dominion of the Portuguese crown: emeralds, tourmalines, rubies, aquamarines, topazes, and amethysts of unusual size. This continuous influx was even apparent to foreign visitors who remarked in surprise upon "the new mines which the Portuguese discover daily."[1] The gold and gems from Brazil were to produce a period of exuberance and luxury in Portugal, eminently represented in spectacular combinations of precious metal and stones of the highest standard of execution.

Two trends have always been apparent in Portuguese jewelry. The first, the preference for extensive use of gold with diamond decoration (as opposed to an emphasis on stones with the metal serving strictly as a support), is perhaps because gold was discovered before diamonds in Brazil. Examples are the famous bow pendants that are characteristically Portuguese, expertly executed in chased gold and enhanced by diamonds, to match earrings, necklaces, and rings (cats. 42, 43). The second trend is exemplified by another typical style of Portuguese jewelry: pavé-set with stones, normally set in silver, following the European fashion of the day.

Bows and ribbons were widely used in Portugal, creating typical motifs that were interpreted and disseminated in infinite variations, both in high-quality and in popular jewelry. Numerous pieces bearing such bow motifs, executed in gold or precious stones, have survived to the present day. The glitter of faceted stones provided the ideal finishing touch of sophistication to the highly stylized and elaborate productions of the century. Women became the principal clients of jewelers, who rose to artistic heights that have rarely been equaled

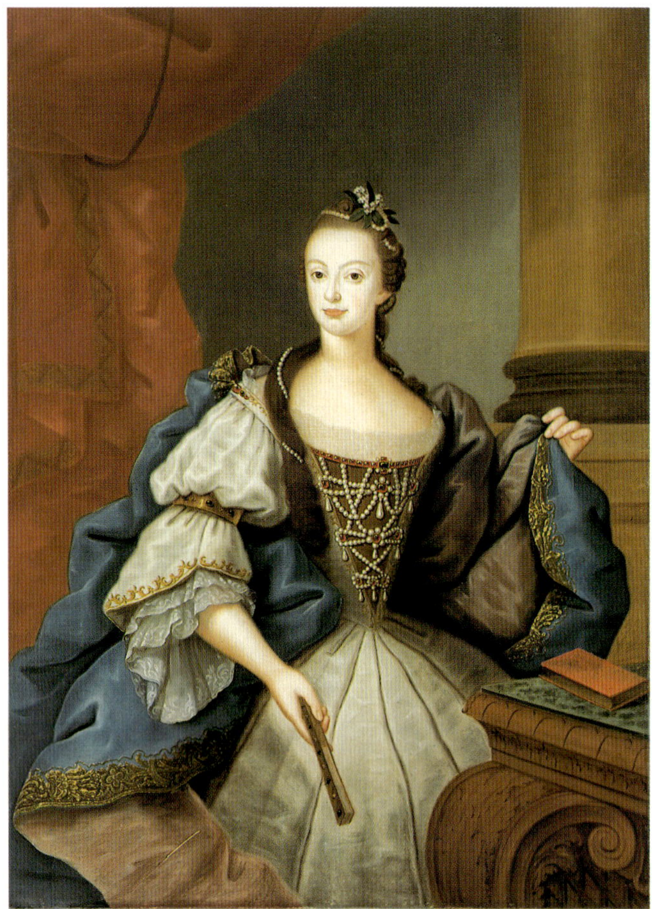

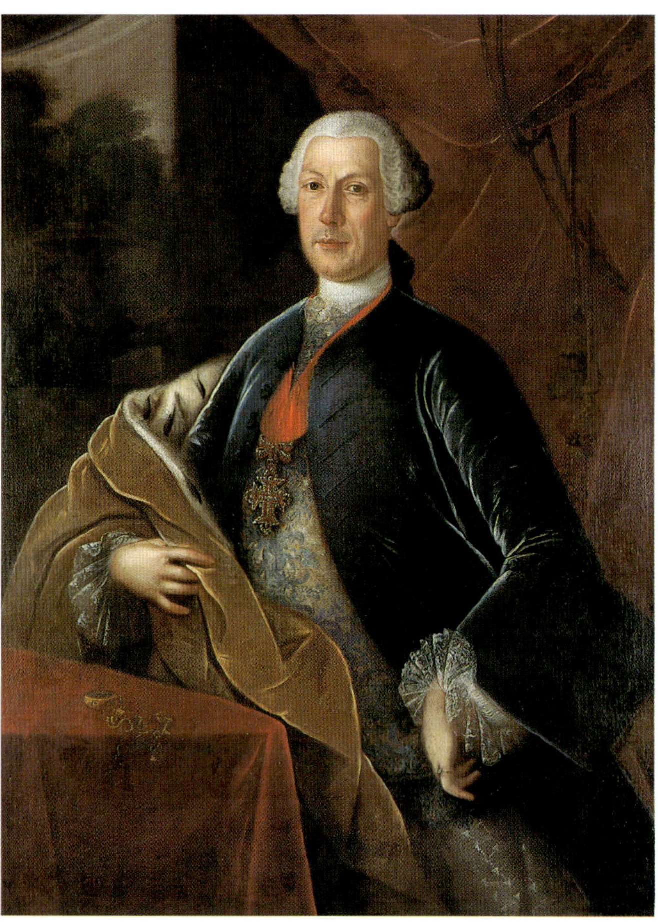

fig. 2. Attributed to Francisco Vieira Lusitano, *Portrait of the Princess of Brazil, Dona Maria Francisca, the Future Rainha Maria I*, 1753, oil on canvas. Palácio Nacional de Queluz

fig. 3. Anonymous, *Portrait of the Infante Dom António*, c. 1740, oil on canvas. Museu Nacional de Arte Antiga, Lisbon

since (fig. 2). The French influence continued to be apparent in design, led by well-known masters such as Pouget, Duflos, and Bourget who were copied throughout Europe, while traveling jewelers disseminated the French manufacturing processes abroad. The Portuguese goldsmiths, jewelers, and gem cutters, either creating their own designs or copying foreign masters, attained such perfection of form and technique that, in some cases, it is difficult to distinguish between imported jewelry and that executed in Portugal.

Catering to the demand for opulence that arose during this period, jewelers created compositions of magnificent decorative effect. New ways of cutting stones set off their beauty by enhancing their brightness, while designs ensured maximum reflection of light, thus emphasizing the color of the gems, which were particularly brilliant when viewed in the flickering light of candles. To further this effect, gems were sometimes mounted in mobile or flexible structures that allowed them to move and maximize the play of light.

This taste for ostentation and dramatic impact that had arisen in Portugal was also evident in the sophistication of insignia of the military orders of Christ, São Tiago, Aviz, and Malta. These were created with high-quality gems, which became part of the range of decorative ornaments worn by this class-conscious and worldly society. The proliferation of such insignia and the frequency with which they were worn led jewelers of the eighteenth century to turn such items into magnificent pieces of jewelry pavé-set with diamonds, keeping abreast of changes in styles of jewelry design. The large number of such pieces that have come down to us indicates the extent to which they were appreciated and demonstrates the sophisticated quality of their execution (see cats. 51-53, 57).

The wearing of an insignia (fig. 3) was a mark of prestige and honor, and that of the Order of Christ became extremely prominent in Portugal, which accounts for the impressive number and continued display of such insignia throughout the eighteenth century. Numerous portraits of the period bear witness to this practice, as do chronicles by foreign travelers such as Twiss and Saussure, who made specific reference to this fact: "Not only are the king, the royal princes and a large number of noble knights of the Order of Christ; countless members of the gentry, officers and even merchants are also members."[2] Those invested in an order could have their insignia made in keeping with their financial means, encouraging jewelers to turn these insignia into veritable pieces of jewelry. The numerous designs and models created over the years demonstrate the evolution of taste and artistic trends during this period. Most were executed in silver, garnets, and *minas novas* (colorless quartz), occasionally combined with topazes, aquamarines, or light amethysts. During this period there were as yet few examples in gold with diamonds and rubies.

Diamonds were the preferred stone. Colored gems such as sapphires, emeralds, and rubies were also esteemed, as were semiprecious stones, which, although less costly, nonetheless achieved great decorative effect. Such stones existed in vast quantities in Brazil and remained fashionable for a long time, particularly rock crystal, known as *minas novas*, which was used in place of diamonds but cut in the same manner, creating a similar but brighter effect. Mention may be made of certain typically Portuguese pieces, beautiful compositions in *minas novas*, chrysolites, imperial topazes, and amethysts that clearly demonstrate the quality and variety of national production (cats. 48, 55, and 58).

For the most part, eighteenth-century jewelry was composed of various elements that could be separated and reassembled in different ways according to personal preference or adapted to particular garments. This was a typical feature in this period. There was a passion for sets of jewelry: necklaces, earrings, bracelets, brooches or hair ornaments, rings, pins, and buckles were included in these parures, in which the various elements can be mixed and matched.

Most of these pieces were decorated with plant motifs, scrolls, and leaves surrounding a frame of ribbons. This was the basis of the structure of jewelry created virtually to the end of the century, the pieces becoming less dense and lighter as the century progressed (cat. 58). As styles succeeded each other, imperceptible improvements were made to the metallic supports for the stones.

Both real and imitation gems were set in cradle-shaped sockets with structures in silver that were closed at the back and lined with very fine, shiny foil of silver or copper, which was sometimes colored to enhance the tone or brightness of the stones. The underside of the pieces was generally left smooth, in contrast to the previous century when it was generally enameled or engraved.

The creation of imitation jewelry arose as a parallel art that became extremely sophisticated and was made possible by the appearance of new technologies. A growing need arose to adorn clothing, and all sectors of European society used imitation jewelry. As early as the mid-seventeenth century there were references to the manufacture of artificial stones and pearls in Venice and Paris, where, in 1767, a guild of artificial gem cutters existed, of which some three hundred craftsmen were members, and reproductions of all kinds of precious stones were available.

However, there was such an abundance and variety of semi-precious stones streaming in from Brazil that, in Portugal, artificial stones were rarely used. Instead, the Portuguese jewelers employed natural stones of great decorative effect in place of those of higher intrinsic value, thus showing prodigious imagination in design and the total technical mastery of their materials.

The jewelry selected for this exhibition consists of early pieces created for the high nobility or wealthy bourgeoisie or belonging to the former monasteries and convents that were closed down by the liberal law of 1834. The latter constitute an unusual collection, including gifts or dowries from noble ladies who took the veil and divested themselves of their personal jewelry when they entered their convents. Since these pieces were thus removed from the social scene, many remain in their original settings. This is valuable to the historian, as jewelry is an ephemeral art and pieces of the greatest intrinsic value were often remounted; few families resisted changes in fashion or survived financial difficulties. Thus, these gems from convents and monasteries are an interesting testimonial. And, in their technical and decorative quality, they reflect some degree of the wealth and variety of Portuguese jewelry during the eighteenth century.

1. Castelo-Branco Chaves, *O Portugal de D. João V, visto por três forasteiros* (Lisbon, 1983), 73.
2. Chaves 1983, 270.

The Silver Table Service of Dom José I of Portugal

Leonor d'Orey

*P*ortugal's unique collection of eighteenth-century French silverware, particularly the work created by the great goldsmiths Thomas Germain (1673-1748) and his son François-Thomas Germain (1726-1791), is especially significant because such works are, paradoxically, rare in France. Few of the objects executed in the famous Parisian workshops between 1689 and 1790 have survived, as the great silverware belonging to the king and high aristocracy alike was virtually all melted down to finance the wars of Louis XIV and Louis XV and, later, after the revolution in 1789, to solve the newborn republic's financial problems.

It is only because large orders were placed by foreign sovereigns, including the Portuguese and Danish monarchs and the czarinas of Russia, that such examples of the craftsmanship of the period have survived at all. Thus the Portuguese collections have double value, as documents of unsurpassed virtuosity and elegance in the working of silver and as examples of artistic achievement otherwise unavailable. Lisbon today possesses the world's largest collection of royal silver, the core of the huge orders placed with the French royal goldsmiths by João V (r. 1706-1750), José I (r. 1750-1777), and Maria I (r. 1777-1792). The pieces are therefore priceless for their style, form, and technique and for the historical and cultural context within which they were commissioned.

From the late seventeenth century, European fashion was created in the French court at Versailles. Royal and noble patrons throughout Europe saw Paris as the source of taste and elegance. The aristocracy ordered decorative and practical objects from France, secure in the knowledge that their accoutrements were in the style used in the Parisian court.

Dom João V of Portugal was no exception. He enjoyed pomp and splendor, particularly at the table, as it was customary at state banquets to display a profusion of ornaments in a theatrical demonstration of wealth and power. Chronicles of the period relate that hours at a time were spent at table, not exclusively for pleasure or amusement, since it was here also that policies were discussed for treaties of state. The king was duty-bound to dine frequently in public to offer his people the opportunity to see him in the flesh, engaged in an activity that was distinguished in those days by the utmost refinement and solemnity.

The dawn of the eighteenth century had seen the development of output from the enormous deposits of gold, silver, and precious stones that had been discovered in Brazil. Portuguese mining interests and companies operated in what was at that time a colony, giving Portugal the means to become a major importer of manufactured goods from Europe. The king collected one-fifth of each mine's production, which poured enormous sums into the state treasury to the benefit of both the public works and the royal household. By mid-century, the quantity of gold coming through Portugal into the European markets was such that it led to a drop in the international price of the precious metal, causing great upheaval in the banking circles that had controlled international trade since the days of the republics of Venice and Genoa.

João V preferred Italy as the source for his ecclesiastical silver and for a while ordered his domestic items in London, where in 1724 he seems to have made his last purchase, a solid gold bathtub weighing 900 marks (456 pounds). As French gold- and silversmiths were the most sought after by European courts, the king of Portugal redirected his patronage to Paris and placed an order with Thomas Germain, Sculpteur Orfèvre du Royaux Galeries du Louvre, the best-known goldsmith of the age, for a lavish silver service and numerous other objects weighing 6,000 marks (1½ tons).[1]

Over the next fifty years, Thomas Germain and his son, François-Thomas, who inherited not only his father's workshop in the Louvre but also his register of clients, produced more than three thousand pieces for the Portuguese monarch and nobility. This Portuguese royal preference, initiated by João V and perpetuated by his successors José I and Maria I, was to provide these goldsmiths with the opportunity to create some of the most accomplished French works in silver of the eighteenth century that have survived to the present day.

Details of how this great collection was assembled can be gleaned from the voluminous correspondence between Lisbon and Paris testifying to a comprehensive program of artistic commissions for the Portuguese crown. One letter describes how the king in 1726 requested full reports regarding the silver services from his personal purchasing agent.

You will seek to inform yourself with the utmost accuracy in the court of the king of France of the tableware he uses when he sups in public. . . . If on such occasions there is what the French call "buffet"; what quality, size, form, and quantity of plates are used; what salvers; what type of water containers (ewers and basins); what baskets etc. . . . You will make the same examinations of the occasions on which the king dines in company, that is to say with the queen alone, or the princes and princesses of the royal household, and you will seek to discover if in these cases they use the same tableware with additional items, or another separate set. . . . Of these and other functions you will find information, not through intermediaries but on your own account at first hand, speaking with the goldsmith who makes them and with the officials who safeguard them, and of each and every one of the functions you will write an individual report with all the particularities you are able to ascertain.[2]

This document reveals that for the Portuguese court, as indeed for many of the sovereigns of northern Europe, the monarch's personal commissioner was sometimes as important, and certainly far busier, than the political ambassador. This letter also reveals that a certain amount of artistic espionage took place, as when in 1760 Empress Elizabeth I of Russia was advised to order a silver service as comprehensive as the one that had been commissioned by the king of Portugal, which indeed she proceeded to do. By singular coincidence, several pieces of the service executed by François-Thomas Germain for the Russian court, in particular two magnificent tureens in gilded silver with a design almost identical to those in the Portuguese service (but with the Russian coat of arms), can be seen today in Lisbon at the Calouste Gulbenkian Museum.

Even the king of France himself was not above curiosity about what was being ordered from abroad; the Portuguese purchasing agent wrote to Lisbon in gratified surprise to relate that "the large toilet set is going to Versailles tomorrow because the king wishes to see it," which was unprecedented for a work that was to be exported.

Thomas Germain, that most outstanding of Parisian master goldsmiths, was held in the highest esteem by contemporary artists, writers, and even monarchs. His reputation in Portugal was such that, on learning of his death in 1748, João V ordered a memorial service, paid for out of his own pocket, to be celebrated for Germain in Lisbon cathedral. This service was attended by numerous artists and goldsmiths of the capital.

On 1 November 1755 Lisbon was struck by a terrible earthquake that destroyed a large part of the city, including the royal palace by the Tagus (see Maxwell essay in this volume). Virtually all of the original work made by Thomas Germain was lost, and Dom José I, João's successor, did not delay in ordering a splendid new silver service from the great master's son. Thus the present dinner service of the Portuguese royal house was created by François-Thomas Germain and his assistants. According to the document of 24 June 1756 in which the fabulous order was placed, four sets were planned, for which the goldsmith submitted designs. The first of these consisted of four tureens, four *pots-à-oille* (serving vessels for a type of stew), sixteen large dishes, one dish for the table center, highly ornamented, each with respective cover. The second service was composed of twenty-five dishes of varying size and design, with small plates for such things as hors d'oeuvres, and endpieces. The third was virtually identical to the second.

The fourth and largest should have included a *corbelha* (large dessert centerpiece) to cover the table entirely, with decorations all round, and at one end of the table, a group depicting America offering her products to the monarch. In the center of the table, His Majesty King José I would give his orders for the rebuilding of Lisbon to personifications of Architecture and the Arts. The other endpiece would represent Pedro Álvares Cabral's discovery of Brazil, including indigenous figures.

Also part of this table setting were twenty-four dozen plates with laurel leaf border, eight dozen plates in vermeil, forty-eight branch candelabra, six wine coolers, 144 sets of cutlery in six cases, seventy-two of the same in silver gilt in three cases, six cruet stands, six mustard pots, six salt cellars, six pepper pots, forty-eight large spoons, six olive spoons, two large and two medium coffeepots, two milk jugs, two teapots with salvers, two large kettles with spirit lamps, two large dessert salvers, four dish warmers, four ewers with basins for washing the hands, six large carving knives and forks, six bread baskets, eight serving salvers, and remaining pieces deemed necessary for the table and for serving purposes.[3] Each item was to display the Portuguese royal coat of arms as well as its weight and serial number to facilitate inventory taking.

The size of the order was such that on 13 December of that same year, the Portuguese ambassador in Paris stated in a letter to Lisbon that "more than one hundred and twenty craftsmen are engaged on Your Majesty's silver service but, since this is one of the finest services of its kind ever made, the work is taking longer than expected, and it is hoped that Your Majesty will do them the honor of not supposing that they have been remiss."[4] And indeed, sixteen months after the commission was placed, the items making up the first service were dispatched from Le Havre. The objects listed in the order were successively dispatched in fourteen shipments in twenty-five numbered cases over a period of nine years, until the goldsmith's workshop went bankrupt in 1765.

The failure of François-Thomas Germain's workshop brought deliveries to an end, for which reason the entire service was never completed. Thereafter, correspondence between Paris and Lisbon took on a more severe tone, which reveals that disputes had arisen because of undue payments, missing consignments, unfulfilled contracts, and the like.

The goldsmith demanded such an exorbitant sum to complete the fourth service that the king objected, and thus the enormous centerpiece, or *surtout*, "of a fairly ridiculous and monstrous pretentiousness" in the words of Ambassador Vicente de Souza Coutinho, did not progress beyond the stage of lead and plaster models. Louis XV even intervened in the matter, but François-Thomas Germain never returned the more than two million pounds he had received in advance payments from the king of Portugal.

The bill submitted by the younger Germain to the king allows precise identification of the objects in question by their weight and serial numbers, while the confirmation of receipt mentions some 1,270 pieces. It may be concluded from these documents that, even though unfinished, this order must have been one of the largest in Europe. The design of the silver pieces reveals a sometimes capricious elegance brimming with fantasy, exuberant shapes in which symmetry yields to endlessly undulating movement.

Dom José I also commissioned an exquisite solid gold luncheon service with nine pieces bearing François-Thomas Germain's mark, which was delivered after the goldsmith's bankruptcy. By reason of its material and its quality, the salt cellar (fig. 1) was described in the *Avant-Coureur* of 8 September 1766: "the shape of the salt cellar is highly ingenious. It is composed of two fish seeming to rise up out of the water, draped in seaweed-like leaves on which the shell containing the salt rests."[5]

Moreover, other objects that did not originally belong to the dinner service but are among the best-known French creations, such as the famous Thomas Germain *surtout de table* (centerpiece) of 1729-1731 (fig. 2) and the sixteen superb vermeil statuettes by Ambroise Nicolas Cousinet of 1757-1758 (see cats. 75-80), commissioned by the duque de Aveiro, were incorporated into the royal collection after the duke's execution in 1759. These items clearly demonstrate the sophistication and elegance with which affluent people of the period lived. The centerpiece is the clearest example of the ultimate aim of such spectacularly sumptuous objects.

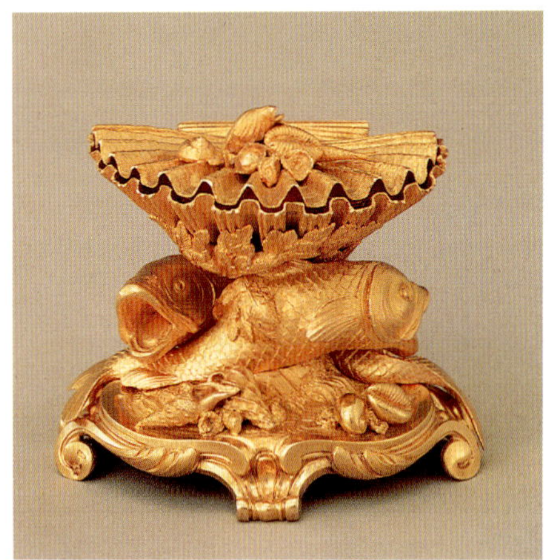

fig. 1. François-Thomas Germain, *Salt Cellar from the Luncheon Service of Dom José I*, 1764–1765, gold. Museu Nacional de Arte Antiga, Lisbon, inv. 1718

fig. 2. Thomas Germain, *Table Centerpiece,*
1729–1731, silver. Museu Nacional de Arte
Antiga, Lisbon

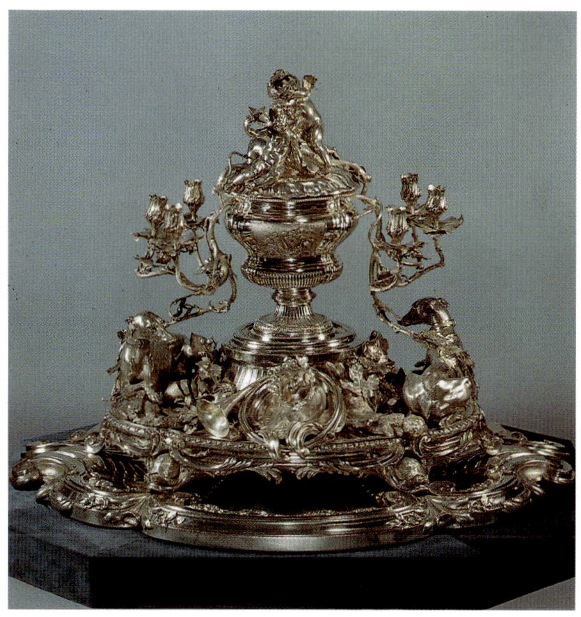

The official presentation of the French service at the state dinner given to
mark the accession of José I's daughter, Maria, was such a significant event that
it is mentioned in the "Acto de Aclamação e Juramento da Rainha D. Maria e
do Rei D. Pedro III" on 13 May 1777:

The magnificent hall could be seen in which Their Majesties and Highnesses were to
dine, where a table was set . . . and a further two tables . . . these three tables were laid
with a rich and extensive silver service recently made in the Parisian court by Germain,
the famous goldsmith, on the special orders of Dom José I, and this was the first time
it was used and displayed in public, to the great admiration and applause of all the
Portuguese and foreign guests who were privileged to enjoy this gratifying and brilliant
spectacle never before witnessed at such a function.[6]

What would the menu have been for a banquet served in this silver? Would
it have been strictly French to match its Parisian source? It is more likely that,
as the recipe books of the royal chefs and descriptions by foreign visitors attest,
French cuisine would have been prominent, but that certain exotic influences
arising from Portugal's many links with distant regions overseas (as evoked in a
number of the items belonging to the service, see cats. 68, 71, and 72) would
also be represented. Dishes of Asian origin would certainly have been served,
such as rice, sweetmeats, curry, and desserts originating from Goa and Macao
that were famous in Portugal as well as fruits and other wondrous tropical delicacies from Africa and Brazil.

William Beckford, the eccentric and witty aesthete who spent some time in
Portugal in 1780, left vivid descriptions of the social life, customs, and meals
enjoyed by the Portuguese aristocracy of his day. In the wealthy abbey of Alcobaça, Beckford was honored with a banquet of "rarities and delicacies of past
seasons and distant countries: exquisite sausages, potted lampreys, strange
messes from the Brazils, and others still stranger from China (edible birds'
nests and sharks' fins), dressed after the latest mode of Macao by a Chinese lay
brother . . . . bearing cassolettes of Goa filigree, steaming with the fragrant va-

por of Calambac, the finest quality of wood aloes." Another passage states: "Still sweeter than the sweetmeats ever confectionized, a preparation of the freshest eggs ever laid, with the richest sugar ever distilled from the finest canes ever grown in the Brazils for private consumption."[7] The French service of which the court was so rightfully proud traveled with the Portuguese royal family to Rio de Janeiro in 1807 just before the arrival of the Napoleonic troops. When Brazil became an independent empire with its own sovereign Pedro I (r. 1822-1831), the son of João VI, the dinner service was divided. Part of it remained in Brazil and became the property of the new emperor and was dispersed when his son, Pedro II, was deposed in 1889. Thus pieces of French silver bearing the Portuguese royal coat of arms and the imperial insignias of Brazil gradually found their way into foreign museums or private collections. Among such items are the coffeepot in the Metropolitan Museum of Art in New York, two basins and an ewer by François-Thomas Germain and Robert-Joseph Auguste respectively in the Musée des Arts Décoratifs in Paris, and a pair of gilded silver salvers, Dom José's large hunting "surtout," and four candelabra by François-Thomas Germain today in the Louvre.

Meanwhile, the larger part of the collection returned to Portugal in 1821 with João VI, the son of Maria I, and continued to be the pride of Portuguese sovereigns until the fall of the monarchy in 1910. Thereafter it was used in official receptions in the former royal palaces. In 1926 some three hundred pieces representing every type of object sent to Portugal from the eighteenth-century workshops of Paris were gathered for purposes of study and exhibition in the Museu Nacional de Arte Antiga. The remainder is kept in the Palácio Nacional da Ajuda and is still brought out on important state occasions.

Thus Portugal still owns the impressive number of 1,370 pieces of gold and silver from this sparkling century, including not only the superb dinner service but also components of gilded silver toilet sets likewise ordered by the royal family.

With the Germains, other names of well-known master silversmiths of the period such as Dennis Frankson, Louis Joseph Lenhendrick, Pierre Germain, Henri Allain, Simon Leveque, Alexis Jacob, Jacques Ballin, Nicolas-Martin Langlois, François Joubert, Sebastian Durand, and Robert-Joseph Auguste are represented in works with the Portuguese royal coat of arms. In terms of quality, quantity, and variety, it is undoubtedly the finest single collection of eighteenth-century French silver in existence today.

1. Cesar Saussure, "Cartas escritas de Lisboa no ano de 1730," in *O Portugal de D. João visto por tres forasteiros,* Biblioteca Nacional (Lisbon, 1989), 268.

2. Letter from Diogo de Mendonça Corte Real to Francisco Mendes de Goes, Lisboa Occidental, 4 November 1726 (ANTT MNE box 1, bundle 5).

3. "Relaçam da prata encomendada a Germain, por ordem de sua Magestade debaixo da direiçam do Senhor Pedro Antonio Virgolino em 24 de Junho de 1756" (AHMF XX/2/71).

4. Letter from Antonio de Saldanha to Luís da Cunha, Paris, 13 December 1756 (ANTT MNE box 564 no. 357).

5. Germain Bapst, *L'Orfèvrerie française à la cour de Portugal* (Paris, 1892), 16.

6. "Auto do Levantamento, e Juramento, que os Grandes Titulos Seculares, Ecclesiasticos e mais pessoas, que se acharao presentes, fizerao a muito alta. muito poderosa Rainha D. Maria I, Nossa Senhora na Coroa destes Reinos e Senhorios de Portugal, sendo exaltada e coroada sobre o regio throno juntamente com o Senhor Rei D. Pedro III. Na tarde do dia treze de Maio. Anno de 1777."

7. William Beckford, *Excursion à Alcobaça et Batalha* (Paris, Lisbon, 1956), 54, 166.

Court Festivities at Queluz

Simonetta Luz Afonso

*I*n 1746[1] Príncipe Pedro (1717–1786) began the major reconstruction project that was to transform the small hunting lodge at Queluz into a magnificent summer residence (see Wohl, fig. 3) for the family members of the Casa do Infantado. Príncipe Pedro, the son of Dom João V and younger brother of Dom José I, was the heir to the property of the Casa, constituting a sizable inheritance that always went to the second child of the Portuguese monarch. Son of one king, brother of another, and royal consort through his marriage in 1760 to his niece, the future Rainha Maria I, Pedro was to expend considerable sums, in enthusiastic fashion, in the construction and decoration of this palace and its magnificent gardens.[2]

When the earthquake of 1755 destroyed the center of Lisbon, the royal palace, and the royal treasury, life at court lost the glitter that characterized it during João V's reign, becoming austere and monotonous. Dom José I was terrified by the effects of the earthquake and had a palace constructed of wood in the district of Ajuda, which had to be made habitable as quickly as possible. In 1786, the French ambassador noted the extensive use of crimson damask and gold braid in the interior decoration of the new palace, writing that "…for the same expense one could have indulged in a type of ornament in better taste and more substantial."[3]

Free of the many concerns and difficulties besetting his brother, the king, and the prime minister, the marquês de Pombal, Príncipe Pedro made Queluz an oasis of sophisticated leisure and entertainment. It was frequently visited by Dom José and the court, particularly to celebrate royal birthdays or the feast days of Saint John and Saint Peter.

Documents describe the first celebration in Queluz in 1755, for which a temporary theater was erected above the tile-lined canal and the gardens were illuminated with numerous tin lanterns.[4] The feasts of saints John and Peter in 1758 and 1760 were praised in the *Gazeta de Lisboa,* a publication that reported on horse races, bullfights, fireworks produced in Lisbon and Italy, and other entertainments.[5] Music played an important part in leisure activities: recitals, concerts, balls, and sung masses, alternating with copious dinners, teas, or suppers, which were held in ever-changing scenarios.

Details of these activities appear in the accounting records that have emerged from a systematic examination of the Queluz archives. To a certain extent, these records confirm or complement the information contained in a document of June 1755 from the court of José I entitled *Ceremonial que se praticou na Hospedagem e Audiências Públicas do Conde de Bachi* (Ceremony observed for the stay and public audiences of the count Bachi). Drawn up in June 1755 on the basis of instructions from Sebastião José de Carvalho e Melo, the future marquês de Pombal, the *Ceremonial* of 1755 reflects the cosmopolitan tastes he had acquired in the courts of Vienna and London where he had served as ambassador.[6]

Of particular interest in the Queluz accounts are the numerous imported products, such as Parmesan cheese, pepper, nutmeg, cloves, cinnamon, coconut, wines from Reims, burgundy, bordeaux (Chateau Lafite), champagne, Côte-Rotie, coffee, green tea, and Milanese chocolate.[7] At court the four meals of the day were breakfast, luncheon, *merenda*, a light meal served in the late afternoon, and supper. The *Ceremonial* of 1755 relates that tea, coffee, and hot chocolate were served at the first meal of the day, in silver teapots, coffeepots, and chocolate jugs or in delicate porcelain services. A Queluz inventory of 1763 includes twenty-three services "…in ware of Saxony and Japan, as well as India, Macau, Holland, and France." These drinks were served again after luncheon which, with its various *couverts*, or services, and dessert, was the most substantial and lengthy meal.

The *merenda* was, of necessity, light. According to the *Ceremonial* of 1755, only *orchatas* (refreshments) or ice creams would be served, the latter in silver "sorbet flasks." The same document indicates that supper consisted of a single service composed of twenty-seven dishes; the 1765 reprint of a well-known cookbook, in a passage referring to the "…first supper… which may be served to an ambassador…" features a larger number of services, but reduces the number of dishes to five, not including the serving plates known as "traveling dishes."[8]

The place of honor of the first service was occupied by a "triumph in the center of the table" and "four table corners," in addition to dishes for salad, hams, sausage, melons of all kinds, oranges from China adorned with sweet lemons, dishes of "raised and decorated" butter, with others for parsley and capers. The second and third services consisted of soups, roast or fricasseed beef, veal, pork, mutton, hare, rabbit, chicken, pigeon, partridge, thrushes, and "little birds" adorned with "chicory eyes," and lettuce or stuffed turnips or fried apples. The fourth service was composed of meat pies, meatballs, "savoy cakes," and puff pastry containing various types of meat. The fifth service was dessert, with sweets made by nuns taking pride of place, accompanied by quince jellies and crystallized fruit. The sixth and final service consisted of cheese and fresh fruits, including different kinds of pears, grapes, and watermelon, ending with salvers of sweet biscuits and hot chocolate.

The table setting varied in accordance with the rank of the guests; hierarchy dictated not only the number of services and dishes served, but even the type of food, and there were certain types of dishes, for example stews, which the *Ceremonial* of 1755 stated could not be served to an ambassador, only to his retinue. In this regard the *Ceremonial* mentions that the tables at which the wardrobe masters and valets were seated were not to be served with silver but with Chinese porcelain.

The Queluz inventories of 1776 (an updated copy of the inventory of 1762) and of 1763 record a dinner service in Saxony porcelain, another in Japanese porcelain, and five Chinese export services, including the famous service bearing Príncipe Pedro's coat of arms, delivery of which was documented in 1773. Numerous pieces have survived, not only of the dinner service but also of the tea, coffee, and chocolate service (see cats. 81–85).

It is thought that the finest of these services must have been used at the principal tables, though perhaps only for meals taken in private. An enormous quantity of blue and white "ordinary French ware" existed for the secondary tables, together with a large number of pieces of Portuguese faience, called "factory ware" (from the Fábrica [factory] do Rato [see cat. 32]),[9] which was protected by a law of 1770 banning the import of all foreign ceramic ware except that from China.

Few witnesses have left firsthand accounts of the private life of the royal family or their immediate circle and attendants. This fact lends particular interest to a dispute between the administrator of the Palácio de Queluz and a valet that led to the former's producing a written justification, dated 8 December 1757.[10] This document provides an insight into the world of the servants who maneuvered to serve their majesties' table, a privilege that entitled the servants to the leftovers. Afterwards the servants would discard the valuable silver platters in the palace corridors or even in a nearby tavern. To put an end to such abuse, when it was discovered that some nine hundred plates were missing, the administrator determined who would serve each table and took an inventory. This document also relates that six valets were appointed to place the dishes on the table of the crown princess and her consort, with only two remaining to serve until their majesties rose from the table.

In February 1767 the ceiling of the dining hall of Queluz[11] was completed, decorated with paintings depicting bucolic picnics and still lifes. However, a number of accounting records[12] indicate that the great banquets were held in the "Long Hall of the Columns," also known variously as the Recitals Hall, the Ambassadors' Hall, or the Hall of the Pitchers, because it was decorated with Chinese porcelain vases or pitchers placed in niches and on pedestals. On these occasions, the dessert was set in the Round Hall decorated with scenes from the adventures of Don Quixote and Sancho Panza, perhaps in ironic allusion to the vices of temperance and greed. This hall, known today as the Don Quixote Hall, was completed in 1768 and at that time was called the "New Dessert Hall,"[13] which suggests that the custom of setting rooms specifically for dessert already existed.

Documents describing the decoration of the dessert service indicate that it constituted a grand finale to the meal.[14] The Queluz inventories of 1763 and 1776 mention an extraordinary dessert in "Saxony ware" that was six feet, eight inches in length, a veritable garden including a country house, small temples with cupolas supported by Atlantes, balustrades, fountains, flower vases, and a pleiad of Olympian divinities accompanied by the Muses of Parnassus and the Liberal Arts, the whole mounted on mirrors surrounded by a broad border of porcelain supported on bronze legs. A series of separate pieces completed this scene, such as fruit, flowers, vines, candlesticks, and two-branched candelabra.

New pieces of Meissen porcelain arrived in 1773, including four groups of mythological figures seated on clouds with twenty-nine figures of shepherds, gardeners, grape pickers, knife grinders, students, a dancing master, and allegorical figures representing agriculture, trade, and astronomy. All these pieces, together with various items in silver, were displayed in ever-changing temporary sets in combination with perishable materials such as papier mâché painted in polychrome or coated with silver, gold, and even silk to create leaves and flowers, requiring the supervision of an architect and three or four painters and other craftsmen.

The inauguration of the opera theater at Queluz in 1774 gave rise to an order for many yards of flower garlands ("twenty ells [a measure of length] of strings of foliage for the dessert"), over two hundred dozen silk flowers and a thousand palm fronds, and more than two thousand three-leafed sprays.[15] Glittering celebrations also accompanied the inauguration of the equestrian statue of Dom José I in June 1775 in the Praça do Comércio in Lisbon (see França, fig. 1), and a few pieces from the Chinese export service that was commissioned for the banquet on that occasion have survived, together with a curious document outlining the form to be followed by the six masters of ceremonies responsible for overseeing the festivities, consisting of fireworks, an open-air concert, a ball, and supper announced by the orchestra playing a march. After supper, the coaches began to depart while other guests made their way to the gaming tables.[16]

A painting of a garden party from that period depicts a stage covered by a red and gold canopy and two rows of arcades with numerous groups of people in which figures from the *Commedia dell'Arte* may be identified, including musicians, acrobats, and masked figures,[17] constituting a valuable pictorial record, which corresponds to contemporary written accounts, of the court's entertainment during balmy summer evenings.

On 31 August 1793, the *Gazeta de Lisboa* treated its readers to a description of an evening party held in the gardens of Queluz, describing the Chinese pavilion that was constructed on the river, the Chinese lanterns, the panes with transparent paintings positioned before the facade, a large waterfall depicting marine divinities, transparent devices that moved around the garden, and, finally, the launching of illuminated balloons bearing the royal coats of arms of Portugal and Spain. This celebration marked the birth of the first daughter of Dom João VI and Rainha Carlota Joaquina de Bourbon and demonstrated the magnificence that could be marshaled by a society that would soon be ravaged by the Napoleonic invasions and their aftermath.

A.H.M.F: Fundo do Arquivo Histórico do Ministério das Finanças, incorporated in the Arquivo Nacional in the Torre do Tombo

A.N.T.T.: Arquivo Nacional in the Torre do Tombo

B.A.N.B.A.: Boletim da Academia Nacional de Belas Artes

B.A.: Biblioteca da Ajuda

M.N.E.: Ministério dos Negócios Estrangeiros

1. Simonetta Luz Afonso and Angela Delaforce, *Palace of Queluz: The Gardens* (Lisbon, 1989).

2. A.H.M.F. box 338, document 11, February 1796 (celebration marking completion of construction).

3. Marquis de Bombelles, *Journal d'un Ambassadeur de France au Portugal, 1786–88* (Paris, 1979), 73.

4. A.N.T.T., Casa do Infantado, bundle 582, 26 April 1755; A.N.T.T., Casa do Infantado, bundle 1, box 2, doc. 29, 25 March 1755.

5. *Gazeta de Lisboa,* 6 July 1758; *Gazeta de Lisboa,* July 1760; A.N.T.T., Casa do Infantado, bundle 582, 7 September 1758 (Dom Pedro's thanks to the architect Mateus Vicente de Oliveira for his considerable work for the celebrations of Saint John and Saint Peter in the Quinta de Queluz); A.N.T.T., Casa do Infantado, bundle 580, 4 July 1760.

6. François, comte de Bachi, was the ambassador of the king of France to Portugal between 1752 and 1756. An earlier *Ceremonial* had been composed in 1753. A.N.T.T.-M.N.E. Memorials, entries, overnight stays, farewells 1713/53 Ceremonial... Conde de Bachi... 1753 L° 149, sheet 154–156v, and A.N.T.T.-M.N.E., Ceremonial Conde de Bachi, 1755, L° 148. (Special thanks to Dr. Nuno Vassalo e Silva and Dr. Olivia Vasques for drawing attention to this unpublished document.)

A comparison of the two documents indicates that the *Ceremonial* of 1755 introduced certain innovations in table etiquette, for example the practice of changing rooms prior to serving dessert, which is confirmed in numerous accounts from the following decades on the subject of halls and dessert tables in the palace of Queluz (see notes 10–12 below). The word *decer* in Portuguese, a corruption of the French *dessert,* is used in the Queluz documents to refer to the room or table intended for serving dessert and also to the objects in silver or porcelain that were incorporated into decorative structures, sometimes of monumental proportions, used for the service of dessert.

7. We cite a few of the hundreds of accounts dealing with expenditures for food for the celebrations: A.N.T.T., Casa do Infantado, bundle L, box 2, document 20, 2 June 1758; A.N.T.T., Casa

do Infantado, bundle 582, 560, 1764 and 1765; A.N.T.T., Casa do Infantado, box 263, 1767–69; A.N.T.T., Casa do Infantado, box 316, 1770 (expenditure on fish for the king's dinner and supper).

8. Domingos Rodrigues, *Arte de Cozinha* (Lisbon, 1765). The author was head of the royal kitchen during the reign of Dom Pedro II, and this popular Portuguese cookbook was regularly reprinted and updated after its publication in 1680. The 1765 edition quoted contains a section dealing with the art of preparing tables in the French style.

9. A.N.T.T., Casa do Infantado, bundle 493, 19 July 1771 (purchase of tableware from the Real Fábrica de Louça warehouse for the Royal Quinta of Queluz).

10. A.N.T.T., Casa do Infantado, bundle 1, box 2, doc. 37, December 1767.

11. A.N.T.T., Casa do Infantado, bundle 493, February 1767.

12. A.N.T.T.-A.H.M.F., box 265, August 1774 ("small expenses incurred by João Bap. Robillion in this Quinta de Queluz. Paint for two dessert tables in the round Hall and the long hall with columns").

13. A.N.T.T., Casa do Infantado, bundle 494, document 13, September 1768 ("eight-sided table I made for the new Dessert Hall...").

14. A.N.T.T., Casa do Infantado, bundle 494, July 1770, bundle 495, May-June 1772 ("Expenses incurred by J. B. Robillion—turned balls of the dessert; paint for the desserts; 50 dozen flowers for the dessert; 28 bouquets for same"); A.N.T.T., Casa do Infantado, bundle 496, doc. 9, June 1773 ("Leaf baskets in the production of the new dessert, supervised by J. B. Robillion, 4 carpenters, painter and one stonemason..."; "...gold leaf for the St. Peter dessert"); A.N.T.T., box 265, July 1774 ("Surveyor/Guardian of the dessert and silver table center...").

15. A.N.T.T.-A.H.M.F., Casa do Infantado, box 265, docs. 16, 19, 24, 30, 31, June, July, August 1764.

16. B.A. 54–X–7 (118), 7 June 1775 (Instruction... Masters of Ceremonies).

17. The painting, which is in a private collection, bears an inscription describing the festivities depicted that is, unfortunately, extensively damaged, obliterating all but the following: "Record of the Festivities Celebrated... Betrothal of the Serene Prince and Princess of Brazil in the year 1786... Drawn and Invented by Muzi." The scene is certainly one of the celebrations on the occasion of Prince João's marriage to Princess Carlota Joaquina de Bourbon, inscribed with the date of 1786, while the marriage actually took place in 1785.

AUTHORS OF ENTRIES

Luísa Arruda 31

Rafael Salinas Calado 32, 34, 36, 37, 39

Teresa Lima de Campos 27

A. Ayres de Carvalho 99–103

Francisco Clode 28–30

Leonor d'Orey 26, 40–58, 65–70, 72–80

Décio Ruivo Martins 60–64

Jennifer Montagu 107

João Pedro Monteiro 28–30

Maria Helena Mendes Pinto 4

Miguel Soromenho 1

José de Monterroso Teixeira 2, 3, 5–19,
    21–25, 33, 35, 38, 59, 71, 81–98, 104–106,
    109–119

Nuno Vassallo e Silva 20, 108

Luís Alte da Veiga 60–64

NOTE TO THE READER

Dimensions are in centimeters,
followed in parentheses by inches.

Catalogue

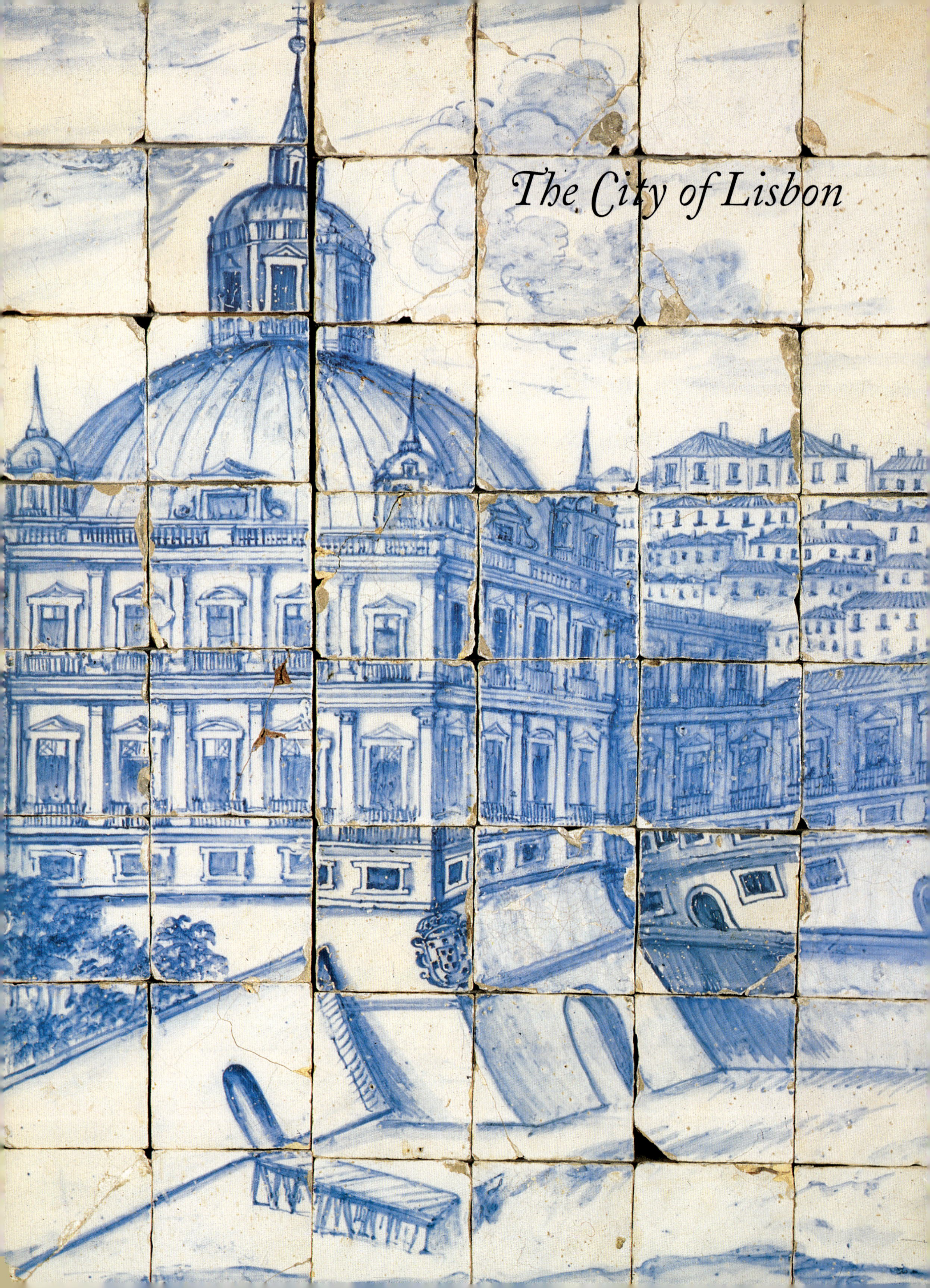

The City of Lisbon

The appearance of Lisbon during its golden years in the early eighteenth century is preserved in occasional paintings and other views. The most important of these documents is a panorama executed in blue-and-white painted tiles that shows the city as though seen from a ship sailing down the Tagus River. A massive earthquake that struck Lisbon in 1755 on the morning of All Saints Day destroyed many of its best-known monuments and changed its aspect forever. Afterward the center of the city was reconstructed on an entirely new plan during the ascendancy of Dom José I's powerful minister, the marquês de Pombal.

1

View of Lisbon
Portuguese
1st quarter 18th century
blue and white tile
111.5 x 2017.5 (43⁷/₈ x 794⁵/₁₆ [66 feet])

Museu Nacional do Azulejo, Lisbon, inv. 1, from the Palácio dos Condes de Tentúgal, Lisbon

Silva 1960; Carvalho 1971; Meco 1991; Brussels 1991:2; Guibbini 1992

This tile panel is the most nearly complete general view of Lisbon to survive from the early eighteenth century. The composition was originally larger, and although it has been truncated at both ends, the impression of the space surrounding the city remains undiminished. The effect is highly decorative, and the artist combined a detailed analysis of construction with a skillful handling of effects of mass and volume, thus endowing the whole with a unity of expression. The composition is by no means rigorous and the draftsmanship is imperfect, but the principal cause of the unquestionable naivete of the whole and of a certain lack of definition is the absence of a single viewpoint: some elements on the riverbank are depicted virtually head-on, while other buildings are seen from a bird's eye view.

It is not immediately evident who painted this panel. In a recent study (1989), José Meco suggested that the view was the work of the tile painter Gabriel del Barco, despite the fact that a previous monograph devoted to this artist did not include the panel in his oeuvre. Meco's hypothesis has subsequently found general acceptance. The tentative and schematic nature of Barco's drawing, combined with a highly developed decorative sense, may indeed be compared with the graphic style of the *View of Lisbon*, but attempts to match buildings as they appeared during Barco's lifetime with those depicted in the panel tend to contradict this possibility. For example, the wooden cupola to be seen on the dome of the church of Santa Engrácia would suggest that the panel was painted in the second decade of the century (Carvalho 1971) and could therefore not have been painted by Gabriel del Barco who died prior to 1703. Of course, the church in the panel could have been based on the architect João Antunes' original plans, with which Barco was very likely familiar.

In terms of decorative motifs, the panel falls into a fairly well-known tradition of *vedute* (views) of Lisbon. While this tradition may be traced back to the fifteenth century, it was not until the final quarter of the sixteenth century that a sizable series of views was produced that laid the foundation for certain of the more enduring artistic conventions in representing the city. While the panorama of Braun and Hogenburg (1572) was of prime importance in its day in conveying the image of Lisbon to the European world, it nonetheless depicted the city in an excessively northern style. Renderings that are believed to be more accurate appear in the view produced by Simão de Miranda de Távora (1575) and the large anonymous drawing now in the Leiden University Library (c. 1570) attributed to the Flemish draftsman Anton van den Wyngaerde. Both give a clear impression of sixteenth-century Lisbon, with its medieval urban structure still very much in evidence, including numer-

ous churches and with a large proportion of the city consisting of buildings related to shipping activities and administration of the empire. In both works, small vignettes offer the viewer brief glimpses of daily life set against an ever-present background of heavy river traffic.

Later, seventeenth-century views reveal a new approach. The object now was to depict the city itself and the ways in which Dom Filipe, the king, had changed it, making the royal palace the city's hub, with the tower built to architect João de Herrera's plans occupying pride of place. The image of the city was enhanced by a royal dimension, apparent for instance in the immense square before the palace. This is true of the view drawn by Domingos Vieira Serrão (1619), which is of particular interest since it shows the temporary architectural structures erected for Filipe III's entry, and is likewise true of the animated canvas by Amaro do Vale (1619), two artists who successively occupied the position of royal painter.

Thus, as an image, this *View of Lisbon* does not add anything new to the *vedute* tradition with the exception of greater possibilities inherent in such a large surface. The fact that so few other views of Lisbon are known from this period may be attributed to the developing nature of the production and collecting of works of art in Portugal. It is also true that, as has been pointed out with regard to other contemporary cases, this virtual absence of views also may be accounted for by the very nature of urban growth: the *vedute* is only justified by the concept of the city square (Guibbini 1992), and the compact medieval structure of Lisbon prevailed until the Pombaline reconstruction of the city. Therefore, while constituting a transition between the two time periods, the tile panel from the Palácio Tentúgal clearly demonstrates the paradox of baroque Lisbon, the capital of a court but still lacking any major points of urban focus.

In the early eighteenth century, what remained of the medieval town was defined by two points of reference: the São

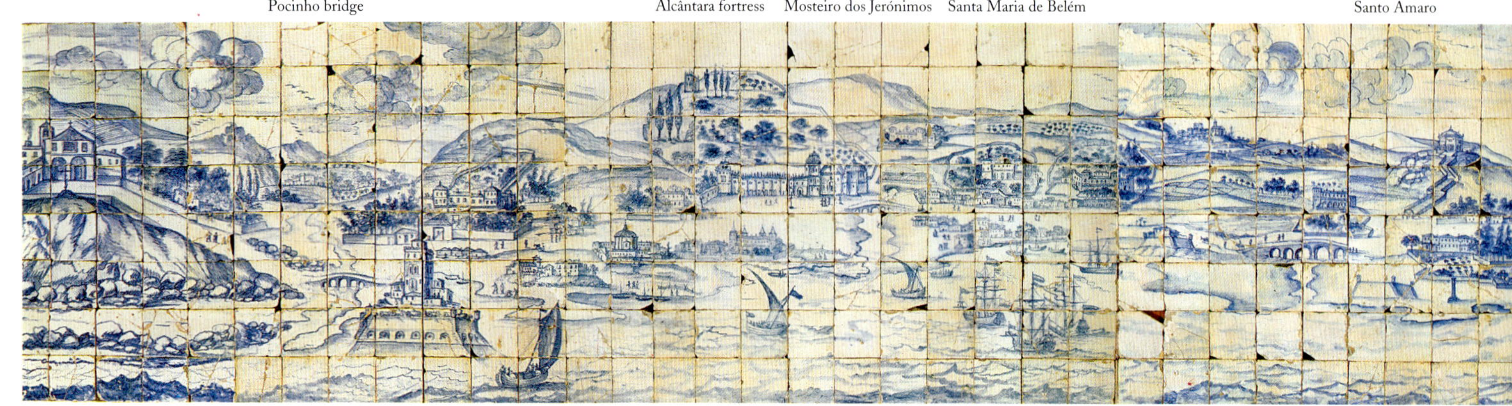

Jorge castle, a large walled area and a royal residence until the sixteenth century occupying the crown of a strategic hill; lower down and almost swallowed up in the compact web of the town is the church of Santa Maria Maior, the cathedral of Lisbon, made prominent by its towered facade and the imposing tower erected by Afonso IV over the chancel.

In the *View of Lisbon,* the great projects executed during the reign of Dom Manuel I still lie beyond the confines of the city: the church of Santa Maria de Belém and the adjacent Mosteiro dos Jerónimos and, farther afield, the recognizable structure of the Torre de Belém; in the center of the composition, the Casa dos Bicos, built in 1521 by the son of the viceroy of India, Afonso de Albuquerque, with its unique facade of diamond-cut blocks, and the adjacent church of the Misericórdia, which was built during the same period. The position of the buildings on the riverbank, which is apparent in this composition, also corresponds to the stage of development attained by the city during the Manueline period. This was a strategic area for services related to shipping, and located here were the Casa da Índia (abutting the royal palace), the Casa da Pólvora, the Alfândiga Nova (new customs house) and, farther to the right, the Taracenas Novas (arsenal) as well as a number of shipyards, some depicting ongoing work on vessels in drydock.

The city of Filipe's day is remarkable for the extensive rebuilding of the old palace, the Palácio da Ribeira. Also from the same period are the imposing Palácio Côrte-Real, obviously of Spanish inspiration, taking full advantage of the river with one of its courtyards opening onto the riverbank, and the monumental silhouette of the royally sponsored church of São Vicente de Fora, crowned by the

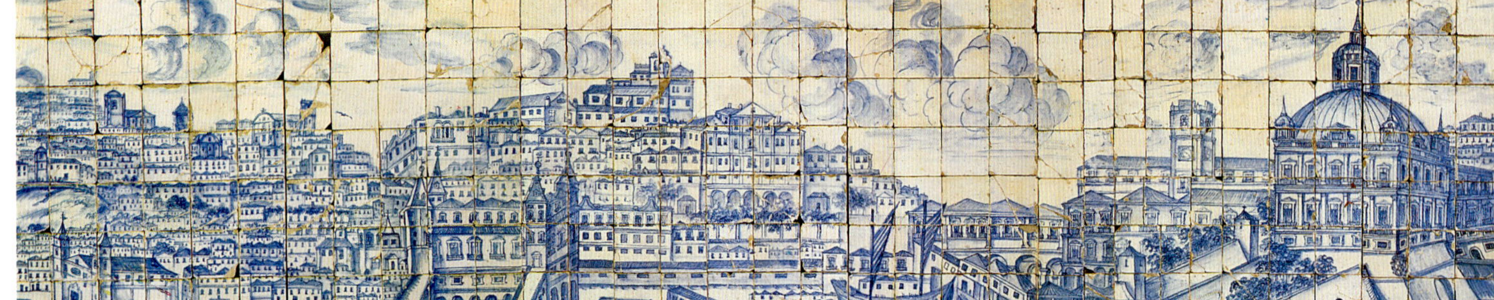

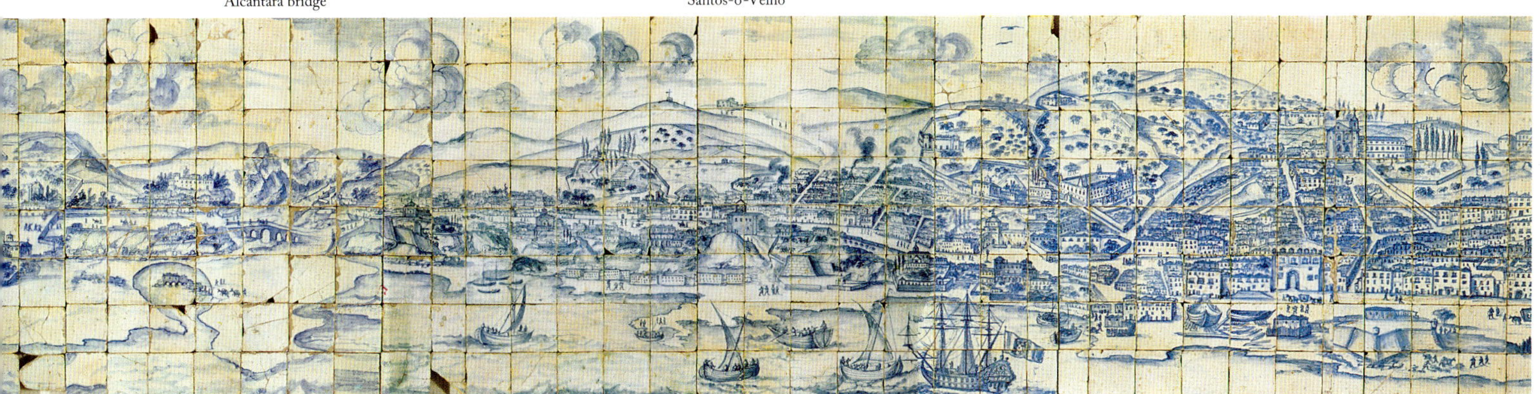

magnificent eight-sided cupola that collapsed in the earthquake of 1755.

Thus, during the early days of the baroque period, Lisbon was an amalgam of a number of periods. The church of Santa Engrácia, with its centralized design surmounted by a cupola visible immediately beneath the church of São Vicente de Fora, constituted the sole attempt in the city to construct a building of modern design. Other religious structures that are prominent in the appearance of the city include the convent of Nossa Senhora da Graça, immediately below the castle, the monastery of São Francisco da Cidade, the churches of Santos-o-Velho, the Paulists, São Roque, Loreto, Santa Catarina, São Paulo, and the Mártires.

On the outskirts of the city, the concentration of the center yields to sparser settlement, with a large number of typically Portuguese *quintas*, a combination of recreational stately home and working farm. One such example, at the extreme left behind the Torre de Belém, is the Palácio dos Condes de São Lourenço, later called "da Praia," replete with towers and surrounding wall, and the Quinta de Baixo, belonging to the Condes de Aveiras, opposite the Mosteiro dos Jerónimos. The area around Lisbon along the Tagus River was also a traditional site for convents and monasteries: São José de Ribamar to the left of the Torre de Belém and, immediately to the right, the octagonal structure of the Irish Dominicans' convent of Nossa Senhora do Bom Sucesso (founded in 1639), which exemplify the trend of expansion toward the west. On the eastern side of the city is the monastery of Santos-o-Novo with its small loggia serving as a vantage point and, behind it, the convent of Santa Apolónia and, finally, the convent of Madre de Deus.

Other prominent features in the panel are certain defensive structures of the city, such as the Estrêla fort, the Alcântara fortress and the Terreiro do Paço, the Santo Cristo and São Jerónimo chapels, both within the enclosed space around the Mosteiro dos Jerónimos, the round sixteenth-century chapel of Santo Amaro, with its winding stairway, and the Alcântara, dos Gafos, and do Pocinho tributaries with their respective bridges. The expressive character of the view can be attributed to the attention the artist paid to the images of everyday life in the city, such as the eminently realistic details of beasts burdened with sacks of flour returning from the water mill, laborers hard at work in the shipyards, coaches passing, and ships sailing up and down the river.

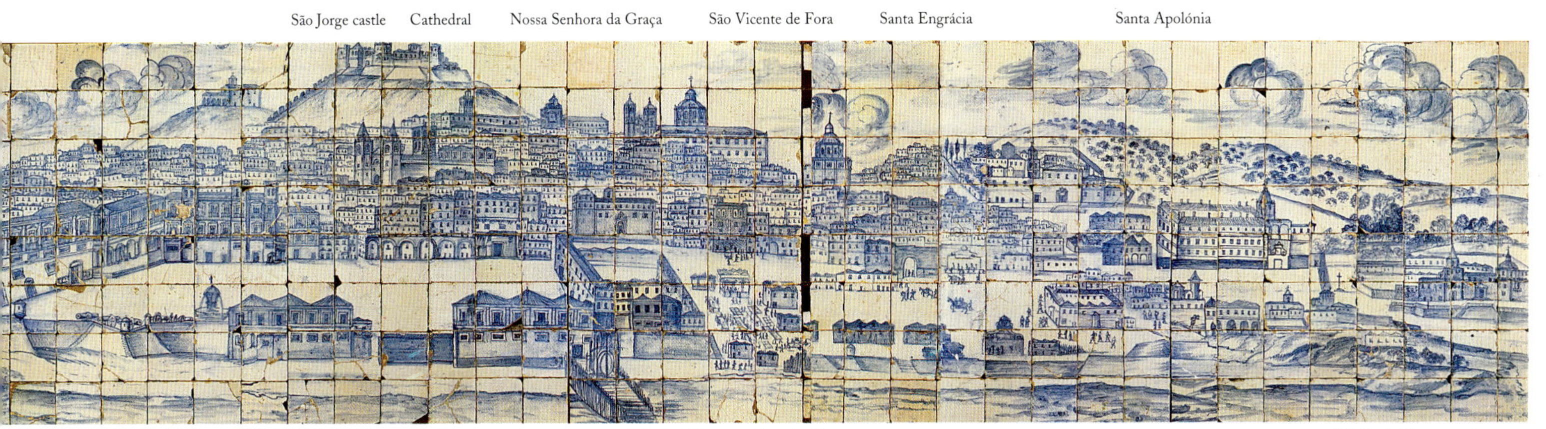

2

View of Lisbon before the Earthquake

c. 1693

oil on canvas

109 x 239 (42¹⁵/₁₆ x 94⅛)

Insc. (on plaque at lower right corner):
INGRESSO ALLA PRIMA UDIENZA DI
MONS. GIOGIO CORNARO, NUNCIO APOS-
TOLICO ALLA MAESTA DEL RE PIETRO
SECONDO IN LISBONNA IL DI JUGLIO 1693
(entry to the first audience of Mos.
Giorgio Cornaro, Apostolic Nunzio to
His Majesty Dom Pedro II in Lisbon,
July 1693)

Jorge de Brito Collection, Cascais

Castilho 1893; Carvalho 1960–1962; França 1966;
Brussels 1991, III.58

The large square tower and the adjacent
building extending to the right dominate
the large square known as the Terreiro
do Paço (palace square). The tower, built
around 1581, was designed by Filippo
Terzi (1520–1597), who had moved to
Portugal after accompanying Dom Sebastião as military engineer on his disastrous Moroccan campaign in 1578. The
fortification-like design echoes the functional nature and purpose of the previous
construction, the palace built by Dom
Manuel I during the early sixteenth century, which was intended to demonstrate
that Lisbon had expanded beyond the
medieval limits of the city walls and to
keep abreast of the new Renaissance
style of urban planning. The main purpose of the original palace, however, had
been to celebrate the Age of the Discoveries, while incorporating the new construction into the military plan for the
defense of the Tagus estuary, since the
palace stood on the beach. The symbol
of royal power embodied in a fortress introduces a military theme conveying in-
vulnerability, prestige, and authority.
The tower accommodated the Royal Library and the Hall of the Ambassadors,
symbolizing knowledge and power at the
international and diplomatic level.

The inscription indicates that the subject of the painting is the solemn procession accompanying the apostolic
nunzio's entry into Lisbon in 1693. It is
known from descriptions that this cor-
tege passed by way of the gate formerly
known as the Arc das Paz (arch of
peace), which appears in views of the city
painted during the Manueline period.
The royal guard stands at attention in a
double line extending the entire width of
the square, as coaches and litters advance
between the two files of soldiers.

3

LOUIS MICHEL VAN LOO
French, 1707–1771

**Portrait of Sebastião José de Carvalho e
Melo, 1st Marquês de Pombal**

1766

oil on canvas

233 x 304 (91¾ x 119¹¹/₁₆)

Câmara Municipal de Oeiras

Machado 1823; Sousa Viterbo 1903; Costa 1935;
Soares 1940; Soares 1947–1960; França 1966;
Brussels 1991, III.1

Van Loo was commissioned to execute
this painting in 1766 by two powerful
merchants, the Englishman Gerald
Devis and a Swiss named Purry. The
painter had returned to Paris in 1752 after
spending fifteen years in Madrid in the
service of Philip V's court, achieving
fame for his portraits of members of the
royal family and of the nobility. This
made him an obvious choice when the
Portuguese diplomatic representative
was instructed to contract a portraitist.
Claude-J. Vernet (1714–1789), who specialized in marine scenes, participated in
painting the background. On the basis of
sketches sent to Lisbon by António
Joaquim Padrão (c. 1731–1771) and J. S.
Carpinetti (1740–1800), Van Loo and

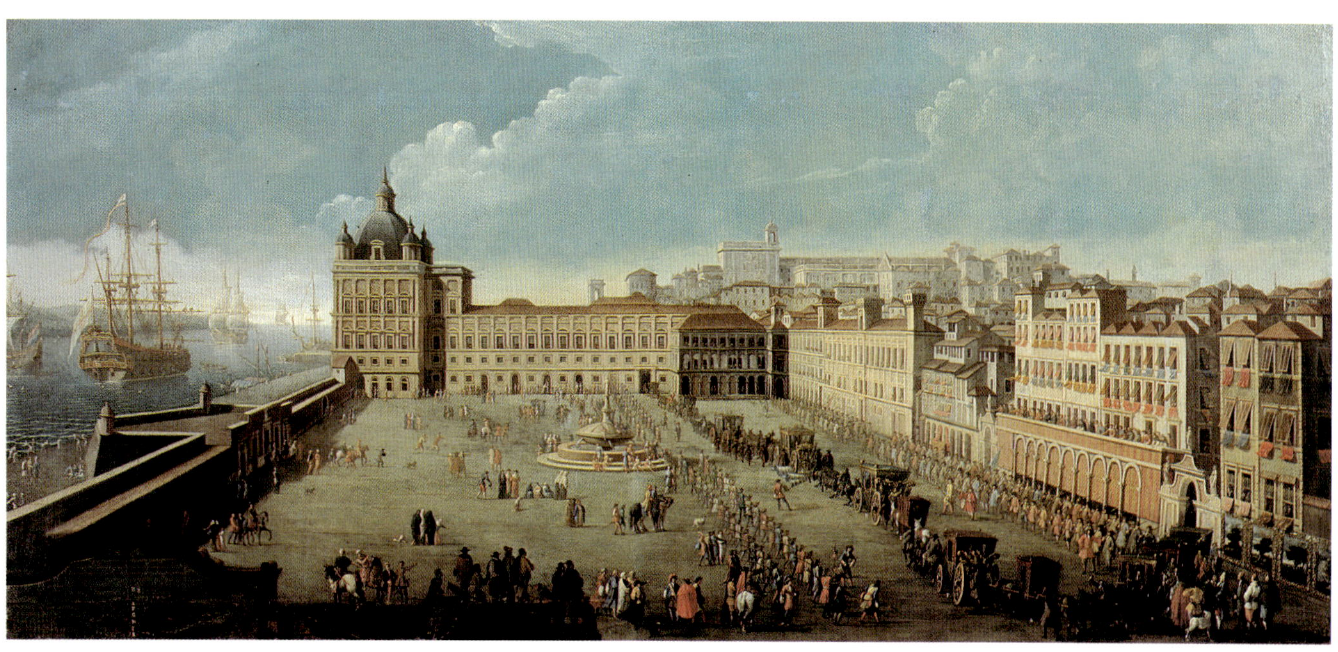

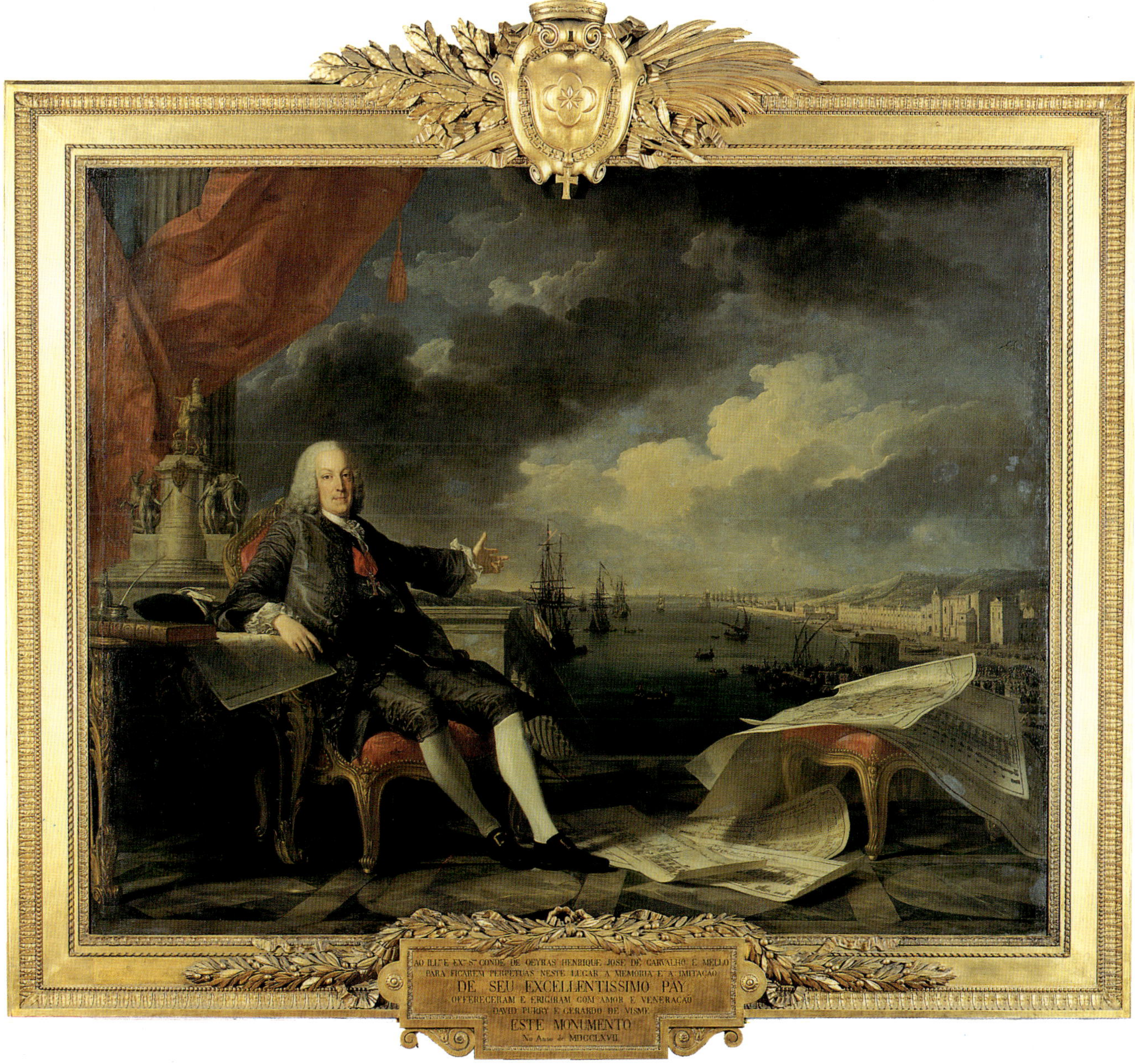

Vernet planned a composition that was approved by Pombal. The usual title, *The Marquis of Pombal Expelling the Jesuits,* implies that this harsh decision represents his personal ideology. However, this allegorical painting, which was widely disseminated in an engraving (1772) by J. Beauvarlet (1731–1797), cannot be confined to a single interpretation. The inscription explains: "Sebastião Jozé de Carvalho e Mello, 1st marquês de Pombal, on the occasion of the expulsion of the Jesuits and the establishment of Trade, Industry, and Art and for the Reconstruction of Lisbon."

Additional aspects of Pombal's actions in government are evoked to enhance his image and policy, particularly the rebuilding of the city after the earthquake, are alluded to by the ground plans spread over a footstool and spilling onto the floor in the bottom right-hand corner. The establishment of Trade, Industry, and Arts is appropriately incorporated in the model for the equestrian statue of Dom José I to be erected in the Praça do Comércio. The fleet at anchor opposite the Jerónimos Monastery and the Praça de Belém alludes to Portugal's maritime dimension and to a belief in navigation

as an essential element of economic and commercial activity, which also found expression in the establishment of trading monopolies in Brazil and Portugal.

The top of the frame bears the coat of arms of Sebastião José de Carvalho e Melo, then conde de Oeiras, the title he was awarded in 1759. He did not become marquês de Pombal until three years after the portrait was executed.

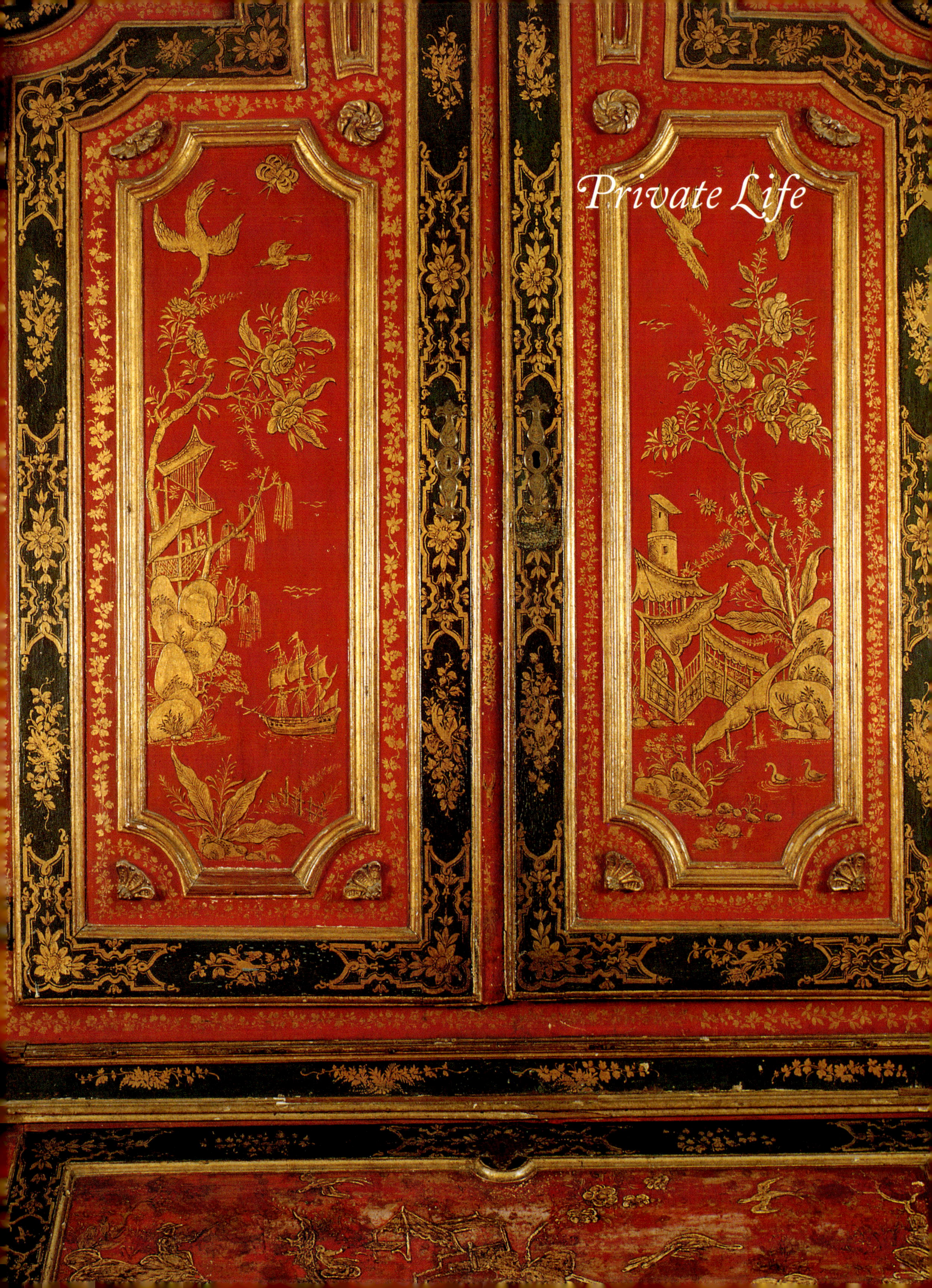

Private Life

Wealthy Portuguese in the eighteenth century furnished their households with domestic objects purchased and commissioned from a variety of local and foreign sources. Ready supplies of hardwoods and silver from Brazil, as well as the ability of Portuguese craftsmen to adapt diverse styles and make them their own, ensured the excellence of furniture and silverware production. Uniquely Portuguese were the compositions in hand-painted blue and white tiles, with which interior walls were decorated, as well as utilitarian works in faience executed in a lively vernacular style. Portugal's worldwide trade gave jewelers access to the widest possible variety of precious and decorative gemstones.

4

Cabinet on Stand *(contador)*
Portuguese
1st quarter 18th century
light ebony with handles in chased brass
146 x 94 x 48 (57¹/₂ x 37 x 18⁷/₈)

*Museu Nacional de Arte Antiga,
Lisbon, inv. 979 Mov*

Langhans 1745; Santos 1953; Smith 1962;
Pinto 1979; Gonçalves 1984

The cabinet is one of the most typical items of furniture in seventeenth-century Portugal. Such cabinets were to become prominent during the mid-seventeenth century, with a balanced and austere construction enhanced by decorative elements on the front of the drawers, on the sides, and frequently on the frame of the stand, which itself developed from an incidental support to become a structural element.

The decoratively shaped and chased brass appliqués, which are a typical feature of seventeenth-century cabinets, had a functional as well as decorative significance. While adorning the front of the drawers they also served to protect the keyholes, corners, and sides from being scraped by the key rings, a function that is emphasized by the ornately edged escutcheons. Additional metal elements decorate the joints of the stand, giving the ornamental screws better purchase.

By the end of the seventeenth century, when Portuguese furniture was tending increasingly toward the French style, such cabinets fell into disuse and, during the course of the following century, they were removed from drawing rooms and offices to other less important rooms, although one finds occasional references to them in inventories and other registers. The cabinet on display is a relatively late example. In the manner of earlier models, it is composed of a chest and a stand, both far removed from the original baroque style. The chest has a protruding molding, which frames nine identical drawer fronts that in reality cover six drawers of different sizes. This body of drawers is flanked by composite twisted columns with Corinthian capitals. The columns appear to join brackets on the rim of the stand that flank a drawer occupying the entire width, the front of which is divided into three drawer fronts to maintain the same visual effect as the drawers above.

The elaborate decoration follows the baroque style that prevailed in the early eighteenth century. The legs are composed of voluminous fluted bulbs and double twisted columns, within a framework in which these twisted elements are interrupted by disks and flattened balls. As though this complex decoration did not suffice, the apron, as this decoration was called, is covered with elaborate plant motifs. The exuberant scrolled foliage, symmetrically arranged on either side of a center occupied by a floral composition, supports two putti, rather like Atlantids raising their arms as though to hold up the body of the cabinet.

The master carver responsible for this cabinet repeated this model or a very similar version in a number of other pieces of furniture, in frames for mirrors, and in altar reredos, taking advantage of the privilege of repeating his designs accorded to him by the regulations governing his profession.

In addition, very similar if not identical motifs appear in silversmiths' works, as is apparent in the decoration of the urns commissioned by the abbess of the Mosteiro do Lorvão from the Oporto goldsmith Manuel Carneiro da Silva (1705–1715) to contain the mortal remains of Rainha Dona Teresa and Princesa Sancha, who died in the thirteenth century and were subsequently beatified. The similarity between the decoration of the apron of the cabinet and that of the urns and the fact that we can date the goldsmith's work allow us to date this item of furniture to the early eighteenth century.

5

Secretary
c. 1720
English
lacquered and gilded wood
212 x 103 x 64 (83⁷/₁₆ x 40⁹/₁₆ x 25³/₁₆)

Private Collection, Lisbon

Branco 1868; Guimarães 1872; Branco 1875; Borges 1889; Symonds 1935; Symonds 1940; Symonds 1941; Pimentel 1946; Huth 1971; Mendes Pinto 1973; Honour and Fleming 1977; AA.VV 1987; Brussels 1991, I.32

The secretary on display was purchased by Dom João V with a special purpose in mind. It was a gift to Soror Paula Teresa da Silva (1701– ?) of the Convento de Odivelas, whose scandalous love affairs caused a great deal of ink to flow at the time and were severely judged by many historians. There came a time when the king's frequent visits to the nun could no longer be tolerated by the community, prompting Dom João to build chambers for her adjoining his own, which he had decorated in the most lavish style: doors of precious woods from Brazil and cast gilded hinges and handles, ornate ceilings with gilded carving, marquetry floors and tile wainscoting depicting *fêtes galantes* in communicating rooms and corridors.

The bedroom was paneled with mir-

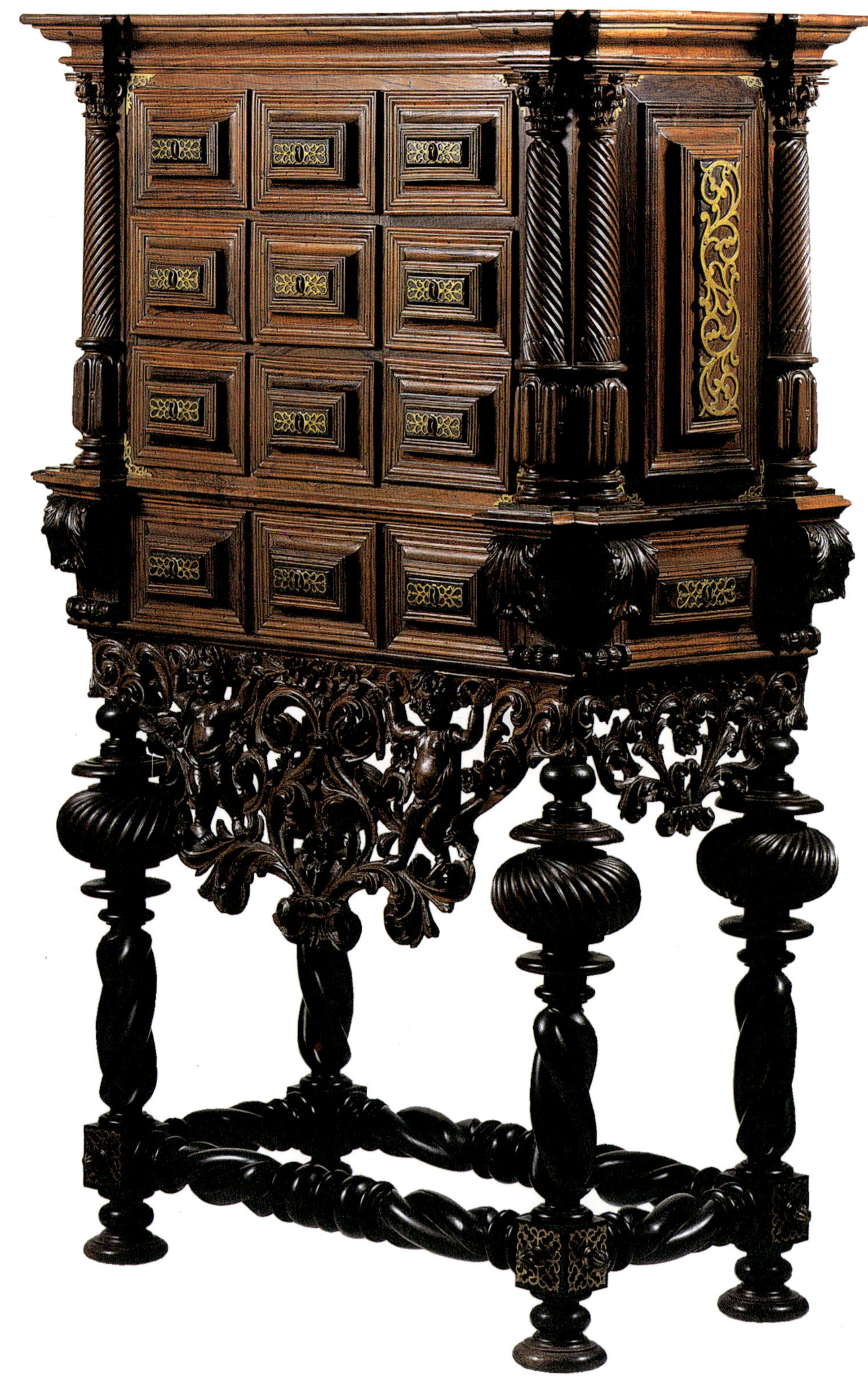

4

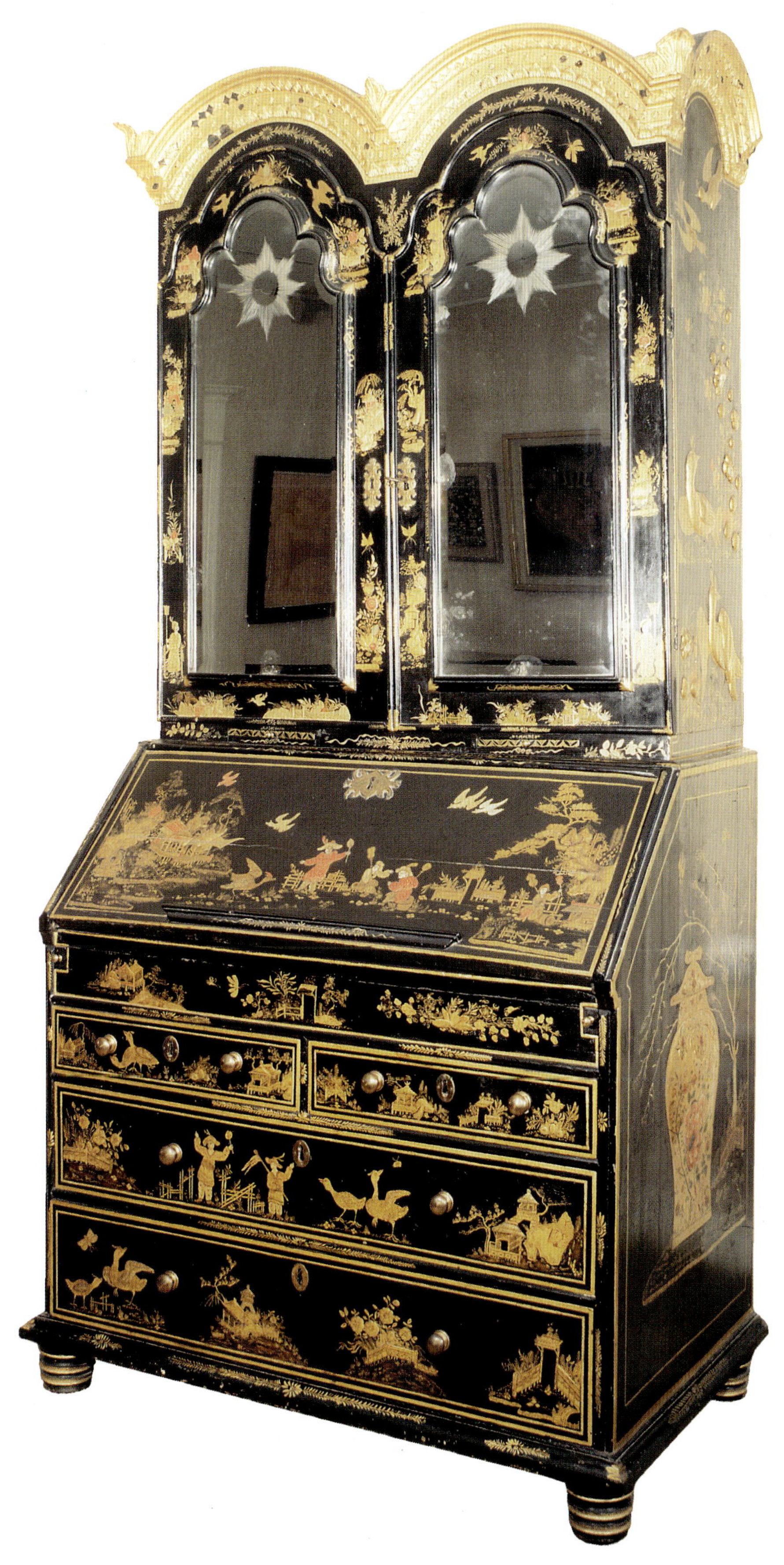

rors that reflected the gleam of the chandeliers; carved gilded chairs upholstered in crimson velvet matched gilded tables and complemented the lacquer and gold secretaries. Inscribed on the inside of the doors of this secretary are the names "Dom João V" and "Paula" encircled in ribbons. The existence of a similar secretary, dating from the same period and perhaps by the same manufacturer, suggests that the two were ordered as a pair, which was customary when making purchases for the court or for large residences. The beveled and engraved glass is typical of the period.

Lacquered furniture became especially popular in Europe during the later seventeenth and eighteenth centuries. For example, the cargo manifest of the vessel *Feu* in London in the early eighteenth century includes "thirteen lacquer trunks and fourteen secretaries." The capitals of Europe were fascinated by Oriental exoticism, and craftsmen had access to original examples, enabling them to analyze and reproduce the lacquer technique. As a result, production began in Europe, originally in France and England, of furnishings and small objects that borrowed freely from Oriental models and imitated the lacquer processes, as revealed in *The Treatise of Japanning and Varnishing* (London, 1688).

In England the technique became so widespread that it was even used in yachts, such as on the vessel presented by the queen of England to the conde de Vilar Maior on his trip to escort Maria Ana of Austria, the future bride of Dom João V, back to Portugal. Frei Francisco da Fonseca, the embassy's secretary, described the vessel: "The prow was decorated with ingenious figures and foliage in gold; the state room was all in the most delicate lacquer from China, intermingled with mirrors and cristal" (Embaixada 1716).

Documents have survived pertaining to the extensive importation of English furniture to the Iberian Peninsula, and it is known that certain models sent to Spain and Portugal differ from those executed for the British market; the most

sought-after pieces were looking glasses and "the English Japanned furniture was also popular with the Portuguese especially when of bright and light colors, such as scarlet and yellow" (Symonds 1940, 234).

6

attributed to GASPAR FERREIRA
and MANUEL DA SILVA
Portuguese
Secretary-Oratory
1st quarter 18th century
japanned and gilded oak
268 x 72 x 44 (105½ x 28⅜ x 17⁵/₁₆)
Museu da Fábrica da Vista Alegre, Ílhavo

Santos 1970; Sandão 1979; Mendes Pinto 1979; Pimentel 1987; AA.VV 1989; Brussels 1991, no. I.33

Since this exceptional secretary-oratory bears the Portuguese royal coat of arms in the center of the front panel, it may be supposed that it was commissioned by the king himself, for it is unlikely that the escutcheon was introduced purely as an ornamental motif. This possibility, as well as the meticulous execution of the decoration, suggests that the carving (or indeed the entire piece) and the painting and gilding may have been executed by Gaspar Ferreira and Manuel da Silva, who in 1719–1723 also produced the elaborate bookshelves for Coimbra University Library (see Wohl, fig. 4), which brought them considerable prestige. Because there were few skilled craftsmen in Portugal at that time other than Ferreira and da Silva, one may assume that it was they who were honored with such a commission.

Similarities with the decoration at the Coimbra library are apparent in the flame motifs surmounting the shelves and the flame finials on the upright section of the secretary as well as the outline of both upper sections. The position of the volutes on the upper corners of the secretary and of those supporting the architrave of the porticoes inside the library suggest a common origin. The

attribution to Ferreira and da Silva is strengthened by the fact that, in 1727, Dom João V commissioned da Silva to paint a series of panels depicting the life of Santa Clara for the church of that name in Coimbra. The type of decoration he produced bears a close resemblance to that of the coromandel screens of Chinese origin (Henan), which were purchased in trading ports along that coast of India (see the compilation of motifs assembled by Jean Antoine Fraisse, an artist who specialized in copying Chinese lacquer work and vases, entitled *Livre des Desseins Chinois* [Paris, 1735]). Chinese porcelain also served to spread the vogue for chinoiserie, opening the way to rococo design with a preference for flowing and asymmetrical compositions.

Attempts were also made in Portugal to imitate the exoticism, sheen, and solidity of lacquer of "Chinese varnish," since the country was a traditional importer of lacquered objects and even of the raw material (the plant Rhus vernicifera), which had long been brought back from the Far East by the vessel *Nao do Trato*. Hundreds of pieces of lacquered furniture were produced in Portugal, including wardrobes, tables, dressing tables, commodes, chests, and benches, bearing witness to an enduring appreciation for Oriental objects.

The Ílhavo secretary-oratory is distinguished also by the fine architectural structure of its interior, which takes the form of a miniature reredos. The inner panels are painted with scenes of Christ's Passion, although these are of indifferent artistic quality.

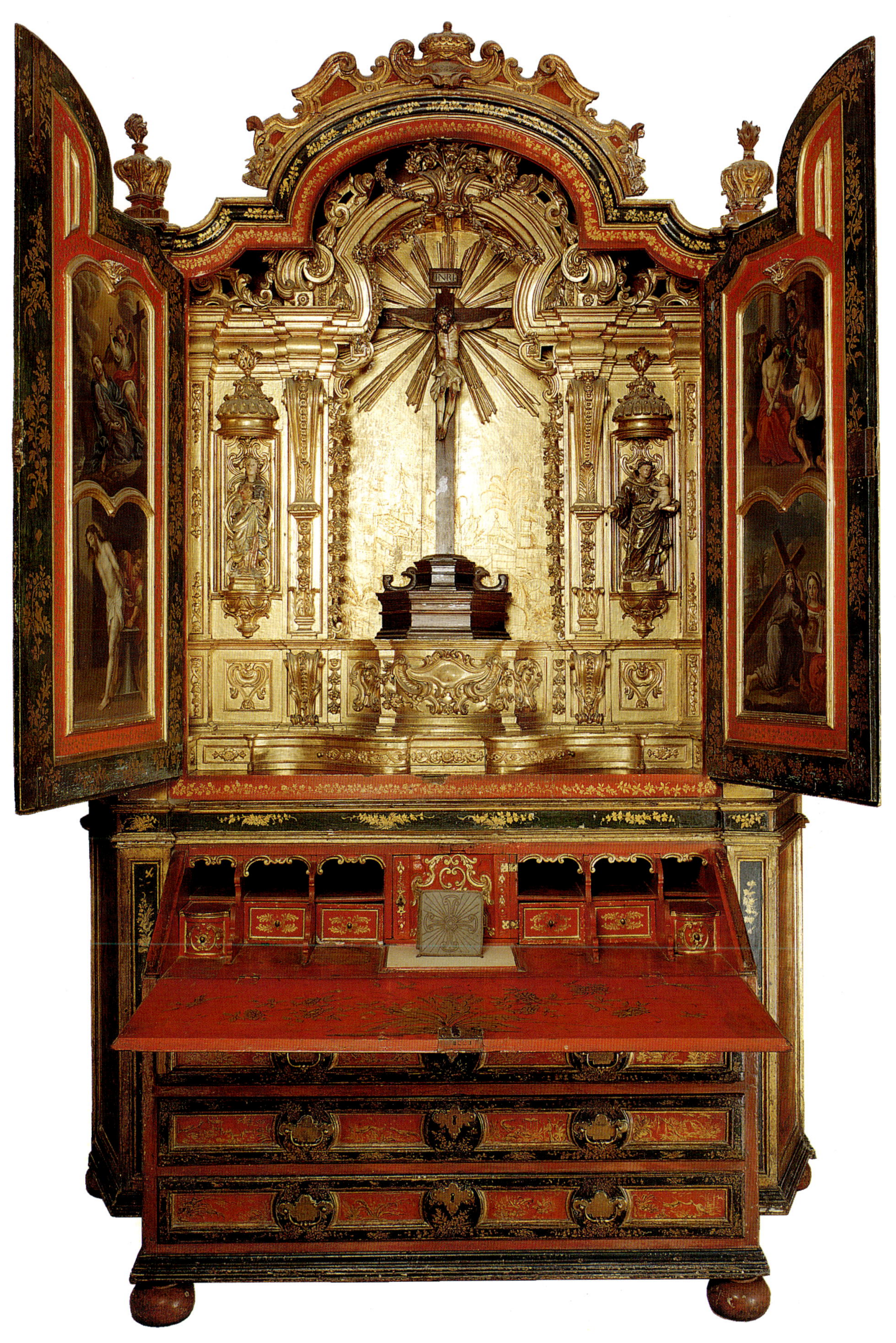

7
Pier Table

c. 1740–1750
Portuguese (?)
carved and gilded myrtle wood with
marble top
91.2 x 136.2 x 65 (35⅞ x 53⅝ x 25⁹/₁₆)

Palácio Nacional de Queluz, inv. 287

Caldeira Pires 1925, 1: pl. xxxvii; Morazzoni 1940;
Viale 1963; Honour 1969; Gonzalez Palacios 1969;
Brussels 1991, 1.56

This is one of six identical pier tables
that may have been ordered as a set: one
pair in the Palácio Nacional de Queluz,
another pair in the Palácio de Belém,
currently the official residence of the
president of the Portuguese Republic,
and a third pair in the throne room of
the Palácio Nacional de Mafra.

The tables in Mafra bear the label
"R P C," signifying either Real Paço de
Cintra (palace at Cintra) or Real Paço de
Caxias, while those in Queluz bear the
initials "R P B" (Real Paço de Bemposta), indicating the practice of distributing furniture among the royal properties. The court moved frequently from
one palace to another, making seasonal
sojourns for such activities as hunting
and bathing. It is known that these tables were present in the Sala das Meren-
das in the Palácio de Queluz, a chamber
adjoining the private dining room of
Rainha Dona Maria I and Dom Pedro
III, chosen no doubt on account of the
refinement of their design, which was
particularly appropriate to such an intimate setting.

The table's design and the elegance of
its construction, enhanced by the angular
scalloping of the top and the graceful
curve of the legs, remind one that
French cabinetmakers are known to have
taken up residence in Portugal during
this period as the Louis XV style became
increasingly popular.

An Italian influence is also present in
the sophistication of the hanging cartouche at the center of the table and the
theatrical effect produced by the cary-
atids. This influence may be explained by
the links between the Spanish and Italian courts, including the kingdom of
Parma and that of Naples and Sicily,
where Charles III reigned for twenty
years before becoming the Spanish
monarch in 1759. Cultural and artistic
influences were regularly exchanged, particularly after the improvement of political relations between Spain and Portugal, to which the marriages in 1729
between the royal children of the two
countries contributed. Closer diplomatic
contacts likewise encouraged artistic
collaboration.

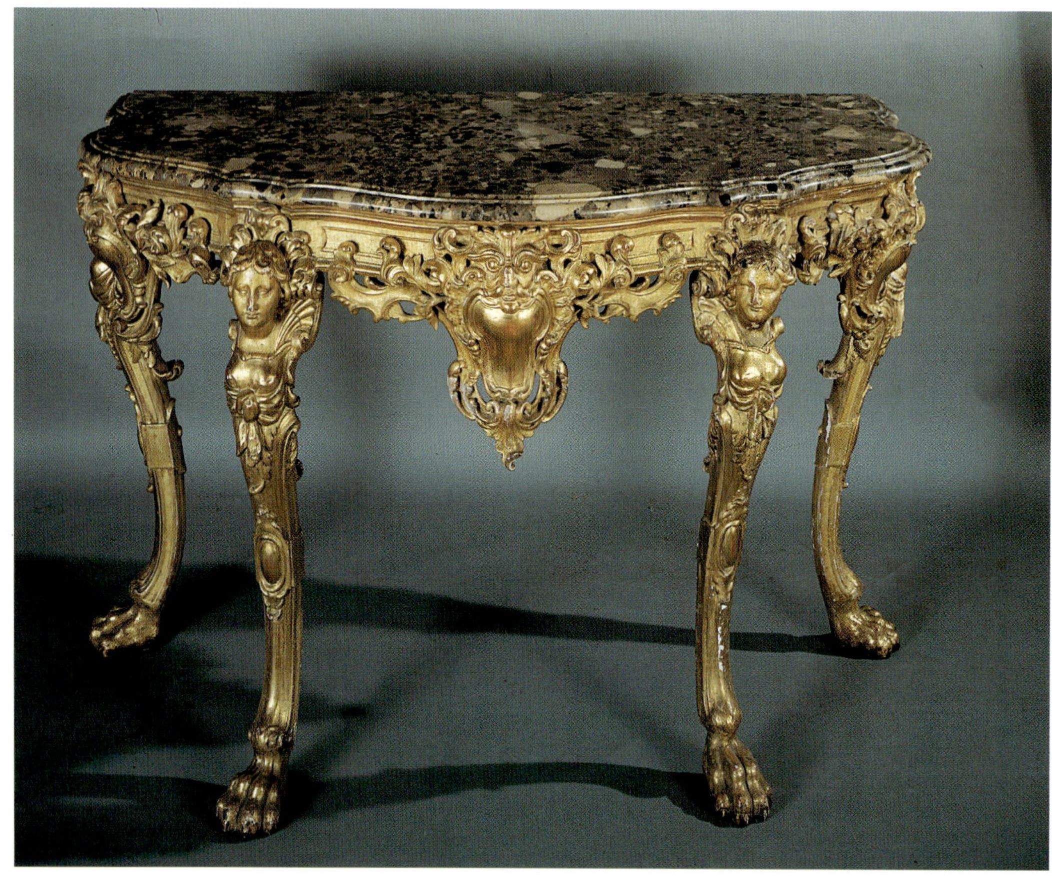

8
Mirror
mid-18th century
Portuguese
gilded carved wood
109 x 75.5 x 19.5 (42^{15}/$_{16}$ x 29^{3}/$_{4}$ x 7^{11}/$_{16}$)

*Museu de São Roque, Santa Casa da
Misericórdia, Lisbon, inv. 39*

Willis 1965; Smith 1966; Mendes Pinto 1979; AA.VV
1989; Brussels 1991, I.57

It is known that numerous mirrors were
imported into Portugal and Spain from
England, particularly during the first half
of the eighteenth century. The large volume of imports was clearly prejudicial to
manufacturers of mirrors in Portugal, as
is indicated by the pervasive influence of
the rococo style, with its characteristic
asymmetrical designs and extensive use
of scrolls. On the example exhibited,
which is one of a pair, the use of such elements, combined with leaves and "broken" scalloping in the central part of the
frame and in the raised upper section,
clearly demonstrates that the carver had
surrendered to the new taste, likewise
apparent in his use of small flower-
strewn trunks and randomly entwined
ivy.

The Real Fábrica de Coina, which
was probably the first mirror factory in
Portugal, was founded by John Beare in
1719. His English experience stood him
in good stead in establishing a high
standard of manufacture, and he was assisted by decrees designed to protect the
industry.

Luxurious mirrors of this type were
the accoutrements of reception rooms,
dressing rooms, and bedchambers, which
played a very important part in daily life
in eighteenth-century Portugal. Here
social life and etiquette were enshrined
amid luxury and magnificence; clothing,
accessories, jewelry, and even hairstyles
contributed in no small degree to creating their owner's social image. As one
contemporary writer put it, "less beautiful mirrors would not suffice to reflect
such grandeur" (Manuel Leão, *Triumpho
Luzitano, Applauzos Festivos*
[Lisbon, 1688]).

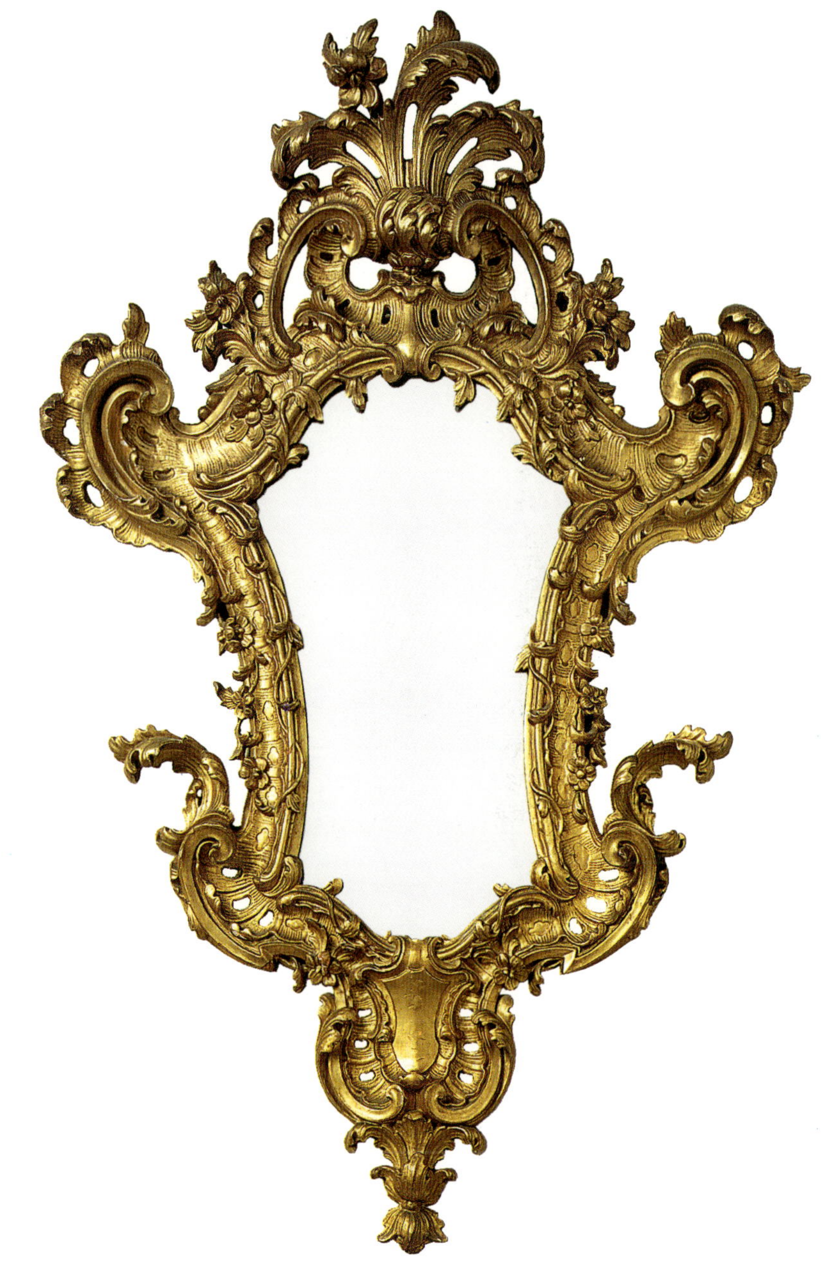

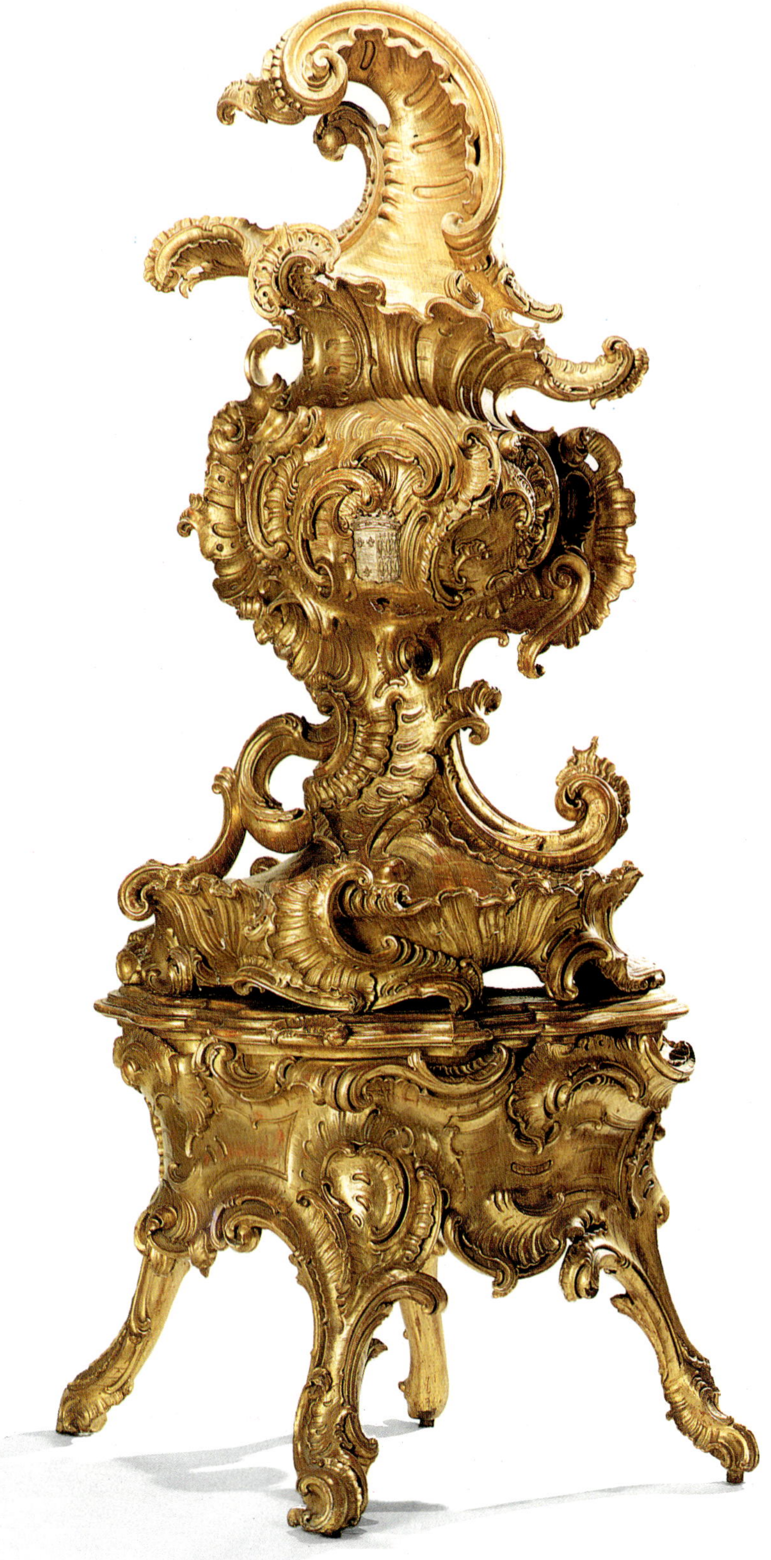

9
Font/Washbasin
German (?)
c. 1760
carved and gilded wood
218 x 126 (86 x 49½)

*Museu Nacional de Arte Antiga,
Lisbon, inv. 1512*

MNAA 1956; Smith 1968; Mandroux-França 1973;
Victoria and Albert Museum 1984; Brussels 1991,
IV.3

This exceptional object, a tour de force
of rococo style, was acquired from a private collection in 1954 for the Museu Nacional de Arte Antiga by the friends of
the museum. Although its emphasis is
almost entirely on decoration rather than
function, the piece was designed to serve
as a washbasin, presumably to be used in
a dining room for washing tableware
during the course of the meal. Stylistically, especially in the extravagant scale
of its decorative elements, it is related to
mid eighteenth-century furniture from
Berlin and northern Bavaria, particularly
Bamberg and Würzburg.

The fountain bears the coat of arms of
the grandson of Louis XV, the dauphin
of France (1729–1765), although the armorial plaque appears to have been
added after the work's creation. It is not
known how or when the piece came to
Portugal.

10
Armchair
3rd quarter 18th century
Portuguese
carved and gilded walnut
102 x 71 x 59.5 (40³/₁₆ x 27¹⁵/₁₆ x 23⁷/₁₆)

Private Collection, Lisbon

Pinto 1952; Santos 1970; Mendes Pinto 1979;
Brussels 1991, IV.66

Like certain chairs of the period of Dom
João V, which were strongly influenced
by the Queen Anne style from Britain,
this armchair is decorated with gilding
on the back, seat, and legs. According to
some authorities, this was a typical feature of items produced by the cabinetmakers of northern Portugal (see nos. 41
and 42, *Catálogo des Artes Decorativas
Portuguesas,* Museu Nacional de Arte
Antiga [Lisbon, 1979], the first chair belonging originally to the Convento de
Santa Ana de Viana do Castelo, and the
second to the Convento de Jesus in
Lamego [both in northern Portugal]).

The chair on exhibition is highly inventive in its design and outstanding in
its technical execution, a very free rendering of English Gothic motifs, particularly the characteristic design of the
chair back. It is similar to models produced during João V's reign, specifically
in the pronounced countercurve of the
legs tapering into volutes, a design
echoed in the arms, which is not a feature of Chippendale's furniture. The effect created by picking out the decorative
elements in gold, in conjunction with the
quality of design, lends this chair particular distinction.

A Portuguese prototype for this chair
appears in Pinto 1952, fig. 93, with the
symmetry of decoration and use of ball
and claw feet leading that author to date
the piece during the reign of Dom João
V. The chairs that appear in figs. 107 and
108 (Pinto 1952) are also decorated with
gilding, but have considerably higher
backs, which are a feature of ceremonial
chairs during João V's reign.

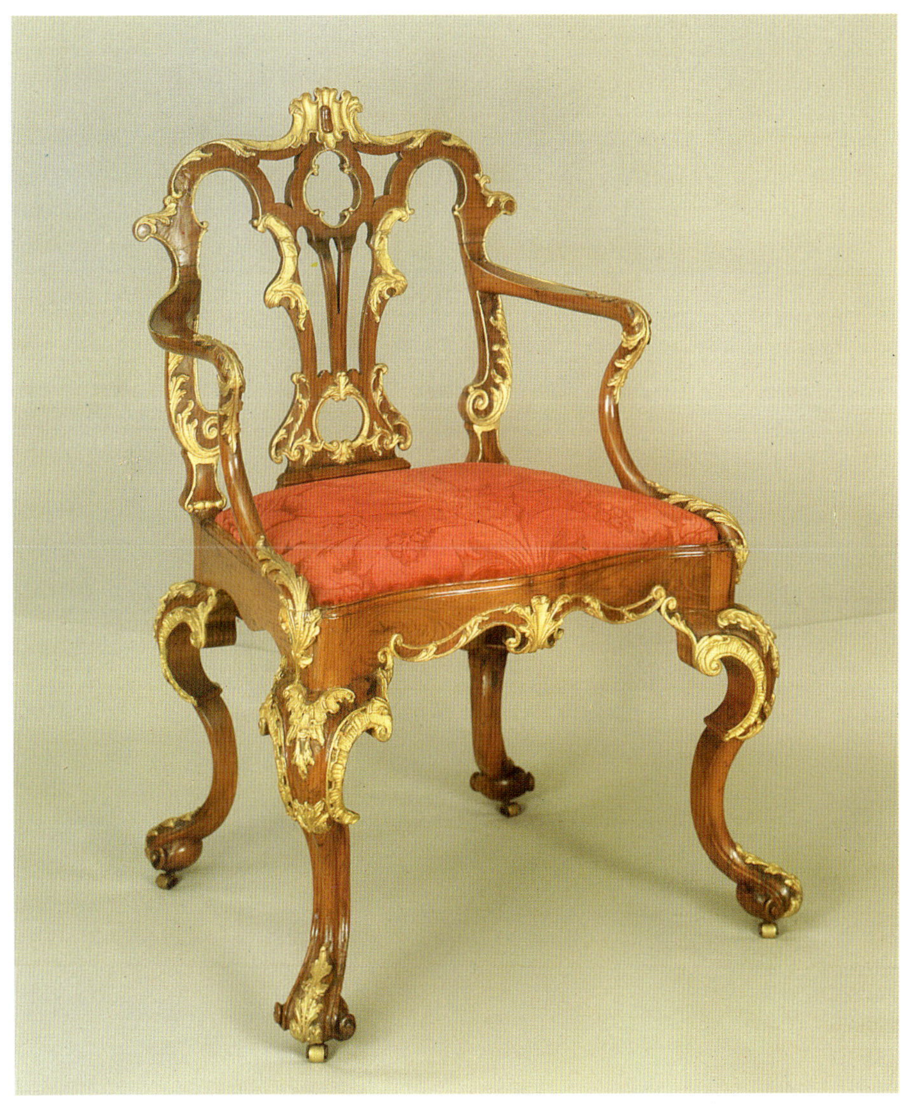

11
Secretary
Portuguese
c. 1760
carved rosewood with gilded bronze
handles
124 x 162 x 71.5 (48¹³/₁₆ x 63¾ x 28⅛)

Private Collection, Paço de Arcos

Chaves 1951; Aguiar 1955; Santos 1970; Mendes
Pinto 1979; Brussels 1991, IV.63

The cabinetmaker who created this extraordinary piece of furniture employed his highly energetic style to take maximum advantage of the physical and textural qualities of the wood itself. Showing his complete assimilation of the range of rococo design, the artist exuberantly decorated surfaces that are traditionally left unadorned, such as the sides, on which are carved large cartouches consisting of very deep scalloping, thus creating an area decorated with meticulous bas-relief. There are also other more obviously rococo elements of design that are, nonetheless, perfectly integrated into the whole, with the scale maintained throughout.

The exuberant decoration is concentrated on the front and back pilasters as well as on the feet and apron. The scrolls end in elongated *S*-curves, linked to other small scrolls interspersed with shell motifs and acanthus leaves, this typical decoration of the period giving the piece a protruding "belly." The feet are in keeping with the general quality of the piece, indeed enhance it, and are a prodigy of carving in themselves. The high degree of artistry is likewise apparent in the raised surround broken by semicircles and in the emphasis given to convex surfaces.

The carving of the top of the secretary is concentrated in the center and corners, stressing the decorative nature of the object. The bronze handles are a good example of the metal work produced by Portuguese workshops, the gilded finish enhancing their impact.

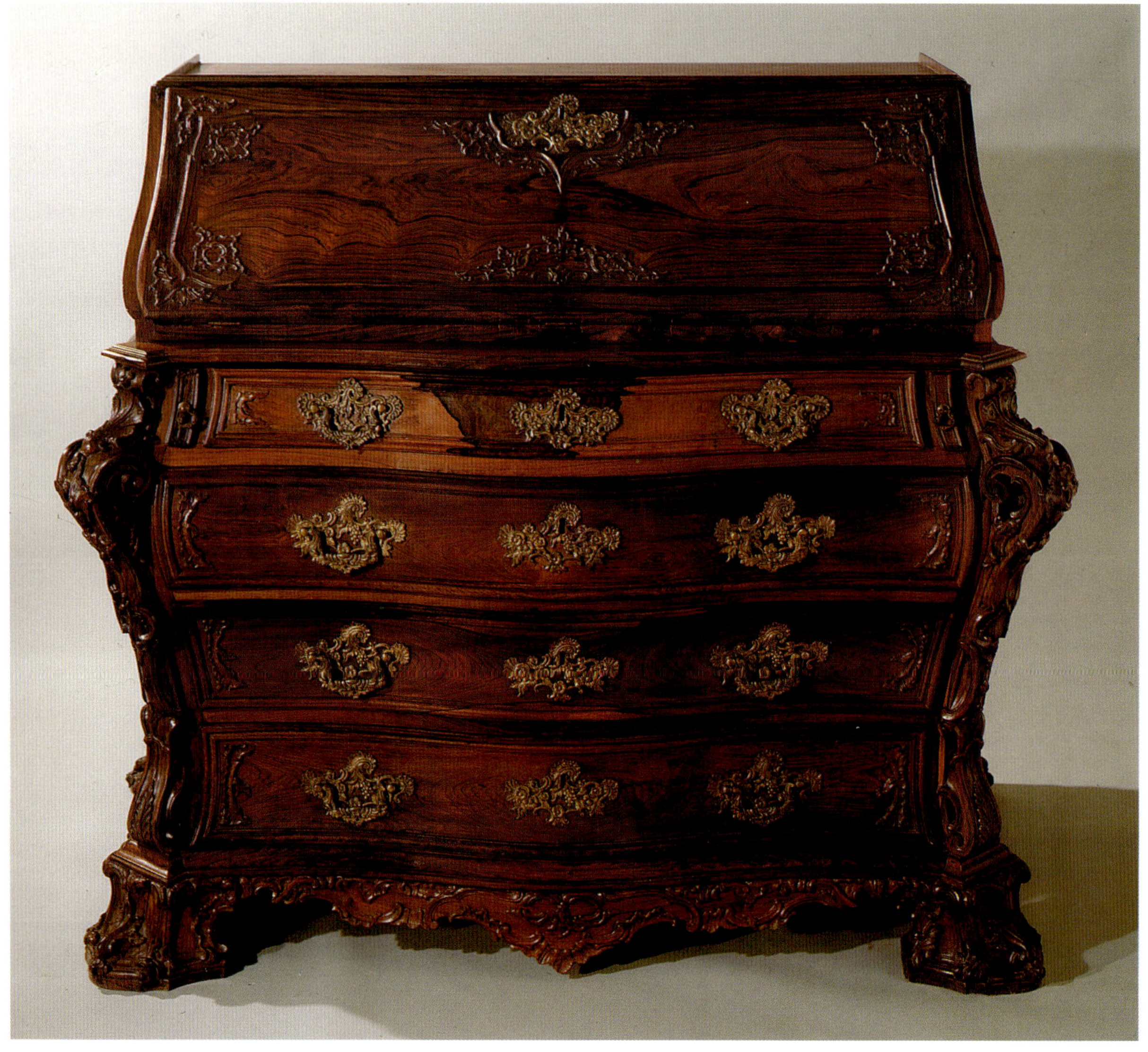

12
Cutlery Case
c. 1750–1770
Portuguese
carved rosewood
35 x 33.5 x 19.5 (13³/₄ x 13³/₁₆ x 7¹¹/₁₆)

*Museu Nacional de Soares dos Reis, Oporto,
inv. 103 our, bought by Manuel da Silva
Correia, 1940*

Oporto 1949, no. 71; Aguiar 1955; Smith 1968, pl.
253; Mendes Pinto 1979; Victoria and Albert 1984;
Mendes Pinto 1987; Brussels 1991, IV.67

This cutlery case is of outstanding craftsmanship. The emphatic decoration, in
keeping with the piece's dynamic shape
and undulating surfaces, is divided into
panels with raised borders. The decorative motifs on the front border of the lid
and the front of the body are similar, and
this scheme is carried through to the
projecting feet and sloping top of the lid.

Only a remarkably talented cabinetmaker could have achieved the undulating effect within the panel divisions on
the sides and front. The interlinking
scrolls emerging from the pilasters and
developing into stylized palms create a
frame for the mask and escutcheon on
the lid and the front.

The cutlery case recalls the miniature
secretaries that were executed by furniture makers to establish their status as
masters. The nature of the task demanded the utmost virtuosity. The mask
that appears on the front of this piece is
unusual in rococo decoration. It may
have been adopted from the English
practice of placing such masks on furniture fittings.

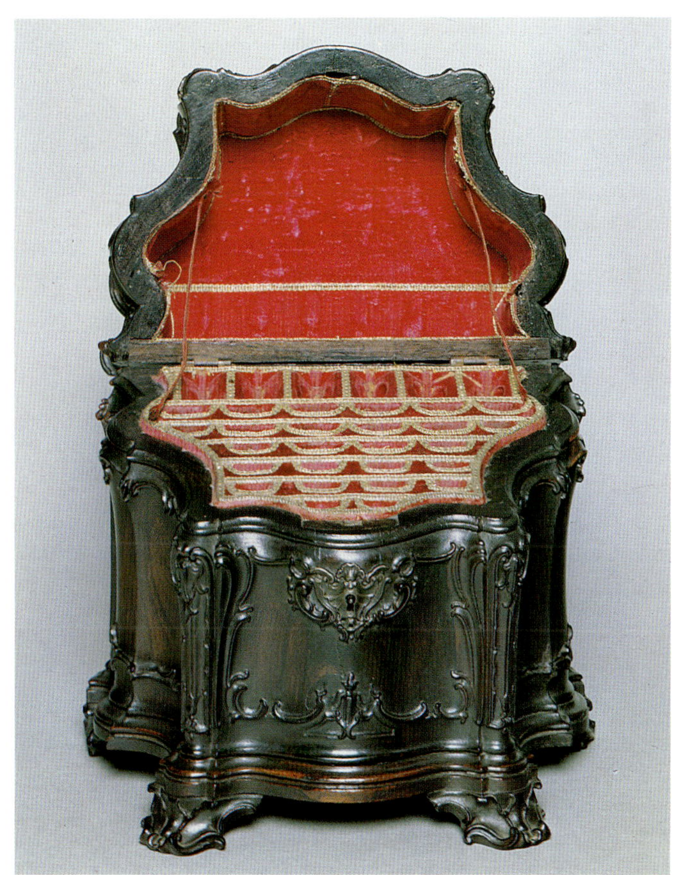

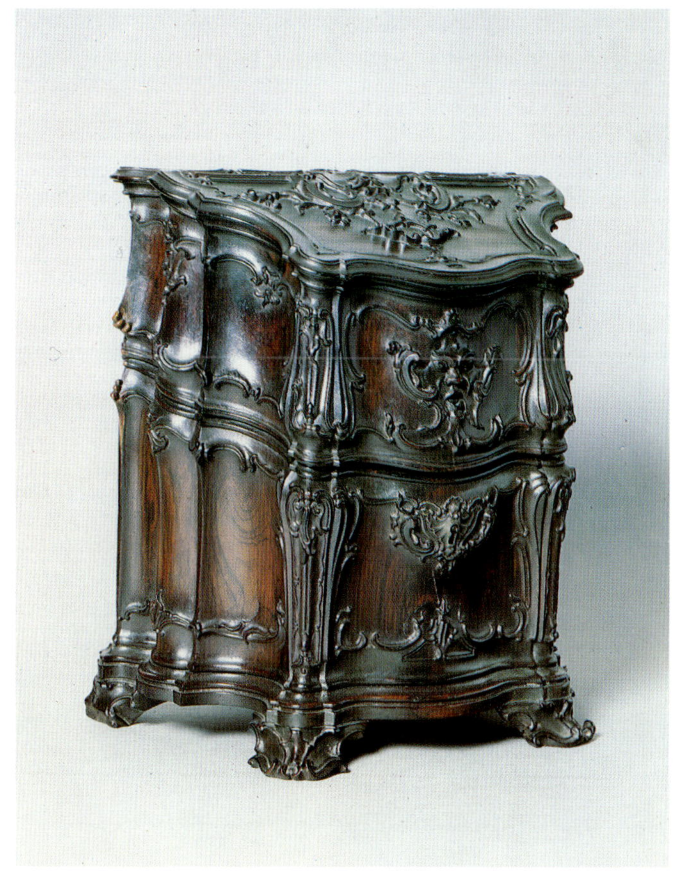

13
Table
Portuguese
c. 1770–1775
carved rosewood
82 x 140 x 69 (32⁵⁄₁₆ x 55⅛ x 16³⁄₁₆)

Private Collection, Lisbon

Guimarães and Sardoeira 1924; Chaves 1951; Chiechonowiecki 1965; Smith 1968, pl. 68; Santos 1970, fig. 591; Brussels 1991, IV.58

Tables of this type were used to display beautiful or valuable objects in the salon, the center of social life in noble households of the period. Their grandeur and stagelike character recall the credenza; one need only compare the pronounced curve of the foot, which is of manifest elegance. The craftsman's skill is revealed in the remarkable balance of smooth surfaces, showing a characteristic Portuguese proclivity for the play of texture and sheen in the broad rosewood panels.

The sophisticated technique of the carving and the abundant ornament have created an especially choice example of Portuguese cabinetmaking. The undulating movement created by the broad *C*-curves is heightened by the raised edges and delicate acanthus leaves. Inscribed in the central section, which forms a cartouche, is the same type of grotesque mask that decorates the curve of the two rear feet. The interrupted convex form of the drawers, which extends through the upper and lower sections, the various moldings, and the broken profile of the overall design are distinctive characteristics of this piece.

Also of interest are the treatment of the gold *rocaille* ornament and the finesse of the gilded bronze fittings. These indicate a taste for rococo design, which was well established in northern Portugal. The delicacy of this particular example was made possible by the hardness of the exotic wood of which it is crafted.

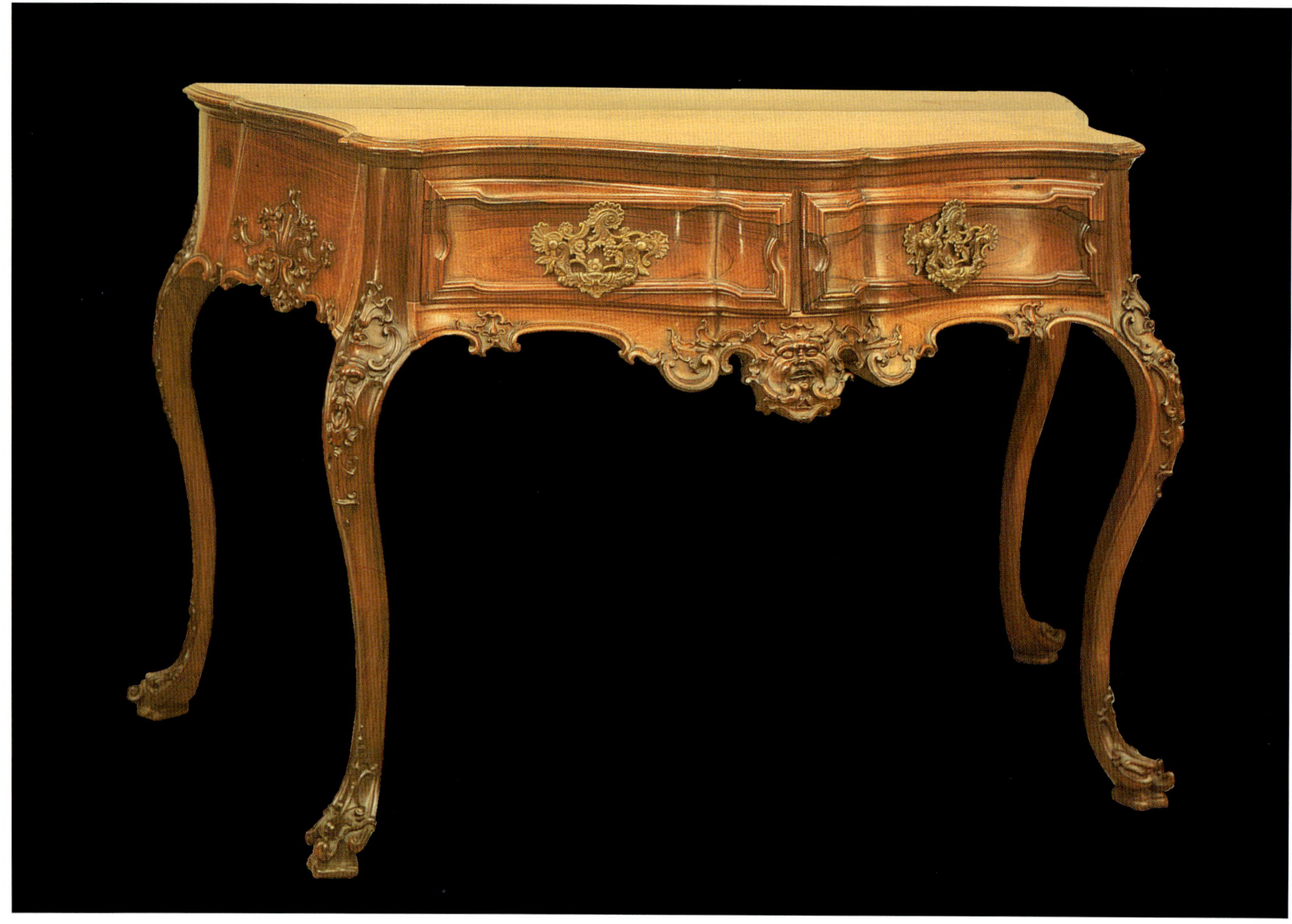

14
Desk Chair
3rd quarter 18th century
Portuguese
Brazil wood with embossed leather seat
94.5 x 71 x 58 (34³⁄₁₆ x 27¹⁵⁄₁₆ x 22¹³⁄₁₆)

Museu Nacional de Arte Antiga,
Lisbon, inv. 970

Chaves 1951; Pinto 1952; Aguiar 1955; Lisbon 1979,
no. 57; Carita 1983; Mendes Pinto 1987; Brussels
1991, IV.59

The large number of secretaries, desks,
and similar items of furniture surviving
from the baroque period is an indication
of the ever more important social role
played by writing, as is the quantity of
desk sets, many in silver (see cat. 24),
being produced during the period.

Desk chairs such as this one offered
Portuguese cabinetmakers an opportunity to explore new avenues of invention
and experimentation in construction.
The striking chair back, which branches
around into the arms, lends cohesion
and definition to this piece of furniture,
while the large shoulder support gives it
solidity. Anyone sitting in this chair ac-
quires an air of solemnity and authority.
The vigorous and elegant armrests reveal
the exceptional quality of the design,
drawing the best from traditional rococo
asymmetry, enhanced by the extremely
meticulous carving that extends to the
seat. This projects sharply in front where
it is decorated with carving in the form
of volutes. The cabriole legs lend the
final decorative touch to this energetic
piece, enhancing the overall effect of
lightness.

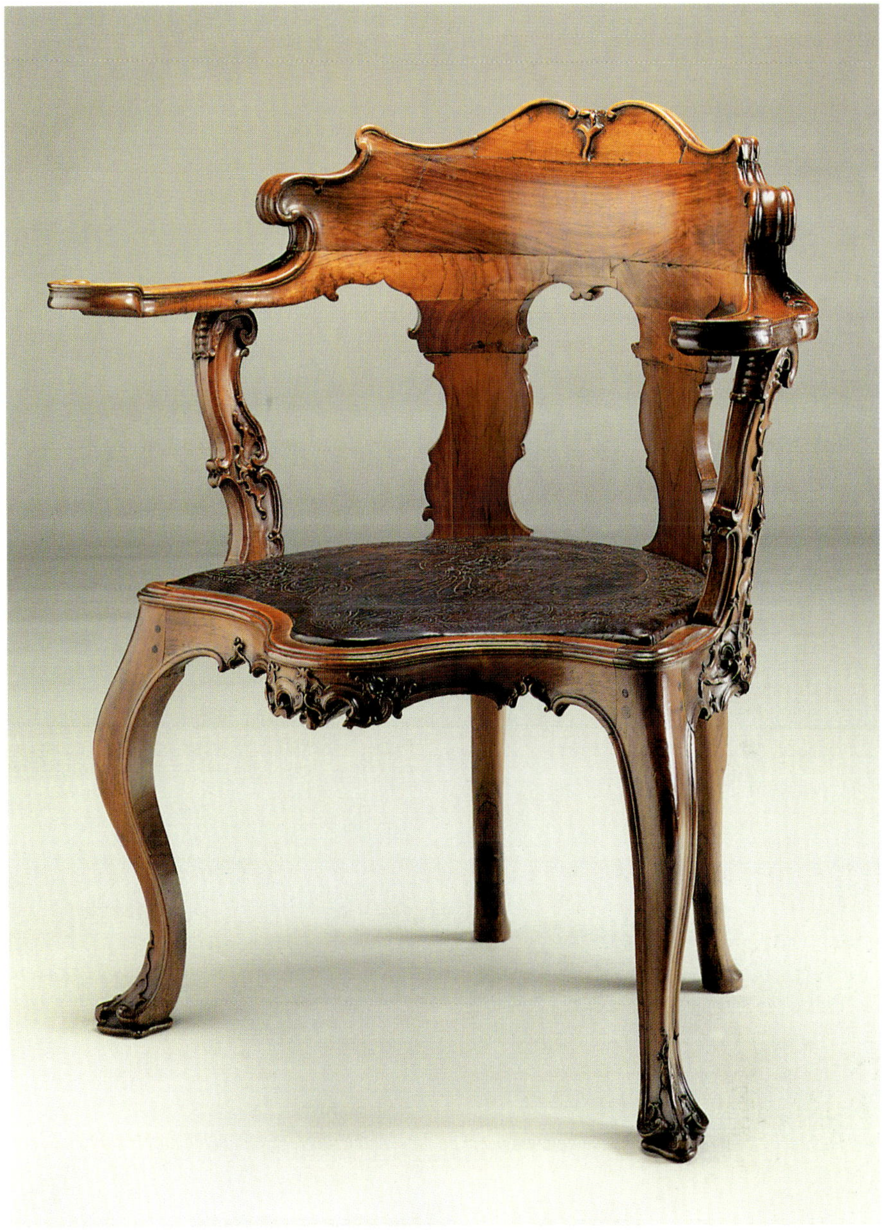

Gaming or Dressing Table
Portuguese
2nd half 18th century
ebony with marquetry in thorn and ivory
with silver handles
72, top 103 (28⅓, 40⁹⁄₁₆)

*Fundação Ricardo do Espírito Santo Silva,
Lisbon, inv. 302*

Chaves 1951; Aguiar 1955; Chiechonowiecki 1965;
Santos 1970; Carita 1983; Baptista 1988; Brussels
1991, IV.64

The *Inventories and Items Confiscated
from the Távora and Atouguia Properties
in 1759,* the collections of the families implicated in the in the assassination attempt against Dom José I, mention a
"folding bench with its writing desk and
set of draughts," appraised at an extremely high amount. While the inventory's calculation of the value of this item
may not have been very accurate, the
folding bench may well have been similar to the work on display, and the reference to the game of drafts lends weight
to this possibility.

This table has been described as
demonstrating "Portuguese craftsmanship at its best: graceful proportions are
combined with superlative carving." A
feature of the furniture produced during
the reign of José I was its individuality
that is amply demonstrated in this piece,
fully justifying the above description in
the quality of the rococo carving, which
approaches the delicacy of a work of the
jeweler's art, a parallel that is underscored by the silver handles. The fine
scalloping is also reminiscent of the style
of carving of pier tables.

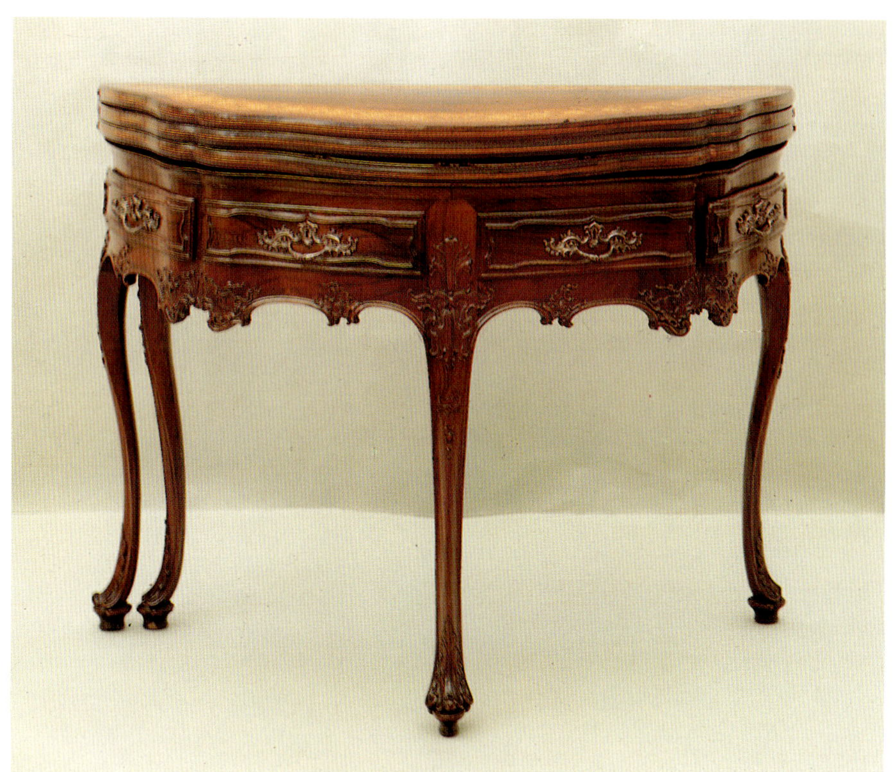

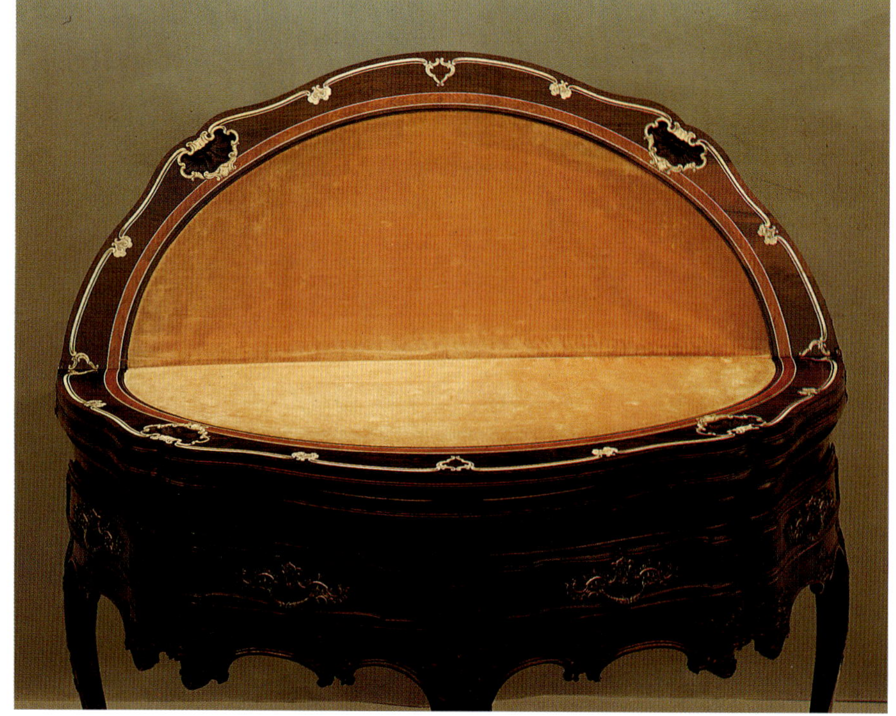

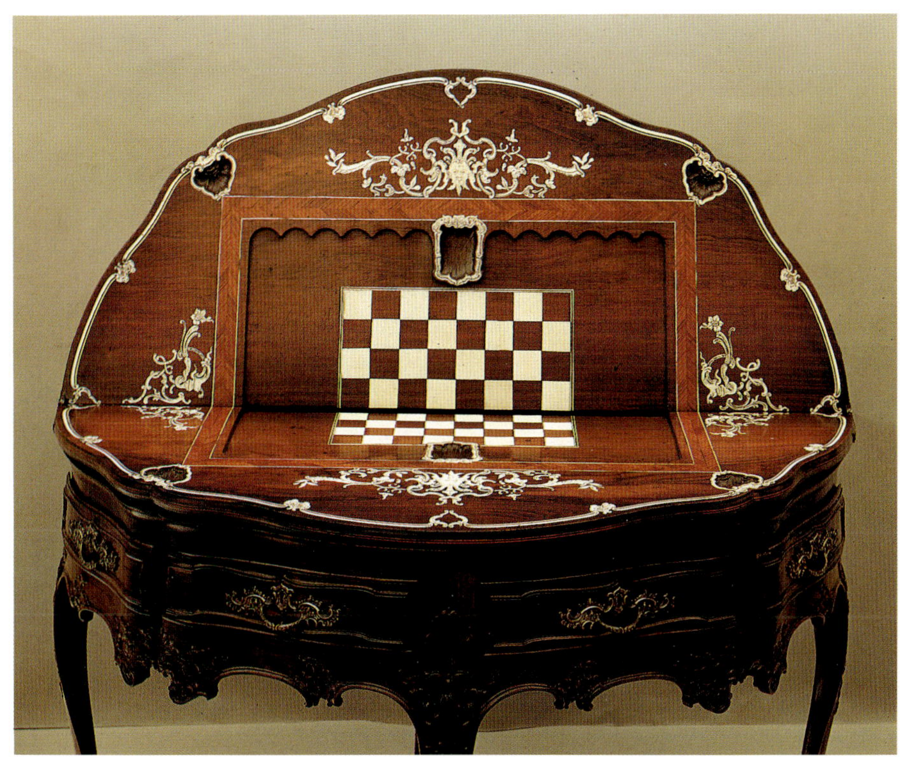

The marquetry work of the tabletop, creating cartouches in the mannerist style, revives a traditional technique that is evident in the Indo-Portuguese furniture created in Goa, which was very much in vogue in Portugal during the seventeenth century. The piece incorporates three folding tabletops, allowing it to serve as a pier table, a gaming table, a tea table, or a dressing table since it is also equipped with an adjustable mirror. The table is a unique example in the multiplicity of its functions and in the creativity of its design.

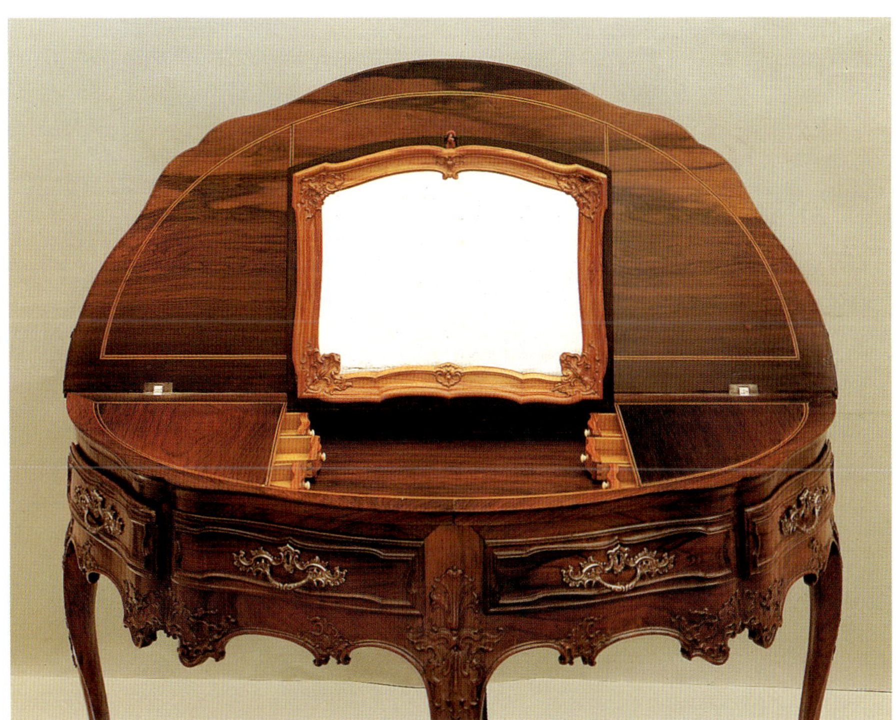

Console

c. 1775
Portuguese
gilded and carved wood with marble top
341 x 109 x 49 (134¼ x 42¹⁵/₁₆ x 19⁵/₁₆)

*Palácio Nacional de Queluz,
inv. 12 M, bought 1948*

Pires 1925; Chiechonowiechi 1965; Santos 1970,
3: fig. 594; Mendes Pinto 1979; Brussels 1991, IV.56

This piece of furniture is a product of the late rococo style, which continued to be popular in Portugal throughout the second half of the eighteenth century. This circumstance reveals the declining effectiveness of training methods and suggests that the leading cabinetmakers of the day were no longer producing new ideas, while less sophisticated clients, who were inclined to frivolity and entrenched in their taste for the rococo, continued to order such pieces.

The elliptical shape of the mirror and the urn surmounting it, as well as the frieze around the body of the console above the festoons and oval medallion, indicate that a neoclassical influence was also present. These elements are clearly in the Louis XVI style. Indeed, French influence is evident in Portugal in jewelry and objects in silver and gold, as well as in the furniture of the period. R. J. Auguste and Roettiers became suppliers to the Portuguese royal household and nobility at this time. The style associated with Rainha Dona Maria I adapts such foreign creations to Portuguese cultural models while making use of local materials, whereas English furniture and Portuguese decorative arts treatises also contributed to this blending of influences.

This console, which is thought to have been commissioned for the palace of Queluz, may be compared with another in the possession of the Museu Nacional de Arte Antiga, Lisbon (inv. 986), which displays a purer development of contemporary styles that may already be seen in a hybrid form in the Queluz console. However, it should be noted that the scalloping linking the

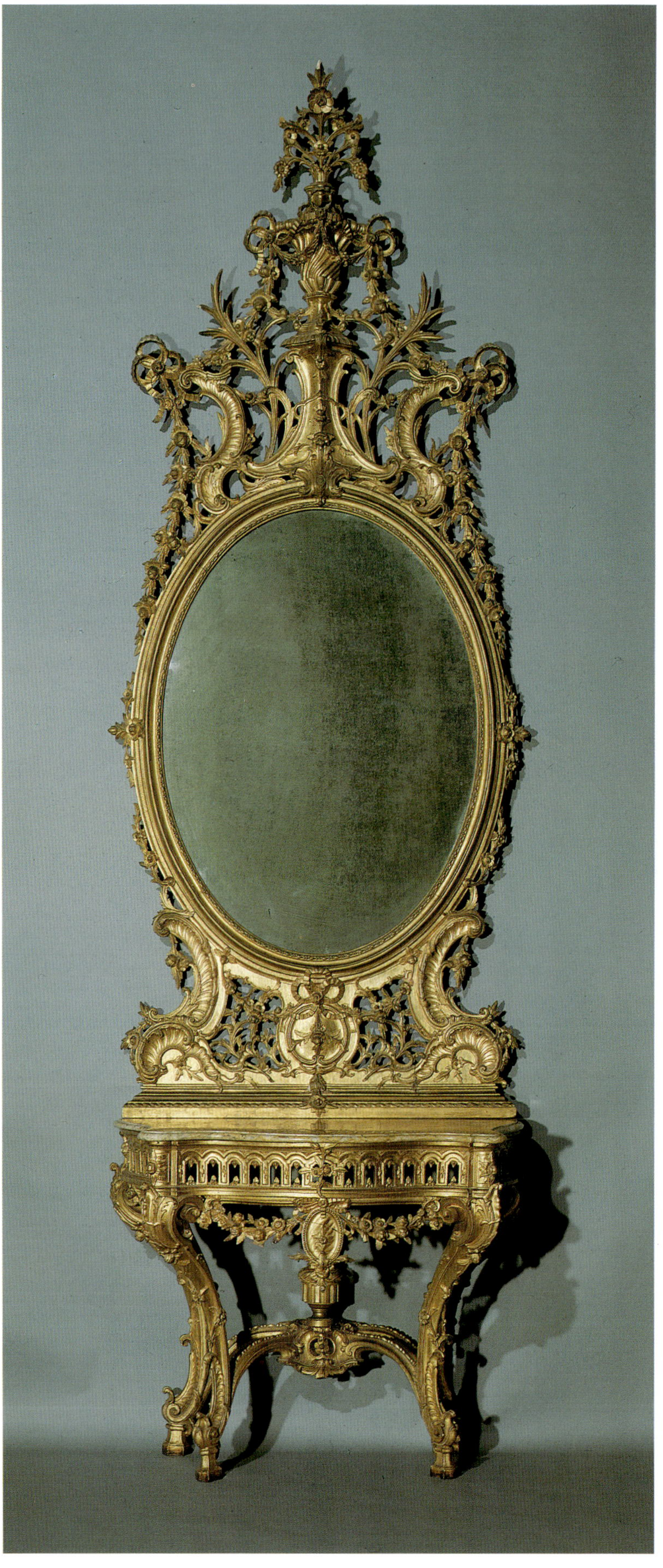

mirror to the top of the exhibited console and flanking the pedestal bearing the urn above the mirror, as well as the markedly Louis XV style itself, are retardataire elements.

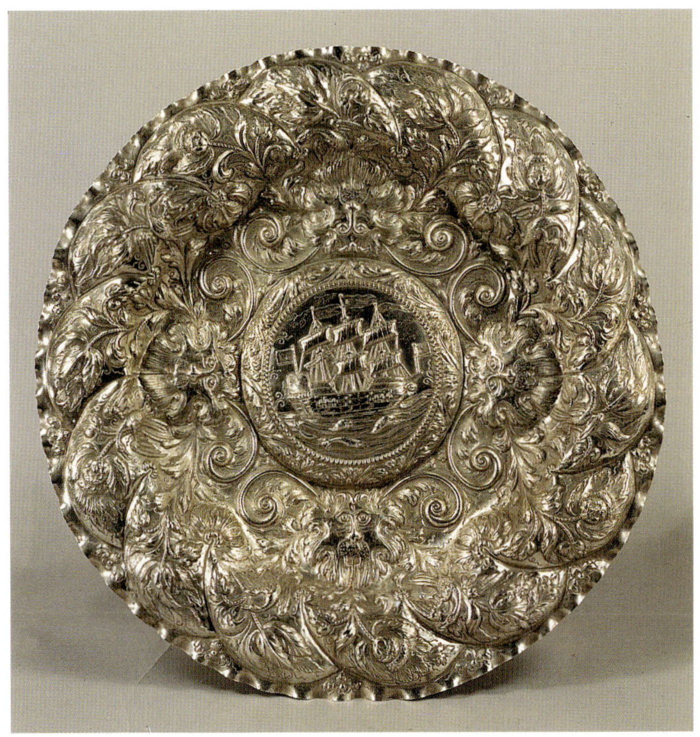

17
Salver
late 17th–early 18th century
Portuguese
repoussé, chased, and engraved silver
60 (23⅝)

Lisbon Cathedral Chapter, inv. 758

Lisbon 1947, no. 124; Couto and Gonçalves 1960, ill 110; Oman 1965; Santos and Quilhó 1974; Brussels 1991, 1.61

The central medallion is decorated with the representation of a large Portuguese ship, following a sixteenth-century formula that became very popular and widespread. It had been fashionable to celebrate Portugal's maritime achievements and, with the discovery of gold in Brazil leading to the launching of new vessels, the Portuguese fleet was growing considerably larger, yet another reason to continue to employ such designs.

The four masks that surround the central frame are also archaisms in a baroque salver, since they were one of the leitmotifs of the mannerist style. These masks are partly hidden by acanthus branches and are joined by scrolls that themselves link to create their own formal and rhythmic counterpoint.

The undulating rim, with its vessel and the underlying allusion to the sea, continues the maritime theme. The consecutively superimposed sections create a noticeable spiral effect and serve as a base for exuberant floral decoration, predominantly of tulips.

This salver may be compared with the two silver urns (cats. 18, 19) that aim at the same sumptuous effect with bold repoussé and chasing, revealing a preference for symmetry and heavy decoration with a powerful impact. The conventional floral motifs take on a spirit of baroque realism in a composition that shows a marked freedom in reinventing traditional forms. (For a similar though smaller salver, see Santos and Quilhó 1959, no. 9).

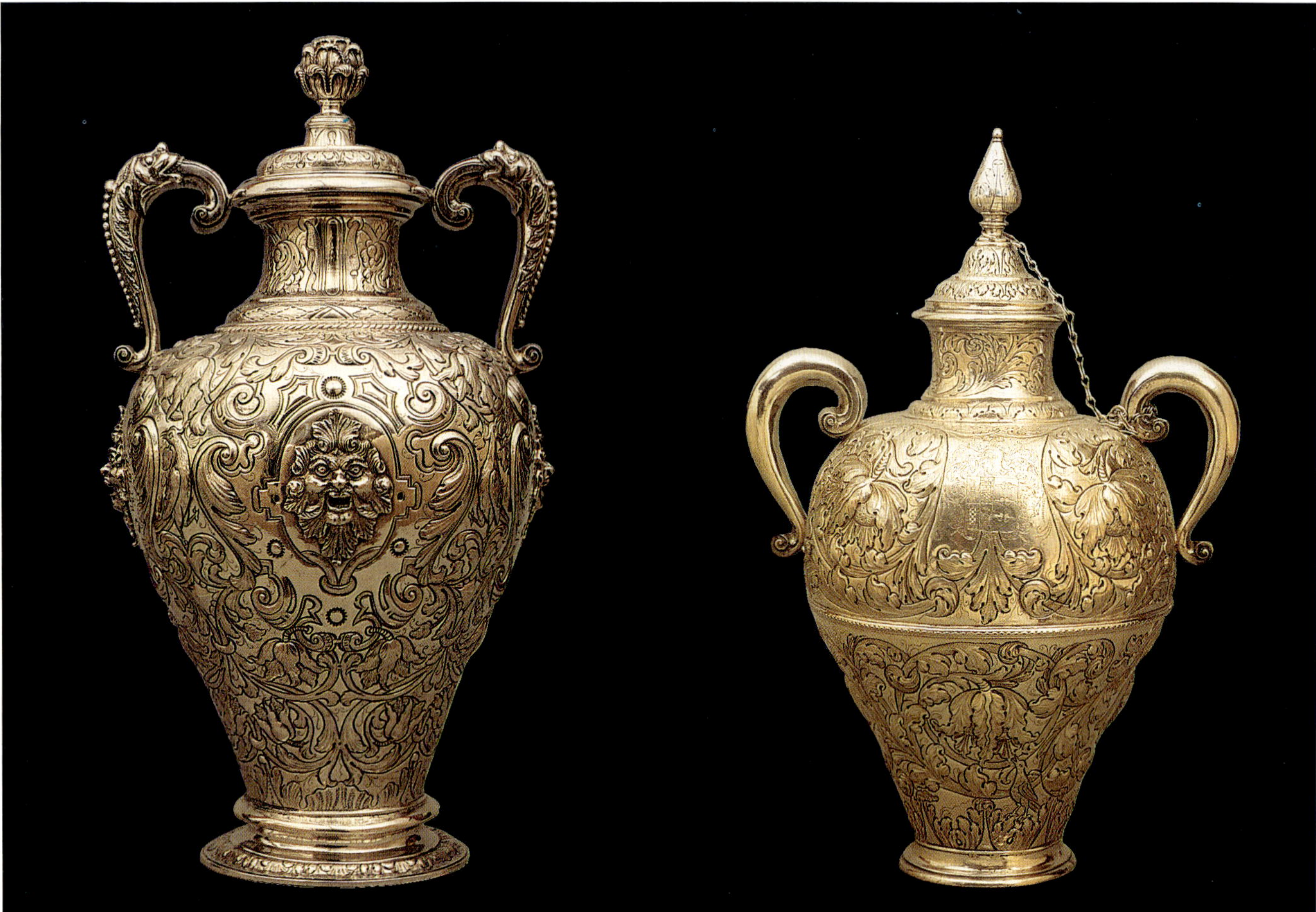

18   19

18

Urn
Portuguese
c. 1720
cast, chased, repoussé, and engraved
silver
57.5 (22⅝)
Private Collection, Lisbon

Couto and Gonçalves 1960; Santos and Quilhó
1974; Oman 1965; Brussels 1991, 1.58

This lidded urn is among the most impressive works in silver produced in eighteenth-century Portugal. The entire body is covered with acanthus leaves incorporating a wide variety of shapes and manners of execution, from the robust character of the repoussé work to the subtlety of the engraving. Four oval frames containing masks adorn the sides, a design typical of the type of decoration carried over from the previous century.

The rhythmic effect produced by the fluting and plant motifs around the neck lends the piece a singular elegance, underscored by the band of laurel leaves. The handle is composed of two *S*-curves in the shape of dolphins with beading creating a stylized fin. The lid is bell-shaped, surmounted by a pine-cone finial. The energy of the decoration reveals the hand of an exceptionally talented craftsman, fully in command of a style that was popular throughout Europe and particularly admired by the Portuguese. Portuguese-made luxuries competed with objects produced abroad, for which the Portuguese always showed a marked preference.

This type of ostentatious vessel recalls descriptions of the embassy of 1708 of the third conde de Vilar Maior (later first marquês de Alegrete), Fernão Telles da Silva, who traveled to Vienna to escort the Archduchess Maria Ana of Austria, daughter of Emperor Leopold I and future wife of Dom João V, to Lisbon. His embassy was invariably described as lavish. The palace in Vienna, which he adorned with furniture and tapestry he had brought from Portugal, certainly fitted this description, while his silverware and Chinese dinner service dazzled even the sophisticated Viennese aristocracy. In the main hall, one display cabinet contained "smooth, worked, and gilded silver" and, on the left, there were "three credences, the first with silver vessels and large basins, the second with a silver vase five 'spans' high and its basin of proportionate size" (Fonseca 1717). One can imagine the exhibited vase in this context.

19
Urn
1st half 18th century
Portuguese
repoussé and chased silver
52 (20½)
Marks: P, municipal assayer of Oporto
1st half 18th c.; I, unidentified
silversmith's mark (Vidal and Almeida
1974, no. 303)

Private Collection, Lisbon

Santos and Quilhó 1974, 119; Franceschi 1988;
Brussels 1991, I.59

This vessel shows the influence of two
traditions of ceramic art. The shape is
identical to that of vases of Dutch origin,
called ginger jars, that were also widely
produced and used in England. This
type also derives from the ornamental
Chinese porcelain that was available in
Europe throughout the seventeenth century, the shape of which was adopted for
objects in silver with such splendid results that they were displayed as domestic decoration on mantelpieces and in
collectors' cabinets.

Another evident source of influence
are the religious vessels with handles for
holy oils, which are frequently encountered in the plain Portuguese silverware
style of the seventeenth century, inspired
by the traditional forms of Portuguese
ceramics. Comparable pieces are to be
found in the collection of the duques de
Palmela (Santos and Quilhó 1974, 119,
no. 140, dated 1682, with a conspicuously
similar handle), and in the Museu da
Irmandade do Sanctissímo Sacramento
da Candelária, Rio de Janeiro (Franceschi 1988, 68).

The repoussé decoration of the piece
is vigorous, incorporating typical seventeenth-century motifs: tulips, irises,
acanthus leaves, and birds, which cover
the entire surface of the pitcher, subdi-
vided by a fretted band. The rhythm created by the repetition and entwining of
the circular foliage motifs creates a lively
sense of movement. The lid is bell-
shaped and crowned with a finial in the
form of a stylized urn.

20
Tomás Correia
active 1698–1728
**Traveling Toilet Set Comprising
31 Pieces**
early 18th century
chased gilded silver
45 x 52 x 80 (17¹¹⁄₁₆ x 20½ x 31½)
Marks: L, municipal assayer of Lisbon,
c. 1700–1720, and TC, Tomás Correia
(Vidal and Almeida 1974, nos. 4, 2293)

*Fundação Ricardo do Espírito Santo Silva,
Lisbon, inv. 520*

Viana 1896, no. 86, fig. xv; Santos and Quilhó 1974,
181; Heitmann 1979, 55; Brussels 1991, I.18

This service, which was purchased in
Italy, is composed of thirty-one elegant
pieces in gilded silver still in their original case. The service was probably part
of the dowry assembled by a Portuguese
noble family, in which works in silver
were particularly highly prized. A dressing table set included mirror, containers,
ewer and basin, brush, and a table service
composed of salvers, bowls, candlesticks,
and trays.

The style of this set is in keeping with
seventeenth-century baroque models,
prior to the introduction of the rococo
motifs typical of French and Italian
works in gold and silver that the Portuguese court was beginning to import.
This service is unique in Portuguese secular silver in that it is complete and the
pieces are in their original case, which is
faced with red leather and lined with
green velvet, with clasps and hinges in
gilded bronze.

Tomás Correia, who signed this set,
was one of the most brilliant goldsmiths
in Lisbon at the turn of the eighteenth
century. His mark "TC" has only recently been identified. The fine set of
altar implements belonging to the Convento das Chagas in Lamego, with a design of broad polished surfaces with

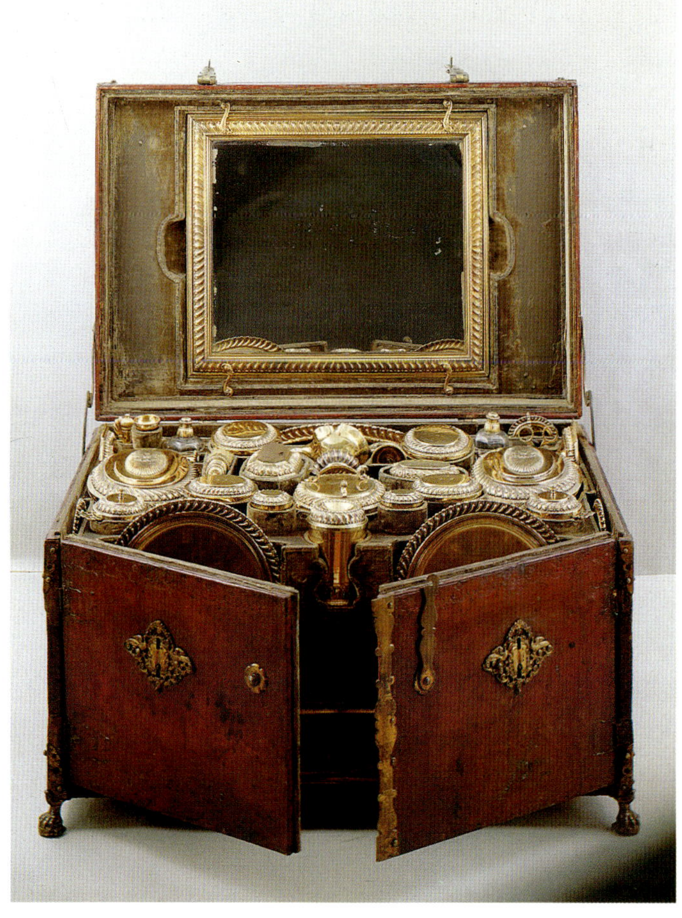

gadrooned edges and rims, was produced
in his workshop and is very similar to
this traveling set. Records exist of
Correia's career between 1698 and 1728. In
1698 he was engaged in Lisbon in selling
the silver belonging to the late bishop of
Braga, Luís de Sousa, who had probably
commissioned the goldsmith to execute
the altar set for the Convento das Chagas
when he headed the Lamego diocese.

In 1705 Correia was among the ap-
praisers instructed by the Jesuits to value
the silver sacrarium executed by João
Frederico Ludovice that belonged to the
Colégio de Santo Antão in Lisbon. The
sacrarium was one of the most famous
examples of the goldsmith's art of the
reign of Dom João V. By 1717, Correia's
reputation was such that he was commissioned by the chapter of Évora cathedral to execute a pair of candlesticks.

In 1728, he appraised the silver in
the dowry of the condessa de Castelo
Melhor, which, according to its description, included a traveling case composed
of a number of pieces in gilded silver.

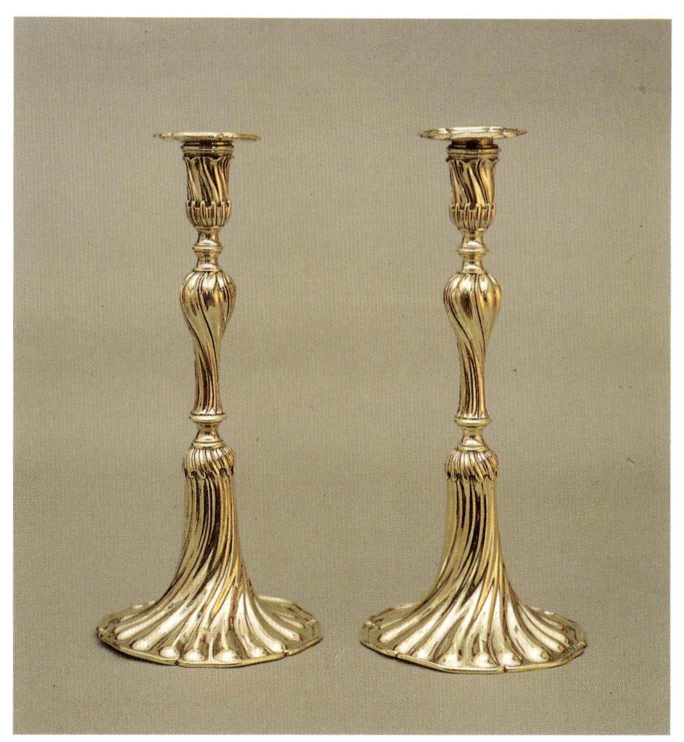

21

Two Candlesticks

c. 1750–1770
Portuguese
chased and repoussé silver
31.5 (12⅜)

Private Collection, Oporto

Poldi Pezzolli 1959; Santos and Quilhó 1974; Hernmarck 1977; Beaudouin 1988; Brussels 1991, IV.50

These trumpet-shaped candlesticks are
highly representative examples of Portuguese silversmiths' work during the second half of the eighteenth century. They
owe their designation to the splayed base
that is subtly emphasized by the raised,
undulating rim. The fluted spirals create
a sense of motion, swirling downward in
the lower section and upward in the central section, with an oblique movement
in the base of the socket beneath the
candle ring that attains its maximum
force in this type of design.

The unusual height of these candlesticks gives the shaft a particular elegance, which is further emphasized by
the distension created by the two nodes,
the upper one double. This virtuosity indicates that these candlesticks were executed by one of the great silversmiths of
the period; their similarity with the candlesticks in the collection of João Teixeira
Júnior (Santos and Quilhó 1974, no. 274)
suggests that they may be attributed to
the same as-yet unidentified master who
signed that piece with the initials "BP."
This ability to create very sophisticated
tensions of form with smooth surfaces is
also evident in the tea service belonging
to the conde de Galveias (Santos and
Quilhó 1974, no. 302). The exhibited candlesticks may also be compared to a pair
in the Casa Museu de Guerra Junqueiro,
Oporto (M. Luz Marques, *Ourivesaria
Civil Portuguesa da Casa Museu Guerra
Junqueiro* [Oporto, 1984], 14, fig. 14).

It is thought that the trumpet-shaped
candlestick type originated in Italy and
in French-speaking Switzerland
(Grüber) and then spread to Flanders
(see Baudouin 1988, nos. 178 and 235 for
the same spiral effect) as well as to Spain
and Portugal, where numerous examples
are to be found.

22
JOÃO COELHO SAMPAIO
Portuguese, 1710/1720–1784
Kettle and Trivet
c. 1758–1768
cast, chased, and repoussé silver with
ivory
44 (17⁵⁄₁₆)
Marks: P, municipal assayer of Oporto,
c. 1758–1768; ICS, João Coelho Sampaio
(Vidal and Almeida 1974, nos. 65, 2652)

Private Collection, Lisbon

Oman 1965; Viana do Castelo 1967; Ramos 1969;
Santos 1970, fig. 497; Santos and Quilhó 1974,
fig. 83; London 1990; Brussels 1991, IV.46

This is one of the best-known works created by the silversmith João Coelho
Sampaio, who is known to have executed
two other very similar kettles, one formerly in the collection of Pedro Alexan-
drino Baptista, Oporto, and the other in
that of José Lico, Lisbon.

Every English household owned such
a utensil (in copper or other metal, rarely
in silver) for the preparation of tea, and
these English kettles served as models
for those produced in Portugal. For example, Thomas Johnson's *One Hundred
and Fifty New Designs* (1761) of furniture
and household items includes a kettle
and trivet that are very similar to Sampaio's. Even before this, in 1744, Paul de
Lamerie was creating similar works, such
as the exceptionally graceful kettle belonging to the Metropolitan Museum of
Art in New York.

João Coelho Sampaio took his inspiration from such English models. It is
likely that many of the items produced
by this silversmith were acquired by the
sophisticated English colony in Oporto
that was connected with the production
and trade of port wine. The design of the
kettle is admirably controlled, its inverted pear shape set off by the elegant
lines of the spirit lamp and trivet. The
latter is composed of three console legs
of pronounced *C* shape topped by female
busts and standing on ball-and-claw feet,
while the spirit lamp echoes the shape of
the kettle in miniature.

The caryatid motif is carried through
to the handle of the kettle with its ivory
handhold, while the side of the kettle reveals the ornamental treatment typical of
Sampaio. An elegant fluted spout in the
form of a swan's neck emerges from this
lavish ornament. Typically rococo
cockscombs and scrolls lend solidity to
the structure, across which are scattered
realistic flower buds denoting a very personal touch that could only have been
achieved by João Coelho Sampaio.

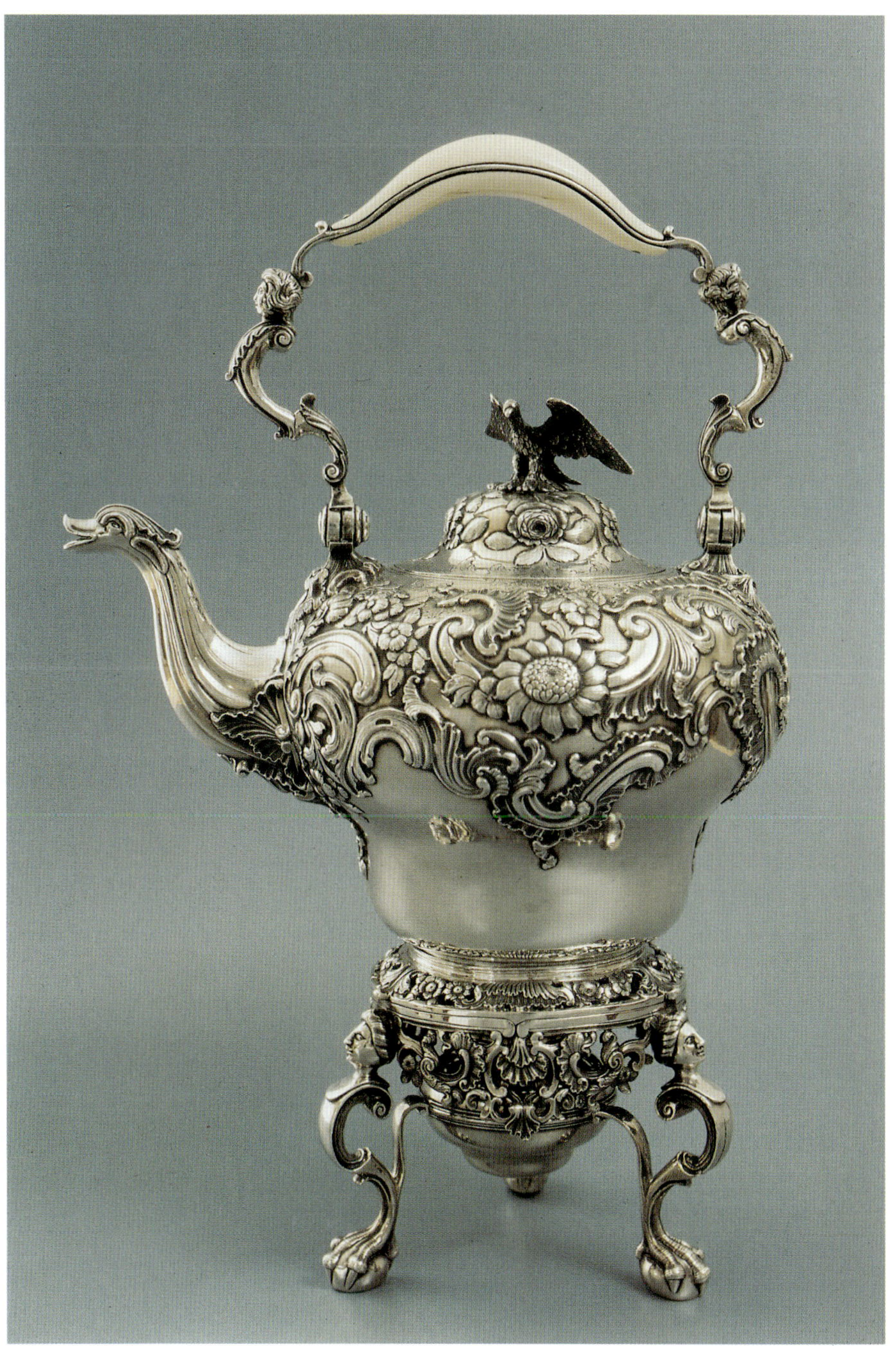

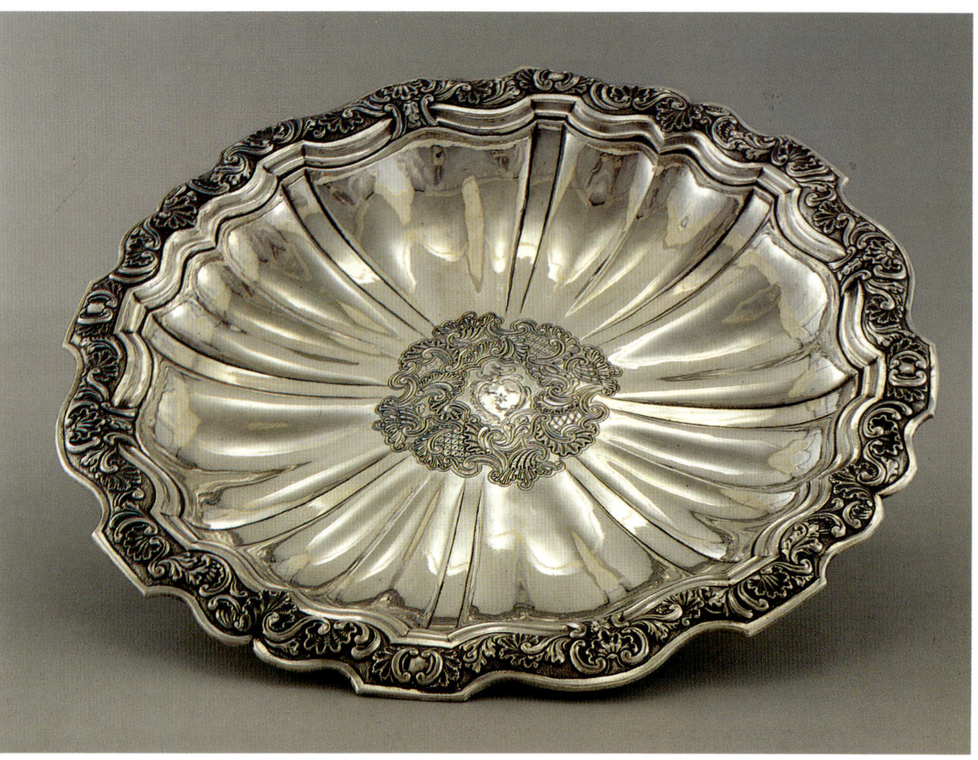

23
JOÃO COELHO SAMPAIO
Portuguese, 1710/1720–1784
Salver
c. 1758–1768
chased, repoussé, and engraved silver
43 (16^{15}/$_{16}$)
Marks: P, municipal assayer of Oporto,
c. 1758–1768; ICS, João Coelho Sampaio
(Vidal and Almeida 1974, nos. 65, 2652)

*Museu Nacional de Arte Antiga, Lisbon,
inv. 1051 our*

Ramos 1969; Santos and Quilhó 1974; Schneider
1980; Luxembourg 1988, no. 29; Brussels 1991, III.56

This salver is one of the finest known
pieces by the silversmith J. Coelho Sampaio (see also cat. 22). Its rim consists of
alternating straight sections and curves,
which are echoed along the inner rims,
and is adorned with small scallop shapes,
C-shapes, leaves, and scrolls. Grooves
run from the outer edge toward the middle at intervals dictated by the design of
the rim, while the coat of arms of the
Van Zeller family, within a highly ornate
frame, adorns the center.

The salver is thought to have belonged to Arnaldo Van Zeller (1702–
1766) of Rotterdam, the son of Luis Van
Zeller and his second wife, Joana de
Harles. He was apparently the first
member of this illustrious merchant
family to take up residence in Oporto,
in a magnificent manor house with an
adjoining chapel that remained in the
family through successive generations. In
1735 he married Ana Francisca Henckel,
daughter of Pedro Henckel, knight of
the Order of Christ, and his wife Ana
Maria Palmer. He was awarded a title by
Dom João V. He left fifteen children including Mauricio Van Zeller, who in his
capacity as businessman was among the
group of parliamentarians appointed to
administer the Real Junta do Comércio,
Agricultura, Fábricas e Navegação destes
Reinos e seus Domínios (1778), replacing
Pombal's Junta do Comércio. The new
organization administered the royal silk
and playing cards manufactories and the
Lisbon aqueduct.

Ratton praised the decision in 1759 by
the marquês de Pombal to establish a
class in commercial studies to teach
folded-page bookbinding and weights,
measures, and foreign currency as well as
exchange rates and monetary parity, stat-
ing that this was necessary "because the
Jorges, Polyarts, Despiers, Vanzelleres,
Crammers . . . were all the offspring of
foreign parents who had [been] educated
abroad." As regards Pombal's economic
policy, the deterioration of wine production in the Alto Douro and the lack of
organization in this trade led to the establishment of the Companhia de Agricultura das Vinhas do Alto Douro (1756),
which breathed new life into activities
that became extremely profitable for
Portugal. The Van Zellers were part of
this dynamic trading entity. A member
of that family was appointed first president of the prestigious Associação Comercial Portuguesa in 1834. The Van
Zellers, like the Kopkes who had become wealthy through their trading relations with the Baltic and Brazil, had
taken Portuguese nationality and extended their activities successfully to include the port wine business. "The Van
Zellers exported an insignificant twenty-
nine casks in 1769, but within a few years
they had become one of the city's largest
exporters" (Schneider 1980).

MANUEL PIRES DE AZEVEDO
Portuguese
Inkwell/Desk Set
c. 1758
cast, chased, and repoussé silver
24 x 28 (9⁷/₁₆ x 11)
Marks: P of Oporto, first half 18th
c./1758; MP, attributed to Manuel Pires
de Azevedo (Vidal and Almeida 1974,
nos. 64, 1461)

Private Collection, Elvas

Vidal and Almeida 1974; Hernmarck 1977; Gruber
1989; Brussels 1991, 1.29

The desk set stands on a three-lobed tray
on three sculptured feet in the shape of
free-standing lions. On the tray, three
cartouches reminiscent of the mannerist
style contain scallop shells of perfect balance and size, which are placed near the
triangular projections of the fretted rim.

Three more scallop shells project from
the shaft above the base, harking back to
the customary triple arrangement of the
drinking spouts of baroque fountains (see
the same design in the well-known two-
handled cup in the Victoria and Albert
Museum, London). This allusion and
suggestion is borne out by the masks similar to gargoyles as well as the ampulla-
shaped finial on which an unidentified female figure, perhaps Minerva, stands.

The sides of the inkwell, sand con-
tainer, and sealing-wax jar are exuberantly engraved with acanthus leaves and
irises in repoussé, which alternates with
smooth surfaces between the leaves and
around the necks of the containers. The
movement conveyed by the finials in the
form of putti with raised arms echoes
this dynamism.

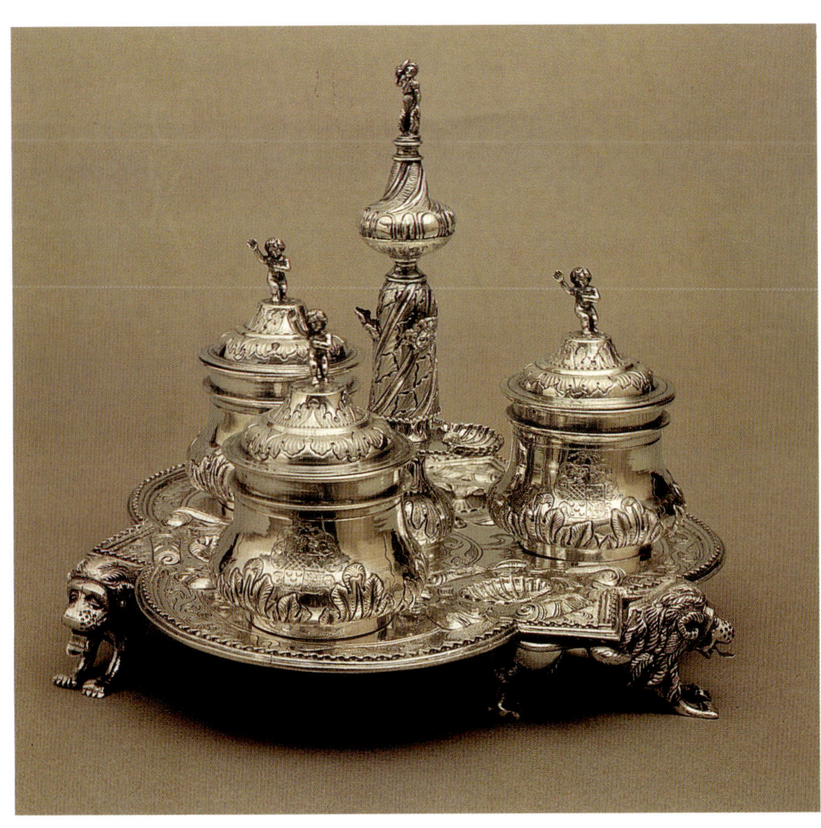

25
Samovar
Portuguese
1750–1770
cast, chased, repoussé, and engraved
silver
65, diam. 23 (25⁹⁄₁₆, 9¹⁄₁₆)
Marks: XI DENIERS (c. 1720–1804);
BP (unidentified silversmith, 1750–1770);
(Vidal and Almeida, 1974, nos. 253, 313)

Private Collection, Lisbon

Couto and Gonçalves 1960; Oman 1965; Santos
1974; Brussels 1991, IV.48

These vessels for serving tea first appeared in Portugal during the middle of
the eighteenth century. The work on
display, in the form of an urn resting on
a quadrangular base, is a splendid example of the original type from which subsequent models were derived.

The samovar is part of a full silver tea
service. Its size lends it a sculptural quality that is enriched by the virtuosity of
the engraving. On the lid, delicate fluting alternates with scalloped rails; two
tiers of projecting palm leaves form a
bell-shaped flower that is crowned with
putti in dancelike postures. Double
grooves spread across the pot with extraordinary movement; garlands provide
balance as well as an organic naturalism
that allows the structure of the decoration to dominate. The pedestal is imposing, with pierced surfaces resting on the
scrolled feet in a sequence of multiple
frames. Double inverted *C*s complete the
elaborate design: curving, striated wings
that end in acanthus leaves. The tap, its
mouth decorated with botanical motifs,
is attached to the ebony handle by encrusted notches.

Pieces of this type in precious metals
are extremely rare, and the scholar
Reinaldo dos Santos recorded only one
like it, dating from the nineteenth century. Another example is pictured on a
table in *Interior Scene,* a painting by
J. Zoffany (1733–1810) reproduced in
Gruber 1982, no. 114.

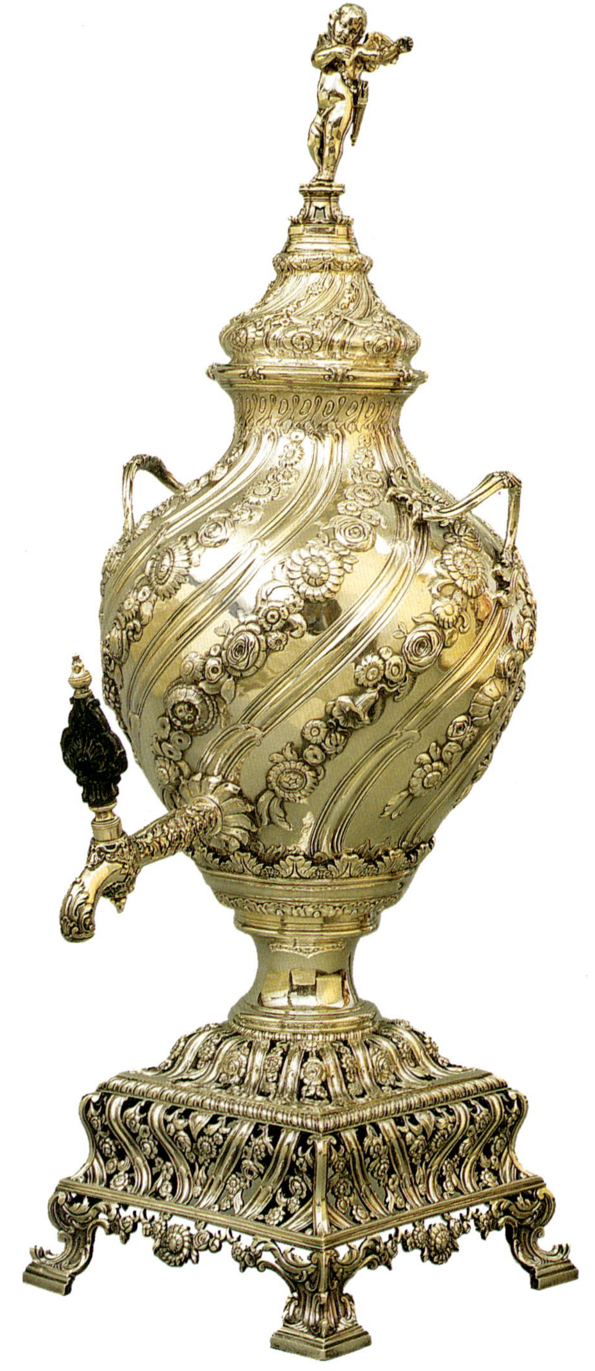

26
Sebastião José de Sousa Pinto
Portuguese
Ewer and Basin
c. 1768–1784
cast, repoussé, chased, and engraved
silver
ewer 32.4 x 11.6 (12¾ x 4⁹⁄₁₆); basin 57 x
40.7 (22⁷⁄₁₆ x 16)
Marks: P (municipal assayer of Oporto
1768–1784); SI (goldsmith Sebastião José
de Sousa Pinto, registered 1768); (Vidal
and Almeida 1974, nos. 69, 1618)

*Museu Nacional de Arte Antiga,
Lisbon, invs. 1072, 1073*

Vidal 1974

This striking ewer is decorated with a
satyr's head on the lip; the handle is in
the shape of a winged dragon perched on
the rim as though about to drink. The
ornate molded rim of the deep basin
traces curves and countercurves chased
with baroque scalloping, while the concave bottom is embellished with an engraved design. The set is impressive not
only in its size but also in the sophistication of the chasing in high relief in the
Italian style.

Ewers and basins for washing hands
were essential components of a table service for banqueting, reflecting the degree
of the owner's predilection for ostentation. For this reason the goldsmiths of
successive eras used these items as vehicles to display their art and virtuosity.

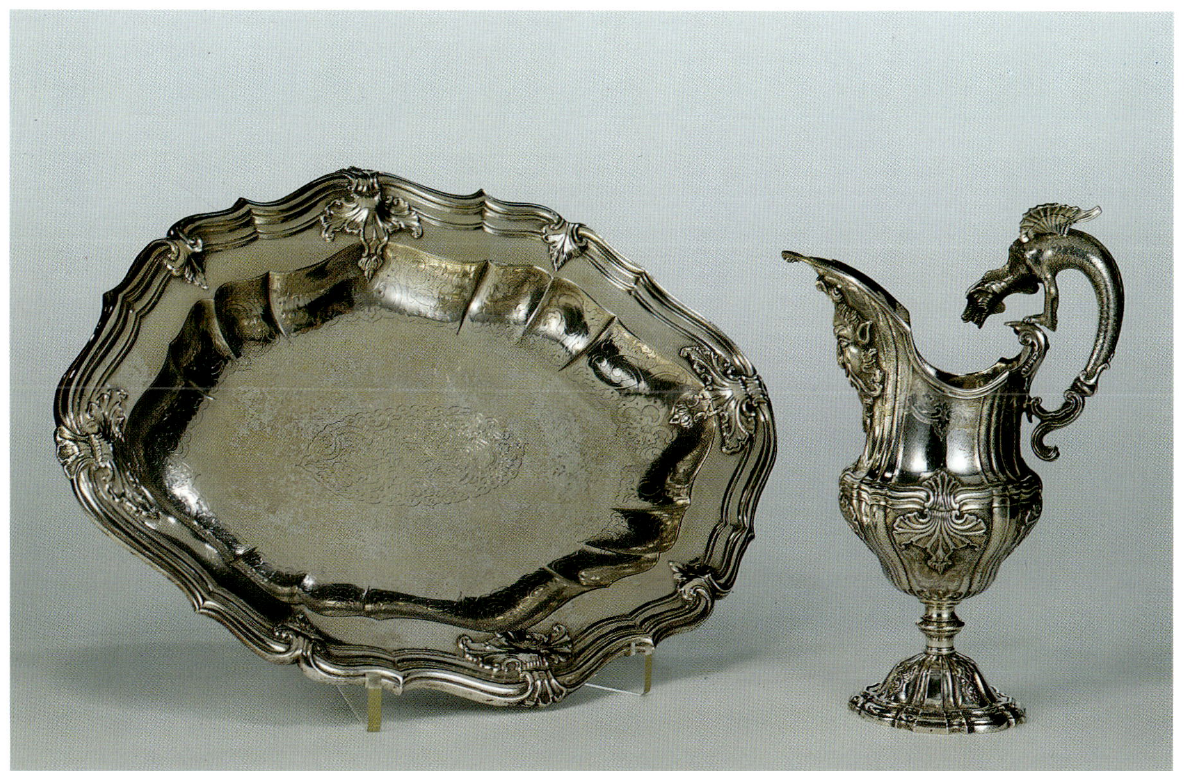

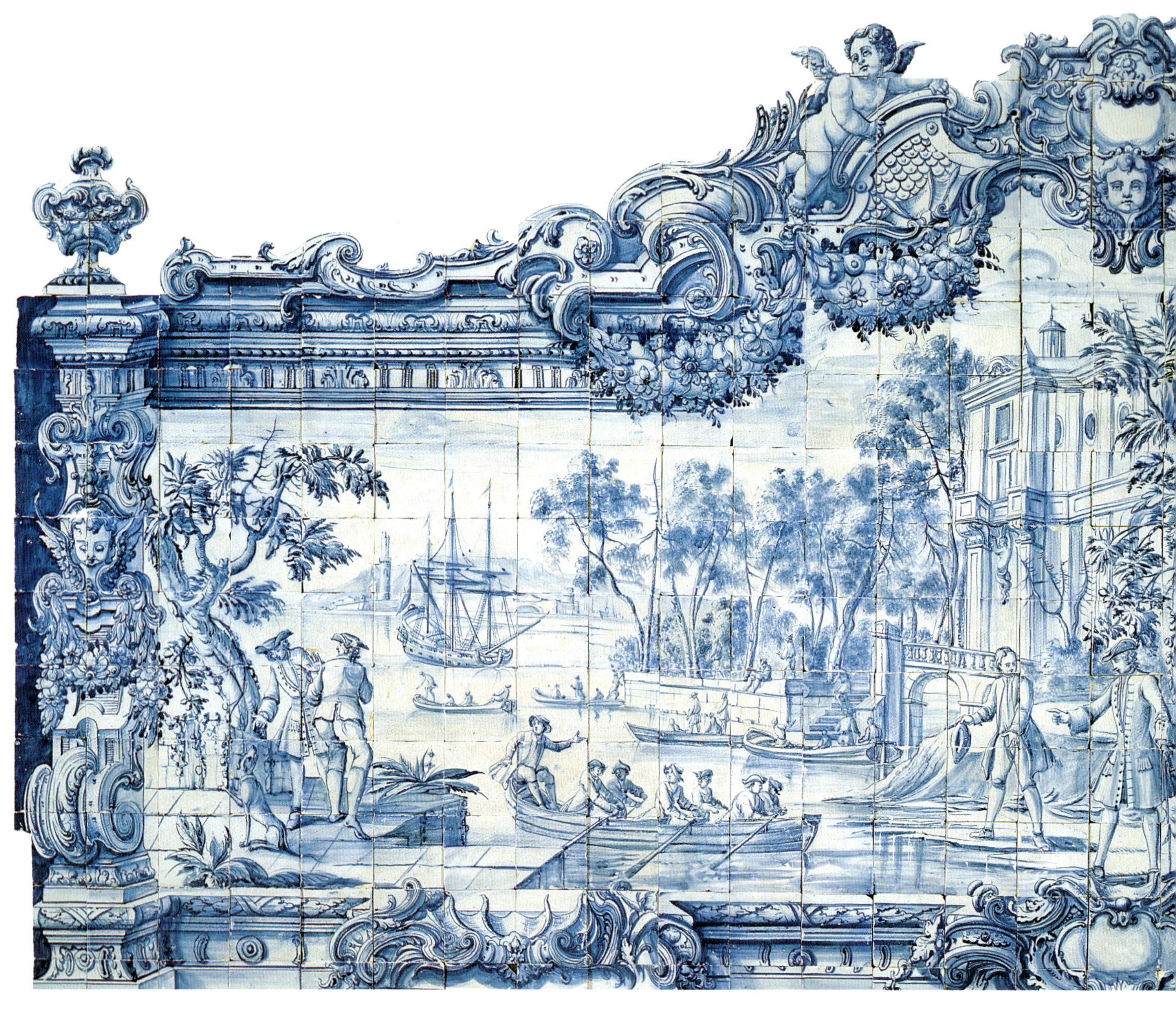

27
Maritime and Country Scenes
2nd quarter 18th century
Portuguese
tiles painted blue and white
199 x 440 (78⅓ x 173¼)

*Museu Nacional do Azulejo,
Lisbon, inv. 709*

Brussels 1991:2, no. 74

At the time these tiles were made, artists
were generally commissioned to create
panels to decorate a specific space which,
in the case of this panel, was very likely a
large wall of a room in a palace. It is evident that models from two decorative
engravings were combined in this panel.
Books with examples of decorative styles
and manuals of landscape composition
were being imported into Portugal, and
the scenes they contained were adapted
by tile painters to the spaces to be decorated and to the preferences of the
clients.

In the foreground of the maritime
scene, forming the central axis of the
composition, are figures of noblemen
with attendants. Boats large and small
fill the scene. On the bank is what appears to be the facade of a palace or
manor house reached by a stairway.

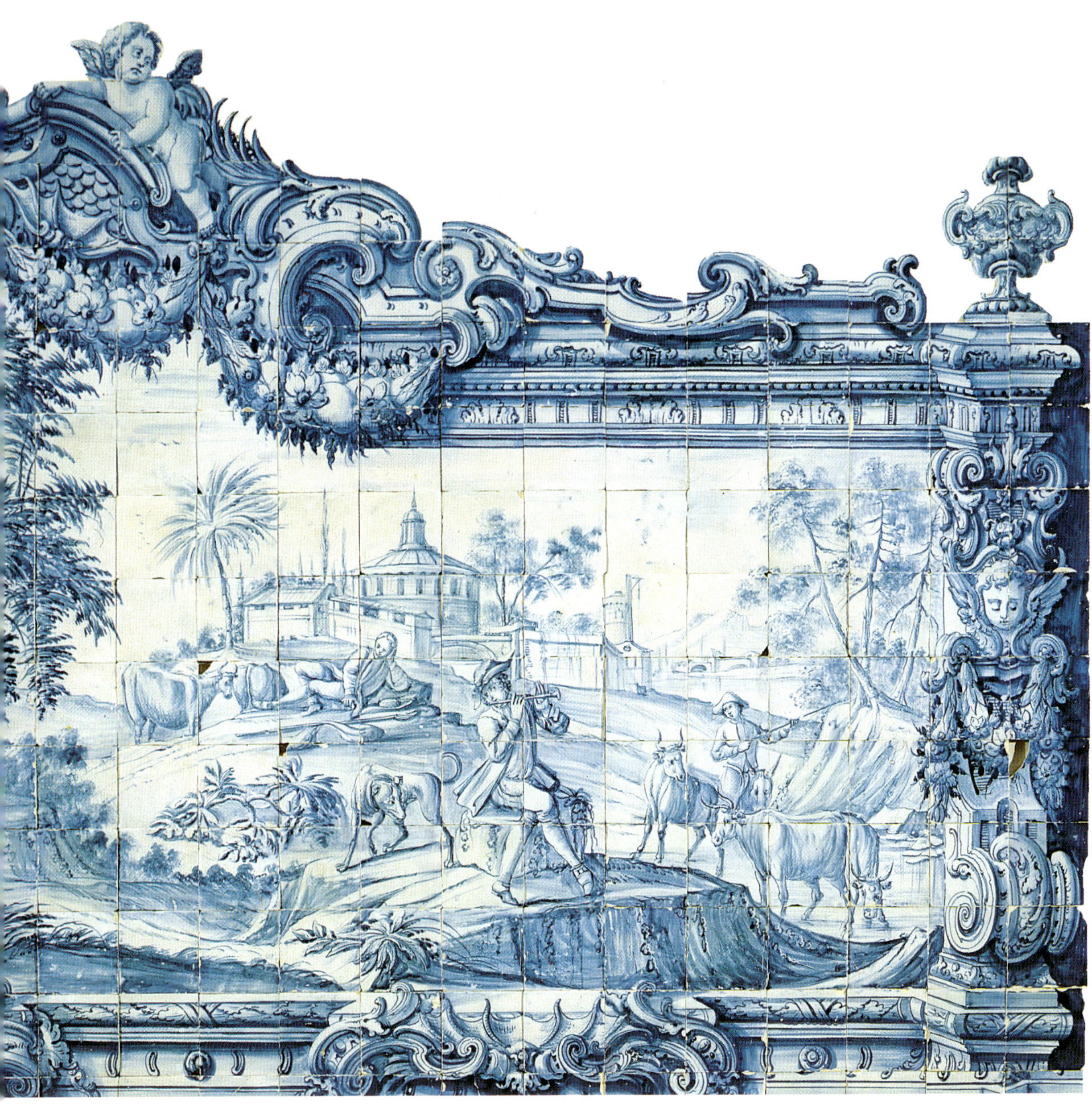

Behind are mountains, a watch tower, and trees.

The pastoral scene on the right depicts a shepherd, cowherds, and animals with buildings and trees in the background. The whole is enclosed in a symmetrical frame with angels, garlands, and fruits, volutes, and cartouches in the center, surrounded by trompe l'oeil side pilasters with putti. This is a fine example of specifically baroque scenography. This panel demonstrates that the monumental scale of such Portuguese creations in tile even influenced the development of architecture.

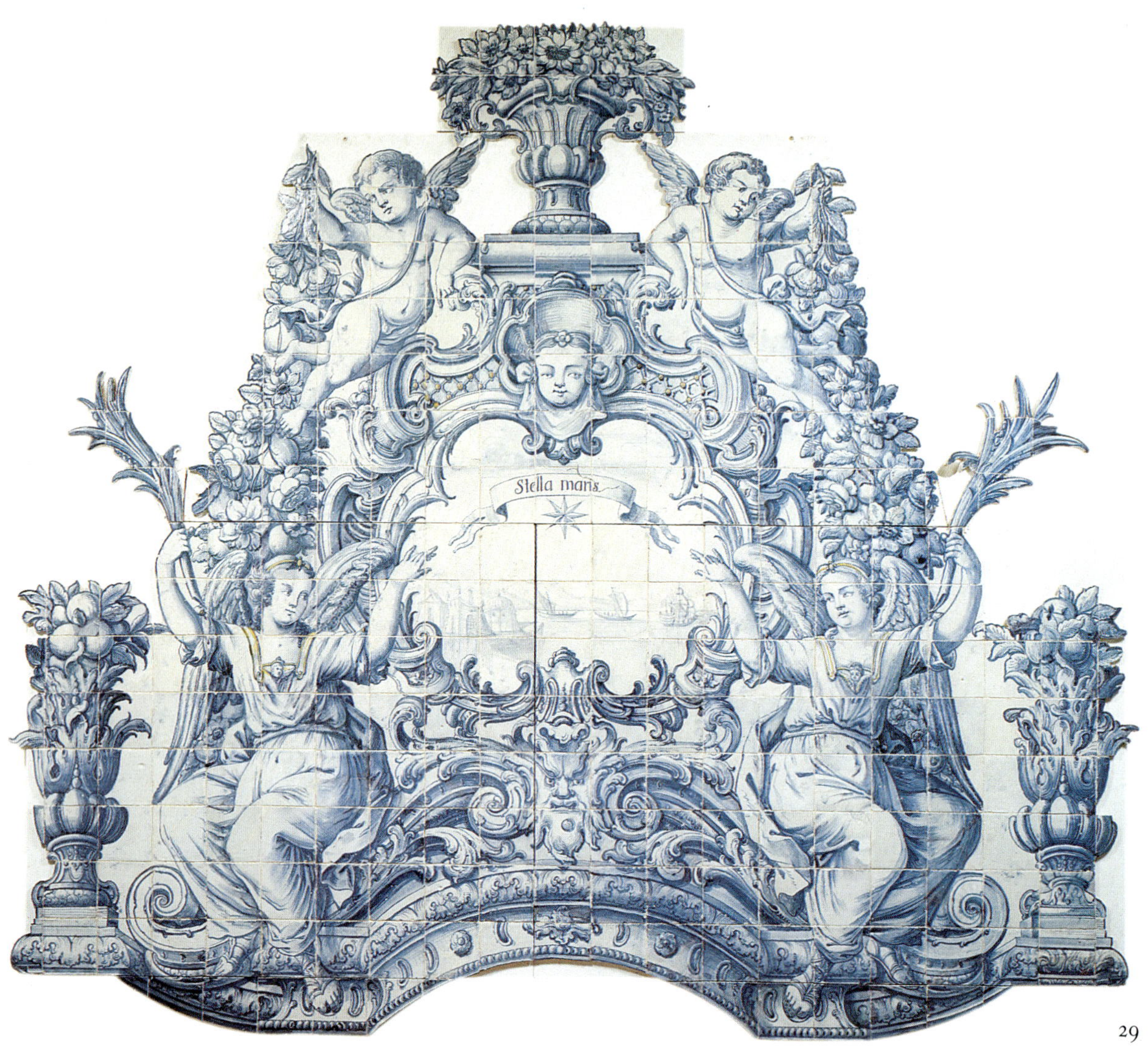

29

28–30
Three Tile Panels
Portuguese
c. 1740
tiles painted blue and white with yellow
accents
nos. 28, 30, 310 x 294 (122$^1\!/_{16}$ x 115$^3\!/_4$);
no. 29, 257 x 294 (101$^3\!/_{16}$ x 115$^3\!/_4$)
Insc: ELECTA UT SOL (cat. 28); STELLA
MARIS (cat. 29); PULCHRA UT LUNA
(cat. 30)

nos. 28, 30, *Fundação Berardo, Funchal,
Madeira;* no. 29, *Solar Collection, Lisbon*

These three silhouetted tile panels depict
the theme of the Litany of the Virgin.
The same subject was rendered in tile
panels in the Ermida da Porto Salvo
(Oeiras), Portugal, by the tile painter

Bartolomeu Antunes (1685–1753). In the
early 1730s, the first signs of a reappear-
ance of polychrome in tile manufacturing became apparent with the use of
yellow. This panel may possibly be attributed to the workshop of Nicolau de
Freitas (1703–1765). This artist was a disciple of António de Oliveria Bernardes
between 1720 and 1724. In 1726, Nicolau
reappeared as painter attached to the
Irmandade de São Lucas in Lisbon. He
entered into partnership with Bartolomeu Antunes, and in 1745 married his
partner's daughter, Joana Caterina Rosa.

Each of the panels is structured as a
pyramid, with, in the case of the two
larger panels, a base of architectural elements creating a lively movement of
concave and convex shapes and produc-

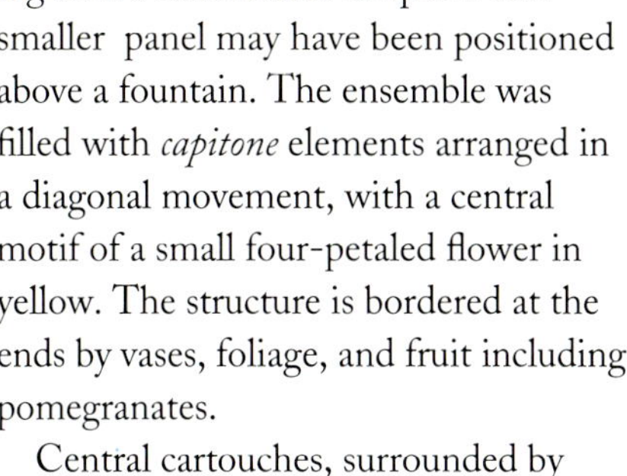

ing fictive continuities of space. The smaller panel may have been positioned above a fountain. The ensemble was filled with *capitone* elements arranged in a diagonal movement, with a central motif of a small four-petaled flower in yellow. The structure is bordered at the ends by vases, foliage, and fruit including pomegranates.

Central cartouches, surrounded by shell shapes, volutes, and scrolls, contain landscapes with inscriptions: *Pulchra ut Luna* (lovely as the moon); *Electa ut Sol* (chosen as the sun); *Stella Maris* (star of the sea) beneath a star. At the base of the two larger panels, dynamic volutes are arranged around a gargoyle. Each composition is brought into balance by two angels carrying palm fronds in their left hands. The whole is surmounted by two cherubs holding a garland of flowers beneath a crest in the form of a vase of flowers. The composition clearly denotes the influence of decorative motifs from French engravings, rugs, and woodwork of the day.

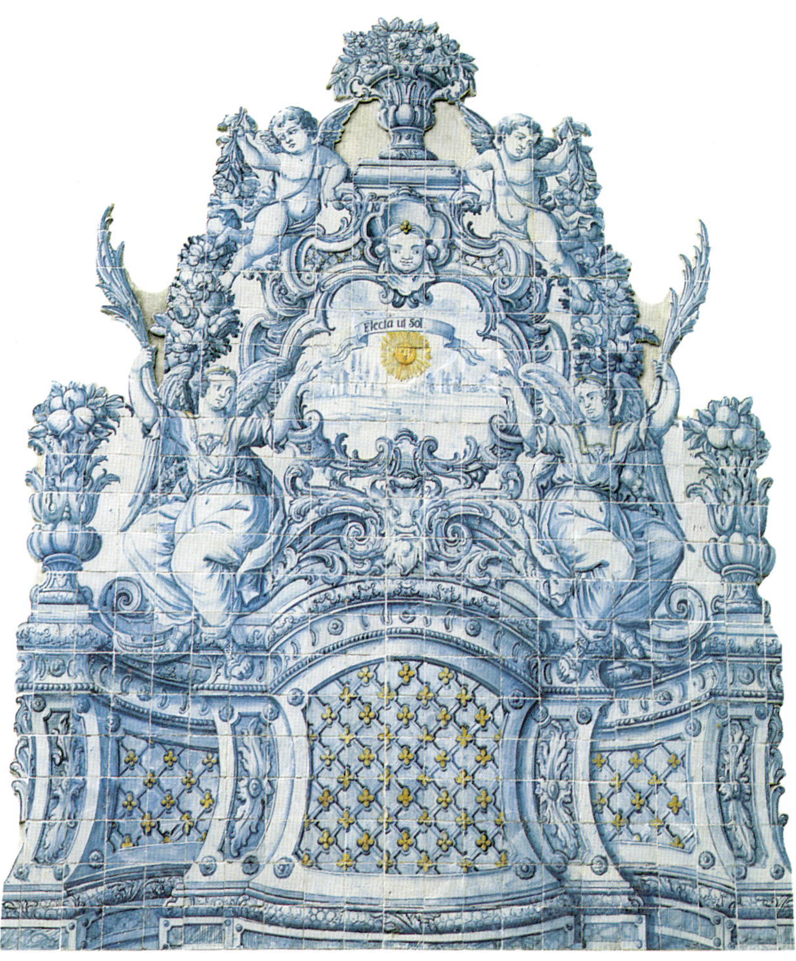

28

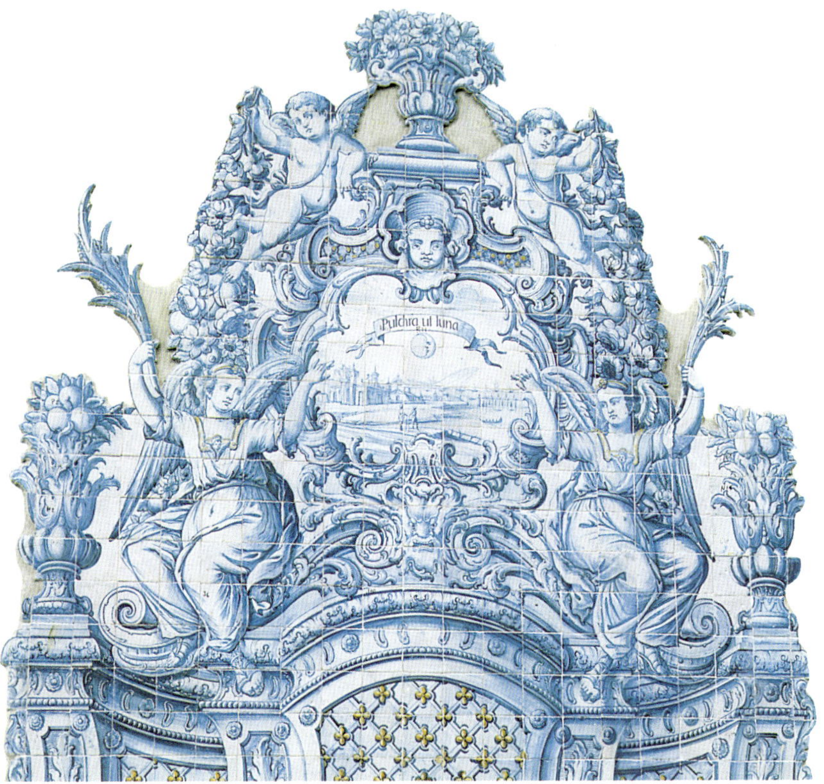

30 detail

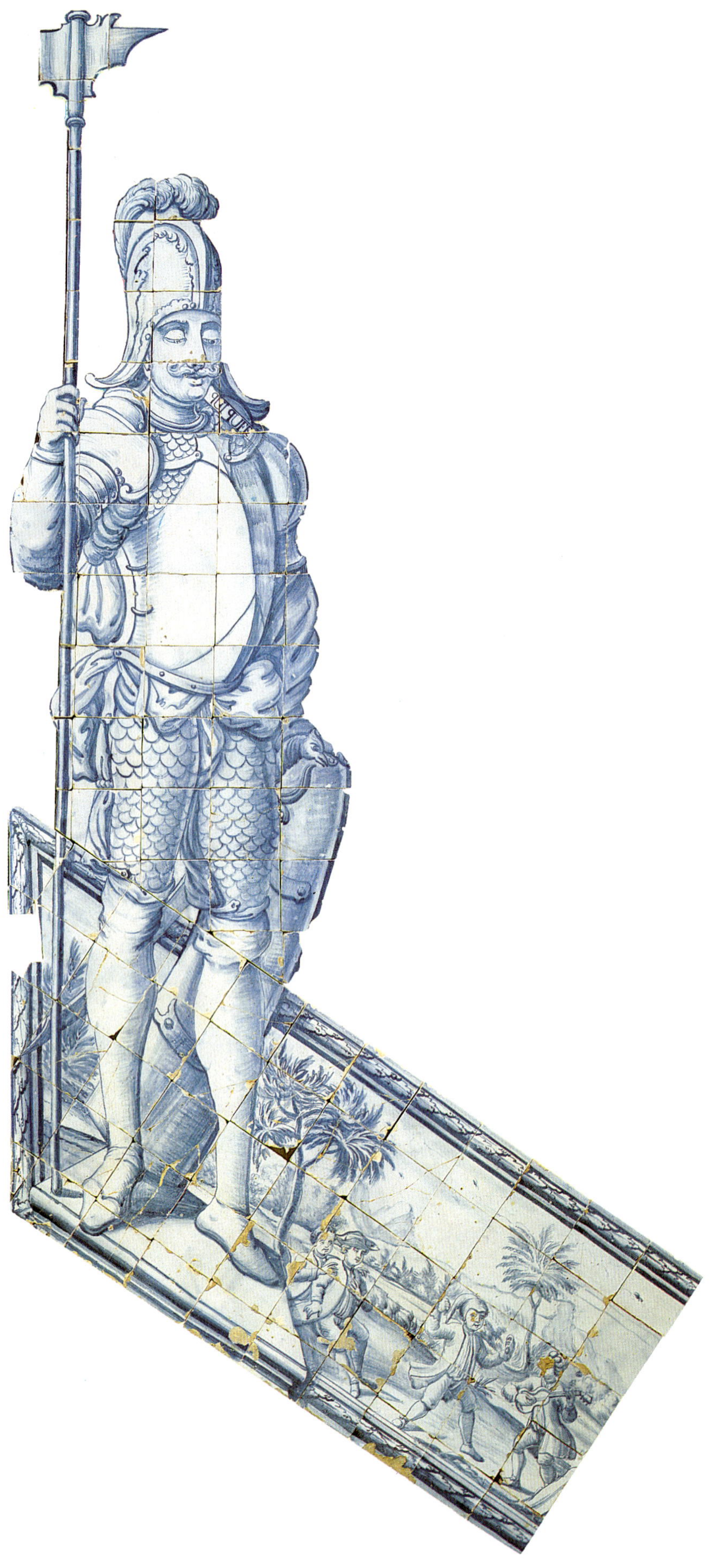

Halberdier
Portuguese
c. 1750–1760
tiles painted in blue and white
285 x 144 (112³⁄₁₆ x 56¹¹⁄₁₆)

Private Collection

Arruda 1979; Brussels 1991:2, no. 62

This figure and the band of decoration
next to which it stands, of which a frag-
ment is displayed, are from the Quinta
das Leiteiras, also known as Quinta da
Vitória Pequena, one of the many estates
located in the outskirts of Lisbon. The
gardens and decorations of the house
suggest it was intended for recreation,
but we may assume that at this time it
also was a working farm.

The courtyard serves as a reception
area, with a flight of steps leading up to
the main floor of the residence. The outside area and the house are integrated by
plantings, a tile fountain, panels of tiles
on several walls, and two silhouetted tile
figures adorning the wall of the exterior
stairway. These figures were the principal elements of the decoration of the
stairway. The figures guarded the stairs,
one at the foot and the exhibited figure
at the top of the stairs beside the front
door. Other tile decoration included a
wainscoting panel on a smaller scale depicting childhood scenes and games.

The two standing figures are warriors,
one a Roman with moustache and the
other, the present figure, a medieval warrior. Both are armed with halberds, lending them the appearance of personal
bodyguards to the owner of the house.
The decoration of the courtyard combines fantasy with humor and irony,
adapting a tradition that was intended to
enhance baroque pomp and ceremony
with the new rococo sensitivity. This
style also catered to new clients, a bourgeoisie who mimicked the nobility and
even demanded the status of stately
homes for their residences.

The execution of figures and landscapes is of high quality, although they
cannot be attributed with certainty to

any known artist. The legs of the exhibited figure seem larger than normal to compensate for the viewpoint from which the halberdier was seen in its original position.

32

REAL FÁBRICA DO RATO
period of Thomaz Brunetto, 1767–1771 (?)
Neptune
white faience with blue decoration
90 x 29 x 28 (35⁷/₁₆ x 11⁷/₁₆ x 11)
Museu Nacional Machado de Castro, Coimbra, inv. C 623

Sandão 1976, fig. 68

This statuette in faience, meticulously modeled in light clay glazed in white, is a vigorous rendering of the mythological figure of Neptune, god of the seas. His venerable crowned head with curling hair and beard is inclined, with a stern yet attentive expression on his features. The right arm is thrust forward, with the hand in a position to hold the trident, which is missing but was most likely of metal.

The quality of the material and of the modeling suggests that this figure belongs to the early period of manufacture of the Real Fábrica do Rato. This large Portuguese company was founded in 1767, during the reign of Dom José I, by the marquês de Pombal, his prime minister, and was initially managed by the Italian master, Thomaz Brunetto. This is an exceptional statuette that was probably intended for exterior decoration. It belonged to a private collection and was purchased by the museum in 1918.

There is no similarity between the statuette and the statue of Neptune in the lake of Praça D. Estefania, in Lisbon, which is thought to have been produced by the workshop of the sculptor Machado de Castro.

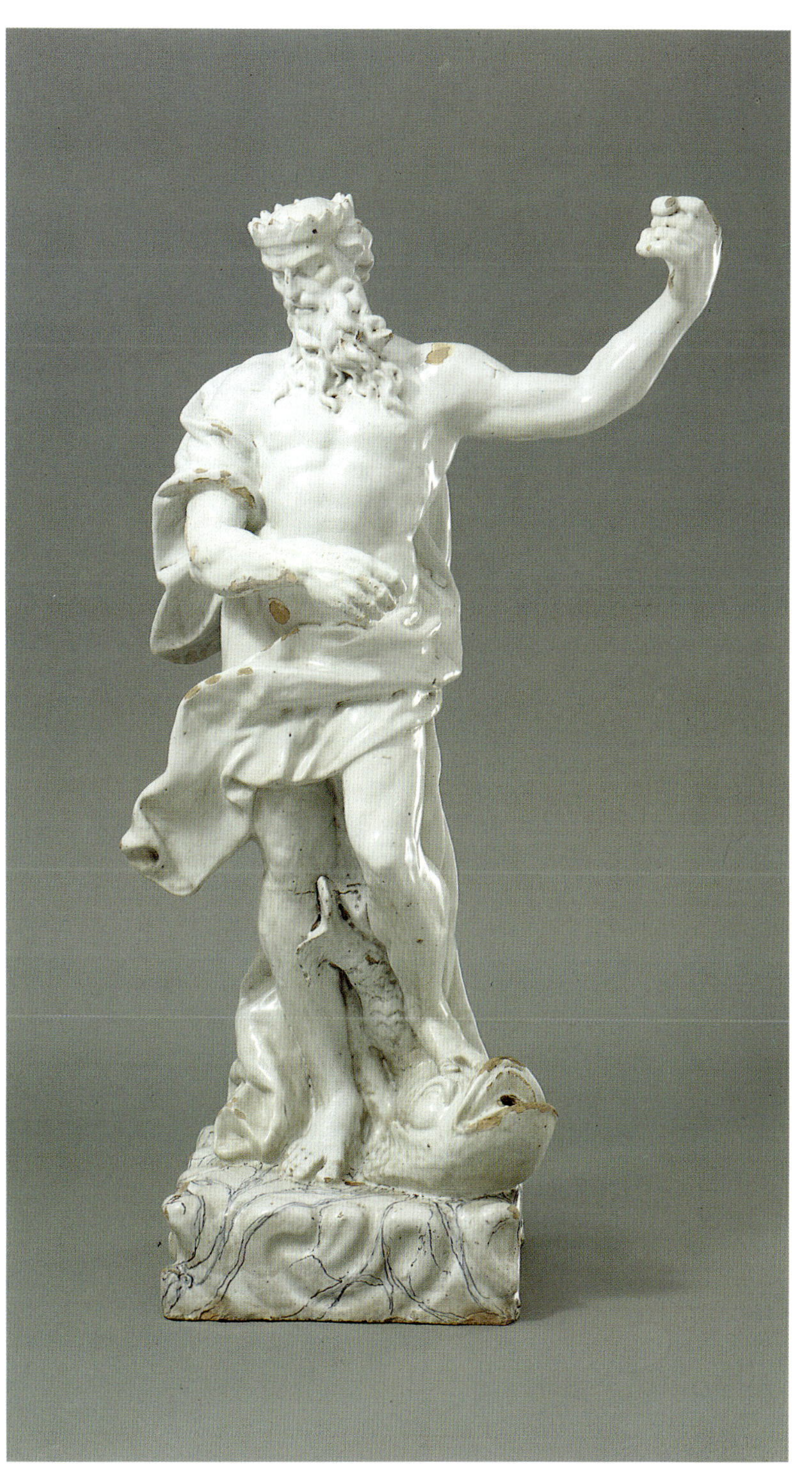

33

REAL FÁBRICA DO RATO
period of Thomaz Brunetto, 1767–1771 (?)
Allegory of Spring
white faience
69.1 (27³⁄₁₆)

*Ministry of Foreign Affairs, Palácio das
Necessidades, Lisbon*

Queiros 1948; Santos 1970; Sandão 1976;
Brussels 1991, III.53

"Even today, what I saw seems to me to
have been a dream." These were the
words of António Arroio, connoisseur of
Portuguese porcelain, when he saw this
piece in the collection belonging to Dom
Fernando, housed in the Palácio das Necessidades, consisting of two sculptural
groups from the Fábrica do Rato including this allegorical figure believed to represent Spring.

Although it does not bear the mark of
the Fábrica do Rato Brunetto, this figure
would appear to date from that company's golden era, when Thomaz
Brunetto ran the factory. He was a well-
known artist and had worked for some
time in the Santo Amaro china factory
before moving on to the Fábrica do
Rato, where he played an active part in
establishing the company's fortunes.

The superb base of the figure is of rococo design, in line with models popular
throughout Europe that originated in
Meissen and had in turn influenced the
Italian ceramics with which Brunetto
was familiar. The open design of the
base enhances its sense of dynamism
through the tension between open spaces
and volute and scallop forms. The figure
is clad in unusual garments consisting of
superimposed layers hung with bells, in
keeping with the rococo preference for
non-European styles, which is likewise
apparent in the peaked hat that also adds
to the figure's charm.

The curving rhythm created by the
supple twist of the body lends the figure
a grace that is typical of this style, child-
like rather than sensual, which is in
keeping with the spirit of miniatures that
is apparent in the work's conception.
The milky-white coloring creates the illusion of evanescent contours, presenting
the viewer with a multiplicity of glittering and sparkling surfaces that are admirably enhanced by the glaze.

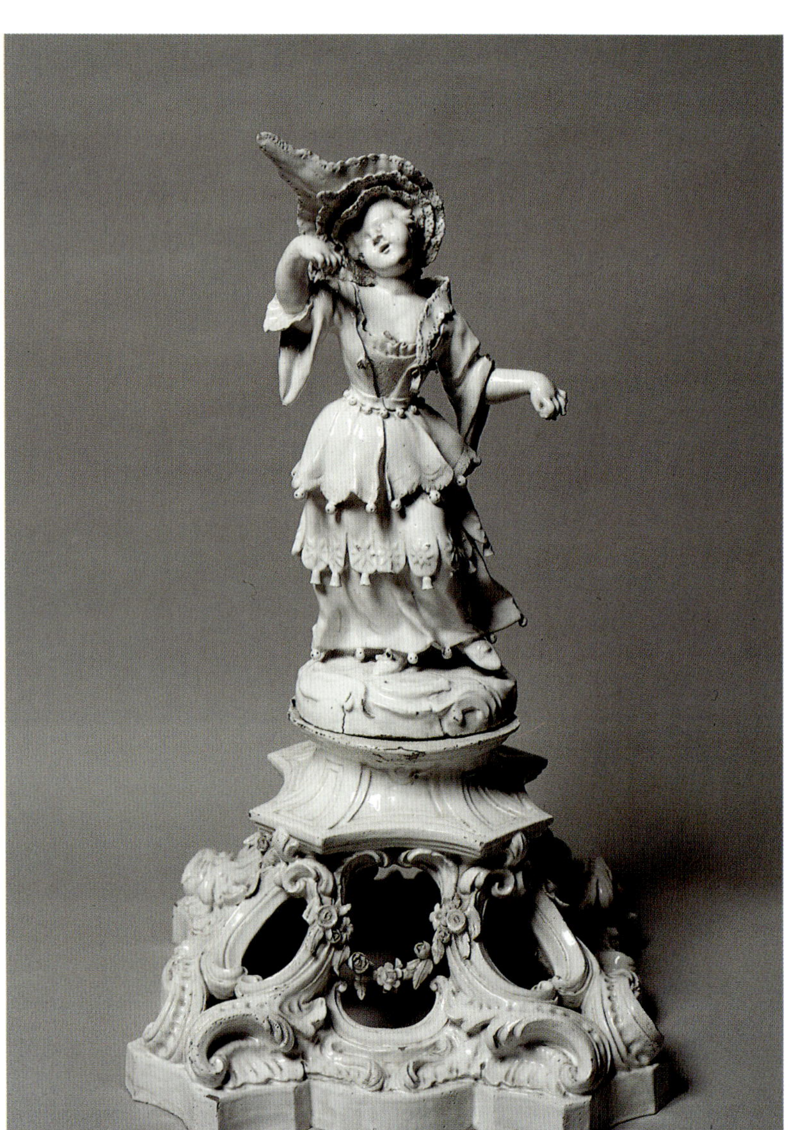

34
REAL FÁBRICA DO RATO
period of Thomaz Brunetto, 1767–1771
Tureen in the Form of a Goose
white faience with blue decoration
33 x 33 (13 x 13)
Museu Nacional de Arte Antiga, Lisbon

Sandão 1976, fig. 81

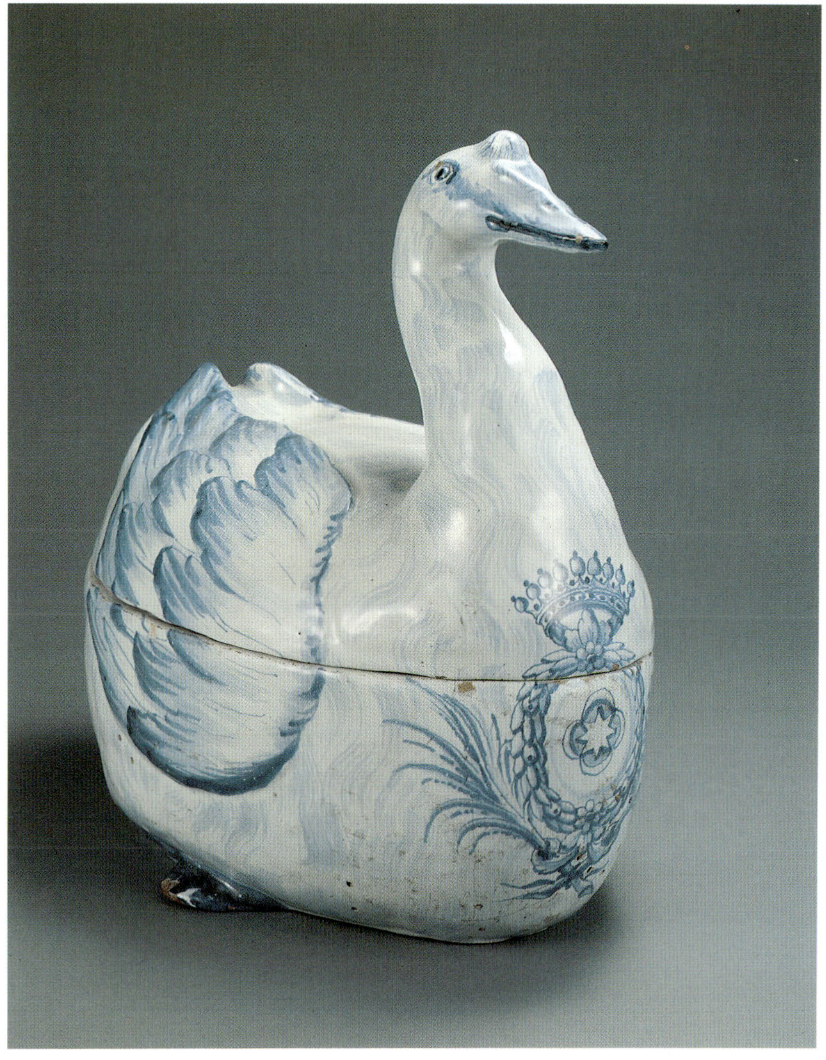

This substantial lidded tureen is modeled in the shape of a crouching goose, with its wing tips raised slightly. A striking piece of complex execution, it is decorated in monochrome tones of blue. Against a light blue background wash suggesting the plumage, strong dark blue strokes define the feathers of the wings, the eyes, the separation of the beak, and the feet. The marquês de Pombal's coat of arms is delicately painted on the breast of the goose, incorporating the front of both the tureen and the lid. The interior is glazed in the same bluish white and bears the mark "F. R.," identifying the Real Fábrica do Rato, above the monogram of Thomaz Brunetto. The high quality of execution of the painting is reminiscent of the fine Portuguese tiles produced during the same period.

Both the form and proportions of this model were inspired by Chinese porcelain tureens of the contemporary Quianlong period c. 1760–1770. It is similar to the Chinese porcelain tureen made to order during the Quianlong period that belonged to the collection of the royal household and currently is in the Palácio de Queluz collection, inv. 1013.

At least two similar tureens from the same service, owned by the Pombal family, are known to exist in Portugal. This item was purchased by the state in an auction in 1947. It is damaged at the front near the escutcheon, and the crack and marks from the metal clamp applied are visible.

REAL FÁBRICA DO RATO
period of Thomaz Brunetto, 1767–1771
**Tureen and Lid in the Form of
a Boar's Head**
Portuguese
white faience with brown and blue
decoration
26 x 26.5 x 77.3 (10¼ x 10⁷⁄₁₆ x 30⁷⁄₁₆)
Marks: F.F.T.B.

Private Collection, Mafra

Queiroz 1948, 63; Sandão 1976, 92

Some of the animal-figure tureens with
lids produced by the Rato factory, such
as this imposing boar's head, have as
their prototypes works in Chinese export
porcelain. The factory produced, in the
words of José Queiroz, a "veritable
menagerie" of such shapes, including
stag's heads, chickens, ducks, and fish.
This group of exuberant pieces found
acceptance because the marquês de
Pombal persuaded the principal noble
families to buy them, thus supporting
the national factory.

REAL FÁBRICA DO RATO
period of Thomaz Brunetto, 1767–1771
Tureen in the Form of a Barrel of Fish
white faience with polychrome
decoration
30 x 27.5 (11¹³⁄₁₆ x 10¹³⁄₁₆)

Museu Nacional de Arte Antiga, Lisbon

Sandão 1976, fig. 79

This round tureen with lid is a naturalistic rendering of a wooden barrel full of
fish. This piece was clearly inspired by
the utilitarian forms with animal figures
produced by the French ceramic workshops of Strasbourg, Mennecy, Sceaux,
and Nevers. The piece is of molded
white faience and is decorated in a range
of tones of antimony yellow, cobalt blue,
and manganese dark violet. The lid bears
the mark "F. R." of the Real Fábrica do
Rato above the monogram of Thomaz
Brunetto.

Other tureens of this type exist in
Portugal. This one originally belonged to
the collection of the Casa Real.

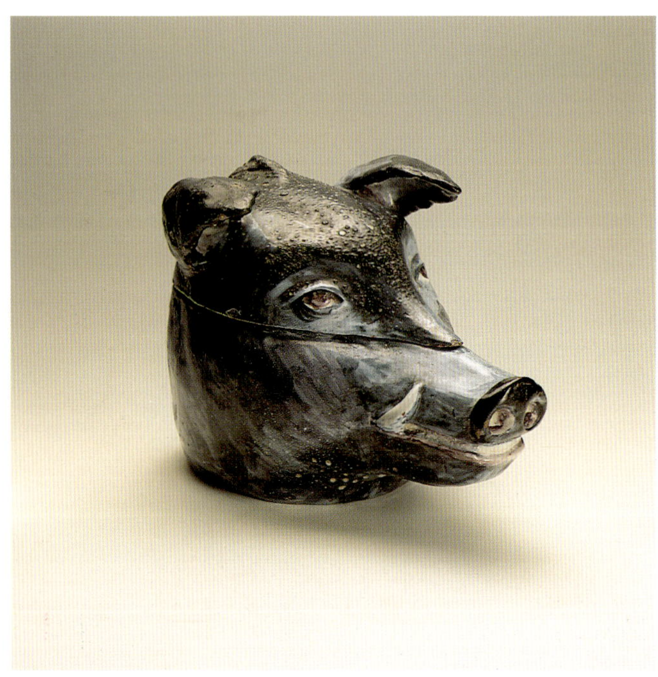

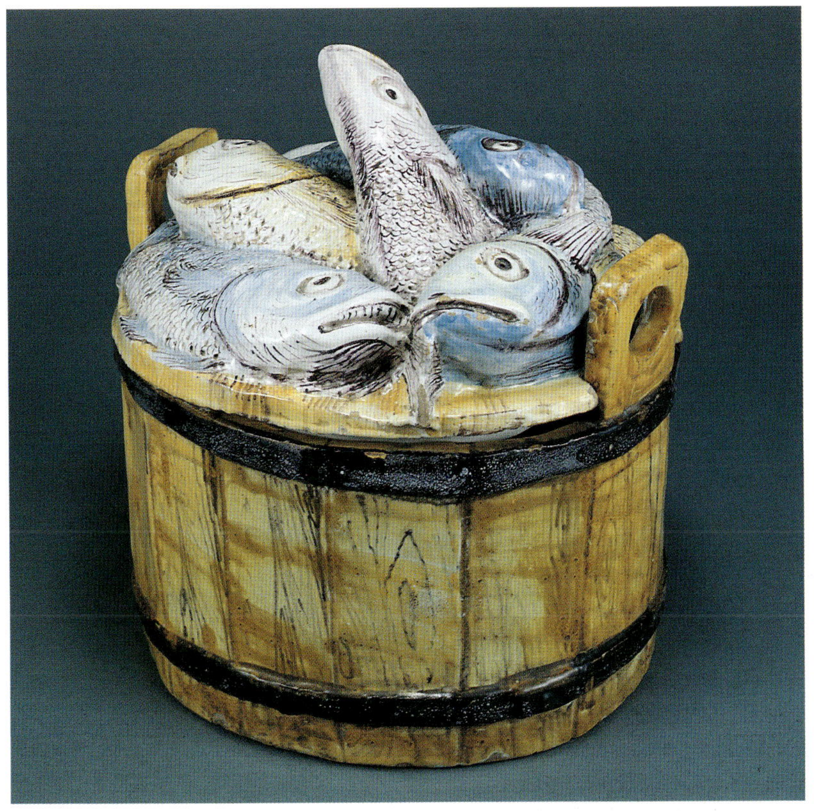

36

37

MANUEL DA COSTA BRIOZO

Tank for a Washbasin

1781
white faience with polychrome
decoration
36.8 (14½)
Insc: 1781/BRIOZA/COIMBRA

*Museu Nacional Machado de Castro,
Coimbra, inv. C 363*

Sandão 1976, fig. 108

This receptacle for water was originally
mounted above a wash basin, which is
now missing. The rectangular tank is of
faience, adorned with scrolls and shells at
the top of the front and back and a gargoyle into which the tap was inserted. It
is painted in bright yellow, blue, and
green, the colors picking out the grooves
of the molding and emphasizing the
naive marbling of the frame around the
gargoyle's mask. Delicate strokes in
manganese burgundy color the shell
shapes and define the eyes, eyebrows,
and beard of the gargoyle. The date and
signature appear on the right side, which

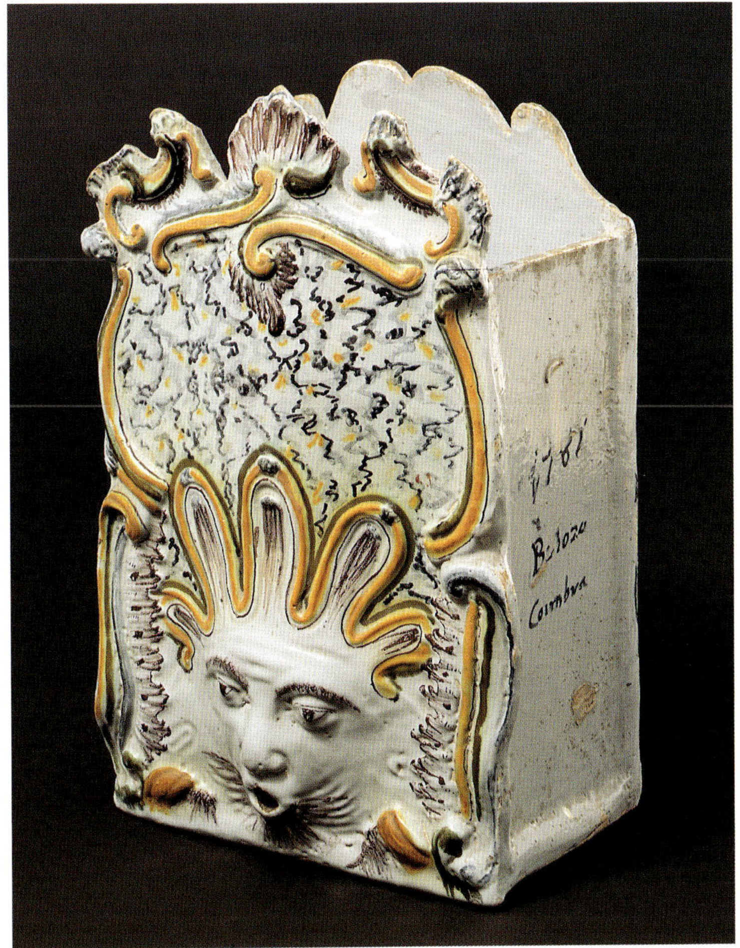

37

is painted blue over the white glaze. The piece is a popular interpretation of the rococo style, handled here with great spontaneity though somewhat clumsy technique. This item comes from the collection of the well-known professor and ceramics expert, J. M. Teixeira de Carvalho. The Museu Nacional de Arte Antiga owns an identical washbasin tank, which has the mark "Briozo/Coimbra" on the back but no date.

Manuel da Costa Briozo, who lived in Coimbra during the second half of the eighteenth century, was a well-known potter, producing pieces that can be divided into two stylistic phases. He began by producing ceramics of popular origin, most in a single color, drawing maximum expression from an exuberant baroque style of decoration in the early 1770s. In the following decade his works became more sophisticated, enhanced by the introduction of polychrome, with rococo tendencies. Briozo's ceramics, which always incorporated the traditional features of the local production of Coimbra, had a marked influence on faience produced throughout the nineteenth century.

38–39
COMPANHIA DAS INDIAS
Qianlong Reign, 1735–1799
Tureen with Platter and Two Plates
Chinese
c. 1775
tureen 32, diam. 29.5 (12⅝, 11⅝); platter, 30.5 x 41 (12 x 16⅛); plates, diam. 24 (9½)

Private Collection, Lisbon

Beurdeley 1962; Howard and Ayers 1978; Boulay 1984; Castro 1987; Brussels 1991, III.31

The Chinese export porcelain tureen reflects the large tureens designed by the workshops of the most prominent French goldsmiths. When Chinese porcelain began to compete with European silver in size and ostentation, familiar Western types with new subjects were ordered from Chinese factories in order to satisfy the demands of Western clientele. This tureen is very close to an example in silver by J. Nicolas Roettiers (1736–1784) in the Musée Nissim de Camondo in Paris, which evinces an almost nostalgic return to the splendor of the age of Louis XIV. Each piece has four feet, although they are differently arranged. The most significant difference between the two is the design of the handle of the porcelain tureen, which is inspired by the scrolled feet of the silver one, while the grotesque mask beneath the handle is clearly influenced by Meissen porcelain. The foliated motif on the

porcelain pot is close to that on a tureen in the Espírito Santo collection (Beurdeley 1962, ill. x), which is quite similar in general to the present piece. The scalloped border of the exhibited pot is also repeated on the periphery of the tray. The handle of the lid is composed of vegetables: cauliflower, French garlic cloves, beans, and mushrooms, giving it a vigorous sculptural quality.

At the center of the tray, a motif of carnations identifies the work as belonging to a well-known service of the same name. Both the tureen and the platter are adorned with the heraldic device of Joaquim Inácio da Cruz Sobral (1725–1781).

Sobral had been a wealthy merchant in Bahia (Brazil) and in 1768 assumed the important position of administrator of customs in Lisbon. He was chairman of the board of trade of the Companhia de Grão Pará, the trading company active in the far north of Brazil, advisor to the royal house, and was elevated to the rank of nobleman in 1773 as lord of Vila do Sobral. A number of pieces belonging to the seven sumptuous Chinese porcelain dinner services owned by this prosperous nobleman have been identified.

The meticulously painted coat of arms of the house of Sobral appears on a shield on the front of the tureen and in a space expressly left vacant for this purpose on the pierced rim of each of the two plates exhibited, which are also from the carnation service.

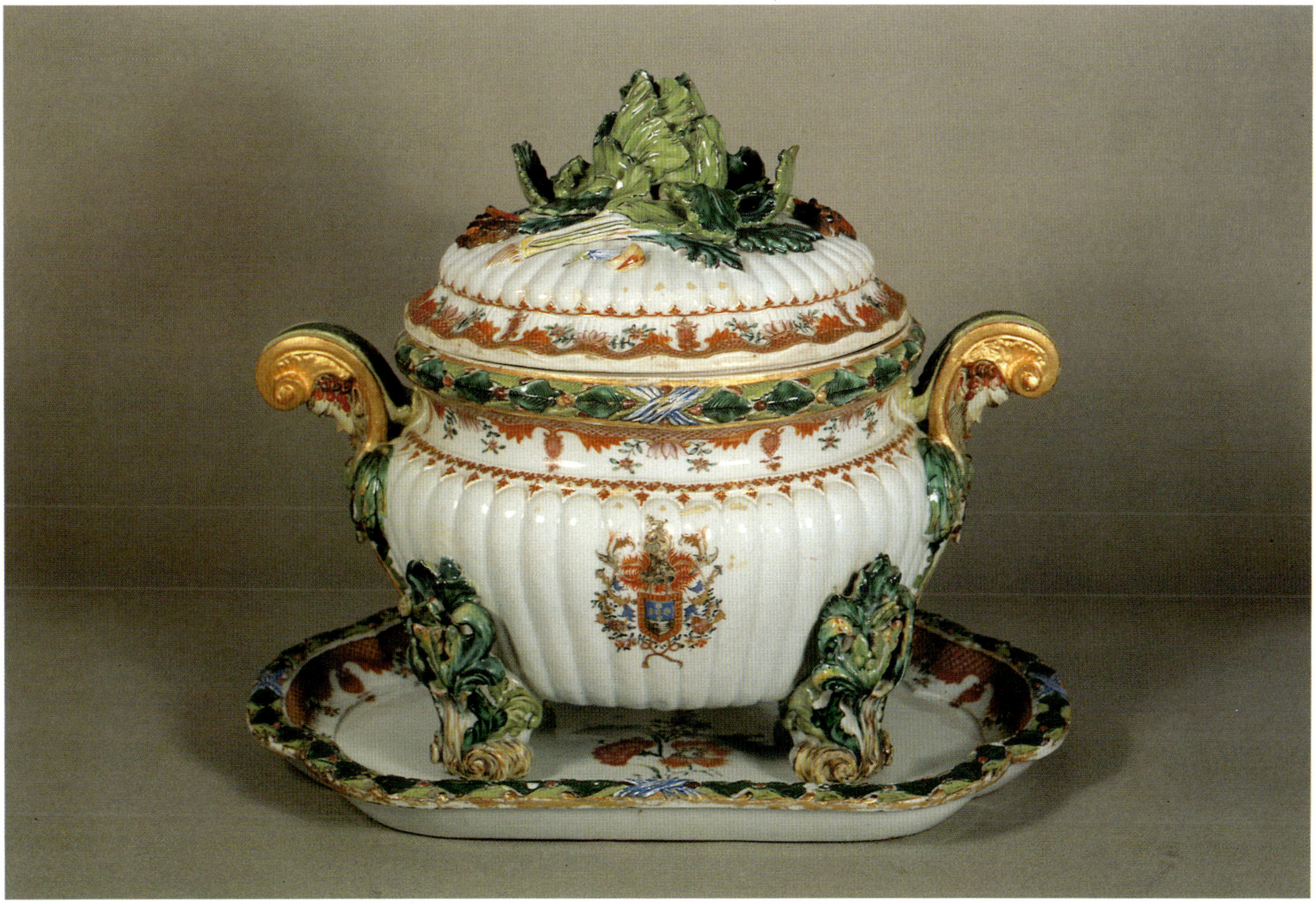

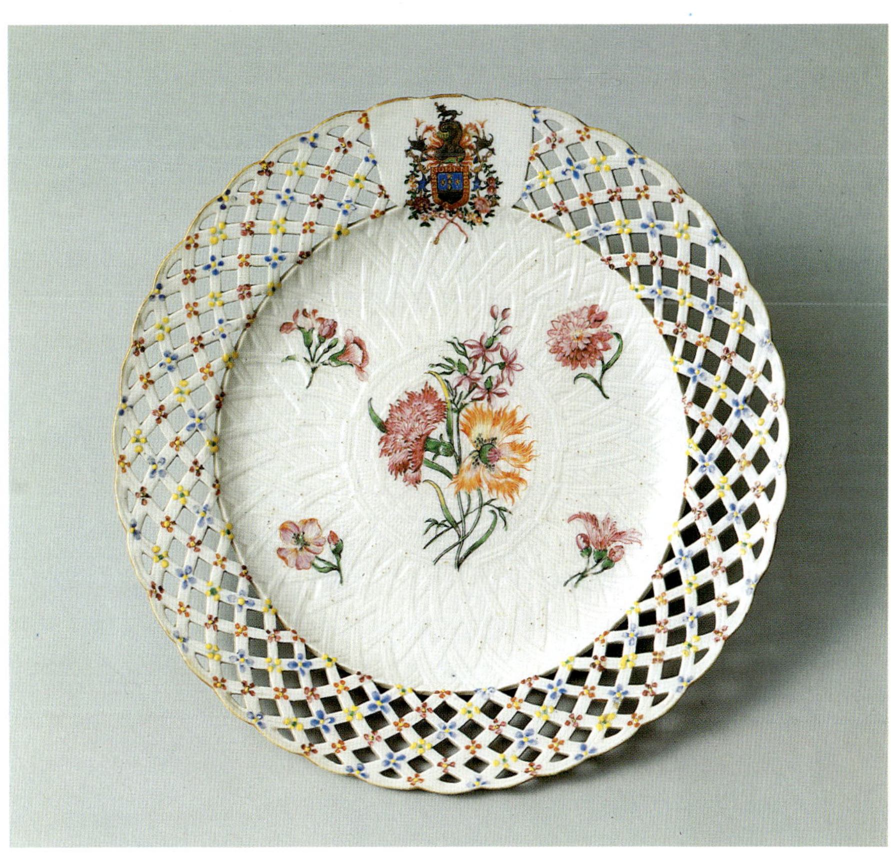

40
Breast Ornament
Portuguese
1st quarter 18th century
gilded silver and gold with diamonds
12.9 x 17 (5^{1}/$_{16}$ x 6^{11}/$_{16}$)

*Museu Nacional de Arte Antiga, Lisbon,
inv. 875 Joa*

Lisbon 1974, cat. 185; Brussels 1991:3, cat. 87;
Copenhagen 1992, cat. 87

This large triangular silver ornament is
set with rose-cut diamonds, with chased
gold feathers above and below. It has
pierced decoration of volutes and plant
motifs, with an elegant basket surmounted by a large diamond mounted
on a mobile structure. The underside of
this piece, in gilded silver, reveals the
complexity of the mount, which was executed with extraordinary technical mastery. The elaborate design of this outstanding piece of Portuguese jewelry
reveals French inspiration.

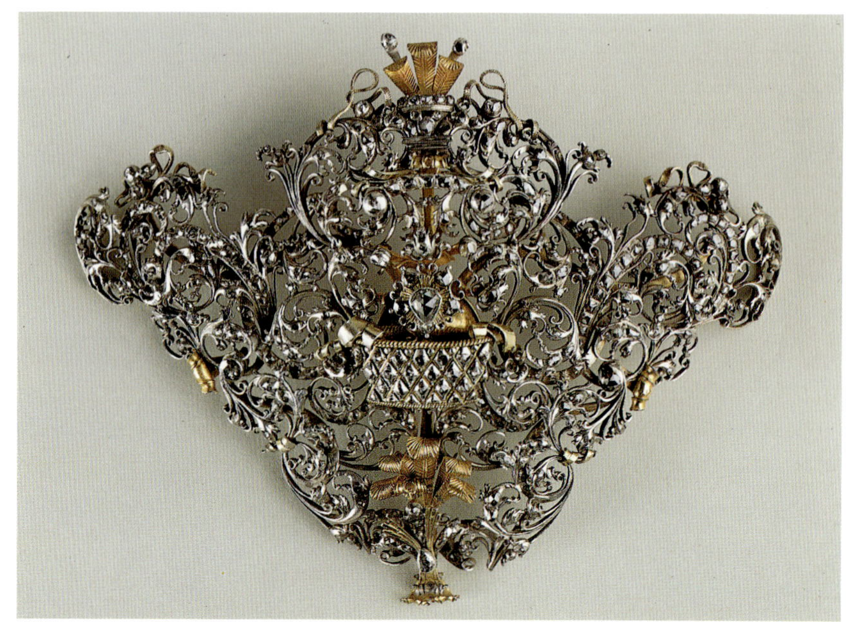

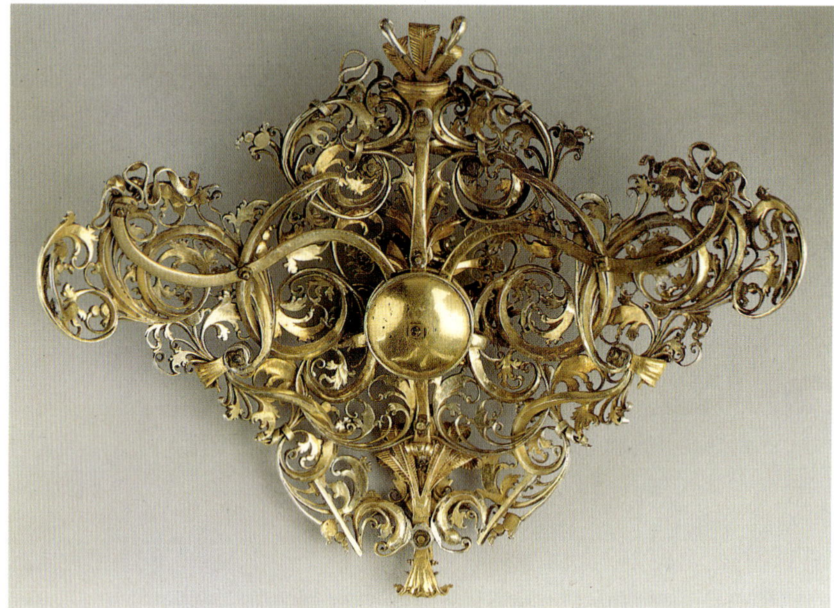

Necklace with Bow Pendant
Portuguese
1st half 18th century
gold with diamonds
29.1 x 5.8 (11⁷⁄₁₆ x 2⁵⁄₁₆)

*Museu Nacional de Arte Antiga,
Lisbon, inv. 707 Joa*

Brussels 1991:3, cat. 89; Copenhagen 1992, cat. 89

This fine necklace is composed of a
series of linked sections of alternating
design, executed in gold set with diamonds with a central pendant in the
shape of a bow.

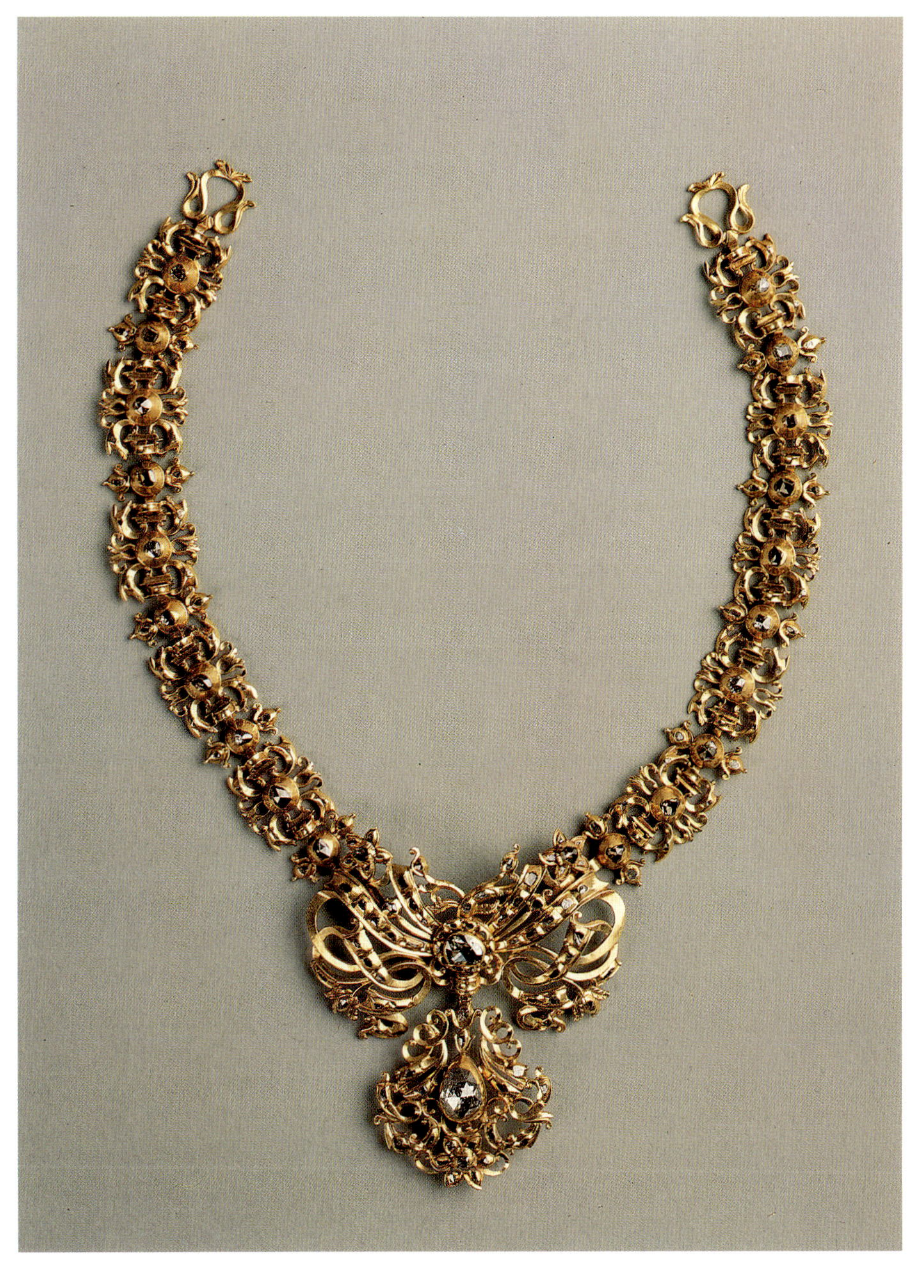

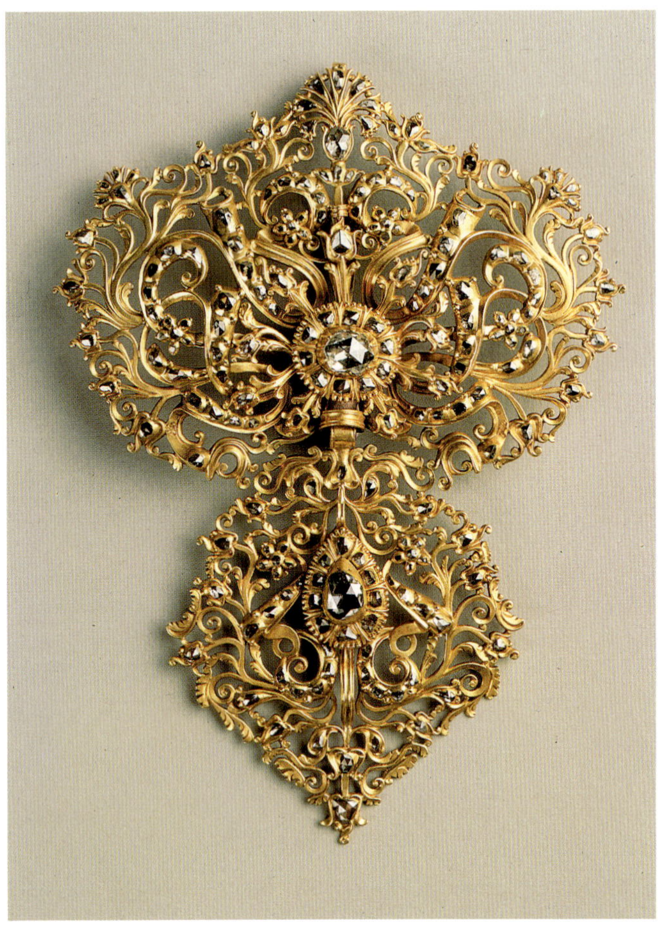 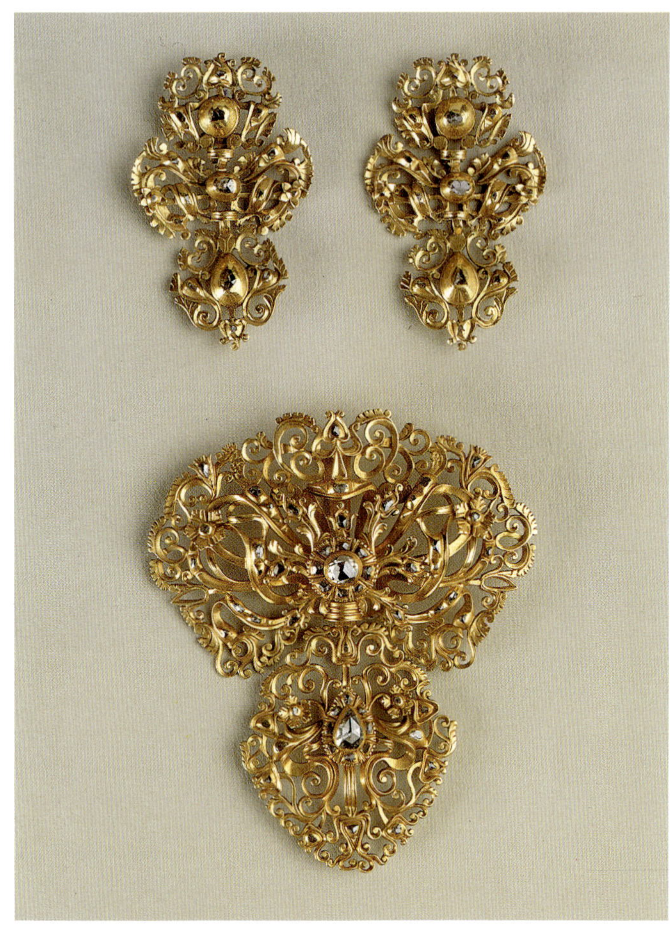

42
Bow Pendant
Portuguese
2nd half 18th century
gold with diamonds
13 x 9.65 (5⅛ x 3¹³⁄₁₆)
Marks: x, municipal assayer of Oporto, 1784–1794 (Vidal and Almeida 1974, no. 81); initials of unidentified jeweler

Museu Nacional de Arte Antiga, Lisbon, inv. 723 Joa

Lisbon 1974, cat. 181; Brussels 1991:3, cat. 91

43–44
Bow Pendant and Pair of Earrings
Portuguese
2nd half 18th century
chased gold with diamonds
pendant 7.1 x 6.1 (2¹³⁄₁₆ x 2⅜);
earrings 4.6 x 2.9 (1¹³⁄₁₆ x 1⅛)
Marks: pendant, x, municipal assayer of Oporto 1784–1794 (Vidal and Almeida 1974, no. 81); Initial of goldsmith Damião José Ferreira, registered in the Guild of Santo Eloy in 1769 (no. 1812); earrings, 1, Municipal Assayer of Oporto 1732–1776 (Vidal and Almeida 1974, no. 63); Initial of goldsmith João Pinto, registered in the Guild of Santo Eloy in 1758 (Vidal and Almeida 1974, no. 1713)

Museu Nacional de Arte Antiga, Lisbon, invs. 300, 299 Joa

Brussels 1991:3, cats. 92–93

These pendants, in chased gold inlaid with diamonds, are a typical example of such bow-shaped jewelry that is characteristically Portuguese. The motif extends to a wide variety of models known for their high technical quality. In older pieces the design of the bow was somewhat rigid, but gradually, during the course of the eighteenth century, the designs acquired movement and the dangling ribbons appeared to flutter. Scrolls and foliage were incorporated, to the extent that it was sometimes difficult to distinguish the bow from the exuberant rococo designs enlivening the composition. This is true of the present sophisticated bow, of elaborate design and accompanied by a decorative profusion of ribbons and swirling plant motifs, with emphasis on scattered tulips and marigolds, worn with matching earrings or necklaces that were generally secured by a narrow ribbon. Such pieces continued to be produced and worn throughout the nineteenth century.

45
Brooch or Pendant
Portuguese
mid-18th century
silver and gold with diamonds, topazes,
emeralds, and rubies
2.9 x 12.2 (1⅛ x 4¹³⁄₁₆)

*Museu Nacional de Arte Antiga, Lisbon,
inv. 275 Joa*

Brussels 1991:3, cat. 123; Copenhagen 1992, cat. 123

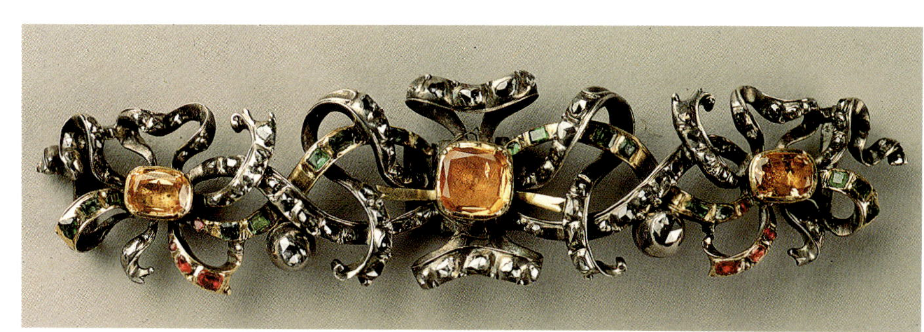

The design of this unusual piece is composed of an elegant combination of ribbons and bows mounted in silver and
gold. The bows in silver are set with diamonds and the ribbons in gold are inlaid
with emeralds and rubies, surrounding
three large topazes that accentuate the
center and the axes of the composition.

46
Pendant
Portuguese
mid-18th century
silver and gold with diamonds and
topazes
7.5 x 7 (2¹⁵⁄₁₆ x 2¾)

*Museu Nacional de Arte Antiga,
Lisbon, inv. 415 Joa*

Brussels 1991:3, cat. 125; Copenhagen 1992, cat. 125

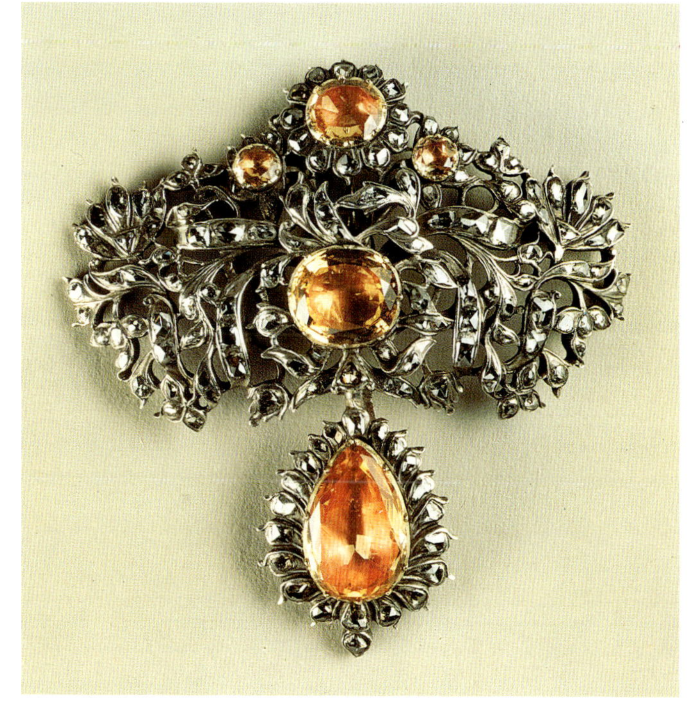

The elements of this magnificent composition include ribbons, foliage, tulips,
carnations, and marigolds. While the
overall structure appears to be symmetrical, the interior arrangement is asymmetrical, lending a great dynamism to
the design. The drop is a superb pear-
shaped topaz, framed in stylized foliage
set with diamonds. The contrast between the darker gleam of the diamonds
in silver and the brighter topazes in gold
throws the gems into relief.

47
Breast Ornament
Portuguese
2nd half 18th century
gilded silver with topazes
12 x 13.6 (4¾ x 5⅜)

*Museu Nacional de Arte Antiga,
Lisbon, inv. 63 Joa*

Brussels 1991:3, cat. 151; Copenhagen 1992, cat. 151

This unusual brooch has a spectacular
decorative effect. It is composed in a tri-
angle and decorated with stylized flowers
and foliage. The gilded silver is set with
fine topazes backed with varying shades
of foil from yellow to gold and pink to
salmon, creating striking variations of
light and color.

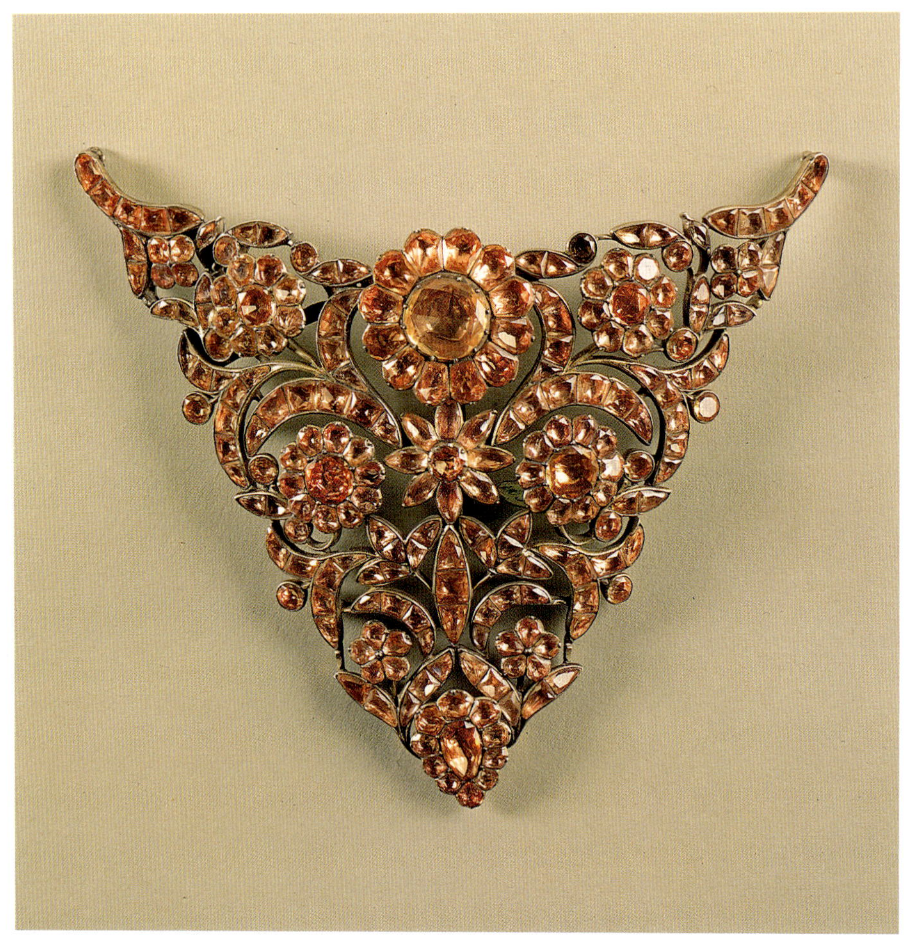

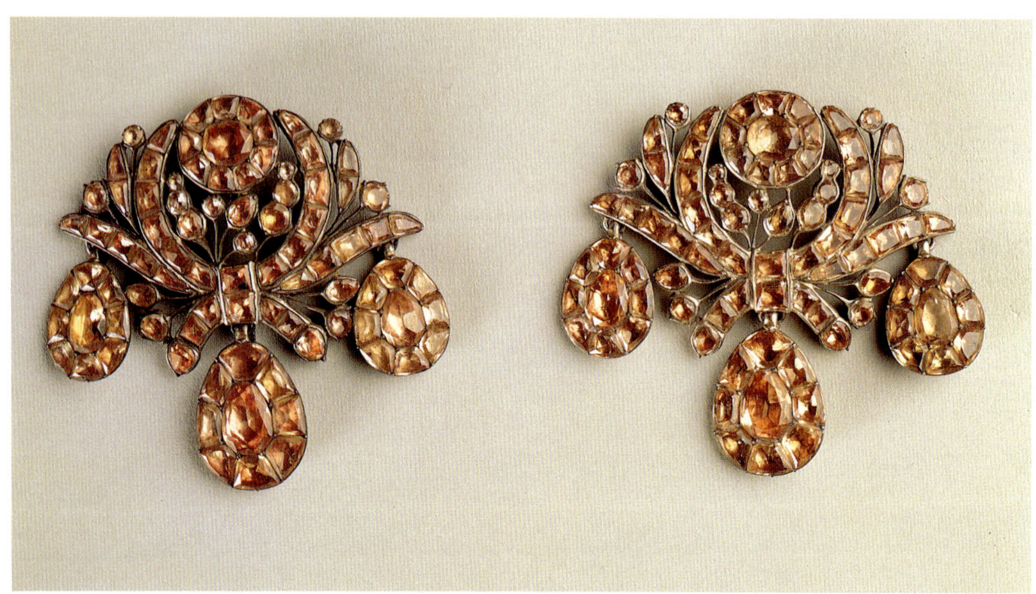

48

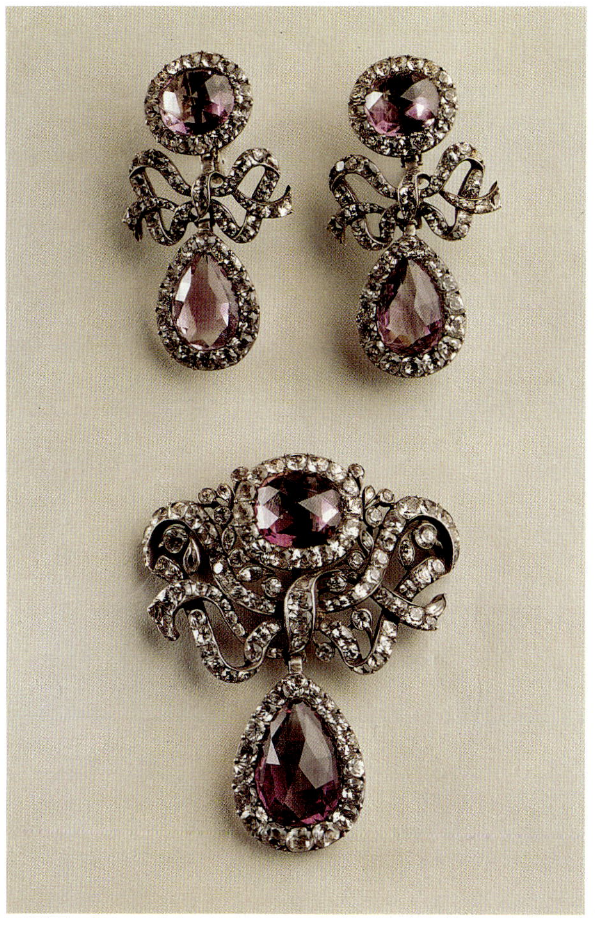

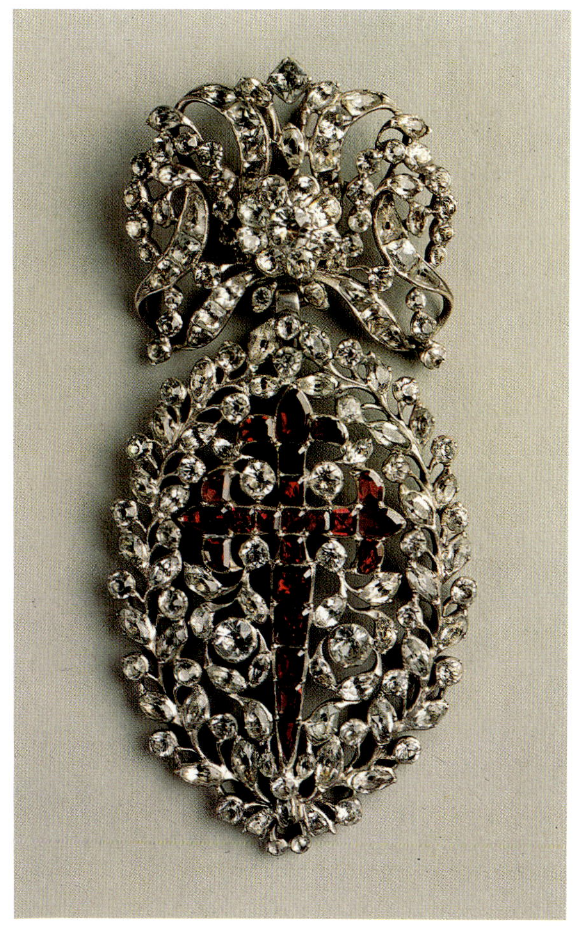

49, 50

51

48

Pair of Pendants
Portuguese
2nd half 18th century
silver with topazes
7.3 x 7.8 (2⁷⁄₈ x 3¹⁄₁₆) and 7.8 x 7 (3¹⁄₁₆ x 2³⁄₄)

Museu Nacional de Arte Antiga,
Lisbon, invs. 168 and 435 Joa

Brussels 1991:3, cats. 153–154

These two pieces of virtually identical
design, incorporating stylized leaves,
flowers, and bows with three drops in a
girandole (radiating) arrangement, illustrate the popularity and variety of such
pieces of jewelry, a fairly large number of
which have survived to the present day.

49, 50

Pendant and Pair of Earrings
Portuguese, mid-18th century
silver with quartz and amethysts
pendant 6.8 x 5.8 (2¹¹⁄₁₆ x 2⁵⁄₁₆);
earrings 5.6 x 5.3 (2³⁄₁₆ x 2¹⁄₁₆)

Museu Nacional de Arte Antiga,
Lisbon, invs. 873, 874 Joa

Brussels 1991:3, cats. 223–224

This *parure* is composed of three gems of
exceptional quality. The rococo composition of bows and ribbons is of a precise
elegance, suggesting a degree of movement that is not excessive. The combination and cut of the stones—the rose-cut
colorless quartz (known as *minas novas*)
and the large *brioleta*-cut amethysts—
and the perfection of the mounting
closed on the back for the quartz, open
to enhance the transparency of the colored stones, demonstrate the consummate skill of Portuguese jewelers during
this century.

51

Insignia of the Order of São Tiago
Portuguese
2nd half 18th century
silver with quartz and garnets
9.2 x 4.4 (3⁵⁄₈ x 1³⁄₄)

Museu Nacional de Arte Antiga,
Lisbon, inv. 879 Joa

Oporto 1989, cat. 5; Palmela Castle 1990, 261;
Brussels 1991:3, cat. 228

This piece is composed of a bow-shaped
loop with hanging ribbons entwined
with floral motifs. From it hangs an oval
composition in which a profusion of foliage set with quartz surrounds the cross of
the order of São Tiago in garnets.

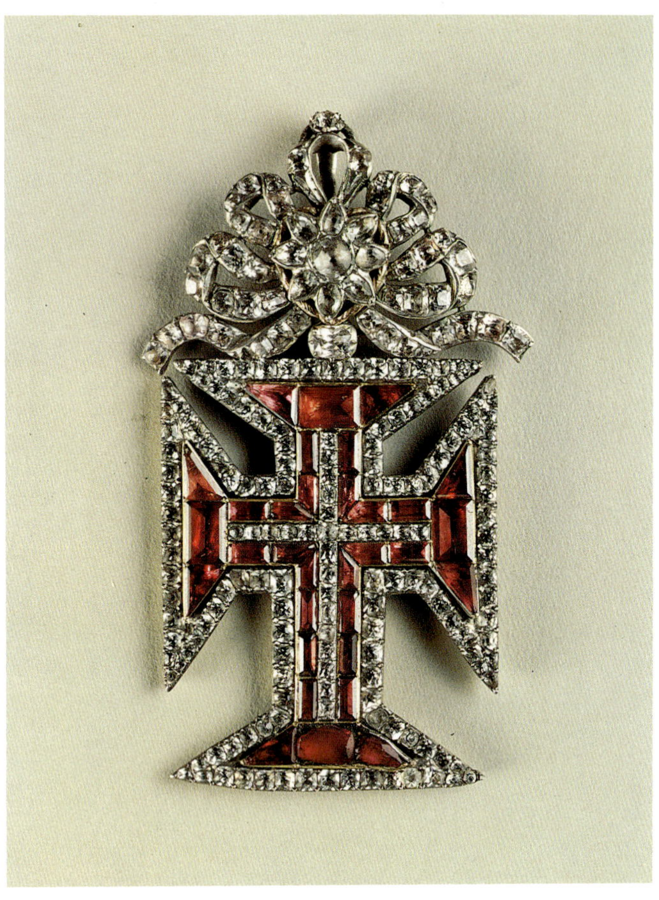 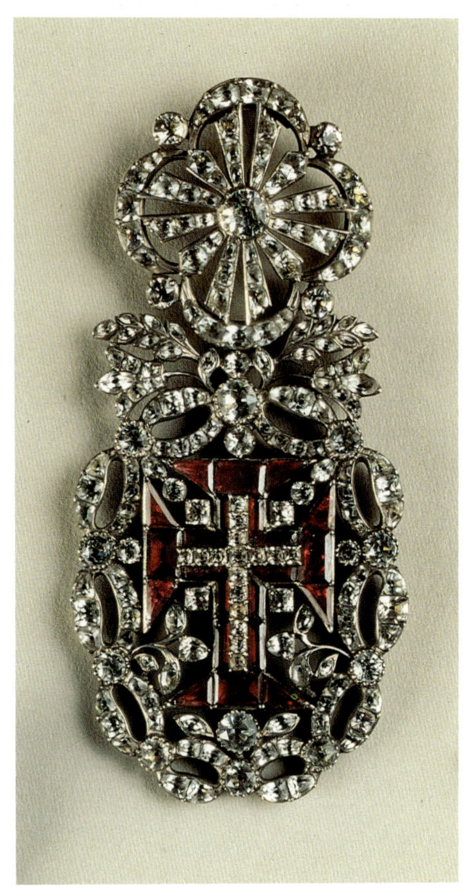

52
Insignia of the Order of Christ
Portuguese
2nd half 18th century
silver and gold with quartz, garnets, and
pink topaz
8.1 x 4.9 (3³/₁₆ x 1¹⁵/₁₆)

*Museu Nacional de Arte Antiga,
Lisbon, inv. 719 Joa*

Brussels 1991:3, cat. 229

The Cross of Christ in garnets, bordered
by a frieze of colorless quartz and topaz,
hangs from an exceptionally fine double
bow that is also set in colorless quartz.

53
Insignia of the Order of Christ
Portuguese
2nd half 18th century
silver with quartz and garnets
9.25 x 4.6 (3⁵/₈ x 1¹³/₁₆)

*Museu Nacional de Arte Antiga,
Lisbon, inv. 770 Joa*

Brussels 1991:3, cat. 230

This insignia of the Cross of Christ in
garnets is encircled in an oval garland
surmounted by plant motifs, hanging
from a floral motif of geometric design
in colorless quartz.

54
Necklace with Pendant
Portuguese
1st quarter 18th century
silver with chrysolites
necklace 25.2 (9$^{15}/_{16}$); pendant 13.3 x 6.8
(5$^{1}/_{4}$ x 2$^{11}/_{16}$)

*Museu Nacional de Arte Antiga, Lisbon,
inv. 391 Joa*

Lisbon 1974, 186; Brussels 1991:3, cat. 237

This large necklace is mounted in silver
and entirely set with chrysolites. It is
composed of a series of jointed floral elements and a large central pendant in the
shape of a double bow from which hangs
a bird. This piece is of outstanding design and finish in the European style of
the period.

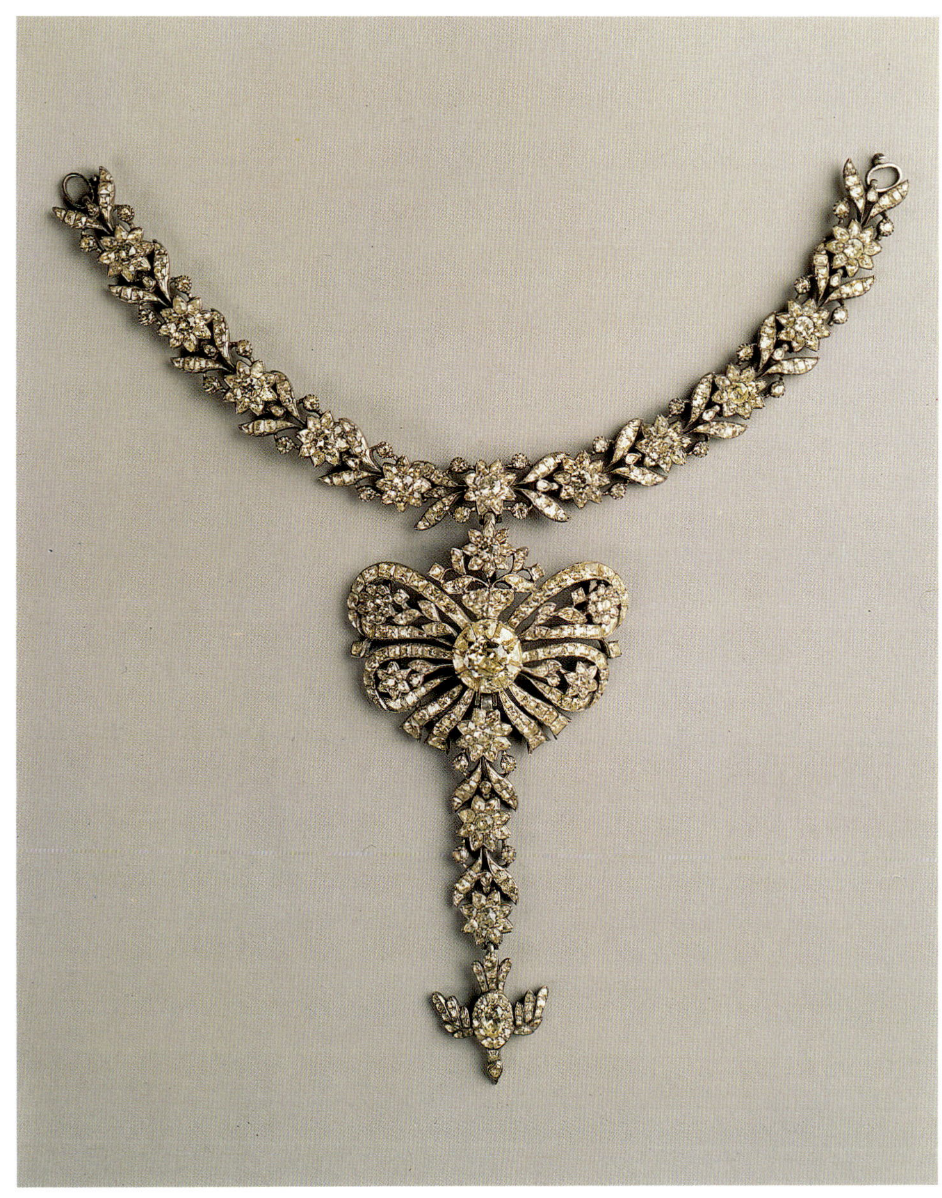

55
Pendant
Portuguese
3rd quarter 18th century
silver with chrysolites
9.1 x 10.8 (3⁹⁄₁₆ x 4¹⁄₄)

*Museu Nacional de Arte Antiga, Lisbon,
inv. 615 Joa*

Lisbon 1994, cat. 184; Brussels 1991:3, cat. 239

From this impressive ornament, in the
form of a branch with stylized leaves,
hangs an arrangement of three large
girandole drops. The whole is master-
fully executed in chrysolites of exceptional quality.

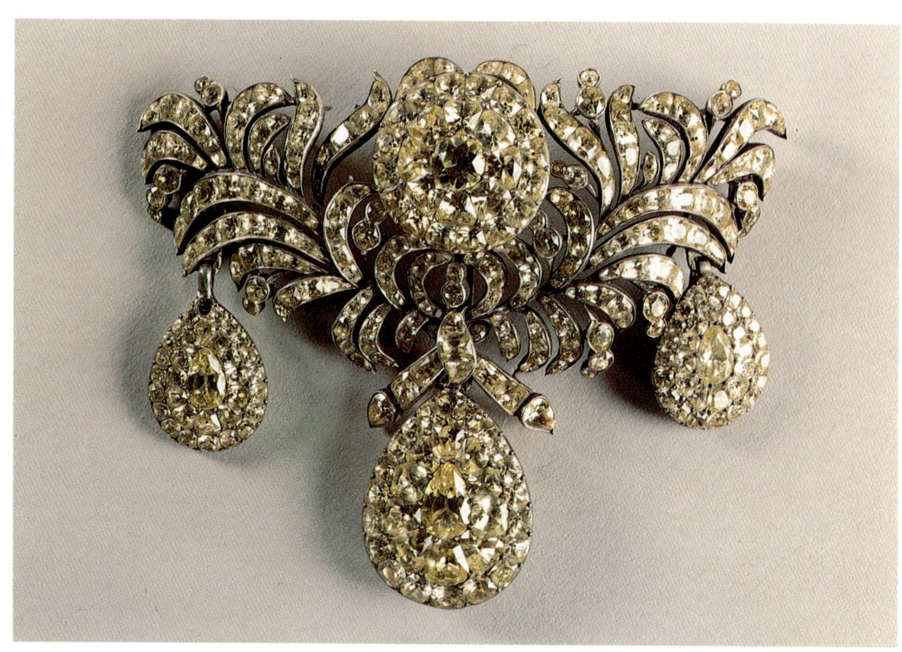

56
Pair of Earrings
Portuguese
3rd quarter 18th century
silver with chrysolites
5.3 x 2.8 (2¹⁄₁₆ x 1¹⁄₈)

*Museu Nacional de Arte Antiga, Lisbon,
inv. 690 Joa*

Brussels 1991:3, cat. 240

The earrings are composed of three elements: a rosette loop, bow, and drop
matching cat. 55. These stones, which
appear to cluster together independently
of their metal support, clearly demonstrate the high quality of pieces produced
in Portugal during the period.

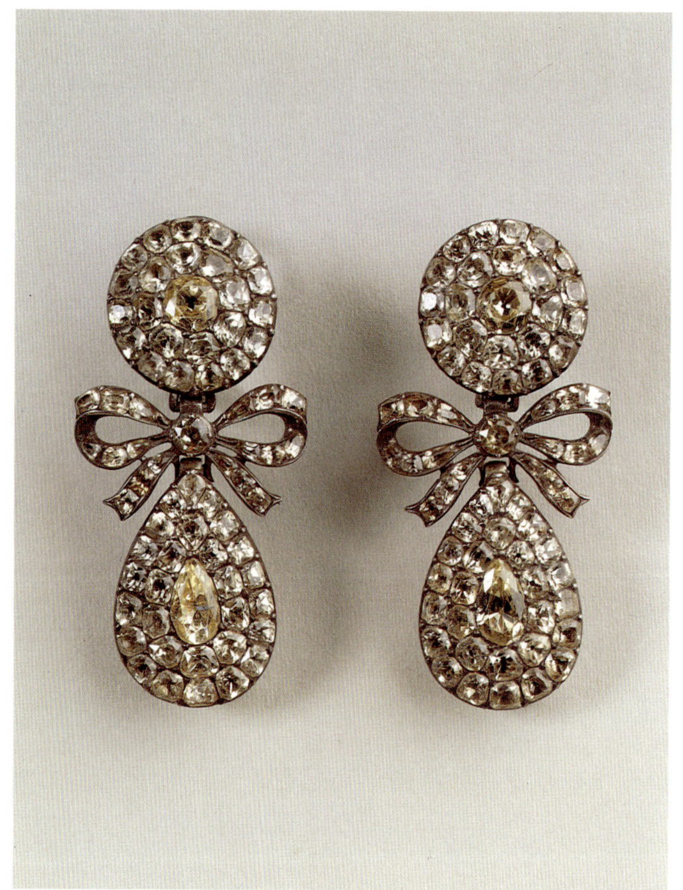

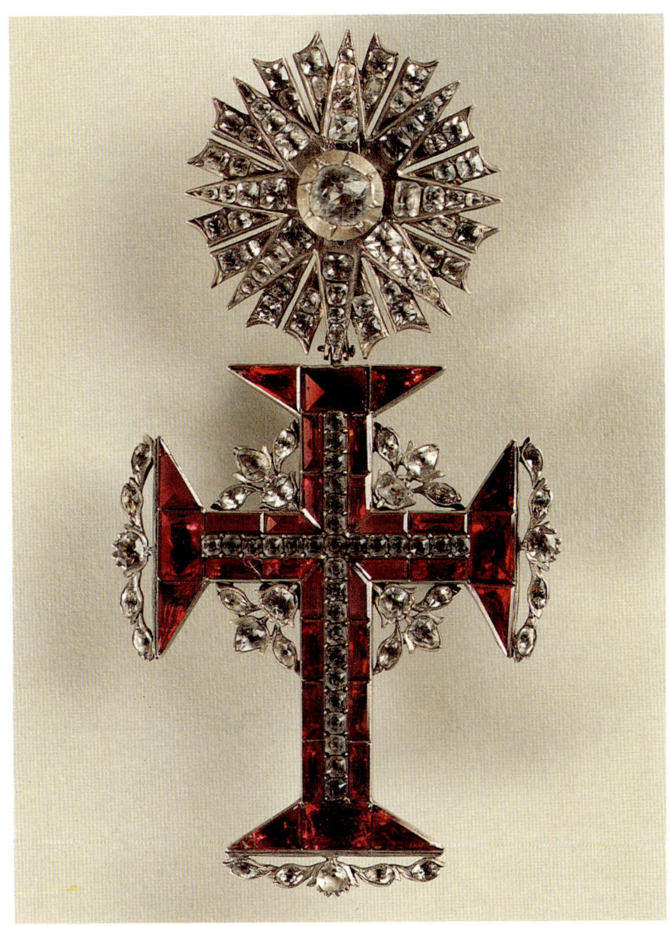

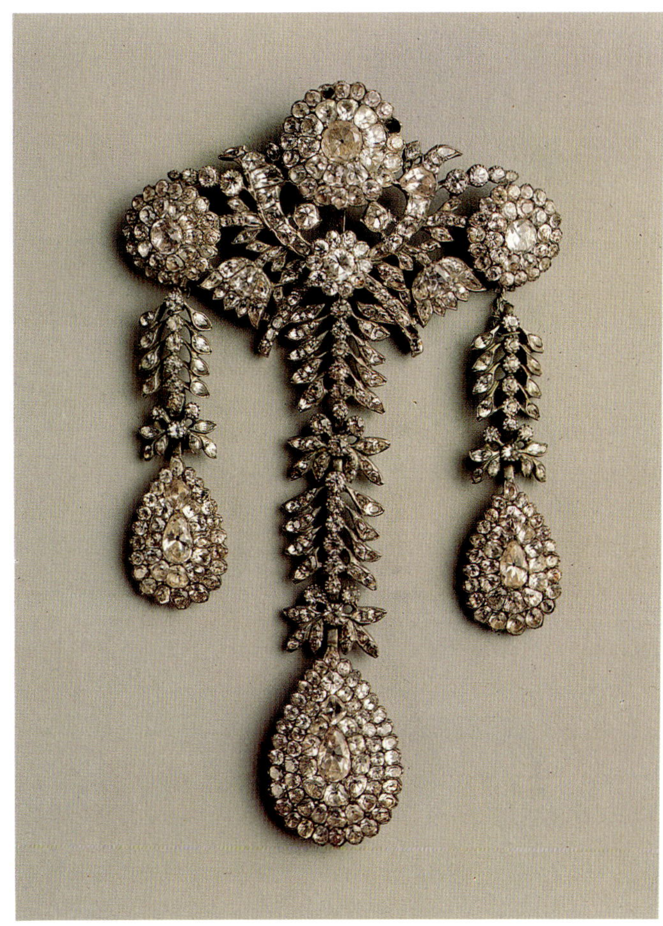

57
Insignia of the Order of Christ
Portuguese
mid-18th century
silver with quartz and garnets
11.4 (4½)

*Museu Nacional de Arte Antiga, Lisbon,
inv. 775 Joa*

Brussels 1991, v.10

58
Breast Ornament
Portuguese
2nd half 18th century
silver with quartz and pink topaz
12.7 x 7.5 (5 x 2¹⁵⁄₁₆)

*Museu Nacional de Arte Antiga, Lisbon,
inv. 361 Joa*

Brussels 1991:3, cat. 267

The Cross of Christ in garnets is set off
by a second inner cross in quartz. The
tips of the arms and center of the cross
are decorated with pierced floral motifs.
The cross hangs from a star-shaped pin
also in quartz.

This magnificent brooch is in the shape
of a stylized bow surrounded by floral and
plant decoration, with emphasis on a pair
of striking tulips. Three long drops ending in girandoles complete this creation of
original design and novel craftsmanship.

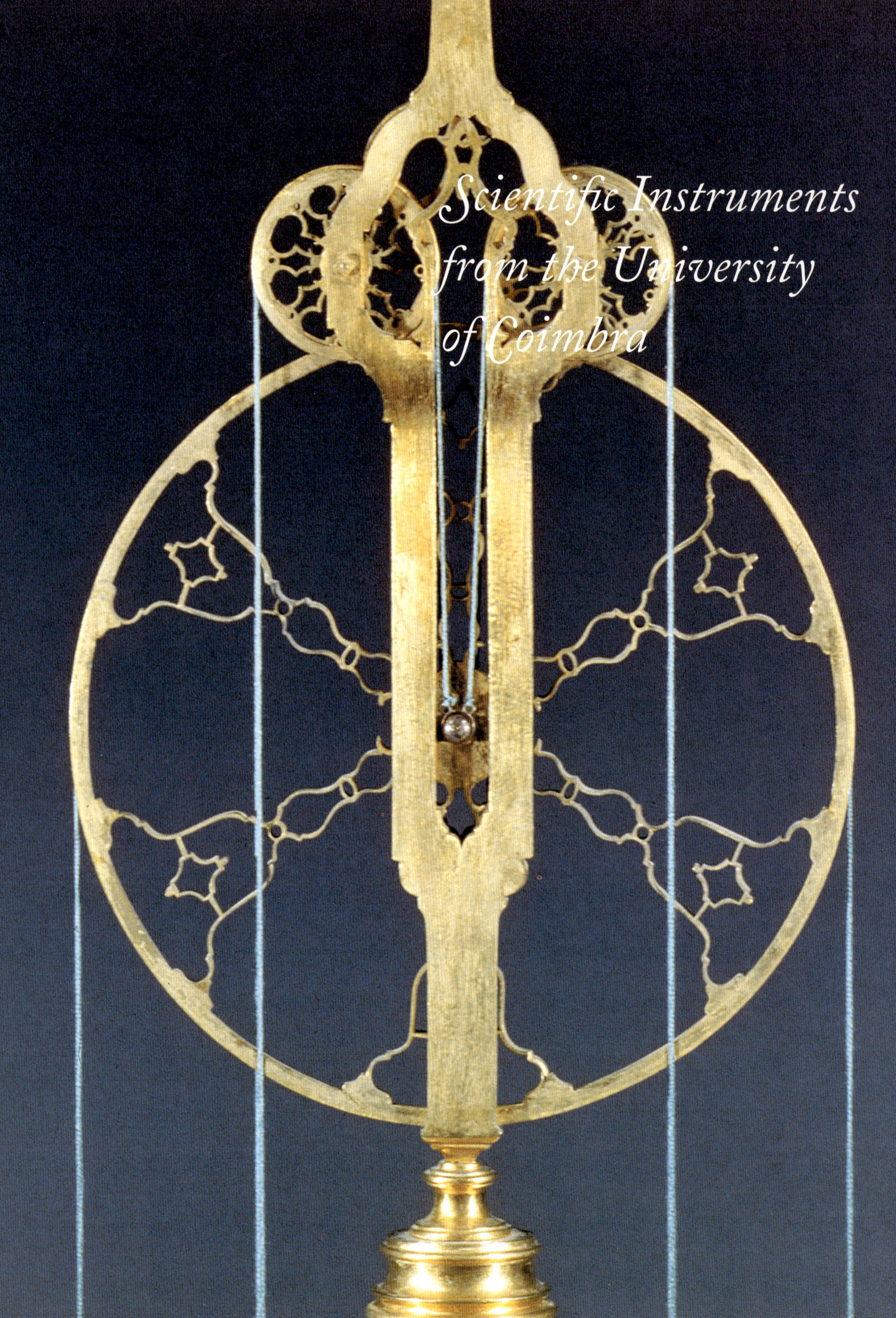
Scientific Instruments
from the University
of Coimbra

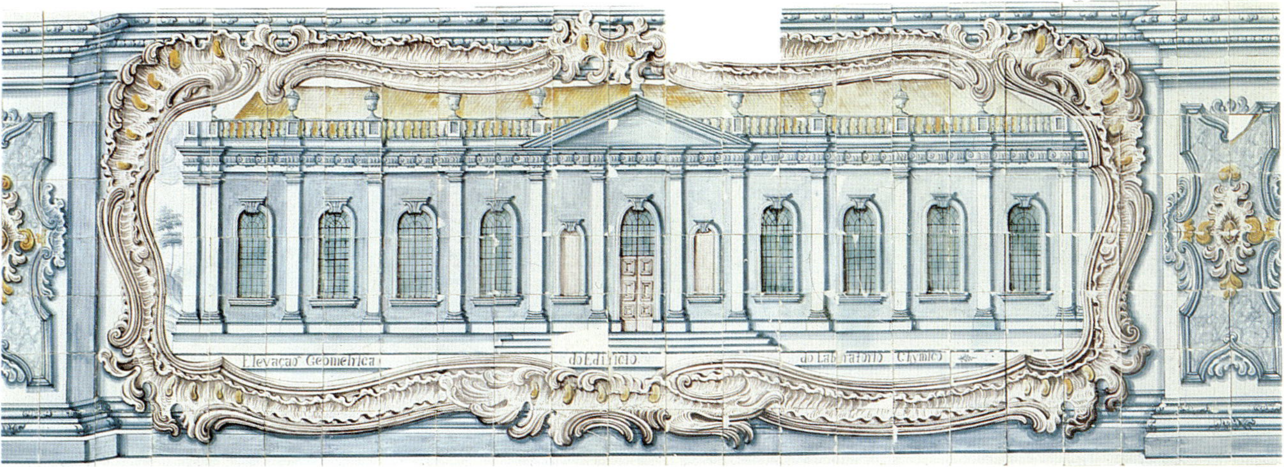

The Cabinet of Experimental Physics at Coimbra was created in 1772 as part of the marquês de Pombal's reform of the university. Its collection of pedagogical instruments was soon enriched by the addition of those belonging to the college of nobles in Lisbon. An inventory of 1788 lists 580 instruments or "machines," as they were then called, in the Coimbra collection. The works exhibited here indicate the astonishingly sophisticated design and fine craftsmanship that was often lavished on these early pieces.

59

REAL FÁBRICA DO RATO (?)
Portuguese
Tile Panels Depicting the Chemistry Laboratory of the University of Coimbra
c. 1773–1777
painted tiles
104 x 296 (40^{15}/$_{16}$ x 116^{9}/$_{16}$)

Museu Nacional Machado de Castro, Coimbra, inv. secção C-1682, from the Old Archbishop's Palace

Rómulo de Carvalho 1978; Soares 1983; Meco 1989; Brussels 1991, III.45

Tiles of the Pombaline period may be divided into three types, the first portraying historical scenes, the second developing decorative compositions, and the third containing simple repetitive patterns. One may conclude that, although mass production of tiles had been introduced to keep pace with the reconstruction of Lisbon after the earthquake, a market remained for decorative tiles to create luxurious and ostentatious interiors. In practice—as revealed in the numerous palaces and noble houses of the period that retain their interior tiles, some with Chinese motifs and borders of highly decorative effect—the compositions do not encompass the full range of grandiloquent baroque images known from the first part of the century. On the other hand, they do not adhere to the economic and creative restrictions imposed by the waist-high tile surrounds of repetitive geometric patterns. Thus they represented a compromise solution, although some of these later tile compositions attained an enviable degree of vivacity and subtlety.

The panel on display reflects this trend; it was designed to celebrate the reform of Coimbra university initiated in 1772 under the auspices of the marquês de Pombal. It incorporates a massive border of rococo scalloping with, at the bottom, an unadorned band of tile edging. Within the scalloped frame is the chemistry laboratory designed by Guilherme Elsden (active 1763–1777).

Elsden, as head of construction projects and responsible for remodeling the original university buildings, was able to establish a modern school of architecture, which trained countless professionals. The Palladian influence apparent in the facade of the chemistry laboratory reveals a marked English influence, while the large windows are generally typical of Portuguese architecture.

JOAQUIM JOSÉ DOS REIS, woodwork
PEDRO SCHIAPPA PIETRA, brass
Device to Demonstrate Equilibrium
Portuguese
18th century
carved wood, brass
77 x 21.5 (30⁵⁄₁₆ x 8⁷⁄₁₆)

*Museu de Física da Universidade de
Coimbra, Gabinete de Física Experimental,
inv. 56 (Colégio dos Nobres, inv. 168)*

Index Instrumentorum 1788, 11-1-179;
Charleroi 1991, no. 32

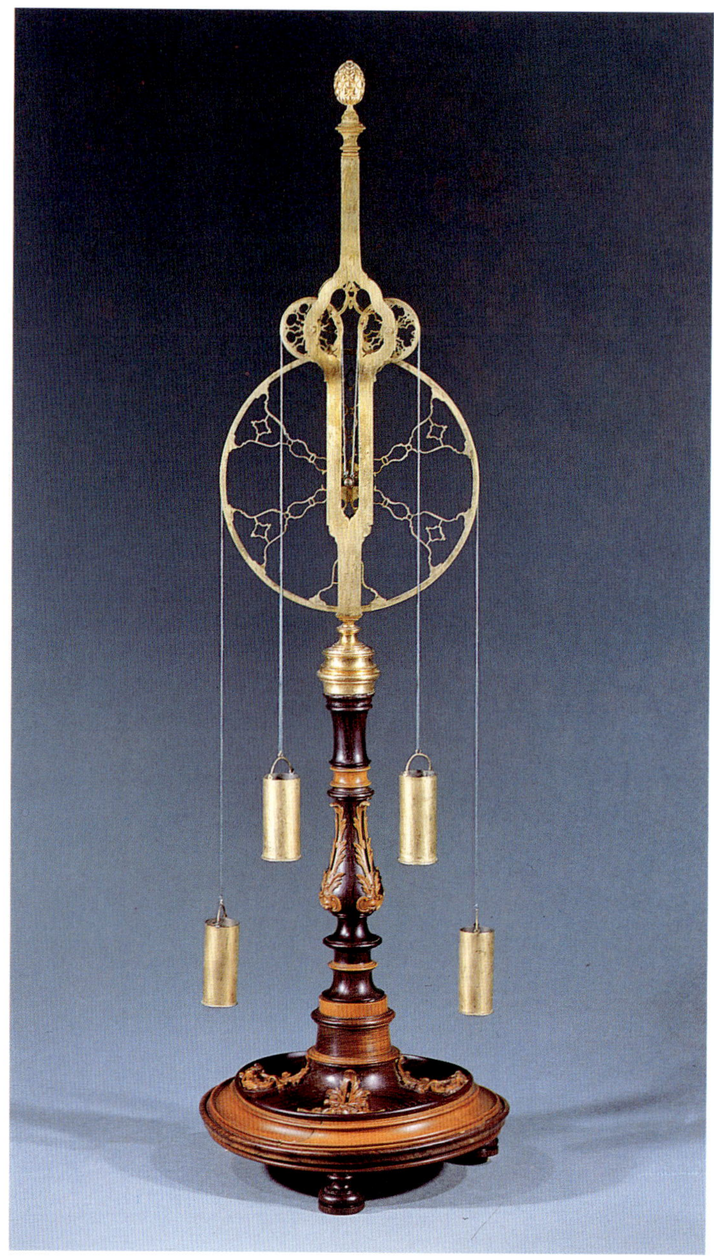

This device consists of a pulley with an
axis that can be moved both horizontally
and vertically. Two metal rings are attached to the axis of the pulley, with a
cotton thread tied to each ring. These
threads pass through the groove of a
fixed pulley. There are four of these fixed
pulleys altogether, all of the same size
and smaller than the first one situated
toward the top of the device. The
threads attached to the rings on the axis
of the mobile pulley are attached in
pairs, with one end of each element of
the pair linked to each end of the axis of
the mobile pulley. A hollow brass cylinder like a small bucket hangs from each
of these threads. A thread passes
through the groove of the mobile pulley,
with another two identical buckets hanging from each end. Small weights were
placed inside the four buckets, distributed to maintain the equilibrium of the
system, so that the mobile pulley remained suspended by the force created
by the four threads attached to its axis.

This device, mounted as described,
serves to demonstrate that if the direction of one of the forces applied to the
mobile pulley is altered while the inten-
sity of each force is maintained, the equilibrium is destroyed. This can be done by
merely bending one of the threads passing through the neck of the mobile pulley, pulling it in a vertical direction. The
sum of the forces applied to the pulley
would then cease to be zero despite the
fact that the strength of the forces on it
continues to be the same. This would

cause its axis to begin to rise, producing
a rectilinear movement. As the pulley
rises, it rotates.

The device is lavishly decorated. The
pulleys are all of brass, the largest of
them bearing six decorative motifs
arranged in a radial formation and serving to link the axis with the ring on the
pulley. The four fixed pulleys are decorated with four motifs similar to those of
the pulley of the mobile axis. The fixed
pulleys are mounted on a vertical column
divided into two parallel branches. Each
of these branches has a central groove,

scored longitudinally from end to end.
The axis of the mobile pulley moves
along these grooves.

The device stands on a round base,
from which the column rises that is surmounted by the support for the pulleys.
The base and the column are of wood,
with fine decorative motifs in relief.

61

JOAQUIM JOSÉ DOS REIS, woodwork
PEDRO SCHIAPPA PIETRA, metal work

Tightrope Walker Illustrating Balance
Portuguese
18th century
carved, painted, and gilded wood with
brass and copper
62.1 x 22.5 x 20 (24$\frac{7}{16}$ x 8$\frac{7}{8}$ x 7$\frac{7}{8}$)

*Museu de Física da Universidade de
Coimbra, Gabinete de Física Experimental,
inv. 32 (Colégio dos Nobres, inv. 87)*

Index Instrumentorum 1788, B-IV-95;
Charleroi 1991, no. 34

The tightrope walker is holding a bent
pole with a brass sphere at either end.
The device was used in physics lessons to
demonstrate the importance of the position of the center of gravity of an object
in relation to its base of support when in
balance. The tightrope walker is supported on a small round brass disk by
means of an iron spike emerging from
beneath its left foot. This disk surmounts a richly carved wooden column.

The stability of the figure is achieved
when the vertical passing through its
center of gravity intersects the point of
support of the spike on the disk. This
point of support is above the center of
gravity of the whole system consisting of
the tightrope walker, pole, and spheres.

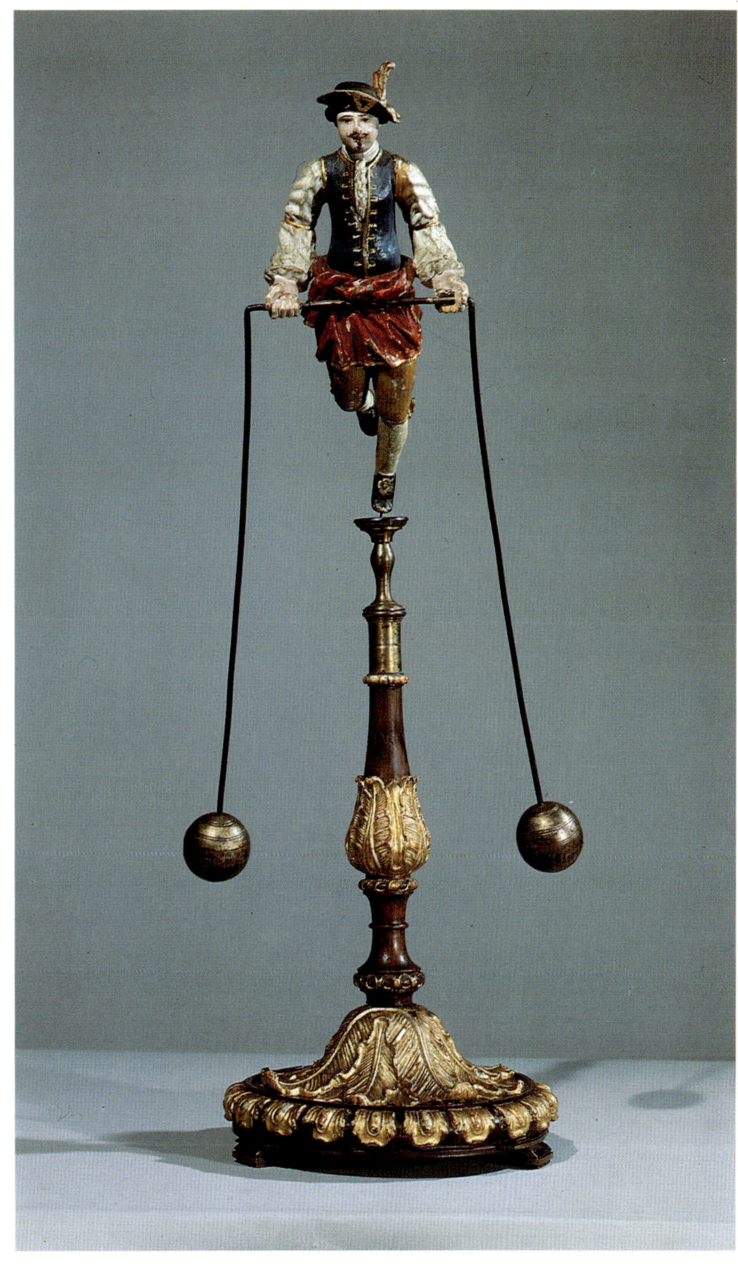

62

JOAQUIM JOSÉ DOS REIS, woodwork
PEDRO SCHIAPPA PIETRA, brass
Desaguliers Tribometer and Table
Portuguese
18th century
carved and inlaid wood, brass
35.4 x 36.1 x 22.5 (13^{15}/$_{16}$ x 14^{3}/$_{16}$ x 8^{7}/$_{8}$)

*Museu de Física da Universidade de
Coimbra, Gabinete de Física Experimental,
inv. 102 (Colégio dos Nobres, inv. 154)*

Nollet 1764, vol. 3; Index Instrumentorum 1788, G-
III-164; Charleroi 1991, no. 36

This splendid example of a Desaguliers
tribometer was designed to study the effect of friction on the axis of a rotating
wheel. The device is mounted on an inlaid eight-legged table with octagonal
lid. The brass device consists of four
wheels mounted on the curved prongs of
two vertical supports attached to the
table at opposite vertices of an octagon

inlaid in the tabletop. Two wheels are
mounted on each support, with the projections from the circular planes inter-
secting without the wheels touching. A
horizontal axis effecting a rotating movement is supported at the upper points of
intersection of the wheels. This axis
moves in conjunction with another
somewhat larger wheel that is slightly removed from the central point of its axis.
A helical spring acts on the axis of the
wheel. When compressed, the spring
causes the wheel to rotate. The friction
thus exerted on the axis is fairly limited.
As a result of the action of the spring, an
alternation occurs in the direction of the
wheel's rotating movement, which results from the successive compression
and release of the spring, as in a watch
mechanism. The whole device revolves
around a position corresponding to the
configuration of balance of the spring,
the movement being damped by the friction. In a demonstration to a physics

class, this effect would be compared with
what would occur if the pointed ends of
the axis were to be inserted in the two
small holes in the vertical supports,
thereby supporting the four wheels with
no contact between the axis and the
wheels. When the axis is supported in
this way, friction becomes much greater,
and it would be clearly apparent that the
number of swings of the wheel produced
by the same initial movement is considerably less than in the previous case.

This experiment shows the compara-
tive advantages of one particular form of
support. The system of supporting the
axis on the points of intersection of the
two wheels placed at the ends of their
axes was widely used in the Atwood machine, whereby friction between the
moving pieces was made minimal.

This machine also permits study of
the damping effect of a lever applied to
the axis of rotation of a wheel during os-
cillatory motion. For this purpose, a
jointed plate is placed at the end, func-
tioning as the fulcrum. This plate is kept
in the horizontal, supported on the device's axis of rotation, with a weight
hanging from the end. This device considerably increases the friction on the
axis, with a resulting increase of the
damping effect on the system's swinging
movement.

The table on which the device stands
is made of lignum vitae, blackwood, and
boxwood and is based on a design appearing in *Leçons de Physique Expérimentale* by Abbé Nollet. It may be concluded
from documents in the Arquivo Nacional in the Torre de Tombo in Lisbon
on the subject of the Colégio dos Nobres
(book 154, 94, 95) that this and similar
tables were executed in Lisbon by
Joaquim José dos Reis who worked in
the library of that Pombaline institution.

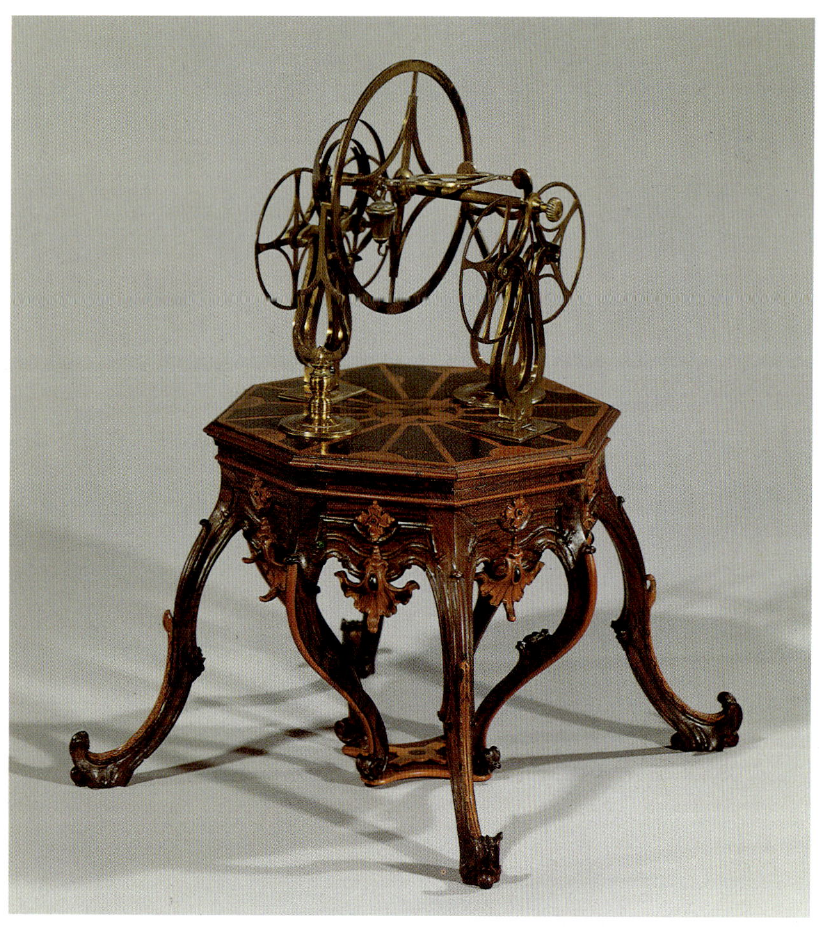

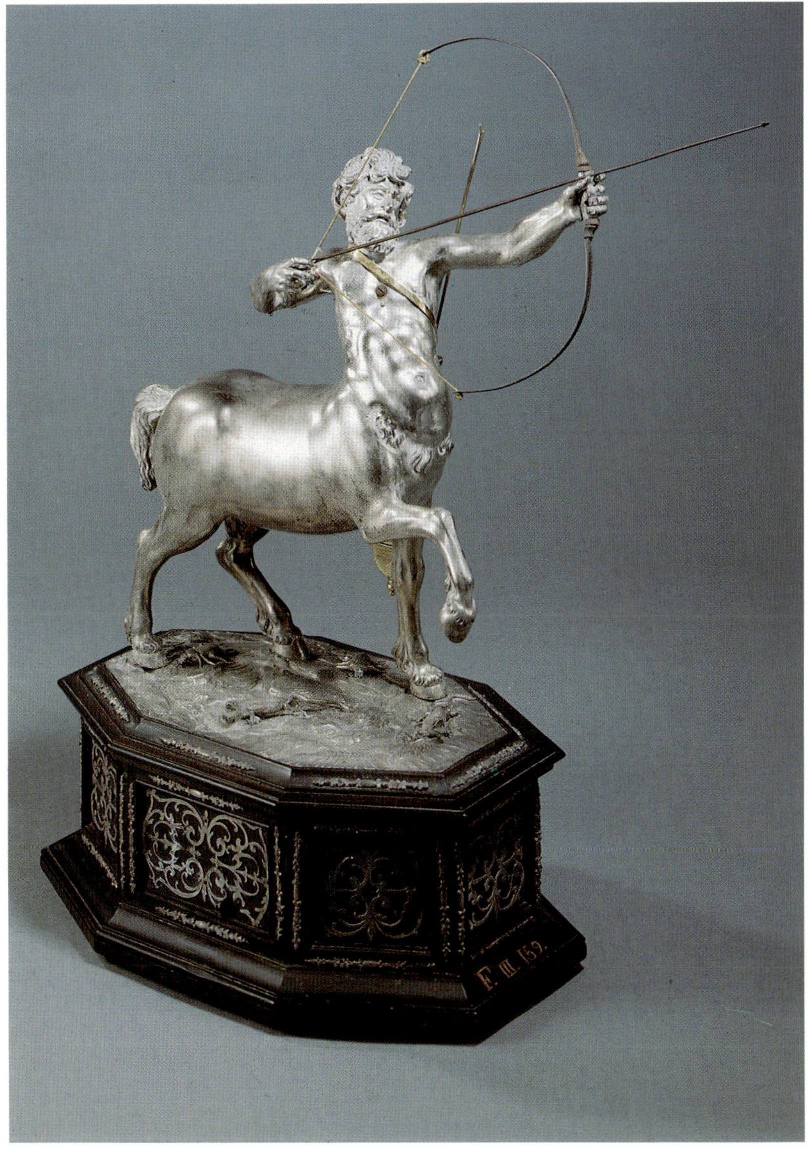

ment of wheels allows the centaur to move and even to change direction.

The automaton does not appear in the list of instruments belonging to the Colégio dos Nobres. It was purchased by António Dalla Bella to add to the collection of mechanisms for studying simple and compound machines. This is an example of a compound machine.

Silvio Bedini of the Smithsonian Institution has suggested that the device is of south German manufacture, dating from the early seventeenth century; he notes the resemblance of the form of the base and its decoration to those of a number of south German automata (see Maurice and Mayr 1980, 278 and elsewhere).

63
Automaton
silver, brass, steel, ebony
39.3 x 16 x 25 (15 1/2 x 6 5/16 x 9 13/16)

Museu de Física da Universidade de Coimbra, Gabinete de Física Experimental, inv. 97

Carvalho 1978; Charleroi 1991, no. 37

This apparatus consists of a silver centaur equipped with a mechanism for firing arrows. The centaur is mounted on an eight-sided ebony box with silver appliqués on each side and on the top. The box is decorated with lizards and insects in relief. The centaur holds a flexible iron bow and stands with his left arm extended and his right arm drawn back to release an arrow. He is further equipped with a baldric and a quiver containing two arrows.

The box contains a mechanism that can be wound by a key, causing the centaur's arm to move by means of a transmission system that passes through his left front leg. The mechanism inside the wooden box was designed to have three wheels, which would stand on the floor. One of the wheels is located beneath the left leg of the centaur, and it is apparent that a second wheel is missing from the other side, beneath the right leg. There is a third wheel, smaller than the other two, at the back of the box. This wheel is attached to a vertical axis. This arrange-

64
**Mirror for Observing
Anamorphic Images**
18th century
wood, polished steel, and watercolor
on card
33.7, 86 (13¼, 33⅞)

*Museu de Física da Universidade de
Coimbra, Gabinete de Física Experimental,
invs. 699, 699/10 (Colégio dos Nobres inv.
375)*

Index Instrumentorum 1788, Y-IV-382; Charleroi
1991, no. 81

The mirror, mounted on a cylinder of
dark wood, permits the observation of
anamorphically distorted illustrations
painted on cards. The mirror is semi-
cylindrical in shape, and is made of a
thick sheet of polished steel, which is
attached to the wooden cylinder.

An undistorted view of the anamorphic painting can be observed when the
cylinder is placed in the correct position
on the illustration.

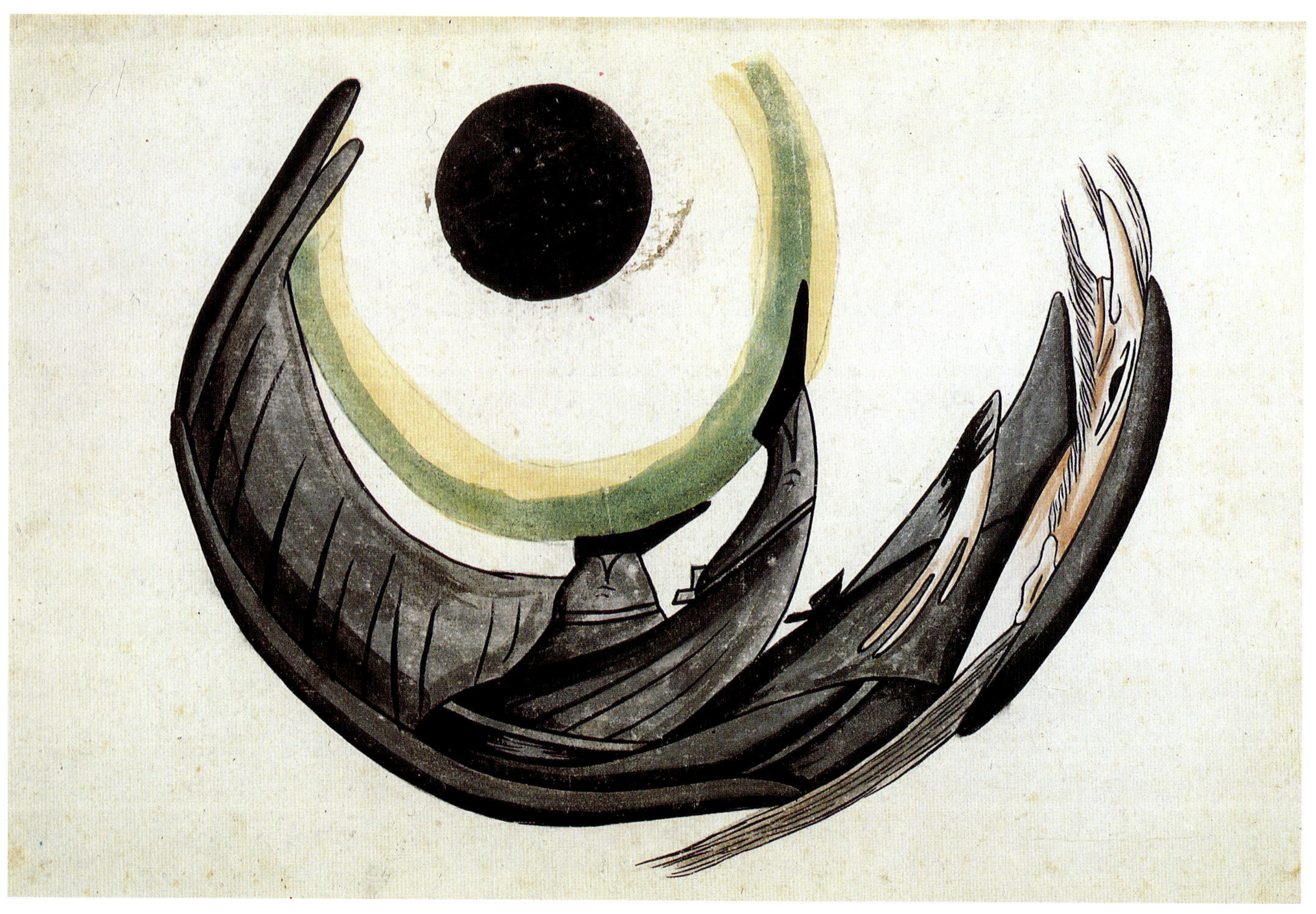

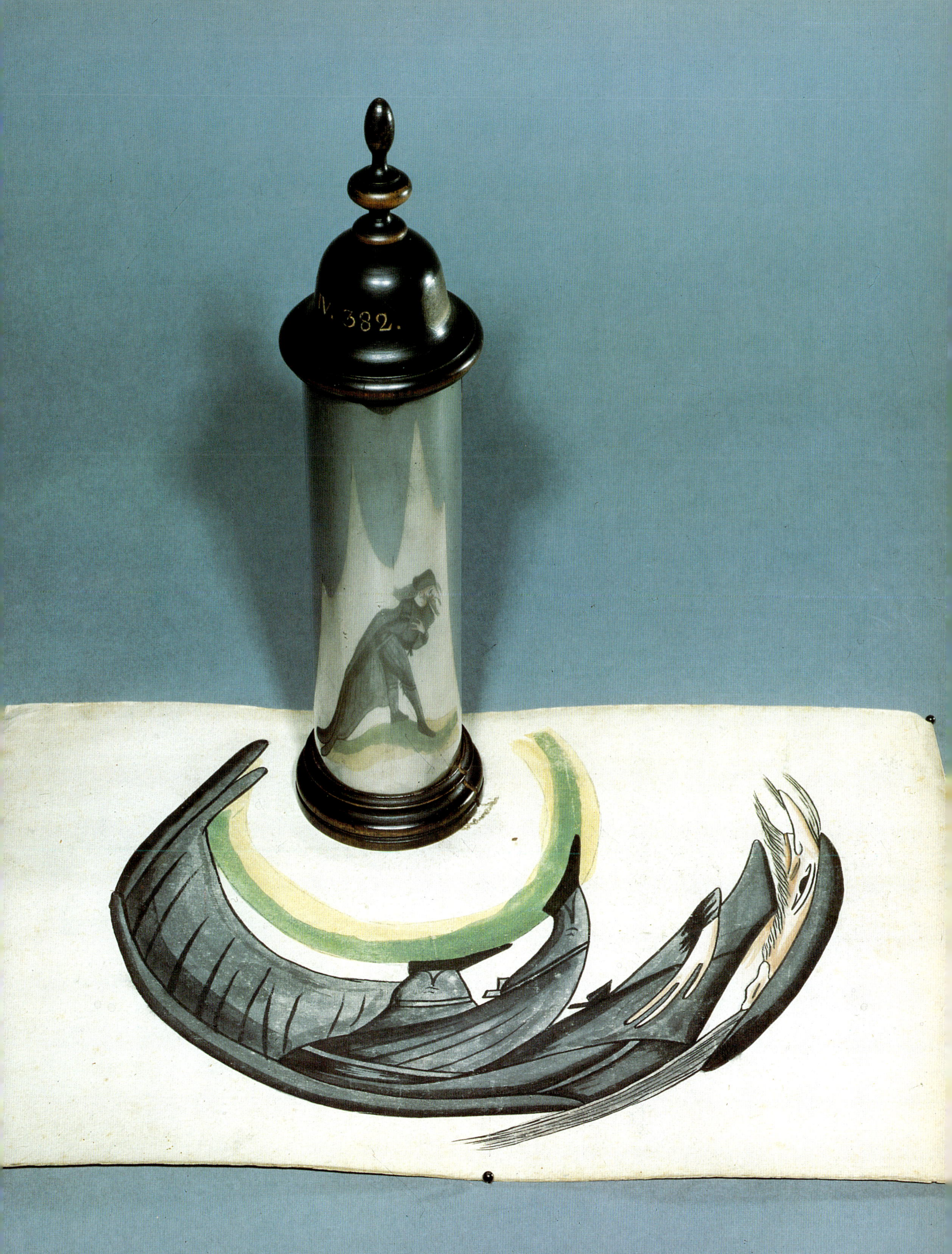

N.º 382.

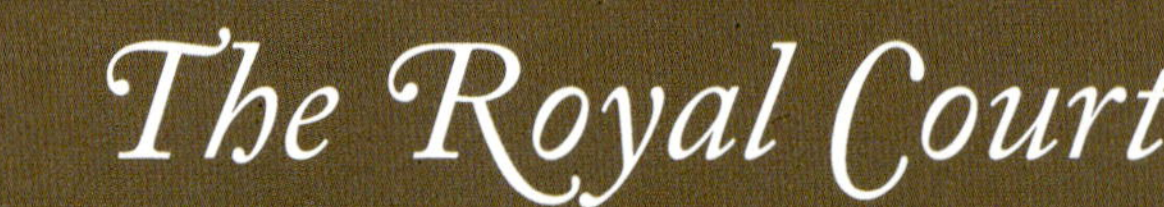
The Royal Court

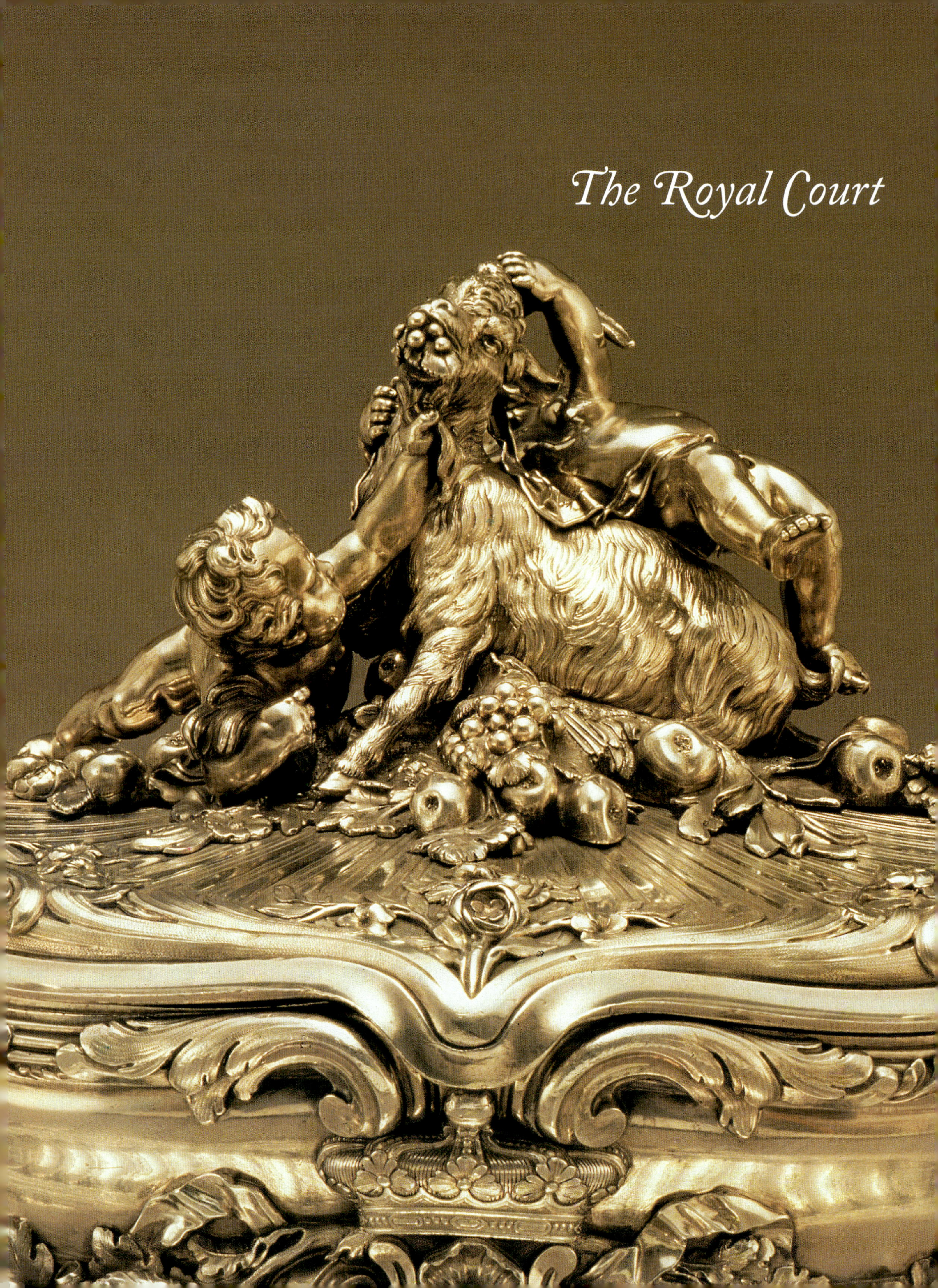

Many works from the royal collections dis-appeared in the Lisbon earthquake of 1755, when the royal palace was destroyed. Active patronage during the reigns of Dom José I and Rainha Dona Maria I, however, have left us splendid examples of royal taste, including luxurious silver tableware from France, particularly the great service ordered from François-Thomas Germain, specially commissioned Chinese export porcelain, and jewelry from the smartest Parisian goldsmiths.

65

FRANÇOIS-THOMAS GERMAIN
French, 1748–1791
Tureen on Stand
1756–1758
cast, beaten, engraved, and chased silver
tureen 29.1 x 50.5 x 25.7 (11⁷⁄₁₆ x 19⁷⁄₈ x 10¹⁄₈);
stand 10 x 58.4 x 43 (3¹⁵⁄₁₆ x 23 x 16¹⁵⁄₁₆)
Insc: FAIT.PAR.R.F.T.GERMAIN.SCULPR.
ORFRE.DU:ROY:AUX.GALLERIES.DU.
LOUVRE.A.PARIS 1757 on underside of

stand; DU N°.2 on inner dish and underside of tray, DU N°2-68M-2°-2 base of tureen, DU N°3 base of liner. Portuguese royal coat of arms on inside lid, base of liner, underside of stand and chased on side of tureen
Marks: Maître (FT/G, fleece) François-Thomas Germain under lid, tureen, liner, and underside of stand; Charge (crowned A) Paris 1750–1756, local id.; Maison Commune (crowned Q) Paris 1756–1757, on lid, tureen, and stand, (crowned R) Paris 1757–1758, underside of liner; Export (cow) Paris 1756–1775, outer rim of lid, underside of liner, base of tureen

Museu Nacional de Arte Antiga, Lisbon, inv. 1833, from the table service of Dom José I

Bapst 1887; Bapst 1892; Costa 1928; Foz 1926; Mabille 1984; Lisbon 1990–1991; Brussels 1991, IV.15

This oval tureen, with removable liner in plain silver, stands on four scroll feet decorated with acanthus leaves, palm fronds, and oak sprigs. On each side of

the tureen appear the embossed Portuguese royal coat of arms, encircled with the chain of the Order of Christ amid sprays of laurel and oak leaves and ribbons. The handles at the sides are in the shape of fauns holding draperies. A reed and leaf tie motif follows the undulating movement of the upper rim of the tureen. The top of the lid is grooved and fluted and decorated with bunches of flowers and fruits, crowned by a sculpted group of two children playing with a goat. The stand *(présentoir)* echoes the oval shape of the tureen and stands on six scroll feet. It is decorated with raised grooves radiating from the Portuguese royal coat of arms engraved at the center. The royal silver service includes four identical tureens forming two pairs that differ only in the sculptured groups adorning the lids. Germain repeated this grandiose type of tureen for the imperial Russian court of Elizabeth I, although the Russian tureens are gilded silver and of course have a different coat of arms.

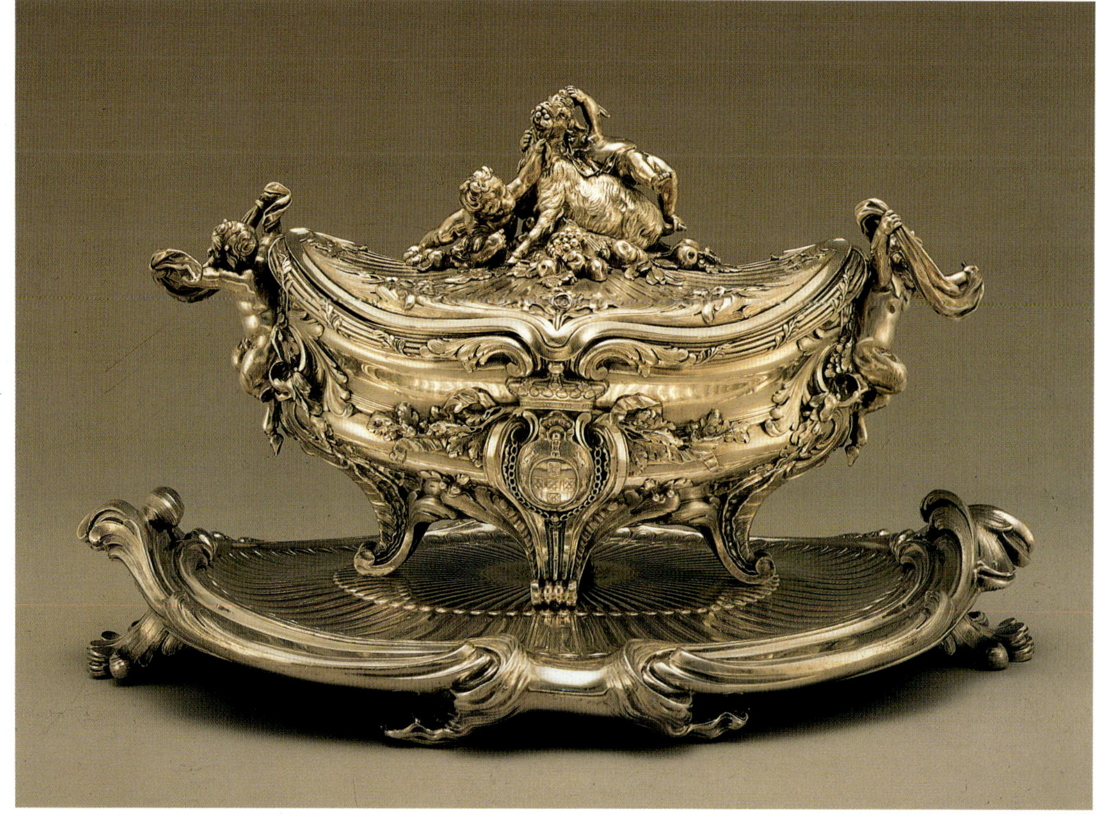

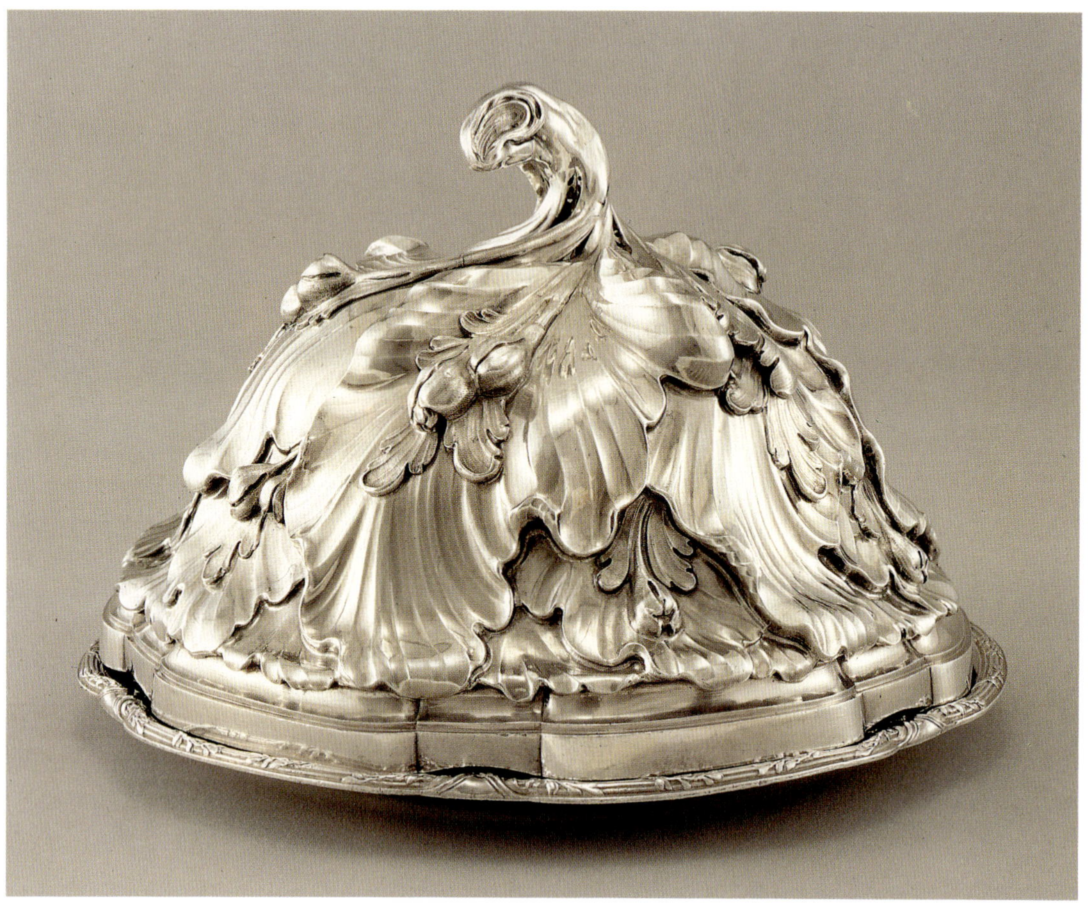

66

FRANÇOIS-THOMAS GERMAIN
French, 1748–1791
Large Round Covered Dish
1756–1758
cast, chased, and engraved silver
dish 42 (16⁹⁄₁₆)
lid 22.4 x 38.5 (8¹³⁄₁₆ x 15³⁄₁₆)
Insc: DU Nº 10, inside edge of lid; DU Nº
10-45ᵐ-3º-3ᵍ, underside of border of dish.
Portuguese royal coat of arms engraved
in center of dish and inside lid
Marks: Maître (FT/G, without fleece)
François-Thomas Germain, inner edge
of lid; (crowned R) Paris, 1757–1758,
inside lid; Export (cow) Paris 1756–1775,
outside edge of lid

*Museu Nacional de Arte Antiga, Lisbon,
inv. 1854, from the table service of Dom José I*

This round dish, with six indentations in
its rim, is edged with a reed and leaf tie
effect and finished with flowers and
scrolls; the rim is engraved with plant
and tapering leaf motifs. The royal coat
of arms of Portugal is engraved in the
center of the plate. The bell-shaped lid is
composed of enormous, overlapping
cabbage leaves with an undulating rim
echoing the shape of the dish. The handle of the lid, which is pierced around
the base to allow steam to escape, is in
the shape of a twisted stalk. This is one
of four large covered dishes that adorned
the sides of the royal banquet table.
The silver service also included twelve
medium covered dishes and four covered
square vegetable dishes or salad bowls
(see cat. 67) decorated to match the endpieces and the medium covered dishes
that were normally positioned at the
sides of the formal banquet table.

67

FRANÇOIS-THOMAS GERMAIN
French, 1748–1791
Square Covered Dish
cast, chased, and engraved silver
dish, 1759–1760
3 x 26.6 x 26.6 (1³/₁₆ x 10½ x 10½)
lid, 1757–1758
18.5 x 23 x 23 (7⁵/₁₆ x 9¹/₁₆ x 9¹/₁₆)
Insc.: (dish) DU Nº 14, inside lid and on
underside of rim of dish. Portuguese
royal coat of arms engraved in center of
dish and inside lid
Marks: Maître (FT/G, fleece) François-
Thomas Germain, underside of rim of
dish, (FT/G) inner rim of lid; charge
(crowned A) Paris 1756–1768 on underside
of edge; (grill) inner rim of lid; Maison
Commune (crowned Q) Paris 1756–1757,
underside of edge, (crowned R) Paris
1757–1758 inside lid; Export (cow) Paris
1756–1775, underside of edge of dish and
outer edge of lid

*Museu Nacional de Arte Antiga, Lisbon,
inv. 1858, from the table service of
Dom José I*

Lisbon 1992, no. 472

The square bell-shaped cover is decorated with overlapping cabbage leaves.
Its handle is composed of twisted stalks,
pierced around the base to allow steam
to escape. The deep square dish has indented corners creating a ridge and curving edges rimmed with a reed and leaf
tie effect.

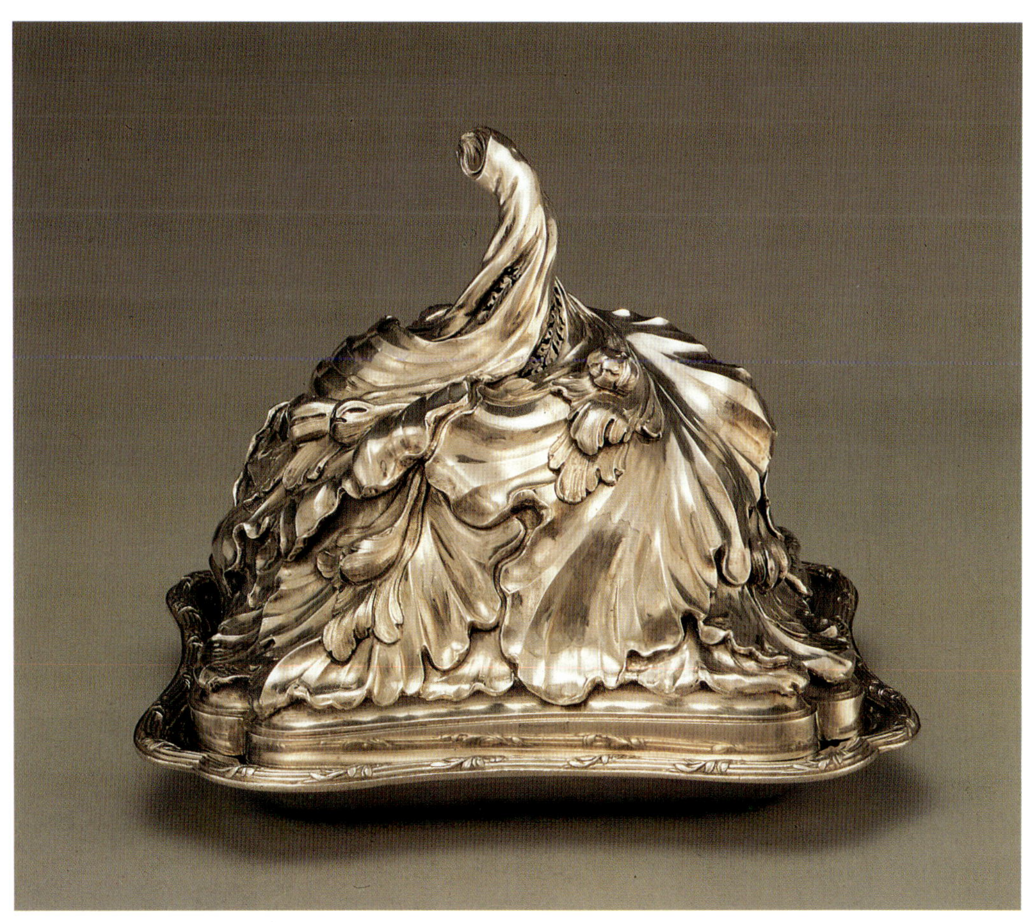

FRANÇOIS-THOMAS GERMAIN
French, 1748–1791
Kettle, Stand, and Spirit Lamp
1756–1762
cast and chased silver with ebony
kettle 30 x 29.2 x 22 (11¹³/₁₆ x 11¹/₂ x 8⁵/₈);
stand 16.2 x 36.2 x 22.8 (6³/₈ x 14¹/₄ x 9)
Insc.: FAIT.PAR.F.T.GERMAIN.SCULPR.
ORFRE.DU.ROY.AUX.GALLERIES.DU.
LOUVRE.A.PARIS.1762 on inner edge of
lid; Portuguese royal coat of arms on
base of kettle and spirit lamp
Marks: Maître (FT/G, fleece) François-
Thomas Germain, base of kettle,
triangular stand, inner side of foot under
handle; Charge (crowned A) Paris
1756–1762, stand, underside of spirit
lamp, and inside wick-holder; (grill)
Paris, 1756–1762 inner side of foot above
handle; Maison Commune (crowned Q)
Paris 1756–1757, underside of spirit lamp,
inside wick-holder; (crowned Y) Paris
1762–1763, stand, inner side of foot under
handle; Export (cow) Paris 1756–1775,
inner rim of kettle, outer edge of lid
base, trivet, underside of spirit lamp,
outer edge of wick-holder

*Museu Nacional de Arte Antiga, Lisbon,
inv. 1847 our, from the table service of
Dom José I*

Bapst 1887; Bapst 1889; Bapst 1892; Ilustração
Portuguesa 1906; Figueiredo 1926; Foz 1926;
Ilustração 1926; Nocq 1926–1931; Réau 1927; Costa
1928; Saraiva 1934; ANBA 1935; ANBA 1936; Sousa
1951; Guerra 1952; Brault and Bottineau 1959;
Dennis 1960; Lopes 1963; Beuque 1964; Bottineau
and Lefuel 1965; Guedes 1971; Hernmarck 1977;
Gruber 1982; Mabille 1984; D'Orey and Teague
1986; Mabille 1987; D'Orey 1990–1991; Brussels
1991, IV.27

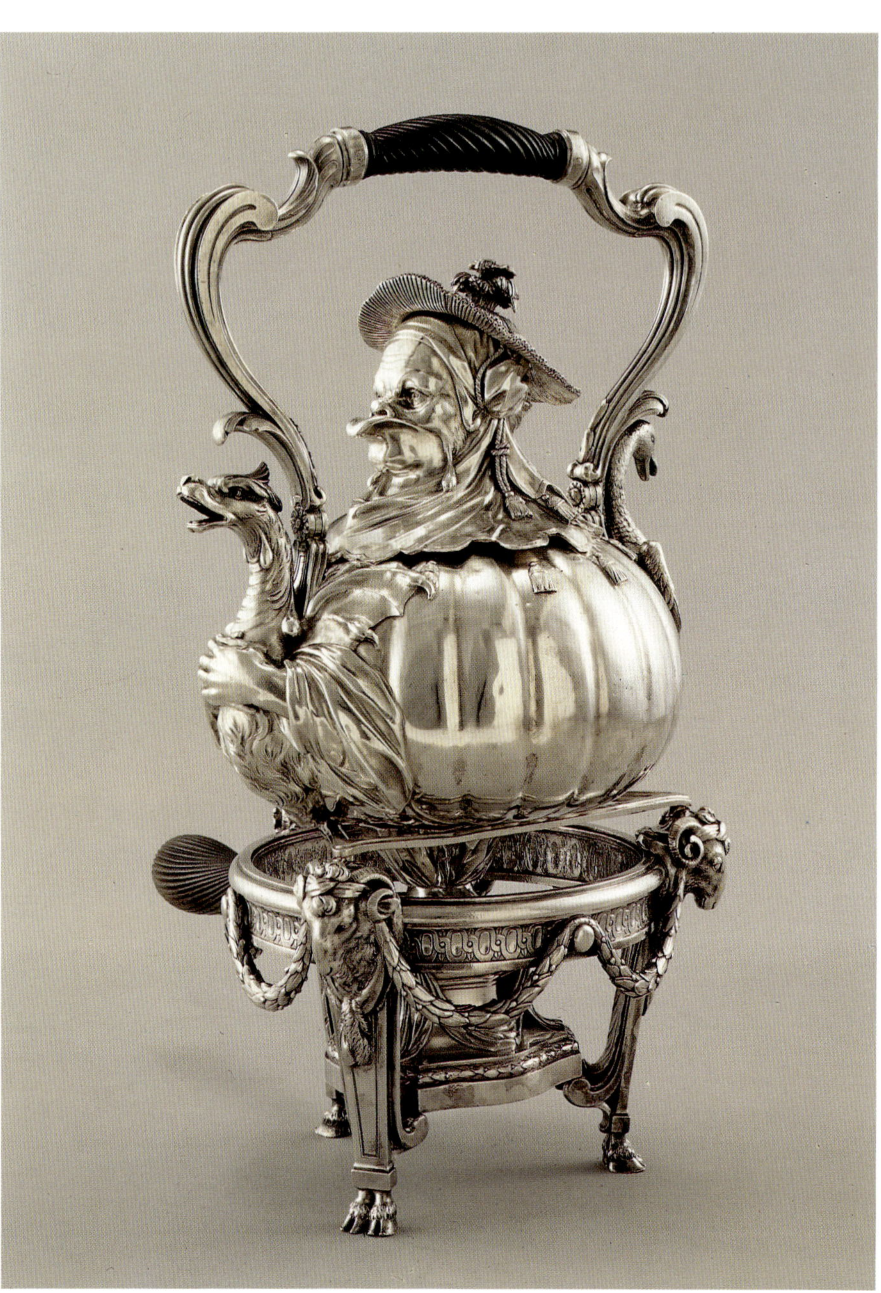

The kettle is pumpkin-shaped, with the
lid composed of the head of a fanciful
Chinese man wearing a broad-brimmed
hat. His hands fold over the breast of a
dragon, the mouth of which forms the
spout of the kettle. The vessel is adorned
on the opposite side by a fine swan with
spread wings. The handle, in the form of
scrolls linked by a carved ebony handhold, is hinged. As opposed to the
rococo style of the kettle, the stand is
neoclassical, with pilasters, surmounted
by rams' heads around which laurel

festoons are looped, tapering down to
two cloven hoofs. The figure's feet serve
as a lid for the spirit lamp.

The Museu de Arte Antiga in Lisbon
owns a pair of these exceptional pieces.
Both belonged to a luncheon set ordered
by Dom José I from François-Thomas
Germain together with the royal silver
service. The set originally included two
kettles, two trivets and spirit lamps, two
teapots (in fact, three are known to exist),
four sugar bowls (three have survived),
four milk jugs (see cat. 70), and four

salvers. Unlike other items in the royal
silver service, they bear no serial number,
but all the objects in the set bear identical
inscriptions and the date 1762.

FRANÇOIS-THOMAS GERMAIN
French, 1748–1791

Coffeepot
1759–1761
cast, repoussé, and chased silver with
ebony
28 x 29 x 17 (11 x 11⁷⁄₈ x 6¹¹⁄₁₆)
Insc.: FAIT.PAR.F.T.GERMAIN.SCULPR.
ORFRE.DU.ROY.AUX.GALLERIES.DU.
LOUVRE.A.PARIS.1760; DU Nº 66,
engraved on base; Portuguese royal coat
of arms engraved on base
Marks: Maître (FT/G, fleece) François-
Thomas Germain, on base; (FT/G, without fleece), on inner rim of lid; Charge
(crowned A) Paris 1756–1762, local id.;
Maison Commune (crowned v) Paris
1761, on base and inside lid; Export (cow)
Paris 1756–1775, on upper edge of lid

*Museu Nacional de Arte Antiga, Lisbon,
inv. 1865, from the table service of Dom José I*

Bapst 1887; Bapst 1892; Costa 1928; Foz 1926;
Mabille 1984; D'Orey 1990–1991; Brussels 1991,
IV.29

This pear-shaped coffeepot with a
projecting grooved handle in ebony
stands on three feet of scrolls and
acanthus leaves. Asymmetrical fluting
traces the curve of the body, lending the
piece an elegant sense of movement. The
lid is engraved with small decorative
motifs and crowned by a finial in the
form of sprigs of the coffee plant. The
lip and the joint of the handle are also
decorated with delicately embossed
leaves and coffee beans. The order for
the silver service mentioned six
coffeepots. Only four such royal pots, of
different sizes, have survived in Portugal,
three in the Museu de Arte Antiga and
one in the Palácio da Ajuda. Another
coffeepot from the Portuguese service,
with a replaced handle, can be seen in
the Metropolitan Museum of Art in
New York.

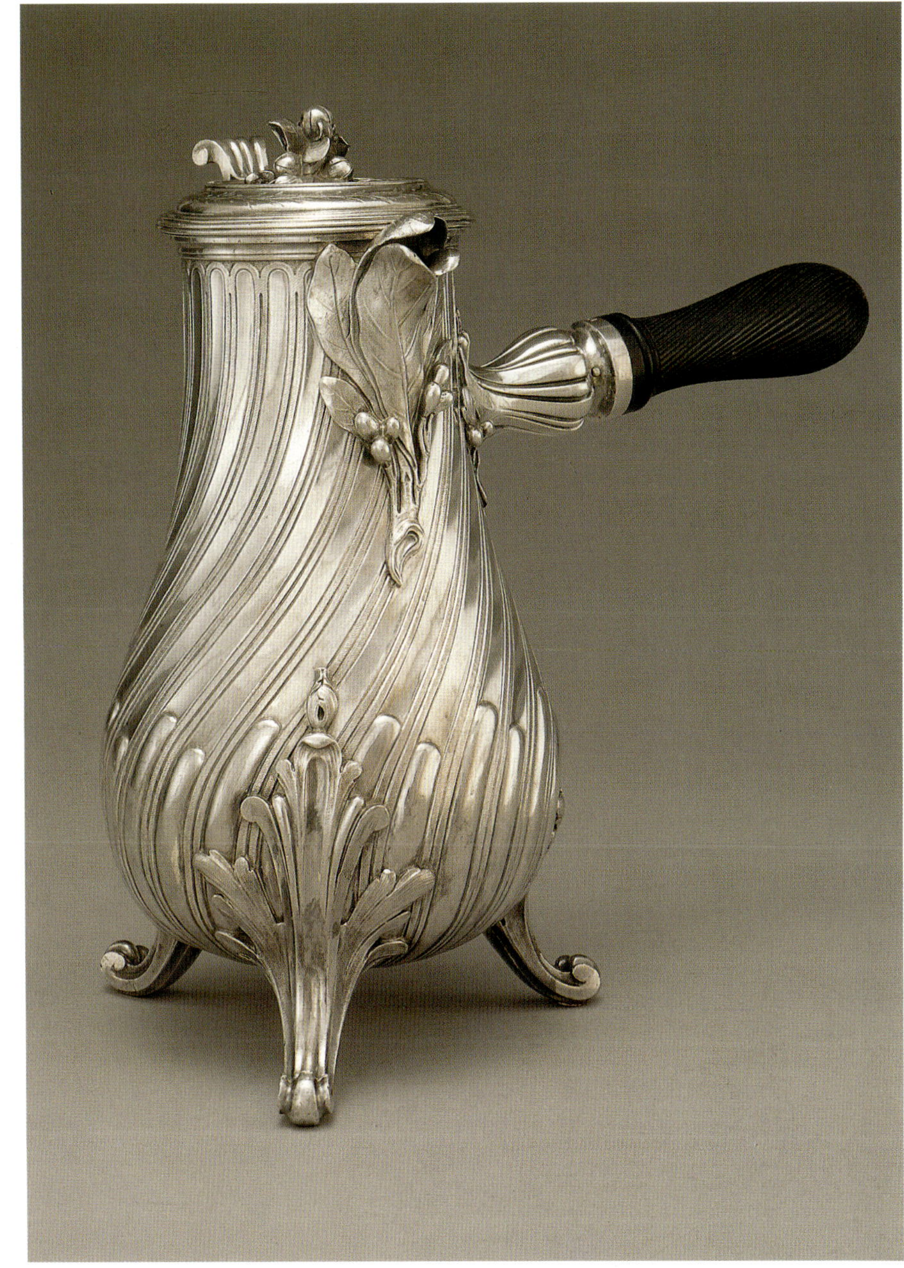

70
FRANÇOIS-THOMAS GERMAIN
French, 1748–1791
Milk Jug
1759–1760
cast and chased silver
21.6 x 17 x 11.2 (8½ x 6¹¹⁄₁₆ x 4⁷⁄₁₆)
Insc.: FAIT.PAR.F.T.GERMAIN.SCULPR.
ORFRE.DU.ROY.AUX.GALLERIES.DU.
LOUVRE.A.PARIS.1762, engraved on base;
Portuguese royal coat of arms
Marks: Maître (FT/G, fleece) François-
Thomas Germain, on base; Charge
(crowned A) Paris 1756–1762, local id.;
Maison Commune (crowned T) Paris
1759–1760, local id.; Export (cow) Paris
1756–1775, on outer edge of base

*Museu Nacional de Arte Antiga, Lisbon,
inv. 1867 our, from the table service of
Dom José I*

Brussels 1991, IV.31

This milk jug is shaped like a baluster
and decorated with embossed spiral
buds, looped draperies, and garlands
suspended between two exotically
plumed masks, the hair and beards of
which are decoratively knotted over the
swelling sides of the jug. The hinged lid
and spout are composed of overlapping
leaves; an elegant arrangement of stems,
leaves, and berries in high relief forms
the handle. This jug is part of a luncheon
set ordered from Germain (see cat. 68).

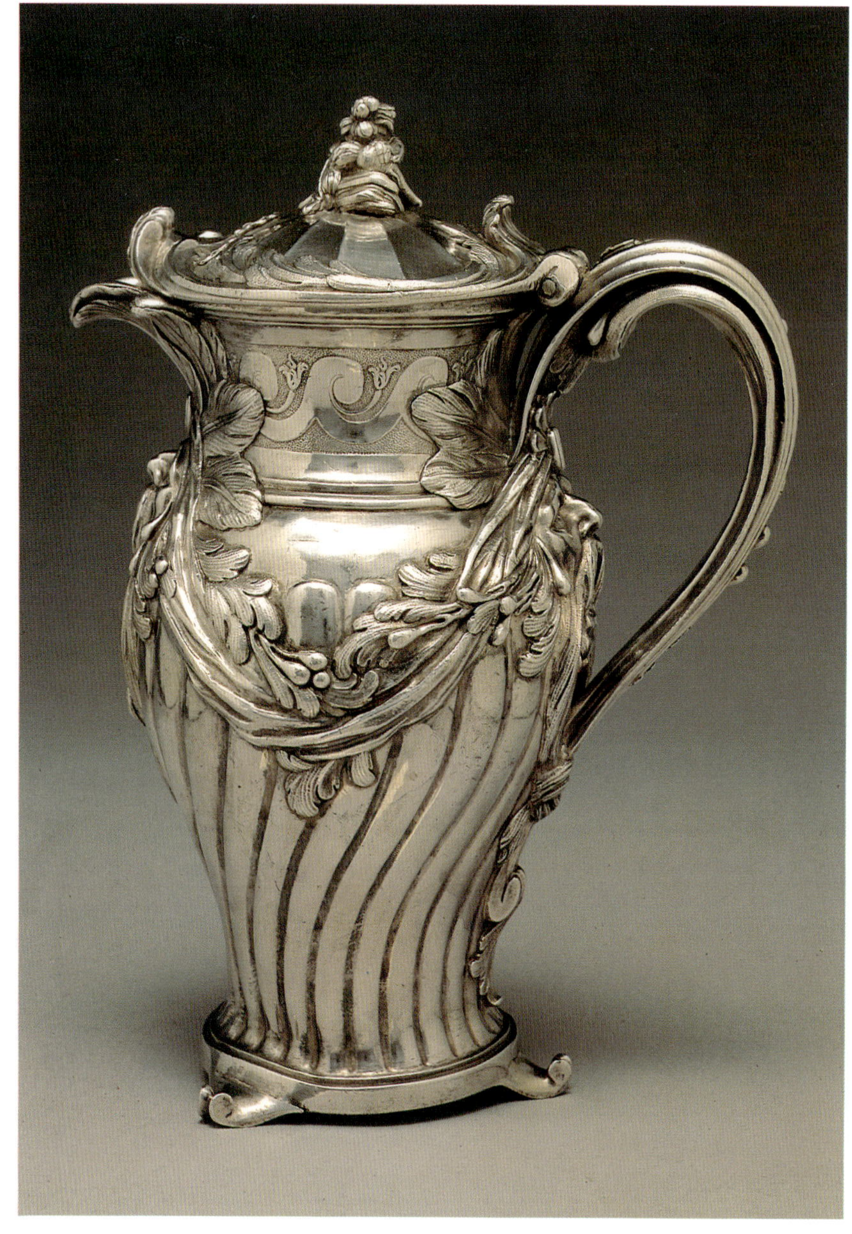

71

FRANÇOIS-THOMAS GERMAIN
French, 1748–1791

Two Salt Cellars
1756–1761
silver and gilded silver
19.2 x 11.4 x 9.7 (7⁹⁄₁₆ x 4¹⁄₂ x 3¹³⁄₁₆)
Insc.: FAIT.PAR.F.T.GERMAIN.SCULPR.
ORFRE.DU.ROY.AUX.GALLERIES.DU.
LOUVRE.A.PARIS.1760 on base of P.N.A.
5384; DU Nº 62 on base of each; Portuguese royal coat of arms engraved on
inside of bases and underside of inner
dishes
Marks: (Maître FT/G, fleece) François-
Thomas Germain, on bases and on inner
dishes; (bars) Paris 1756–1762, on bases;
Maison Commune (crowned R) Paris
1757–1758, on bases, (crowned V) Paris
1760–1761, on inner dishes; Export (cow)
Paris 1756–1775, on bases and inner dishes

*Palácio Nacional da Ajuda, Lisbon,
invs. 5384, 5385, from the table service of
Dom José I*

D'Orey 1990–1991

Each of these salt cellars is in the form of
a Brazilian Indian boy clad in a head-
dress and belt of feathers. The figure
leans forward slightly, grasping the tapering sack on his back. The sack contains a removable gilded silver liner intended to hold salt. The figure stands on
a square pedestal with rococo decoration
and four scroll feet. The salt cellars belong to a set of twelve virtually identical
pieces from the royal silver service, varying slightly in the position of the hands
and angle of the bodies.

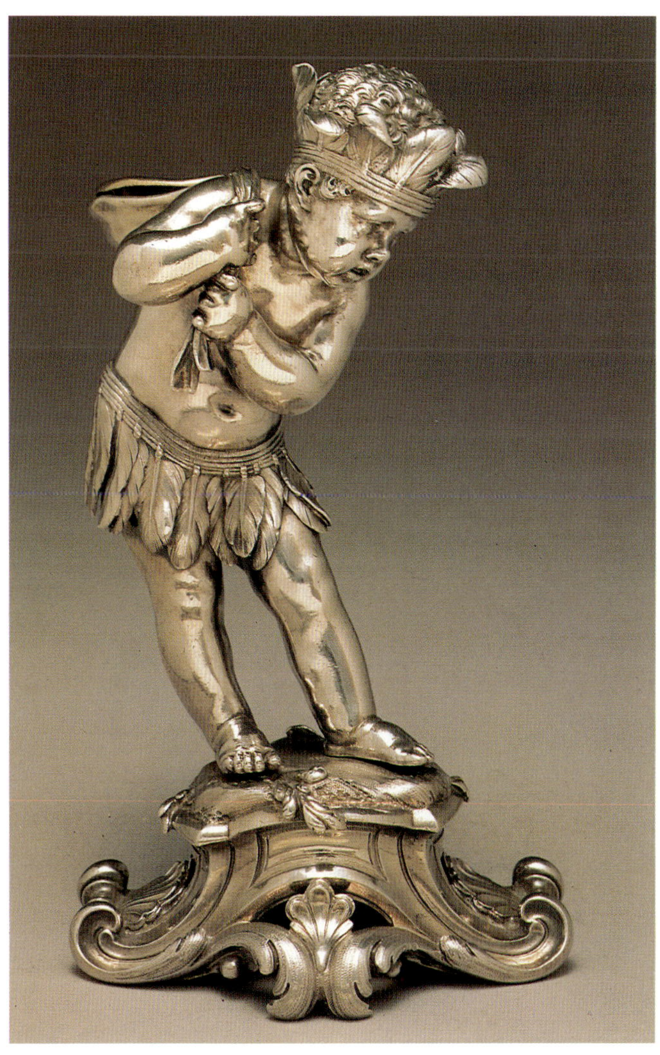
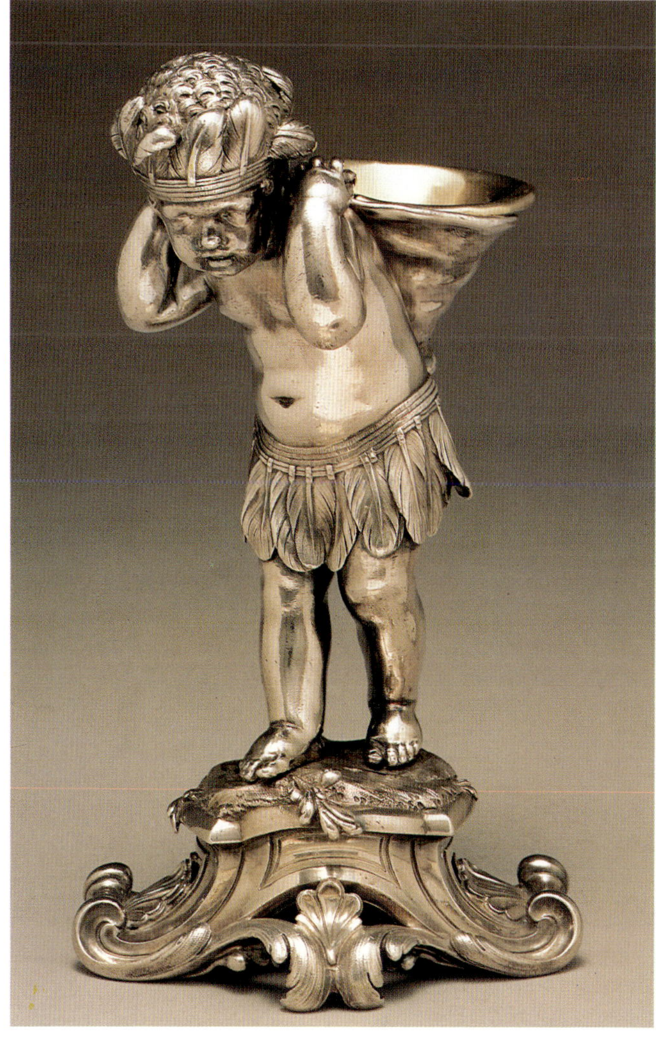

72

FRANÇOIS-THOMAS GERMAIN
French, 1748–1791
Spice Holder
1757–1760
chased, repoussé, and engraved silver and
gilded silver
24.6 x 30.6 x 8.5 (9¹¹/₁₆ x 12¹/₁₆ x 7⁵/₁₆)
Insc.: FAIT.PAR.F.T.GERMAIN SCULPRE.
DU.ROY.AUX.GALLERIES.DU.LOUVRE.A.
PARIS.1760; DU Nᵒ 61 inside bases;
Portuguese royal coat of arms on base
and underside of inner dish
Marks: Maître (FT/G, fleece) François-
Thomas Germain, on base and underside
of inner dish; Charge (crowned A) and
(grill) Paris 1756–1762, on base and inner
dish; Maison Commune (crowned T)
Paris 1759–1760, (crowned V) Paris 1760–
1761, on base and inner dish; Export
(cow) Paris 1756–1775, on outer edge of
base

*Museu Nacional de Arte Antiga, Lisbon,
inv. 1841, from the table service of
Dom José I*

Foz 1926; Saraiva 1934; Bottineau 1958;
Mabille 1987; Brussels 1991, IV.22

This spice holder, or endpiece as it is
called in the document by which the silver service was commissioned, consists of
a pair of Indian boys, clad in feather
headdresses and belts, seated on sprigs of
pepper and nutmeg. With their raised
left arms the figures balance a tropical
fruit, the upper part of which forms a lid.
With his right hand each figure holds a
basket on his lap, containing a gilded silver liner intended to hold condiments.
The boys are seated on a highly ornate
and elegant rococo base. This piece is
one of a series of six identical spice
holders from the royal service.

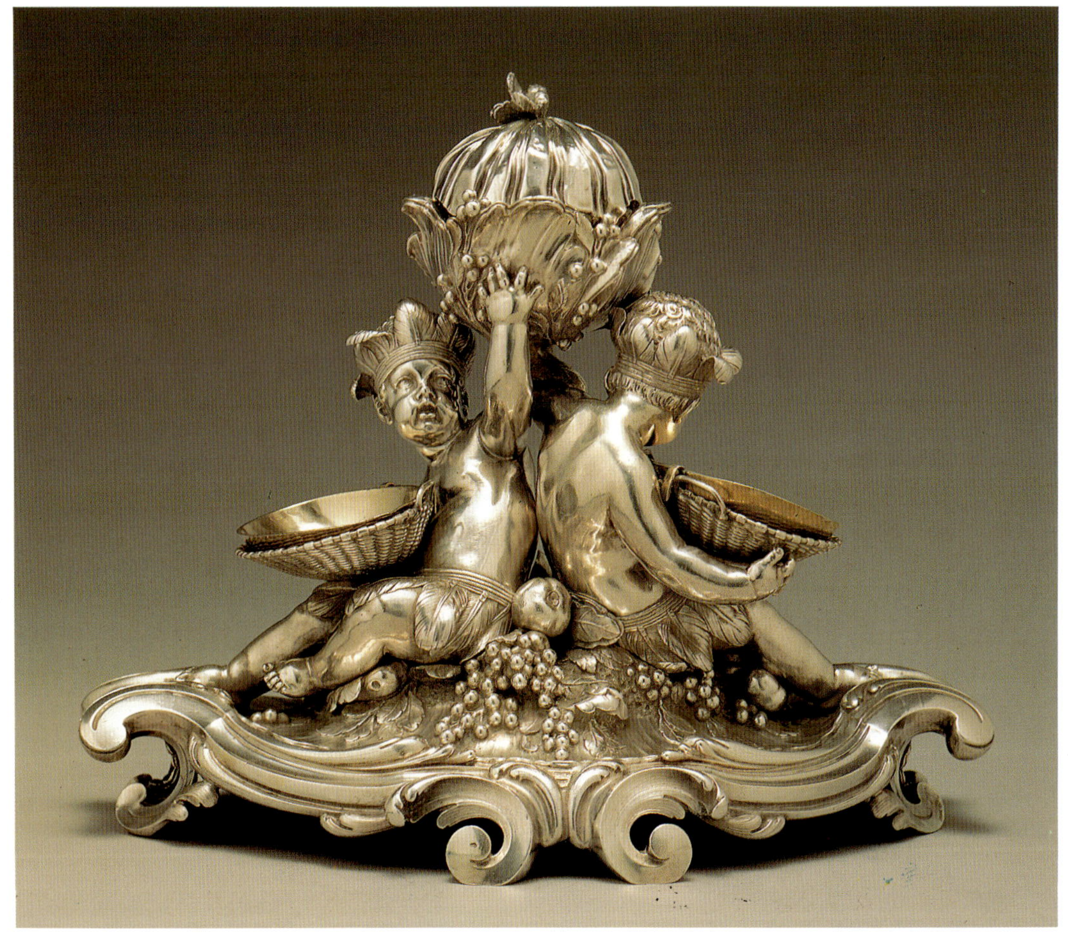

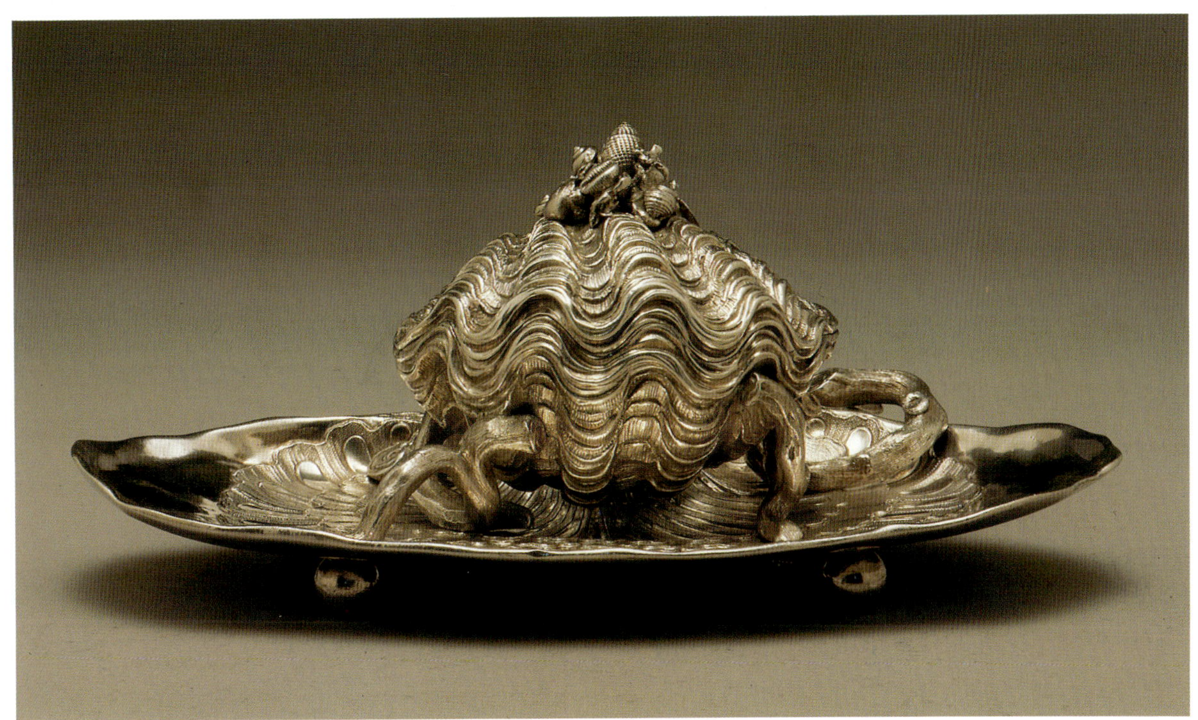

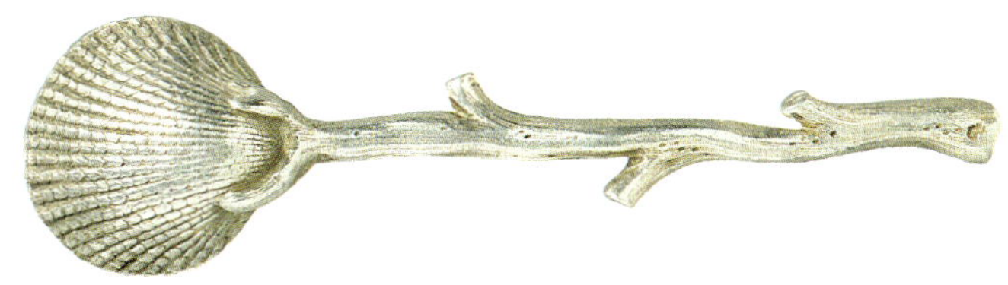

73–74

FRANÇOIS-THOMAS GERMAIN
French, 1748–1791
Salt Cellar and Spoon
1760–1761
cast, engraved, and chased silver and
gilded silver
salt cellar, 9 x 22 x 13 (3⁹/₁₆ x 8⁵/₈ x 5⅛);
spoon, 10.8 x 1.2 (4¼ x ½)
Insc.: DU Nᵒ 59 on underside of base and
inner dish; Portuguese royal coat of
arms; local id.
Marks: salt cellar, Maître (FT/G, fleece)
François-Thomas Germain, underside of
base and liner; Charge (crowned A) Paris
1756–1762, local id.; Maison Commune
(crowned V) Paris 1760–1761, local id.;
Export (cow) Paris 1756–1775, edge of
base and liner; spoon, Export (cow)

*Museu Nacional de Arte Antiga, Lisbon,
salt cellar inv. 1845, spoon inv. 898, from
the table service of Dom José I*

D'Orey 1990–1991; Lisbon 1992, cat. 479

The salt cellar is in the shape of a jointed
oyster shell, the upper part of which may
be raised, and is surmounted by highly
realistic whelks and seaweed. The shell is
supported by a branch of coral resting on
a shell-like oval base. It contains a removable plain gilded silver liner in which
the condiment is placed. The identification of this piece as a mustard pot has
been accepted to date, although this description may not be accurate, as its
shape and decoration are not entirely
suited to that function, whereas the
French goldsmiths were scrupulously
careful in this regard in the other articles
of the silver service. There are four of
these in the Portuguese silver service.

A small spoon in the form of a mussel
shell, with the handle decorated with a
branch of coral, accompanied the salt
cellar.

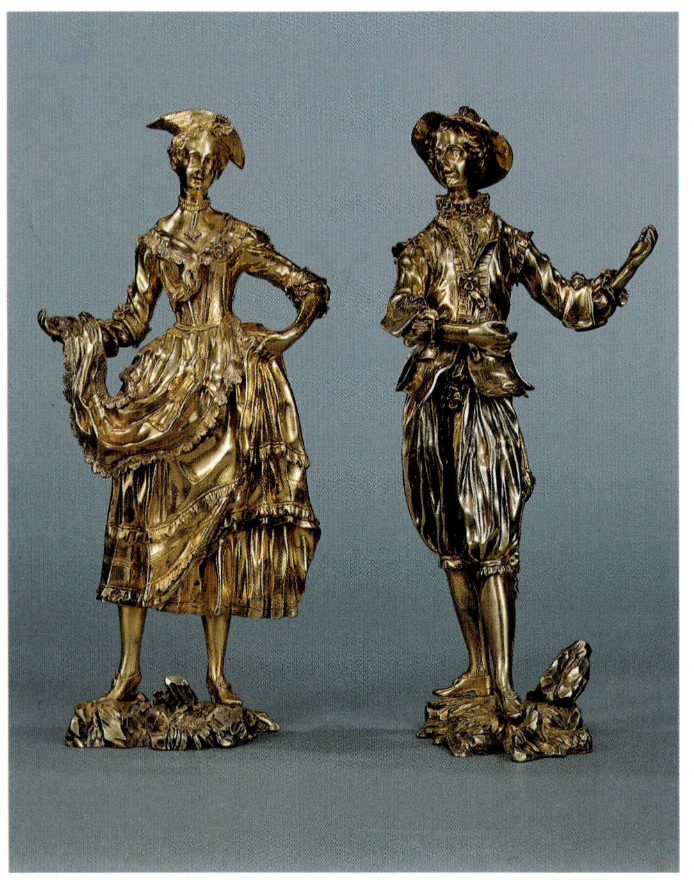

75, 76

75–80

AMBROISE-NICHOLAS COUSINET
French, 1745–1788
Six Statuettes

1757–1758
cast, chased, and engraved gilded silver
38.9 to 40 (15⁵⁄₁₆ to 15 ¾)
Marks: Maître (AN/c, snake) Ambroise-
Nicholas Cousinet, on figures and inside
bases (illegible or non-existent on figure
nº 1812 and 1817); Charge (crowned A)
Paris 1756–1762, on figures nº 1811, 1812;
(grill) Paris 1756–1762, on figures 1813 to
1814 and inside bases; Maison Commune
(crowned R) Paris 1757–1758, on figures;
Export (cow) Paris 1756–1775, on outer
edge of bases

*Museu Nacional de Arte Antiga, Lisbon,
cat. 75, inv. 1811; cat. 76, inv. 1818; cat. 77,
inv. 1817; cat. 78, inv. 1812; cat. 79, inv.
1813; cat. 80, inv. 1814; from duque de
Aveiro to Dom José I*

Bapst 1892, 33; Réau 1927, 17–26; Boletim ANBA 1935;
Brussels 1991, IV. 19; Lisbon 1992, nos. 458, 491–492

These unique vermeil statuettes by
Ambroise-Nicholas Cousinet belong to
an extensive set of sixteen male and female figures composing eight couples in
fancy European and Oriental dress.
They stand on simple bases that contrast
with the meticulous finish of the figures.
Scholars such as Bapst, Foz, and
Figueiredo have attempted to identify
the national origin of each couple as
French, English, Spanish, Italian, Polish, German, Hungarian, and Chinese
(Bapst 1892, 33). It is more likely that the
statuettes represent picturesque figures of
popular origin such as peasants, shepherds, flower girls, and idealized images
of exotic civilizations. Such portrayals
were very popular during this period and
appear frequently in drawings by the
great painters and sculptors that served
as models for the manufacture of porcelain. Cousinet's figures can legitimately
be called translations into precious metal
of the amorous couples usually produced
in soft-paste porcelain, which appear to
be dancing with arms extended as
though holding things in their hands. A
list of the silverware belonging to the
Portuguese royal household, dated 1795,
indicates that each Cousinet figure originally held a basket, possibly designed to
contain flowers or sweets ("Prata,
loiça … que estavam no Paço da Quinta
de Belém e foram para o Paço das Necessidades," 23 October 1795, in Boletim
ANBA, series I [Lisbon, 1935], III–117).

Porcelain figures became extremely
popular during the eighteenth century
and were highly valued as decoration.
Figures in silver were more unusual,
however, and this superb group is certainly the most important such set that
has survived. Despite their imposing
size, the statuettes are unquestionably a
product of the same rococo spirit as the
delicate porcelain figures made fashionable by the Meissen factory, which were
so successfully imitated by the manufacturers of Vincennes and Sèvres. The
part-Oriental, part-Parisian exoticism of
Cousinet's statuettes, though fleeting,
reflects one of the most original aspects
of the spirit of that period. The figures,

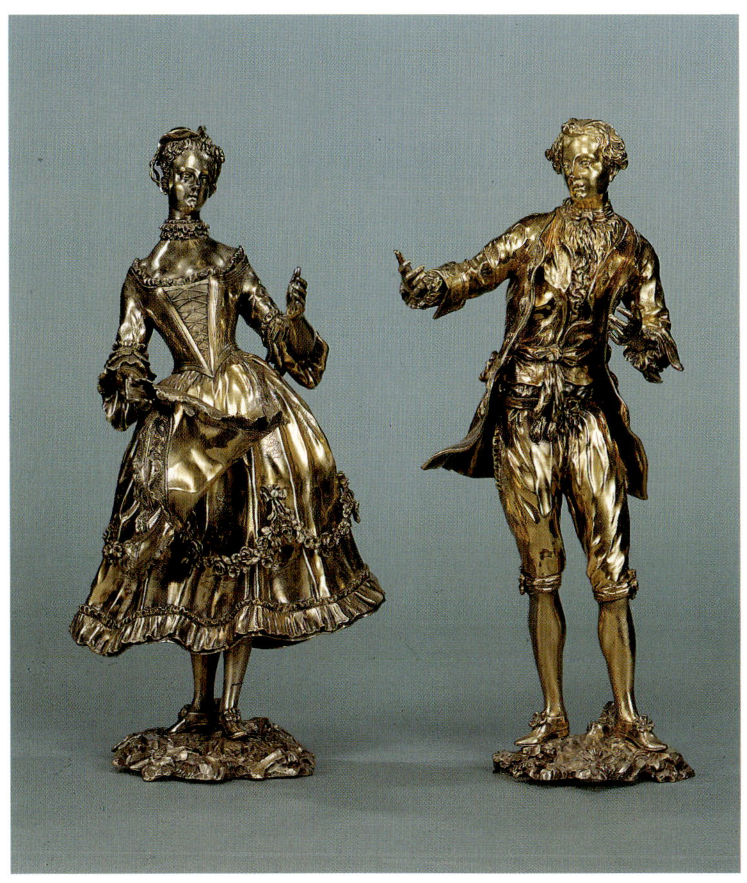

77, 78

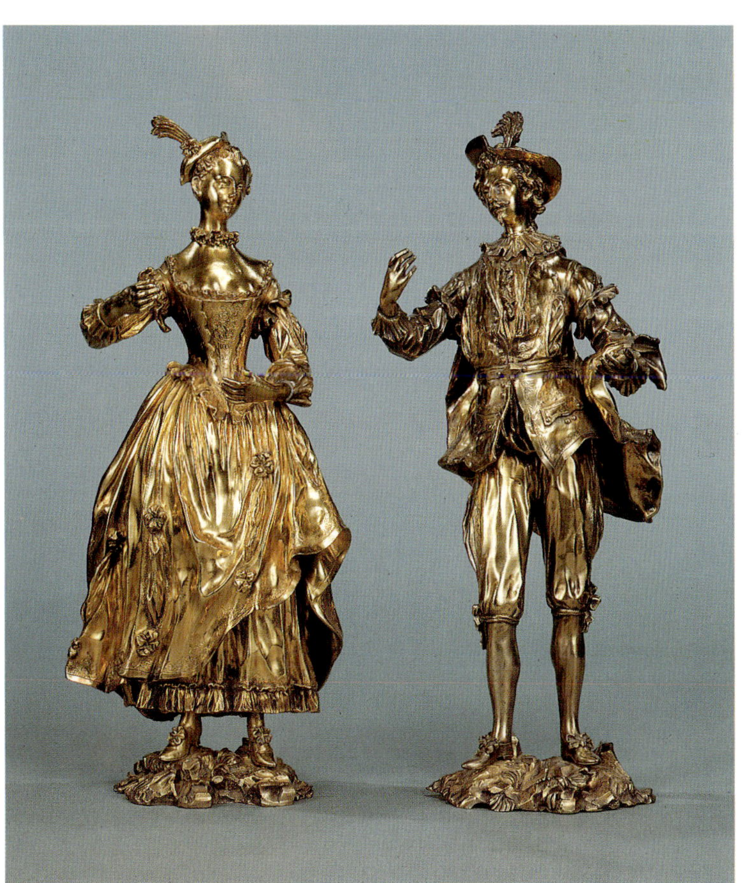

79, 80

faces, and gestures, as well as their swirling garments, as though immobilized in mid-step while dancing, reveal the artist's thorough knowledge of the sculptural expression of movement (d'Orey 1991, 58). As has been suggested, the lifelike and delicate modeling may reflect not only the deft hand of the goldsmith, but perhaps also an underlying design by a contemporary sculptor or painter. Names such as Falconet or Pigalle, Boucher or Watteau have been put forward. However, Louis Réau ascribed the statuettes to the authorship or collaboration of the goldsmith's brother and sculptor to the prince of Condé, Henry Cousinet, who also modeled figures in porcelain (Réau 1927, 17–26). Whatever the case, Ambroise-Nicholas Cousinet's meticulous garments and hairstyles, executed with great delicacy and masterful realism, bear eloquent witness to the extraordinary refinement of the goldsmith's art of eighteenth-century France.

The figures were commissioned from Cousinet by the duque de Aveiro in December 1757. However, the unfortunate duke was to have little time to enjoy his figures, since he was accused in September 1758 of being involved in a conspiracy and assassination attempt against Dom José I, leading to his imprisonment and, finally, execution on 13 January 1759. The sentence of death also ordered the confiscation of his worldly goods, whereupon his statuettes became the property of the Portuguese crown, together with the grand silver table centerpiece (see d'Orey silver essay, fig. 2) by Thomas and François-Thomas Germain, which had also belonged to the duke.

COMPANHIA DAS INDIAS
Chinese, Qianlong Reign, 1735–1799
**Royal Dinner Service: Sauce Boat and
Plate, Two Spoons, Sugar Bowl,
Candlestick**
c. 1750–1760
sauce boat 14 x 17 (5 ½ x 6¹¹⁄₁₆); plate 21.5 x
18 (8⁷⁄₁₆ x 7¹⁄₁₆); spoons 21 (8¼); sugar bowl
14 (5½); candlestick 19 (7½)

Palácio Nacional de Queluz , inv. 31 A

Pires 1925; Solla 1928, pl. cxi; Brancante 1950;
Beurdeley 1962; Picard 1966, fig. xv; Boulay 1984;
Castro 1987; Silvano 1987; Brussels 1991, iv.9

The coat of arms featured on this dinner
service is identical to that appearing on
the first coins of the reign of Dom José I,
engraved by Bernardo Jorge from a
drawing thought to be by Vieira Lusitano. These are believed to have been
minted in 1750. Curiously, the crest was
copied upside-down on the porcelain,
which unintentionally introduces a note
of imbalance.

The crown continued to make extensive purchases of porcelain during this
period, and royal inventories reveal that
Príncipe Dom Pedro (1717–1786), the
younger brother of Dom José I, particularly admired Chinese ware and had
acquired a considerable collection of
"dishes from India and Macau," a somewhat inaccurate reference to Chinese
porcelain. Records indicate that in 1755
he received a large order cleared by a
customs agent named Oldemberg.

The timing of the first orders for
porcelain was no doubt intended for the
royal wedding between Princesa Maria
and her uncle, Príncipe Dom Pedro,
which took place on 6 June 1760 in the
chapel of the Real Barraca da Ajuda.
Dom Pedro, who had already given the
first of his famous parties in Queluz,
closely followed the work on the building of the palace and, in the year following the wedding, invited members of his
entourage to attend a performance there
of David Perez' opera *La Vera Felicità*, a
metaphor for the idyllic times in which
they lived.

In the inventory of 1767 the dinner
service is called "a set of china from
Macau, white background, encircled by
fret-work in red and shades thereof,
highlighted in gold; escutcheons bearing
the royal coat of arms and those of Malta
appear on every piece," a description that
corresponds to the set here on display.
The design of the exhibited dinner service, particularly the sauce boat reminiscent of a ship with vigorous volutes on
the bow and stern, is in keeping with a
Western model that was used for a number of services executed in China for a
sizable European clientele.

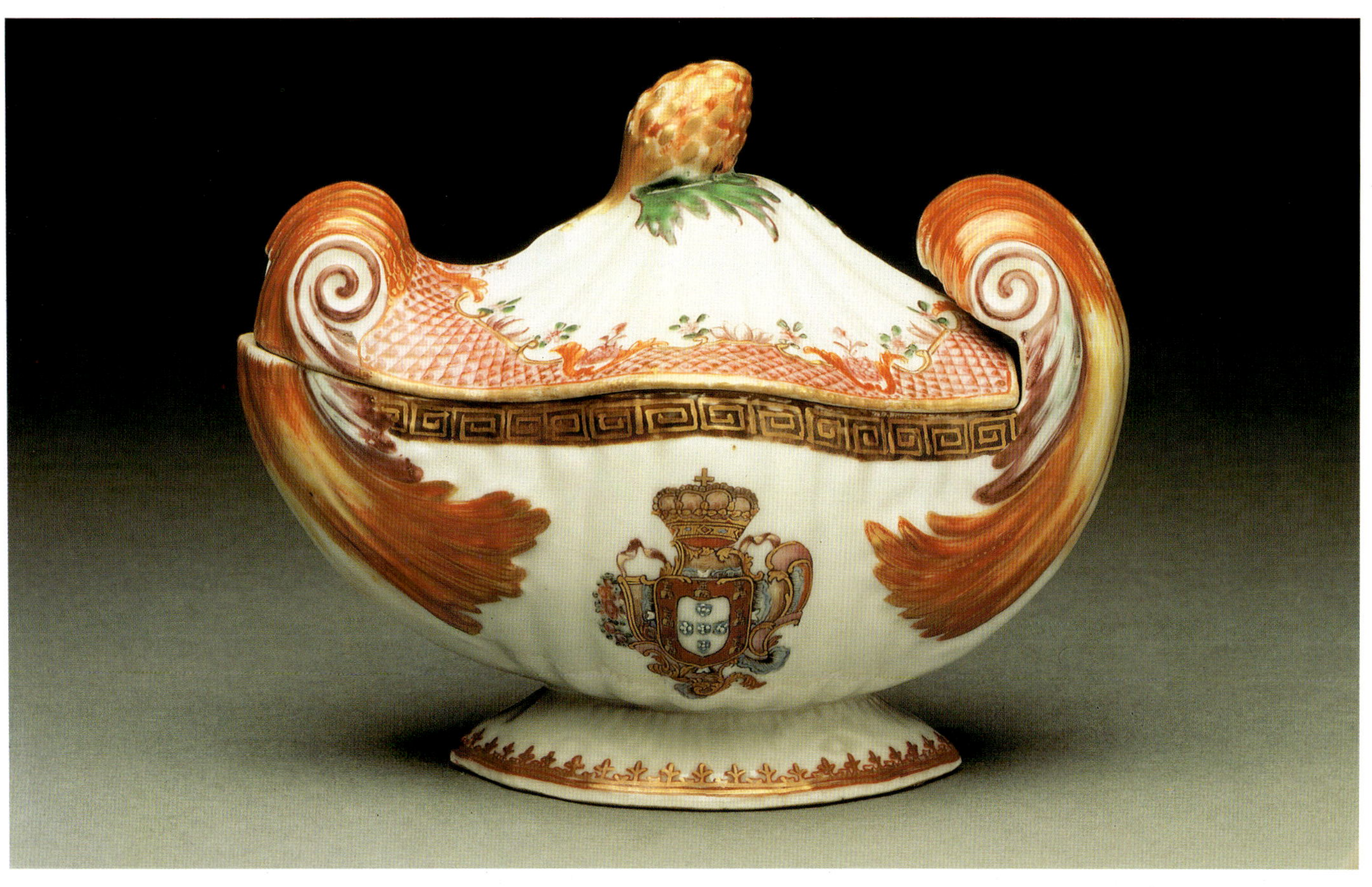

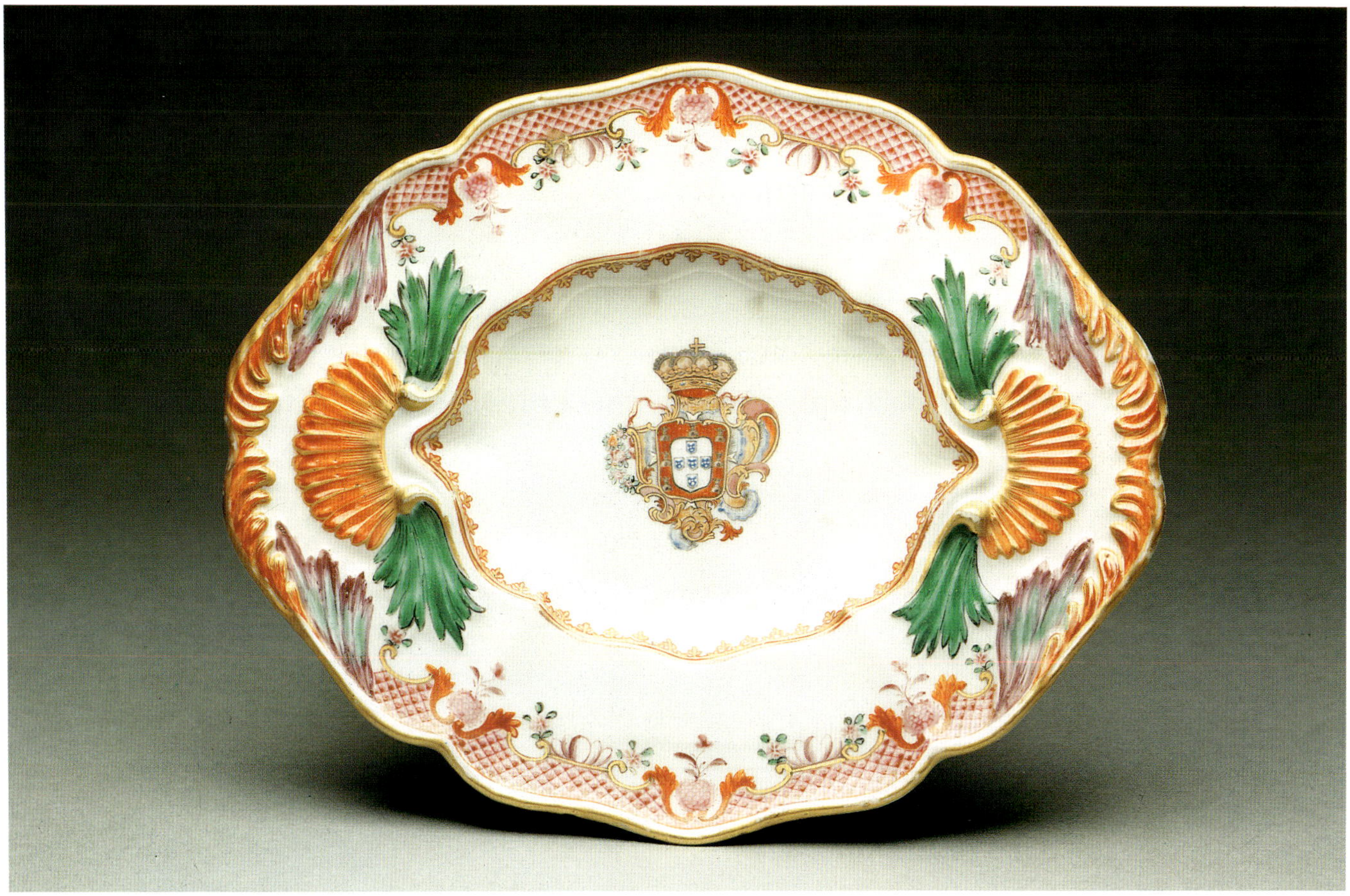

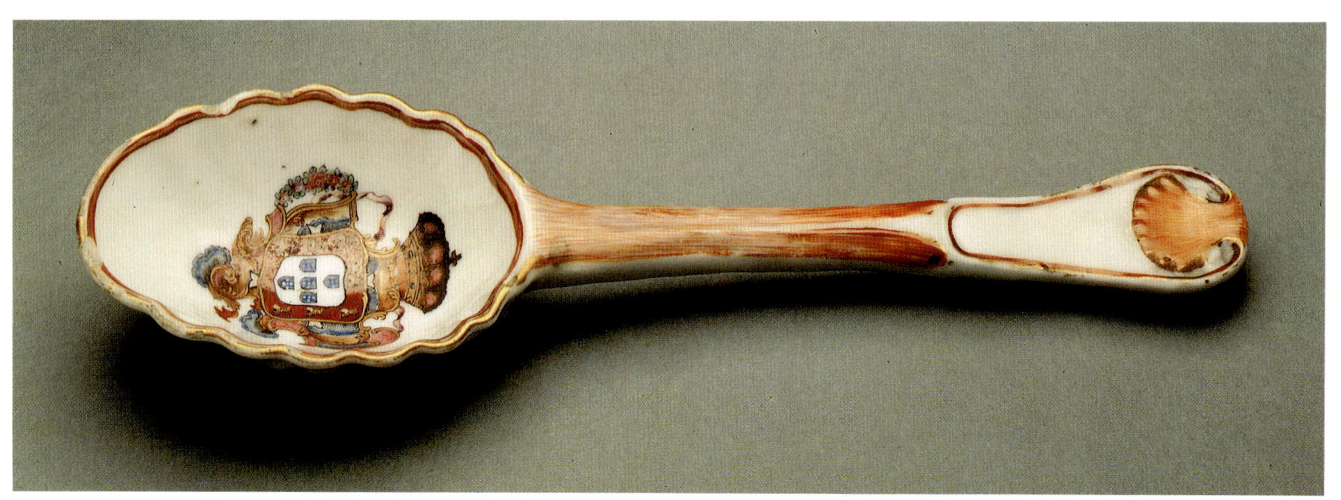

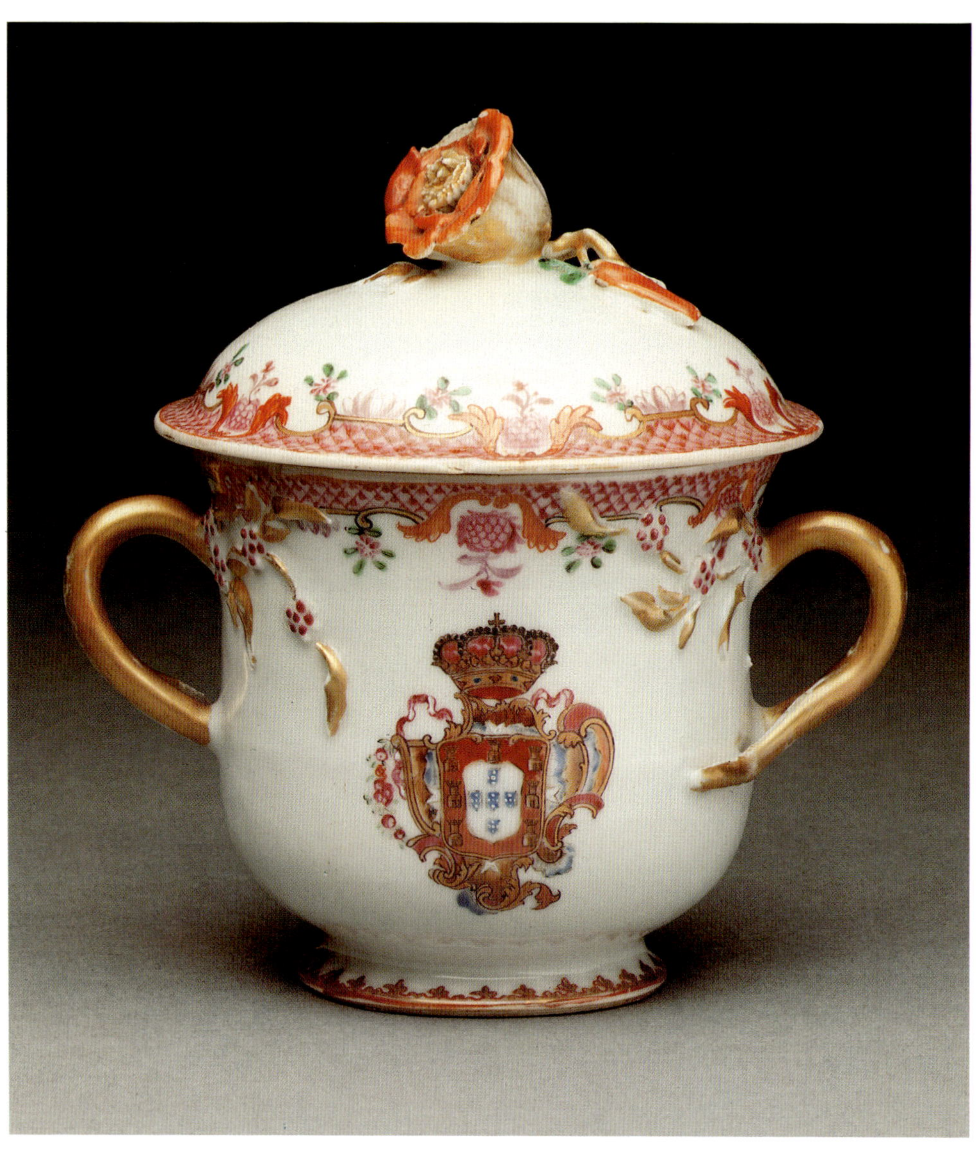

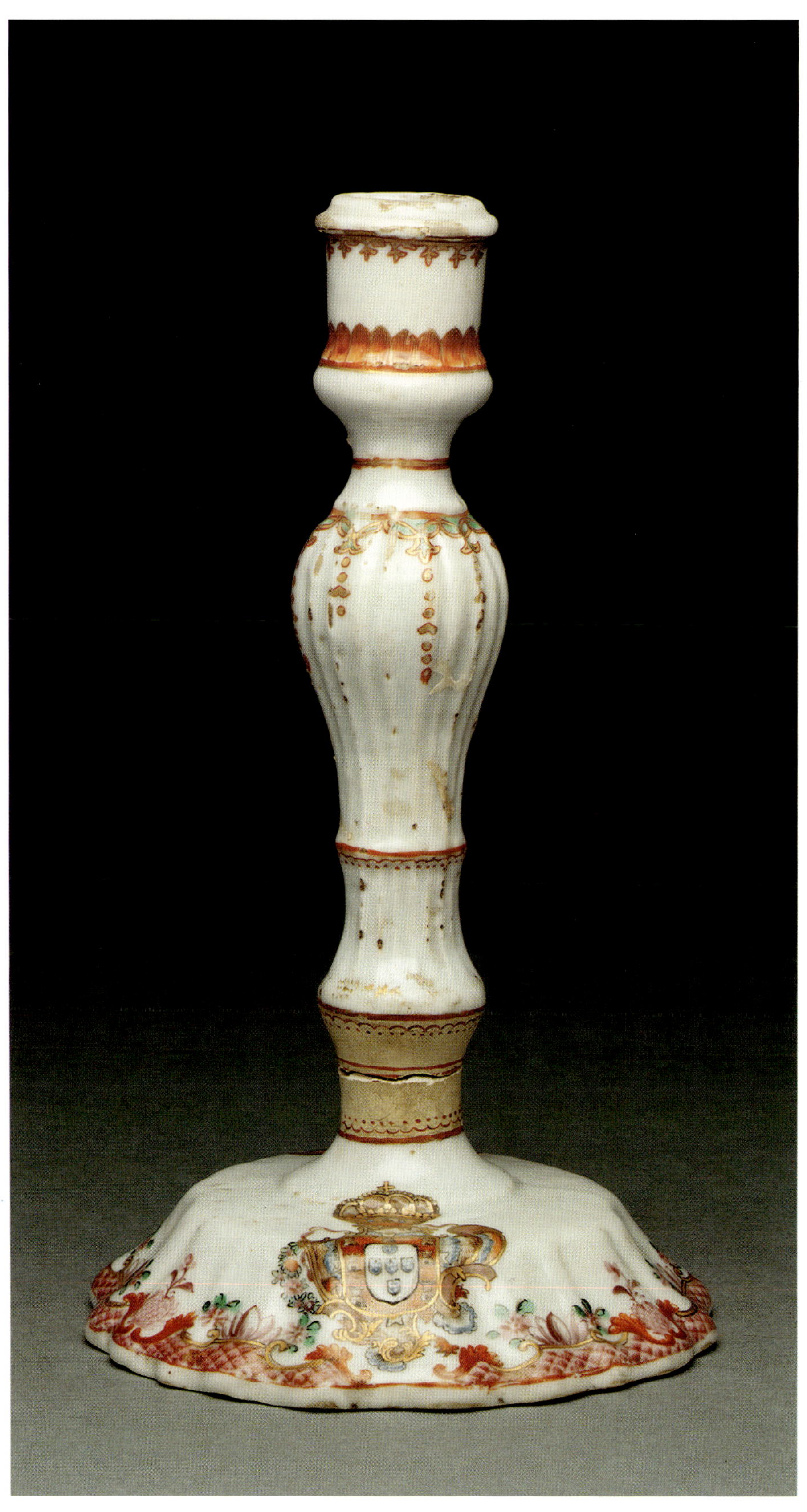

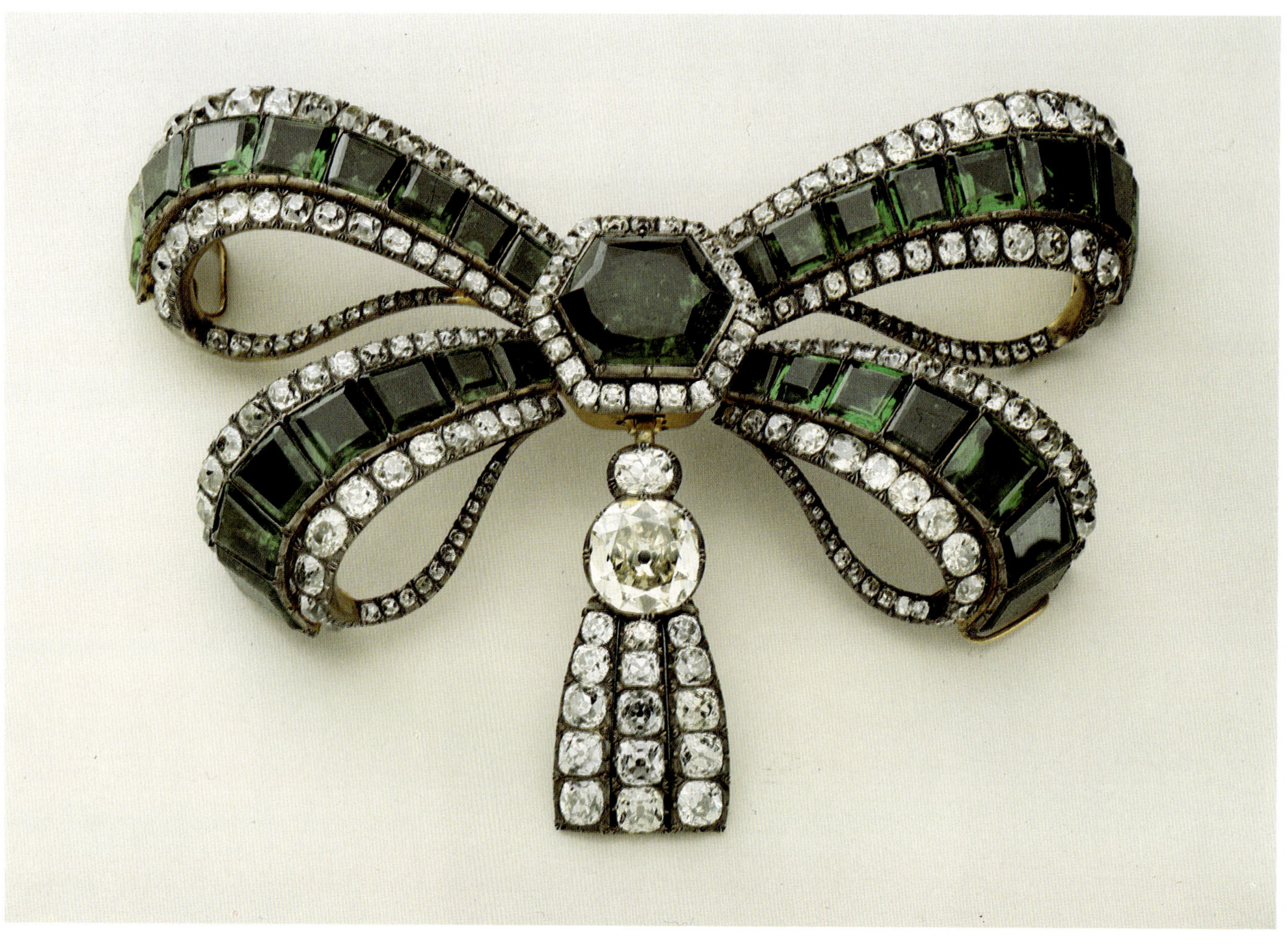

86

Corsage Brooch
1st quarter 18th century
silver, gold, diamonds, and emeralds
12.4 x 18.5 x 4.1 (4⅞ x 7⁵⁄₁₆ x 1⅝)

Palácio Nacional da Ajuda,
Lisbon, inv. 4779

ANBA 1942, nos. 30 and 31; Steingräber 1957;
Muller 1972; Black 1974; Tait 1986; Brussels 1991,
V.2; Lisbon 1992, no. 11

This bow-shaped stomacher, mounted
in silver and gold, consists of 216 diamonds and thirty-one emeralds cut in
the manner of the first half of the eighteenth century. The emeralds, of exceptional size and color, are probably from
Colombia. The hexagonal emerald
forming the bow knot weighs almost
forty-eight carats and is framed in diamonds; the ribbons, edged in diamonds,
are composed of graduated quadrangular
emeralds; and from the central knot
hangs a tassel-shaped pendant topped by
a large twenty-four-carat diamond.

The stomacher belonged to the Infanta Mariana (1736–1813), sister of
Rainha Dona Maria I (1734–1816). It is
known that the infanta ordered the sale
of this piece in order to finance the
founding of the Convento do Desagravo.
However, the piece was never actually
sold, perhaps through Príncipe Dom
João's intervention, and it appears in the
patriarchal treasure after the court's return from Brazil. When the Infanta Isabel Maria had the inventory of Dom
João VI's possessions drawn up in 1826,
the existence of the piece was made
known by Canon Manuel Wenceslau,
who was in charge of the patriarchal
treasure at the time. The infanta, as regent, ordered that the stomacher be deposited in the royal treasury, where it has
remained until this day. During the

reign of Dom Luís I, at the request of
Rainha Dona Maria Pia (1847–1911), the
jeweler Estêvão de Sousa (active 1863–
1878) turned the emerald and diamond
stomacher into a suite consisting of
necklace or tiara, earrings, brooch,
bracelet, and comb.

87

JACQMIN
French, 1718–1770
Snuffbox
1756
chased gold with silver appliqués and
inlaid diamonds and emeralds
4.8 x 9.6 x 7.6 (1⅞ x 3¾ x 3)
Insc.: JACQMIN JOYAILLIER DU ROY-PARIS
L. ROUCEL À PARIS LE 29 JUIELLET 1756
Marks: jeweler (J.D. heart) Jean Du-crol-
lay, date (crowned P) Paris 1755–1756;
charge (horse's head), Paris 1750–1756;
discharge (chicken), Paris 1750–1756

*Palácio Nacional da Ajuda,
Lisbon, inv. 4786*

Nocq 1926–1931; ANBA 1935, docs. CII and CIV;
Snowman 1966, figs. 279, 280; Brussels 1991, v.3;
Lisbon 1992, no. 8

This magnificent rectangular snuffbox in
chased gold, with hinged lid, is studded
with 853 diamonds and 204 emeralds,
with the largest diamond weighing about
twenty-nine carats and decorated with
sprays of flowers and leaves. The base is
adorned with a basket of flowers framed
in floral and shell-shaped ornaments in
low relief. This object, which bears the
signature of Jacqmin, the jeweler of the
court of Louis XV (1710–1774), also bears
the stamp of the great French goldsmith
specializing in such snuffboxes, Jean
Ducrollay (active 1722–1765), as well as an
inscription referring to the renowned
French goldsmith Louis Roucel (active
1763–1787). The piece was commissioned
by Dom José I from the French court
jeweler through António Saldanha, who
was then Portuguese ambassador in Paris
and who, in a letter addressed to Luís da
Cunha dated 11 December 1756, mentioned that he had received "a box, decorated with diamonds," to be delivered to
the Portuguese monarch.

It may be deduced from this document that the diamonds used to adorn
the box were provided by the Portuguese
crown, since the return is mentioned of
"certain diamonds left over from the
commission" on which the jeweler had
already "used twenty-two thousand
livras" (Boletim ANBA I, doc. CV, 60). A
few days later, in a letter to Luís da
Cunha dated 21 December, the ambassador mentioned that "the diamond-
studded box, which His Majesty ordered
me to send to the conde de Ungam who
will deliver it to the court, was dispatched the day before yesterday in the
hands of a messenger from the Madrid
court office who was here awaiting dispatches from his ambassador." Meanwhile the magnificent object had been
seen by the king of France's favorite,
Madame de Pompadour, as the same
document stated: "…I might mention to
Your Excellency that, since Mr. Grenier
did not commend the jeweler who made
the box to secrecy, the latter was led by
the sumptuousness of the snuffbox or by
pride in his work to show it to many
people, and he even took it to Versailles
to show Madame Pompadour sometime
after her arrival at Fontainebleau, as the
jeweler himself admitted to me" (Boletim ANBA, doc. CIV, 61).

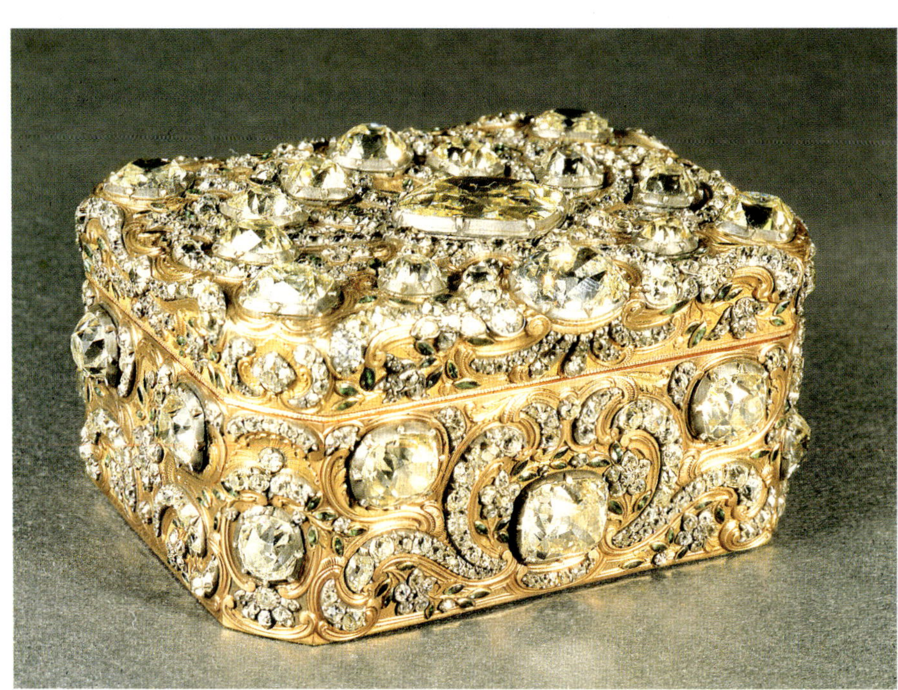

88

Cane Handle
French
1750–1770
chased gold, silver, and diamonds
9.1 x 3.9 (3⁹⁄₁₆ x 1⁹⁄₁₆)

*Palácio Nacional da Ajuda,
Lisbon, inv. 4781*

Boxer 1963; Muller 1972; Brussels 1991, v.4; Lisbon
1992, no. 24

This gold cane handle is decorated with
exotic birds, vases of flowers, and scrolls.
It is set with 387 diamonds mounted in
silver. The stone at the upper end weighs
almost twenty-five carats and can be removed. This piece was made for Dom
José I and appears in the inventories from
the time of Dom João VI to 1842–1844.

In the eighteenth century, diamonds
in Portugal came almost exclusively from
Brazil. In 1753, Sebastião José de Carvalho e Melo, the future marquês de
Pombal, placed the diamond trade under
royal protection, prohibiting all private
parties from mining, purchasing, selling,
transporting, or processing uncut diamonds in Portugal or in the Portuguese
overseas dominions without written authorization. This regulation made the
diamond monopoly enormously profitable for the treasury.

The diamonds decorating this cane
head and those adorning the snuffbox
(see cat. 87) were mined during the 1750s.
This object, which belonged to Dom
José I, was no doubt ordered from Paris
as was the snuffbox, and it is likewise of
the highest technical standard of
execution.

Canes were not a usual accessory,
since it continued to be the custom to
wear swords at court. However, when
a theft was reported at the conde de
Pombeiro's residence near Bemposta in
1731, one of the most valuable objects
stolen was "a cane with emeralds and
diamonds." The many precious stones
imported from Brazil in the eighteenth
century no doubt encouraged the creation of a wide range of accessories that
they could adorn.

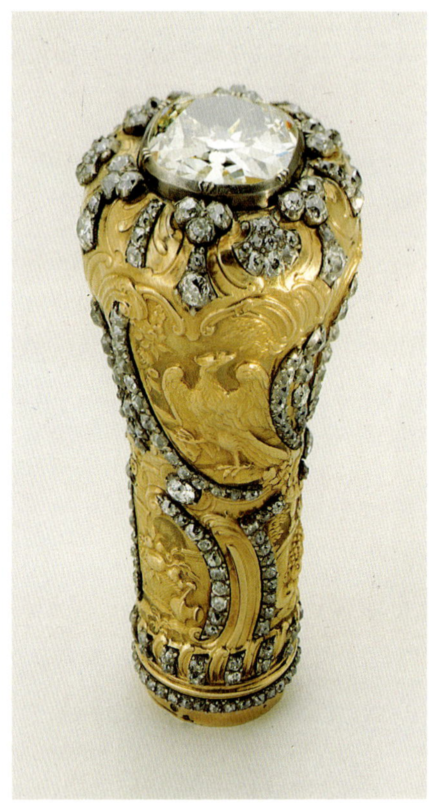

89

DAVID AMBRÓSIO POLLET
French, 1754–1822
**Insignia of the Order of the
Golden Fleece**
1790
gold and silver with diamonds, rubies,
and sapphire
26.7 x 12.2 (10½ x 4¹³⁄₁₆)

*Palácio Nacional da Ajuda, Lisbon,
inv. 4774*

Estevens 1944; Rosas Jr. 1954; Européia-Trésors
1987; Brussels 1991, v.7; Lisbon 1992, no. 251

The Order of the Golden Fleece was
created by Philip the Good, duke of
Burgundy and count of Flanders, to celebrate his marriage to the Infanta Isabel
of Portugal (1397–1471), daughter of
Dom João I. Its name refers to the legendary golden fleece of a lamb hanging
from a tree in Colchis that was imbued
with magical powers and was the goal of
the mythical expedition of Jason and the
Argonauts. The order represented a final
bid of the House of Burgundy to create a
supra-national elite of knights. Only

thirty members were admitted to the
order, since this number evoked the two
naval ships that made a lavish embassy to
bring the princess from Lisbon. On the
day of his marriage the duke adopted the
motto: "Aultre n'aray [que] dame sabeau
tant que vivray" (I will have none other
than Dame Isabel for as long as I live).

This decoration was created for
Príncipe João, later to become Dom João
VI, on whom the order was conferred on
3 May 1785 in Vila Viçosa (A.N.T.T., C.F.,
109, doc. 1). The goldsmith and keeper
of the French royal jewels, Ambroise
Pollet, received payment for this piece
on 10 May 1790 (B.A.N.B.A., 5, *Documentos* [Lisbon, 1948], 88–89). The work is
decorated with some four hundred diamonds, 102 rubies, and a large sapphire.
This last gem is a replacement obtained
in Paris by the goldsmith José Rosas Jr.
in 1945 as a substitute for the existing
stone, which was false (José Rosas Jr.,
Catálogo das Jóias e Pratas da Coroa [Lis-
bon, P.N.A., 1954]). Insignia of this type
were worn over garments or uniforms,
hanging from a ribbon; given the requirements of fashion, however, the
statutes of the order permitted the insignia to be worn around the neck without the ribbon, which, unlike the pendants, belonged to the order. Only the
lower part of the gem maintained the
characteristics of the insignia: the flam-
ing "fire stone," symbolized by the sapphire from which horizontal rows of diamonds and rubies emanate in a realistic
representation of tongues of flame, and
the "golden fleece" (hanging from one
ring) set with diamonds. The bow and
stylized floral design beneath it, admirably setting off four large pear-
shaped diamonds, have a purely ornamental function.

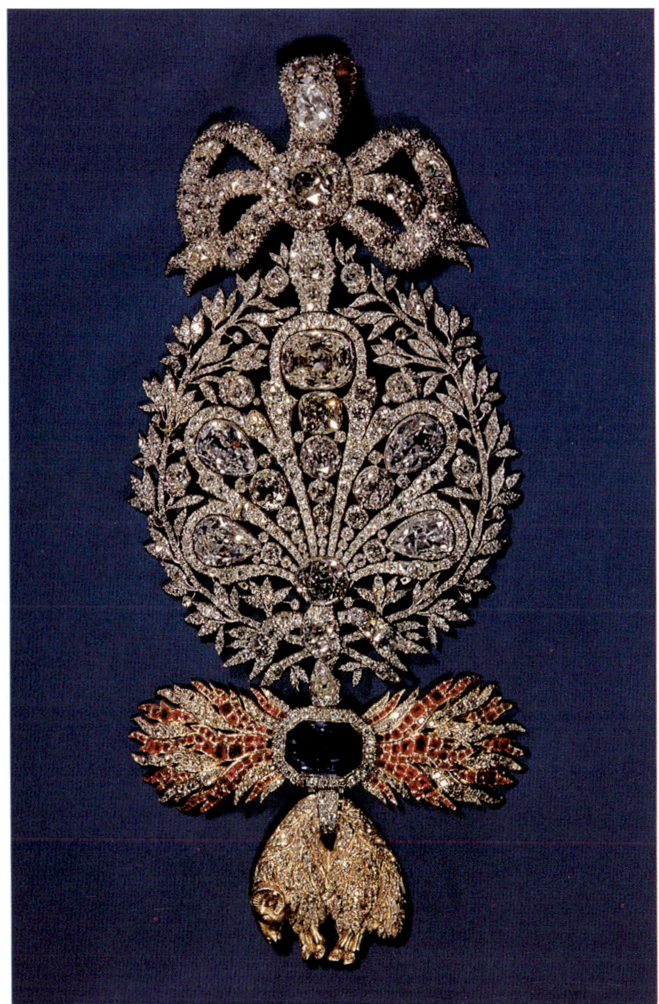

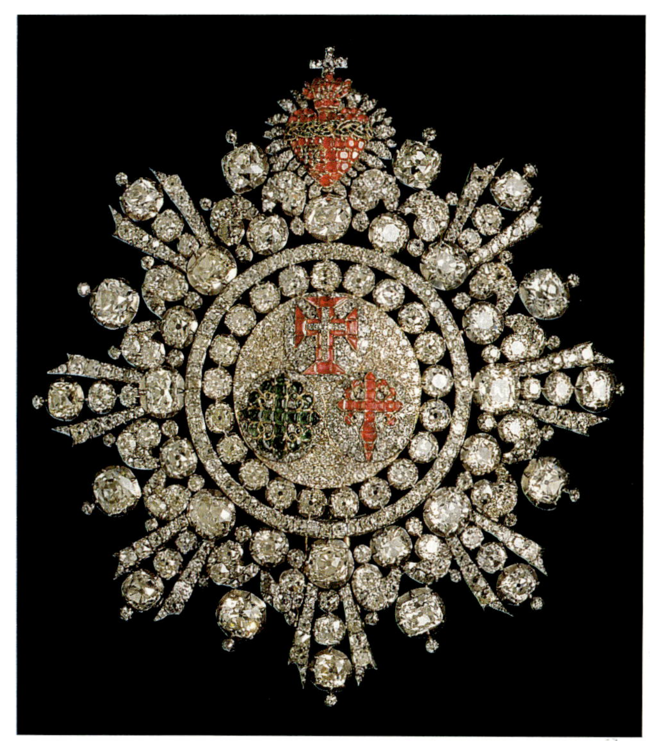

89

DAVID AMBRÓSIO POLLET
French, 1754–1822
Badge of the Three Military Orders
1789
gold and silver with diamonds, rubies,
and emeralds
12.9 x 12.2 (5$\frac{1}{16}$ x 4$\frac{13}{16}$)

*Palácio Nacional da Ajuda, Lisbon, inv.
4777*

Rosas Jr. 1954; Lisbon 1986; Lisbon 1990; Brussels
1991, v.8; Lisbon 1992, no. 248

The badge is set with diamonds, emeralds, and rubies in an open, linked setting in gold and silver. The center of the
badge contains the symbols of the orders
of Christ and of São Tiago in rubies and
of the order of Avis in emeralds. The
total number of diamonds exceeds six
hundred, with an estimated weight of
116.50 carats. Most of the diamonds already belonged to the royal house and
were valued by the goldsmith Pollet in a
receipt dated at Lisbon, 14 November
1789.

The order was the result of a decision
by Rainha Maria I in 1789 to combine
the orders of Christ, Avis, and São
Tiago of the Sword in a single insignia,
surmounted by the Sacred Heart of
Jesus, to which the sovereign was especially devoted. In this way, the queen not
only simplified the use of the decorations
of the three orders by making them into
one, but also made it a more lofty distinction, not only for the Portuguese
sovereigns, but also for foreign heads of
state who were the only persons eligible
to become members besides the grand
master of the order (D. Luís I Duque do
Porto e Rei de Portugal, P.N.A., 76).

The Arts in the
Service of Religion

91

Processional Altar
1689
Indo-Portuguese
chased, repoussé, and engraved silver

Igreja de São Domingos, Macao

Couto 1938; Couto and Gonçalves 1960; Santos 1974; Brussels 1991, II.27

This magnificent processional altar, the style of which indicates that it was created in Portuguese India, has its formal prototype in the tabernacles reproduced in Western art from the fifteenth century onward. This tradition, creating models that circulated throughout Europe, showed a preference for the centralized designs revived in the Renaissance, following the theory that centralized spaces are the most propitious for man's relationship with God, a notion of sacred space that ultimately looks back to Solomon's Temple.

As worship of the eucharist became more widespread, the Catholic church commissioned a wide variety of processional altars, allowing free rein to the artist's imagination and leading to the appearance of new types. The origins of the exhibited piece are therefore highly eclectic, including such major Renaissance monuments as Bramante's Tempietto in Rome and the multifaceted dome of Brunelleschi's cupola for the cathedral in Florence. The pyramid-shaped pinnacles are typical of the mannerist period

and were first used in Portugal by Filippo Terzi; this motif also appears in the original monstrance of the new cathedral in Coimbra of 1598. Another formal influence is the bronze baldachin created by Bernini for Saint Peter's in Rome (1633), in the four spiral columns that were repeated so frequently in baroque designs.

The São Domingos processional altar also reflects the tendency of Indo-Portuguese art to incorporate architectural structure in its church furnishings, as is apparent, for instance, in the Vidigueira reliquary or in the reliquary chest belonging to the condes de Nova Goa, which employs a style of decoration identical to the exhibited piece. As is often the case in Indo-Portuguese art, the processional altar combines Oriental imagination and Western elements, for example the cherubs' heads with Indian facial features and the acanthus leaves intertwined with Indian flora. This combination of motifs gives the piece a special charm arising out of the mixture of cultural elements and artistic styles.

92

attributed to MARCELIANO DE ARAÚJO
Portuguese, 1690–1769
Angel Candle Holders
1726
carved, painted, and gilded wood
Inscs: LAUDATE EV/OMNES VIRTUTE, PS. 147 (This sculpture was commissioned with devotion by Marianna da Glória) ANNO 1726; LAUDATE DOMINUM OMNE ANGE EJUS (This sculpture was commissioned with devotion by Mother Catharina Luiza) DO CEO ANO 1726

Private Collection, Lisbon

Santos 1950; Kubler and Soria 1959, 96, plate B; Smith 1968; Smith 1970; Brussels 1991, II.1

Candle holders of this type were frequently placed at the entrance to the chancel of a Portuguese church to draw attention to the consecrated space while simultaneously protecting it and provid-

ing illumination. In this case, the angels are attired in stylized armor, the upper part partially concealed by a bow with dangling ends while the lower part is hidden by fluttering draperies that soften their military aspect. The armor reflects a tradition dating back to medieval times when angels supplied a primarily protective presence.

Martin Soria (Kubler and Soria 1959) called this pair of angels "the most original achievement of rococo wood carving in Portugal." The lightness, grace, and ambiguous nature of the angels, created by the dexterous rendering of the garments and the life-size scale of the figures, give them a lighthearted and secular dimension and make them a part of the rococo tradition. Soria also noted that "the stylized features are reminiscent of the manner of Josefa d'Ayala" (or Josefa d'Óbidos, c. 1630–1684), probably the most important Portuguese painter of the seventeenth century, who was well known for her still-lifes and paintings of historical and religious subjects in which she sought to achieve an almost naive sense of the sublime. This somewhat contrived archaism recalls the sculptures of the late mannerist style, some of whose features reappeared at the zenith of the rococo period. The shields held by the angels and the cornucopias, also elements of this style, support this assessment.

Although these masterly sculptures are known to have been executed in 1726, the identity of the artist has not yet been established with certainty. The inscription notes that one angel was donated by Soror Mariana da Glória, but we know little more about her than that she was elected abbess of the Convento de Nossa Senhora da Conceição de Marvila in Lisbon on 8 March 1753 (L. Caetano de Lima) and that she wrote a book published in 1750, of which not a single copy has survived, entitled *Fundação do Convento de Nossa Senhora de Marvila.* These details suggest that the angels were commissioned in the south of Portugal; and yet a similarity of style is evident with the work of Marceliano de Araújo, the

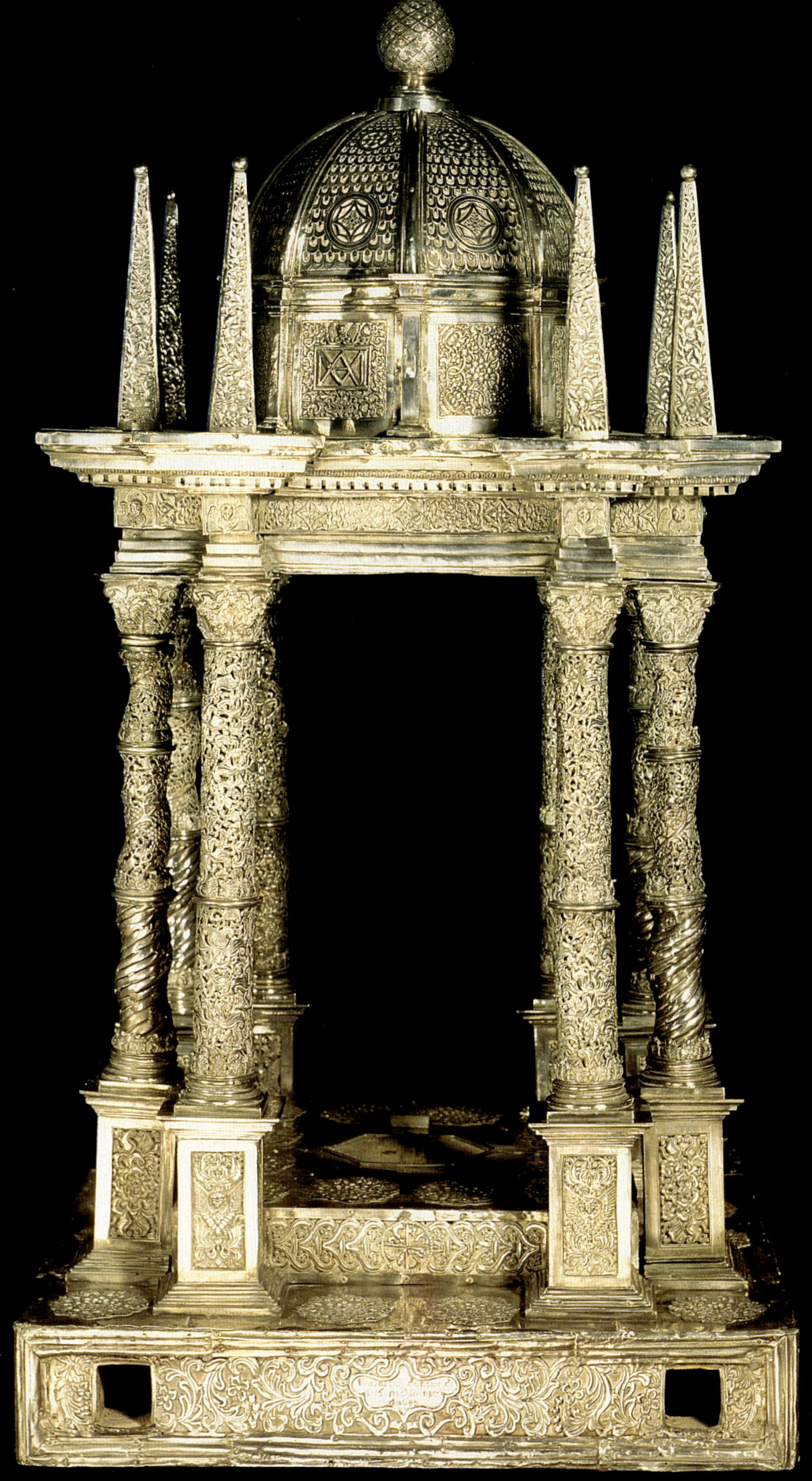

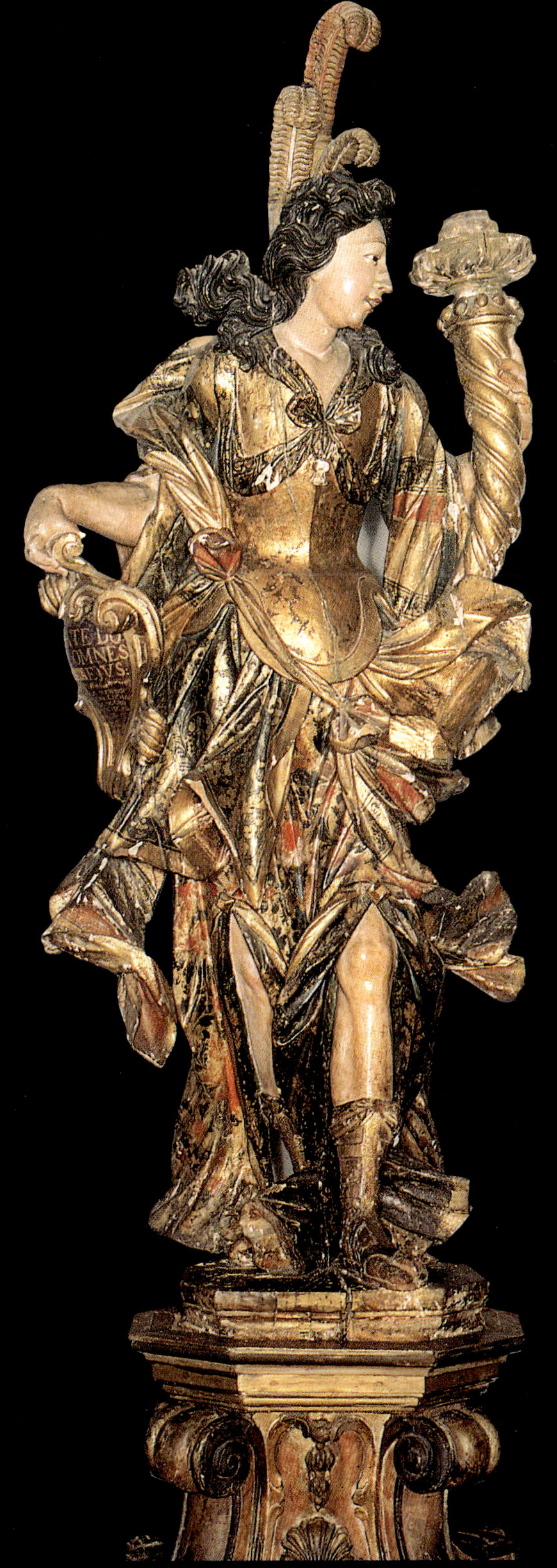
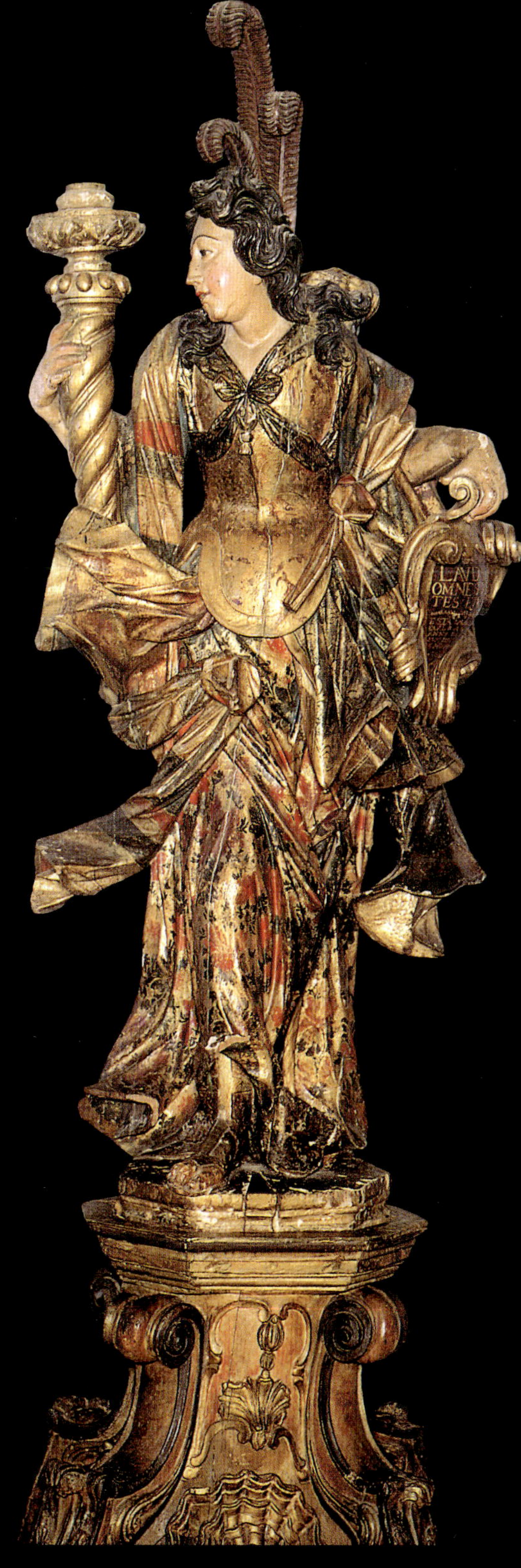

wood carver, sculptor, and cabinetmaker from Braga. This is particularly striking when one compares them with the series of sculpted allegories (such as Strength), which Araújo executed in 1737–1738 for the impressive organ cases in Braga cathedral, "forming a set with the adjacent choir stalls creating a dazzling impact of splendor, which is virtually unrivaled in wood carving" (Smith 1970).

93
Reredos with Canopy
Portuguese
reredos c. 1725, canopy c. 1775
carved and gilded wood
681 x 376 (265 x 147)

Igreja de São Francisco, Évora

Costa 1941; Bazin 1953; Moniz 1959; Smith 1963; Espanca 1966; Louro 1967; Alves 1989; Brussels 1991, II.2

The sculptural and architectural impact of this imposing piece was reduced when the Irmandade da Penitência chapel of the Ordem dos Terceiros in the church of São Francisco was rebuilt and reduced in size between 1937 and 1942, causing the reredos to be moved to the space beneath the arch that had originally divided the chapel. The rebuilding of the chapel was carried out to provide free access to the church's north door, which became the main entrance, and the current arrangement of the reredos within the chapel is the result of this alteration.

The reredos, dating from the 1720s, was installed in the chapel reserved for the Ordem dos Terceiros during a period when the order enjoyed economic prosperity. It adheres to the so-called national style typical of the reredos produced in Portugal between 1675 and 1725. Distinguishing features of this style are spiral columns entwined with vine leaves and tendrils, bunches of grapes and birds, and semi-circular supporting arches that are frequently of the same design and decoration. The term national style was coined to distinguish it from the previously predominating mannerist models in which Italian architectural elements were much in evidence.

There are reredos similar to this one in a side chapel of the Paulist church in Lisbon dating from about 1685, behind the high altar of the São Bento da Vitória church in Oporto of about 1704, and in the Nossa Senhora dos Cardais church in Lisbon dating from 1693. Thus the present Évora reredos is a late example of the type.

Two majestic pilasters, carved with high-relief motifs of acanthus leaves and strings of rosettes, mark the outer edges of the reredos, constituting a masterful and technically impressive structural base for the architrave supported by the pilaster capitals. The emblem of the Ordem Terceira de São Francisco appears in the center of the upper section, supported by two cherubs. Beneath it is the niche, which originally contained a statue of Our Lady of the Immaculate Conception, set against a beautiful aureole with swirls of clouds visible between the radiating rays.

The curved canopy was added in 1775 at the same time as the mural decoration of the walls and ceiling of the chapel and a series of adornments above the windows and niches. The asymmetry of the scalloping, held in check by the draperies, creates a fine rococo effect and admirably fulfills the requirements of the new vocabulary of design. The quality of the carving and gilding is maintained in the addition, contributing to the perfect balance of the whole.

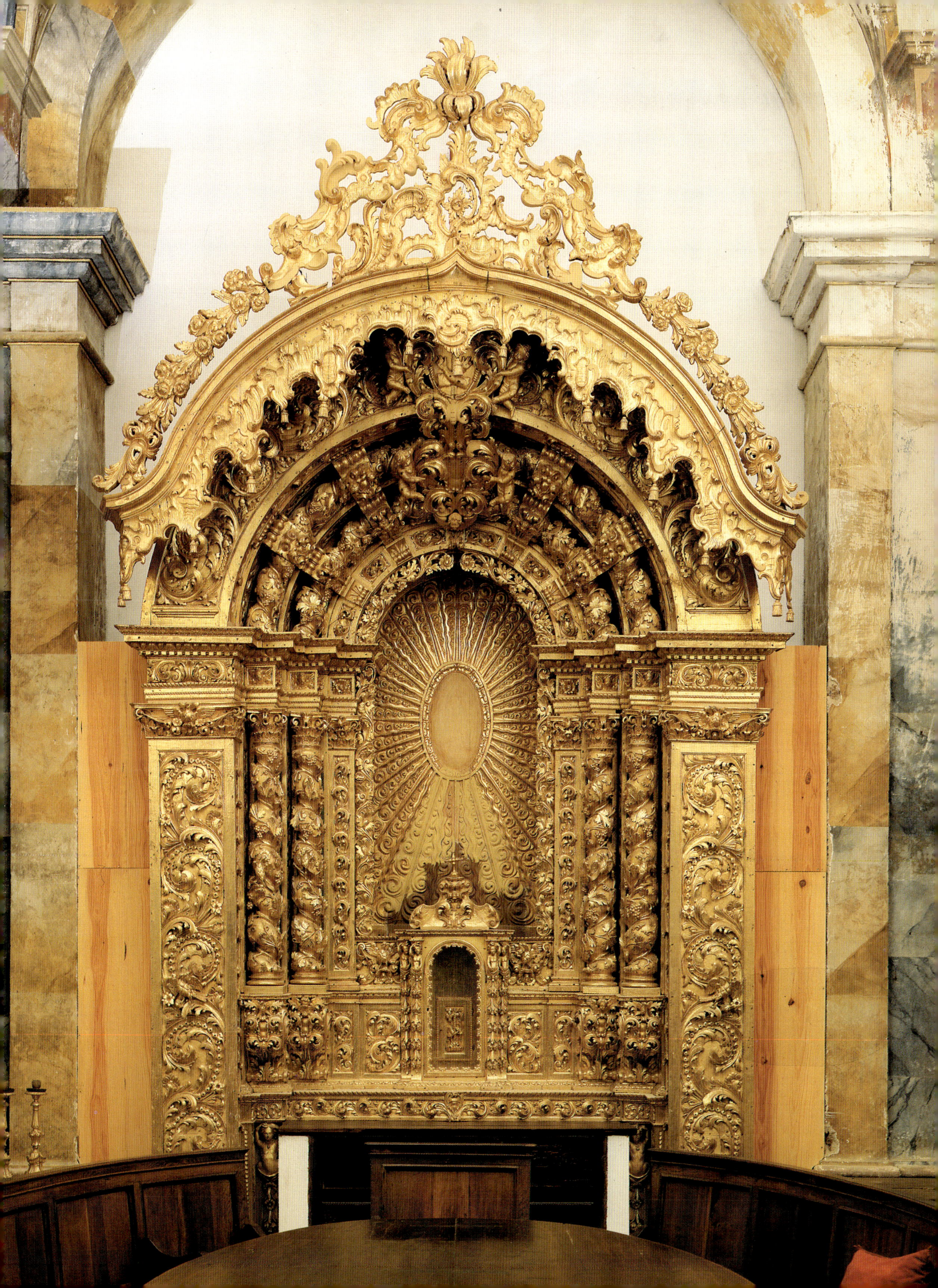

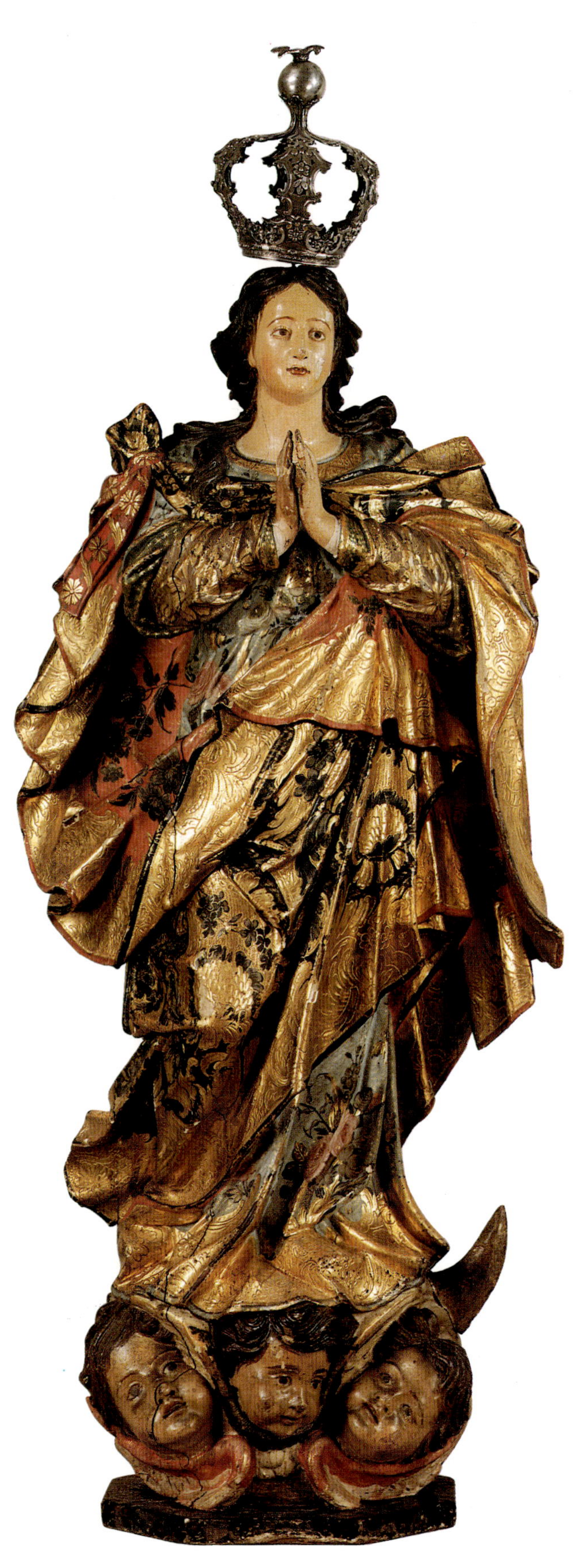

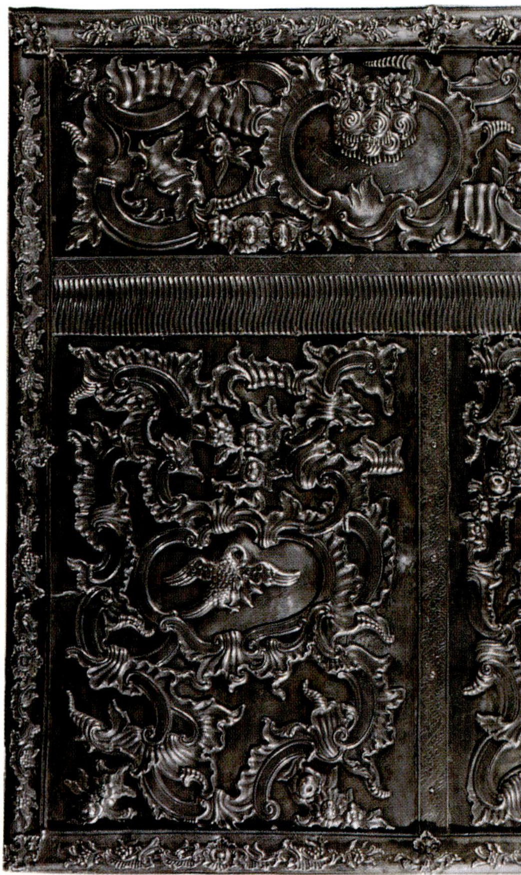

94
**Our Lady of the
Immaculate Conception**
Portuguese
c. 1760
sculpted, gilded, and painted wood
120 (47 ¼)

*Igreja de Nossa Senhora da Conceição dos
Cardais, Lisbon*

Macedo 1945; Santos 1950; Moura 1987;
Brussels 1991, II.16

The earliest known reference to worship
of Our Lady of the Immaculate Conception dates back to the Middle Ages. In
the fourteenth century, Queen Saint Isabel founded the chapel of the Immaculate Conception in the Santíssima
Trindade Convent in Coimbra. A
church dedicated to the Misericórdia da
Conceição Velha was built in Lisbon
during the sixteenth century under the
reign of Dom Manuel I "the Fortunate,"
while the Order of Nossa Senhora da

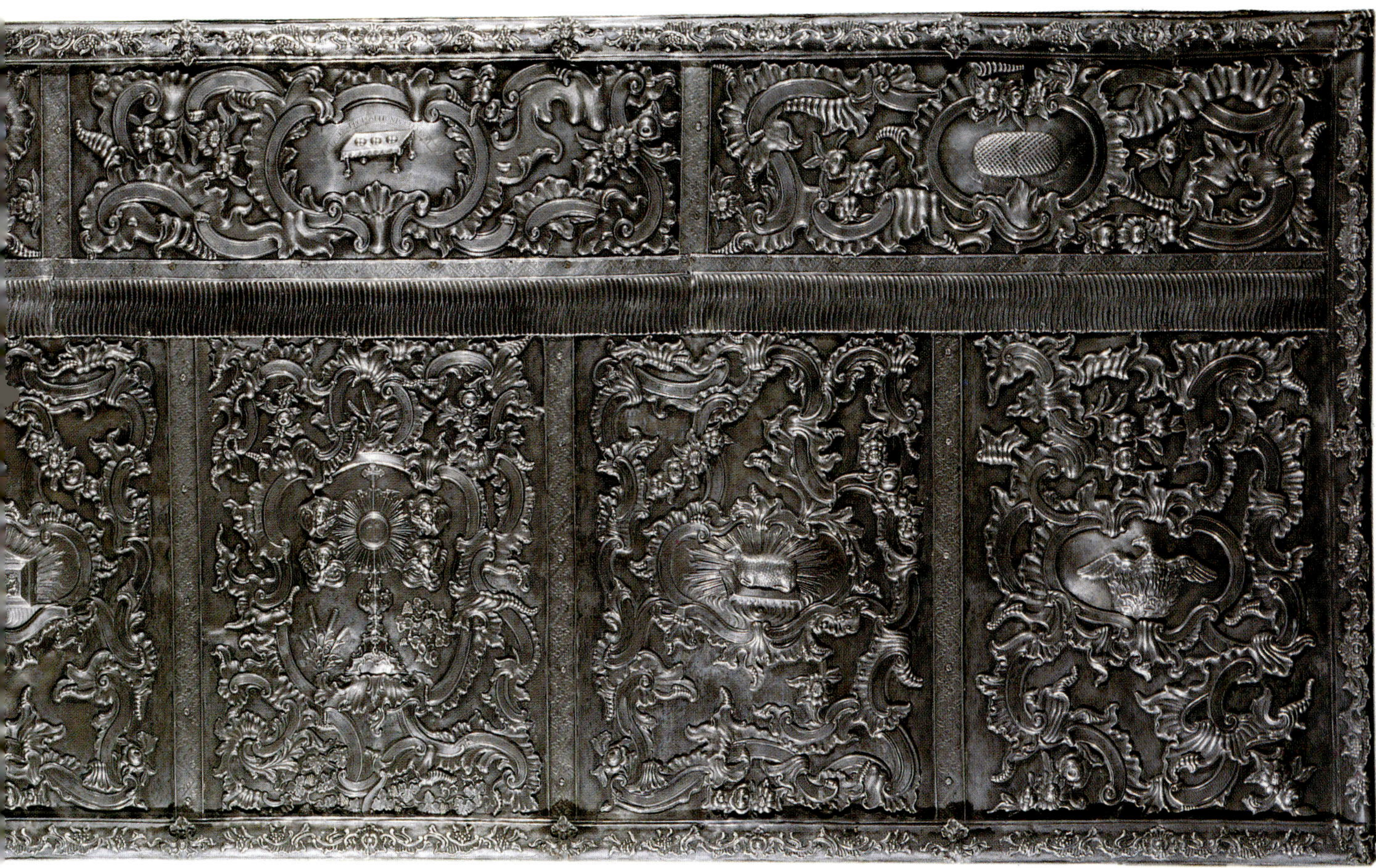

Conceição was established in the royal palace under the protection of the court.

During the days of great patriotic fervor of the restoration of the monarchy (1640), when Portugal asserted its independence from the royal house of Austria, Our Lady of the Immaculate Conception became inextricably linked with Portuguese history. When João, eighth duke of Bragança, was acclaimed first king of the fourth Portuguese dynasty, he offered a mass in her honor and named her patron of Portugal, which was subsequently endorsed by the parliament of 1645–1646. The royal crown was presented to the Virgin, and thenceforth Portuguese monarchs never again wore crowns.

The worship of the Immaculate Conception has continued throughout Portugal to the present day. Its most representative iconography evolved during the sixteenth and seventeenth centuries. The statues produced during the eighteenth century, including the exhibited work, adhere to Roman prototypes, combining them with elements from secular art including the swirling movement of the garments reflecting in part the experiments of modelers in clay.

The works of the Spanish painter Murillo were much admired throughout the Iberian Peninsula, and his type of Virgin, exalted by her beauty and purity, constituted another source of inspiration for the Cardais statue. The arrangement of the garments and the sculptural exuberance of the cloak are designed to create a presence with theatrical and emotive effect. The Virgin, with her hands clasped in a meditative pose and her expression beatific, furnishes a model of piety that the believer may contemplate with empathy. Heaven appears to be within the grasp of the praying Virgin and likewise of the faithful; her expression communicates hope and tranquility and summons spiritual commitment, quite unlike the less contemplative emotions associated with the rococo style.

Comparable images are *Saint Anne and the Virgin* (see Brussels 1991, IV.75), the *Virgin of the Rosary* (1753–1760) in the Mosteiro de Alcobaça, and *Our Lady of the Stairs* in the Igreja de São Domingos in Benfica.

95
Altar Frontal
Portuguese
3rd quarter 18th century
chased, repoussé, and engraved silver
98.5 x 230.5 x 8.5 (38½ x 89⅞ x 3⅜)
Marks: P, municipal assayer of Oporto, 1758–1768; MFG, unidentified silversmith's mark (Vidal and Almeida 1974, nos. 68, 2343)

Lamego Cathedral Chapter

Santos 1974; Aiorn 1984; Brandão 1984; Brussels 1991, II.5

The altar of Lamego cathedral was commissioned by Bishop Feliciano de Nossa

Senhora (b. 1741), who sponsored an extensive campaign of improvements in the church, especially the organ cases in the chancel (1754) and the magnificent choir stalls.

The silver frontal reflects a long-standing tradition of using a variety of materials to adorn the front of the altar, with a preference for textiles, tiles, wood carving, and, to a lesser extent, leather. During the eighteenth century, a style in tiled altar frontals developed in Portuguese India incorporating Oriental motifs. On these frontals the structure of the ornament is netlike, emphasizing the upper transversal bands and trimmed along the lower edge with a simulated tasseled fringe. Like those tiled frontals, the Lamego frontal is netlike in its composition and features the simulated tasseled fringe, although its decoration is in the rococo style, which was prevalent in secular goldsmith's works.

Within the frames created by markedly asymmetrical scrolls, there are eucharistic symbols such as the table on which the show bread (Exodus 25.30) is laid out. The design of the table shows that the craftsmen were under a clear English influence, but they gave it a Portuguese stamp in the solidity of the cabriole and in the ball and claw feet as they did in the monstrance at the center of the lower register of the altar frontal, which displays cherubs around the aureole and bunches of grapes and ears of wheat around the base.

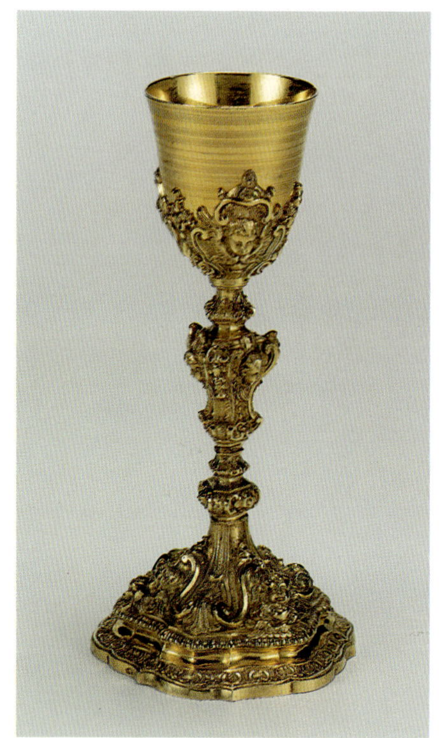

96
Chalice
Portuguese
2nd half 18th century
cast and chased gilded silver
26.7, diam. 8.5 (10½, 3⅓)
Marks: L, municipal assayer of Lisbon c. 1750–1770; M.R/G, Lisbon goldsmith, 2nd half 18th century, attrib. Manuel Ribeiro Gomes (Vidal and Almeida 1974, nos. 14, 483)
Museu Nacional de Arte Antiga, Lisbon, inv. 22

Couto 1927

This ornate and elegant chalice, with the base, central section, and cup profusely adorned with scrolls, foliage, shell motifs, and cherubs' heads, demonstrates the influence in Portugal of Italian religious objects in precious metal. Two virtually identical chalices without marks, originally from Paço São Vicente de Fora, are also found in the collection of the Museu Nacional de Arte Antiga, demonstrating that this model was well known in Portugal. No doubt there are also other versions of the same design.

97
Pyx
mid-18th century
Portuguese
repoussé, chased, and engraved gilded
silver, leather case
36 (14³⁄₁₆)

Lisbon Cathedral Chapter, inv. 767

Vasconcelos 1914–1915; Couto and Gonçalves 1960;
Brussels 1991, II.58

A pyx is a receptacle for the consecrated
host for the eucharist. In Portugal it is
called the sacrarium vessel and in Brazil
the *âmbula.* This particular form of pyx
became usual in the seventeenth century,
evolving out of the original round box
with a lid that, over time, acquired the
form of the eucharistic dove.

A pyx is in effect a lidded chalice, for
which reason it is also called a ciborium.
The pyx on display has a circular base
decorated with a band of oval shapes and
grooves in relief, and four female figures
symbolizing Faith, Hope, Charity, and
the Church. On the body of the pyx, angels hold instruments of the passion and
of the eucharist against a background of
rays emanating from clouds. On the lid,
twelve cherubs' heads and symbols of the
eucharist emerge beneath a finial in the
form of a cross.

Like so many other Portuguese religious objects, this pyx owes much to
Italian models, which it follows very
closely. Dom João V had decreed that
religious objects should adhere to accepted models as required by the church,
for which reason those executed in Portugal were based on types that had received official approval. In 1729 three silver pyxes were ordered from Rome,
while "a beautiful monstrance standing
four 'spans' high," also in gilded silver,
was commissioned the following year.

Documents indicate that in 1730, Frei
José Maria da Fonseca e Évora, the
king's agent in Rome, was urged to exer-
cise the utmost care in having the design
of the ciboria copied from those in the
following churches: "Saint John Lateran,
the chapel in which the Holy Sacrament
is always present, the chapel of the crucifix; Saint Peter's, the Gregorian
Madonna, the Santo Spirito, in Sassia"
and many others (letter dated 24 May).

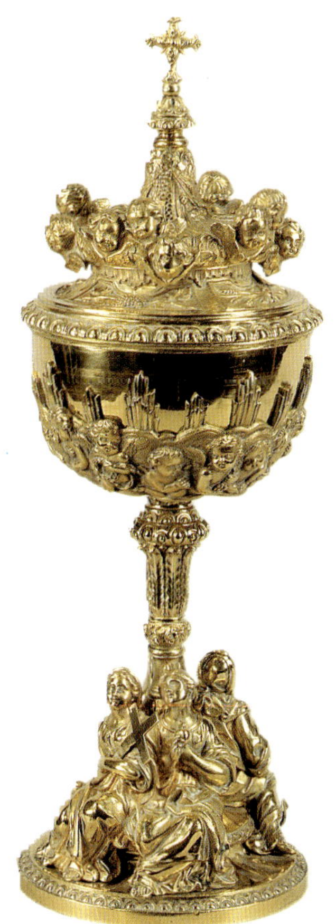

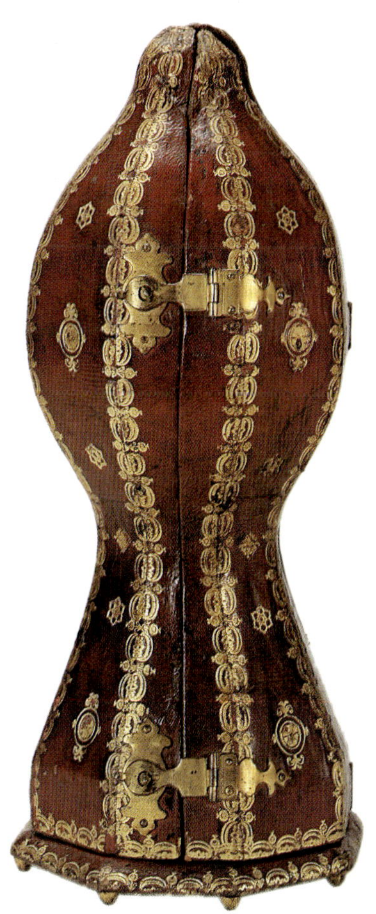

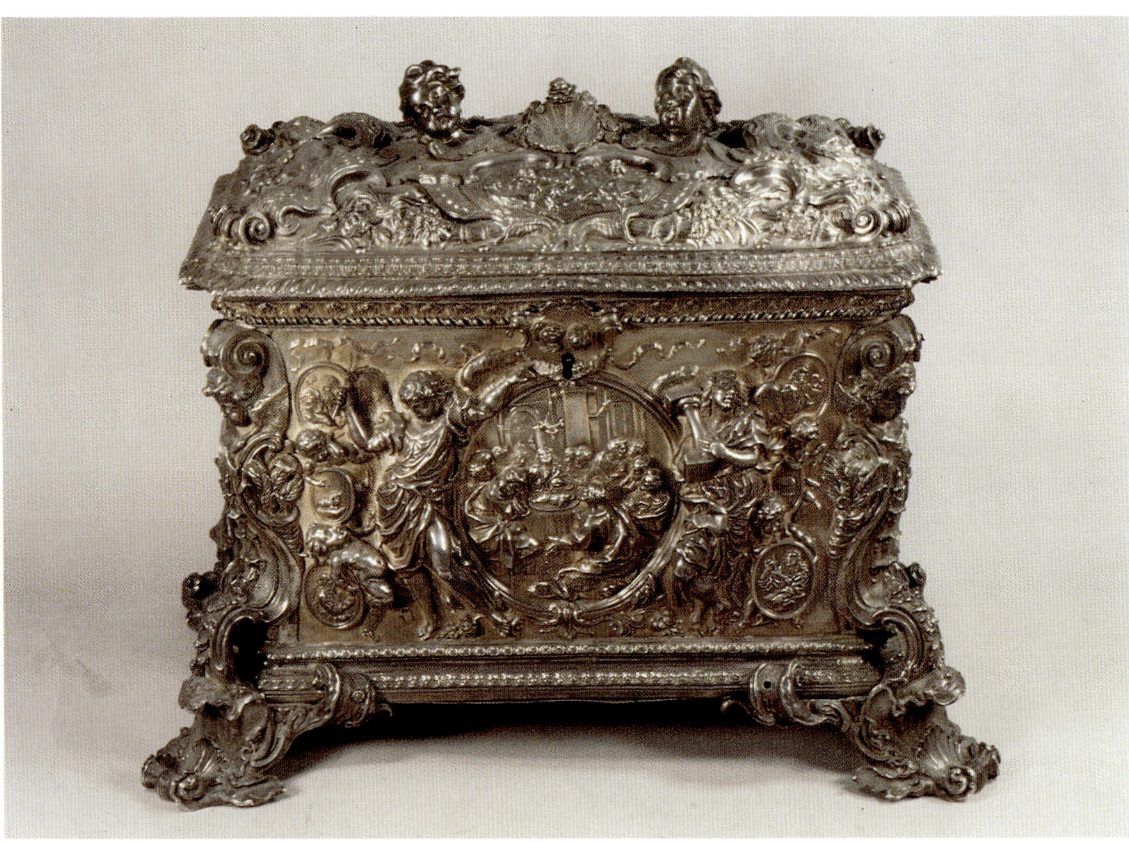

98
attributed to MANUEL ROQUE FERRÃO
Portuguese, active 2nd quarter 18th
century
Casket for the Holy Sacrament
1720–1750
repoussé, chased, and engraved silver
70.8 x 95 x 58.2 (27⅞ x 37⅞ x 22¹⁵⁄₁₆)
Marks: XI DINHEIROS, municipal assayer
of Lisbon, 1720–1750 (Vidal and Almeida
1974, no. 2384); F/MR, silversmith
Manuel Roque Ferrão

Lisbon Cathedral Chapter

Sequeira 1916-1934; Coelho 1950; Couto and
Gonçalves 1960–1962, fig. 118; Santos 1970;
Montevecchi and Rocca 1987; Brussels 1991, II.59

To commemorate Christ's passion and
death, mass is not celebrated and hence
the eucharist is not consecrated on Good
Friday. Therefore, hosts that have been
consecrated the day before must be kept
for communion on Good Friday. By tradition this was an observance of great
solemnity. A magnificent shrine was
erected and a precious opaque casket
equipped with a lock was placed on the
altar (or on a throne) to receive the eucharist. According to the Bishops' Ceremonial, the decoration of the chapel
should be conducive to contemplation,
for which reason monstrances, relics,
symbols of the Passion, black veils, and
images were not permitted (with the exception of worshiping angels). Perma-
nently lit candles stood on this altar, also
called the monument or sepulcher, and
the faithful worshiped until the end of
the ceremonies on Good Friday.

These caskets followed baroque forms
and decorative conventions, while certain
elements were incorporated from the vocabulary of furniture, apparent in this
piece in the splay of the feet required by
the exceptional size of this casket. The
Lisbon cathedral casket reflects the influence of the numerous Roman baroque
works in silver and gold that were in
Portugal, particularly those kept in the
patriarchal see, largely as a result of the
efforts of J. F. Ludovice to popularize
such traditions.

On the corners, the heads of angels
surmount the *S*-shaped brackets, which
resemble the legs of desks, decorated
with garlands and supported by cornucopias executed with masterly chasing.
The Last Supper is depicted on the
front, within a circular frame flanked by
two angels in the Roman style.

The stamp of the municipal assayer
reveals that this piece is datable between
1720 and 1750. It was probably executed
by the goldsmith Manuel Roque Ferrão,
who is known to be the author of a lamp
(Museu Nacional de Arte Antiga, inv.
361) bearing identical marks and originally belonging to the Paço de São
Vicente in Lisbon.

99
Crucifix
Indo-Portuguese
3rd quarter 18th century
ivory and carved, gilded, and painted
wood
204 x 108 x 28 (80⁵⁄₁₆ x 42¹⁄₈ x 11)

Lisbon Cathedral Chapter

Santos 1950; Silva 1966; Ferrão 1983;
Brussels 1991, IV.70

This exceptional representation of the
crucified Christ dates from the end of
the baroque period. The structure of the
long-limbed figure demonstrates a
markedly naturalistic treatment, creating
a sentimental and highly emotional effect. This dramatic quality is emphasized
by the unusually prominent veins and
the rivulets of blood, following an icono-
graphic tradition introduced during the
eleventh century wherein Christ was no
longer portrayed in his death agony but
as a corpse, with limp body and head
slumped forward.

Other details that contribute to the
impression of pathos are the curling hair
beneath the crown of thorns and the
curled beard, which is arranged to give a
remote expression to the features. The
tightly knotted loincloth enhances the
effect of suffering, while the aureole behind the cross lends an evangelical symbolism to the ensemble. As an ultimate
representation of the Passion, the figure
manages to combine the biblical inter-
pretations of mystics and theologians
with the creative imagination of painters
and sculptors, an amalgam frequently
encountered in art created in Portuguese
India during of the reign of Dom José I.
The arms of the walnut cross are tipped
with carved and gilded elements in the
rococo style. In high relief at the base of
the cross are the instruments of Christ's
Passion: two goads, tongs, hammer,
whip, ladder, sponge, and lance.

There are similar crucifixes in the
Museu Nacional Machado de Castro,
Museu Nacional de Arte Antiga, Museu
de Beja, and other Portuguese collections, while the national collection of
Brazil possesses notable examples of the
same type of work.

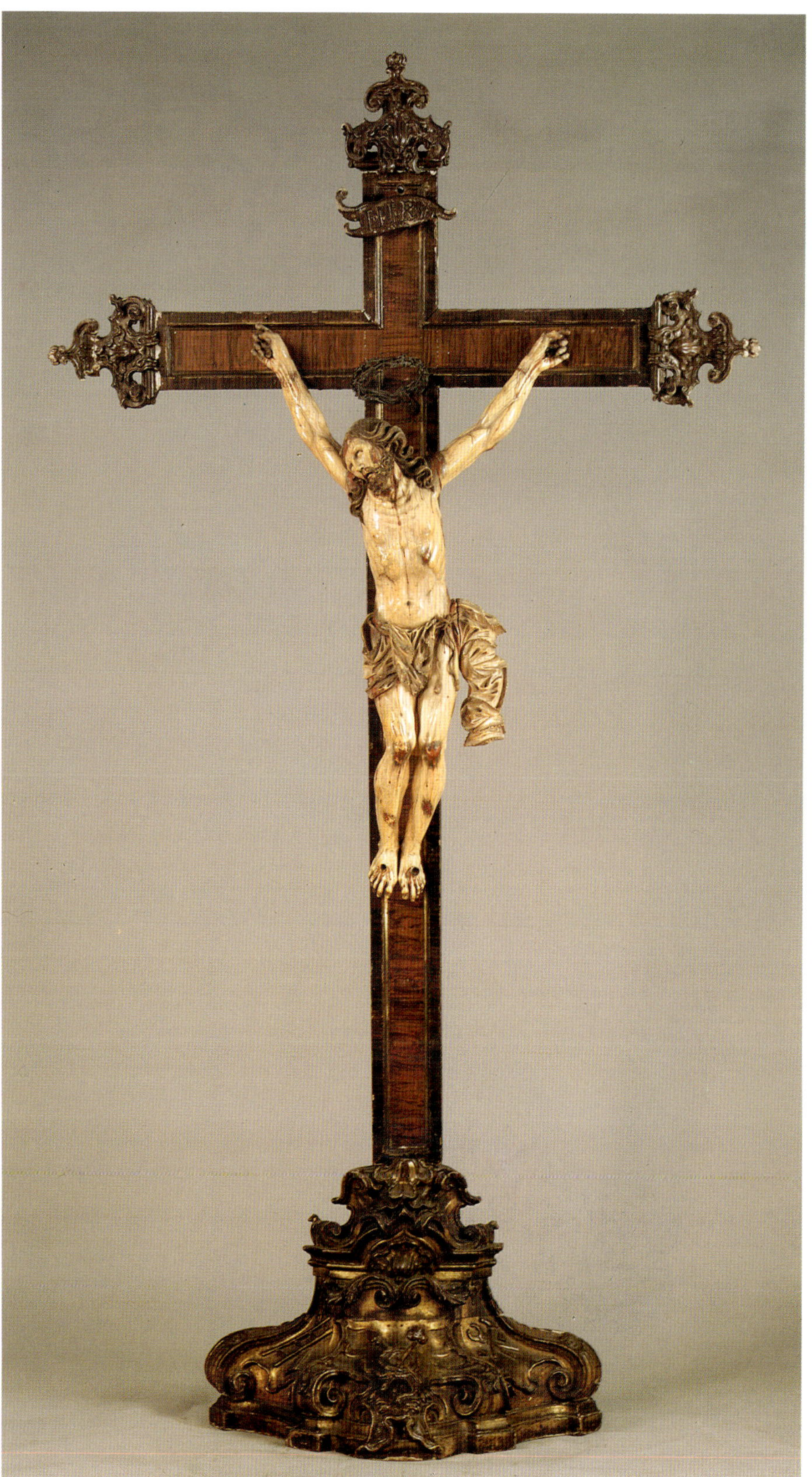

100–103
design attributed to
JOÃO FREDERICO LUDOVICE
1670–1752
ANTÓNIO NUNES NEVES, goldsmith
active 1717–1762
Altar Ensemble of Coimbra Cathedral
1st half 18th century
chased, repoussé, cast, and engraved
silver
Saint Catherine 77 (30⁵/₁₆); Saint
Anthony 76 (29¹⁵/₁₆); crucifix 202.2 (79⁵/₈);
candlesticks 103.5 (40⁹/₁₆)
Marks: L, municipal assayer of Lisbon,
1720–1750; AN, silversmith António
Nunes Neves

*Museu Nacional Machado de Castro,
Coimbra, figures of saints invs. 1949/E 301,
2995/E 302; Coimbra Cathedral Chapter,
crucifix and candlesticks*

Sousa Viterbo 1900; Couto and Gonçalves 1960;
Carvalho 1960–1962; Nogueira Gonçalves 1984;
Brussels 1991, II.70

The silver altar ensemble of the old
cathedral of Coimbra, one of the most
beautiful of its kind, was produced, like
many other of these precious sets, during
the period of Dom João V. It miracu-
lously escaped both the earthquake of
1755 and pillage by Napoleon's troops.
The set was executed at some point in
the period 1717–1741. António Nogueira
Gonçalves has studied these items and
attributed them to the famous German
silversmith and architect João Frederico
Ludovice.

Professor Nogueira Gonçalves' study
and the inventory of the city of Coimbra,
published by the Portuguese national
academy of fine arts, indicate that in 1742
this set consisted of the following pieces:
"Roman cross with the image of Christ
crucified with aureole in proportion," "six
tall, Roman-style candlesticks all identi-

cal, worked with foliage and flowers in
relief, bearing the silver assayer's marks
on their bases which are identical to the
hollow base of the cross," "six half-length
figures of saints standing on pedestals
with their identifying emblems, the
pedestals adorned with angels in relief,
and other elements mounted with
screws." "The total weight of these figures with their pedestals is five hundred
and eighteen marks, six ounces and
seven eighths." All of these pieces have
survived; the remaining statues, which
are kept in the new cathedral of Coimbra, represent saints Peter, Paul, Lucy,
and Francis.

The half-length figures of saints on
their pedestals are clearly identifiable by
their attributes and emblems. With the
exception of the statues, the bases of all
the items are marked with an L sur-

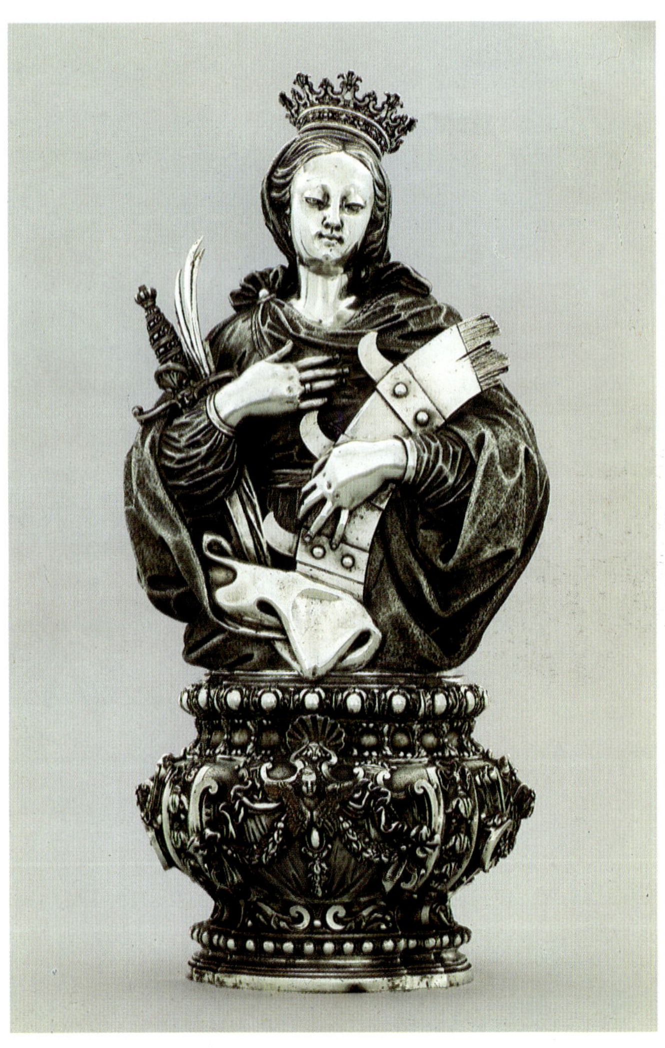

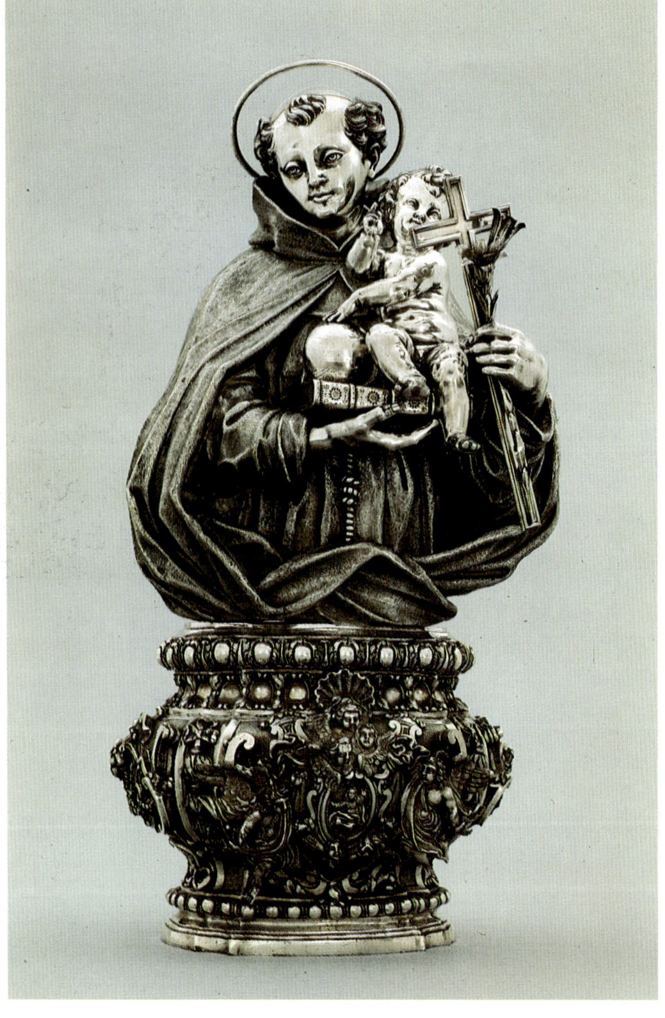

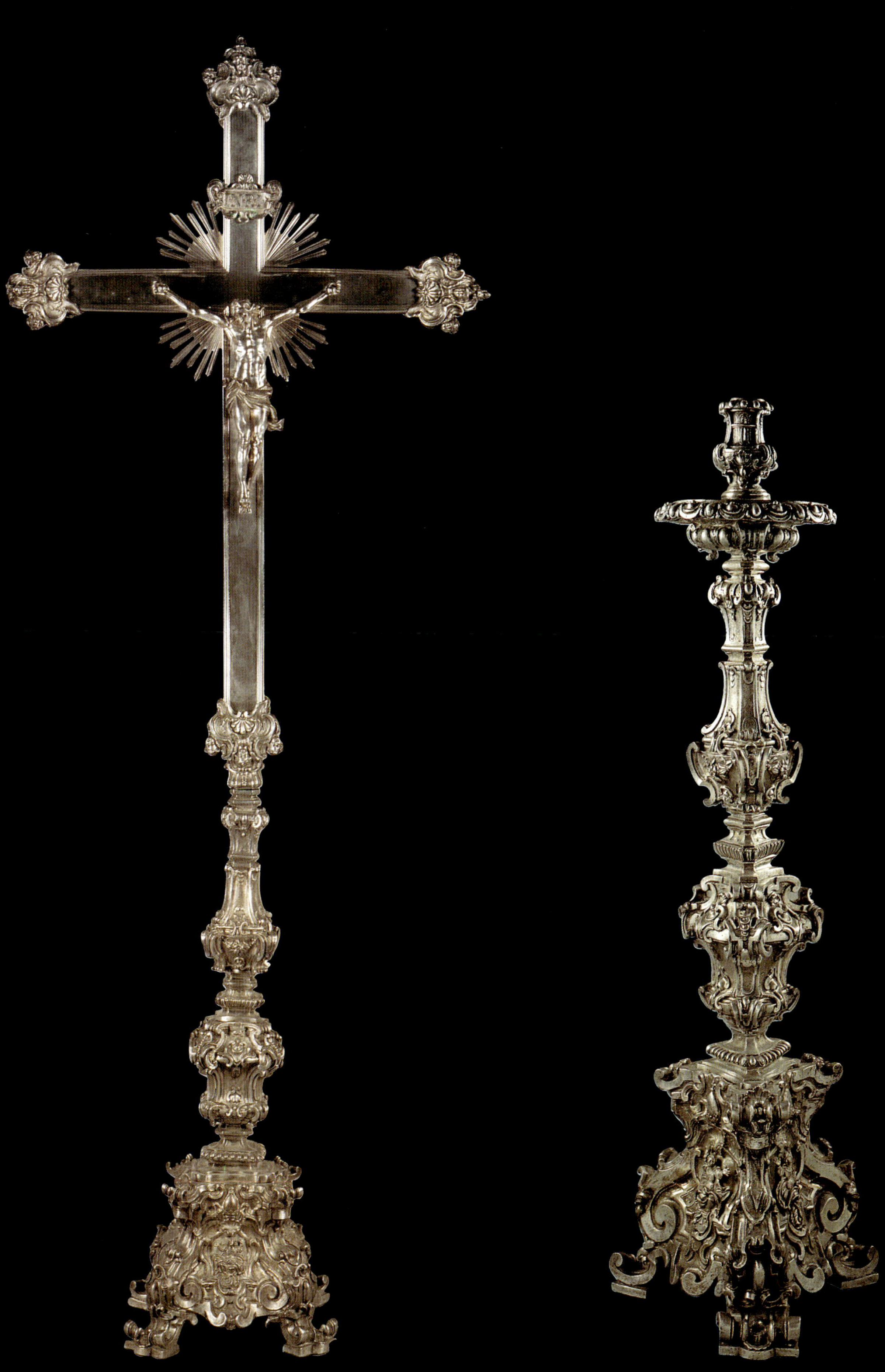

mounted by a crown, indicating that they were produced in Lisbon during the first half of the eighteenth century. The cross, the candlesticks, and the pedestals, which are sculpted with delicate and graceful motifs, bear the mark "A.N.," which surely refers to the famous goldsmith António Nunes Neves, who, in about 1762, restored some of the items belonging to the altar set of the patriarchal church in Lisbon that were damaged in the earthquake. The pedestals for the figures are decorated in low relief with a depiction of the Assumption of the Virgin enclosed in a medallion. The Virgin is carried to heaven with her arms outstretched and surrounded by a host of cherubs and seraphim, the composition surmounted by a shell. This motif, which is repeated on the base of the candlesticks, may allude to the Assumption of the Virgin represented in the central section of the reredos in the chancel of the old cathedral of Coimbra.

It is apparent that the sculpted figures —the saints, the Christ on the crucifix, and the graceful figural decoration of the pedestals, including the Virgin surrounded by angels—were initially modeled in clay or perhaps carved in wood by an outstanding artist. As Nogueira Gonçalves pointed out, the period 1717–1725 corresponds exactly to the restoration of arts under Dom João V, and we should seek the identity of this sculptor among those active during these years. He was likely to be a goldsmith as well. As the author noted: "the sculptures are in the Italian style and so, since it is unlikely that they were commissioned abroad, it would appear probable that they were executed in Portugal by a foreign artist residing here."

The Jesuits of the church of Santo Antão in Lisbon, for whom Ludovice designed a monstrance, now lost, in 1701, had no doubt informed the king of Ludovice's fame, which preceded him from Rome, and pointed to his talent as demonstrated by his magnificent monstrance. This is probably why he was first invited to the royal palace as a goldsmith and engraver rather than as an architect. Ludovice's work in Santo Antão and possibly in the royal palace, as well as his patronage by the German nobility and the Society of Jesus, put the goldsmith in an ideal position to demonstrate his talents to the Portuguese clergy and court, and particularly to attract the attention of the young Dom João V, who was always eager for novelty.

While the Coimbra altar set and that of the chapel of Saint John the Baptist in São Roque in Lisbon (see cat. 106) are the most lavish ensembles from the period of Dom João V that have survived, documents record two other splendid sets, both imported from Italy and both since destroyed, that once adorned the patriarchal church in Lisbon. As we are told by the contemporary historian Batista de Castro, the king spared no expense in acquiring liturgical objects, ordering and commissioning items from all over the world to adorn Portugal's churches regardless of cost. Prominent among these objects were the nine sumptuous candlesticks and the exquisite and unusual cross that he commissioned from Florence and Rome in 1732, designed and executed by Antonio Arrighi (see cat. 104) in Rome. "And his incomparable liberality was not satisfied with this splendor . . . jewels of incalculable worth, the finest settings, items in gold and silver, were showered on the *sé patriarcal* [seat of the patriarch], to ensure that religious ceremonies were celebrated with the greatest possible magnificence. The cross and candlesticks are so unique that they were intended to adorn the altar of the chancel only on royal occasions such as weddings, baptisms, acclamations of new monarchs, and any other occasion ordained by the king" (Castro 1762–1763).

Thus another altar set had to be ordered from Rome for daily use. On 3 May 1735, José Correia de Abreu wrote to Rome to Frei José Correia da Fonseca e Évora: "do not forget to proceed with the task that has been entrusted to you concerning the silver statues and busts." The "book of receipts and payments from petty cash of the Holy Church of Lisbon beginning January 1762" in the archives of Lisbon cathedral, together with the "Inventory of all the precious Jewels, Items in Gold, Silver Gilt, and Silver belonging to the Holy Church of Lisbon on August 1, 1762, kept by Father Mateus Simoens, Treasurer of this Holy Church," allow us to reconstruct the later history of this second altar set. (The discovery of these documents was made with the kind assistance of Canon João de Castro and Father Botoreu.)

The earthquake of 1755 evidently caused extensive and virtually irreparable damage to this magnificent ensemble, which came from Rome and consisted of statues of the Apostles, together with figures of the Virgin and Saint Joseph, all on pedestals and all in silver. The carver José de Almeida was summoned, and from 1762 to 1765 he reconstructed the figures and pedestals in wood. Expenses relating to this task appear in existing records.

Subsequently, numerous receipts are made out to the master silversmith Domingos Fernandes, who from 1762 to 1766 cast and engraved all the silver statues as well as an additional two pedestals for the Virgin and Saint Joseph and those for saints Andrew and James. The work on the pedestals for the remaining saints was distributed among the following silversmiths: Luís dos Reis, José da Fonseca, António Nunes Raposo, Crispim dos Santos who executed two pedestals, Luís José de Almeida and, finally, António Nunes Neves, who executed the pedestals for saints Peter and Matthew, and, in 1762, made a "repair and addition to Saint Peter, giving him a new arm and leg." This is surely the goldsmith whose initials "A.N." appear on the altar ensembles of Coimbra and Évora cathedrals.

In 1769 this ill-fated altar ensemble was damaged again, this time in a fire. It was subsequently moved to several other churches in Lisbon before disappearing completely during the Napoleonic invasions.

104

ANTONIO II ARRIGHI
Italian
1687–1776
Bishop's Crozier
c. 1740–1760
chased and gilded silver
32.5 x 16 (12¹³⁄₁₆ x 6⁵⁄₁₆)
Marks: Lion's claw with sphere (1734–
1744); quartered shield with arms of
Dom Frei António de Sousa

*Museu Nacional de Soares dos Reis, Oporto,
inv. 32*

MNSR 1942, no. 4; Valente 1948; Guerra n.d.;
Carvalho 1962, 2:416; Lopes 1971; Bulgari 1980;
Brussels 1991, II.50

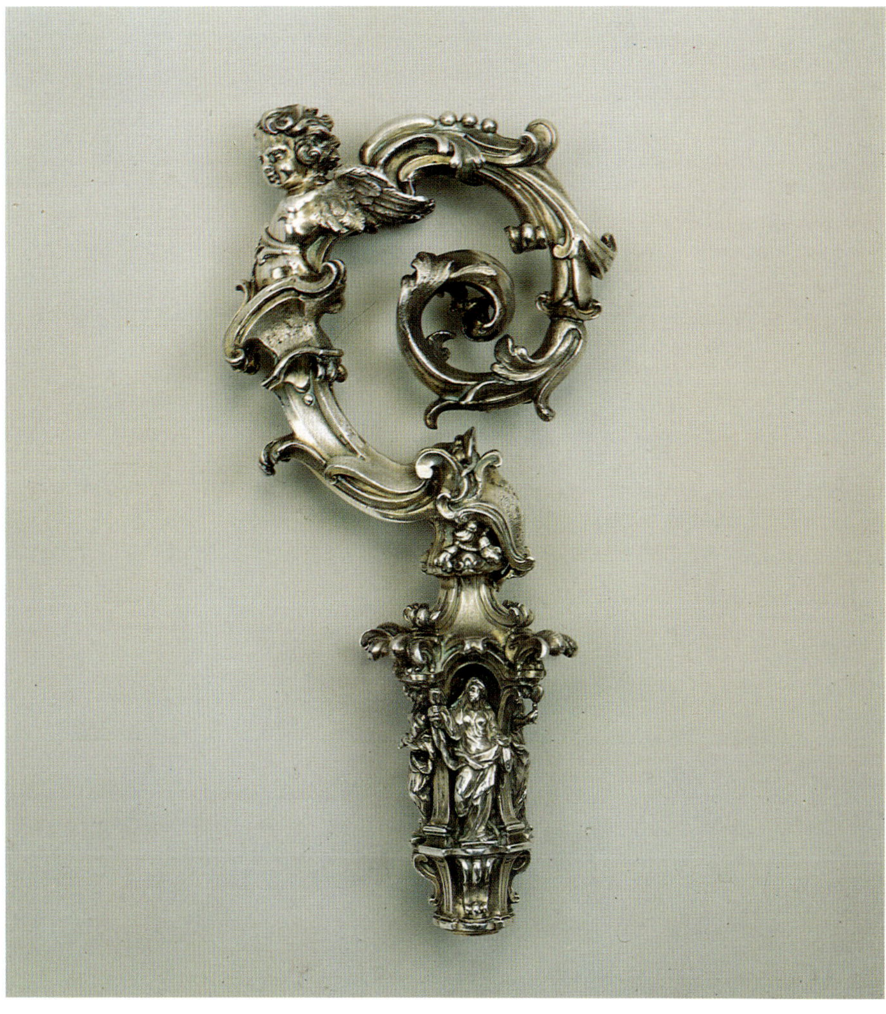

This crozier follows the conventional
form of the coiled episcopal staff, but its
exuberant style distinguishes it from its
prototypes, recalling instead the extravagant designs typical of certain medieval
and, more particularly, Roman examples.
The evocative asymmetry of the crozier's
sweeping curve and the floral motifs reflect the assimilation of rococo style into
Roman art, yet the piece nevertheless remains faithful to the baroque vocabulary
of the age of Bernini, a heritage that is
also evoked by the delicate putto.

The crozier has been definitively attributed to Antonio II Arrighi, the celebrated Roman goldsmith, thanks to an
accurate reading of the goldsmith's
stamp. Nonetheless, some questions remain with regard to the coat of arms that
is engraved within a small cartouche located on the lower curve of the crozier.
The armorial device is that of the bishop
of Oporto, Dom Frei António de Sousa
(1690–1766), named to that position by
Pope Benedict XIV in 1756. It is, however, superimposed over another device
that has been effaced. This bishop was
the son of the second marquês de
Távora, Dom António Luís de Távora.
That family was condemned in 1759 for
having been implicated in the assassination attempt against Dom José I, and
thus was prohibited from bearing this
name and coat of arms. This suggests
that the first set of engraved arms were

those of the disgraced Távora family.
Arrighi's authorship suggests another
possibility, that the crozier was ordered
by Dom Frei José Maria de Fonseca e
Évora, who died when he was bishop of
Oporto in 1752, and that it originally bore
his arms. He had accepted the invitation
of Dom João V in 1739 to govern the
diocese of the northern capital. His entry
into Oporto was a solemn affair, full of
pomp. He liked the ostentation of liturgical objects from Rome and he was well
acquainted with such pieces, having
served as the king's agent in Rome in assembling the extraordinary collection of
religious works that was acquired for the
Portuguese court during his thirty years
in residence there. One of the altar sets
he obtained for the patriarchal church in
Lisbon was by Arrighi (1732); these objects disappeared in the earthquake of
1755. That commission had been the re-

sult of contact between Fonseca e Évora
and Arrighi, and it may be that, some
years later, the bishop placed a personal
order with the same goldsmith.

105
attributed to

João Frederico Ludovice
1670–1752
Bemposta Monstrance
c. 1740–1750
gilded, chased, and engraved silver; gold,
diamonds, rubies, sapphires, amethysts,
topazes, and other gems
97 (38³⁄₁₆)

*Museu Nacional de Arte Antiga,
Lisbon, inv. 1 our*

Vasconcelos 1914–1915; Caldeira Pires 1925;
Estevens 1944; Couto 1951; Moita 1954; Couto and
Gonçalves 1960–1962; Smith 1968; Santos 1970;
MNAA 1975; Bulgari 1980, 2:62; D'Orey 1988.1, 33;
Teixeira 1989; Pedro 1989; Brussels 1991, II.57

The earliest written reference to the
Bemposta monstrance is probably that in
the last will and testament of Dom
Pedro III, who died 25 May 1786 (ANTT
drawer 16, packet 3, no. 1). In it he left
the "Quinta de Queluz" to his son, the
future Dom João VI, and urged him "to
be meticulous in the religious obser-
vances offered to God in the chapel of
Bemposta, to which I leave my magnificent monstrance," thereby requiring that
it remain in the Casa do Infantado. This
identification is supported by documents
in the historical archives of the ministry
of finance (*Casa Real*, part 1, cx. 273).
One of these, an inventory entitled *Relação das Pratas e Joyas que vão da Real
Capella da Bemposta, por ordem de Sua
Magestade,* includes two altar sets, one
for the high altar and the other for the
altar of the Holy Sacrament, while the
last item on the list is an "elaborate monstrance" (Estevens 1944, part 1, doc. DL).
The fact that this list was found among
documents concerning Queluz suggests
that these items were to be sent there.

There is controversy about the identity of the author of the monstrance, but
it is usually attributed, with reservations,
to João Frederico Ludovice, the German-born Italian-trained goldsmith and
architect who dominated the Portuguese
building projects of his day and was a
prominent member of Portugal's artistic
community during the almost fifty years
of his professional activity there.

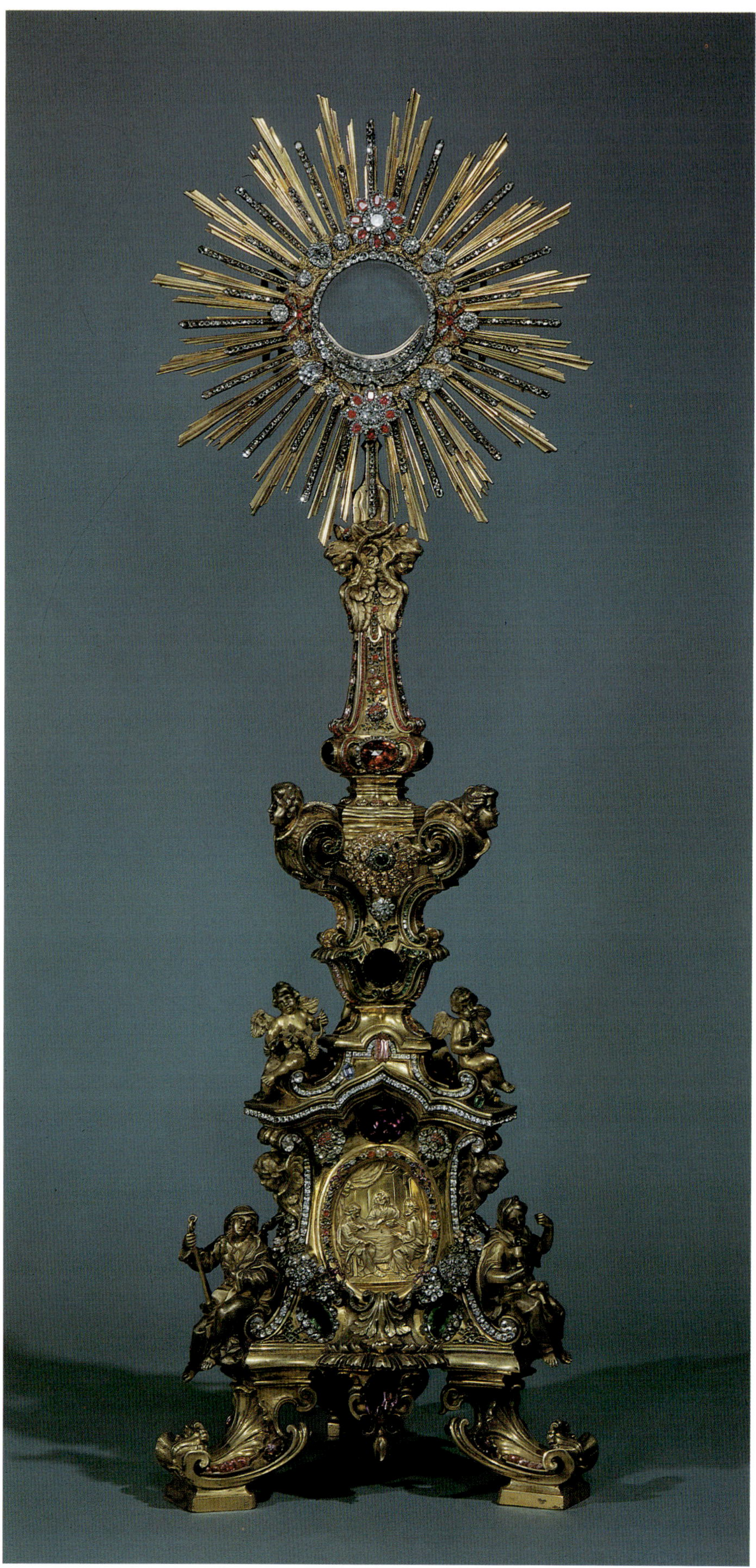

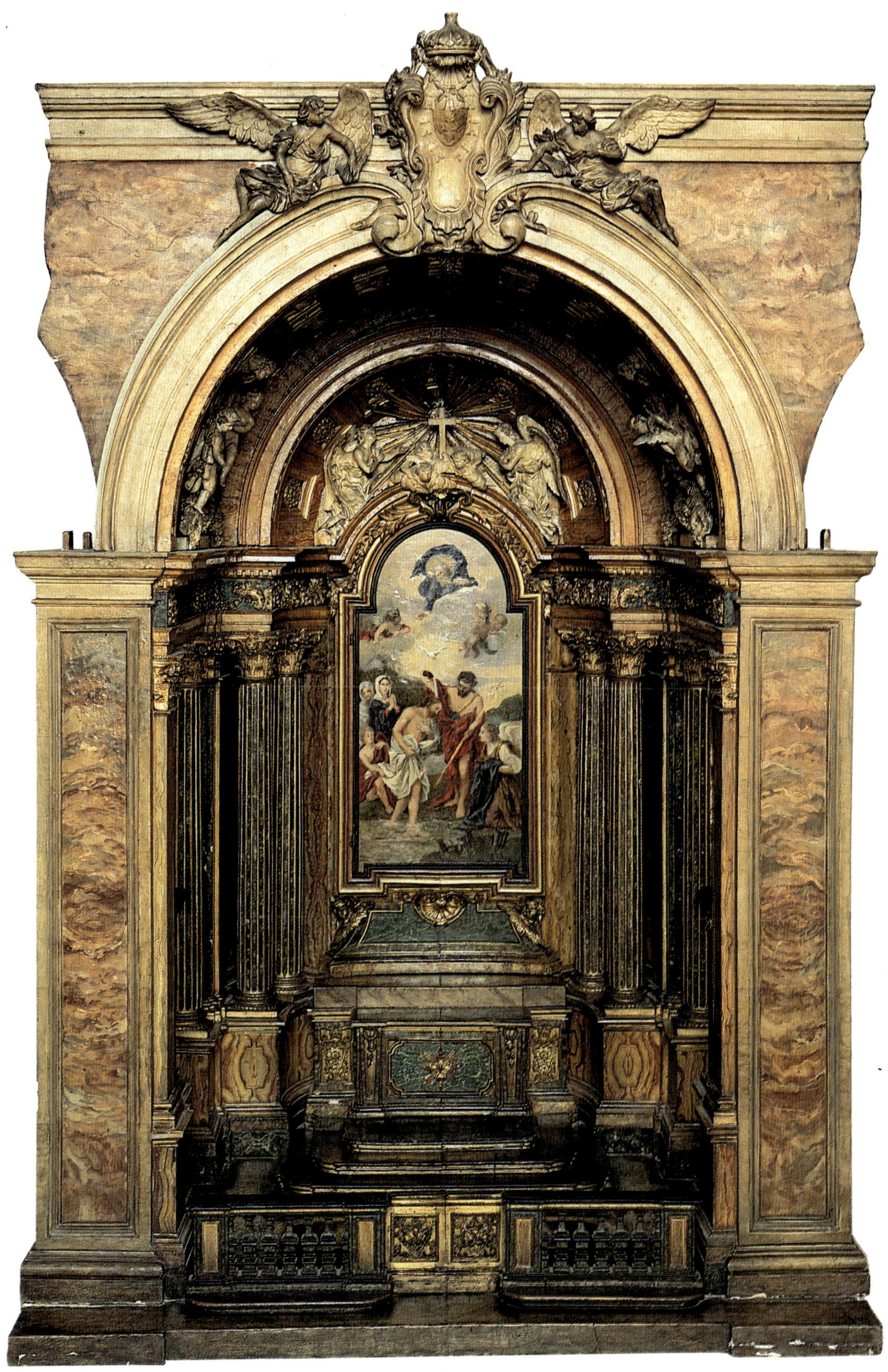

106

It is known that Ludovice was intent on winning the commission to create the altar ensemble for the high altar of Évora cathedral, just as he had been asked to submit designs for the candlesticks and crucifixes of the altar of the Oporto cathedral. It is assumed that he made sketches for the monumental altar set of Coimbra cathedral (cats. 100–103). The only commission he failed to win was that of the patriarchal church, which commissioned two altar ensembles, one from Antonio Arrighi and the other from Thomas Germain. However, Ludovice would not have ventured to request this commission outright at the time when he was already heavily engaged in the construction work at Mafra.

Ludovice was, nonetheless, the goldsmith in Portugal best equipped to execute a Roman-style work, since it would appear that chasing was his specialty, and his experience in Rome gave him an advantage over local goldsmiths. The king's explicit protection and Ludovice's favor with the queen, Maria Ana of Austria, no doubt influenced Príncipe Francisco (1671–1743) who, disposing of the considerable revenues of the Casa do Infantado, commissioned Ludovice to execute this magnificent monstrance. Although unsigned, a design for a monstrance in the Gabinete de Estampas of the Museu Nacional de Arte Antiga (inv. 473), which appears to be in Ludovice's hand, is almost slavishly faithful to Roman prototypes. His authorship of this drawing is confirmed by other signed sheets that closely resemble the sketches of the sacring tablet in Évora cathedral.

In its structure, the Bemposta monstrance resembles a four-sided candlestick base supporting powerful sculptural elements. The lower section represents Faith, Hope, and Charity, and at the foot of the shaft three cherubs hold symbols of the eucharist. The three oval medallions depict biblical themes: the Supper at Emmaus, a bunch of grapes symbolizing the blood of Christ, and Christ in the Garden of Gethsemane.

106

GIUSEPPE PALMS
Italian, active mid-18th century
**Model of the Chapel of
Saint John the Baptist**
1742–1744
painted and gilded walnut and painted copper
140 x 93 x 86 (55⅛ x 36⅝ x 33⅞)

Museu de São Roque, Santa Casa da Misericórdia, Lisbon, inv. 1 our

Sousa Viterbo 1900; Smith 1936; Castro 1939; Bulgari 1980; Rocca, Borghini, and Ferraris 1990; Rodrigues 1988; Brussels 1991, II.66

In this project for a sumptuous chapel in the church of São Roque in Lisbon, in which Dom João V "the Magnanimous" was as closely involved as he had been in the construction of Mafra, the king gave free rein to his preference for things Roman when he entrusted the commission to Luigi Vanvitelli (1700–1773), a young architect working in the Eternal City, and Nicola Salvi (1697–1751). Vanvitelli was known for his adherence to classicism and had executed the first neo-Palladian interiors by 1732 in the church of San Domenico in Mantua. The chapel of Saint John the Baptist was executed in Rome and then transported to and reassembled in Lisbon. Its marbles, lapis-lazuli, and bronzes rivaled those of the church of the Gesù in Rome, the headquarters of the Jesuit order, and in fact was intended to adorn one of the side chapels in the Jesuit church in Lisbon.

Padre J. B. Carbone's correspondence indicates that this influential Neapolitan Jesuit, well read in astronomy and mathematics, was appointed by Dom João V to monitor the progress of the commission from Lisbon. In Rome the Portuguese ambassador, Manuel Pereira de Sampaio, was also active. João Frederico Ludovice, in his capacity as the senior architect at court, was requested to give his technical opinion of the architectural merits of the project, leading to one of the most heated artistic controversies of the eighteenth century. Ludovice's intransigence, rooted as he was in baroque orthodoxy, caused him to be quite unprepared to tolerate Vanvitelli's updating of this style.

The model differs in only two details from the chapel that was eventually assembled in São Roque, first in the twin spiral columns that link the balusters to the pillars, and second in the mosaics that replaced the paintings by Agostino Masucci. This model was executed by the woodworker Giuseppe Palms who created the structure, while G. Focchetti and G. Voyet executed the marbling and Gennaro Nicoletti painted the miniatures of the paintings for the altar and side elevations.

The chapel was consecrated in Rome in 1744 by Pope Benedict XIV and transported to Lisbon where it was reassembled in the church of São Roque. Dom João V died shortly before the completion of the work on the chapel in 1750 and was therefore not present at its consecration ceremony. This magnificent event was enhanced by fabulous vestments (cat. 108) and sumptuous religious objects in gold and gilded silver belonging to the altar set (cat. 107), one of the most lavish in the world, which had been ordered in Rome for use in the chapel.

107
GIUSEPPE GAGLIARDI
Italian, 1697–1749
Torchère
1744–1749
gilded silver on a base of gilded bronze
285 (112³⁄₁₆)
Insc.: JOSEPH GAGLIARDI ROMANUS
INVENTOR FU(N)DIT ET FECIT
Marks: Umbrella and crossed keys;
Gagliardi (two "G"s separated by
a sun)

*Museu de São Roque, Santa Casa da
Misericórdia, Lisbon*

Ajuda MSS. 49-VIII-6, fols. 203, 254; 49-VIII-28,
f. 24v; 49-VIII-35, f. 82; 49-VIII-21, f. 133; Chracas
1749, no. 5025, 4.10.1749, p. L4; ASV, Sacra Rota,
Iura diversa, 493, 1756; Lavagnino 1940, 113; Bulgari
1958, 480–481; Lipinsky 1961, 74–78; Malory 1974,
172; Hernmarck 1977, 337; Rodrigues 1988, 83–101;
Quieto 1988, 28; Brussels 1991, II.67

This torchère is one of a pair. The triangular base of each is borne by six kneel-
ing near-naked figures, and within
niches flanked by cherub heads are
seated (on the one exhibited here) saints
Jerome, Thomas Aquinas, and Ambrose,
and (on the other) saints Gregory,
Bonaventura, and Augustine. Six
cherubs kneel on the elaborately molded
top of each base, flanking the royal Portuguese coat of arms and supporting a
triangular-sectioned knop, surmounted
by three pairs of cherub heads and decorated in high relief with three pairs of
putti holding flowers. The baluster above
is of six faces, and three cherubs seem
about to fly from its summit, below the
drip pan and candle holder. Apart from
the figures, the whole is richly ornamented with swags of flowers and
berries, masks, cartouches, shells, and a
variety of moldings and is variously bur-
nished and punched. Each stands upon a
gilded bronze base decorated with laurel
leaves, acanthus leaves at the corners,
and an empty cartouche in the center of
each of the three sides.

In March 1744 these two grandiose
torchères were ordered for the chapel of
Saint John the Baptist to be installed in

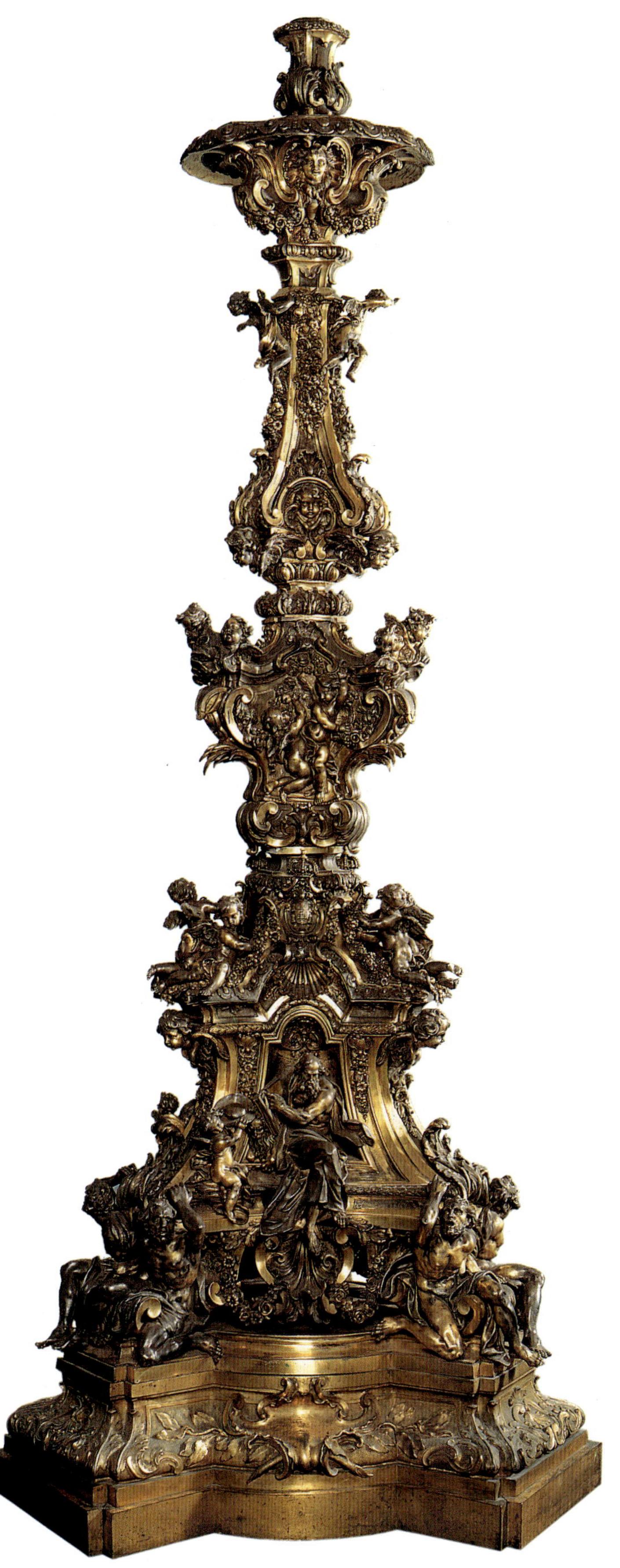

São Roque in Lisbon. On January 1745 Sampaio sent the drawings for approval, and payments began on 30 July 1745. By 1748 only one was in a fit state to be exhibited in the Palazzo Capponi, but it was not yet gilded, and some of the putti had had to be added in silvered wax; the other was even less advanced. At this stage it was judged that, while the drawing and the model of a single face had appeared satisfactory, substantial changes (even to those parts already finished) and additions would be required, Sampaio apparently assuring the artists involved that "non badava alla spesa, purche l'opera fose riuscita bene" (the cost should not be a cause for concern provided that the work turns out well). By 1749 they were finished and stamped by Paolo Alexandri and Bernardo Birelli, and, in October, together with the other goldsmiths' work for the chapel, they were blessed by Benedict XIV. The description of the torchères on this occasion by Chracas merits quotation: "Due nobilissimi Torcieri di argento dorato di altezzi pal. 12 in circa, non compresovi il zoccolo (…), lavorati con grand'artirizio, e di finissimo gusto. Ognuno di essi sostenuto nel suo piede da sei figure di rilievo, et è ornato di vari Angeli, palme e fiori, oltre delle sue Cornici, le quali nella parte inferiore lasciano l'intervallo a tre Statue de'Dottori di S. Chiesa nelle sue Nicchie. Tutte dette eccellenti Opere lavorate con disegno del celebre Gio. Batt. Maini Scultore, furono principiate dal fu Giuseppe Gagliardi Argentiere, e terminate dal Sig. Leandro suo Figliuolo con tutta perfezione tal che ne ha riportato molto applauso" (Two very noble gilded silver torchères approximately twelve palms high not including the base crafted with great skill and of a highly refined taste. Each of them is supported by feet that have six figures in relief and [is] decorated with a variety of angels, palms, and flowers, in addition to cornices, and these decorations leave space in the lower part for three statues of the Doctors of the Holy Church in niches. All these excellent works made on the designs of the famous sculptor Giovanni

Battista Maini were begun by the late silversmith Giuseppe Gagliardi and completed by his son Leandro with a total perfection that has brought them much praise [Quieto 1988, 28]).

The torchères were appraised three times, first in May 1749 after the death of Giuseppe Gagliardi (by G. B. Maini and C. Giardoni), and again on 27 September (by F. Juvarra, G. B. Maini, C. Giardoni, and M. Pirolli) after they had been completed in their more elaborate form by Gagliardi's son Leandro. In 1750, when they had been loaded aboard ship at Civitavecchia, Padre Cabral, S.J., who had taken over control after the death of Sampaio, had them appraised again by F. Tofani, G. Burroni, A. Vendetti, and S. Miglie, without informing the Gagliardi heirs and without any expert acting on their behalf; on this occasion they were valued at a substantially lower sum, s.39156.27 as against s.61726.55.

This lowering of the value led to a lawsuit by Gagliardi's heirs against those of Sampaio, eventually won by the Gagliardi family due to the irregularity of the final valuation and the fact that Matteo Pirolli, who had made a statement claiming that he had overvalued them, admitted that he had been compelled to do so by the threat that he would not be paid for his own work for the chapel.

The depositions provide fascinating information on the work done by the assistants in Gagliardi's workshop: that G. Francisi had been largely responsible for the chasing, though, as he stated, "non hò mai cisellato alcun pezzo, senza che prima ne approvasse la pelle (…) Gagliardi, il quale perciò voleva, che facessi prima più Mostre, frà quali sceglieva egli quela, che più gli gradiva" (I never chiseled a single piece without Gagliardi first approving the surface… but he always wanted me to make several models from which he would choose the one he liked best), and that Carlo and Pietro Pacilli had made the drawing of the torchères "secondo le precise direzioni, gusto, e volonta" (following the precise directions, taste, and wish) of

Gagliardi, as well as many of the models for the additions. We also learn that the work was done in great haste, the artists having to work through the night and (with papal dispensation) on feast days, especially toward the end when the torchères had to be ready for the papal blessing, and so that, as well as paying for the larger number of workmen required, Gagliardi had to pay extra for this overtime.

They also provide evidence that, as Chracas believed, the design was, at least in part, due to Giovanni Battista Maini. That he was responsible for the parts changed and added after 1748 is attested to by the Pacilli, who described them as "fatti dal Sig. Giambattista Maini gia mro di me Pietro." But there is also a feature of the original design to which this same deposition by the Pacilli draws attention, with the insistence that the torchères are infinitely richer than the candlesticks by Spinazzi (those of the set known as the *muta nobile*), and the claim that the designs for those had not been seen until both were completed and shown together in 1749; the necessity for such a declaration becomes evident when one compares the drawing with the *muta nobile*, for it is evident that the base and knop of those candlesticks correspond almost exactly to the original drawing for the torchères. This drawing is certainly not by Maini, and the *muta nobile* candlesticks are said to have been designed by Spinazzi himself, yet their similarity demands an explanation, the most probable being that (despite the Pacillis' claim to have made the drawing according to the instructions of Gagliardi) both depend on a sketch provided by a third artist. That this artist was Giovanni Battista Maini becomes the more likely when one recalls that he was highly regarded by the authorities in Lisbon (Sousa Viterbo, doc. VI, 115). Finally, Maini himself, giving evidence regarding a conversation with Tofani after the third appraisal, said that Tofani assured him that the work was good, "e che veramente se conosceva che era stato fatto coll'assistenza mia" (and that he knew that the work had really been done with my assistance); although this conversation concerned the *Immacolata* (unquestionably made on Maini's designs) as well as the torchères, it seems from the context that this judgment applied to both. It is sufficient to look at the figures of the Doctors of the Church to concur. As for the Atlantes below, clearly inspired by Algardi's Titans below the fire dog of Jupiter (casts of which were owned by Maini's pupil Innocenzo Spinazzi, together with a number of models by Maini), they have a sculptural power that, as has always been recognized, would be wholly exceptional in the unaided work of a silversmith; if there are no comparable nudes among Maini's certain works, these do display a marked interest in the sculpture of the preceding century.

There are morphological similarities between these specifically sculptural details and many of the cherubs who proliferate among the decoration. More significant is the manner in which the figures are integrated stylistically into the design as a whole, which suggests that the entire complex structure was conceived and elaborated by a single mind.

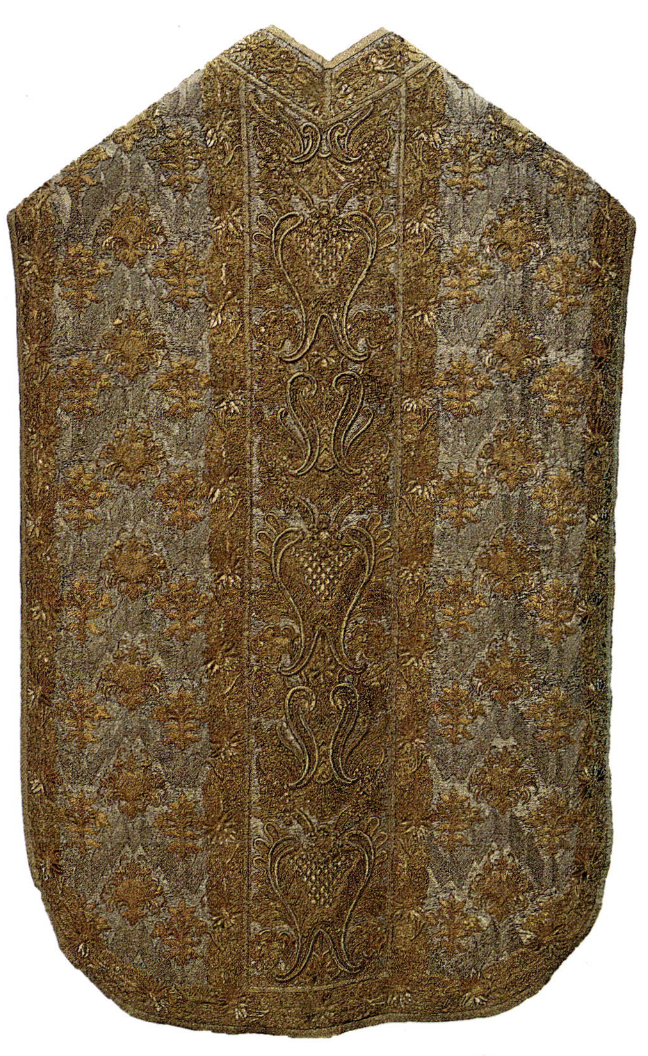

108
NICOLO BOVI
Italian
Chasuble for Feast Days
1744–1747
silver lamé embroidered in gold
106 (41⅜)

Museu de São Roque, Santa Casa da Misericórdia, Lisbon, inv. MT 113

Sousa Viterbo 1900, 56; Rodriguez 1988, 202

This beautiful chasuble is part of a set of six vestments from the Roman collection presented by Dom João V to the Jesuit church of São Roque in Lisbon. The set has become known as the treasure of the chapel of Saint John the Baptist.

The vestment was embroidered in Rome by Nicolo Bovi, as was the entire set of purple vestments for the sacrarium of the chapel. This chasuble and all other items in fabric for the chapel were ordered in Rome in 1744. The chapel inventory taken in 1784 notes that the vestment showed signs of wear, suggesting that it had been used frequently.

According to oral reports, which have not, however, been verified, Pope Benedict XIV blessed the chapel of Saint John the Baptist in Rome in April 1747 wearing white vestments, before it was transported to Portugal.

Following the expulsion of the Jesuits from Portugal in 1759, all the assets of the Casa Professa de São Roque were handed over to the Santa Casa da Misericórdia in Lisbon, including its entire treasure. For this reason, the Museu de São Roque is today one of the main centers for the study of precious religious objects and vestments produced in Rome during the 1740s.

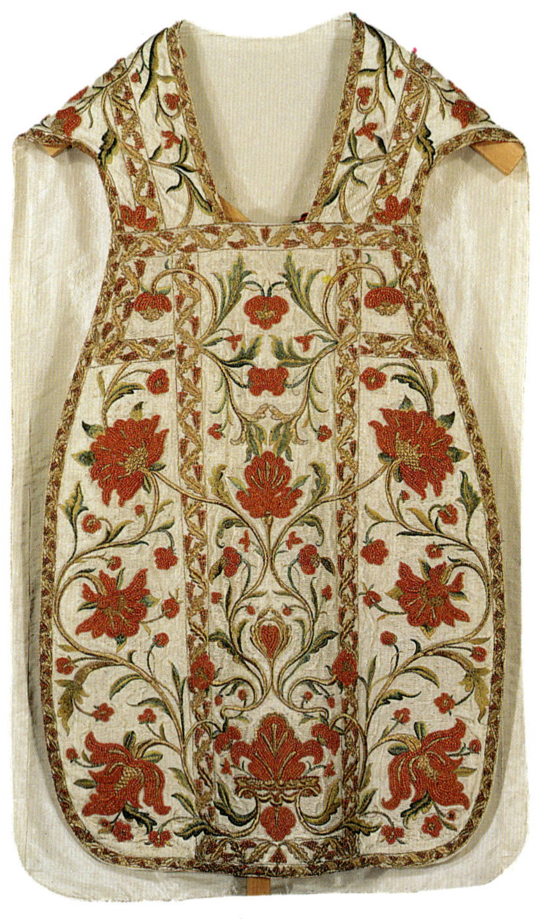 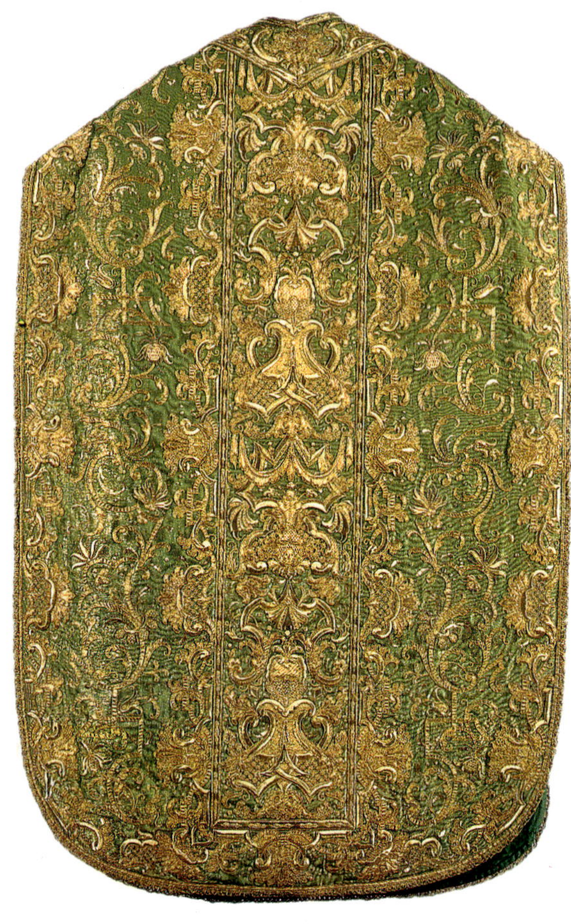

109
Chasuble
Portuguese
1st half 18th century
white silk lamé embroidered in gold
thread, multicolored silk thread, and
coral beads
107 (42 ⅛)

*Museu Nacional de Soares dos Reis,
Oporto, inv. 31*

Sousa Viterbo 1903.1; Vasconcelos 1914–1915,
fasc. 1; Coelho 1950, t. 2; Mayer-Thurman 1975;
Brussels 1991, II.54

The type of chasuble that is still in use
today became current during the seventeenth and eighteenth centuries. During
the Middle Ages, such vestments had
been conical in form with an opening for
the head in the center, reminiscent of the
Roman *paenula* that was, basically, a
wide cape covering the entire body, providing a tent-like shelter (Latin: *casula*).
This shape was subsequently modified to
free the celebrant's movements, at the
same time reducing its weight.

The chasuble is one of the most
solemn vestments, for which reason
church regulations specified that it
should be of fine-woven silk with embroidery in silver or gold thread, which
implied considerable cost. During the
eighteenth century, vestments became
more decorative in nature, losing a great
deal of the symbolism inherent in earlier
garments whose embroidery often depicted subjects from the Scriptures.

During the eighteenth century, the
vogue for observing nature and botanical
study influenced decorative plant motifs
in works of art. Here the stems of flowers are picked out in gold thread and the
leaves are embroidered in many shades
of silk thread, while the flowers themselves are composed of coral beads, reflecting a long-standing tradition in
Western art of incorporating exotic materials. Coral was also widely used in
jewelry, evoking the Oriental exoticism
that was introduced by the Age of Discovery. As coral became increasingly
fashionable, it was much coveted as a
gift. The fact that coral is used here to
decorate a religious vestment suggests
that it may have belonged to a church
dignitary in some way connected with
the Portuguese government in India.

110
Chasuble
Portuguese
mid-18th century
green silk lamé embroidered with gold
and silver
100 x 87 (39⅜ x 34¼)

Lisbon Cathedral Chapter

Bastos 1954; Mayer-Thurman 1975; Brussels 1991, II.55

Green vestments, symbolizing life and
hope, are worn during services from the
eighth day of Epiphany to the third
Sunday before Lent and from the eighth
day of Pentecost through Advent.
Three sets of such green vestments exist,
known as "carnations," "roses," and "ears
of wheat." The vestments also differ in
their edging, which ranges from an un-
broken undulating line to a straight line
broken into sections of varying length,
while the fringe takes several forms. In
this chasuble a number of bellflowers,
daisies, violets, and forget-me-nots can
be seen among intertwined leaves. The
sheen of the lamé cloth is emphasized by
the gold and silver embroidered foliage,
fringes, and arabesques. The sumptuousness of this vestment is further emphasized by the trimming along its edges, a
touch of great refinement.

The interlaced design of the lively
naturalistic floral motif marks a departure from the baroque classicism that
was customary in objects of this type
produced in Italy, where it indicated a
restrained acceptance of rococo influence. In fact, since the Portuguese royal
factory of silks, founded by Dom João V,
is known to have manufactured gold
lamé cloth between 1734 and 1766, it may
be presumed that this vestment was produced in Portugal. Documents recording
delivery by the Cathedral Chapter of numerous bars of gold to fill an order for
vestments support this possibility.

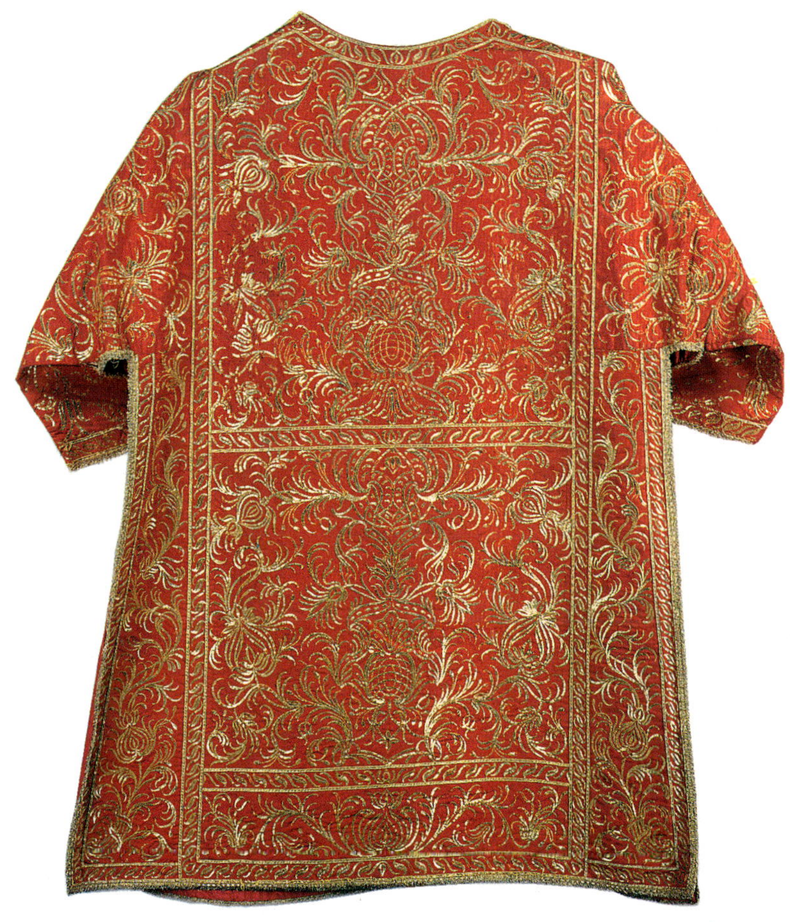

111
Dalmatic
Portuguese
1775–1800
115 x 147 (45¼ x 57⅞)
silk grosgrain embroidered with gold and
silver

Lisbon Cathedral Chapter

Bastos 1954; Mayer-Thurman 1975;
Brussels 1991, II.56c

With its abundance of gold embroidery,
this dalmatic is a stunning example of an
eighteenth-century religious vestment.
Stylized plant motifs are interwoven
across the entire surface of the garment,
creating a field of scattered gold that
sparkles magnificently. Garlands of fruit
accentuate the effect of a labyrinth,
which underlies the ornamental scheme.

Dating to the beginning of the reign
of Rainha Dona Maria I, this vestment
bears witness to the elegance of baroque
liturgical celebrations. It is part of an ensemble that includes a chasuable, a
gremial, and an immense cape (*magna*).

The dalmatic is a vestment that was
adapted by the church from a long-
sleeved garment introduced into Rome
from the province of Dalmatia. By the
middle ages it had become the correct
outer vesture for deacons, while it was
worn beneath the chasuable by bishops.

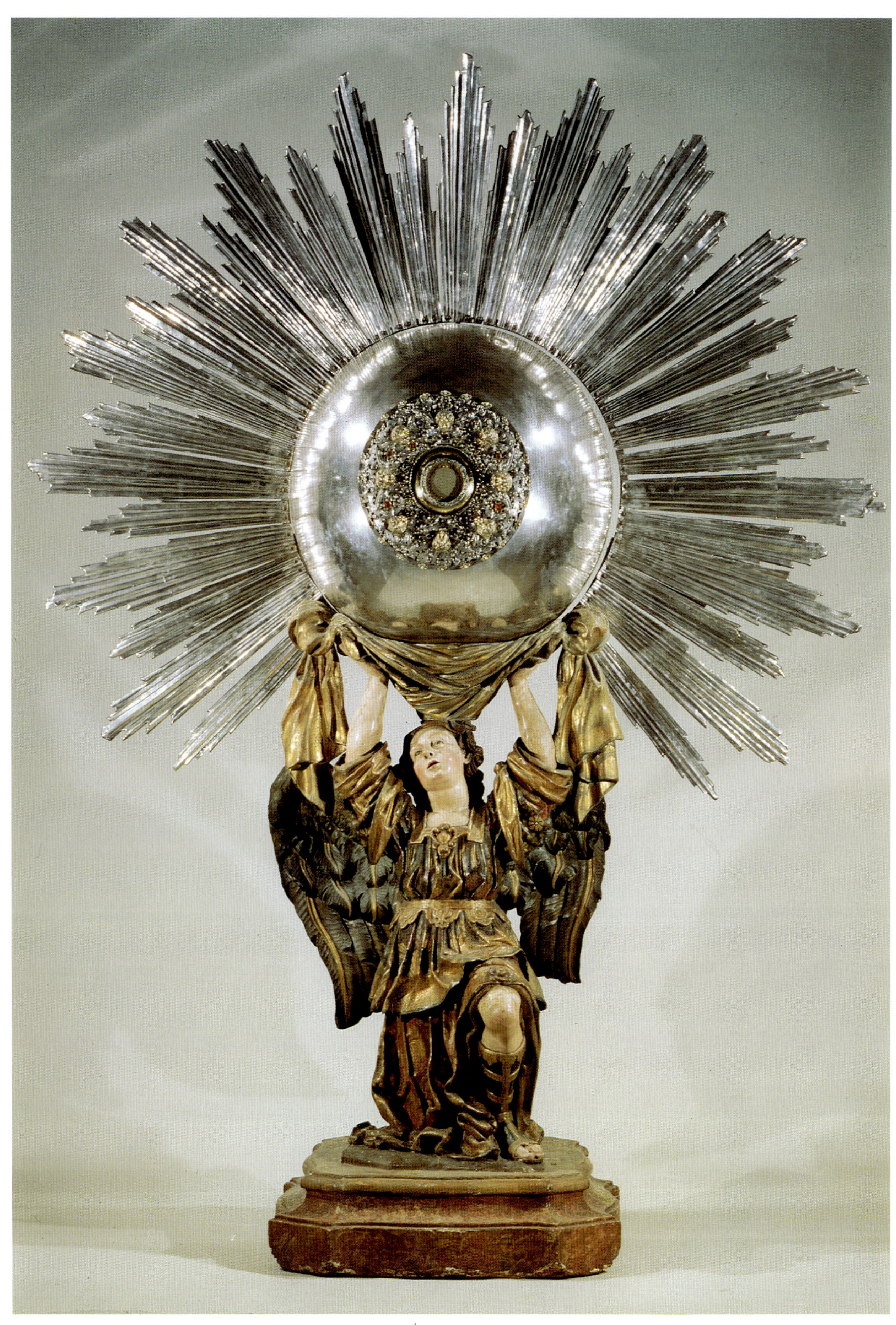

Sacramento Monstrance
Portuguese
c. 1760
receptacle: chased, repoussé, and
engraved silver, 222 (85¾); pedestal:
gilded and painted oak, 162 (63⅛)
Marks: L, municipal assayer of Lisbon,
1750–1770; BP, unidentified silversmith's
mark (Vidal and Almeida 1974, nos. 17,
313)

*Museu Nacional Machado de Castro,
Coimbra, inv. 3456/E 337, from Igreja do
Sacramento, Lisbon*

Smith 1936; Santos 1950; Santos 1974; Moura 1986;
Teixeira n.d.; Brussels 1991, 11.6

Like a figure of Atlas, who is usually depicted holding the world on his shoul-
ders, a genuflecting angel holds aloft a
large silver sphere surrounded by an aureole of tapering rays, to which is attached the door of the receptacle fitted
to the sacrarium for the host.

The formal inspiration for this extraordinary monstrance looks back to the
forms of architectural reliquaries, in particular the *tempietto* type. It also recalls
the pedestals on which relics or sacred
statues are temporarily displayed. There
are parallels to ostensories for the eucharist and, more particularly, to a
lunula, a name deriving from the half-
moon shape of the stand on which the
host is placed inside the glass receptacle
of an ostensory, sometimes supported by
a cherub.

The impact of this ensemble is over-
whelming, and the fact that the sphere is
composed of well over four hundred
pounds of silver places it in a class by
itself among religious works of the goldsmith's art. The author of this piece was
active during the second half of the
eighteenth century and, although he has
never been identified, his mark appears
on a variety of secular pieces of great
sophistication.

In this work, the goldsmith emphasized smooth surfaces by raising the decorated areas, creating sensitively
arranged formal tensions—the rays emanating from the sphere are admirably
suited to this technique. The design of
this monstrance is related to that of a famous monstrance once in the church of
Santo Antão in Lisbon, which was created in 1701 by João Frederico Ludovice
(1673–1752) for the Jesuits, the first of his
works to be executed in Portugal. A de-

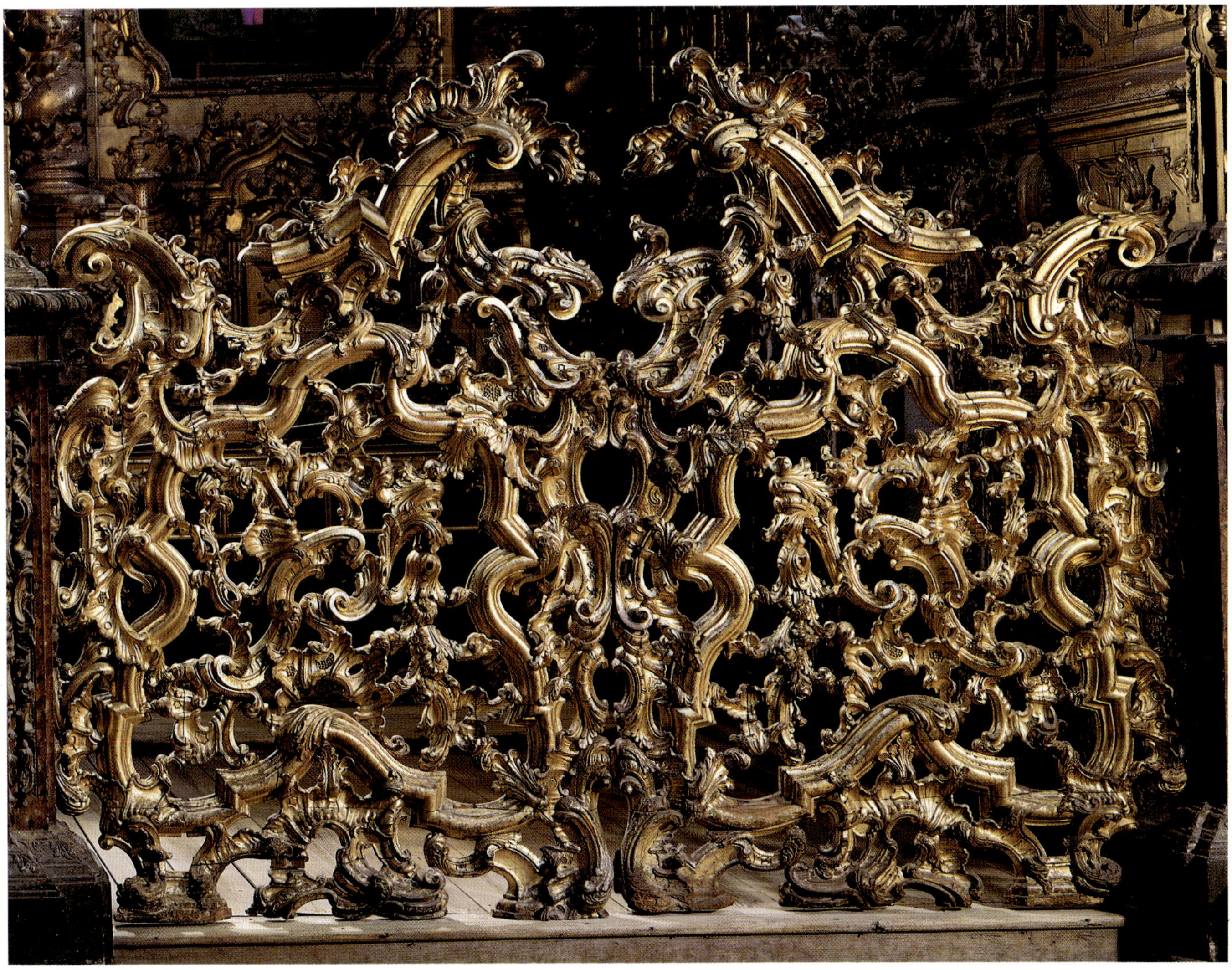

scription of the church written shortly after it was completed states that two angels "prostrate in worship of our Lord who is within the monstrance" were displayed on the altar *(História dos Mosteiros* [1950], 448). Although Ludovice's original monstrance was lost in the earthquake of 1755, the memory of such an inventive work of art must have remained vivid for Portuguese artists, amplified as it would have been by the goldsmith's standing in Rome and the great tradition of the Roman baroque that he represented.

113

FRANCISCO PEREIRA CAMPANHÃ
(?–1776)
Portuguese
Gates from the Chapel of Nossa Senhora da Soledade
1764–1765
gilded carved wood
272 x 295 (107 $^1\!/_{16}$ x 116$^1\!/_8$)

Igreja de São Francisco, Oporto

Basto 1957, 1962; Smith 1963; Smith 1963.1; Oporto 1963; Smith 1968.1; Santos 1970; Alves 1989; Brussels 1991, II.3

The church of São Francisco in Oporto is one of the most splendid examples of the so-called "golden churches," its effect being enhanced by its monumental size. Different parts of the church follow different styles, the result of a variety of commissions and donations by individual patrons. The reredos of the chancel, the side chapels, and the nave constitute a showcase of different artistic styles.

The reredos for the chapel of Nossa Senhora da Soledade is among the most impressive works of organic rococo carving in Portugal. The carver Francisco Campanhã, whose identity is established by the contract for the reredos, was well acquainted with the decorative prints produced by Augsburg engravers, which were present in the collections of the Benedictine monastery libraries in the north of Portugal and circulated among

the workshops of sculptors, carpenters, and architects.

Campanhã made his name with the reredos of the chancel of the church of Nossa Senhora da Vitória, another of his masterpieces commissioned by the bishop of Oporto, António de Sousa. Campanhã appears as master sculptor in the contract for the gates.

Robert Smith evocatively described Campanhã's work in the chapel of Nossa Senhora da Soledade as follows: "the space is filled with a web of asymmetrical scrolls combined with an infinite variety of snowflakes, executed with a delicacy suggesting the anatomy of a bat's wing. Nervous and full of movement, it seems to sweep in constant movement within its narrow confines. This form of decoration, which became associated with Oporto, might be compared with the supreme fantasies of French rococo." Indeed, this pair of gates might well be adduced as an illustration of one definition of rococo design in general: the "infinite interlinking of individual curves."

114

JOAQUIM MACHADO DE CASTRO
1731–1822
The Holy Family
c. 1770–1780
polychromed terra cotta, painted wooden niche
Saint Joseph, 90 (34$^1\!/_2$); the Virgin, 85 (33$^1\!/_2$); the infant Christ, 54 (21$^1\!/_4$)

Museu de Aveiro, inv. 133 B, from Convento das Carmelitas, Aveiro

Vasconcelos 1914–1915; Santos 1950; pl. CLXV; Macedo 1953; Bazin 1968, fig. 925; Brussels 1991, IV.71

If one compares this Holy Family with the figures in the crib in the Estrêla basilica in Lisbon by Machado de Castro, it is evident that the sculptural style of this group is more vigorous, having no doubt been executed during a more creative period of the artist's career. The

difficulties endured by Machado de Castro when executing the equestrian statue of Dom José I in 1777 account to some extent for a subsequent decline in his work, which is reflected in the stance of the figure of Saint Joseph in the Estrêla basilica executed in 1782: head bowed, his cheek resting on his hand, he appears to be standing aloof from the scene.

By contrast, the Aveiro group has an eminently extroverted character, an effect that lends itself admirably to modeling in clay. The group recalls the work of Bernini in the characteristic exuberance of the garments, while the child's gaze and his outstretched arms demonstrate the artist's successful assimilation of his Roman models. Machado de Castro's use of gold leaf to create an effect that is at once vernacular and imposing, a technique that was borrowed from the vocabulary of wood carving, enhances the range of floral and shell motifs on the figures' costumes, giving the design a secular stamp.

The joyful atmosphere of the group is appropriately framed by a niche of multicolor imitation marble against a rococo background of simulated fabric reproduced from the contemporary designs in silk. Unlike the figures in a typical Nativity group, this Holy Family was created for a specific small space, permitting the group a more coherent balance and sense of interconnection.

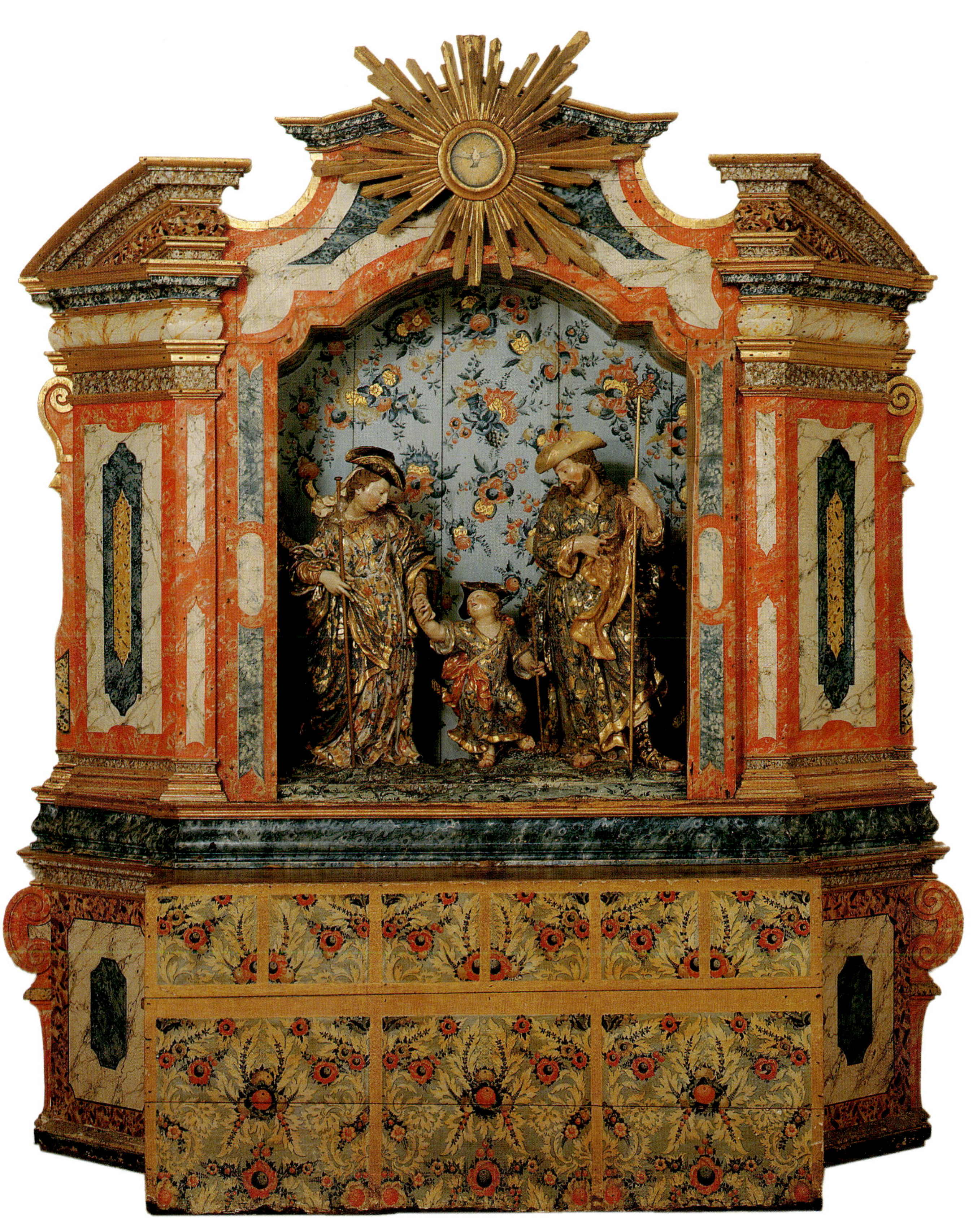

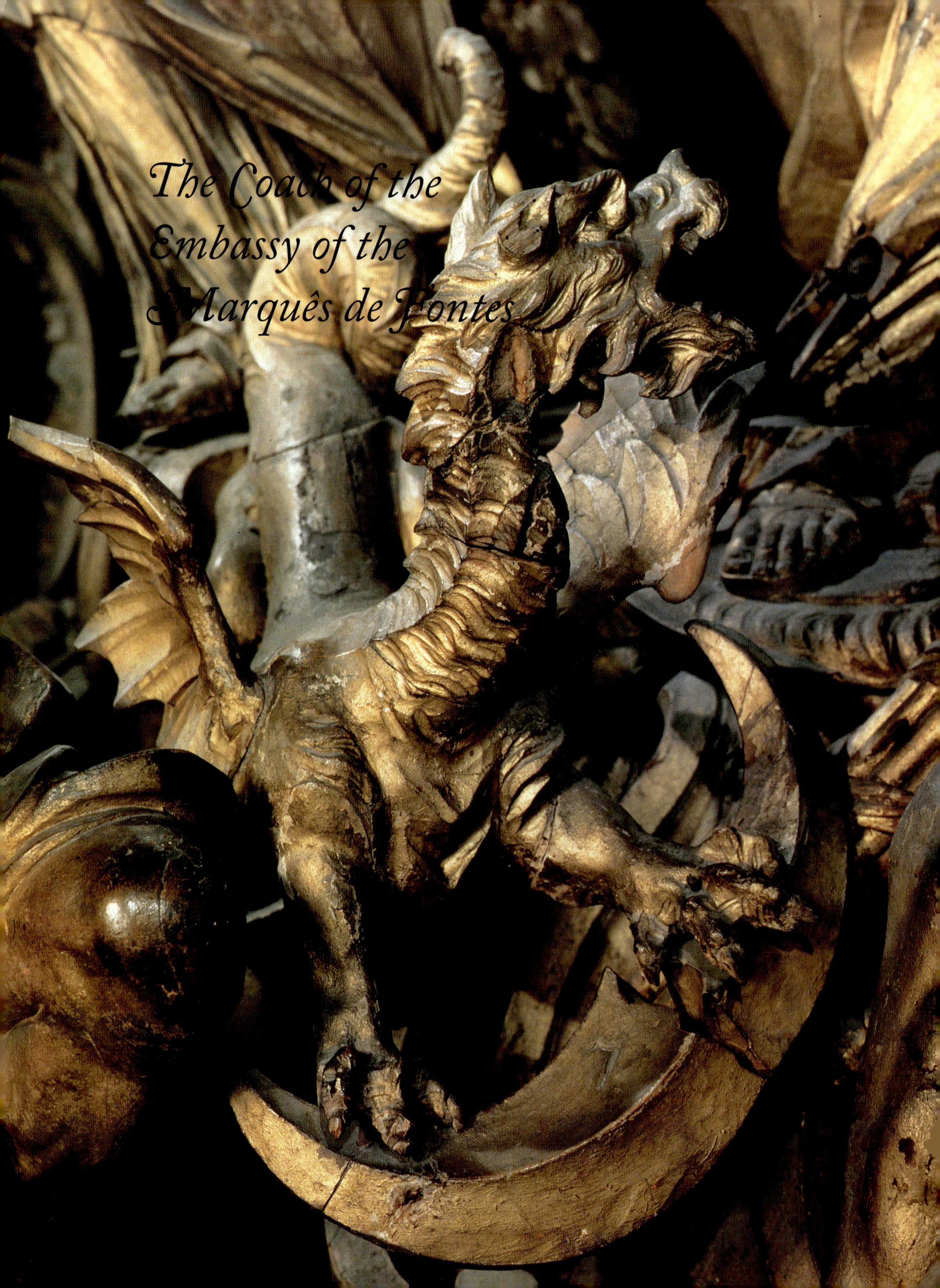

The Coach of the
Embassy of the
Marquês de Fontes

The marquês de Fontes was entrusted by Dom João V with the delicate mission of obtaining special privileges and concessions for the monarchy from Pope Clement XI. The "First Noble Coach" is one of three sumptuously decorated carriages surviving from the procession that took place in Rome in 1716 marking Fontes' official entrance as Portugal's ambassador extraordinary to the Holy See.

115

First Noble Coach of the Embassy of the Marquês de Fontes to the Papal Court
Italian
1713–1716
iron, gilded iron and gilded copper, leather, carved and gilded wood frame with wood and crimson velvet body embroidered with gold thread and with gold fringe
325 x 237 x 728 (127 $^{15}/_{16}$ x 93 $^{5}/_{16}$ x 286 $^{5}/_{8}$ [11 x 7 $^{3}/_{4}$ x 24 feet])
Museu Nacional dos Coches, Lisbon, inv. 10

This splendid coach was commissioned as part of an entourage of four coaches for the official entrance in 1716 of the ambassador extraordinary of Portugal, the marquês de Fontes. Subsequently given by the marquês de Fontes to Dom João V and transported from Rome to Lisbon, the coach remained from that time in the royal collection until the creation of the Museu Nacional dos Coches.

This coach is of the traditional Roman type, which was established around the middle of the seventeenth century and remained unchanged until the beginning of the eighteenth, when a more modern model originating in France began to be used also in Rome, even for ceremonial purposes. (In the newer model the coach body was no longer suspended by large straps from the high protruding ends of the frame but was attached to it using iron suspensions.)

In the exhibited coach, the velvet-lined body with gold embroidery and decorative fringe now lacks the curtains that completed the decorations. The interior is lined with damask. On the four corners of the roof are four ornaments, called "vases" at the time, shaped as shell-like scrolls made of wood and wire and lined with velvet. At the top of the four poles or mounts holding up the top of the coach are four carved monstrous beast heads to which were tied the ropes that held back the curtains so the interior of the coach could be seen. The body is suspended from the frame using four large straps attached to the front and rear.

The gilded wooden sculptures adorning the front and rear of the coach are arranged as follows. In front of the frame, just underneath the driver's footrest, a cherub points the way. Four small Zephyrs at the top hold a long garland with laurel leaves and berries, repeating the same motif embroidered on the coach body. Leaning at the sides of the driver's box are two figures, on the left a half-dressed young man crowned with laurel who probably held a laurel garland, now lost, in his hands. On the right is a woman wearing a diadem of rays of light; a radiant sun is carved on her breast and a serpent biting his tail encircles her waist. These represent "the love of heroic virtue" and the immortality of the name of Portugal, where the sun and its rays stand for brightness, clarity, and luminous fame and the serpent stands for eternity.

At the center of the rear, which was the most important part of these triumphal coaches, is the most complex and conclusive symbolic representation of the entire program. The City of Lisbon sits majestic, wearing classical armor, covered with the mantle of royalty and holding a scepter. A civic crown, formed of walls interspersed with towers, is held above her head by a female figure standing on her right. This figure, half-dressed, holds in her left hand a trumpet signifying fame, and is indicated as "the glory of princes." On the left is Abundance with her cornucopia. At the feet of Lisbon are weapons piled up, symbolizing spoils of war, and a small dragon, symbolic of the royal house of Bragança, tearing apart a Turkish crescent. Below, in the posture of conquered and imprisoned enemies, are a Turk and a Moor.

The concept of the sculpture at the back of this coach, beyond its particular meaning linked to the glories of Portugal, is found again very similarly in a plate from the decorative repertoire of Filippo Passalini *(Nuove invention… utili ed argentieri, intagliatori, ricamatori et altri professori delle buone arti del disegno… [Rome, 1698], plate 22)*, where the back of a triumphal coach, invented for the entrance of an ambassador of the Order of Malta, represents an armed goddess seated above a trophy of weapons piled on the prow of a ship with two Turkish prisoners in chains below her. This type of allegory was in the air when Pope Clement XI was promoting his war against the Turks. In the same year as the embassy of Fontes, the Accademia del Disegno in fact proposed as the theme for second-year students "a cart loaded with spoils, and trophies, with some Ottoman slaves tied behind it" (see *Le Tre Belle Arti in lega coll'Armi per difesa della Religione, mostrate nel Campidoglio dall'Accademia del Disegno… [Rome, 1716]*). See also the winning drawings published in "I Premiati dell'Accademia 1682–1754," *Catalogo della Mostra*, ed. Angela Cipriani [Rome, 1989], nos. 51 and 52). This coach seems to respond to that theme in an inimitable manner.

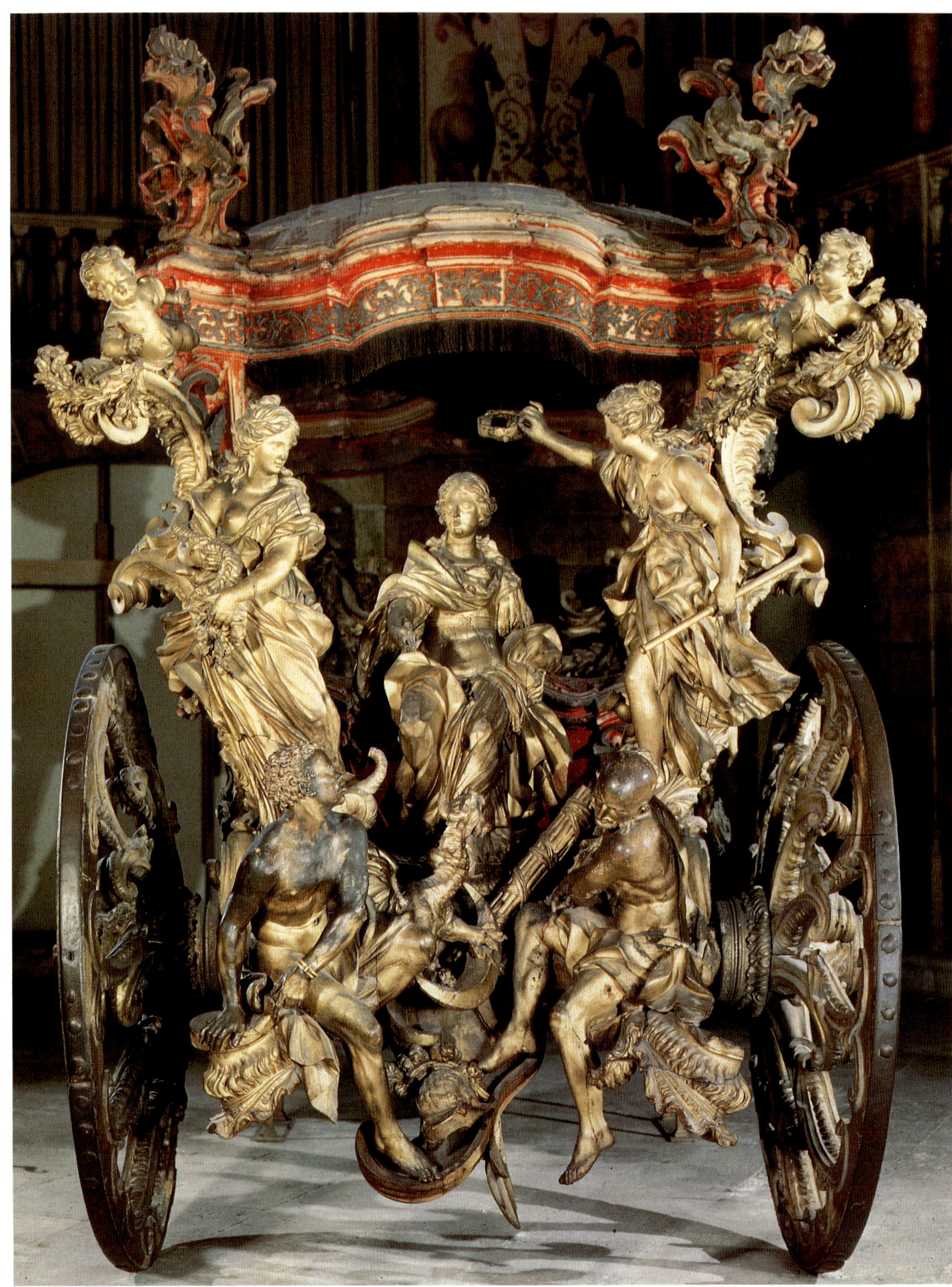

115

Caparison

c. 1738-1739
velvet with silver appliqués
162 x 188 (63¾ x 74)

*Fundação Ricardo do Espírito Santo Silva,
Lisbon, inv. 555*

Rosa 1738; Freire 1923; ANBA 1935; Brussels 1991, 1.42

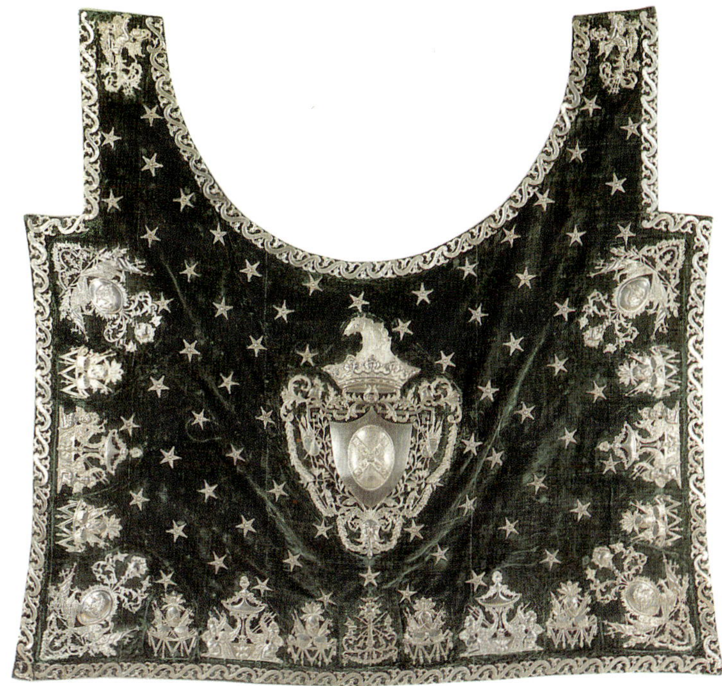

This splendid caparison, a decorative
covering for a horse, bears the coat of
arms in silver of Dom Jaime Álvares
Pereira do Melo, third duque de Cadaval
(1684-1749) and chief equerry to Dom
João V. The Cadaval coat of arms is very
similar in design to that appearing in an
engraving by Pierre Antoine Quillard
(1701-1733) in the book by Padre António
Reis, *Joanni V. Epigrammatum Libri*
(1728), and on the frontispiece of the
book *Últimas Acções do Duque D. Nuno*
(1730).

As the king's chief equerry, the duque
de Cadaval had an important role to play
in court ceremonies. Much depended
upon him and the functions in which he
participated, since they were seen as
structuring elements denoting grandeur
during a period in which the monarch
was at the hub of a mighty orchestration
of power and public spectacle.

The caparison would have been
designed for use on these grand occasions, quite possibly for the magnificent
bullfights that were held in 1738 in Junqueira, a suburb of Lisbon, to celebrate
the twentieth birthday of Mariana
Vitória, princess of Brazil. An enormous
bullring was built of Flemish pine, on
which 345 carpenters were engaged full-
time for a period of two months. The
arena was decorated with allegorical statues representing the Continents and
other lavish adornments, attracting an
enormous crowd. Some twelve thousand
people were unable to enter, while a
lucky few could watch the entertainment
from the towers of Belém and the Búgio.
Some four thousand coaches awaited
their occupants near the bullring and a
similar number of ships lay in attendance
on the river. The event was supervised by

the princess' chief equerry, the visconde
de Vila Nova da Cerveira, while the
duque de Cadaval was responsible for
the bullfight. He had formed four groups
(or strings) of nobles, and himself acted
as *guide* for each of them. Dom Jaime
became famous in the history of Portuguese bullfighting for requesting and
receiving the king's authorization to fight
the bull without the protective pads on
its horns, thereby reintroducing a practice that had been discouraged by Dom
Pedro II at the request of his queen.

The first person to enter was the duke
himself, dazzling the spectators with the
extraordinary lavishness of his attire and
the jewelry he wore, following a plumed
horse carrying two sacks of clay pellets
and covered by a green saddle cloth bearing the duke's coat of arms. Five servants
in green livery with silver frogs led horses
in harnesses encrusted with precious
stones, tassels of gold thread, and their
"caparisons embroidered with coats of
arms," very likely including the present
exhibit.

No effort was spared in making this
event as magnificent as possible, and
many of the items used were ordered
from Paris. Records exist in the archives

of the Germain workshop in Paris to the
effect that, in 1736, work was progressing
satisfactorily on production of "all
caparisons and necessary preparations for
the Arreyos Hunt" (ANBA doc. cv) and,
as the bullfighting season was approach-
ing, there is a comment to the effect that
Germain was devoting a great deal of his
time to the court and "also that blankets,
bags, cloths, and harnesses for horses
were being produced, of great magnificence and which cost a great deal of
money" (ANBA doc. xxxvii, 2 Sept. 1736).

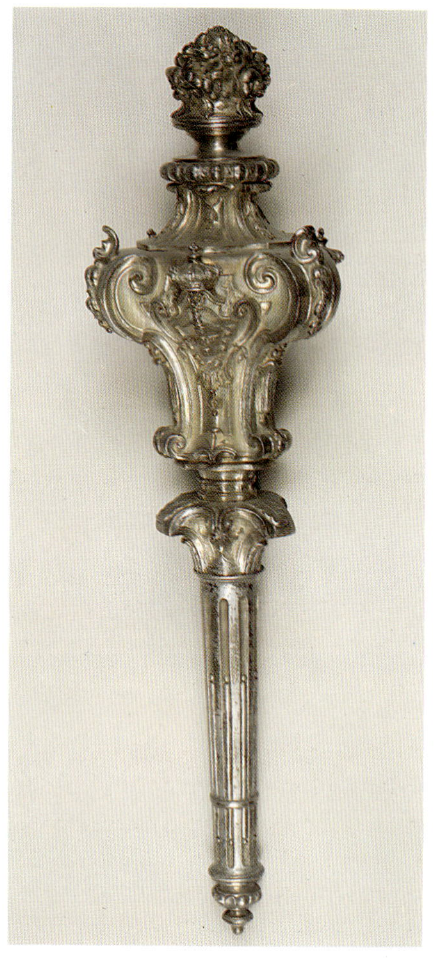

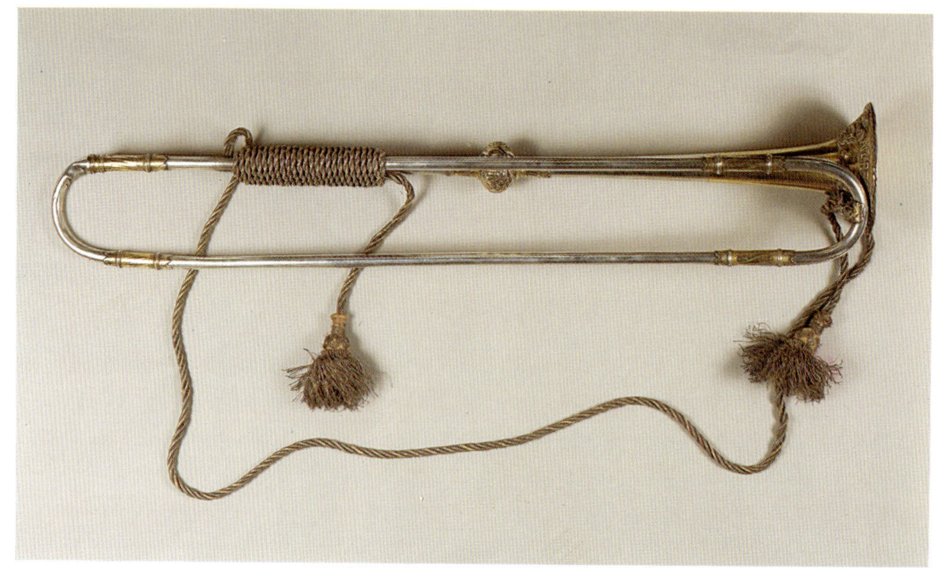

117
Two Maces
1750–1770
Portuguese
chased, repoussé, and engraved silver
80 (31½)

*Museu Nacional dos Coches, Lisbon,
invs. Av. 13, 14*

MNC 1943, 57, no. 244; Silva 1977, 126, fig. 99;
Brussels 1991, IV.11

The mace is one of the most representative symbols of royal power, a variant on the rod carried in ancient times by the doorkeepers at court and in the processions that assembled when members of royalty appeared in public. Ushers and kings of arms preceded the procession on horseback.

These maces from a set of six may well have been part of a royal order for trumpets and drums placed in 1761, since maces complemented the musical instruments by enhancing the visual manifestation of royal power. The principal hallmark on these items permits the maces to be dated between 1750 and 1770. The chasing is of the same high artistic quality as other Portuguese works in silver and gold from this period, a consequence of the kingdom's prosperity and the growing taste for the ostentation of valuable works in silver.

The baluster-shaped shaft broadens at the top into a form resembling the inverted triangular pyramids of the processional lanterns, the corners decorated with an elongated *S* with scroll. This design probably repeated that of an order placed in Paris in 1729 for "silver maces, as normally carried by ushers in public functions" (ANBA, doc. xxix, 1935).

118
Two Trumpets
1761
Portuguese
chased, repoussé, and engraved silver,
green velvet banderole
62 x 13 (24⁷⁄₁₆ x 5⅛)

*Museu Nacional dos Coches, Lisbon,
invs. IM 39, 40*

MNC 1943, 58, no. 250; Silva 1977, 126, fig. 97;
Brussels 1991, IV.10

During the reign of Dom João V, major changes were introduced in the manner in which the royal guard functioned. For the festivities in Caia in preparation for the royal weddings of 1729, the monarch ordered that the green and silver livery of the house of Bragança be replaced by the red livery that had been traditional during the first and second Portuguese dynasties. The Caia procession, composed of more than forty coaches, was accompanied by "a group of fifteen horsemen and their officers, twenty-four drummers and trumpeters of the Royal Household attired in scarlet velvet with gold frogs." Frei Francisco Costa, who recorded the journey of the escort that had traveled in 1708 to Vienna to accompany Ana Maria of Austria, Dom João V's bride, related that when the twenty decorated vessels set sail, "the trumpets and trumpeters" regaled the ears and eyes of the crowd, enhancing the visual impact with their silver cords and embroidered banderoles. And in 1750, during Dom José I's acclamation ceremony on the balcony of the Terreiro do Paço, the appearance of His Majesty was greeted by "minstrels, trumpeters, and drummers who played with charming delicacy and harmony" (*Júbilos de Portugal* 1750).

The trumpets on display, manufactured in 1761, were played during the festivities attending the inauguration of the equestrian statue of Dom José in 1775. They bear an engraved inscription and the crowned Portuguese royal coat of arms within a frame of plant motifs. The cord of plaited silver thread is decorated with a fringed tassel. The banderoles are embroidered in gold and silver, picking out the royal coat of arms flanked by two figures representing Fame on a background of green velvet, confirming that this color replaced Dom João V's preferred red.

In 1787, upon the death of João da Bemposta, the Casa do Infantado received "six trumpet ensembles, consisting of plaited silver cords and tassels on green banderoles" (Pires 1923, 210), indicating that, like the royal household, this high-ranking family also had its own group of trumpeters.

119
Tabard
1761
Portuguese
silk brocade with silver gilt appliqués
128 x 104 (50 ³/₈ x 40 ¹⁵/₁₆)

*Museu Nacional dos Coches, Lisbon,
inv. 4866*

Sousa 1741; Castro 1763; Sousa Viterbo 1912;
Keil 1943; Silva 1977; Alves 1985; Brussels 1991, IV.13

The tabard on display, one of a surviving set of four, was probably created in 1761, during Dom José I's reign, as were the maces of the kings of arms (see cat. 117). It is decorated with embroidered frogs and heraldic castles in applied silver gilt and is further enhanced by a collar also of silver gilt hanging outside the tunic. Similar costumes appear in a description of the baptism of the princesa da Beira, in 1793, as being worn by the kings of arms, ushers, and heralds who advanced in pairs, attired in their "tunics of white silk, with lining and piping of scarlet silk, embroidered with castles of the realm, in accordance with ancient custom" (*Memórias Históricas* [Lisbon, 1793]).

It is clear from historical records that heralds and other costumed officials who appeared in royal processions played an important role in the mechanism of government. For example, in 1707, upon the completion of the oath during the ceremony of acclamation of Dom João V, in the wooden theater erected next to the tower of the Paço da Ribeira in Lisbon, the chief equerry of the kingdom and standard bearer intoned: "Real, Real, Real por El-rey D. João Quinto" (royal, royal, royal for the King Dom João V). This refrain was taken up by the kings of arms, ushers, and heralds, after which the royal trumpeters played a fanfare. These officials performed an active role in the political confirmation of the new

monarch, in addition to the extensive list of court functions for which they were responsible.

In the kings of arms regulations introduced during the early sixteenth century, Dom Manuel I had decreed that in future there would be three kings of arms, three ushers, and three heralds, who would generically be called officials of the nobility. Their principal responsibilities were to verify the authenticity of titles and honors of the nobility and to maintain the register of nobles, containing records of coats of arms and the kings of arms' book.

The kings of arms had the symbolic names Portugal, Algarve, and India, the first being the Principal; the ushers were known respectively as Lisbon, Silves (capital of the Algarve), and Goa, corresponding to the titles of Portugal, Algarve, and India; the heralds were called Santarém, Tavira, and Cochin, the names of cities in these three regions.

Investiture in any of these positions involved a ceremony of great magnificence, in which the king sprinkled water on the head of the new official and intoned the name he would use in the future. It was even stipulated that these officials' insignia was to be a green silk tunic with gilt decorations and a shield bearing the arms of Portugal. It is known that ushers headed processions whenever the monarch appeared in public, symbolizing the authority of the court, and it was they who announced the arrival of anyone entering the royal residential chambers.

The kings of arms preceded all the other officials, and the ostentation of their maces and collars and the castles embroidered on their tunics attested to their role as magistrates responsible for verifying the authenticity of titles of nobility, based either on monarchic legality or on national identity.

Chronology

1699
arrival in Lisbon of first shipment of gold from Brazil

1700
Clement XI becomes pope

1703
Methuen Treaty on trade relations between Portugal and Britain

1706
death of Dom Pedro II

Dom João V proclaimed king

1708
marriage of João V and Maria Ana of Austria

1711
birth of Princesa Maria Bárbara de Bragança, first child of Dom João V

1712
birth of Príncipe Pedro, son of Dom João V

1714
death of Príncipe Pedro, birth of Príncipe José, sons of Dom João V

1716
Dom João V authorizes construction of library for University of Coimbra

the splendid embassy of the marquês de Fontes received by the pope in Rome

1717
birth of Príncipe Carlos, son of Dom João V, the future Dom Pedro III, consort of Dona Maria I

Portuguese fleet takes part in Battle of Matapan against the Turks

Portuguese royal chapel awarded status of patriarchal church by the pope

work begun on Mafra

1720
foundation of Royal Academy of History

1722
construction begun on stairway of Bom Jesus do Monte, Braga

1725
Dom João V places orders with silversmith Thomas Germain

1728
Dom João V suspends relations with the Holy See

1729
discovery of diamonds in Cerro Frio, Brazil

1730
Clement XII becomes pope

consecration of the basilica of Mafra

orders given for the construction of the chapel of Saint John the Baptist, church of São Roque, Lisbon

1732
end of conflict with Holy See

diamonds discovered in Bahia, Brazil

1734
birth of Princesa Maria to Dom José and Marie-Anne Victoire de Bourbon

gold discovered in Mato Grosso, Brazil

1737
patriarch of Lisbon becomes cardinal

1740
Dom João V becomes ill

1747
construction of palace at Queluz begins

arrival of chapel of Saint John the Baptist from Rome

1749
construction of aqueduct in Lisbon completed

1750
death of Dom João V

Dom José I proclaimed king

Sebastião José de Carvalho e Melo appointed secretary of foreign affairs and war

1753
Carvalho e Melo places the diamond trade under royal protection

1755
Lisbon earthquake

1756
Carvalho e Melo becomes secretary of domestic affairs

1757
royal silverware service ordered from François-Thomas Germain

1758
assassination attempt against Dom José I

1759
execution of the men accused of attempting to assassinate Dom José I

expulsion of the Jesuits

1760
Princesa Maria marries Príncipe Pedro

1767
birth of Príncipe João (future Dom João VI)

1769
Carvalho e Melo made marquês de Pombal

1772
reform of the University of Coimbra

reform of the Inquisition

1773
end of the distinction between new and old Christians

1775
inauguration of the equestrian statue of Dom José I in the Praça do Comércio, Lisbon

1777
death of Dom José I

Dona Maria I proclaimed queen

Pombal dismissed and exiled

1792
incapacity of Dona Maria I by reason of mental illness

1799
regency of Príncipe João formally declared

Bibliography

AA.VV 1952
AA.VV. *As artes Plásticas no Brasil.* Rio de Janeiro

AA.VV 1989
AA.VV. *Meubles de laque et Goût extrème oriental au XVII° et XVIII° siècles.* Bibliothèque Nationale, Paris

Aguiar 1955
Aguiar, António de. "Mobiliário português do século XVIII." *Ocidente* 201. Lisbon

Alcouffe 1985
Alcouffe, Daniel. *Musée du Louvre: Nouvelles Acquisitions du département des objets d'art 1980-84.* Paris

Alves 1985
Alves, Ana Maria. *Iconologia do Poder Real no Periódo Manuelino.* Lisbon

Alves 1989
Alves, Natália Marinho. "Araújo, Marcelino de." *Dicionário da Arte Barroca em Portugal.* Lisbon

ANBA 1935
"Documentos relativos à ourivesaria francesa encomendados pra Portugal." *Boletim da Academia Nacional de Belas Artes* 1. Lisbon

ANBA 1936
"Documentos relativos à ourivesaria, pintura, arquitetura, coches. . . ." *Boletim da Academia Nacional de Belas Artes* 2. Lisbon

ANBA 1942
Personagens Portuguesas do século XVII. Exposição de Arte e Iconografia. Exh. cat. Academia Nacional de Belas Artes. Lisbon

Arruda 1989
Arruda, Luisa. *Figuras de Convite na azulejaria portuguesa do século XVIII.* Lisbon

Babelon 1946
Babelon, Jean. *L'Orfèvrerie Française.* Paris

Bapst 1887
Bapst, Germain. *Etudes sur l'orfèvrerie française au XVIII° siècle: Les Germain-Orfèvres-sculpteurs du Roi.* Paris

Bapst 1889
Bapst, Germain. *Catalogue raisonné des pièces d'orfèvrerie française composant la collection du Marquis da Foz.* Paris

Bapst 1892
Bapst, Germain. *L'orfèvrerie française à la Cour de Portugal au XVIII° siècle.* Paris

Baptista 1988
Baptista, António Alçada. *Fundação Ricardo do Espírito Santo Silva.* Lisbon

Barbosa Élogio
Barbosa, D. José. "Élogio." National Library in Lisbon, Coleção Pombalina, cód. 418

Basto 1957, 1962
Basto, Artur Magalhães de. "Apontamentos para um Dicionário de Artistas e Artífices que trabalharam no Porto do século XV ao século XVIII." *Boletim de Cultura da Câmara Municipal do Porto* 20 (1957), 25 (1962)

Bastos 1954
Bastos, Carlos. *Subsídios para a história da arte ornamental dos tecidos.* Oporto

Bazin 1949
Bazin, Germain. *L'Architecture religieuse au Portugal et au Brésil à l'époque baroque.* Lisbon

Bazin 1950
Bazin, Germain. "Reflexions sur l'origine et l'évolution du baroque dans le Nord du Portugal." *Belas Artes*

Bazin 1953
Bazin, Germain. "Morphologie du Retable Portugais." *Boletim da Academia Nacional de Belas Artes* 5. Lisbon

Bazin 1968
Bazin, Germain. *Le Monde de la Sculpture.* Paris

Beaudouin 1988
Beaudouin, P., P. Colman, and D. Goethals. *Orfèvrerie en Belgique, XVI°, XVII° et XVIII° siècles.* Tielt

Beuque and Frapsause 1964
Beuque, E., and M. Frapsause. *Dictionnaire des Poinçons des Maitres-Orfèvres Français du XVI° siècle à 1838.* Paris

Beurdeley 1962
Beurdeley, Michel. *Porcelaine de la Compagnie des Indes.* Fribourg

Black 1974
Black, Anderson. *Histoire des Bijoux.* Paris

Borges 1889
Borges, Figueiredo. *O Mosteiro de Odivelas.* Lisbon

Bottineau 1958
Bottineau, Yves. *Catalogue de l'orfèvrerie du XVII°, du XVIII° et du XIX° siècles.* Musée du Louvre et Musée Cluny. Paris

Bottineau and Lefuel 1965
Bottineau, Yves, and O. Lefuel. *Les grands orfèvres de Louis XIII à Charles X.* Paris

Botto 1909
Botto, Joaquim Maria Pereira. *Promptuario analytico dos carros nobres da Casa Real Portuguesa e das carruagens de gala,* vol. 1. Lisbon

Boulay 1984
Boulay, Anthony du. *Christie's Pictorial History of Chinese Ceramics.* Oxford

Boxer 1957
Boxer, C. R. *The Dutch in Brazil, 1624–1654.* Oxford

Boxer 1969
Boxer, C. R. *The Portuguese Seaborne Empire 1415–1825.* London (1st ed. 1965)

Brancante 1950
Brancante, Eduíno da Fonseca. *O Brasil e a Loiça da India.* São Paulo

Branco 1875
Branco, Camilo Castelo. *Caveira do Mártir,* vol. 1. Lisbon

Branco 1868
Branco, M. Bernardes. *As minhas queridas freirinhas de Odivelas.* Lisbon

Brandão 1963
Brandão, Domingos de Pinho. "Retábulos de Talha Dourada e Painéis de Igrejas e Capelas da cidade do Porto." *Alguns Retábulos e Painéis de Igrejas e Capelas da cidade de Porto.* Oporto

Brault and Bottineau 1959
Brault, Solange, and Yves Bottineau. *L'Orfèvrerie française du XVIII° siècle.* Paris

Brazão 1937
Brazão, Eduardo. "D. João V e a Santa Sé." *As Relações Diplomáticas de Portugal com o Governo Pontifício de 1706–1750.* Coimbra

Brussels 1991
Triomphe du Baroque. Exh. cat. Europalia

Brussels 1991:2
Azulejos. Exh. cat. Europalia

Brussels 1991:3
La magie des couleurs et des pierres. Exh. cat. Europalia. Also exhibited and published in Copenhagen as *Aedele Stene og Magiske Farver*

Bulgari 1958–1959/1980
Bulgari, Costantino. *Argentieri gemmari e orafi d'italia . . . ,* part 1, *Roma.* Rome (2nd ed. 1980)

Bury 1956
Bury, John B. "Late Baroque and Rococo in North Portugal." *Journal of the Society of Architectural Historians* (Oct.)

Carita and Cardoso 1983
Carita, Hélder, and Homem Cardoso. *Oriente e Ocidente nos interiores em Portugal.* Oporto

Carvalho 1956
Carvalho, A. Ayres de. "O Pintor Cirilo Wolkmar Machado (1748–1823)." *Boletim do Museu Nacional d'Arte Antiga* 2. Lisbon

Carvalho 1960–1962
Carvalho, A. Ayres de. *D. João V e a Arte do Seu Tempo.* 2 vols. Lisbon

Carvalho 1963
Carvalho, A. Ayres de. "A Escola de Escultura de Mafra." *Belas Artes* 19

Carvalho 1971
Carvalho, A. Ayres de. *As Obras de Sta. Engrácia e os seus artistas.* Lisbon

Carvalho 1978
Carvalho, Rómulo de. *História do Gabinete de Física da Universidade de Coimbra.* Coimbra

Castilho 1893/1940
Castilho, Júlio de. *A Ribeira de Lisboa* (2nd ed. 1940). Lisbon

Castro 1762–1763
Castro, Pe João Baptista de. *Mapa de Portugal Antigo e Moderno.* 3 vols. Lisbon

Castro 1939
Castro, José de. *Portugal em Roma*, vol. 1. Lisbon

Castro 1987
Castro, Nuno de. *A Porcelana Chinesa e os Brasões do Império*. Oporto

Chaves 1951
Chaves, Luís. "O Mobiliário." In Barreira, João. *As Artes Decorativas* 1:359–394. Lisbon

Chiechonowiecki 1965
Chiechonowiecki, A. "Furniture of Spain and Portugal." *World Furniture*, ed. Helena Hayward. London

Chracas 1716
Chracas, Luca Antonio. *Distinto Ragguaglio del sontuoso Treno delle Carrozze con cui ando all'Udienza di Sua Santita il 8 luglio 1716 l'Illustrissimo, ed Eccellentissimo Signore Don Rodrigo Annes de Saa, Almeida e Meneses, Marchese di Fontes*. Rome

Chracas 1749
Chracas, Luca Antonio. *Diario ordinario*, n. 5025 (Rome, 4/10/1749), 14

Coelho 1950
Coelho, Dom António, O.S.B. *Curso de Liturgea Romana* (2nd ed.). Braga

Colombo 1966
Colombo, Giulio. "Lo Scultore Giambattista Maino." *Rassegna gallaratese di storia e d'arte* 25, no. 96, 29–45

Correia and Gonçalves 1947
Correia, Verílio, and Nogueira Gonçalves. *Inventário Artístico de Portugal*. Vol. 2, *Cidade de Coimbra*. Lisbon

Costa 1928
Costa, Luís Xavier da. "Notas sobre a Baixela Germain da Antiga Corte Portugesa." *Arqueologia História*, vol. 6. Lisbon

Costa 1935
Costa, Luís Xavier da. *As belas-Artes plásticas em Portugal durante o século XVIII*. Lisbon

Costa 1940
Costa, Luís Xavier da. "A Escultura Portuguesa em Madeira no sec. XVIII." *Revista de Guimarães*. Lisbon

Costa 1941
Costa, Lúcio. "A Arquitetura Jesuítica no Brasil." *Revista do Patrimônio Histórico e Artístico Nacional* 5. Rio de Janeiro

Costa 1945
Costa, Agostinho Rebello da. *Descrição topográfica histórica da cidade do Porto* (2nd ed.). Oporto

Couto 1927
Couto, João. "Os calices na Ourivesaria portuguesa, do sec. XII ao XVIII." *Esmeralda* 24–30. Lisbon

Couto 1951
Couto, João. "A Arte da Ourivesaria em Portugal. Elementos decorativos." In Barreira, João. *As Artes Decorativas* 1:15–74. Lisbon

Couto and Gonçalves 1960–1962
Couto, João, and A. M. Gonçalves. *A Ourivesaria em Portugal*. Lisbon

Dennis 1960
Dennis, Faith. *Three Centuries of French Domestic Silver: Its Makers and Marks*. 2 vols. Exh. cat. The Metropolitan Museum of Art. New York

d'Orey 1988
d'Orey, Leonor. "Ourivesaria portuguesa." *Revista Clube Edições de Arte*, vol. 1. Lisbon

d'Orey 1990–1991
d'Orey, Leonor. *A Baixela da Coroa Portuguesa*. Lisbon

d'Orey and Teague 1986
d'Orey, Leonor, and Michael Teague. "In the King's Service." *House and Garden* 158 (November), 182–188

Embaixada 1716
Fonseca, Francisco de. *Embaixada do Conde de Villarmayor Fernando Telles da Sylva de Lisboa à corte de Vienne e Viagem da Rainha (…) D. Maria Anna de Austria*. Vienna

Enggass 1966
Enggass, Robert. *Early Eighteenth-Century Sculpture in Rome*. State College, Pa.

Espanca 1966
Espanca, Túlio. *Inventário Artístico de Portugal. Concelho de Évora*. Lisbon

Estevens 1944
Estevens, Manuel Santos. "Subsídios para a história da Ourivesaria Portuguesa," vol. 1. (thesis, Museu Nacional de Arte Antiga, Lisbon)

Ferrão 1983
Ferrão, Bernardo. *Imaginária Luso-oriental*. Lisbon

Ferreira 1970
Ferreira, Teresa Gomes. "L'Argenterie Gulbenkian." *Connaissance des Arts* (Dec.)

Figueiredo 1926
Figueiredo, José de. "A Baixela Germain." *Lusitania* 3. Lisbon

Foz 1926
Foz, Marquês da. *A baixela Germain da antiga Corte Portuguesa*. Lisbon

França 1965/1988
França, José-Augusto. *Une ville des Lumières: La Lisbonne de Pombal* (2nd ed. 1988). Paris

França 1966/1978
França, José-Augusto. *Lisboa Pombalina e o Iluminismo* (2nd ed. 1978). Lisbon

Franceschi 1988
Franceschi, Humberto. *O Ofício da Prata no Brasil*. Rio de Janeiro

Freire 1923
Freire, Luciano. *Catálogo Descrito e Ilustrado*. Museu Nacional dos Coches. Lisbon

Fusconi 1984
Fusconi, Giulia. "Per la storia della scultura lignea in Roma: le carrozze di Ciro Ferri per due ingressi solenni." *Antologia di Belle Arti*, n.s., 80–97, nos. 21–22

Gonçalves 1967
Gonçalves, Flavio. "The Architecture and Wood Sculpture of the North of Portugal, 1750–1850." *Portugal and Brazil in Transition*. Minneapolis

Gonçalves 1984
Gonçalves, António Nogueira. *Estudos de Ourivesaria*. Oporto

Gonzalez Palacios 1969
Gonzalez Palacios, A. *Il mobile nei secoli: Paesi Bassi, Paesi Iberici, Russia*. Milan

Gruber 1982
Gruber, Alain. *L'argenterie de maison du XVIe au XIXe siècle*. Fribourg

Gruber 1989
Gruber, Alain. *Silverware*. New York

Guedes 1971
Guedes, Natália Correia. "Terrina da Baixela Germain." *Observador*

Guerra 1952
Guerra, Luíz José Bivar de Pimentel. *Inventário e sequestro da Casa de Aveiro em 1759*. Lisbon

Guibbini 1992
Guibbini, Guido. "La città rappresentata." *Genova nell'età Barocca*. Genoa

Guimarães 1872
Guimarães, Ribeiro. *Summário de Varia História*, vol. 1. Lisbon

Guimarães and Sardoeira 1924–1935
Guimarães, Alfredo, and Albano Sardoeira. *Mobiliário Artístico Português (Elementos para a sua História)*. 2 vols. Oporto

Heitmann 1979
Heitmann, B. *Die Deutsche Sogennanten Reise-Service und die Toiletten Garnituren von 1680 bis zum Ende des Rokoko*. Hamburg

Hernmarck 1977
Hernmarck, Carl. *The Art of the European Silversmith (1430–1830)*. 2 vols. London, New York

Honour 1959
Honour, Hugh. "Filippo della Valle." *Connoisseur* 144 (Nov.), 172–179

Honour 1969
Honour, Hugh. *Cabinet Makers and Furniture Designers*. London, New York

Honour and Fleming 1977
Honour, Hugh, and J. Fleming. "Lacquer" and "Japanning." *The Penguin Dictionary of Decorative Art*. London

Huth 1971
Huth, H. *Lacquer in the West*. Chicago, London

Illustração Portugueza 1906
"A Baixela Francesa da Corte de Portugal." *Illustração Portugueza*, 2nd ser. (June)

Illustração 1926
"A Baixela Germain." *Illustração* 11 (June)

Index Instrumentorum 1788
Index Instrumentorum, 1788: Gabinete de Física Experimental, Universidade de Coimbra

Kreisel 1927
Kreisel, H. *Prunkwagen und Schlitten*. Leipzig

Kubler 1959
Kubler, George. "Architecture, Portugal and Brazil." In Kubler and Soria 1959

Kubler 1972
Kubler, George. *Portuguese Plain Architecture between Spices and Diamonds, 1521–1706.* Middletown, Conn.

Kubler and Soria 1959
Kubler, George, and Martin Soria. *Art and Architecture in Spain and Portugal and Their American Dominions, 1500 to 1800.* Harmondsworth

Langhans 1943
Langhans, Franz-Paul. *As corporações mecânicos,* vol. 1. Lisbon

Lavagnino 1940
Lavagnino, Emilio. *Gli Artisti in Portogallo (l'Opera del genio italiano all'estero).* Rome

Leite 1979
Leite, Maria Fernanda Passos. "Ourivesaria." Museu Nacional de Arte Antiga. *Artes Decorativas Portuguesas.* Lisbon

Lipinsky 1961
Lipinsky, Angelo. "Il Tesoro di San Giovanni in Lisbona." *Fede e arte,* 56–89

Lipinsky 1963
Lipinsky, Angelo. "Gli Arredi sacri di Benedetto XIV per S. Pietro di Bologna." *Fede e arte,* 186–208

Lisbon 1934
Exposição de Arte Francesa. Exh. cat. Museu Nacional de Arte Antiga. Lisbon

Lisbon 1955
Exposição de Ourivesaria Portuguesa e Francesa. Exh. cat. Fundação Ricardo do Espírito Santo Silva

Lisbon 1974
O trajo civil em Portugal. Exh. cat. Museu Nacional de Arte Antiga

Lisbon 1987
Pinto, Maria Helena Mendes. *Os Móveis e o seu Tempo.* Exh. cat. Museu Nacional de Arte Antiga

Lisbon 1992
Tesouros Reais. Exh. cat. Palácio Nacional da Ajuda

London 1990
Paul de Lamerie: At the Sign of the Golden Ball: An exhibition of the Work of England's Master Silversmiths (1688–1751). Exh. cat. Goldsmith's Hall, London

Lopes 1963
Lopes, Carlos da Silva. "Baixela Germain." *O Primeiro de Janeiro.* Oporto

Lopes 1971
Lopes, Carlos da Silva. "O Retrato do Senhor D. João." *Museu* 14 (Aug.–Dec.)

Mabille 1980
Mabille, Gérard. "Les Surtous de table dans l'art français du XVIIIᵉ siècle." *L'Estampille* (Oct.)

Mabille 1984
Mabille, Gérard. *Orfèvrerie Française des XVIᵉ, XVIIᵉ et XVIIIᵉ, catalogue raisonné des collections du Musée des Arts Décoratifs du Musée Nissim de Camondo.* Paris

Mabille 1987
Mabille, Gérard. "Germain, Durand, Auguste: L'Orfèvrerie Française dans L'Europe des Lumières" and "La table et ses usages au XVIIIᵉ siècle, ou le service à la française." *AAFA. La table d'un roi,* 56–70 and 87–92. Paris

Macedo 1945
Macedo, Diogo de. *A Escultura nos séculos XVII and XVIII.* Lisbon

Machado 1823
Machado, Cyrillo Volkmar. *Coleção de Memórias relativas às vidas dos pintores, e escultores, arquitetos e gravadores portugueses.* Lisbon

Malory 1974
Malory, Nina A. "Notizie sulla scultura a Roma nel XVIII secolo (1719–1760)." *Bollettino d'arte,* series V, 59:172

Mandroux-Franca 1973
Mandroux-Franca, Marie-Thérèse. "Information artistique et 'mass media' au XVIIIᵉ siècle: La Diffusion de l'ornement gravé rococo au Portugal." *Bracara Augusta* 27, no. 64, 412–445. Braga

Maurice and Mayr 1980
Maurice, Klaus, and Otto Mayr. *The Clockwork Universe.* Washington

Mayer-Thurman 1975
Mayer-Thurman, Christa C. *Raiment for the Lord's Service: A Thousand Years of Western Vestments.* The Art Institute of Chicago

Meco 1985
Meco, José. *Azulejaria Portuguesa.* Lisbon

Meco 1989
Meco, José. *O Azulejo em Portugal.* Lisbon

Meco 1991
Meco, José. "Barco, Gabriel del." *Dicionário da Arte Barroca em Portugal,* 66–69. Lisbon

Memoriale 1716
Memoriale al Papa Clemente XI presentato dall'Ambasciatore Straordinario del Re del Portogallo Marchese de Fontes, con cui si offre per parte del Re del Portogallo Joao V la dote per tre nuovi vescovati in Cina [Rome, c. 1716]

Mendes Pinto 1973
Pinto, Maria Helena Mendes. *José Francisco de Paiva, ensamblador e arquiteto do Porto (1744–1824).* Lisbon

Mendes Pinto 1979
Pinto, Maria Helena Mendes. "Móveis." *Artes Decorativas Portuguesas no Museu Nacional de Arte Antiga. Séculos XVI-XVIII.* Lisbon

Mendonça 1951
Mendonça, Maria José de. *Tapetes de Arraiolos.* In Barreira, João. *As Artes Decorativas* 3: no. 1, 265–320. Lisbon

Merveilleux 1983
Merveilleux, Charles Frédéric. "Memórias Instrutivas sobre Portugal, 1723–1726." *O Portugal de D. João V vista por três forasteiros.* Lisbon

Millon, Henry A. *Filippo Juvarra. Drawings from the Roman Period 1704–1714.* Rome

Minor 1984
Minor, Vernon Hyde. "Filippo della Valle as Metalworker." *Art Bulletin* 66, 511–514

Moita 1954
Moita, Luís. "A custódia cujo desenho é atribuido a Ludwig (o arquitecto de Mafra)." *Olissipo* 17, no. 65. Lisbon

Moniz 1959
Moniz, Manuel Carvalho. *O Convento e a Igreja de S. Francisco.* Évora

Montagu 1989
Montagu, Jennifer. *Roman Baroque Sculpture.* London

Montevecchi and Rocca 1989
Montevecchi, Benedetta, and Sandra Vasco Rocca (coord.). *Dizionari terminologici: Suppellèttile ecclesiastica* 1. Florence

Morazzoni 1940
Morazzoni, G. *Il Mobilio Italiano.* Florence

Moura 1986
Moura, Carlos. "Uma poética da refulgência: a escultura e a talha dourada." *História da Arte em Portugal.* Lisbon

Museu De Aveiro 1960
Roteiro do Museu de Aveiro

Museu Nacional De Arte Antiga 1956
Ofertas de Obras de Arte. Boletim do Museu Nacional de Arte Antiga 3: no. 2. Lisbon

Museu Nacional De Arte Antiga 1975
Roteiro de Ourivesaria. Lisbon

Museu Nacional de Soares dos Reis 1949
Catálogo-Guia. Jóias, Pratas, Relógios, Miniaturas, Esmates e Diversos. Oporto

MNC 1943
Keil, Luís. *Catálogo do Museu Nacional dos Coches.* Lisbon

Nava Cellini 1982
Nava Cellini, Antonia. *La Scultura del settecento (Storia dell'arte in Italia).* Torno

Nollet 1764
Nollet, Jean-Antoine. *Leçons de Physique Expérimentale,* vol. 3. Paris

New York 1960
Three Centuries of French Domestic Silver. Exh. cat. The Metropolitan Museum of Art. New York

Nocq 1926–1931
Nocq, Henry. *Le poinçon de Paris. Répertoire des maitres-orfèvres de la jurisdiction de Paris depuis le Moyen-Age jusqu'à la fin du XVIIIᵉ siècle. 5 vols.* Paris

Oman 1965
Oman, Charles. *English Silversmith's Work, Civil and Domestic.* London

Oporto 1984
Brandão, Domingos de Pinho. "Tesouro da Sé do Porto." *Ourivesaria do norte de Portugal.* Exh. cat.

Oporto 1989
S. Tiago. Exh. cat. Museu Nacional Soares dos Reis

Palmela Castle 1990
O Castelo e a Ordem de S. Tiago na história de Palmela. Exh. cat. Palmela Castle

Paris 1954
Les Trésors de l'orfèvrerie du Portugal. Exh. cat. Musée des Arts Decoratifs

Pedro 1989
Pedro, Constança. "Ourivesaria." *Dicionário da Arte Barroca em Portugal.* Lisbon

Pesci 1938
Pesci, C. Gradara. "Due opere dello scultore Pietro Bracci in Portogallo." *Roma* 16, 234–236

Pessanha 1905
Pessanha, José. "Tapetes de Arraiolos." *O Archeologo Português.* Lisbon

Picard, Kerneis, and Bruneau 1966
Picard, R., J. P. Kerneis, and Y. Bruneau. *Les Compagnies des Indes. Route de la Porcelaine.* Paris

Pimentel 1946
Pimentel, Alberto. *As Amantes de D. João V.* Oporto

Pimentel 1987
Pimentel, António Filipe. "O Gosto oriental na obra das estantes da casa da Livraria da Universidade de Coimbra." *IV Simpósio Luso-Espanhol de História de Arte, Portugal e Espanha entre a Europa e Além-Mar.* Coimbra

Pinto 1952
Pinto, Augusto Cardoso. *Cadeiras Portuguesas.* Lisbon

Pires 1925
Pires, António Caldeira. *História do Palácio de Queluz,* vol. 1. Coimbra

Poldi Pezzolli 1959
Argenti italiani dal XVI al XVIII sécolo. Cat. Museo Poldi Pezzolli. Milan

Pometti 1899–1900
Pometti, F. "Studi sul Pontificato di Clemente XI, 1700–21." *Archivio della Società Romana di Storia Patria* 2, XXII, 1899, 109–179; 3 and 4, XXIII 1900

Queiros 1948
Queiros, José. *Cerâmica Portuguesa.* Lisbon

Quieto 1988
Quieto, Pierpaolo. *Giovanni V di Portogallo e le sue committenze nella Roma del XVIII secolo (la pittura a Mafra, Évora, Lisbona).* Bologna

Raczynski 1847
Raczynski, A. *Dictionnaire Historico-Artistique de Portugal.* Paris

Ramos 1969
Ramos, Maria da Glória Magalhães de Sousa. "Os Coelho Sampaio e a sua Arte". *Museu,* 2nd series, 12. Oporto

Réau 1927
Réau, Louis. "L'argenterie française du XVIIIᵉ siècle au Musée de Lisbonne." *Gazette des Beaux Arts,* 17–26

Rodrigues n.d.
Rodrigues, Maria João Madeira. *Metais do Museu de S. Roque. Catálogo.* Lisbon

Rodrigues 1988
Rodrigues, Maria João Madeira. *A Capela de S. João Baptista e as suas coleções.* Lisbon

Rosa 1738
Rosa, F. A. *Relaçam das insignes festas, que se fizerão no Sitio da Junqueira.* Lisbon

Rosas Jr. 1954
Rosas Júnior, José. *Catálogo das Jóias e Pratas da Coroa, no Palácio Nacional da Ajuda.* Oporto

Sandaõ 1976
Sandaõ, Arthur de. *Faiança Portuguesa. Séculos XVIII-XIX.* Oporto

Sandaõ 1979
Sandaõ, Arthur de. *O Móvel pintado em Portugal.* Oporto

Santos 1950
Santos, Reynaldo dos. *A Escultura em Portugal,* vol. 2. Lisbon

Santos 1953
Santos, Reynaldo dos. *História de Arte em Portugal.* Oporto

Santos 1970
Santos, Reynaldo dos. *Oito Séculos de Arte Portuguesa,* vol. 3. Lisbon

Santos and Quilhó 1959/1974
Santos, Reynaldo dos, and Irene Quilhó. *Ourivesaria portuguesa nas coleções particulares,* 2 vols. (1st ed. 1959). Lisbon

Saraiva 1934
Saraiva, José da Cunha. *A Baixela Germain. Subsídios para a sua história.* Lisbon

Schneider 1980
Schneider, Susan. *O Marquês de Pombal e o Vinho do Porto.* Lisbon

Silva 1960
Silva, Augusto Vieira da. "Panorama de Lisboa em azulejos existente no Museu Nacional de Arte Antiga." *Dispersos* 2. Lisbon

Silva 1977
Silva, Maria Madalena de Cagigal e. *O Museu Nacional dos Coches.* Lisbon

Silvano 1987
Silvano, Eduardo Rangel Pamplona. *O Enigma da Coroa Real.* Lisbon

Simões 1963
Simões, J. M. dos Santos. *Azulejaria Portuguesa nos Azores e na Madeira.* Lisbon

Simões 1979
Simões, J. M. dos Santos. *Azulejaria em Portugal no século XVIII.* Lisbon

Smith 1936
Smith, Robert C. "João Frederico Ludovice, an Eighteenth-Century Architect in Portugal." *Art Bulletin* 18, no. 3

Smith 1963
Smith, Robert C. *A Talha em Portugal.* Lisbon. See also Smith, Robert C. "A Talha no Porto." *Documentos e Memórias para a História do Porto. XXXII, Alguns retábulos e Painéis de Igrejas e Capelas do Porto.* Oporto

Smith 1966
Smith, Robert C. "Dated Looking Glasses." *Connoisseur*

Smith 1968
Smith, Robert C. *The Art of Portugal 1500–1800.* London. See also Smith, Robert C. *Cadeiras de Portugal.* Lisbon

Smith 1970
Smith, Robert C. *Marceliano d'Araújo, Escultor Bracarense.* Oporto

Smith 1973
Smith, Robert C. "The Building of Mafra." *Apollo* (April)

Snowman 1966
Snowman, A. Kenneth. *Eighteenth-Century Gold Boxes of Europe.* London

Soares 1940
Soares, Ernesto. *História da Gravura Artística em Portugal.* Lisbon

Soares and Lima 1947, 1948, 1950, 1954, 1960
Soares, Ernesto, and Henrique de Campos Ferreira Lima. *Dicionário de Iconografica Portuguesa,* vols. 1–5. Lisbon

Soares 1983
Soares, Mário O. *Técnicas de Decoração em Azulejo.* Coimbra

Solla 1928–1930
Solla, Conde de Castro e. *Cerâmica Brazonada.* 2 vols. Lisbon

Sousa 1741
Sousa, António Caetano de. *História Genealogia da Casa real Portuguesa,* vol. 7. Lisbon

Sousa 1775
Sousa, António Caetano de. *Memórias históricas e genealogicas dos Grandes de Portugal.* Lisbon

Sousa 1951
Sousa, J. M. Carneiro de. "Notícia da proveniência da mais volumosa peça de Baixela Germain." *Olissipo* 56. Lisbon

Sousa Viterbo 1900
Viterbo, Francisco Marquês de Sousa. *A Capella de S. João Baptista.* Lisbon

Sousa Viterbo 1902
Viterbo, Francisco Marquês de Sousa. *Artes Industrias e Industrias Portuguesas. Tapeçarias.* Coimbra

Sousa Viterbo 1903
Viterbo, Francisco Marquês de Sousa. *Notícia de alguns pintores portugueses e outros que, sendo estrangeiros, exerceram a sua arte em Portugal.* Lisbon

Sousa Viterbo 1912
Viterbo, Francisco Marquês de Sousa. *O Rei das charamelas e as charamelas reses.* Lisbon

Sousa Viterbo and Almeida 1900
Viterbo, Francisco Marquês de Sousa, and Vicente de Almeida. *A Capela de S. João Batista.* Lisbon

Steingraber 1957
Steingraber, Erich. *Antique Jewellery, Its History and Art.* New York

Symonds 1935
Symonds, R. W. "Giles Grendey (1693–1700) and
the Export of English Furniture to Spain." *Apollo*
22, no. 132, 12

Symonds 1940
Symonds, R. W. "A Royal Scrutoire. English
Furniture in Portugal." *Connoisseur* (June)

Symonds 1941
Symonds, R. W. "English Eighteenth-Century
Furniture Exports to Spain and Portugal."
Burlington Magazine (Feb.)

Tait 1986
Tait, Hugo. *Seven Thousand Years of Jewellery.*
London

Teixeira 1987
Teixeira, José. *D. Fernando II, Rei Artista, Artista
Rei.* Lisbon

Teixeira 1989
Teixeira, José. *Exposição Comemorativa do
Bicentenário do Ministério das Finanças.* Lisbon

Terrier 1985
Terrier, Max. "La Mode des Espagnolettes,
Oppenord et Juvarra." *Antologia di Belle Arti* 1985,
n.s.

Trebbi 1958
Trebbi, Bruno. *L'Artigianato nelle chiese bolognesi.*
Bologna

Valesio [1978]
Francesco Valesio, *Diario di Roma*, 2:7–8, vol. 4, ed.
G. Scano. Milan

Valente 1948
Valente, Vasco. "O Pratas Armoriadas."
Ourivesaria Portuguesa 3, 4. Oporto

Vasconcelos 1914–1915
Vasconcelos, Joaquim de. *A Arte Religiosa em
Portugal.* 2 vols. Oporto

Viale 1963
Viale, V. *Mostra del Barroco Piemontese.* Cat. Turin

Viana do Castelo 1967
Exposição de Arte Ornamental do Distrito de Viana.
Exh. cat. Museu Municipal

Victoria and Albert Museum 1984
Rococo, Art and Design in Hogarth's England.
London

Vidal and Almeida 1974
Vidal, Manuel Gonçalves. *Marcas de contrastes e
ourives portugueses, Complementos e anotações às
marcas antigas de pratas portugueses e brasileiras por
Fernando Moitinho de Almeida.* 2 vols. Lisbon

Vieira Lusitano 1780
Vieira de Matos, Francisco. *O insigne pintor e leal
esposo Vieira Lusitano, história verdadeira que ele
escrive em cantos lyricos....* Lisbon

Wohl 1973
Wohl, Hellmut. "Carlos Mardel and His Lisbon
Architecture." *Apollo* (April)

Wohl 1975
Wohl, Hellmut. "Recent Studies in Portuguese
Post-Medieval Architecture." *Journal of the Society
of Architectural Historians* (March)